GW01143913

Teaching, Learning and Other Miracles

TRANSGRESSIONS: CULTURAL STUDIES AND EDUCATION

Series Editors
  Shirley Steinberg, *McGill University, Canada*
  Joe Kincheloe, *McGill University, Canada*

Editorial Board
  Heinz-Hermann Kruger, *Halle University, Germany*
  Norman Denzin, *University of Illinois, Champaign-Urbana, USA*
  Roger Slee, *McGill University, Canada*
  Rhonda Hammer, *University of California Los Angeles, USA*
  Christine Quail, *SUNY, Oneonta*

Volume 1
An Unordinary Death…The Life of a Suicide Bomber
Khalilah Christina Sabra
Paperback ISBN 90-77874-36-4 Hardback ISBN 90-77874-37-2

Volume 2
Lyrical Minded
The Critical Pedagogy of Hip-Hop Artist KRS-ONE
Priya Parmar, City University of New York, USA
Paperback ISBN 90-77874-50-X Hardback ISBN 90-77874-64-X

Volume 3
Pedagogy and Praxis in the Age of Empire
Towards a New Humanism
Peter McLaren & Nathalia Jaramillo
Paperback ISBN 90-77874-84-4 Hardback ISBN 90-77874-85-2

Volume 4
Dewey and Power
Renewing the Democratic Faith
Randall Hewitt, University of Central Florida, USA
Paperback ISBN 90-77874-92-5 Hardback ISBN 90-77874-93-3

Volume 5
Teaching, Learning and Other Miracles
Grace Feuerverger, Ontario Institute for Studies in Education, University of Toronto, Canada
Paperback ISBN 90-8790-000-7 Hardback ISBN 90-8790-003-1

Volume 6
Soaring Beyond Boundaries
Women Breaking Educational Barriers in Traditional Societies
Reitumetse Obakeng Mabokela (ed.), Michigan State University, USA
Paperback ISBN 90-77874-97-6 Hardback ISBN 90-77874-98-4

Teaching, Learning, and Other Miracles

Grace Feuerverger
OISE, University of Toronto, Canada

Foreword by
William Ayers

SENSE PUBLISHERS
ROTTERDAM / TAIPEI

A C.I.P. record for this book is available from the Library of Congress.

Paperback ISBN: 978-90-8790-000-7
Hardback ISBN: 978-90-8790-003-8

Published by: Sense Publishers,
P.O. Box 21858, 3001 AW
Rotterdam, The Netherlands

Printed on acid-free paper

All Rights Reserved © 2007 Grace Feuerverger

No part of this work may be reproduced, stored in a retrieval system, or transmitted in any form or by any means, electronic, mechanical, photocopying, microfilming, recording or otherwise, without written permission from the Publisher, with the exception of any material supplied specifically for the purpose of being entered and executed on a computer system, for exclusive use by the purchaser of the work.

For all the children

*There is a crack in everything;
That's how the light gets in.*
    -Leonard Cohen

CONTENTS

Acknowledgements		ix
Foreword *William Ayers*		xi
Introduction	For Love of Teaching	1

PART ONE

Chapter one	A Pilgrimage	9
Chapter two	Living in Two Worlds	17
Chapter three	Return to Fielding	27
Chapter four	Reading for Live	37
Chapter five	A Call to Teach	45

PART TWO

Chapter six	University Teaching	65
Chapter seven	Reclaiming ESL Voices	87
Chapter eight	My Yiddish Voice	103
Chapter nine	Of Wars and Wonderland	111
Chapter ten	Adolescence and Trauma	119
Chapter eleven	The Term They Cancelled Halloween	129
Chapter twelve	I [too] Have a Dream	141
References		153

ACKNOWLEDGEMENTS

This work was a labour of love.

Two locations played important roles in the writing of this book. Firstly, I am grateful to have been able to spend a half-year sabbatical in the serene atmosphere of the Berkeley City Club where I wrote the first draft of this book and later spent more time there, working on subsequent drafts. Writing in its magnificent library was a cherished privilege and I am convinced that the spirit of its architect, Julia Morgan – the first woman to study at the *Ecole des Beaux Arts* in Paris – was right there accompanying me as I sat at an exquisite antique desk with my laptop. The tranquility there was other-worldly.

But it is the second location – the Montreal in which I was born and raised – that will forever be in my heart. In part, this book is a gift to my place of birth, one of the great cities in the world, and one which, in a variety of ways, saved my life.

This book is also a way for me to "give back" to an institution that offered me so much sustenance: School, my place of safety and comfort. I am filled with gratitude for those teachers of my childhood years who bore silent 'witness' and helped me find a path toward the life force. I wonder if any of them will ever see this book; I wonder how many of them are still alive.

To my next-door neighbour Françoise and her family of so long ago I would like to say: *Je vous remercie de m'avoir donné un premier chemin vers la vie, vers la joie, vers la beauté de la culture canadienne-française.*

I also want to thank the children in all my classrooms who taught me more than I ever dreamt possible, especially to my young student Mandy whose words "Express yourself, Mrs. Feuerverger, you have a right to," became a part of my mantra forever.

I was blessed to have been given the opportunity to teach, and to be nourished by my bright and devoted students at OISE in the University of Toronto – most of whom are teacher-practitioners in the field.

A big 'thank you' goes to all my participants whose courage and perseverance I will always admire.

I also count among my blessings the generosity of spirit that led Bill Ayers to write the Foreword for this book. How fitting it is that he was the one to write it. Given our greatly different life experiences, it is wondrous that we were brought to the same place: a deep devotion and commitment to children and their families within the context of education. I also would like to thank Rick Ayers (Bill's brother) – another generous soul – who welcomed me into his classrooms at Berkeley High School.

Many thanks to Shirley Steinberg who believed in this manuscript and helped me to find its "home." And to Andy Hrycyna and Ellen Reeves who offered very

ACKNOWLEDGEMENTS

positive suggestions. I am also grateful to Richard Rodriguez and to Maxine Greene for their encouraging words.

And, for many other reasons, I thank Sandra Acker, Shirley Brower, Jim Cummins, Judy Farqhuarson, Matthew Fox, Sarah Freedman, Jim Gifford, Zehavit Gross, Nancy Johnson, Trevor Johnson, Joe Kincheloe, Herbert Kohl, Jonathon Kozol, Anne Michaels, Marla Morris, Normand Labrie, Robert Lecker, Evelin Lindner, Jose Lopes, Mariana Masterson, Rosanne Morris, Jack Miller, Carol Mullen, Lisa Richards and Roseann Runte.

I also thank Michel Lokhorst of Sense Publishers for making the publication of this book such a joyful experience.

I am grateful to the Social Sciences and Humanities Research Council of Canada (SSHRC) for funding various parts of this project.

Very special thanks go to Michael Connelly who opened a new professional door for me when he hired me into the Joint Centre for Teacher Development at OISE in 1991. I walked through that door into an extraordinary narrative journey.

I will be forever thankful to the late Benjamin Geneen who taught me the true meaning of faith, love and compassion. He was and always will be "*in loco parentis*" for me.

Finally, words cannot express the feelings in my heart for Andrey, the greatest of all the miracles in my life.

FOREWORD

By William Ayers

Here is a book about teaching as it could be, about democracy and freedom as aspirations yet to be achieved, about childhood as a lived and storied experience teetering precariously between propulsive power and utter vulnerability. Here, indeed, is a book about miracles – written by a miracle-maker for the miracle-workers teachers might yet become.

We need, of course, more than hope and inspiration if we are to rescue teaching from its many discontents, its welts and its wounds. We will need courage and collective hard work in order to create something truly decent, something authentically human, something notably better for all children and families. In truth we need both: determination alone cannot take us where we need to go, not even over the next hill; vision without rolling up our sleeves and linking arms for the messy work ahead is mere idle dreaming. We need to nourish the dialectic of determination and dreams – of values, vision, and gritty effort.

All teaching is enacted in a specific here and now, all of it brought to life in the mud and muck of the world as we find it – this prairie or that field, this street or the other one. We don't choose the world as such; rather, we are thrust into a world already there, going, going, going, up and running. We need to take the world as it is to start, unvarnished, and plunge forward as participants if we are to live fully, deeply, purposefully – if we are to see both the beauty and the pain of it, if we are to add our little weight to the balance.

It is in this sense that teaching is both an intellectual and an ethical enterprise, requiring thoughtful and caring people to carry it forward – not some disembodied head without a heart, nor some vaguely smiling flame without a brain. As teachers we need to both think and feel our way into what we are doing. In fact, it's at the crossroads of the intellectual and the ethical where teachers begin to truly find their bearings. It's here that we crawl toward love – not love as a romantic longing or a sweet confection, but love as a call to action, an impulse that insists that all human beings matter, even when law or custom or social practice or brutality or invasion or restriction says otherwise.

We teachers are increasingly de-skilled and hammered into interchangeable cogs in a bureaucracy, pressured to reduce teaching to a set of manageable and easily supervisable tasks, and to sum up all our efforts on the basis of a single and simpleminded metric, to strip teaching of any moral purpose or intellectual engagement or creative action whatsoever. In these circumstances, and at this moment, it becomes even more important to find ways to resist, to fight back, to rescue teaching from the gathering forces of mindlessness and carelessness. We must think, and we must fight.

Grace Feuerverger understands this, and she knows that when we speak up and speak out we are often afraid, but that remaining silent in no way ameliorates our fear. It is best, then, to take a chance, to speak out and to act up. Since all life is a risk, stepping forward affords at least the possibility of a different perspective, the hope of something better. If what is before us is out of balance, if some part of what we see stands as an obstacle to our fullest humanity or if it is in some way unacceptable or offensive, we are called to say "no." It is in the spirit of resistance and hope that Feuerverger goes in search of a more fully humanistic pedagogy.

And it is here that we face a contradiction: the humanistic ideal and the democratic injunction tell us that every person is an entire universe, that each can develop as a full and autonomous person engaged with others in a common polity and an equality of power; the neoliberal imperative insists that profit is the center of economic, political, and social progress, and develops, then, a culture of competition, elitism, and hierarchy. An education for democracy fails as an adjunct to neoliberalism just as an education for neoliberalism fails to build either a democratic ethos or a participatory practice – something must change.

This book can be read as a series of challenges. The first is the challenge of democracy itself: what is democracy? What does schooling in a democracy actually look like? How might we build democratic communities in our classrooms and in our lives?

Another challenge is the problem of childhood itself: how do we build good environments and communities for children, as opposed to test factories where children are judged and sorted in narrow ways? How do we create schools that align themselves with children and build upon their deep capacities for imagination, expression, and experimentation? How do we resist the tendency to insist that children align themselves to schools that themselves function as factories or prisons?

And of course, the challenge of inclusion: how do we create an educational project that invites the full participation of all? How do we break down barriers to full participation of historically oppressed or excluded groups, and offer everyone an intellectually robust and honest learning experience?

Joined with these challenges and at the center of things is the challenge to see larger society as it really is – riddled with injustice, burdened by racism, disfigured by imperial ambition, with schools at least partially maimed as they're pressured to become sites that reinforce inequalities. Our task, then, is to link democratic possibilities in our own classrooms to fresh opportunities in our larger social and political lives.

While totalitarianism demands obedience and conformity, hierarchy, command-and-control, and royalty requires allegiance, democracy invites free people to come together voluntarily as citizens capable of both self-realization and, at the same time, full participation in a shared political and economic life. Democracy is a form of associative living in which people embrace a level of uncertainty, incompleteness, and the inevitability of change. Democracy thrives on difference: there are no immutable, fixed standards, the same for all, that will ultimately serve democratic purposes.

Grace Feuerverger is in every sense a 'mensch' – someone who, in Rosa Luxemburg's memorable definition, is able to both love the details of everyday life, and at the same time someone who is willing to put her shoulder on history's great wheel when required.

Teaching, Learning, and Other Miracles, asks us to reflect on fundamental issues of teaching and learning. It asks us to consider, who we want to be as teachers, where we want to stand in relationship to children and their families, how we want to interact with the larger communities that we are each a part of. It invites us to see ourselves in solidarity with, rather than in service to, the people we work with. A book of inspiration and practical guidance, it will awaken in teachers, parents, and students a unique way of thinking about the classrooms we have and the schools we deserve.

William Ayers
University of Illinois at Chicago

INTRODUCTION

For Love of Teaching

It is up to each of you to work out your own liberation.

- Siddhartha

This book is an exploration of teaching and learning in schools as a sacred life journey, a quest toward liberation. It seeks to pay tribute to one of the greatest gifts we can offer all children in our society — a really good public education. I want this book to speak especially to and for teachers who wish to make a real difference in the lives of their students. Each chapter concerns, in different ways, the act of creating and of being in classrooms as sites of cultural encounters and spaces for dreams and friendship and knowledge. I wrote this book because School for me, as a child, was a magical place where miracles happened. I was given unimaginable treasures: the caring of several teachers, their genuine interest in the betterment of my life. Perhaps I was simply lucky, but that isn't simple at all. Teaching and learning within the embrace of cultural and linguistic diversity became a road toward recovery – an odyssey of hope in the midst of darkness.

This book is autobiographical to the extent that I offer my own particular and perhaps idiosyncratic view of education; it is about sharing an everlasting quest toward a more compassionate way of understanding teaching and learning in the world. I hope that this book will speak to other teachers – and students – who find themselves, as I did, on winding and often treacherous paths, longing to discover meaning and a glimpse of their own potential in their lives at school. While I share some personal stories about my school teaching years, about my university teaching and about my research work, underlying all of these is the story of how language, culture and school serendipitously came together in my childhood to offer me a way to survive. My childhood school journey tells me that teachers can and do make a profound difference in the lives of their students. I hope that each chapter that follows will offer inspiration and direction to anyone who appreciates the priceless opportunity that a good public education can offer to students of all backgrounds, cultures, races and religions.

I also wrote this book for the many children in our classrooms today who have experienced violence, war, abuse, poverty, and other traumas and oppressions, and for the many teachers who teach them. Some of these students may fall by the wayside – too weary to continue on their journey toward the life force, beaten down by the brutality of it all. As a child of Holocaust survivors, I too grew up in the shadows of horror. As a teacher I remember seeing bewilderment, even terror, on the faces of many of the children in my classrooms. And I remember asking myself: "Did they suffer as much or more than I did?" What is the purpose of one's life as a teacher and educator? Surely it is to lighten the load of our students. And perhaps we can then lighten our own. We in the field of education, either as practitioners or administrators or theorists, need to honour and respect the struggle of all students and their parents who are trying valiantly to overcome personal difficulties. We need to reserve our greatest respect for them. And we need for them to know that we care. We need to offer them a meaningful and pluralistic curriculum in a trusting environment.

But perhaps what motivated me most to write this book was that School really became my childhood salvation, just as later, teaching became my life's work. A long time ago I needed to reach out to those who could offer me sustenance, and now I seek to return this gift to others who are seeking renewal, as I once did. And for me this takes place in classrooms and in schools – sacred spaces of possibility and of transformation. My vision of an inclusive, culturally responsive educator is one who brings to the classroom a new story, his or her *own* story, a kindred spirit who offers students a pathway toward wholeness. Perhaps this may sound lofty but I know it to be possible because I lived it. The title of Parker Palmer's book "The Courage to Teach" describes it completely and holds a simple but powerful truth: teaching is not only about "information and technique"; it is about the "capacity for connectedness" – what Paul Tillich calls "the courage to be." It is, as Emily Dickinson has put it, "the thing with feathers", or as Bill Ayers describes it, "an act of hope for a better future."

One of the main goals of this book is to explore the ways in which teaching *as an act of courage and beauty* forms the basis for creating a spirit of community within the classroom and beyond. In the end it is really about courage and love. The word *courage* derives from the Latin root for *heart*. It comes from the support of our fellow human beings, and so from creating connections. School should be a meeting place continually reinventing itself so that there is always room for more "others", for more choices, for more dreams – a path toward repair and restoration. The power of the teaching-learning experience lies in its potential to connect us to our selfhood, to cultivate our own identities as well as our integrity, talents, and inner passions and drives which lie at the very core of our being.

I have always searched for a sense of "home" within the protective layers of my 'professional' life. Teaching became my way of sharing hope – creating and being in community, the sense of safety of the classroom, the love of learning, the dialogic relation with all those bright-eyed and those not yet so bright-eyed young beings looking up to me for guidance and for direction. On some unconscious level I must have longed to share their space so that I might get a second chance at repairing my own unfortunate childhood. And indeed in some ways this wish, miraculously, was granted to me. As an elementary schoolteacher I shared my sense of wonder at the magic of language, of story, and of the imagination that creates them.

Teaching became a pilgrim's journey for me, filled with challenges and wonders. It became an act of faith, an act of restoration of a marred canvas. My students enjoyed coming to school because I enjoyed teaching them about the way the world was showing itself to me – about the sanctity of literature, of language, of culture; about the pleasure of reading a good book, of hearing a healing story, of learning a new language, solving a math puzzle, or of observing a different way of life; about the salvation that lies within all of those activities. Do we not all bring our personal lives into our professional worlds? The key is to respect the lives of others, as well as our own. Each soul is a sacred entity, and as a teacher I tried to the best of my ability to communicate this to my students. I wanted my students to know that lived experience of deprivation, abuse, violence – of any kind of oppression – does not have to become a life sentence.

A teacher who teaches for the love of it knows that miracles are a dime a dozen in a classroom where peace and hope reign. Why have so many policymakers, politicians, test makers and scorekeepers lost track of this simple truth? We are continually told that education is in crisis all over the world. And therefore, in the name of greater accountability, the icons of evaluation and assessment have become sacrosanct – to the detriment of other, more informal, ways of measuring the progress of children. Accountability is indeed important and we certainly need to "hardline" it with many students, but it cannot *only* be about balancing a budget or about high stakes testing, no matter how persuasive such arguments may sound. Such discourse *must* be placed within a context of justice, fairness, creativity and peace – a respect for one another in our schools, our communities, and in our world. The kind of tests that are being given to students in schools at the present time does not necessarily measure such development and such aspirations.

A teacher can be a messenger of disdain and indifference or of hope and freedom to his or her students. I believe that most teachers desire to be the latter. They seek to inspire and to build confidence in their classrooms, where all children can learn a sense of agency and purpose and thus discover their inner gifts. Teachers want to create an atmosphere where passion for discovery is kindled. And they dream – dare we say it – to create excitement, fun and laughter in the midst of all the learning. If only they were also *encouraged* to do so! Students want to hear about heroes and buried treasures and dragons and quests, not only about what needs to be "covered in the curriculum." Teachers and students need a sense of adventure in their classrooms – something more than merely trudging through lessons and preparing for those high stakes tests. What happened to encouraging the joy of good discussions, the abandon of listening to a great fairy tale or folktale, or spreading the wings of imagination during a science lesson?

My experience tells me that work needs play for creativity to be truly unchained. Students need drama performances; songfests, quizzes, storytelling events, the creation of "books" about their families and about their cultural and linguistic backgrounds. Each student standing in front of a class, or up on stage in the auditorium reading or performing, represents a triumph in the face of adversity. Certainly, curriculum needs to prepare students for the 'real world' and the "global economy," but above all it needs to be grounded in the dignity of the human being. The one important 'benchmark' in education – and this surely is a timeless truth – is the extent to which every student can be helped to understand that he or she does have value in the world, no matter how unfortunate their initial circumstances may seem. Each classroom calls out for a witness. Each student is an angel in disguise. Each lesson is a work-in-progress. Each teacher is both an artist and a muse. Perhaps such reflections seem like fantasies, but the greatest achievements derive from fantasy, from dreams, and from what seem to be insurmountable obstacles. Perhaps this seems like romanticism, but how can one appreciate the mystery and the majesty of teaching without it?

I believe that next to parenting, teaching may be the most demanding and important work on earth. A teacher must enter the labyrinth of School with a deep personal as well as professional desire for making life more meaningful and more just. I knew early on in my own life that I had a vision of myself connecting with others, all kinds of others, from all kinds of backgrounds. I saw School, and later school teaching, as an opportunity to share knowledge and different ways of looking at the world – to communicate with people of many cultures and languages, and to offer and to receive ideas. To be involved in the teaching-learning enterprise means entering into a dialogue, the kind of dialogue that Martin Buber describes as a "communion," allowing us to listen to both the spoken as well as the silent voices of the classroom, and to have a conversation about not only what is said but also what may be *felt* even without its having been expressed in words.

I have always thought of education as a genuine dialogue, one that acknowledges the longing of many students for what may not be possible in their family lives – an opportunity for "inclusion" and for finding a way to breathe between the cracks and crevices of 'outsiderness', difference, or even of despair. I hoped that in the classroom created by me, there would be justice and respect for diversity, and encouragement of inner talents. I would nurture my students and they would nurture me. We would enter into each other's worlds; we would break down barriers. I would rescue my students from their prisons and together we would free each other from all sorts of tyrannies.

What happened to training our teachers to love teaching? What happened to teaching and learning for the sheer joy of it? Educational theorist Nell Noddings (2003) argues that we must think about the idea of happiness as being an educational aim. She claims that if that idea were taken seriously then we would actually establish very different guidelines for teaching. In the present climate with its relentless focus on testing, teachers are leaving the profession in large numbers out of discontent. When I now describe my earlier years of teaching as "thrilling" and "filled with wonder" to my own university graduate students (most of whom are themselves teachers) the new ones look at me with confusion and perhaps even suspicion. They simply cannot fathom such apparent freedom. They are bewildered by it. They are busy trying simply to survive in the midst of bureaucratic tyrannies.

But any caring teacher – even in our constrained educational times – instinctively understands that teaching is not merely a question of mastering technical skills. It is relational and interactive. As in any profession where there develops over time an intimate relationship between practitioner and client, teaching is as much an art as it is a science. There is a well-known adage that even the best curriculum will fail if teachers' hearts are not in it. Bill Ayers (1993, p. 18) captures the essence of the profession when he states that "teaching is primarily a matter of love." Thich Nhat Hanh, the Vietnamese Buddhist monk, acknowledges the teacher as a healer and views education as a holistic and spiritual practice. As teachers, we need to be truly present in our work; teaching is work of the soul and we need to approach it with awe and with wonder. The poet and novelist Anne Michaels (1996, p. 121) says that "the best teacher lodges an intent not in the mind but in the heart", a view consistent with Paulo Freire's notion that pedagogy has "as much to do with the teachable heart as the teachable mind, and as much to do with efforts to change the world as it does with rethinking the categories that we use to analyze our current condition within history."

This sense of ethical action in education — by which I mean enabling our students to fulfill their potential as part of our responsibility in teaching – symbolizes for me the profound links between public and private worlds in the teaching profession. No matter how much schools are increasingly bent toward narrow agendas of efficiency and control, a central message of this book is this: that if teaching is to be truly meaningful we must talk of difficult moral dilemmas with our students, of the absolute necessity to find a way for us to learn to live together peacefully. And we must also pose the question: *"why does one go into teaching in the first place?"* It is a matter of acknowledging our struggle to make sense of our own lives as we confront the lives of our students in classrooms every day.

I firmly believe, as an educator devoted to working for cross-cultural understanding, that the authentic educational debates are those in which theory and practice are sculpted into a discourse devoted towards the striving for conflict resolution and peace – moral integrity and a true respect for diversity – a respect for **all** humanity in the name of those who have suffered and those who continue to suffer at the hands of oppression all over the world. We must come together to teach and learn about how to find an end to violence, poverty, oppression and war, no matter what colour of the rainbow we happen to be, and no matter where we are coming from. The ultimate goal of this book is to bear witness to the courage of teaching and learning within a context of vulnerability – or as Elliot Eisner put it, "on the edge of incompetence." In such an atmosphere we begin to teach with true compassion. I am afraid to think of where today's children of difference, of poverty, of abuse, and of war will be if we do not offer them an education open to the rainbow of diversity and mindful of the challenges of a "humanity in ruins", in Samuel Beckett's words.

I also wrote this book because I believe that it is crucial to recognize that education is about creating an attitude of reverence, passion and a love of learning in each child: what Joshua Heschel calls "radical amazement." This is what we really require in order to uplift the human spirit both within as well as outside of the classroom. And we need to teach that the human spirit is meant to be uplifted. Worthwhile education is soulful education. Soulful education seeks to share, not to impose. It offers loving authority by setting reasonable boundaries, not brute discipline denying personal choice. In the end it is not so much about technique as it is about presence, about the awareness of our frailties and of our splendid potentials – about creating a world more joyful, more creative, more articulate, more caring, more loving, and more peaceful than it is now. We are, after all, wanderers of the desert, and it is the majesty of the educational enterprise to find a purpose for our wanderings and turn it into an aesthetic, affirming endeavour. Again quoting Beckett, the contemporary artist in responding to "the chaos of experience" must "find a form that accommodates the mess." This is just as true for the contemporary teacher who must find artful ways in the classroom to offer a road toward redemption and coexistence.

Teaching and learning are a shared enterprise which demand acknowledgement of the bright and dark sides of humanity — a space in the continuum of time where we give one another permission to listen, liberate, respect, transform, and to heal one other. I took the treasures that were given to me by some teachers and in turn gave them to my own students when I became a teacher. And now as a professor of education I continue to share this message with as many teachers, students and parents as I can, because I know that *"there, but for the grace of God, go I."* Only love and compassion can guide us through the hardships of our lives – perhaps now more than ever – and onto the other side where we can live in safer places of hopes and dreams. I found such a 'promised land' in the classroom – that is my safe place in the world, in spite of any of its shortcomings. Indeed, I discovered early on in my career that teaching is not merely about curriculum objectives or pedagogical strategies, or subject matter, or lesson plans or state or provincial guidelines. It is first, foremost and always about *saving lives*. This is what a "culturally responsive" education must ultimately address. Nothing more or less really matters.

PART ONE

CHAPTER ONE

A PILGRIMAGE

Our original guiding stars are struggle and hope.

-Pablo Neruda

As I emerged from the taxi, I stared silently at the building in front of me. It was in late December, a Thursday, the day before the school term was to end. The weather that day was unusually mild – especially for Montreal. Fielding[1] School – what was I doing returning here, so many years after I had said goodbye to this place, a place, which had been my school, my shelter, my home, my refuge? I had just arrived off a flight from Toronto, and was about to begin a research project here.

It happened unexpectedly. I had been to a conference in Ottawa on "Immigration and Diversity" that fall, and by chance I had sat down next to an older woman at lunch the first day and we began to talk. I told her about a multicultural literacy project for immigrant and refugee students which I was conducting in Toronto. The woman, who turned out to be a Catholic nun, said she knew of a school in Montreal in which a similar project was taking place. Soeur Marie Monette is the director of a social organization serving newly arrived families in Montreal and works with immigrant school populations. I asked her which school this was in Montreal and she answered: "*Ecole Fielding.*" I was quite unprepared for this answer, and she herself seemed startled when I told her that I had gone to that very school as a child, a child of survivors of World War II. We looked at one another for a few moments and she then declared in a decisive tone: "*But you must go back. I can arrange it for you.*" And so began my journey back to an ancient time, a time of miracles and of sorrows in my life...

The brick school building before me was exactly the same as I remembered it. Snow was falling lightly onto the ground as my eyes took in the scene. There were children in the playground with their colourful winter jackets running and jumping and laughing. Some mothers were walking away and waving good-byes. The 1:30 p.m. bell ushering in the afternoon was just about to ring. I stood there not really wanting to move, wanting the moment to last forever. But the bell rang and I knew the time had come for me to re-enter this lost world. *Lost once and now found again.* One might say that I was returning in a *triumphant manner*. I had left this place many years ago, as a child of Holocaust survivors, almost as weary and as wounded by *that war* as my parents had been.

Many memories greeted me while I stood there. But I set them aside as I entered the school looking for the office of Geneviève Durocher, the coordinator of the literacy program for the school, who was waiting to meet me. The familiarity of the

CHAPTER ONE

surroundings surprised me. After so many years Fielding School looked exactly the same! I was wearing an elegant black winter coat with a soft lining. As teachers and students walked past me, what they saw was a woman with a burgundy velvet beret on her head and carrying the dark brown leather briefcase that she had bought in a bazaar ("shuk") while at a conference in Morocco a year earlier. Could any of them really understand that what they were seeing was a phantom who had returned from another era, from a time *very* long ago? No, they would not be able to guess it. I fooled them just as I could now fool anyone. I looked like a well-dressed professional, a visitor with a purpose. I felt my feet carrying me toward the office and in my daze I sensed a woman extending her hand toward me. This, I thought, must be Geneviève.

Geneviève! How many times did I use exactly that name when I wrote my make-belief stories about exciting French-Canadian families who were enjoying life and who had relatives and who celebrated Christmases and birthdays and summer holidays. I wrote those stories when I was a pupil at this very school, trying then desperately to hold onto the life raft of a French-Canadian fantasy that I had manufactured and had woven into a shattered life. Those blessed stories of make-belief saved me. I wish I had kept them; in my heart they will always be there. And now, here I was, shaking hands with an adult version of the French-Canadian girl whom I had then so very much longed to be.

Geneviève. I doubt that she would have wanted to be me: a forlorn child in a second-hand dress afraid of life, frightened of everything. A little girl who at much too young an age knew that her world was a dangerous place – a place where Hitler and his Gestapo lurked always in the shadows. "Don't turn around, even if your shoelaces are undone. Keep running with your colouring book and crayons and your Dick and Jane reader. Even if your heart is beating too fast. Just keep running."

Geneviève escorted me into her office and introduced me to her colleagues. I was the professor of Education from l'Université de Toronto. Did the ghost of my former self understand that I had come back today to reclaim her? Did she know that I had not yielded to the demons of despair? Did she know that I had survived in spite of the bleakness of my family life? Was she surprised to see me now, looking confident, poised and professional? How could such a transformation have happened?

It has been said that imagination is more important than knowledge and I could have been a poster child for this notion. I had no choice but to re-imagine my story and try to lift it from the defiled into the sacred. Do you know how much obscenity, how much desecration there is in the shock of learning that your relatives are a mountain of corpses in that land of war and nightmares from where your parents had come? To be confronted with such profanity at so young an age puts one in danger of losing sight of the sacredness and beauty in life. Losing sight: I was always terrified of going blind. I was always terrified of lights going out and yet I could sit in the darkness for hours rocking myself for comfort. Menacing darkness had engulfed me then but for some inexplicable reason it did not extinguish the fire within me – the desire to discover my true path. I became a little wayfarer preparing myself for the journey toward my "sacred story" – as Crites (1971) or as Connelly & Clandinin (1999) might describe it – waiting for a knock on the door of my battered soul, for the call of the wild in the winter winds, for the sound of the bells from the church nearby, or for the words of fairy tales that would lift me onto a rock and give me restful shelter there. For me that rock was School.

For me, Fielding School became that place where heaven and earth would meet every day to shed light onto my darkness. I paid attention to everything that happened there, to my teachers, to my fellow students, and to my books. I was mindful of what was expected of me, and of what it looked like to be normal. School, miraculously, held out a promise of restoration and of transformation. I knew when I was reading stories or listening to the ones my teacher would read out to us that there was something in them that was trying to reach me – an interesting phrase, a joyous message, a lesson to be learned. In the classrooms of my childhood, every word, every gesture, every lesson, and every story was ripe with meaning. I sat in my seat savouring such moments, feeling guilty, and yet also stunned at the possibility of a future different from the past – of an end to slavery, a beginning of freedom.

Geneviève brought me to the classe d'accueil (the "reception class" for newly arrived immigrant children) where a visible diversity of children aged 8, 9, and 10 were working on a lesson in arithmetic with their teacher. Geneviève introduced her to me. The teacher had a face that was bright with good intentions. Her name was Sylvie and she was *d'ancien souche* – a descendant of the original French settlers to New France in the 1600s. Sylvie – another name from out of my childhood stories!

I was invited to speak to her class, and the first thing I told the children was that I had been a pupil in this very school when I was the same age that they were now. They looked very surprised at this. And it was indeed a surprising piece of news – hard to believe. What was I doing there? Was I coming back from the dead? The students seemed to sense that there was something unusual – and yet very familiar – about me. I felt that they knew instinctively that we all had something important in common. I also told them that at that time we spoke English in this school and not French. (Of course it would certainly not have been appropriate then for me to go into any of the history of the Separatist movement and how the Parti Québecois who were voted into power in 1976 transformed the social, political and linguistic landscape of Quebéc forever.)

Later on I sat as an observer at the back of Sylvie's class next to a brown bunny rabbit, the class's mascot, which hopped around in its cage. I looked out of the large windows which lined the far wall of the classroom and onto the old brick apartment buildings across the street. How many times had I drawn pictures of those very same rundown apartment buildings imagining children sitting on the balconies and flowers on the entrance lawns? Hoping for a better tomorrow. The pure snow continued falling softly outside; it looked very 'Christmassy.' In turns the children stole glances at me. Some of them smiled at me and I smiled back at them. We had already formed an invisible bond that was rooted in a common suffering. Some of these children had clearly been through hell; one could sense that from a mile away. While the children were working on their arithmetic, the teacher came over to me and told me that some of the black children spoke French patois and were from Haiti. Others were from Ghana, Guyana, Somalia, the Sudan, Sri Lanka, Rwanda, and the Congo. Some of the children looked Slavic – I found out that they were from parts of the former Yugoslavia – Bosnia, Croatia and Serbia. One was from Romania. There were also some children there from China. Others were from Iraq, Iran and Afghanistan. One child, sitting a little apart from the others, was from Russia and had lived in Israel for several years. What were their stories, I wondered? They probably wondered about mine. But one thing seemed clear: we were all children that had come from the Land of War.

After a time, the teacher told the children to put away their arithmetic books. Suddenly we were in a leçon de français. She wrote some nouns on the board: Pupitre. Horaire. Ecole. Garçon. Fille. Magasin. And then she asked, "Quelle est la définition d'un article?" ("What is the definition of an article?") Thus began a lesson on the definite and indefinite articles in French. As the children brought out their cahiers de français, I was transported back to the French classes I had taken in that very school, perhaps even in that very same classroom.

My French classes had been my salvation and my French teacher the Fairy Godmother I had longed for. Her name was Madame Simon and she was truly beautiful. She was originally from Morocco but had lived in Paris for many years before emigrating to Montreal. This was in the mid - to late 1950s and she wore clothes I had never seen before. They were the latest styles and they quite astonished me. She was a slender and tall woman with cobalt blue eyes and jet-black hair done up in a chignon. She wore high heels which made a pleasant clacking sound as they touched the floor when she walked around the classroom dictating words for us to write into our cahiers during Dictée. Her soft voice, mingled with her perfume, travelled through the air. I felt blessed to be in her elegant presence. And I became her disciple although I never told her so – I was too much in awe of her. She was a goddess that I could worship only from afar. I always had the right answer to any question she asked of us in class. Puzzled by my enthusiasm, she came over to me early on in the year and asked me whether I had a French-speaking mother. (One other child in the class did.) I had to tell her "no" wishing that I could have said "yes."

What I couldn't explain then to Madame Simon was that my mother was the very opposite of her – a woman driven by the guilt of survival from the concentration camp where she had been interned for three years along with my father. My mother would weep about her two brothers who had been sent off to the death camp at Treblinka. She was supposed to have taken care of them. How are you supposed to take care of someone in a Nazi concentration camp? Yet those were the final words to her from her own mother as they stood gathered in the main square of their city, Czestochowa, in Poland, being herded onto the railway cattle cars: "Take care of your brothers. Don't lose sight of them." Nobody could have understood then that was to be an impossible demand. One day my mother had lost track of them. There had been an "action" (deportation) and the two young boys were forced into the long line for the train bound for Treblinka. They likely were sent directly to the gas chambers upon their arrival. My mother was grief-stricken when she discovered they were gone. She never really recovered from this loss.

Verschwinden – lost forever. I hate that word, Verschwinden. It smells of burnt flesh and blood-soaked fields in bleak windswept landscapes. The blood of my relatives. Corpses piled one atop the other in deep pits. I am sure the fields at Auschwitz, Treblinka, Maidanek, Sobibor, and all the other concentration camps are very fertile now. I am told birds sing there now and that the fields are covered in flowers. There were no birds or flowers then when the prisoners there were being systematically incinerated. My mother and father knew all about hatred and anti-Semitism in pre-war Poland and in Nazi-occupied Poland. They were forced out of their homes into wretched ghettos and then into concentration camps. In my mind I still see pictures of little children in the ghettos, emaciated, their eyes searching for God. Many starved in those humiliating places, places infested with rats and lice and bodies rotting in the streets. And then in 1942 they were all deported to the various camps. What became of the teddy bears of the children who were suffocated in the gas chambers? When I was a child, I believed that God had suffered with them. I was afraid to think of any other possibility.

Because my mother and father had been young and able-bodied they were sent to a prison just outside their hometown as slave laborers for the Nazis – a prison that became a labour ammunitions "factory." With meager food rations and with lice infestation everywhere, disease was rampant. Many people in that camp died of typhus. When anyone looked ill, they were either shot immediately or transported to a death camp. My father had saved my mother's life a number of times there. One day he lost track of her and rushed out to the area where the "line-ups" took place. There were Nazis everywhere shouting, pointing guns, standing in black boots and shiny uniforms. My father saw her amidst this cacophony – in that long line toward Hell. He decided that he didn't care then whether he lived or died, he wanted to be with her. He ran towards the line and pulled her out. "For some unfathomable reason", he would later tell, "they didn't shoot me. Maybe they didn't notice or maybe for that one moment they just couldn't be bothered. Who knows? I just didn't want to live without her." I guess you could call that a love story – a love story in slavery.

But enough about Hell for now. I want to go back to Hope. This is what I always struggled toward as a child – toward the Land of the Living. And my Land of the Living was in fact this very place, Fielding School. What I did not fully realize back then was that living in Montreal offered me the chance of a lifetime: the chance to escape into somebody else's cultural and linguistic landscape, and thereby the chance to hold fast onto life. School – and especially my French classes – became my refuge. It was my imaginings of belonging to French-Canadian culture that lit up my heart and changed the destiny of my soul. Learning French, in Fielding School, became my foster home – a place where I could navigate among communities that were full of life and energy and continuity. The childhood stories which I wrote there describing the lives of French-Canadian families, nourished me through their dynamic relation to the world. I felt safe at my desk in class immersed in these writings because they opened an escape route from the six

CHAPTER ONE

million ghosts that haunted all of my everyday conscious as well as unconscious moments. I wrote then, as I do now, as a means of reclaiming my personal and professional territory: "along the path of discovery ... from mourning and in the reparation of mourning ... one writes from death towards death in life" (Cixous p. 21, in Sellers, 1996).

I brought myself back to the present as I sat at the back of Sylvie's classroom and began to read the posters on the wall. There were signs saying;

Donne un coup de main à ta planete. (Give your planet a hand.)

Un bel environnement pour notre futur. (A beautiful environment for our future.)

Evitons le gaspillage. Réutilisons nos vieux papiers. (Avoid waste. Recycle your old papers.)

These posters make sense for children who are fortunate enough to live in a land of plenty. But do they make any sense for children who have just barely escaped poverty, oppression, and war? Some of them have never even been to a school before now. Some have never had enough to eat before now. And some of them are trying very hard to look "normal" and to hide any signs of trauma. I know something about that. I've been trying to hide woundedness all my life. I probably always will. It was in Fielding School that I had written in my diary: *"Put a smile on your face. Try to look as "normal" as you can. Try to look like you belong. Maybe one day you will."* At least when I was at school I was surrounded by other children (both Jewish and non-Jewish) some of whose parents had also been through *that war*. This certainly gave us an unstated bond of camaraderie. We never talked about it. We didn't have to. But it was comforting to somehow know that we were not alone. When I spoke with some of the children later, I learned that their desires were very similar to what mine had been – to escape their traumatic pasts toward the dream of a better future.

Then I noticed a calendar hanging on the wall near to where I was sitting. The calendar had been a joint class project with an elementary school a few blocks away from Ecole Fielding. Tears filled my eyes as I read the inscription underneath.

A L'Ombre de L'Arbre de Paix
Mon monde de paix, c'est:
Un, des gens fiables, bien aimables;
deux, sans vandalisme, sans racisme;
trois, violence et mépris
    bannis pour la vie!
quatre, ne plus de pollution, population à l'unisson!
Un monde de paix,
C'est quand les insensées guerres
S'éffacent de la merveilleuse cité de la Terre;
Les enfants, le coeur rempli d'amour,

14

Riront avec beaucoup d'humour.
Dans ce monde de paix
Les parents reconnaîtront de leurs enfants
De multiples talents;
Ils les accepteront tels qu'ils sont;
Et ils les aimeront sans condition. (décembre 2001)

Sylvie gave the children another written assignment to work on. With an expectant look, she then came over again to speak with me at the back of the room. We stood and talked quietly. Her eyes seemed filled with sadness as she spoke about the pain that these children carry into the classroom. She told me that she feels their loneliness but feels powerless to change their personal circumstances. "They have been through so many changes, so many problems, so many disappointments; but now they are in a better place. Why can't they call this place home? Sometimes it's all too much for me. I am taking on their anxieties and I feel weary." She told me that as a child she had gone to St. Mark's, an English Catholic school nearby, and always thought of Fielding School as being "very ugly." Even though she is French-Canadian, her parents had sent her to St. Mark's to learn English because, she explained: "Bilingualism, as Prime Minister Trudeau's vision for Canada, became very important in the late 1960s when I was going to school." And she added: "So I knew how difficult it is to learn a new language even though I didn't have to leave my home, or my country. I just can't imagine what these children have been through."

Indeed, learning a new language is difficult enough without the loss of one's cultural context. To be torn away from one's culture and from one's homeland, as was the case with these children, creates a situation where they don't believe that their stories are worth very much. Sylvie confessed to me that when she passed Fielding School on her way to St. Mark's every day in her childhood, she would notice that "all those immigrant kids looked so unhappy and foreign that I never really wanted to know them." "I was one of those kids at an earlier time," I told her. "I know", she answered, "but you look so different now. That is why I am telling you this. I came back here as a teacher and am now faced with the immigrant kids that I avoided when I was young. And now they have all piled into my classroom and I feel helpless – and also guilty," Tears welled in her eyes.

I surveyed the class. The children were all busy working at their desks. None of them looked up. The late autumn light was beginning to dim as the end of the school day approached. Sylvie told me about how for the first three months after their arrival the girls just cry and the boys hide their misery by acting out or by shutting down. "There is so much anger, frustration and despair in them. I just don't know if I can go on because I feel so exhausted by their pain. My husband suggested that I create some distance emotionally between myself and these children."

Sylvie proceeded to point out some of the different pupils and to tell me about the particular brand of suffering of each of them. I knew that I didn't have much time left with her but I wanted to leave her with some kind of gift, something concrete to hold onto. I sensed that she was a caring teacher searching for some sign of hope. She waited for me to respond to what she had said. Why is it that people think that just because I had suffered as a child of Holocaust survivors, I will necessarily have some magic wand that can 'absolve' them of all their fears? And yet at certain times I do. I said to her: "Before you give up on what you are doing here in this classroom and in this school, remember that you are a witness to the suffering of these children. Maybe they have nobody else who can serve that purpose. And do you have any idea of how important that role really is? It could make such a difference in their lives. For many of these children, this school is the safest place that they have ever known. And your compassion is having a healing effect on them whether you realize it or whether you don't."

I looked into her eyes and continued: "I was lucky enough to have had a teacher like that right here in this school a long time ago when you had still not entered St. Mark's and when I was struggling to survive. This teacher didn't say very much to me personally but she did take me in her arms sometimes and held me as I wept after class. It was a blessing and I have not forgotten it. Don't be afraid to look into the heart of the pain of your pupils. The challenge is to make them feel worthwhile and loved and respected. It is in fact these children, these strangers, these "others", these unwanted beings who can remind a teacher of what the real meaning and the real purpose of their profession actually is." The bell rang; it was the end of the school day. Sylvie and I hugged each other and she said gratefully that this for her was *"un retour au passé"* (a return to the past) and I answered her: *"pour moi aussi"* (for me as well).

Forty years ago when I was a small child at Fielding School my personal life was shrouded in veils of sorrow. School was my only ray of hope. And here I was, back into the past, to nurture this teacher who as a child had not wanted to be anywhere near someone like me. But I was one of the lucky ones who had been given sustenance and I wanted to share the gift of this good fortune. This doesn't happen to every lost soul but it happened to me. This is the story that I wish to share with all teachers. A classroom is both a dangerous and a wondrous place. It can destroy students or it can save them. I wanted this teacher, Sylvie, to be open to the mystery and the possibilities inherent in her classroom, a classroom full of diverse faces and voices and life stories. But most of all, I wanted her to realize that teachers are indeed capable of making a difference.

It was still snowing softly outside as I left the school building. Memories began to swirl around me as I walked about in the crisp air. I needed to wander through the streets of the neighbourhood. Suddenly I felt like a little child again...

NOTES

[1] In this book many names are pseudonyms, including names of schools.

CHAPTER TWO

LIVING IN TWO WORLDS

I learn so as to be contented.

-Tsuk Ubai stone wash basin in the Ryoanji Temple

EARLY YEARS

"Language is the only homeland," writes poet Czeslaw Milosz. But for me it was not the language of my homeland that saved me; it was the language of strangers. The challenge I faced was to re-invent my life, and language offered me the tools to accomplish this task. I was four years old when I discovered French-Canadians, and I will forever be grateful that I grew up in their midst. It was in the early 1950s in the Province of Québec, and Maurice Duplessis, an ultra conservative, populist premier was in power. He was not interested in the cosmopolitan nature of Montreal nor in the great influx of immigrants and refugees from World War II who were arriving with languages and cultures that were foreign to Québec. Who were those people anyway arriving with so little material baggage and with so much pain? And the "Anglostocracy" (the English-Canadians of high socio-economic status) who were really in charge of Montreal at the time simply ignored us. Sometimes in my imagination I could see them holding their noses. We must have seemed like quite bedraggled beings to some of them, and like poor souls to others. I didn't know any Anglo kids until I went to school and when I finally met them, they seemed to me to be as distant as the moon.

But I am getting ahead of things. We lived in a very low-income working-class area at the east end of the city –- half immigrant and half French Canadian. Although these early years were a time of distress for my family, they were, for me, also a time of wonder as I witnessed the vitality and laughter of our French-Canadian neighbours – even though they too were all struggling to put food on the table. It must have seemed obvious how desperate our circumstances were. I was terrified of the rats that congregated in the cellar. There was little problem of discipline in our home. All my parents had to say was that they would put us in the cellar if we misbehaved. I never stepped out of line nor would it have occurred to me to do so. To be rebellious first requires a certain degree of security and confidence and that was not a part of our vocabulary. I tried to capture the desolation which engulfed my childhood when I wrote the following piece several years ago.

CHAPTER TWO

Searching for Home

There is a yearning in my soul that may never be quenched. A sense of loss so huge that it swallows me. I used to feel helpless and hopeless in its thrall. How do I describe this longing for light and love and hope and justice? Where people are fortunate enough to believe in a world that makes sense, and in the continuity of families through the generations; and that good will triumph over evil.

What do you think it does to a child to know that her native language, the language of her home, her ancestors, is dying a bloody death? To know that this language and the culture it represents has been cut in its prime. Killed. Mutilated. Tormented. Humiliated. Brutalized.

To know that if she had been born ten years earlier, in the place where her parents had been born, that she would have been exterminated. What do you think it does to such a child? To enter the last scene of a macabre dance of death. What lay ahead for her? Where would her life fit? Her parents had survived an unthinkable catastrophe, but to what purpose? Was the world a better place for it? Nobody wanted to hear about the tragedy. They were embarrassed by it. Or they preferred to ignore it.

Her parents had come to a new land of immigrants, refugees, and survivors. The only reality she knew was that she was not safe, and that her parents could not protect her. Hitler was always out there. Waiting. She had to be ever vigilant. She was alone and afraid. No fairy tales to keep her warm. In her desperate search for meaning, she was forced to re-invent her life. She held on for a miracle, and remarkably the miracle came. And that miracle was language – a new language, a new home, and a new beginning.

There is a longing in me for "normalcy"– what others take for granted… To be able to teach your children your home language because there is a homeland where they may use it and feel pride. To know that there is still a physical link between you and that Old World. That you can visit the place where your parents grew up, that little town in which their stories lived. Or, at least, to be able to visit the gravestones of your ancestors there.

I cannot take such things for granted because I cannot have them. They are gone with the winds of the War. Winds that still blow with hatred and racism and evil. Even as we enter a new century, a new millennium.

When I first wrote this I was elated because it had been embedded in me like shrapnel for a long, long time. When these words finally found their way onto paper I recognized consciously and for the first time the extent of the pain and I therefore also realized the magnitude of the respite that I was offered from it. I am not certain about the possibility of healing; that may be too grand a hope. But I do have faith in the mystery of one's own destiny. And my destiny was tied up in the powers of language and cultural diversity which restored my faith in living. Now, as an adult, I understand the presence of larger forces – of the Divine so to speak, of Angels, and of Providence (*Mazal,* in Hebrew) – which must certainly have directed my every thought and movement. But back then, when I was merely a child, I only sat in silence and waited for whatever might come by and enable me to survive. I was waging my own private battle against *that war* which still sought to devour the surviving remnants of the genocide. I didn't know it then, but I know it now, that in the shadows of those twilights of the Montreal evenings of my childhood, I was asking for deliverance. And someone listened...

My father brought home a mysterious object one evening. It looked like a bulky piece of furniture with a dark screen and several knobs. I turned the knobs expecting to hear words as I had from our radio. But instead something incredible happened. There were moving pictures on the screen and I could *see* the images *speaking*. There were all sorts of stories, and shows with puppets and dolls and with real live people. How did they all get into the box? There was Channel Six for English and *Canal Deux* for French, but where else in the world in the mid-1950s (other than in Montreal and in its environs) could you turn on a television and discover the amazing Channel Seven, which offered programs in French for several hours each day and then magically transformed itself and offered English programs. You didn't even have to turn any knob; it happened all by itself.

I will never forget the sense of adventure that I felt as I would turn to that channel and wonder which language and which culture would greet me. The whole experience had a mysterious feel to it – like 'forbidden fruit' – and I watched those programs intensively. Channel Seven became my role model for "bilingualism within a multicultural context"[1] well before that concept entered the Canadian national discourse. How effortlessly one could traverse from one culture into another and (somehow hope to) be accepted by both of them. I became a joyful traveler, a border-crosser. For me this became an everyday reality. This love affair began the moment I heard the glamorous sounds of French over the radio when I was a very small child and it completely swept me off my feet a few years later as I watched Channel Seven and stepped over into the fantasy of a New World – or should I say *"un nouveau monde."* This fantasy grew to become the pathway to a recovery of passion and of meaning and of hope in my life. My longing to be in the French Canadian milieu became an act of devotion so complete that I found my source of healing there. And only now, many decades later, do I really understand the extent of the divine intervention that took place there, in that sacred Montreal of my childhood dreams. But before French there were other languages...

PUBLIC AND PRIVATE WORLDS

The Private World

Is it possible that the experience of language is the only teacher of language? For me there was language *inside* and there was language *outside*. Language at home was language *inside*. And there were two of them. Polish was spoken between my parents as their language of communication. It had a melodious sound to it and even today when I hear Polish it seems to me as soft as a springtime breeze. But this was stolen pleasure. Using the Polish language was a highly ambivalent communicative activity for my parents after World War II. It was the language they had spoken in the mainstream society in Czestochowa where they had lived. But at their homes they had spoken Yiddish with their families. They were schooled in Polish but also took Yiddish and Hebrew lessons at *'Cheder'* – afternoon educational programs which focused on Yiddish literacy as well as the learning of Hebrew (the language of the Bible), and also Torah studies. Bilingualism (and indeed often multilingualism) has been an integral part of the Jewish experience throughout the millennia. Hebrew was always the sacred language of liturgy no matter what the lingua franca, the spoken language, might have been. Jesus, for example, spoke in Aramaic but he wrote in Hebrew. Since the State of Israel was founded in 1948, Hebrew has become the vernacular as well as the sacred. But again I digress.

The realm of Polish in my home was reserved exclusively for my parents' use. There seemed to be a fence around it, which we as children were not permitted to penetrate. There was nothing seemingly unusual about this; it just was the way it was and this never had to be stated in an overt manner. We knew that Polish was their domain and all that was important to us at the time was just to try to figure out what it was that they were saying to each other. I cracked this code quite early on but knew that my knowledge of that language would have to remain passive. Something was very wrong with that language and only later, when I was of school age, did I discover exactly what it was. I knew that this wasn't a mere matter of communicative competence. My parents were able to discuss literally anything using that language as medium. They read and they wrote in that language. They enjoyed literature and poetry in that language. And I loved to hear my mother speak on the telephone with her friends in Polish or to listen to radio during the Polish hour. I had plenty of opportunities to become familiar with it. But this was where it had to end. And I never questioned this.

We had another language in our home that was in fact the medium of communication between my parents and us their children. It was Yiddish, and it too was beautiful – but in a very different way. I think I understood the Whorf-Sapir hypothesis long before I was literate. Language and culture were inextricably bound but other issues were involved as well. I instinctively knew that the notion of identity was omnipresent in this duality and that it mattered very much. Who was I really? And where did I belong? One thing I sensed well before my parents actually put any of it into words: Polish and Yiddish were not friends with one another. In fact the tension between the two languages was distressing and oppressive. They inhabited the same space in my home but powerful, invisible borders held them apart. Only by means of listening could I transcend those borders and enjoy the 'dangerous' presence of Polish at home. But my own spoken words found their expression in Yiddish, which was the acceptable means of communication at our home because Yiddish was *our* language, that of the Jewish people of Eastern Europe. There were no rules either spoken or unspoken to prevent Yiddish from entering the space of conversation between my parents and their children. And Yiddish was such a gentle language. But unfortunately it was a very fragile one because it had survived an unspeakable catastrophe. Yiddish was a bird with a broken wing.

This is how I knew, so very long ago – well before I knew how to read or write – that the language of Yiddish was not merely a language and that the same as well was true for Polish. These languages had people who spoke them and they each represented thoughts, ideas, a history, a collective consciousness, a way of looking at the world, a *culture*. Some people (like my parents) could speak both languages but that did not mean that they were accepted in both cultures. This was a mysterious and confusing revelation which led me to understand the complexity of language learning and the fluidity of 'culture' at a much earlier age than my monolingual friends. And, most importantly, I came to understand that the intertwined realms of language, culture and identity had been violated by *that war*. Most of the people in the concentration camp where my parents were incarcerated spoke both Yiddish and Polish. But my young mind understood well enough that it was mainly because they spoke Yiddish that they were forced into that place – with perhaps a few exceptions. That, at least, is how I explained it to myself.

Many of the Polish people my parents knew before *that war* were hostile to them. They had lived in a city which was a Catholic pilgrimage site. Many of their non-Jewish neighbours openly considered Jews to be Christ-killers. One story, which although minor in terms of the hideous persecution that took place during the war, has always stayed with me. It took place in the mid-1930s in a very anti-Semitic Poland. My mother's little brother (who would later be killed) was walking home from school. He was about six years old at the time and he wore glasses. Suddenly a bunch of older boys overwhelmed him and beat him unconscious all the while yelling that he was the anti-Christ. His eyeglasses were shattered beyond repair. The family was so poor that they didn't have the money needed to replace his glasses and so he had to miss school. I don't know whether he ever got a new pair of glasses; I hope that he did…

I got my first pair of glasses in Grade Four at the age of nine and felt quite excited about them. The frames were a beautiful shade of blue and I felt very grown-up as I walked out of the optometrist's store. But then I remembered the story about my mother's little brother and guilt overcame me. In a moment all my excitement vanished. Years later, when I saw the Alfred Hitchcock film "The Birds" the scene in which the birds attack the children on their way home from school was too much for me. What frightened me most was the moment when one boy's glasses are knocked off his face and become shattered amidst the chaos. It was just too real for me. To me this wasn't just a young actor in a horror film. This was my little uncle. In my young mind Polish became a shadowy menace while Yiddish was deeply wounded. And the Nazis, who were even more evil and who callously rounded up Jews and sent them to their deaths, spoke in yet another language altogether. It was German, and I came early to the conclusion that it was the Devil Himself who had chosen to speak that language.

However although I was born into their sorrow, I found that I could not remain forever with the dead. Had I done so, I too would eventually have died spiritually, if not also physically. So I really had no choice. I abandoned my tortured Yiddish and went out into the world of Montreal where I made friends with two new languages: French and English. In my heart I wept for the lost and fragile bird named Yiddish, but its ghosts always remained to comfort me.

The Public World

Ma Chère Françoise. Françoise Leduc, who was my next-door neighbour, is etched in my memory forever. She was about the same age as I, but that is where any similarity between us ended. Her large blue eyes always shone with life and laughter. My brown eyes were clouded with sorrow and with shame. She had ever so many relatives who would come over to her house and visit on Sundays after church. I sat alone on my stoop watching them hug and kiss one another on both cheeks (the French way) carrying pots and pans filled with deliciously smelling cooked foods. My mouth may have watered then but my eyes never did. Tears came only many years later when as an adult I became healthy enough to face the pain. My traumas were just too great at the time.

All I could do was watch and wait. There are a few black and white photographs of me as a child, although not very many. My parents could not afford such luxuries. There is one picture of me holding a skipping rope, wearing a disheveled dress which was torn at the elbows. Françoise actually took that photo. In it I am trying to smile but cannot quite make it. My eyes have dark circles under them. I looked like Raggedy Ann. Françoise always looked fresh, like a little princess with pink bows in her blond hair. Her bows were not necessarily all that new and neither were her clothes, but they looked so much better than mine – at least that was my perception at the time. However, oddly enough, Françoise liked me. I couldn't quite figure out why, but what surprised me more was that somehow we were able to communicate even though I could not yet fully speak in the magnificent language that rolled off her tongue so effortlessly.

Ma chère langue française! It was the French language which offered me the first glimpse of any real hope in this world. I remember the excitement – the adrenalin "rush" – which I experienced the very first time I heard the sounds of French coming out of a radio. Different, Foreign, Enticing, Unknown. More interesting, more cheerful. Songs in French seemed full of life and French life seemed full of songs. I ran into the arms of the French language like an orphan child seeking its warmth and shelter. And there she was for me – *la langue française* – lovely and so accessible. I was in heaven, transfixed; I *knew* that I had found my foster home. *I believed* in French just as a devout Roman Catholic might believe in salvation. And I knew that I could have all of the keys to its kingdom. All that I had to do was just to hang around with Françoise. I started to spend a great deal of time at her place.

My mother seemed relieved at this development. Looking back, I realize now that it must have taken some of the everyday pressures and responsibility off her mind. I now understand that she was utterly imprisoned in her grief and in her guilt, alternating between weeping hysterically and then silently about her losses. Sometimes I felt that my ghostly uncles who had been killed in Treblinka were more real to her than I was. And secretly I hated her for that. But I also hated myself for being so ungrateful, after everything she had suffered. How dare I have expected her to be able to mother me? And how dare I even to have had such forbidden feelings? She herself needed someone to care for her. But I was a small child in need of a mother. Yet the Holocaust reigned supreme. There was no space for the neediness of an emotionally bereft little girl who rocked herself to sleep at night, terrified that Hitler might come at any time and carry her off to the lands of her parents' nightmares.

I always felt safe in Françoise's home. The lights seemed brighter there and none of Hitler's Gestapo seemed to be hiding in any corner or under any bed there. I remember my first invitation for dinner to her place. I was excited at this but also nervous that I might do or say something wrong and that they would not want to see me again. But finally when the moment arrived and I was seated at their arborite table with its chrome trimming and padded chairs, I was able to relax. Theirs looked pretty much the same as our kitchen set except that it was newer. Françoise had two older brothers and one baby sister. In the midst of all the savoury food being offered and amidst the pleasant sounds of easy-going conversation, I could make out many of the words spoken but these were the ones that struck me most: *"La pauvre petite; ses pauvres parents; c'est pitoyable ce qui est passé aux Juifs là-bas; Quelle horreur; Seigneur, donnez-leur Votre misericorde."* Even at that young age I realized they were pitying my family and asking the Lord to have mercy on our souls, us, the Jews. As I grew older I knew that I did not want to be pitied and that I did not want to feel "deviant", but at that time I felt safe in the midst of their genuine sadness and somehow, at the time, this seemed to me to be good enough.

I remember also that they all clasped their hands together at the beginning of the meal, bowed their heads and mumbled some prayer to the *Vièrge Marie.* A strange feeling of being a traitor then overcame me. Was I, a Jew, really supposed to be involved in this? These were *"goyim"* (a word which means "gentiles" in Hebrew) and didn't their religion condemn the Jews for having killed somebody very important to them, somebody named *Le Seigneur*, somebody whom they loved very much? A sense of unease swept over me. I knew that by being involved here I had done something bad but didn't understand fully what it was. All I knew was that this man whom they called Jésus had (like my parents and like my other relatives) also suffered terribly. Was there any connection here? I was too afraid to ask.

Sometime during the meal I looked up at the wall and saw an image hanging there of a half-naked man on a large wooden cross. He had thorns in his hair and his head was slumped to one side. Is that a red gash in his rib? Was he dead? I somehow understood in an instant that he was the one they loved so much; the one they had accused the Jews of having killed. Many confusing thoughts ran through my young brain. But one thing was clear to me. If he had suffered so much (and just looking at him up there on that cross it was obvious that that was the case) then he *must* have been Jewish. This was a startling revelation to me and yet I knew in my heart that it must be true. Maybe I had once heard my parents say this; or maybe I had only dreamt it – I had no clue as to how this information had come to me. But I did know. And somehow I was also just as certain that Françoise had no idea at that time that Jesus was in fact a Jew. What a strange secret had just been given to me! I guarded that secret carefully and began to feel closer to that poor man hanging there so sadly. Did he by any chance know any of my relatives who had also been killed in a terrible way? I was afraid to bring up this line of discussion with my parents. Somehow I understood that this would hurt them and that they could not take on any more pain. So I just silently carried with me that magical piece of knowledge.

Next to Jesus, high on a shelf, stood a statue. It was of a woman in a long white robe, white veil, and a sky-blue cape. Her arms were outstretched and a halo of stars surrounded her head. How peaceful she appeared, although she had a faraway look in her eyes. After the Leduc family (except for their baby Lisette) finished their prayers they crossed themselves from the top of the head to the heart and then to each shoulder and up to the mouth. Madame Leduc then went over to that statue and crossed herself again. So this was the *Vièrge Marie*. For me on that warm July evening, only a few weeks before my fifth birthday, it was a love at first sight. *Un coup de foudre*. This was the Holy Mother Mary, *la Sainte Mère*. Françoise wore a pretty gold medallion around her neck with an image of this woman engraved on it. Earlier, when we had been playing hopscotch in the afternoon, I had asked her about her necklace as I had never seen one like it before. My friend's face had a smile on it as she explained to me that *La Sainte Mère* was the Mother of God and that she had great powers of healing for anyone who believed in Her[2]. She could perform miracles and cures. She could comfort even the most downtrodden. She would take you into her arms even if you had committed a *sin*. She would help you get back onto the right path. She was especially mindful of those in deep suffering and was called by many other names: Our Lady of Sorrows, of Perpetual Help, of Peace, of Miracles, of Charity, of the Sacred Heart, Queen of Heaven, Queen of Angels, Queen of the World, and so on. And many churches in Montreal were named after Her, such as the beautiful Basilica in Old Montreal *Notre Dame, (Our Lady)*. And then Françoise looked at me quite seriously and said, "She has your name too: *Notre Dame de Grâce.*"

At this I was taken aback. "How could that be?" I asked her earnestly. We both sat down on the grass and thought about it. Françoise too was intrigued. "Maybe there is a Catholic in your family," she said to me, her eyes glittering at the possibility that perhaps I was a part of her religious world after all. "No, I don't think so," I replied with considerable conviction. But Françoise did not seem at all convinced by my answer, while for my part I was fascinated that I too had something special in common with this powerful woman – a name, a holy name – Grace. Salut *Marie, pleine de Grâce, priez pour nous*. Hail Mary, full of Grace, pray for us.

Mary, full of Grace. For perhaps the first time in my young life, a sense of joy overcame me and transported me out of the dreariness of my own family story. An awesome thought tugged at a corner of my mind: Could Mother Mary be my Holy Mother too? Could she take me, psychological orphan that I was, and put her arms around me in the stillness of night? Could she feed me with her love? Could she protect me? I knew that my older brother had been born under the icon of the Black Madonna – the *Matka Boska* – at the monastery of the *Jasna Gora* in Czestochowa, my parents' hometown, immediately after the end of the war. A part of the monastery had been turned into a makeshift hospital at the time. My mother described for me how the Polish women who were also there delivering their own babies whispered in hushed tones that my mother was a "Jew" – as if she had come from some far-away planet. And I guess this had in a sense really been true: she had come back from the dead. And there she was about to give birth to a new life. I think that my brother may in fact have the distinction of being the first and perhaps the only Jewish child to have been born at the *Jasna Gora* where the *Matka Boska* was "in attendance."

The *Matka Boska* story filled me with wonder and in my young mind I interpreted it to mean that Mary had saved my brother's life. She became my only hope and I decided to adopt her. But I didn't breathe a word of this to anyone. I felt as if I finally had an ally, a guardian angel, a powerful friend. I was taking my first tentative steps toward the life force yet my heart oscillated between excitement and a guilt-ridden foreboding of punishment to come for so heinous a crime. I have been waiting for a thunderbolt to strike me ever since. But at the time I needed my *Sainte Mère* (Holy Mother Mary) and that took precedence over other considerations. I had found a way to survive. In the years to follow I became more and more serious about "studying" the lifestyle of the Leduc family, and of the French-Canadian culture more generally, its language and its religion. I had no idea that I was at the time already in training to become the disciplined sociolinguist and educational ethnographer that was eventually to become my professional work as a university professor.

But well before my university career I became an elementary schoolteacher and in my heart I will never be far away from the classroom – from any classroom. Because School, and especially French classes, saved my life, and the classroom became my true and only home.

NOTES

[1] Prime Minister Pierre Elliot Trudeau enshrined this concept in federal law in 1971.

[2] It goes without saying that Françoise had surely no awareness of the fact that the historical Mary was actually a devout Jewish woman.

CHAPTER THREE

RETURN TO FIELDING

The market value of the very young is small. Only in the sight of God is the apple blossom worth as much as the apple; Green shoots as much as a field of ripe corn.

-Janusz Korczak

My second visit to Fielding School took place during a hastily planned trip to Montreal in December almost exactly one year after the first one. My husband and I were preparing to leave for a six-month sabbatical in Berkeley, California. This visit to Montreal was not a formal research trip and I did not tell anyone in advance that I was coming. This time I did not arrive to the school in the triumph of professorship and this time I did not arrive there in a taxi. This time I had walked a great many blocks, starting from my hotel, in biting cold and snow to get there. It was a time for wandering, a moment for returning to a shadowy past, alone. It was a moment for returning to the safety of a hiding place that can never be forgotten: SCHOOL.

This time I came with the innocence of a child's soul. This was *home*. Fielding School will live in my heart forever. The words of Augustine in his *Confessions* (10: 6, 215) describe aptly the near hallucinatory nature of that visit: "Memory affords a bridge between time and eternity. It is a brilliance that space cannot contain; a sound that time cannot carry away; a perfume that no breeze disperses; a taste undiminished by eating; a clinging together that no satiety will sunder." I was staying at a small hotel near the Université de Montréal because my husband had some work obligations there. In spite of the fact that I was exhausted from what had been a busy term and that we were about to go on sabbatical (all that packing!) I decided to come along. I wanted to see Fielding School again.

I had slept in and awoke to the sublime beauty of a Montreal snowstorm. It was actually fairly tame, as Montreal storms go. In the distance from the window I saw a silvery church spire, so ubiquitous in the Montreal of my childhood. I could also see people "slip-sliding" about on the sidewalks. I went outside and into a *librairie-bistro* – a bookstore and bistro combination – as beautiful as any that one might find in Paris. What scenes of jollity greeted me there! People were coming in for lunch taking off wet coats, hugging and kissing one another. Many of the get-togethers were related to the Christmas season. Many of the tables there had *Réservé* signs on them. I sat down in a corner and surveyed the scene. The waiter was young, good-looking and French-Canadian. I was immediately drawn back into my childhood fantasy and decided to succumb to it.

And who knows – maybe Françoise, my first little friend, was one of the people sitting at the other tables. It's not completely outlandish. As far as I could make out, these patrons were all connected with the *Université de Montréal* – either as faculty, students or staff. And there I was anonymous and ghostlike, just as I had been many years earlier looking in at the brightly lit lives near to my home. It seems that I am never too far away from the chaotic quilt of my past. Once again nobody could see behind my façade of a well-dressed woman, ordering a meal of *quiche aux épinards* and *soupe à l'ognion.* And of course *café au lait.* A woman who had an air of confidence about her. How could anyone possibly tell that she was about to embark on a second pilgrimage to her beloved refuge: *School.*

After this meal I started walking, block after block after block, trying in the swirling snow from memory to find the way and retrace my childhood steps to Fielding School. I had forgotten its exact location but was determined to find the place just as a lost child might have done. And I needed to *see* her, and to *be* that lost child once again. And I needed to ask her to forgive me. The street signs began to seem familiar after a while. I stopped to ask a taxi driver for directions. He told me I was on the right track but that there were still several more blocks to go. I passed the hospital where I was born. There was a lot of comings and goings on at a bus stop nearby by people who were busy living their own lives; I was just an anonymous being, a passer-by in the snowy landscape. It was only a few days before Christmas. It occurred to me that this was turning out to be a walk back into my childhood. I had to be careful not to slip on ice because I was now heading downhill.

I tread gingerly during this *promenade* – as a child whose heart was stronger than her feet. But the more I walked, the closer the loneliness became. Loneliness, my old companion. We carried each other towards the school. I passed young mothers with children in their strollers, all bundled up. They were of many colours: Black and Brown and Yellow and White. So many languages could be heard in the air. Suddenly I found myself back in a land of immigrants and refugees. The snow-crunched ground upon which I stood seems to have remembered me. But this time I looked "Canadian." What does it mean to look like a Canadian? The snow was falling fast and hard now. The last few steps were harrowing – ground so icy that I practically ended up on hands and knees as I descended a small staircase leading onto the school's playground. The area was deserted because the students were inside now. I must have just missed their recess.

What a 'homecoming' this was — desolate and unkempt, just as that lost child had been. But I felt that I was on sacred territory now. In my mind's eye, I saw my younger self waiting silently for me at the side of the building in a corner where she once used to console herself. I moved toward her with a sense of longing. In my mind I reached out to embrace her and to tell her that she was alone no longer, that she was a shabby and unwanted outsider no longer. I had come now to take her away from this place of hiding and into the light of second chances, of new identities, and a more fruitful existence. And in this reverie my mind wandered back to the time at the beginning of my salvation.

SCHOOL

It began in kindergarten. It was in the mid-1950s and I was one of those children who couldn't wait to start school. I already knew that there was a world outside of my home that was filled with possibilities and I knew that I needed to find my place there. School was my ticket out of the emotional devastation that hung above me like the sword of Damocles. I was, however, very disappointed when I found out that I would not be allowed to attend the same school in which Françoise was to be enrolled. This came as quite a shock to me, and it deeply shaped my future professional life. In those days, the English and French Canadians of Montreal lived in their "two solitudes"[1] while immigrant communities struggled to learn English in order to be able to survive economically. English Canadians definitely held the purse strings then; there was little question of that. The educational system of Quebec was a confessional one, that is, religiously based, and reflected the original historical realities of Canada's English-French hostility. The Quebec Act, which was drawn up by the English "victors" of the 1759 battle on the Plains of Abraham, divided public education into Catholic for the French, in order that they be permitted to maintain their language and religion, and into the Protestant system for the Anglos. Immigrant non-French kids who were Catholic would choose to attend separate English-speaking Catholic schools because clearly English was the language of power. By the late 1800s, and especially in the early 1900s, immigration brought Jews to Quebec and this became an issue for the province's confessional (i.e. Christian) educational model. So in order for Jews to have a place in schools, a by-law was created in the early 1900s which allowed Jews to be Protestants "for educational purposes." Nice logic! However, for me, this was the bane of my existence. I had desperately wanted to go to the French-speaking Catholic school around the corner with Françoise. There I would have learned French in an authentic atmosphere. But that option was not allowed to me by the authorities. I therefore had to create other authentic ties to French language and culture.

I remember trudging off to my first day at school as if I were going to a different planet –linguistically as well as culturally. And I wondered why this fate had befallen me. I was probably one of the only non-French Canadians who adored the French world in complete innocence. It seemed like a terrible injustice, in my child's mind, to be denied access into their educational system. Indeed this was symbolic of the complex animosity and suspicion — the site of historical struggle – between English and French Canadians, a struggle which still holds Canadians hostage to this day. In any case this was the lot of this immigrant child, a Holocaust urchin just trying survive. But school was SCHOOL be it Protestant or be it Catholic. In the end it didn't matter all that much. What did matter was that *School* brought me into the light of life. It became my sacred space and in it the desert in my soul began to bloom.

CHAPTER THREE

Education became my road to liberation and for this I will always be grateful. Even if on that first day I had very mixed feelings about where I was heading and even though it turned out to be a most difficult day on my long journey to the Land of the Living. But on that very first day of school I was made well aware that I was not part of either majority culture – neither English nor French.

In fact I almost didn't make it to my first day of school. There had been so many children of kindergarten age that year that enrollment had to be cut off by date of birth, and July 1 became the divisor. Since I was born on July 30 it was decided that I would not be admitted that year. Haze of memory has not dulled the tear in my heart when I first learned of this news. And then, a few weeks into the school term, as I was walking around unconsolably at home I heard the telephone ring and my mother repeating words that were being told to her: that a boy was having trouble in class and needed to be taken out of school, that I was next on the waiting list. To this day I have faith in waiting lists. I was nervous and excited that morning half a lifetime ago when I was getting ready for my first day at school. I don't remember what the weather had been like but I do know that a sun was shining in my heart. I also don't remember what I wore that day, but I do know that it couldn't have been fancy. But I felt that it was fancy, and something inside me was bursting with excitement – a feeling both foreign and yet filled with expectation.

When I entered the inner sanctum of the kindergarten classroom on that first day, I believed that all would be well with the world from now on – the hope of a child who had placed all of her gambling chips on a fantasy world called *School*. Yes, there was disappointment that *School* would have to be the English one many blocks away and not the French one just around the corner where all of my friends were going. But no matter. At least I would be there. I felt my heart beating as I was shown to my seat in the long row. It was intimidating to be in an English environment although I was not fully conscious of what I was really feeling at the time. All I knew was that everything that had been familiar to me was now gone, had now vanished by a linguistic sleight of hand. I was quiet as a mouse when the teacher began roll call. I wasn't the most confident child to begin with, given my background. And then came a sense of foreboding. Many family names slid easily off my teacher's tongue. Those were "Canadian" names: names that were easy for the teacher, names that were part of the same club. Some names were a bit different but those she could handle. I felt dread rising within me with each passing letter of the alphabet. And then finally she came to S. There was a Smith before me – I could only imagine such good fortune. And then the inevitable: SREBRNIK. The ultimate tongue twister, the perfect name of not-belonging, a label of outsiderness.

But still I was unprepared for the cruelty to follow. As my teacher stumbled over the three consonants in a row, her face became redder and more upset. I wished she would have asked me how to pronounce my name. That would have ended her agony at once. As I was just about to say my name, she threw the list down on her desk, glared at me and said: **"When you immigrants come to this country, why can't you just shorten your names to make it easier for us?"** I might as well have been hit by a truck. The question reverberated in my ears like a thunderclap. I felt sick; I wanted the floor to open up in front of me and to just disappear. Instead, a sea of little faces all stared at me: some were smirking, but others were as just as frightened as I was. They too had "strange" names; it was just that mine came toward the end of the alphabet and by then the teacher had lost any patience she may have had. I took some comfort in the realization that I was not the only immigrant child in the class. There were other children there of displaced persons from the War. In fact playing in the schoolyard at recess meant being immersed in a multitude of languages and cultures – at that time primarily from Eastern and Central Europe. Multiculturalism to me was as natural as breathing. Those of us who were "different" formed an immediate and unspoken alliance which would carry us through many difficult times.

When I got home that evening I approached my father and, trying to sound nonchalant, I asked him whether we could shorten our family name. He looked genuinely puzzled for a moment and then asked me whether my teacher had suggested this to me. I nodded and burst into tears. My father was usually a prisoner to his silent rage about *that war*. But every so often a ray of sunshine would peer through his sorrow and one could witness what he might have been. And this was one such moment. Stepping outside of his woundedness for a while my father put me on his knee and gave me a hug. "You tell your teacher", he said, "that our name is as good as anybody else's and we're not going to change it – it's our name." His act of defiance gave me back my dignity, and when I walked into class the following day I told the teacher what he had said. She looked annoyed but she never bothered me about my name again. I tell this story for all children in classrooms who understand how easy it is for a teacher or for others to steal their sense of self with a careless indifference. An action doesn't necessarily have to be monstrous to end up causing havoc and or injustice. It can start out very simply with not allowing you to hold onto your name.

Most of the teachers at that time, however well meaning they might have been, did not recognize the value of our cultural backgrounds. They made us feel as if we had an unfortunate burden to carry and that the faster we rid ourselves of it, the better it would be for everyone. But what I came to believe is in fact the opposite. (Sometimes "bad" teachers" can teach you as much or more than "good" teachers.) On that first day of Kindergarten I came to understand that a name is a very sacred thing. Maybe if you have never had your name threatened or mocked, you cannot understand the humiliation. It is, like any other violation, an assault on your personhood. Today, as a university professor, I teach my students about issues of language, culture and identity in educational contexts, and I tell the story of my first day in Kindergarten in almost every such course that I teach.

In spite of such negative messages from some of the teachers about our immigrant status, School still truly was a place of refuge. There was order and quiet, and there were toys and books all around. I remember how I felt when I was chosen to play cymbals in the "band" – like being chosen to be a film star. I also discovered that I enjoyed singing. We learned the Protestant hymns and recited the Lord's Prayer every day and sang "God Save the Queen." I liked the continuity of it. My voice rang out loudly every day. Somehow I knew that it was OK to do all those things as long as you didn't say the name "Jesus." And so whenever the word

CHAPTER THREE

"Jesus" or "Christ" or "Saviour" came up in the hymns, I held silent for that moment. There were several other Jewish children in the class and they too all did the same. Had we discussed this amongst ourselves as a little group? I don't think so – but we clearly knew that we were each other's allies. "Onward Christian Soldiers" had an ominous ring to it. I learned early on that (well before the Holocaust) Jewish blood had often been spilled throughout the millennia all in the name of Christianity. By not saying "Jesus" or "Christ" or "Saviour" I knew I was holding steadfast to my Jewishness and this gave me strength. I had nothing personally against Jesus himself who, as I had gathered, was a wonderful teacher and healer. But, according to what I had heard in my religion, the Messiah had not yet arrived and only God the Father was considered to be divine. I also enjoyed playing skip rope with my classmates on the playground at recess. And when the bell rang to signal the end of recess we all rushed into line and stood straight and quiet as the teacher-on-duty would walk by us toward the school door to lead us back into class. The shuffling of our shoes on the pavement and the scrunching of paper were pleasurable sounds to my ears.

But walking to and from school was an anxiety-provoking activity. I had to cross several large streets, sometimes with classmates but oftentimes alone. The trek was fraught with the noises of cars and trucks and sometimes of police sirens. I always felt relief as the street where I lived came into view but there were still trials ahead. What frightened me most was the viciousness with which the bullies at the end of my street would beat up some of the Jewish kids because they were *"maudits juifs"*, "cursed Jews" who had killed their Christ. These bullies often hid at the back of my favourite candy store as I walked to and from school every day. I was always in terror of being assaulted by them although usually they picked on the boys. Every so often the owner of the candy store, a frail old man, would come out to break up a scuffle waving his finger at the bullies, calling them *"vauriens"* "good-for-nothings." I always felt that I was superior to those fat boys. In the final analysis they too came from homes where there was much suffering, but I was disgusted at the way in which they chose to act out their misery. It never would have entered my mind that humiliating someone who is different from you could be a remedy to assuage your own battered soul. I didn't have respect for that. My first lesson in cross-cultural communication came in fact from my father.

MY FIRST LESSON IN CROSS-CULTURAL UNDERSTANDING

It started with a terrible guilt over a new friendship I was forming in Grade One. She was a tall, boisterous and free wheeling sort of kid – a tomboy and I was immediately drawn to her. She spoke what was on her mind and didn't seem to be afraid of anybody. But when she thought nobody was looking her face showed a bruised expression. I could see the fragility beyond her tough exterior and was intrigued by it. I already admired, even at that young age, anybody who could hide their feelings and put on a good act. And she too wanted to be my friend. Her name was Marianne and it turned out that she lived in the apartment building next to mine – in fact her father was the janitor there. His job offered him a wage as well as a rent-free apartment for his family. But on the third day of our friendship I found out that her parents came from Germany and had also arrived in Canada after World War II. When I discovered this, I was heartbroken. She was the 'enemy.' How could I possibly become her friend? A weight descended upon me as I began to devise ways of avoiding her. She didn't understand what was happening. I hadn't told her that I was Jewish – only that my parents had come from Poland. The bruised look of her green eyes followed me. The joy of school suddenly vanished for me and that was too much – School was the only hope I had and I couldn't afford to lose it.

Once again I decided to confide in my father and tell him about this terrible conundrum. Tears ran down my cheeks as I explained my quandary to him one evening before bedtime. I was prepared for any sort of disapproval or even punishment, but what actually happened was life affirming. He looked at me for a time and simply asked: "Is she a nice girl? Do you like her?" And I answered: "Yes, very much. But she is German." And then my father looked at me in a way I had not seen before. He quietly told me that no matter what had happened during *that war* we have to see one another as individuals and to make our decisions in that way. If Marianne is someone I wanted to play with then that was OK. He told me that her father had in fact been a soldier in the German army but that he really didn't have anything to do with humiliating or killing Jews per se. He then told me that Marianne's father had spent *that war* on the Eastern Front in Russia and had been badly wounded there. I understood for the first time the reason for this man's severe limp.

That is the way my father was: someone who could look beyond stereotypes even under heinous circumstances, and go straight to the heart of the matter. Today I would say that he was an educator for social justice and intercultural harmony. But then he was just a human being who longed for peace and who respected humanity in all its glory and frailty. Little wonder that I ended up devoting my professional life to issues of language, culture and identity within the context of social justice and peace education. My father died many years ago – just two months before I received my faculty position. Perhaps I can forgive myself for having been given what was denied to him because of THAT WAR: the opportunity of higher education, and the blessing of a meaningful and respected profession. And perhaps the only way I can deal with the sorrows of my father's thwarted life is to teach and to write. In this way I can keep his dreams alive.

LES CLASSES DE FRANÇAIS

One question I always ask students of education in my graduate courses is: *"Was there a teacher who made a difference in your life?"* My own answer is a YES in spite of the fiasco of my first day in Kindergarten. I had another teacher in elementary school whose presence changed my life. She was my French teacher and I have already mentioned her in Chapter One. But perhaps it is more what Madame Simon *represented* that really changed the direction of my life. Let me try to untangle the pieces that led to this transformation. My mind often wanders back to those French classes because it was there that a true sense of inner peace first came to me. It was there that I first felt joy in the verbal games and in the grammatical puzzles of learning a new language. I felt delight in knowing that I was thereby building a structure, from the ground up. I was discovering new ways to look at the world, new ways to communicate. I was creating a new identity, a new self, a route of escape, and a viable new community. It was irresistible. *La langue française* said to me: "You will always find strength in your love for me. There will always be a home for you here. You are not unwanted in this new place. *Bienvenue*. Welcome." Young as I was, I could recognize such a blessing when I saw one and was overwhelmed by the generosity of its precious gifts. I felt desolate no longer. Even in the English Protestant schools [the Protestant School Board of Greater Montreal (PSBGM) was the official title] French was a compulsory subject of daily instruction from Grade One onwards. However the school board didn't hire French-Canadians to teach it. And a sort of mirror image of this was also true – no non-Catholics were hired in the Catholic system. This was a most effective way to keep English and French Canadians – "the two solitudes" apart.

How I admired Madame Simon! It never ceases to amaze me how this feeling remains untarnished by time, radiant in its intensity. My ears delighted in the sound of her Parisian accent. How chic! That, I vowed to myself, was the way I was going to speak French. I felt that if I could speak French like that then I too would become as elegant as Mme. Simon. And I thought: "so this is what a French teacher looks and acts like!" and tucked that knowledge away for future reference. I always had my hand up in her class and was always answering the questions. I sought out every opportunity to let French words pour out of me. And they poured from pencil to paper as well. I wrote stories in French about an imaginary family with a kind, gentle mother and a cheerful, robust father and with children having names like Chantal and Lisette and Marie-Thérèse who went to ballet classes and wore pretty dresses, and had lots of relatives who brought them gifts and laughed with them. Life, in the French of my imagination, was just wonderful.

They were a great escape and I held onto those stories as to a life raft. I kept embellishing my characters with more and more detail, using my ever expanding French vocabulary. And I continued to watch television shows in English on Channel Six and in French on *Canal Deux*. For a good part of the day the famous logo with the Indian head was on and only later in the afternoon did shows begin to appear. I adored the special bilingual/bicultural quality of Channel Seven, and always felt a spark of excitement when the programming would cross the English-French "boundaries." Here I caught my first glimpse at the possibility of peaceful coexistence within diversity. And I also figured out a neat trick. I realized that certain English television programs (for example, "Father Knows Best" or "I Dream of Jeannie" or Howdy Doody) would appear on the French channel based on the current English episode but dubbed in French. And so I began a self-taught, personalized course in contrastive analysis. I would diligently watch the English language version first and then the French one, figuring out any new words. When I ran into difficulties I would transliterate the words and ask Mme. Simon about their meaning next day in class. She was amazed at my motivation as were my classmates, many of whom were also immigrant children but who were satisfied with their English language curriculum. They didn't see the value of French in their everyday lives. In fairness to them, it is they who were "normal" and I who was the atypical one. French classes at school became a salvation and I loved them in that profound way that only a child can. Such as when you get your first really fancy toy. I never had any fancy toys or dresses. French became my fancy dress, my escape from the bleak world into which I had been born.

The real beauty of the imagination is that it can create something that did not exist before. Before French, I felt homeless and alone and without direction. After French, I became a person filled with purpose and desire. I remember that when I was in Grade Six and eleven years old I participated in a school project to be a "student teacher" for the pupils in the Grade Two French classes. I remember preparing for these classes very diligently and I recall that Madame Simon was impressed. But it came naturally to me and felt so right. There was never any doubt in my mind that I couldn't pull it off. In front of a class – and especially in front of a French class – I truly became the master of my own destiny. I had found a place in the world. I was going to be just like Madame Simon. I was going to become a French teacher. Although these thoughts were not really fully formed at the time, they held out their promise. Such is the power of "modelling."

I was a child who had been marginalized and humiliated by personal circumstances. Where would I have been without the gentle breezes of Madame Simon's lilting French accent that washed over me, or the fruitful writing time in class when I produced those little poems and stories about my beloved French-Canadian families? The words we copied in *"Dictée"* were magnificent flowers that bloomed in the brokenness of my heart. As they floated softly from Madame's lips onto the pages in my notebook I fell madly in love. How could I have survived without this profound seduction? The power and the privilege of teaching lies in its potential to connect with every student's deepest needs. As a pupil in Madame Simon's French classes, I drank from the endlessly deep well of language. My thirst was unquenchable and my dreams of entering a cultural space where my sense of dislocation could vanish was too strong to pass up. Learning French in my childhood was an act of devotion, and teaching it years later was an act of gratitude.

NOTES

[1] This metaphor was born in the novel by Hugh McLellan with the title "Two Solitudes" written in 1945.

CHAPTER FOUR

READING FOR LIFE

My true religion is kindness.

-The 14th Dalai Lama

A REVERIE

I am sitting alone in the library of the Berkeley City Club, built originally as a women's club in 1929 by Julia Morgan – the architect who also designed the Hearst Castle in San Simeon. I am on a sabbatical leave for a few months, writing and reflecting – a tranquil moment. This library is a space of grandeur with Gothic vaulted ceilings, sepia-coloured Greek columns and gloriously decorated wood ceilings and rosettes. It is a splendid and peaceful space, a work of art, and how wonderful it is to experience in solitude the sublime beauty of its contemplative atmosphere. There seem to be friendly muses lurking all about in this noble library and they announce a sense of tradition. As I am writing, I think: Is writing, in one form or another, not what we all long for – especially those who have been uprooted from their place of origin? Maxine Greene (1973) wrote: "For the man who no longer has a homeland, writing becomes home." I look up at the shelves that line the wood-paneled walls around me, shelves filled with books from the late nineteenth and early twentieth centuries. Some of the titles catch my attention: "They Shall Inherit the Earth," "The Coming of the New Deal," "Yesterday's Streets," "One Small Candle," "I Write as I Please" and "Breaking Through." Books everywhere! – just like there were at the first library that I visited when I was a child. And now I, the adult, am surrounded here by books in a library with a pedigree – in this fine place whose architect Julia Morgan[1] had named her "little castle."

For me it seems always to be about language and culture: the aesthetic pleasures of reading and writing. Call it: "Writing as Art." Writing is artful in the same delightful though excruciating manner as is dance or music or painting or sculpting. But art does not start off by being "cultured." It begins from something personal: a profound longing, a sense of woundedness, a passion that can move mountains. It begins as something necessary; an immediate need. Art comes from the depths of the human soul, from a need to be redeemed: a need to forgive oneself in spite of injustices borne. Art comes from moving towards the life force in spite of humiliation or torment or fear. Art also comes from the experience of exile. Art is a joy filled with sorrow, a struggle against despair and toward hope. Art communicates faith in the midst of darkness and nurtures and strengthens those who respond to it.

In this silently graceful literary landscape in which I now sit, alone with my laptop computer, one of the muse spirits of the library seems to have attached herself gently to me. She is not a grand figure but rather a fragile one yet with a powerful message. She is a bedraggled little muse with the name of "Outsider." She is learning to speak English and has come over to me in order to announce her hope that she and I together might eventually bring forth, from this place of letters, something worthwhile to share. As I stare out through the leaded diamond glass windows I realize how fitting it is that here, in this bastion of mainstream privilege, I will write about the first books I ever read and about the first time that my father took me to a public library in Montreal – about my discovery of the world of reading.

"DICK AND JANE"

Right from the start I loved to read. I adored the 'Dick and Jane' series. They made me feel cozy and protected. They took me away from my problems and offered me life. Each pupil was given their very own crisp new copy of the book – what a treat. And all those words in it, as well as the blessed words on the teacher's colourful flashcards: *"Look Jane. See Spot run. Look Dick. Look, look. I see something funny."* They had a baby sister named Sally with curly blond hair, her well-loved teddy bear named Tim, and a dog named Spot who was a black-and-white Springer spaniel, and Puff, an orange marmalade cat, and they lived on Pleasant Street in a quiet neighbourhood with single family dwellings that had white picket fences and green lawns with flowers and shrubs. When it rained they all wore shiny boots and had yellow umbrellas and enjoyed playing in the puddles. They never seemed to feel wet or cold the way I did. Sometimes they got themselves into little scrapes but everything always worked out in the end. In summer they visited their grandparents who lived on a farm and there they played with all the barnyard animals.

Everything about their family life was peaceful and cheery. Whenever I opened my "Dick and Jane" reader I could escape and pretend for a little while that I too lived with them. I could pretend that I was as carefree as they were. I could pretend that I wore pretty clothes just like theirs. That I too had parents who belonged to mainstream society. That I too had all that "social capital." And I could pretend that I too had grandparents. Grandparents! – how unthinkable. And yet for a while I could set my loneliness aside and allow my heart to feel alive. But I knew that Dick and Jane didn't really look like me, and that their family's situation bore little resemblance to my own. I knew that I was an outsider peering into their perfect lives. They were white, Anglo-Saxon, and Protestant. They were always clean, successful, and having a fine time. Their father held a respectable job and their mother enjoyed her role as homemaker and, I imagine, was probably a member of the PTA and did fine volunteer work.

What would I not have given to jump into those pictures and never return to the shabbiness that was my life! But I knew that was impossible and so I had to content myself with only reading about them. How amazing it might have been to have had books in the classroom that would have reflected *my* life as a child of immigrants and refugees – as someone outside of the mainstream. Perhaps then might I have felt less isolated, but this was in the mid to late 1950s so this was not to be. Still, I loved "Dick and Jane" because they represented a sort of haven. And it didn't matter to me that this was only in fantasy. Without such fantasies I could not have survived. So I longed for the 'normalcy' and for the mainstream lives of "Dick and Jane" although actually it was regrettable to me that they were not in fact French-Canadians and that their stories were written in English and not in French. But that perhaps was asking too much. By then I had accepted my fate that I would be learning in an English speaking environment although I never stopped wishing for its French equivalent – surely an unusual example of multiple identity formation and a different approach to learning about majority and minority group relations.

GATINEAU PUBLIC LIBRARY

When I was six years old my father took me to Montreal's Gatineau Public Library for the first time. With my hand in his I discovered that "real" stories were to be found there. I sensed there that I was treading on holy ground. There were colourful posters on the walls, and books. *Books everywhere*! They were stacked high on shelves and people were sitting at long tables and reading. It was so *quiet!* My father took me to the Children's Section. The chairs and tables were smaller there and the books reminded me of school. I was proud that I knew all about reading by then. But I hadn't yet known about the troubles and the triumph of Cinderella, or the transformation of the Ugly Duckling, or the terrible sufferings of the Little Match Girl. These books spoke directly to me and I devoured them with awe. Their messages transcended all languages, all cultures, all religions, and all races. They gave me the greatest gift – a sense of belonging to the family of humankind and a sense of *community*. I felt that I could commiserate with all of the characters in these stories no matter what their place of origin was. It didn't matter – they were all my friends and I understood them.

They spoke about universal issues. They spoke about displacement, about wandering, about fleeing from hardship, about violence, loss, death, about acts of kindness, friendship and courage. They offered me faith in the knowledge that, in spite of all the terrors and injustices, humanity does exist and that I too was a part of it. These stories revealed that there was connectedness to life even in the midst of destruction. They were sites of memory and of eternity. And how else could I have made sense of my own family story? How else could I have survived the darkness – the shifting sands and complex horrors that seemed to threaten my existence at every turn? These books, quite simply, offered me the world and a lifeboat. The realization that reading could be a liberating force was overwhelming. And I was hooked forever.

The greatest thing about this library was that they allowed you to take the books home for a while. This was an amazing concept and I was struck by this good fortune. The lady at the desk was slim and wore a crisp white blouse and blue skirt. Her hair was in a bun and she wore gold-rimmed glasses over smiling eyes. She took a small rubber stamp and stamped the back pages of my books. How I loved to watch this ritual! There appeared a date, and I was told that I had to return the books by then. She was the *librarian* and I felt in awe of her. All those many books in her charge! She was entrusted with so many stories. How excited I was to receive my very own library card with my full name and address typed (correctly) on it. I felt very grown up and my father too seemed delighted. There was always exuberance and joy in his face whenever he was in the presence of books. He had been to the section for adult readers and took out many books on his favourite subject – European history. I knew how precious those books were to him. At home he read all the time, and I knew early in my life that reading was an important escape for him. And it became so for me as well.

I learned of the power of words to create refuge or a sense of adventure or a place of peace. I was following instinctively what Parker Palmer proposes in "Sacredness: The Ground of Learning" that "if we recover a sense of the sacred, we could recover our capacity for *wonder and surprise,* essential qualities in education [his italics]." Indeed, reading for me was a sanctified activity; you could find solace in those pages. There was also much pleasure in reading. That was clear to me as a young child because when my father was reading, his eyes took on a sparkle and all his worries seemed to disappear into his book. I basked in the glow of my father's reading time. On weekdays he worked late but on Saturday afternoon after he came home he would hold his current book under his arm and sit down on a chair in the living room and life became beautiful. I loved to sit near him and bring my own book over, my father and I reading side by side. Sometimes he would look into my book and ask me all sorts of questions. And I asked him about his bigger and more impressive looking book. He said that when I was older I would be reading books like his. But he respected my books as much as he did those that he was reading. He told me: "Each book has a special message. Each one has an important lesson about Life."

Those conversations with my father were the closest thing I knew to Heaven. I believe that he could have been a wonderful writer. He could have been a great teacher. Maybe I became a teacher and a writer in order to tell of his love for reading and for learning about different cultures, languages, identities – a legacy he left me. For example, he enjoyed the cultural and linguistic diversity of Montreal immensely. *"You learn more about yourself when you read about others. And how lucky we are to live in a city where language and culture are so important. How I envy the French-Canadians for their 'joie de vivre.' But it looks really hard to bring them together with the English who have the power,"* he explained to me. He had been reading Hugh McLennan's novel about the "Two Solitudes", as well as some non-fiction works on Canadian history and had gained a keen understanding of the historical dissonances between the these two very different peoples. He described McLennan's book to me avidly. He spoke about the search for negotiation and reconciliation which lies at the core of any dialogic relation. He longed for what Martin Buber referred to as "communion" – a dialogue between cultures that results in mutual validation. My father also taught me that reading stirs the imagination and the imagination carries freedom to our souls. It enables us to mend broken spaces and make them accessible again – what Paulo Freire called "liberation as a mutual process."

Nobody lied in the fairy tales that I read – honesty that was refreshing in the wilderness. What I most appreciated was that I was not being falsely reassured. These authors were not afraid to tell how desperate things were and it was a relief to read the truth, to experience the sense of "reading the word through one's world" in Freire's words. Fairy tales often demonstrated ways to vanquish the doom. And that's why I began to take them seriously. They offered strength and courage and hope in the face of adversity. They suggested that, in spite of the terrors in the darkness, you could transform your sadness into something that will lift you out of the ashes into the sunlight of LIFE. These stories spoke to me as directly, intimately, and truthfully as would a loving guardian. When *Hansel and Gretel* were abandoned by their parents and forced to live in the forest at the mercy of a witch, I sighed relief to realize that they too felt pain and confusion and anxiety and hopelessness. This was something with which I was familiar. In short, they too had to wander in labyrinths and their trials and tribulations were *real*. In the depths of misery they whispered to me: "*We can make it out of this hell; let us find a way together.*" *Hansel and Gretel* overcame their existential crisis by their own wits and labours, and if they could do it then perhaps so could I. It *was* possible to find a solution. It was this essential optimism of the fairy tale's message that spoke to me. Perhaps this is why Lewis Carroll called fairy tales a "love-gift" because a child needs to play with his or her problems in the safe harbour of happy endings.

> Child of the pure unclouded brow
>
> And dreaming eyes of wonder!
>
> Though time be fleet
>
> And I and thou
>
> Are half a life asunder,
>
> Thy loving smile will surely hail
>
> The love-gift of a fairy tale.
>
> C.L. Dodgson (Lewis Carroll in Alice Through the Looking Glass)

Bruno Bettelheim in his book "*The Uses of Enchantment: The Meaning and Importance of Fairy Tales*" says that "as with all great art, the fairy tale's meaning will be different for each person, and different for the same person at various moments in his life." They "illustrate that the [child's] inner conflicts may be solved and may suggest what the next steps in the development toward a higher humanity might be."

The literary qualities of the stories also comforted me. When you witness a genuine work of art you are never alone again. Bettelheim goes on to say that "fairy tales, unlike any other form of literature direct the child to discover his identity and calling and they also suggest what experiences are needed to develop his character further... These stories promise that if a child dares to engage in the necessary hazardous struggles, then benevolent powers will come to his aid and he will succeed." And one might add, within a pedagogical context, that as educators, sharing one's own life stories with children opens the door to liberating and truthful relationships for them.

Here was a magic glue to help put the pieces of life together again – in a new way. The stories told me – yes, I could do that! To go to the source, to be on a personal discovery, to become a seeker. You have to *want* to believe, to have faith in unknown forces. True, you will have to leave home for this journey but know that there will always appear threads and signposts along the way in order to bring you back. These stories always suggest that we must pay attention to what we have lost, to what we need to find in order to recover. I would have travelled anywhere with *Hansel and Gretel*, with *Little Red Riding Hood* or with *Cinderella* in spite of how many witches, and evil stepmothers and stepsisters, and absent fathers or mothers and big bad wolves abounded. Because there was always the good fairy godmother to tell me that I had the power to transcend the realities which imprisoned me. Crites (1971, p. 295) states that "consciousness awakes to a culture's sacred story." That is what all stories aim to do — to transform. By what sacred story are you living? This is a question I ask teachers whom I teach at university. And I share with them how I discovered my own sacred story a long time ago when I read *The Little Match Girl.*

"THE LITTLE MATCH GIRL"

When I was eight or nine years old, I lay in bed recovering from a bad flu one dreary day in late November. I remember the time of year because our teacher had told us that two of the children in our class were going to New York to celebrate the American Thanksgiving with their relatives. It was a late afternoon and the light outside my bedroom window was already fading. There was snow on the ground outside and I was feeling feverish and bored. I opened a small book from my Golden Book fairy tale series which I collected at the check-out counter of the local grocery store where I went with my mother every week "to make an order", as it was called in Montreal at the time.

As I began to read "The Little Match Girl" nothing could have prepared me for her kind of suffering. Here was a beautiful little girl who found herself in the trappings of a homeless urchin, an outcast. Hers was a cold and uncaring universe, yet she held on to the love of a grandmother who was somewhere up in the shimmering sky, in a place called Heaven where God and His angels dance and sing and tell stories; where it is always springtime and nobody has to feel lonely.

She often heard her grandmother's soft and healing words and longed to be up there with her. But instead she found herself slumped on the frozen ground of an alleyway with a handful of shiny matches which she was supposed to sell. But nobody wanted to buy them.

People were rushing past her, coming and going, carrying brightly coloured packages in their arms. It was Christmas Eve and in her distress she sensed the joy of other children getting ready for the celebrations. She could make out a tall Christmas tree through the curtains of a house across the street. A woman and a little boy were putting ornaments on it. They sparkled through the window taunting the little girl. Did she have a name? Where had she come from? Where was her family? I knew her only as *"The Little Match Girl"* and I knew that once upon a time there had been a grandmother who had loved her dearly. As the hours fell away and it became very dark she began to light the matches; her last hope. They shone brightly warming her heart, but their light didn't last very long and she would soon be thrown back into darkness. Yet she could hear the singing from children caroling in the streets and could smell the aromas of Christmas dinners being prepared everywhere. But nobody saw The Little Match Girl who lay like a ghost on an icy patch of snow somewhere outside of where the world should be. A world that should show kindness to a little girl who is alone and hungry and who had never hurt anybody in her life. She wanted only to survive and to live like other children. She would have enjoyed a good meal or a dolly. Or a mother and a father who could care about her. But their hearts had been broken a long time ago in a place far away called "concentration camp"; how could they possibly have been able to hear her?

Tears fell from my eyes as I looked in sadness at the pictures on the pages of the storybook. I hated how familiar it felt, that she looked like me. I hated that I couldn't help her. I hated that she was found in the morning, frozen and dead. Dead. Like my relatives. She was burned by the extreme cold; while they were burned in the ovens of Treblinka. Does it really matter? They too had been left to the devil – just like the Little Match Girl. She probably knew very well what it was like to be in a concentration camp, where you had no food and no toys and nobody to hug you. When you felt so weary, like some of the old people with eyes bulging out of shrunken faces. And you just lay down, because you couldn't walk anymore, because it was time to let go of all the pain and finally close your eyes and be with your grandmother in Heaven. To me the Little Match Girl was one of my cousins, from "over there." When I figured that out, I knew that I would never truly know the warmth of a safe place in the world. *But she did find her grandmother and lived with her in Heaven.* Those final words of her story helped me because I knew that I too might one day meet my grandmother and grandfather and all my relatives who had been put to death in that far away hell that oozed with blood and guts and murdered babies.

"But she did find her grandmother and lived with her in Heaven." That sentence carried me in its arms and we flew away from "over there," into a world where people sang and laughed and spoke in beautiful languages. I could enter this land and then I was safe – even if only in fantasy. And I trusted those words. They

were dressed up as if going to a party, and would never let me down. With those words I was never alone again. Did they know then that I would end up sharing my love of fairy tales and myths with students when I was an elementary schoolteacher? Yes, of course they did. They had made it happen. Every one of those words found their way into all the stories that I read and shared with my students in the years that followed. Some of them needed those stories just as I had needed them to go on living.

Years later I also shared them with my graduate students (most of whom are teachers) in my university course "Children's Literature in a Multicultural Context." This is the first quote in my outline for that course: *"Remember only this one thing," said Badger. "The stories people tell have a way of taking care of them. If stories come to you, care for them. And learn to give them away when they are needed. Sometimes a person needs a story more than food to stay alive. That is why we put these stories in each other's memory. This is how people care for themselves"* (from the folk tale "Crow and Weasel" by Barry Lopez, 1990). Sylvia Ashton-Warner in her memoir "Teacher" refers to Guy de Maupassant who says "Words have souls...But that soul is not manifest until its word is graciously set" (1967, p. 202).

It is the souls of words set in fairy tales and in other stories written from the heart that can save lives in classrooms. When I became an elementary school teacher something magical happened. My heart thawed and I began to tell the tales that came out of my soul. They were like the candy and the desserts and the treats that children everywhere who are suffering will one day eat in Heaven with their grandmothers.

NOTES

[1] Julia Morgan was the first woman to study at the *Ecole des Beaux Arts* in Paris.

CHAPTER FIVE

A CALL TO TEACH

It is impossible to teach without the courage to love, without the courage to try a thousand times before giving up.

-Paulo Freire

A SUMMER LANGUAGE PLAY SCHOOL

The first time I began to share my love of languages and cultures in a professional space was during what could be called my first administrative and teaching position: I was then almost eleven years old. It was summertime. My parents did not have the resources to send me to a day camp, and so I was left to my own devices. Montreal in the summer can be hot and muggy, and that particular summer in Montreal was hot and muggy to the core. For a child, the prospect of an endless chain of stifling days is like seeing infinity but without any of the excitement. Had there been a circus in town I might surely have run away with the clowns. My father was working hard juggling between two jobs and my mother was preoccupied with my baby sister. My brother, five years older, was already in his teens and his social life was well beyond my ken.

There was a small chance that we might all go up north to Val Morin in the beautiful Laurentian mountains – *Les Laurentides* – and rent a room in the house of two spinster sisters. But financially, things were precarious for us. There was little money for such a 'luxury' and if it did happen, it would not be until August. My parents had found out about these two women by word of mouth. When I eventually met them I was delighted in spite of how eccentric and ancient they seemed in my mind's eye because they were French-Canadian and took me under their wing. Their house was a dilapidated place but it was filled with dark mysteries, or so it seemed to me at the time. And they had pictures on the wall of the Virgin Mary and Baby to keep me company. In the end, my parents and the Mesdemoiselles Desrosiers negotiated a sum that was acceptable for all concerned – for they too had very little so the small amount my parents could offer was very helpful to them.

But it was still the beginning of the summer and I longed for *something to do*. I could of course read but that was solitary activity and I needed to play. My friends had all disappeared into their *holidays* (a magical word!) or visits to their relatives somewhere. One hazy afternoon, thick with the promise of thunderstorms, I was hurrying back from a bakery nearby where I had been sent to buy fresh bread and milk. My favourite lemon cupcakes (*tartelettes au citron*) were featured in the window and I was able to buy one. My spirits lifted as my tongue rolled in the refreshing lemon cream. As the winds were coming up I overheard one woman say to another as they passed by me on the sidewalk: *"If only there was a small play school in the neighbourhood where I could send my three-year old for a few hours a week, it would really be a godsend. My four month old baby is a handful."* The other woman nodded in agreement. *"Maybe we should look into this – I am in the same boat as you."*

I almost dropped what remained of my cupcake in utter astonishment. *A play school!* This was Divine Intervention. I loved school and I surely could share my books with younger children. I could be a *play teacher*. Images of my French teacher danced before my eyes. I could teach French and English to little kids. My young mind went into overdrive and I hardly even noticed the first heavy raindrops that were starting to fall. I ran home in joyful reverie as lightning began to tear through the darkening skies. I got home absolutely drenched, changed into dry clothing, sat down at our kitchen table, and began to print up signs in both French and English with colourful crayons on many pieces of paper:

To Parents With Little Children

TO PARENTS WITH LITTLE CHILDREN

AUX PARENTS AVEC DES PETITS ENFANTS

GRACE'S SUMMER PLAY SCHOOL BEGINS ON MONDAY JULY 7!!!

IN HER HOME *** AVENUE MONTCLAIR.

GRACE HAS MANY BOOKS TO SHARE WITH YOUNG CHILDREN.

THERE WILL ALSO BE LESSONS ON LANGUAGE IN ENGLISH AND FRENCH.

GRACE HAS COLOURED CHALK AND A BLACKBOARD.

PAPER, PENCILS AND CRAYONS ARE INCLUDED.

IF YOU ARE INTERESTED PLEASE CALL *********.

And then I watched Nature's spectacular show of sound and light outside our kitchen window. The storm was so fierce that the electricity went out and I later had to finish my posters by candlelight.

I have always loved thunderstorms. Perhaps it has something to do with the sense of joyful purpose that enveloped me during this early experience in a really *huge* thunderstorm – with a child's acknowledgement of forces larger than oneself, forces that can change everything. In the sunlight of the following morning I began to post my hand-made signs. I posted one in the nearby bakery, and I also dropped some through mail slots of homes in the immediate vicinity of my place. I kept my fingers crossed.

That very afternoon I received some responses. Three different neighbours called and asked me how much I was charging. I hadn't even though about money! I basically allowed each of them to set a rate which seemed reasonable to them. By the following afternoon I had recruited five pre-schoolers. They sat outside with me on the gallery off our kitchen. With chalk in hand I wrote my name on my little blackboard. But the children weren't altogether impressed and were getting restless. Suddenly I understood that they couldn't read yet. So I hurried to my bedroom and brought out one of the fairy tales from my now growing collection. I began to read to them. It was "The Little Match Girl." Then we "discussed" the story. I learned very quickly then that you have to be honest with children. Although I was myself a child, they were much smaller still. I had already discovered that fairy tales enrich life and give hope for the future. That even the most difficult story holds out the promise of a decent ending. I had also figured out that the story itself was a "work of art", to use Bettelheim's term, although I would hardly have been able to articulate this at the time. I was intuitively sharing with my small charges the delight of the literary qualities of the story and the universal message that it offered. What would I have done without the Little Match Girl?

A wondrous thing happened to me when I read this story aloud that first time to my little "pupils." Suddenly I found solace in a most unexpected place — in the site of the "classroom." I confided to the little children that my grandmother too was in Heaven and that maybe she was not as far away as I had always thought. Maybe she was looking down at us even at this very moment. They all nodded at me, gravely. There was no sugarcoating in the story. We recognized the starkness out there but we all gained comfort from knowing that The Little Match Girl was able to establish a mighty, liberating and truthful relationship with us, and she embodied a powerful message: that even in the worst of times there is always a way out: a way to see a solution that others may not see. We also drew pictures about the characters, and we enacted little skits based on them. And when the mothers came by in the late afternoon to pick up their children, the little ones handed them their carefully drawn pictures of The Little Match Girl along with their impassioned oral narratives.

I remember the sense of accomplishment I felt that afternoon – my first taste of "success" as a teacher. And with it came a desire to tell and share stories. To me these two things became synonymous: a great teacher is a great storyteller in one way or another. Tom Barone, in his book "Aesthetics, Politics and Educational Inquiry" (2000) says that "a [good] teacher invites students to explore aesthetic experiences that, the teacher hopes, will provide wondrous avenues toward the future." Stories can be, as he quotes from Foucault (1984) "transgressions offering

CHAPTER FIVE

radical alternatives for thinking about the world and acting within it. The teacher plays an important role in making these engagements more likely to occur... she or he must engage in the aesthetic project of empathic understanding, which may become the 'learning event' – the kind of experience Dewey called 'educational', a growth-inducing experience that grants the capacity for having even richer experiences in the future. Key to this capacity is storytelling... a way in which students may discover new options for interpreting the world and new possibilities for living" (p. ix).

On some unconscious level my play school pupils and I were aware of the Divine in the story of the Little Match Girl, just as any child might be. We all have our own great stories to create and to tell. John Taylor said that "imagination and faith are the same thing – giving substance to our hopes and reality to the unseen." (as cited in Kathleen Norris, p.65). When I read Phil Cousineau's (1998) book "The Art of Pilgrimage", I was struck by how similar to this his theme was: "Never doubt that there will be darkness and disappointments on your travels [that is, in your life]. The question is how much courage can we muster to deal with them and to move on? Can we transform painful stories into instructive ones?" In my own child-like way, this is what I shared with my small charges those many years ago: that telling and reading good stories can reinvent one's world. Is it any wonder then that I chose to share fairy tales and myths, years later, when I became a "real" teacher?

BEFORE PRE-SERVICE TEACHER EDUCATION

Languages and cultures, in particular French and Latin, continued to be oases throughout my high school years and later became officially legitimized when I entered my first year at McGill University and became immersed in the Honours French literature program. When I entered McGill I felt a breath of fresh air; things were really going to be different from now on. And they were. I 'cavorted' with authors like Jean-Paul Sartre, Paul Claudel, François Mauriac, Gustave Flaubert, Marie-Claire Blais, Gabrielle Roy, and so many others – and I also had a secret crush on my French professor. My friend and I used to visit him in his office after class and discuss with him, in French, the existential woes of "*la condition humaine*" and "*le péché originel*." Professor Lapointe recognized a certain quality in me and told me that he thought I "ran the risk of being too intelligent for my own good." In that first year I also took courses in Sociology, English, Russian, and German along with French and Latin. I won Highest Marks in German that first year. A heady beginning to my entry into a new world.

In my second year, a new chapter opened up for me when I decided to also study Italian literature. The choice for me had been between Spanish and Italian. But my mind wandered back to the Sunday mornings of my childhood when I would watch local Italian-Canadian singers perform on television. Their songs were magical for me and opened sunny new horizons. Their energy seduced me. Italian has always had that effect on me. When I am amongst Italians, the sun always breaks through the clouds and life suddenly becomes breezy. Many people have commented to me on the fact that when I speak Italian, my voice, my mannerisms and even my spirit seem to transform. This is the magic of languages for me. There was no contest really. Not only did I choose Italian; it also chose me. The following year, as a result of a competition at McGill that I entered, and won, I was awarded a scholarship by the Italian government to study at the *Universià Per Stranieri* in Perugia, Italy.

I graduated from McGill with highest honours and was preparing to go off and do a Masters degree in Comparative Literature at the Hebrew University in Jerusalem. I had visited Israel during the summer in which I had studied in Italy and this had opened up a shimmering new way of connecting me with my Jewish identity. For the first time in my life, it meant something more than just the personal suffering I had known. That first visit to Israel had allowed me to catch glimpse of an opening, a door that would offer something hopeful behind the looking glass that had been shattered by the Holocaust. Life beckoned.

But first I had decided to visit a fellow student whom I had met at McGill. She was from the San Francisco Bay Area and had returned home after graduation, and invited me to come and spend some time with her before my departure for Israel. It was supposed to be only a pleasant interlude but instead turned out to alter the entire course of my life journey. I met my future husband in Berkeley, just across the bay. He was a doctoral student at Cal and also a Montrealer and also a child of Holocaust survivors. We both knew almost immediately that we wanted to be together. So I who had expected to stay in California for only two weeks ended up there for almost two years. I put my graduate program in Jerusalem "on hold" and was 'parachuted' into Berkeley, which was of course known for being the radical college town that it was at that time – a veritable hive of youthful "liberalism" and anti-Vietnam war activism.

But I could not partake of its vitality. I arrived too late to apply for scholarships and so decided instead to work in San Francisco at a department store named *City of Paris*. It had been created by a French entrepreneur who had settled in San Francisco in the late 1800s. The building was quite an architectural delight with a magnificent domed roof and an Eiffel Tower on top of it. I was hired because of my fluency in French and my main function was to walk around different departments in the store in order to chat with Francophile shoppers who were mainly (but not exclusively) women from San Francisco's "high" society themselves looking forward to practicing the French they had learned at university, and more specifically during their junior year abroad in France. I enjoyed this experience immensely although in my heart I knew that I was just marking time. I kept wondering what to do about the graduate program at the Hebrew University which was still "on hold."

I had become confused about my future professional direction. Berkeley was a deeply alienating place in the early seventies unless one was totally immersed in a university program there or in its radical politics. And I was not involved in either. Finally I did end up taking some graduate courses in Italian literature and psycholinguistics there, but the course that transformed my professional life was Professor Robert Ruddell's seminar at Tolman Hall on literacy and bilingual education. I believe that one's personal and professional destinies are intertwined. Mary Catherine Bateson (1990) says that "composing a life involves an openness to possibilities and the capacity to put them together in a way that is structurally sound...We are engaged in a day-by-day process of self-invention – not discovery, for what we search for does not exist until we find it – both the past and the future are raw material, shaped and reshaped by each individual" (p. 28). In the retelling of my story through this narrative, I understand now that the texture and meaning of my life began to take its form and shape at Berkeley. I found both my soul mate in Berkeley and also my ultimate academic interests and goals. But it seemed so vague then and the timing was all wrong. I could have lived many other stories but this is the one that happened. And, of course, it is still unfolding.

We got married in Montreal and returned to Berkeley in order for my new husband to complete his Ph.D. studies. I rejected all my fellowships in Comparative Literature in order to accompany him to his first university position at the University of Alberta in Edmonton. I had been programmed to think that that is what a good wife should do. Upon reflection, I am amazed at how out-of-step with the seventies decade I was. I might as well have been living in a post-World War II DP camp trying to piece my life together. There was free love, Civil Rights and the Black movement, women's lib, ethnic studies, going off to Europe to live in caves in Greece, CUSO, the Peace Corps. Who wanted to hear about the hidden psychological prison of a child of Holocaust survivors? We, these post-Holocaust children, were not yet fully conscious of this immobilizing strait–jacket that we were in and of how it affected us at every step. At least I wasn't. Many of my peers at Berkeley became caught up in drugs and confrontational student politics, but for a sheltered and traumatized young woman this was frightening. I was relieved to get out at the time.

PRE-SERVICE TEACHER EDUCATION

Although I had offers of fellowships from several universities for graduate programs in Comparative Literature, the first job that came through for my husband (at the University of Alberta) was at a place neither of us had previously considered. When we visited Edmonton for his interview, I went to see the people at the Department of Comparative Literature. But it didn't feel right. I then walked by the building that housed the School of Education and thought of how much I had enjoyed the seminar on bilingual education by Professor Robert Ruddell. And his words came back to me: *"You should go into education. You're a natural and it sounds like you could do a lot for bilingual education in Canada. Why don't you try the classroom for a while? Your students would be so lucky!"* And why not, indeed? My Fielding School French classes flickered before me. I walked into the building and registered for the one-year P.D.A.D. program (Professional Diploma After Degree). And so formally began my teaching career.

I had entered the teacher training program at the University of Alberta in Edmonton as an afterthought, as a path of least resistance, with memories of the school experiences of my childhood intertwined with my fantasies about French-

Canadian language and culture. But the university graduate fellowships which I had declined gnawed at me. I staved off these unconscious regrets by the presumption that teaching was only meant to be a temporary stop on a journey toward something I could not yet define. The pre-service teacher education program at the University of Alberta, however, turned out to be a remarkable experience. I do not know whether this cohort program still exists. In it, students were divided into groups of five and each such group was assigned to a mentor who would observe our student teaching stints. The mentor for my group was a professor who was, at the time, already close to retirement. He was a kind-hearted man who always saw the good in people and who never gave up in trying to bring out the best from every one of us. This wonderful man, Roly Ward, had been a superintendent of schools in Edmonton and eventually an adjunct professor in Educational Administration at the University of Alberta. Of all our professors, he had the most "hands-on" experience in the schools and had an extensive network of people and resources in school boards across all of Alberta. He had taught in both rural as well as in urban areas, as well as on a Native reserve.

My chosen specialty was bilingual education and Roly found the perfect school for me in which to student teach. It was a bilingual school in a small Franco-Albertan town called Vimy situated some forty miles north of Edmonton. In the morning subjects there were taught in French, and in the afternoon in English. Being from Quebec, I was viewed as a bit of a celebrity there – as someone who was coming to them from the "home country." They knew, of course, that I was not French-Canadian but my French was so native-like that this little mattered to them. What mattered to them was how genuinely enthusiastic I was about French Canadian culture and – even though I myself was not Catholic – how much I knew about their religion and my appreciation of it. In fact they accepted me to such a degree that I was even allowed to teach religion classes there – surely a first for a non-Catholic! I told them that I was Jewish and they respected my wish to teach from the Old Testament. The children in my Grade Four class there came to love Moses as much as they loved Jesus but were also intrigued by my personal connections to their Virgin Mary. It was an exercise in inter-faith dialogue. For many of the people in Vimy, I was the first Jew they had ever met and I felt like an emissary there. How strange that after yearning for such an experience in my childhood, here I was, finally, in a French Catholic school – although not as a student, but as a student teacher!

Although I was euphoric, my spirits were marred by the unmistakable evidence all around me that the French language was in fact dying in that school and in that town, a realization that burdened my happy weeks there like a dark cloud. Years later my teaching experience at Vimy came back to haunt me when I read Phyllis Dalley's Masters (1989) thesis at OISE focusing on her identity struggles as a child of a French-Canadian mother and an English-Canadian father from New Brunswick. Her thesis is a narrative inquiry of the several years she spent teaching in Alberta and she writes of the "volcanos and war that communicated [her] passionate struggle to keep the French language above water in a small town, in [her] students." Her reflections display much inner personal conflict and turmoil,

CHAPTER FIVE

and it was like "a knife through [her] heart" to see students lose access to their mother tongue, French.

Some years ago, after I was already a professor of education at OISE, I was invited to give a banquet address at the National Conference on Heritage Languages which was being held in Edmonton that year. In going there, I had two items on my personal agenda: 1) What had become of Roly Ward? and 2) what had happened to the bilingual school in Vimy? Roly Ward, thank God, was still alive – a healthy, vigorous, cheerful man well into his eighties. I was grateful to have had that opportunity to thank this kindly man for everything that he had done for me, and to be able to update him on my professional accomplishments since that time. We laughed and cried together for hours over lunch. The second item on my agenda did not have such an outcome. I learned that the bilingual school in Vimy had closed its doors several years earlier. The French language there had died. Did it really have to end? Is this the inevitable story? Must society be forever unable to allow minority experience to represent universality? Such questions continue to haunt me and inform my research work.

MY FIRST TEACHING POSITION

Our stay in Alberta had been hospitable and we enjoyed its 'frontier' character. But, yearning to return to the east, we accepted an opportunity to move to Toronto in the mid-seventies. There, on a warm afternoon in mid-July, I had an interview with the principal of an inner-city elementary school. He was pleased with my teaching evaluations and letters of reference, but warned me that "this is a tough neighbourhood." He talked about subsidized housing, unruly kids, a culturally diverse school and low-socio-economic status. I nodded at this with some enthusiasm saying "I would like a chance to teach these children." He obviously liked my response – or just as likely, he may have been rather desperate to fill that slot – and offered me the position on the spot.

At the end of August as I went in to the school to prepare my classroom I felt higher than a kite. My first year of teaching in the big city! I peered into my Grade Five classroom. It was a little dusty as classrooms always are at the end summer. But there seemed to be an expectant feeling there as if the room were waiting for me to do something. The walls were bare. I had brought in some colourful posters and a few teddy bears. I am an arctophile – a bear collector – and I chose three who seemed eager to visit this new class of mine. One was a Paddington Bear who wore a blue raincoat and large red boots. The other was a little Japanese bear named Naoko, in a bright yellow silk kimono. And the third was "Little Rascal" who wore green and blue plaid overalls and was always getting himself into mischief. As I was arranging these bears on my desk a large woman poked her head through the doorway. "I'm Ann," she said. "You've got the class with Calvin and Armando and Rita and Dolores in it. It's the worst class in the school – I doubt if you'll make it until Christmas." And then she disappeared. She seemed quite a bit older than me and her demeanor indicated: "I've got experience and you don't."

Suddenly my posters that were lying on the counter near the blackboard didn't seem quite so colourful and even the bears seemed to be frightened. I sat down at the desk and suddenly felt very alone. I was still adjusting to life in a new and very large urban center. That morning I had been so excited to be coming to my very own new classroom and in an instant a pin had burst my balloon. At first I became filled with anxiety but then I reasoned: "If I had made it through my first day as a student who was rejected by her teacher because of my immigrant name, then I can surely survive my first day as a teacher, even if my students were to indeed turn out to be a bunch of hellions." This thought buoyed my spirits and I became angry at that brutal introduction from my new colleague. She had been rude and mean-spirited. With renewed vigor I taped my posters on the wall. At the end of the day I went home to our apartment and tried to enjoy the Labour Day weekend – the weekend before the start of the school term.

Sometimes, they say, the first week of teaching predicts the future. I don't necessarily believe this because it is too categorical, but it did turn out to be true in my case. I walked into my classroom at 8 am the day after Labour Day and met a teacher across the hall from my room. He was a pleasant fellow and it turned out that this was his first day at the school too. I had a Grade Five class and he had a Grade Six. Things were looking up! We went into the staff room and chatted with several of the other teachers. This time the atmosphere seemed more welcoming and, happily, Ann was nowhere to be seen. I was starting to feel more comfortable as the bell rang. I made my way through the lines of children in the hallway and entered my classroom. I stood at my desk with a sense of adventure waiting for my students to arrive.

In the mid-1970s when I began my teaching at Laurelea Public School, Toronto was already a very large city with an interesting mix of cultures and races (although it was not nearly as large and diverse then as it is today). In my Grade Five class, for example, no less than ten language groups were represented. I saw their faces as each student shuffled in – faces marked by neglect, by poverty, by not knowing that their lives had meaning. They were good-looking – as children always are. I felt immediately in awe of the possibilities inherent in this new classroom of mine full of its diverse, new faces. I was accustomed to these faces; they reminded me of the places where I had grown up in Montreal. I felt that I had an important role within this classroom and I wanted to respect the complexities of these children's lives. And it was soon apparent to them that I was both an 'insider' and an 'outsider.' 'Insider' because I had grown up in circumstances similar to their own — a child of immigrants and refugees. 'Outsider' because I was not their peer but rather their teacher – an adult, an "authority figure."

Understandably the children were all wary of me because until then their teachers had displayed little interest in learning about the social and economic worlds from which they had come. I could understand how they felt. I too had had teachers like that. But as a teacher I realized that I faced an enormous challenge ahead of me. No sooner had the children settled into their seats than they started jumping out of them. Paper airplanes flew through the air. I somehow got through roll call – names, names from everywhere. I tried hard to pronounce all of them

CHAPTER FIVE

properly. But I became alarmed when I found myself yelling for attention. This was not my vision of the teacher I wanted to become. And it wasn't even an hour into my new career. "It's a tough school... You'll never make it to Christmas." Ann's words echoed in my ears...

I had prepared a reading lesson. It was based on a standardized "basal" reader series. I remember feeling somewhat apprehensive while planning that lesson. The stories in the readers seemed stilted, inauthentic. How would any child be able to relate to such contrived and uninteresting material? It seemed to me that all that these basal readers offered were the most basic skills; *meaning* did not seem to count for anything. At that moment, as total chaos was about to break out in my first class, my eyes turned to the shelf that housed those dreadful readers. And I made an unprecedented decision which I knew would make or break my status as teacher in the minds of these children. With unexpected and steel-like confidence, I marched over to the shelf and gathered up as many copies of those green and blue-covered readers as I could hold. Fortunately my classroom was located on the ground floor and also fortunately it was not raining outside. I strode over to the window, opened it wide, and then I proceeded to throw out the books. I literally <u>threw them out the window</u>. It was a moment in time when everything stands still and waits to be born. The children stopped their running about, quickly returned to their seats, and abruptly sat down. All of their disbelieving eyes were upon me as one could have heard a proverbial pin drop.

This is what I said to my students: "I don't blame you for not being interested in these books. They look pretty dull to me too. I wouldn't want to waste my time with them and I won't waste your time with them either." Their eyes grew larger. They looked bewildered, and I was starting to relax. "Books should be full of stories that catch your attention," I said. "Those are the kind of stories I want to read with you in this class. Have any of you ever heard of Greek myths? I adore them... They are stories about ancient gods and goddesses and about all sorts of things that happen to them." I saw the wonder that began to envelop the children. I don't know whether theirs was wonder at the anticipation of reading things called Greek myths or at the prospect of spending a year with such a strange new teacher! But whatever the reason, this became a sacred moment. It was as if some angel had come down to rescue this very ordinary classroom on a very ordinary first day of school in a large urban center in North America.

There were white faces, brown faces, black faces, yellow faces and red faces staring at me and they all seemed to be transformed by the exciting invitation that had just been offered: "We will read *interesting* stories and they will have *meaning* for all of us." It was a promise. Nobody in school had ever really made such a promise to them before. Suddenly "the thing with feathers, that intangible sense of hope" pervaded our classroom. That, I mused to myself, is what has been missing for them. I had found children's versions of the Greek myths in a bookstore in Edmonton a year earlier and I brought these little treasures with me into class the following day. These children were all well below their reading grade level and some of them had no reading skills at all. So I began to read the stories to them. I wanted this to be a shared love. I tried to create what Bruno Bettelheim called "an interpersonal event in which adult and child enter as equal partners" (p. 147).

I made a pact with my students because we all knew that we were embarking on what might have been called a 'subversive' adventure. Greek myths were not part of the school curriculum and we were entering uncharted territory, certainly as far as the formal Language Arts program was concerned. Of course, things were more flexible in those days. (The Ontario The Ministry of Education's Hall-Dennis Report written in 1969 was a thoughtful and progressive curriculum guideline. Sadly it is just a historical artifact now.) I told my students that it might happen that the principal or the school district superintendent would visit our classroom unannounced one day to watch me teach and that if we were ever in the middle of one of our Greek myth reading times, that they (my pupils) must motion to let me know right away if this were to happen. I would then be able to quickly put my books away and quickly go on to do something considered more "acceptable." In this my students were very willing accomplices. We were thick as thieves and it felt delightful. These students were seeing the pleasures of school now in a way that school itself did not allow. I am reminded of American novelist Flannery O'Connor's observation that "most of us come to the church by a means the church does not allow." In this case, substitute "school" for "church."

And so began a year of sharing stories during Language Arts classes: the Greek myths, fairy tales, and yes, stories about my own childhood. They listened to me and soon they began telling me their stories. And I listened to them. It was an organic grassroots process: building, story by story, a bridge to understanding one another a little better. Of course there were more than a few tough moments, trying discipline problems. There were days when I came home exhausted, feeling like I wasn't getting anywhere with these children. But through it all, I always felt affection for them and I respected their struggles.

One mid-October morning I was reading the story of "Ceres and Proserpina" to my class, the Roman version of the original Greek myth entitled "Demeter and Persephone." There are many themes in this story that related directly to the everyday realities of my students: loss, violence, abuse, a mother's sorrow, a child's being torn away from "home." It is a work of true art and in the sharing of this story I had embarked on a spiritual exploration with my students. The students were all taking this story to heart. There was an air of reverie in our classroom that morning as we were all commiserating with the mother and daughter of the story – a quiet time of many reflections as we all took things in and, as Bettelheim put it, "allowed the story itself be our discovery" (p. 22). BUT SUDDENLY CHILDREN'S HANDS BEGAN FLAILING ABOUT! There was intense anxiety on the faces of the children. I did not understand. And then, in an instant, I sensed the presence of a human being standing right behind me. I turned around and there HE was – the SUPERINTENDENT of the school district. My heart sank. I was not following the curriculum and I had been caught red-handed. Somehow my students understood what this meant and they too were terrified. But I saw in him the face of a kind man, and I remember having heard good things about him. This was to be the test.

CHAPTER FIVE

The superintendent asked me what I was doing and I told him the truth: that the basal readers were very uninteresting, that it simply wasn't fair to foist such meaningless text onto students; I told him how stories need to fire up the reader's imagination, how my students were truly beginning to enjoy reading because these Greek myths really spoke to them. My students' heads were all nodding in agreement. I had said my piece and was now prepared for the inevitable ax to fall. Instead, however, a genuine smile began to spread across the superintendent's face. "Well," he answered, "this is certainly most irregular but I have seen these students in previous years and this is the first time that I see them truly engaged in their work. You are clearly doing something very right and I recommend that you continue in exactly the same manner. I will indeed mention this to your principal." That was the gist of his comments to me. He then shook my hand and at that moment my students all began to clap their hands. I felt pure joy in my heart. I had tasted what Parker Palmer (1991) calls "education at its best – this profound human transaction [which is] not just about getting information or getting a job. Education is about healing and wholeness and transcendence, about renewing the vitality of life. It is about finding and reclaiming ourselves and our place in the world." From that moment onward there was no doubt that teaching was to become my safe place in the world.

Many years later, on a summer Sunday afternoon, I happened to be taking a friend's five-year-old daughter for an outing. It was fourteen years after I had taught this particular Grade Five class. My friend's little girl and I had been at a park and decided to go to MacDonald's for a snack. We were queued in a long line and finally got to the front to place our order. The young lady at the other side of the counter was very pretty. She gave me an unexpected look and asked "Are you Mrs. Feuerverger?" "Yes, I am." I said surprised, "And who are you?" "I'm Rita from your Grade Five class at Laurelea Public School. You know, I never forgot those Greek myths you taught us. I really began to enjoy reading after that. In fact I took all my younger brothers and sisters to the library over the years and I read those same stories to them. And you know I am studying now to be an early childhood educator. It's all because of you, Mrs. Feuerverger. You turned me around and made me feel like I could do it. Thank you."

I was struck. Rita had been the eldest of five children. Her mother had been on welfare and her father in prison. Rita had to become a surrogate mother to her younger siblings. In class she had always looked tired and older than her years. Now I was facing a bright young woman on a summer job and on her way toward an interesting career. What had become of the other students who had been in that class, I wondered? What had happened to Dominic, who had stolen a table lamp from a restaurant in order to be able to bring me a present for Christmas. Or to Calvin, whose father frightened me when he told me: "I love Calvin to death. If he acts up, just tell me and I'll beat the s–t out of him." Calvin carried so much sadness in his eyes. Rita didn't know what had happened to any of them. I hope they are OK. As I write this I calculate that they are in fact all now in their forties. My friend's little girl, who witnessed my conversation with Rita, asked me after we sat down at a table to eat, "Grace, will you read those stories to me too?" "You bet

I will," I replied. This little girl is now a young woman enrolled in a midwifery program but she reminds me now and again of how much she used to enjoy the Greek myths which I read to her each time she would visit.

MANDY

There are many children who touched me deeply during my school teaching years. But one student shines out in my memory with a special light. Her name was Mandy and I met her during my third year of teaching. I will never forget her. She was in a Grade Five class that I taught half a lifetime ago. She had the largest brown eyes one can imagine and flowing raven-black hair. Her skin was pale and her smile was a heavenly gift to the world. When she walked into my classroom on the first day of the school year I somehow knew that she was meant to teach me something very important.

The school was located near a Children's Aid Society home and some of the students in my class actually lived there. In some cases, the abuses they had suffered in their family homes had been so severe that they had to be removed. Typically the abuses had been discovered by someone and these children then became the ones lucky enough to have gotten away. But, instead of being comforted by living in their new quarters, these children were stigmatized by their non-institutionalized peers who looked down upon them as being the dregs of society. I quickly learned that there were three unspoken strata of child society in my class and in my school. The lowest were those in "Children's Aid." Then there were the foster kids – they, at least, were in a family. And at the top were those who lived with their biological parent or parents – which, of course, did not necessarily mean that all was well for them. But they at least could pretend.

When Mandy walked into class on that first morning of the school year she looked like a princess. It turned out that she had been placed in "Children's Aid" after having been shuffled about for several years from one foster family to another. But to me she looked like a princess — a Native Indian princess whose parents had succumbed to alcoholism and drugs. Over time Mandy became a sort of "muse" for me. She was bright and generous although very fragile. She once told me privately that if only she had behaved a little better her parents would have surely kept her. That was her version of reality. After some weeks I looked into her file housed in the school office. The version in her file was this:

> Ten year old child, very cooperative. Brutally beaten by father at age eight. Ribs broken, lacerations, serious bruising. Hospitalized for six weeks. Unsuccessful stays in foster homes. Placed in care.

It was the end of a school day and I was alone in the classroom. I put down the file folder and stared out at the maple trees in the schoolyard which were beginning to flame in the colours of fall – red and yellow and orange. I felt my heart burning as brightly as those leaves.

There were other students in that same class who also had been violated in one way or another, but why is it that I remember Mandy so vividly? She had the face of a goddess and the courage of an angel. She tried hard to do well in school and was even a leader in some games on the playground. Mandy's hand often went up to answer questions in class. At other times she sat sullenly in her seat, immobile and impossible to reach. I was intrigued by her. Mandy's religious background included Christianity, as well as Animism. Along with end of term discussions about Christmas and Hannukah, we learned from Mandy the wonderful Indian story of the Mighty Gitchee Manitou who had created the Universe. And Mandy played the most magnificent Virgin Mary for the Christmas pageant I have ever seen.

Some weeks into the new year, Mandy invited me to be her guest for dinner at the Children's Aid Home. I accepted with anticipation and saw in her eyes a look of pride. It was only a small gesture of compassion but I found out later that no other teacher had ever gone to visit a child in the Home. Later, other such invitations sometimes came and I always went and shared some lovely times with the children there. I related strongly to their suffering. What is compassion, after all, if not, as Rachel Naomi Remen (2001) writes in *The Heart of Learning*, "the experience that all suffering is like our suffering, and all joy is like our joy. When we know ourselves to be connected to all others, acting compassionately is simply the natural thing to do. True compassion requires us to attend to our own humanity, to come to a deep acceptance of our own life as it is."

One day I came back into my classroom, after having been 'on duty' during a bitterly cold recess period, and discovered that my desk had been ransacked. My purse, which had been inside the desk, was gone. I was stunned. Who could have done this? I discussed it with my students. Every one of them was perplexed. Days went by and the puzzle remained unsolved. I decided to give it time. At first I assumed this had been an act of desperation on the part of one of the students. Later the thought occurred to me that perhaps somebody had broken into the school during recess – a different matter altogether. One late afternoon when I had been preparing a lesson plan for the following day I heard a gentle knock on the door. I opened it and there was Mandy, eyes drowning in tears. She was clutching my purse and other items from my desk in her little hands. I brought her inside and closed the door. I dried her tears and put my arms around her. "Why did you do it?" I asked her quietly. "Because I wanted to feel like you," she sobbed. "You have everything I don't have." All I told her that afternoon was that, although I had lived with my parents when I was a child, I had been very alone because they had not been able to take care of me in the way that I had needed. In the way that every child needs to be taken care of. Mandy looked at me, searching my face for any hint of a lie. When she realized that I was really telling her the truth she began to put everything neatly back into my drawer. This incident was never mentioned again. And Mandy never took anything from me again.

Personal boundaries are sacred and when such boundaries are invaded, great harm is unleashed. Mandy's father, the adult who should have cared for her, had almost killed her during an alcoholic rage. And her mother was too high on drugs to take any proper notice. Mandy in this sense was therefore twice assaulted. Even so, after she was released from hospital, she longed to be reunited with her parents.

Such is the tragedy of child abuse and betrayal. The foster homes into which she had been placed, could never live up to Mandy's fantasy of having loving and caring parents. So she behaved badly there. "*If only I had tried harder, my parents would have wanted me.*" This fatal survival mechanism: to believe in one's parents as being good, no matter what. For how else can a child explain such brutality, such injustice, such horror? Nobody seemed able to stop the destiny that happened to be Mandy's. Hers was the journey through fire. In the act of remembering and narrating Mandy's story, I feel humbled by her heroic attempts to transcend the broken shards of her life.

Our classroom however became a space where Mandy could become an artisan of her own healing. Sometimes, she reached out to others in astonishing ways. She helped others who needed attention in the reading circles. Sometimes, however, she would lash out cruelly at someone and then become withdrawn and filled with rage. Sometimes she felt remorse. Mandy's presence cast a large spell in my classroom. I witnessed the holiness of her struggle to escape from the wreckage of her lived experience. How was she able to possess let alone communicate any faith in humanity? And yet she did do this in my classroom. Perhaps it helped her to know that I saw who she really was: a wounded child trying to figure out a way to rebuild and reconstruct a burnt out existence. She was an expert at being abandoned and yet she tried hard not to abandon others. From where did she receive the strength and will to do her good deeds in the classroom?

In my heart I honour Mandy for her belief in the necessity of holding fast. I think she must have known, on some level, that I was a comrade–in-arms. Many of the other children had also seen the "enemy" from up close. They became what Tobin Hart calls "sacred mirrors." When I shared with them some stories of my own childhood, which had been eaten away by the rottenness of war, my students listened. If there was one lesson I wanted to share with them, it was this: that in spite of the violence, there will still be love in the hiding places. The trick was just to find it.

One day Mandy offered me one of the greatest gifts of my professional and personal life. Here is what happened. A racial slur had been uttered by one of the teachers toward a student in a classroom which was right next to mine and I had overheard it. I was beside myself in sadness. This teacher was always at me about the "clannishness" and "stubbornness" and "stinginess" of the Jews and loved to taunt me subtly. I was a new teacher and she had been there forever and felt that she needed to dominate everyone. Trying to stand up to her was like taking on Goliath. I was expected to keep my mouth shut. It would be my word against hers. I had endured her anti-Semitic and racist "jokes" in the staff room. Many teachers laughed with her, while some, like me, were silent.

Schools are not necessarily safe places. We have to fight to make them so. But at that moment I was afraid – a child of people who had been cruelly treated. I had no voice and no song. And I did not yet have my permanent teaching certificate. Then something that I regarded as truly abominable happened. During the month of May this same teacher decided to bar a child from the end-of-year track meet because of some minor offence. This was cruel and unusual punishment and it seemed to me that it had more to do with the colour of his skin than with anything else. (I don't recall his parents ever being informed of this situation, and I doubt if the boy himself understood that he had the right to tell them.)

Some of the teachers in the school were upset about this development but the principal was a weak man who was in fact under the thumb of this teacher, and very close to retirement. The students who belonged to this boy's team were upset because he was a star player. It turned out that Mandy was also on that team. I decided to open up a discussion with my class about this injustice because the details of it had leaked out anyway. The safest thing for me to do would have been to just ignore it but, unexpectedly, I found myself talking with my class about tolerance and inclusiveness and respect for diversity in a multicultural society, long before it had become 'fashionable' to do so. The sense of relief that swept over the children was like a fresh breeze in a heat storm. And then Mandy spoke out with words that arrived like a thunderclap: **"Express yourself, Mrs. Feuerverger. You have a right to."** She might as well have been Moses coming down from Mount Sinai with the Ten Commandments in hand.

There was silence, the kind of silence which speaks the truth. All of the children in the class began to nod their heads. The clarity in Mandy's defiance was astonishing to me. We had been living on the inside of a local tyranny and she had blown the whistle. The sense of community that was created in that little classroom on that afternoon was joyous to behold. And I knew in an instant that I had to live up to Mandy's words. I walked through the small corridor of light which she had opened and I kept on plowing through it until the decision was reversed and that boy was allowed to participate in the track meet. For the first time in my life I discovered a "still small voice" in a place deep within me. It had the kind of quietness that, once heard, can smash all forms of tyrrany. And I understood for the first time the power of a spiritual response to effect change deep in the heart. Mandy's words held out a vision of transformation, and I marvelled at the fact that these words came from a place within her of what appeared to be powerlessness and yet had the authority to transcend all of us and to offer us this blessed gift.

My purpose here is to tell this story so as to allow us to be redeemed by Mandy's words. Her words cried out for a more just society. Mandy's voice liberated me that day, and the children in my classroom had witnessed it. In fact I have been trying to live up to her words ever since. How had she known so exactly just what I needed to hear then? How fortunate I am that Mandy shared her indignation, her soulful call for equality. *Dear Mandy, I hope that you have survived and that you have found love in your life. You deserve it, sweet, heroic child. I will never forget you. Perhaps one day you will come back and tell me about all that has happened to you. In the meantime you are safe in the warm embrace of my memory.*

FROM PAST TO PRESENT

One fall term not very long ago, I shared for the first time the story of Mandy with the students in my graduate course "Multicultural Perspectives in Teacher

Development: A Reflective Seminar." At the end of our last class that fall term, in the midst of all the "goodbyes" and "Happy Holidays," one student handed me her essay. I placed it on my desk along with several other essays. This student was one of the few in that class who was in the Masters of Teaching program which incorporates a teacher training (pre-service) component. So she was not yet a teacher. The following week I was at home packing to leave for the holidays and began to collect up my students' essays from my desk. Her essay happened to be on the top of the pile. This note, which had been handwritten and attached to her essay entitled "The Power of Teaching" fell out.

> Dear Grace,
>
> I remember in one of our class discussions this term you were telling us a story about a little girl who stole your purse in class. After a while that little girl came into the classroom to see you and told you the truth. Throughout your story, all I remember was your telling us that this girl was abused and neglected as a child. You finished off the story by saying how much it affected you as a teacher. The last thing you said before you opened it up for comments was "This child really gave me insights on understanding that the students in our classrooms come from many difficult situations, and that although their family environment may not be safe, they may need only one teacher to make a difference in their life. The last thing you said was: "I feel that I will meet this student again."
>
> And you did! For that child's circumstance resembles my own...
>
> Thank you for allowing me to write this final paper. This is the first time in my life that I felt comfortable and at ease. Your teachings and power have helped me speak and write from the soul. This is what I call "The Power of Teaching." You are the first teacher in my life to give me the energy to remember. You have given me the opportunity to reflect on my past. It has made me appreciate who I have become today.
>
> Best of luck,

I stopped packing, sat down at my desk, and read her final paper right then and there. The paper was a bittersweet testimony to her inner strength in the midst of violence in her own childhood home. Afterwards I looked out of my window at the cold December twilight and wondered at the complexity of human emotions and the soulful forces which are always present (though often hidden) in classrooms all over the world. And a thought struck me: that one can recover one's voice – that one can be healed – only by becoming vulnerable again. Such miracles happen in classrooms where teachers understand that the sources of knowing are in their midst — they are our students. I am reminded of Tom Barone's words: "Each student is, like the rest of us, a person in the midst of writing and re-writing his or her own life story. Each is comparable to an artist in the middle of a creative process that moves toward a resolution that is not preformulated, but gradually emergent. The end of the story of each living human being is yet to be encountered." He goes on to quote the literary critic, Frank Kermode (1967) who describes how we all rely upon the stories of others for guidance in writing our

CHAPTER FIVE

own (p. 126-127). I wrote this email message to my student that wintry evening as the light outside disappeared over the horizon:

Dear ***

I am leaving tomorrow. So I guess I was just lucky that your essay was on top of the pile that had accumulated on my desk. I have just finished reading it, and am sitting here in gratitude. You have given me a precious gift for the holidays with this paper. I feel truly privileged that you chose to share your professional/personal story with me. And I want you to know that, by what you have written, you have given me back a piece of my professional/personal life. Thank you for your courage, my dear. I am in awe.

Please do keep in touch – I don't want to lose track of you. If ever you need a letter of reference, please let me know. I would be honoured to write one on your behalf. I can't wait to see you as a teacher in your own classroom!

With all my best wishes for the holiday season,

Grace

PART TWO

CHAPTER SIX

UNIVERSITY TEACHING

All politics can do is keep us out of war; establishing a lasting peace is the work of education.

-Maria Montessori

MISE EN SCÈNE

After seven years of teaching in elementary schools, I left in order to regain the thread of my graduate work. I had become disillusioned with teaching in spite of how much I loved it and of how precious the students had been to me. I began to feel trapped and wasted and felt stirrings inside me toward the need to effect changes in the field of education. As a classroom teacher I saw no possible route in that direction. In my personal life, I was on the verge of upheaval and metamorphosis. I felt the need to shed my old skin and was itching all over.

It was a tremendously difficult decision to resign. My principal begged me to stay. The parents of my students pleaded with me. Stern voices inside my head shouted "How can you leave a well paying job while others are standing in line for teaching jobs? Who do you think you are anyway to have the nerve to leave such a secure setting to go start studying again? What childish nonsense is this? You will surely pay for such foolishness. And where will a new degree lead you anyway? To an M.A.? To a Ph.D. as well? Unheard of! Do you really have the stamina for this? It is your brother who was supposed to get a Ph.D. – not you. You are committing a betrayal. You surely will be punished for this!" Such were the demons blocking my way, hissing their venomous fires. And I was terrified.

But I was also stubborn. Another voice quietly murmured that this was a new chance for freedom. That if I didn't take this risk, I would end up sitting at my seat in that classroom – an embittered wreck who would have lost all of that passion that had brought her into the teaching profession in the first place. "Have faith", this voice said softly to me, "you will see that this will turn out well. Take the chance. You cannot afford not to. *Feel the fear and do it anyway.* You are becoming bored and starting to feel stale. Something is wrong and you have to find out what it is."

I didn't realize it then but I had just embarked on a quest for meaning in both my personal and professional life. And so I completed my Masters and Ph.D. programs and then started working on a postdoctoral fellowship collecting data from university students regarding their perceptions of minority language learning and

CHAPTER SIX

ethnic identity maintenance in Canada. I was elaborating and extending the work of my doctoral dissertation but feeling somewhat alone in the process. Much time had passed. Then one day I happened to pass by a bulletin board at the Ontario Institute for Studies in Education (OISE) which advertised a seminar in the Joint Centre for Teacher Development (JCTD) with the title: "*The Self I Dream: A Narrative Reconstruction of a Personal Mythology.*"[1] I was intrigued by this topic. I had not known about the Joint Centre for Teacher Development and was surprised to learn that there existed a place in an academic environment that sponsored such work. I attended this seminar and although I knew nobody there, I somehow felt very at home. I remember participating vigorously in the discussions that followed and then meeting Mick Connelly, the founder and head of the JCTD, at the end of the session. A week later I found myself in his office telling him all about my research interests and then suddenly hearing from him an academic rationale which would permit me to change the entire direction of my professional journey.

Unconsciously I had been going through a process of transformation in my professional life. I had intended to continue using the quantitative methodologies which had carried me through my M.A. and Ph.D. theses (Feuerverger, 1983, 1987) but my postdoctoral work was taking on a life of its own and I had begun (surreptitiously!) to conduct in-depth interviews with my participants and to listen to their *stories*. What Mick Connelly told me that afternoon in effect allowed me to realize that my work needed to find its expression in a new way. The narrative mode had in fact suggested itself to me but I had been uncertain and working too much and too long in isolation to fully recognize its validity. Michael Connelly opened the door to a new professional world, and helped give me the permission that I needed to embark on the journey of qualitative inquiry. What he told me was simply this: "*Doing narrative is not a crime.*"

PATHWAYS TO NARRATIVE

I was hired by Michael Connelly into the JCTD in the Department of Curriculum at OISE in the summer of 1991, and that fall I taught a course titled "Multicultural Perspectives in Teacher Development: A Reflective Seminar" for the first time. I have taught this course every year since and each time I have taught it, it has proven to be a gratifying experience. The first time, however, will hold a special place in my heart forever. As I write this, a flood of warm memories sweep over me from that springtime of my university career and I feel privileged to have had those experiences. I had created the syllabus for this course during the hiring process. I remember being quite surprised at how quickly it had come together, as if all of my undergraduate, graduate, and postdoctoral work, as well as all my elementary school teaching years had been a dress rehearsal for this moment. That is how it felt to me at the time. I floated on a cloud of euphoria into that first graduate class in the late afternoon on a Tuesday in September 1991. The sheer delight of walking back into a classroom as the teacher after a hiatus of a decade was intoxicating. This time it was a classroom of graduate students and I felt exhilarated.

The story I am telling of my own beginning university faculty experience is exploratory rather than definitive, summoning to gaze upon the 'real' life behind the role of a teacher. It turned out that in that first year all the students in my "Multicultural Perspectives" course happened to be women. We gathered to share our life stories of dislocation, survival, and triumph over adversity. This emergent spirit was in keeping with the planned objective of the course which was to explore issues of diversity and difference within school contexts. Although we all came from different places around the world we had a similar, albeit implicit, agenda in mind – to discuss our research stories as they interacted with our investigations of multicultural classrooms. An experiential approach to the topic appeared to me to be the only methodology that could do it justice. I felt as if I had awakened from a long slumber and was ready for the first time in my life to experiment with my own voice, and even more importantly at the time, to listen to the voices, inaudible as they might be, of my graduate students.

We were about to embark on an improvisational journey to confront the chaos of our experiences as teachers, or to use Samuel Beckett's term "to find a form that accommodates the mess." And messy it was, and messy it always will be, for that is the stuff of life and we are here to bear witness to it. But the journey we had embarked upon began to point us toward the driving desires which had brought us all into the realm of education. It didn't take us long to figure out that the personal and the professional are so tightly intertwined as to be inseparable. As those evenings of encounter multiplied week by week, my graduate students began, through the sharing of their journal writings, to pay finer attention to the intricacies of home and school for themselves as teachers as well as for the students in their own classrooms. Just as I had tried to do in my own elementary school classrooms, I dared to (re)kindle in these women – teachers all – a passion for discovery of the self and so of the other. We began to appreciate narrative as a process of making meaning of experience by telling our stories of personal and social relevance (Connelly & Clandinin, 1990, 1995, 1999) – by understanding that "we gather other people's experiences because they allow us to become more experienced ourselves" (Van Manen (1990).

I know now that for me this course represented, in part, my never-ending search for "home" in the classroom. And it still does. While cultural and linguistic diversity shaped my personal life, it also became my 'bread and butter.' Multicultural and multilingual education, by its very nature, engenders emotionally intense discussions – situated as it is at cultural crossroads which have been altered so dramatically over the past few decades in Canadian and in other urban centers, and especially in Metropolitan Toronto. It was clear to me that a course focusing on issues of diversity from the perspective of practicing teachers in classrooms was needed in order to develop more effective directions for promoting cross-cultural understanding at all levels of schooling. That is why I had decided to create it.

Because I was hired late in the summer, the description of my course did not appear in the university Bulletin. I remember wondering if anyone would show up.

CHAPTER SIX

The course syllabus of "Multicultural Perspectives in Teacher Education: A Reflective Seminar" indicated that this was to be:

> a hands-on" exploration of how teacher/educators can prepare themselves in a fundamental way to reflect on their underlying personal and professional attitudes towards the multicultural micro-society of their classrooms. We will focus on how teachers can begin to unearth the "unconscious myths" that motivate them in the planning of curricula and in their choice of interpersonal classroom strategies. We will consider how multicultural education provides pedagogical opportunities for students, teachers, and researchers within interactive spaces that engage issues of personal and cultural identity. The intent is to examine the epistemologically complex implications of understanding teacher development as autobiographical/biographical text in the sharing of our own teaching stories (Connelly & Clandinin, 1998; Hunt, 1991; Jackson, 1995). Giroux (1991, 1994) claims that "multiculturalism has become a central discourse in the struggle over issues regarding national identity, the construction of historical memory, the purpose of schooling, and the meaning of democracy." (From the course outline)

Such theoretical notions informed the discussions about multicultural school-based research throughout the term of my first course and very much shaped the relationship that my graduate students and I developed week by week. The central questions for my professional self will always be the ones that I posed in my first graduate course and still pose today: *Why does one go into the field of education in the first place? How is one called to the profession of teaching?* The night before that first class a close friend of mine (who is not an academic) said to me "Just share yourself with them. Let there be joy in the class." And I told her, "Yes, that is exactly what I will try to do." The words of my young student Mandy, from my Grade Five classroom of so many years ago, alsorang again in my ears. "*Express yourself, Mrs. Feuerverger. You have a right to.*"

TOWARDS AN "ENGAGED" PEDAGOGY[2]

In order to make sense of the complex cultural worlds we inhabit, my graduate students and I focused on our autobiographical narratives within the context of our professional lives via the medium of the scholarly articles I provided for them each week. We began to reflect on the sacred force that lies behind the profession of teaching and on the personal contact which connects with this force to create an interactive environment for learning. We emerged from our compartmentalized boxes to find ourselves in what Ruth Behar (1996) termed "a borderland between passion and intellect, analysis and subjectivity, ethnography and autobiography, art and life." In an early journal entry I acknowledged the strong autobiographical thread between myself and my students concurring with Robert Coles (1997) that "...intense self-scrutiny is, one hopes, an aspect of all writing, all research" and further that "the search for objectivity is waylaid by a stubborn subjectivity." I am narrating this pedagogical experience as grounded in the metaphor of the "cultural orphan" who, while feeling dislocated, is also healing herself through a process of relational 'storytelling' within a professional context.

As a child, I always longed to live in a world of harmony, of joy and peace. This is still my driving force. Deborah Britzman (1998) says that one's own telling is informed by the "discourses of [one's] time and place." In fact, my professional life is dominated by my sense of being a border-dweller, someone still searching for 'home.' For the first time in my public life I began to share reflections of myself growing up in a multicultural and multilingual home in Montreal, psychologically scarred and tormented by the events of the Holocaust. This was a way to open a textual space for understanding and honour the struggle of "otherness" without and within ourselves. I remember the very first time I actually uttered the words "I am a child of Holocaust survivors" to my class. We were discussing the obstacles that many immigrant or refugee students in classrooms throughout Toronto have to overcome. One of my graduate students then said: "It's horrible to know how much they have suffered. When I was a child we didn't have to deal with these things because there were no such students in my class. We were Canadian. Now everything is different." The woman who said this was about the same age I was, perhaps a trifle older. So theoretically I could have been a classmate in her childhood classroom.

An intense feeling overcame me. It would have been easier for me to keep silent. But I heard my words gather speed as they emerged: "How do you know that no one in your class had come from elsewhere? Did this ever come up in class? Was there ever any discussion about World War II? You had started school in the mid-50s. Maybe there was one child in your class who said nothing, who just wanted to fit in, who didn't want to be singled out as a child of war or deprivation. Did your teachers ever discuss this?" "No," my student said, "they never mentioned it ... they never did." And I said: "I am a child of Holocaust survivors. There were other children in my classes, Jewish and non-Jewish alike, whose parents' lives had been torn by World War II. None of my teachers in elementary school ever brought this up. Perhaps some didn't know how to approach this issue. I can forgive them. Perhaps others were simply indifferent to our plight. I can almost forgive them. And then there were some who humiliated us in all sorts of ways, making us feel deviant and excluded. I cannot forgive them."

I saw a light go on in the eyes of my students. We became present, really present, to one another. The course began not only to take shape but also to gain soul, an aesthetic of improvisation. Every class was intense; something fresh, something that had never happened to them in a graduate course before: the need to have an authentic voice, the need to find from the heart, the need to care for the soul. We danced on high wires without any safety nets beneath us, dizzying. In one of my journal entries I wrote:

> I feel privileged to have been allowed into the lives and dreams and nightmares of my students ... I sense that we have something deep in common. Many of us have been wounded but we are survivors. We have come together to give each other support in the retelling and rebuilding of our

life stories. We will nurture each other. I think that in a psychological sense we are cultural orphans, all of us. But we are orphans who are determined to succeed. We are orphans who are not alone. We are the lucky ones. I sense anger in my students, but it is a righteous anger. It is a liberating anger...

Throughout that first term my graduate students and I acknowledged the "foreigner" whose language, culture, values and traditions are different from our own. We were, right from the start, involved in a transformative process towards a collective consciousness – a group of individuals with a commonality of purpose – to create a more nuanced, more reflective pedagogical discourse of intercultural understanding and harmony. Our inquiry led to new insights into our personal and professional lives and to a more compassionate understanding of the teaching-learning experience within diversity, and to moral and ethical dilemmas in education. Within this discourse lies Nel Noddings' (1984, 1991) notion that a good education must be based on caring relationships in terms of "how to meet the other morally" and so opens a space for contemplation. We stressed, as Henry Giroux (1991, 1995) does, the development of pedagogical contexts that "promote compassion and tolerance rather than envy, hatred and bigotry, and that provide opportunities for students to be border crossers..." (ibid, p. 508). My students and I focused on the necessity that students and teachers find common ground in the midst of seemingly insurmountable differences. We realized that teachers need to be border crossers too. They need to create bridges filled with communication, with genuine *dialogue*.

VOICES EMERGE: NARRATIVE AND THE FORMATION OF PERSONAL AND ETHNIC IDENTITY

For my graduate students, one theme question will always be "In what ways have our personal stories influenced our research interests and how do these both interact with what we are discovering through observation and conversation in our classroom setting? How is our research story evolving through this process?" Such issues are in keeping with bell hooks' (1994) notion that "progressive, holistic education, 'engaged pedagogy' ... emphasizes well-being... and therefore a process of self-actualization" (p. 15). Jack Miller's (1988, 1995, 2001) work is also dedicated to such visions of a union between mind, body and spirit. Through journaling, my students and I became more familiar with our unique, personal perceptions of our place in society and of the ways in which we may contribute to teacher development. Discussing our subjective perceptions of ethnic identity involved a good deal of personal reflection striking at the core of how we defined ourselves in the world. We discovered that our language and ethnicity were connected to our sense of purpose and self-worth in society. We examined our individual, familial and cultural differences to find that within these differences we had very much in common.

As it happened, we had all come into the course balancing at least two cultural identities and languages. From the start I wondered, as others may have, how these juggling acts informed our personal, practical knowledge in our multiple roles (as women, teachers, researchers, daughters, wives, mothers). We seemed to be located in a "state of liminality… betwixt and between … poised upon uncertain ground… a lack of clarity about exactly where one belongs and what one should be doing, or wants to be doing" (Heilbrun, 1999).

I encouraged my students to construct new meaning for their texts while searching for professional identity. We became fellow travelers in our educational landscapes and journal writing became a shared enterprise. We heard the voices of the "other" within our lived experiences and, as a result of this influence, our own stories became reconstructed and retold from a fresh perspective. A story of collective professional identity evolved as we shared our individual narratives, illuminating our capacity to understand ourselves and to nourish our souls. We explored our life histories of living within and between various cultural worlds, struggling to find voice, meaning and balance. We became involved in a "reflection-in-action" (Schon, 1987) on our own philosophy of teaching and learning and on the search for our personal and collective Canadian identity. Tom Barone (2000) says, "one must always remember that the process of self-creation always comes with considerable human anxiety: one needs a certain courage to dwell in uncertainty over one's self."

Our individual voices began to emerge within a developing dialectical relationship between personal and professional reflections, between theory and practice as a means to our understanding of the "self" in relation to the "other." It was in these painful and yet hopeful pedagogical musings that we felt summoned to, in Maxine Greene's (1988) words, "the tasks of knowledge and action." We realized, from the telling of our own stories, that many of us came from very different places in the world and that for some there was less available light in their lives than for others. We all began to know that the dichotomy between mind and body was an artifice. We had conversations about the well-known debates over objectivity versus subjectivity and of how this directly affects the teaching process in classrooms. What is teaching? What is learning? How do you teach children about freedom when they have lived inside of tyranny all their lives?

We discussed the power of literature, that storytelling is not just an ornament, but an announcement of freedom. I became entrusted with many stories about being the outsider. Some students spoke with confidence. Some more hesitantly. I wanted the stories emerging in my course to be "trangressive", as Foucault (1985) had put it, "offering radical alternatives for thinking about the world and acting within it." Storytelling, whether in an elementary, high school or university classroom, allows students to discover new options for interpreting the world and new possibilities for living" (Barone, 2000). And it is the teacher who plays a valuable role in making such a learning event happen: this idea of engaging in the aesthetic project of "empathic understanding", as Barone calls it. And "empathy can permit one to encounter another's life expression, a process that can deepen the teacher's appreciation of the student's "funded biography" (Dewey, 1963). And I would add, vice versa.

I recall an incident in one class wherein some of my more gregarious students (socialized in Western society which places a premium on "talk") tended to dominate the conversations. I was mindful of the quieter students from Eastern cultures being intimidated by their Western peers. My impulse was to step in tactfully, but I waited hoping that things would sort themselves out. Then when I received an e-mail message from one of the "silent" students complaining that several of her Western peers were "hogging" discussions in class and that she was becoming increasingly frustrated at this, I knew that I had to intervene. And yet, my desire was to avoid offending any sensitive egos, including my own, because as a beginning university teacher I sought very much to maintain a warm rapport with others who were also journeying toward self-knowledge.

But, in spite of this inner tension, I did raise the issue of conversational inequalities and this opened a space for dialogue about the desire to be in the "limelight" and its effects on classroom interactions. One of the students realized for the first time that she was still trying to get the attention of her parents at the kitchen table. The "aha" moment occurred when she realized that she was re-enacting her "family scene" in her role as the teacher who kept a tight lid on the responses of the pupils in her classroom. Another student was so overwhelmed with changes taking place in her personal life that she had simply become too immersed in her own story and so forgot to listen to others. Yet another was grateful that in spite of her father's lack of higher education, he had placed a high premium on learning and had inadvertently shown her the way to a teaching career. She hung onto that professional identity with perhaps too much intensity. This discussion allowed us all to become more sensitive to the complexity of the "other" in the classroom and so to continue on our reflective pedagogical journey.

The discourse of caring and intercultural understanding was exemplified in the students' growing trust in me as facilitator, and was reciprocated in my own actions and journal writing sentiments. As one of my journal entries expresses:

> We are all very compatible. Problems arise and we look for solutions. All issues can be raised because everything is negotiable. What I feel most proud of is the sense of honesty and openness that my students and I share in class. We trust each other. We feel safe in the telling of our stories. And we are striving to find meaning in our stories. Our stories intersect to become new stories with new life and direction. We are in search of our personal identity.

In the spirit of Witherell & Noddings (1991), my students and I enacted a pedagogical "search for enlightenment, responsible choice, and perspective or means to solve a problem considered mutual and marked by appropriate signs of reciprocity" (p. 7). As I experienced these dynamics in my class, I was reminded of Belenky et al's (1986) notion of "real talk" wherein careful listening, emergent ideas, and mutually shared understandings shape pedagogic encounters. I have recently returned to Belenky et al's text only to realize the possibility that the "real talk" in our course discussions released an energy within us. This energy was described by one student who wrote in her journal that she had *"half forgotten what kind of magic really good classes can do to you. They give you confidence in yourself, inspiration, and most of all, energy. One person's story triggers so many other new stories which have been forgotten. No, actually, not forgotten, but waiting to be brought to light, to be 'reconstructed.'* "

A major theme that emerged from this first graduate course awakened us to the power of the "family" narrative which creates "unconscious myths" that drive our professional actions and choices in educational careers. Many of us explored what Belenky et al (1986) call the "epistemological atmospheres of our families" by discussing the kind of discourse used within our families that either nurtured or constrained us as women (p.157). As one of my graduate students put it, this process of intellectual development began for her as a child and extended into her adulthood through journaling:

> I have been a 'loner' during many periods in my life. It might explain why I often feel that I do not belong, even when I am at the hub of activity. I remember escaping, as a child, into the world of books. They were all the companions I needed... And so I went seeking an identity in the magic world of words... Only recently have I begun keeping a journal - more for academic purposes than any personal quest, though the two are intimately intertwined at this stage...

IMAGES OF THE MULTICULTURAL HOME

In our discussions of the assigned readings from scholarly literature on multicultural issues in education, my students and I built bridges to one another initiating a process that challenged others to expand their listening space. I gave the students the freedom to interpret "classroom" for themselves. Several students, who were on leaves of absence from their school boards, expressed interest in inquiring retrospectively into their teaching experiences. These particular students inadvertently expanded the planning of my own curriculum by exploring their own underlying personal attitudes towards their multicultural classroom experiences. They brought to the course a window of opportunity through which the rest of us could more closely examine how our past teaching-learning experiences shaped our present inquiries into classroom sites.

In my own case, the similarities between my first classroom experience as an elementary school teacher and my first teaching experience in this university course became apparent. For example, both teaching experiences had alerted me to the importance of sharing problems openly in a spirit of dialogue and negotiation of meaning. My graduate students shared stories of the teaching-learning experience within a multicultural/multilingual context. Here is an example of a Chinese graduate student's journal writing concerning her participant-observation as a research assistant in an elementary school research project I was conducting, which focused on the sociolinguistic needs of newly arrived children:

> The ESL teacher takes advantage of every opportunity to impart a feel of the language to her students. I watched her speaking English in a very playful and lively way even though most of the students may not yet be able to

understand all the words... Her sensitivity to the ESL students' cultural backgrounds is so clear. Their first language and culture are respected. While introducing the mainstream Canadian culture, she makes sure that learners get a chance to share their own culture with the others and that their identity is not denied. The first time I observed one of her classes, [the teacher] was introducing Halloween stories and touched upon the concept of superstition. As follow-up activities, students were asked to write about superstitions in their own culture and therefore got a chance to share their unique ideas and experiences with their schoolmates... They are encouraged to read in their own language while learning English and to share these readings. This is a very important way for the students to retain their own identity, which is crucial to their self-concept. Consequently, kids also get to know about different cultures and a multicultural awareness is cultivated. For example when the Chinese girl finished telling a story from her culture, I heard an Iranian boy saying that he wished that he could read Chinese. As a result, students learn to admire and respect those who come from other backgrounds and languages, rather than to be prejudiced against them. I believe that this is such an important part of multicultural teaching.

A Japanese graduate student in my course, teaching an after-school heritage language class and reflecting on it in her journal writing, wrote about her own teaching self:

I like using metaphors when I describe my teaching and in this case a metaphor of baking comes to my mind. Being a teacher is like baking a cake. You mix eggs, sugar and flour. What comes out is not like any of the ingredients; yet the quality of the cake depends on the quality of the ingredients. If you use stale eggs, the cake will smell stale too. Teaching is the same: what I do outside of my classroom is not directly related to the activities that I employ in my teaching. However, one can tell from my teacher-self, I believe, the quality of my other "selves." What I bring into the classroom is what I am interested in now, who I am as a whole person.

That same student's later journal writing not only reflected a transformation in her metaphor of "baker" to "shopkeeper" to "shop owner" but also reflected the theme of my own course involving the cultural orphan trying to heal herself by becoming whole:

Over the past few months, the metaphor of shop keeping has become more and more fitting to describe my teaching. I, as a novice shop owner, started off with high ambitions, stocking up all sorts of goods that I thought customers would like. Then realizing that the shop was not selling as well as she had predicted, the owner realized that not everyone has the same taste as she does, that she had to cater more to her customers' different tastes. She started to have more variety, even things she never liked herself. She became more sensitive to the "customers' needs." She started to buy goods that sold well in a larger quantity and diminished the amount of goods that were unpopular.

As a means of improving writing skills within her classroom, this graduate student decided to have her pupils write journals as she herself was doing in our course. The results were more powerful than she had anticipated:

> I never expected that writing would become a tool for communication between my students and me. But some students started to tell their life stories and I felt morally obliged to do the same ... I learnt to respond to my students in narrative [as we were doing in the graduate seminar – my insertion]; I tell my stories to them to illustrate my point. It involves a certain risk. By doing this, I am revealing my private self to them. I become more vulnerable. What if my students show what I write to their parents, other teachers, even to other students? ... They are taking the same risk as I am. They have enough trust in me to know that I would not do such a thing. Then I must have the same degree of trust in them too. You cannot expect someone to tell their lived experience when you are not prepared to commit yourself.

> This all amounts to respecting different voices. I have a voice both as a teacher and as someone with a dual cultural and linguistic heritage. Each of my students has a voice too, each of them just as important as any other, including mine. And what a diversity there is among them. When I realized this, I stopped developing a curriculum that was coherent only in my eyes ... My students made me realize that they are their own people and that they have their own agenda... My idea of teaching shifted more towards the metaphor of owning a shop. Shop owners do not expect every customer to buy everything in the store. They do however hope that once a customer steps into the shop, s/he will buy at least one thing. For this end, they try to be sensitive to the needs of the customers and collect things that they are likely to buy. My teaching is the same. I no longer expect every student to learn every single thing that I teach in class; however, I do hope that I have something to offer every one of them, that they learn at least one or more things in my course, in the real sense of the word.

This student of mine had decided to apply what we were doing in our graduate seminar to her heritage language teaching and it worked.

Our graduate seminar itself became a multicultural home wherein "different voices" were respected and the "whole person" was treated as a significant phenomenon of schooling. A view of the "whole person' emerged from the course as students reflected on and wrote about their participant-observation experiences. Perhaps not surprisingly, then, reflections on childhood dominated as a theme in the journals and certain "narrative threads" – involving tensions and the necessity of resolving tensions – emerged. The first example illustrates an Anglo-Canadian graduate student's personal childhood struggle between "selves" and a new awareness of "torn identities" of the children that inhabit the classrooms of multicultural Toronto:

CHAPTER SIX

> I look back on my childhood. There seems to be two dominant themes that run the course of my life ... narrative threads: intellectual independence fostered by my father, and 'fitting the mould' advocated by my mother - be it the patriarchal one set up by my father, or later the one defined by my husband... The 'dream world' portrayed by my father was far more eloquent than the realities laid down by my mother. Which did I choose? Is it possible that the strife I live as adult stems from the child, from a time in which conflicting messages were impinged on my being at a young and supple age? Is it conflict born of the struggle between the 'self' I am expected to be and the 'other' I want to be? So many children in classrooms in Toronto live this kind of torn identity because of their immigrant status. I now am more aware their cultural conflicts because of the discussions in this course.

A number of other graduate students told me directly that they would never have been able to delve as deeply into their multiple identities had I not opened up my own narrative to them. A South Asian student argues that struggle is part of the healing process and that so is the act of writing:

> One MUST write to discharge the tensions. In seclusion. To channel the excess and diffuse energy. To question beliefs and opinions by learning and refining the art of writing the silent selves. That is strength and growth...To lay bare the pain is part of the process of healing... "We can't imagine what we can face, and we can't face what we can't imagine." It takes courage to imagine! It takes courage to explore, to dig out and to express the repressions of oppression. To recover our own experiences, knowledge and possibilities..

A Chinese student who shared her journal writing with us during the term sensitized us to her experiences during the Chinese Cultural Revolution. Although she was one of the quieter ones in our class, her action of journal sharing provided a catalyst for a deeper level of reflective sharing. She opened up different parts of ourselves as we lived out the mythology of "cultural orphan" collectively. The student had a wonderful and hearty laugh which was contagious. She explained that laughter became her survival mechanism during the hard times of the Cultural Revolution. The choice was between tears or laughter and she chose laughter, the life force. When I looked at her I saw a flower shining with hope. In fact one of her metaphors for the power of teaching was the fragrance of the *osmanthus* blossoms. I do not believe that I have ever seen or smelled this flower but she described it as "*white at the beginning, golden in full blossom, tiny but sweet; the fragrance stays long and spreads a distance.*" When I would look at this student, I could see the *osmanthus*. "*I am lucky to remain positive and optimistic toward life after experiencing so much suppression and such severe disruption as I had*", she wrote. She also told us how she was given a great gift by her father: Taoism.

In the Taoist viewpoint, the world, that web of time and change, is a network of vortices like a moving and dangerous torrent of water; and the ideal Taoist is a person who has learnt to use all their senses and faculties to improvise the shapes of the currents in the world, so as to harmonize himself or herself with them completely. Meanwhile, the person remains an individual, a unique individual, who owns ever-increasing senses, faculties and methods of improvisation. Her laughter was intended to express "*a sadness so deep.*" She laughed because it was the only way in which she could express herself. It was an act of defiance, of dignity and of identity. At the end of term she wore her own ethnic costume to our department's Holiday party, a choice which brought out the tension of herself as stranger who, although feeling "culturally different here", found the strength to share herself with us. In her words:

> 'Open' is the word to describe the class. We are all open to ourselves as well as to others. Both the teacher, Grace, and the students presented their true cultural and personal voices. We could be who we really were. Thus a caring relationship, caring for both others and different parts of our selves was created, where every person was co-operating, supportive, learning and teaching.

A Canadian graduate student from the Maritimes who grew up in a homogeneous society read from her journal in class one evening:

> This is a whole new exploration for me as a teacher. In so many cases these newly arrived students are trying really hard to fit into Canadian society as quickly as possible but it's so tough – trying to be what their parents want them to be culturally. The kids feel like it's holding onto the past and they want to get to the future! How do you bridge the two worlds?

A VISIT FROM AN AUTHOR

The theme of 'cultural bridging' (Stredder, 1998) that our journal writing created was brought to a new level by an author's visit to one of our classes. Mrs. Ibolya (Ibi) Grossman, in her autobiography, *An Ordinary Woman in Extraordinary Times* (1990) which she wrote at the age of 74, enchanted us with her maternal quality, while contributing to and participating in the dynamic of this class. She had begun writing this book as an assignment in a senior citizen's creative writing course and her teacher had recognized her potential. This teacher encouraged her and helped her to rework her assignment into a memoir and then convinced the Multicultural History Society of Toronto to publish it. I met Mrs. Grossman while browsing at a book fair in the fall of 1991. A book cover, which consisted of an old-fashioned sepia-coloured family portrait, had drawn my attention. I was leafing through this book when a small elderly woman next to me started to speak. She had a smile on her face and asked me whether I knew who had written this book. I told her that I didn't. She asked me whether I was going to purchase it and I said, "Yes, it looks really interesting." Her smile widened and then she placed her hands on her hips and said, "I wrote that book and I recommend it." The look of pride on her face was a sight to behold. I wanted to bend down to hug her but, having just met her, I thought that might seem strange. We exchanged telephone numbers and I went home to read her book. I finished it in one sitting and immediately called Mrs.

Grossman to invite her to speak to my class. I also picked up a few copies of her book at her home for my students.

My students enjoyed hearing the story of my chance encounter with Ibi and were taken by her narrative. It is a moving account of a Hungarian-Jewish Holocaust survivor, who faced persecution, loss, and exile, and it is written with such childlike innocence that it can break your heart. She had been branded "stranger" within her homeland. Her husband died in a concentration camp but she and her baby son survived and eventually came to Canada to start their lives over again. I felt very close to Ibi nourished by her strength in the face of all her suffering. The student in my seminar who had endured the Chinese Cultural Revolution identified strongly with Ibi as well. "It is shocking how overnight one can be labeled a stranger and an enemy in one's own country", the student cried when speaking to my class. "How can one come to terms with that?" The foreign students in the class were, by virtue of their status, strangers to Canada: some were visa students, others foreign residents. They too expressed feelings of being 'different' and 'out of step' in the Ontario school system as did even some students who were Canadians but from outside of Ontario.

Perhaps more meaningfully, the personal sense of stranger resonated for us all of us as women who walk the tightrope of multiple cultural lives (Gilligan, 1982). Ibi stayed in our class for the full three hours and she identified strongly with the article *"Stranger's Story"* (1990) by Virginia Shabatay which we also discussed that day. We all recognized this quality of what it means to live on the edge, and of what the stranger, by her very presence, requires of those with whom she comes into contact: an openness towards difference that helps constitute caring relationships between teachers and students. I had come to understand from interviewing newly-arrived elementary students in a multicultural literacy project in an inner-city school in Toronto (which also began in that first year of my faculty position) that the image of "stranger" is central to many immigrants' experiences (see Feuerverger, 1994). As participant-observer in this school, I came to recognize that knowing the existence of the 'foreigner', as Julia Kristeva (1991) puts it, is a central aspect of language awareness which, I believe, can be defined as a sensitivity and a conscious understanding of the myriad languages and cultures in our world and of their role within humanity.

This experience of the 'immigrant as stranger' brought my graduate students together in more or less the same way that immigrants find one another in a new land. They began to create a vibrant sense of community out of their losses and in spite of their woundings. This reminds me of the words of William Pinar (1998) that "living on the margins may be dangerous but at least you can breathe there..." In my own journal writing about my multicultural literacy project in an inner-city school in Toronto, I wrote that: *I could immediately identify with the anxiety in the eyes of many of the participants as they brought back sharp memories of my own parents' post-World War II struggle four decades ago, as refugees and immigrants trying to pick up the pieces of their broken lives in a new land that offered the hope of personal freedom and economic potential.*

UNIVERSITY TEACHING

In another journal entry where I share more of my early tensions as a child of immigrant parents, I explain how I now transcend cultural and linguistic barriers through my classroom teaching and through my school-based research work:

> I, in my role as teacher/educator and researcher, am also retelling and reliving my personal story through this multicultural literacy project. Perhaps this project resonates with me because I sense their confusion and loneliness. Their childhood story is in many ways my childhood story. I too would return home from school to parents who felt totally powerless in their new society and who were intimidated by my teachers and the educational system in general. I never shared any of my school books or lessons with them. Many times I would have to translate what the teacher would have to say about me to them on parents' night. How small and weak my parents would seem in this circumstance. How they were diminished in my young eyes. On some level I must have sensed the injustice of the situation...

My own theme of literacy imbalance within my immigrant family's experiences (documented as a more general phenomenon of the immigrant experience in Feuerverger, 1991, 1994) affected one of my graduate students who came from Portugal. She shared her story of tensions in her family vis-à-vis literacy and higher education:

> I early perceived cultural differences between my parents. My father subscribed to all the papers and was the local news reporter. His barbershop was like a cultural centre; my mother was not part of any discussion. He did not value her opinions and sometimes I heard him calling her "ignorant." It was my father who taught me how to read and I remember him always with a paper or book in his hands. I did not forget two of his favourites - Victor Hugo's "Les Misérables" and Dostoevsky's "Crime and Punishment." There were several volumes and I remember trying hard to read them and finding them very boring. My mother threw the books away when he died. She did not value books... At that time I could not understand why she did that. Now I realize that these books for her might have been obstacles, barriers, walls erected between the two of them. Was she also afraid of losing me when I went to the big city to study? Was that why she was never a great supporter of me pursuing an education?

MOTHERING IN THE WORLD OF TEACHING

That evening with Mrs. Ibi Grossman also unleashed a whole other dimension of exploration deeply embedded in our cells: the mother-daughter relationship involving connection but also separation, uncertainty, and loss. This theme of motherhood was, in part, enacted in our discourse of caring that reflected the "politics of talk" (Belenky et al, 1986) within families. Some of my students displayed ambivalence towards their mothers and sought to learn more about their mothers' lives. Some felt that it was too late to restructure their mother-daughter

79

CHAPTER SIX

relationship but were optimistic that they would do their best to be more fully 'present' to their own children and to their students. It was clear that we had only touched the surface of the complex mother-daughter story as it relates to the teaching story, but we at least had the courage to begin the process. In the following excerpts from two of the graduate students' journals, the theme of mother-daughter relationships is apparent. In the first example, an Israeli student explored the traditional messages her mother communicated and the tension that she, as the daughter, clearly felt:

> So here I am growing up with a vision of personal freedom [gathered from my father's wonderful stories] conquering new horizons as my imagination roams asunder... My mother did not endorse such an outlook on life. As far as she was concerned, a young girl's life led to family, children, community service – the traditional role of women in archaic, patriarchal societies. The message was loud and clear in the example set at home, as well as the preaching that went along with it... I'm not quite sure I know what I am doing. I don't seem to be able to separate my mother's stories from myself. As a matter of fact, the only way I seem to be able to relate to her, now that she is dead, is through images and stories revolving around the mother/daughter relationship, which I immediately turn on its head looking at my own daughters, asking myself what is the message they received over the years and how has this affected my professional life?

In the second example, my Chinese graduate student wished to become like her mother, who was a "well-accomplished person" and professor. But the point remains that this student, too, is trying to understand how her own professional story fits with that of her mother's:

> My mother does not fit the "good" mother model. She used to teach at university before she retired. ... I liked to go to her apartment at university where there was always messiness... My mother is direct, open and has a bad temper... She smokes, plays cards by herself every day and reads novels every day. It is fun to watch her read – laughing and crying with the authors but never bothering to remember the names of the authors or the titles of the books. But I bet she has read all the novels available in the Chinese language (classical, modern and those translated from other languages). She did not mother my brother and me in the way a traditional Chinese mother should have done... She practices Tai Chi every day and loves gardening. She is a well-accomplished person instead of a traditional mother model. I am proud of her because she is not a "good" mother in the usual terms. Because of my mother's mothering, I can see myself on the way to becoming as well-accomplished as she is, in my own way in my career. I don't have to be a "perfect" woman or a "superwoman"...

The theme of motherhood within the context of education was, in part, enacted in our seminar encounter with Ibi, the author. One South Asian student in the class compared our visitor Ibi directly with her own mother and then reflected on my "mothering" in class:

> Ibi was such an addition to the class. I was overwhelmed by her honesty and her motherliness. It made me think of my own mother and how distant she was, really. I could never go to her for any good advice; she was always so critical of me. Ibi made me feel how much I have missed and it saddens me. Her devotion to her son in the midst of all her suffering is so inspiring. She lost her husband in the war but kept on being the best mother she could be. How young she was and how strong! I will never forget her cracked voice when she spoke of losing this man who was her husband for such a short time. The tears were hot and stabbing my eyes. I looked around. We shared this tragic moment together. At the next class, we all began to talk about our mothers and mothering in general. It happened so spontaneously. I heard M. mention that Grace was motherly in her teaching role. The more I think about it the more I agree. She lets us "be"; she lets us grow. She cares about us personally and professionally. She is nurturing.

An enduring image I hold in my memory is when all the students rushed over to Ibi as she was getting ready to leave. She hugged us all as if we were her children. Her embrace made us feel protected and special in a way that we could only marvel at. One student could not hold back tears. Drained by yet another "stranger's" story, we were left feeling shipwrecked but very much alive and one step closer to the wholeness of being at the core of our inquiries. These personal memories brought us closer to a "solidarity with one another" (Delpit, 1992).

In a journal entry by a Québecois student who came from a small farming community, a first encounter with "difference" at school in the mid-1950s was through a young Hungarian girl. In learning about this young girl she was exposed to a different language and culture which helped shape her personal and professional life. Here is an excerpt from her writing:

> One morning a Hungarian girl 'appeared' in our class from behind the nun's layers of skirts ... The teacher introduced her as 'someone very special.' "God has decided to save her and her family from communism." We all sighed in awe. I thought for sure she must have had some special power, in the line of Bernadette Soubiroux. Sooner or later people will start talking of miracles or strange things happening to our village. Visitors will come from everywhere. Mystery was in the air. An exciting lift that carried me to an unexplored, unpredictable place...

> When she started talking in her language, I was lost in wonder... How could it be? Different words to name the same things. I was curious about the new sounds, about her. We invented a game: saying words, isolating sounds, making up new words. No doubt a game influenced by the decoding that was going on in the classroom. But it didn't matter if the words made sense. By the end of grade one she knew how to read as well as I did... But she didn't

> dress like us. She didn't eat like us. She didn't smell like us. She didn't talk like us and she was poor, poorer than us...

As another, perhaps more exotic example of a first introduction to "otherness", there is a sense in the following piece that the Roma (Gypsy) women embody a different way of life, one that also entails magic and enchantment and "wistful dreams":

> In my little Portuguese village, the Gypsies always came in late spring when the bright yellow blooms of acacias contrasted with the blue skies... Was my fascination an unconscious recognition of the difference between their lives and the way my parents were bringing me up? Was I already longing for the independence I now value so much? Most of the time the Gypsy children did not pay much attention to me but once in a while I played with some of the girls. We did not exchange many words. This upset me because I loved the music of their language. I wished I could speak like them. I did not understand everything they said, but I understood there was another linguistic code, another way of communicating. Was this my first encounter with a foreign language? Gypsy women were beautiful, I loved their long skirts and I could not help following them when they went into the village. The owners of the stores feared them because they said the women were capable of stealing things right in front of their eyes. Sometimes the women convinced some adults to have their palms read and I was intrigued by their knowledge. They had come from other places, they must have learned these things somewhere else. When the villagers said the gypsies were witches I did not believe them. They cooked, and took care of the children - I could watch them from the bridge. They were like everybody else - just different because they travelled. The whole summer was enchanted. Groups of gypsies came and went, they never stayed long. I used to watch them disappear down the road and I had wistful dreams of being stolen by them.

Just as Pinar (1988) had suggested, the notion of teaching and learning for us became a search for self-knowledge that actively pursues a construction of self-identification with marginalized social groups. I searched for ways within my teaching to create the sense of a collective cultural home that would thrive in a university setting, shaping personal and professional destinies. The image of the "cultural orphan" added strength to my teaching self. Perhaps I was working towards trying to become not only a caring professor but also, as Belenky et al (1986) describe it, a "midwife-teacher" whose sharing of my life story would support the evolving multicultural consciousness of others.

In the spirit of making a home of the classroom, I held the last class of this course in my house. Everyone prepared a dish representing their own culture – contributing to a multicultural feast. The warmth of our words filled us with emotions that had developed in the sharing of our narratives throughout the term. I wrote a journal entry that evening as a tribute to this educational experience:

Throughout the term, we peeled off the layers of our (cultural) past, week by week, until what we stared at was the potential of our future. A glimpse of paradise; a broken promise made years ago. Within the landscape of our cultural diversity we shared a common goal. We were in the process of discovering our stories. They had been lost in the maelstrom of political, social, psychological violence. Our voices had been silenced in the storm but we survived, shipwrecked but alive. And suddenly we found each other in this course. No wonder that sparks began to fly. We began to write our journals and we shared the grief and pain and anger and joy. This is what education is all about: this gem of community and learning...

TEN YEARS LATER

In the fall of 2001 the first class of my "Multicultural Perspectives in Teacher Development: A Reflective Seminar" took place on September 11th. I had just returned from a conference in Europe on the evening of September 10th. Early the following morning I unpacked the remaining items from my suitcase, still somewhat groggy from the jet lag and began to get myself organized for my first class of the new academic year. I always look forward to the excitement of meeting a new group of students. With every new academic year – and that was my tenth in the Centre for Teacher Development (CTD) – I remember wondering what this fresh new year will bring. At around 8:30 a.m. I had a pleasant telephone conversation with a colleague about our respective summer activities. I got off the phone and went back to work. And then the phone rang. Did it sound more urgent than usual? I picked it up and heard the voice of my husband calling me from work. His voice seemed odd and muted as he uttered bizarre words: "*I'm not sure what's going on but it seems that the U.S. has been attacked. Turn on the radio or TV.*" I felt as though I was hallucinating as I watched the hijacked airplanes tear into the World Trade Center Towers in New York. Fiery explosions; the smoke; confusion on the streets of Manhattan; firefighters rushing into the inferno; emergency rooms waiting for survivors.

I called the CTD and spoke with Mick Connelly who kindly said that if I wanted to cancel my evening class, he would certainly understand and support me. But I wanted to be with my students – although I really had no idea whether anyone would show up. I heard that people in office towers downtown in Toronto were leaving to return home. Everyone became enveloped within this surrealistic moment in time. Everything seemed to go into slow motion. It took me forever to get my course materials together. I walked to the subway station. The weather was beautiful, so incongruous with the grim events unfolding in the U.S. I arrived at OISE/UT at 3 p.m. – well before my class, which was scheduled for 5:30 p.m. The news from New York City was becoming more and more gruesome. I got up to the tenth floor and spoke with people in the CTD.

A sense of disbelief hung over everyone in the building like a strange dark cloud. At 5:30 p.m. I walked into the room on the third floor where my class was to be held and was overwhelmed to see a dozen faces staring at me – in confusion, in shock, in fear, but also in gratitude that I too had arrived. Our class huddled together – lost wanderers in a crazy nightmare. We were all relieved to find ourselves in a safe space where we could share our feelings. The windowless classroom became a zone of privacy – a sacred spot in a world that suddenly had become much more menacing than before. It seemed to me as if we all bonded immediately. We all decided right then to commemorate the shattering loss of that day by putting together a collective piece of our reflections of that horrific event (see Feuerverger, et al, 2001).

During the break, my students went out to a nearby bookstore (as had been planned) to buy my book "Oasis of Dreams: Teaching and Learning Peace in a Jewish-Palestinian Village in Israel" which had just been published, and when they returned I noticed some of them clinging to the book as if for comfort. One student said she was grateful to have this book as a symbol of hope in that terrible moment. Strangely, this catastrophic event clarified even more why I had decided to write this book – the result of a nine-year reflexive ethnographic study about an extraordinary Jewish-Palestinian cooperative village and its unique bilingual, bicultural educational institutions.

Neve Shalom/Wahat Al-Salam (the Hebrew and Arabic words for "Oasis of Peace") is a village that began as an intercultural experiment and it has certainly changed me forever. (My first research sojourn there took place right at the end of my very first term in the Centre for Teacher Development.) Dealing as it does with individuals on an educational odyssey toward peace in the midst of deadly conflict, this book seemed to have become still more timely after the tragedy of September 11th. In the ethnographic research process, I walked through a landscape of spiritual reflection, of pedagogical reveries, of social and political tensions. I listened to painful stories as well as healing ones, and shared narrative portraits of remarkable individuals who, in their attempt at peaceful coexistence, invite us all to become fellow dreamers of peace.

This village is a profoundly sacred space and nourishes me in ways I could never have expected. It comforts me in this time of violence in Israel and in the occupied territories and brings me closer to the reason I came to it in the first place: to bear witness to the power of what these villagers are seeking to accomplish against all odds. At the core of "Oasis of Dreams" – as indeed at the core of all my academic work – will always be that child of the Holocaust searching for a safe place in the world – for a site of refuge, peacebuilding and hope for humanity. That child will never have the luxury of taking life for granted. She will always feel "homeless" – a psychological orphan. The deeper meaning of this Jewish-Palestinian village for me is in its call for reconciliation in spite of the woundedness that surrounds both Israelis and Palestinians. And I am grateful that I was able to reveal the suffering within my own soul to these villagers. And are we not all wounded in our own ways – especially in the aftermath of September 11th? Do we not all need to be rescued by the message which the village of *Neve Shalom/Wahat Al-Salam* offers us – that 'peace on earth' is possible?

I used this book in my course for the first time that Tuesday evening of September 11, 2001 and was gratified by the responses of my students. It opened a whole new space for building a discourse of intercultural understanding. We focused on how these courageous villagers have chosen to engage in true dialogue and thus to become architects in their destinies rather than pawns. We discussed how they may be on the threshold of a liberating narrative which urges us to reflect on its global potential for peacebuilding and social justice – in spite of our present despair, or perhaps even because of it. Perhaps what lies at the heart of this village is only a dream on the larger world stage, but without it we are lost. In fact their moral enterprise may be the only way toward compassion and redemption for us all.

As I put the finishing touches on this chapter, I have relived and retold the story of that halcyon time of my first university graduate course in the fall of 1991. It seems now as if it happened a long time ago and in a different world, one that was more innocent then. Our global village seems to have become a more dangerous place and I believe that now more than ever we as teacher/educators are called to provide for our students a more hopeful view of what the world has the potential to be. This was one of the reasons I originally decided to write *"Oasis of Dreams"* – to share the message that individuals do make a difference and that teaching always will be what Bill Ayers describes as "an act of hope for a better future." I shall always be grateful for that first course and for that first year in the Joint Centre for Teacher Development where I found my academic home among an extraordinary community of learners. This was where I learned something I had always believed in: that the educational enterprise is an art form which transcends social, historical or cultural context. It is about creating connections: voices as a meeting place. In the end, what will matter most is how we treat each other locally and globally – how much respect and care we give each other in and out of our classrooms, in and out of our schools and our cultures, issues that stand as moral and ethical challenges within the larger framework of humanity.

NOTES

[1] This seminar was based on the M.A. thesis of Carol Mullen.
[2] Some of this particular section's material appeared in *Narrative and Experience in Multicultural Education* under the title "Multicultural Perspectives in Teacher Development" (Thousand Oaks, CA: Sage, 2005)

CHAPTER SEVEN

RECLAIMING ESL VOICES

If we do not belong completely anywhere, at least we do in our mother tongue. That is where our identity is."

-Marianne Alopens

In September 1991, when I had just completed the first week in my new faculty position in the Joint Centre for Teacher Development at OISE, my colleague Jim Cummins and I were contacted by a school board official in Toronto who was interested in having us create a school project to complement a new board policy that had been put into place a little while earlier – the Multicultural, Ethnic and Race Relations (MERR) policy initiative. In carrying out this work, Jim and I decided to focus on two basic questions: 1) What does it mean to teach and learn in classrooms filled with students coming from every part of the globe and speaking a multitude of languages, but not yet English? And 2) How do we reclaim the voices of ESL students and build bridges toward cross-cultural understanding and literacy development? We came up with a very simple idea based on the work of Alma Flor Ada at San Francisco State University: the goal of the project was to encourage children from culturally and linguistically diverse backgrounds to develop their literacy skills not only in English, their second language but also, to some degree, in their first language as well; and most importantly to develop pride in their cultural backgrounds.[1]

We received a grant form the Ontario Ministry of Education to purchase dual-track books where on one side of the page the story is in English and on the other side it is in the home languages of the children. The idea was for the children to use these books in their classrooms and then to bring them home to read to their parents. Our intention was to give these students opportunities for reading both in school and at home by providing such books in the school library.

For recently-arrived immigrant children who already have reading skills in their home language the purpose is obvious: to stimulate their continued literacy development while they are acquiring English language skills. A second objective was to bring immigrant parents and the school together and allow opportunities for the parents to be directly involved in their children's education, to give them a voice in the educational process of their children. What was important was to recognize the fact that schools can play a major role in encouraging children's home language and culture development even where intensive first language instruction is not available. It was a question of encouraging schools to welcome parents to participate in their activities.

CHAPTER SEVEN

THE MULTICULTURAL TEXTURE OF A TORONTO SCHOOL

After several planning meetings with a few principals, and school board officials, it became clear that the principal of Somerset Public School was especially keen on this project and he generously offered us a "carte blanche" in our research work. I became the main researcher, when Jim had to turn his attention to another research project and I later applied for another grant to document on film the institutional changes taking place as a result of the project. As an educational ethnographer it made sense for me to interview the students, teachers and parents and to observe what goes on in the classrooms where the dual track books would be used. But first I had to sell this idea to the teachers. I remember that first meeting with them well. Anxiety hung over the staffroom like a thick fog. Most of the teachers were concerned that the project would add to their workload. The last impression I wanted to give was that of a university researcher who had come to impose her agenda onto the teachers. That does unfortunately too happen often, and it is one of the reasons that teachers are so wary of researchers coming into their schools.

For me, if research work is not a partnership between researcher and participants in a naturalistic, interactive, grassroots way, then I do not want to be associated with it. It should always be about soul and not about ego. I wanted this project to be about reclaiming voice and encouraging cross-cultural understanding and harmony. I wanted us all to imagine how to make this school – all schools – more inclusive places for ESL students – all students. The idea was that the dual-track books had the potential to become a vehicle for sharing our cultures, our stories, our humanity: to become part of a creative process. Literary critic Kermode (1967) said that "we all rely upon the stories of others for guidance in writing our own" (p. 126-127). So I simply asked for volunteers. The teacher-librarian and one ESL teacher raised their hands exuberantly. And for me that was good enough. The others sat still. I could tell that many were on the verge of opening up but had decided on a 'wait and see' attitude. I thanked the two volunteers. I hoped that once the others would witness the enthusiasm in the students which I believed the project would foster, then they too would want to come on board. And that in fact was what eventually happened. In the meantime, however, the project was off and running and I sighed with relief.

To record and later be able to convey a sense of the scene and mood of the school and its participants, I kept an ongoing journal. Mishler (1986) says that "telling stories is a significant way for individuals to give meaning to and express their understandings of their experiences" (p.75). Connelly & Clandinin (1990) write that "education and educational research is the construction and reconstruction of personal and social stories; learners, teachers and researchers are storytellers and characters in their own and others' stories." Eisner (1991) too agrees that "schools...have moods, and they...display scenes of high drama that those who make policy and who seek to improve practice should know. The means through which such knowledge is made possible are the enlightened eye – the scene is seen – and the ability to craft text so that what the observer has experienced can be shared by those who were not there" (p. 30). The story of the school, its "high drama", can be read as a "natural psychological unit" (Rayfield, 1972, p. 1085).

In the final analysis, this story about the dual-track multicultural literacy project belongs to all of the participants who helped to re-envision what the process of reading and writing in culturally diverse schools is about. We all became caught up in a project that left lots of room for serendipity to enter. The school library became a little sanctuary where the books began to sit proudly on shelves waiting for little hands to come and caress them. And indeed little hands did begin to roam about the shelves and to discover all sorts of amazing new pictures and languages, and alphabets. One could see the children lose themselves in the pages of these books, eyes open in awe and wonder. Revelations happened: new ways of understanding where their peers had come from, new discoveries about ways of living in the world, new approaches to telling stories – all sharing this affirmation of life lived in a rainbow of different languages, different customs, different traditions. And English was always there on the other side of the page to keep everyone grounded. Not one student fell by the wayside.

THE SCHOOL SETTING

I remember vividly my first official research visit to meet the students. It was an exciting moment in my new professional life and I was filled with anticipation. I felt that there was something very inviting and very real about Somerset right from the beginning. This school is situated in an inner-city, low-income, culturally diverse area with high-rise apartment building complexes near the school that included grocery stores, restaurants, a dry cleaning store, a day care centre, and more. The school's playground sits on a hill overlooking a major thoroughfare in the eastern part of the city. When I think of the school's playground I see the mothers and fathers of the children with faces and dresses of all colours and shapes. It certainly reminded me of my own childhood life at Bedford School decades earlier. Culturally and linguistically, this felt like Babel to me because of its diversity and because of all the languages of the children: Urdu, Hindi, Gujurati, Punjabi, Catchi, Bengali, Chinese (Cantonese and Mandarin), Romanian, Farsi, Vietnamese, Bulgarian, Korean, Japanese, Tagalog, Swahili, Somalian, Arabic, Durie, Pushtu, Tamil, Tigrigna, Turkish, Spanish, Guyanese and Trinidadian English, to name only some. This community is a reception area for most of its residents in the sense that they experience it as the first step in a long and difficult climb. I understood how difficult life is for these new immigrants, economically, socially, and psychologically. I had experienced it all before in watching my own parents eke out a living – that sense of vulnerability, shame, anxiety, and exhaustion.

A delicious aroma of fresh vegetable soup enveloped my research assistant and me as we entered the school that first day of the research project. A huge bowl overflowing with popcorn welcomed us in the staff room where a large pot of tea was also brewing. On the stove was a veritable cauldron bubbling with the soup. As we went upstairs to the library I thanked my lucky stars that this was to be my research school for the year. The library was filled with armchairs, overstuffed sofas and rocking chairs; shelves of brightly-coloured books; children of many different ethnic backgrounds were sitting on the floor sharing some of the dual-track books that had already arrived – all under the maternal gaze of Queen Elizabeth II framed in a 1960s wall portrait.

Judy, the teacher-librarian, became a key player in our project from its inception. One of her responsibilities involved purchasing the first language books and this proved to be an adventure in itself. We were lucky to have her on our side in this: her enthusiasm and devotion were remarkable. Judy grew up in a monolingual town in Northern Ontario and longed for exposure to different cultures. As a child, she became fascinated by folktales from around the globe: they became her bridge to other worlds. So it is not surprising that as an adult she became a professional storyteller in addition to a teacher-librarian. The contribution of her work to our study was invaluable. She spent countless hours tracking down leads to children's books in many languages including languages that were less well-known; and her caring attitude towards the ESL students was evidenced in her boundless enthusiasm about the use of the dual-track books which she shared with the children. Judy's stories about tracking down these books were full of intrigue and passion. They revolve around meeting potential booksellers in various small corner stores or in homes well off the beaten track of mainstream society. Her life history matched with her own philosophy that *"a story is a story, and the more children are exposed to them, the better."* Those backrooms of grocery stores where she found many of the great little dual-track books were the beacons of many ethnic neighbourhoods.

One important aspect of these 'dual text' or 'dual language' books is their ability to instill a sense of inclusive education. As mentioned previously, one set-up is that the story of the home language is presented on one side of the page and told in English on the other. In other dual texts, both languages appear on the same page. The point of the bilingual feature is that it allows **all** children access to **all** books. In this way, children are exposed to cross-cultural appreciation and understanding, and teachers can ensure that no one in the class is left out so that no divisiveness is created. The potential then exists for teachers to foster a climate of enjoyment by making use of these books in the mainstream Language Arts classroom. In librarian Judy's words, "We have Chinese children reading the English part of the Bengali book...because if they can read English, they can enjoy the story."

These books also make it possible for children to share this school activity with their parents. Their parents' English may not be advanced enough to read with ease; but they can participate by reading the first language that to their children and the children can read the English text to them, or they can simply enjoy the illustrations together. The magic comes from the fact that their cultures and languages are represented as well as acknowledged within mainstream schooling. This is very symbolic. Judy helps us to imagine what this sharing is like as she describes the joy on the face of a newly-arrived student upon discovering books in his language:

We have a new student from Iran who just arrived the other day and I knew his class was coming into the library that morning. So I took one of the Farsi books from the shelf and and I just held it like this, in front of me, and the class came in and this child's eyes lit up and he asked "Is that Farsi?" and I said "Yes, do you want it?" and he just looked spellbound. And then another Iranian boy who's been here for a while became his reading "buddy" and they read together.

Her comments illustrate what it feels like for a child to be connected to the warmth and familiarity of one's own language in a new culture. She also describes how disorienting it can be to be surrounded by foreign words and a foreign alphabet:

I have stood in a store where every spine of every book was Chinese, Japanese, Korean or Vietnamese and I can't read the alphabet...You just stand there and you have to have somebody to help you. It's overwhelming. You feel helpless. So I can understand how children feel when they first arrive. Everything is a different alphabet, so to see their own language really means something for them.

Not all of the books are bilingual however. In the case of Farsi and some other languages, the books are single language texts, yet they can still be shared because some of the stories had been translated by the more 'established' children and parents in the school, those who have been in Toronto longer and therefore have reached a certain level of proficiency in English. In any case, the main purpose of this project was not necessarily literacy development in the first language *per se*, but rather to open a space for cross-cultural communication and respect for diversity. The message this project offers to students is that their cultural backgrounds *do* count and that all children have a place in the school and moreover in mainstream society. It proclaims that immigrant children need not give in to the limitations and restrictions imposed on them by their circumstances, but rather that they too have a place in their new classrooms and therefore within Canadian society.

I often saw myself in the eyes of these children. I sensed their confusion and loneliness in many of my interactions with them because my own childhood story is, in many ways, their childhood story. As a child of immigrant/refugee parents, I, too, returned home from school to parents who felt powerless and intimidated in their new society. Knowing that my parents felt alien to the educational system, I never shared any of my schoolbooks or lessons with them. How different my own cultural life might have been if I had had the opportunity to see storybooks in Yiddish in the library of my beloved Fielding School. Instead my two worlds – home versus mainstream school – were situated on different planets. I was obliged to incorporate a humiliating caricature of myself and my parents, as do many immigrant children. What then happens is the gradual loss of a healthy sense of self, of a sense of entitlement in society. Is it any wonder then that I became involved with this Somerset research project?

CHAPTER SEVEN

A STORYTELLING LESSON

While sitting with Judy, the teacher/librarian, and a group of students in the library, I observed a storytelling lesson enacted by children in a Grade Five class. A Persian story was read out by two of the children. One student, Sima, read the story to us in Farsi (the national language of Iran). The second girl, Shiraza, translated the story into English. The first child had come to Canada recently and was still not very fluent in English and yet she appeared to be confident in the rocking chair which is given to the "reader-in-charge." Everyone was fascinated by the sounds of this language. Applause. She felt proud of herself. And there was no question in anyone's mind that she was a fluent reader even though she was a new immigrant.

The story read to us by the girls is called "The Long-Legged Raven" and is about a snake that tries to snatch an unhatched egg from a pair of ravens. During discussion, students asked specific questions about the cultural context of the story. Others asked textual questions. And still others asked about vocabulary, wanting to hear the Farsi word for "snake" or "bird" or "egg." Some shared similar stories from their own culture. Issues about identity, family separation and homesickness, and `belonging' arose during this storytelling lesson. The children all became aware that regardless of their cultural origins, many of them shared similar family dramas. *"I miss my grandmother so much!"* said one boy from Guyana. *"She used to tell me all kinds of stories about my country and people but now I'm here in Toronto with my mom and other brothers. And my mom works all the time and has no time to read to us. But now I'm starting to bring home books to read to her."* This young boy found a way to use literacy to comfort his mother as a substitute for his grandmother.

AN ESL CLASS

After recess I sat in on an ESL class where each student chose a book or poem in their home language and read it out loud. Claire, a Chinese girl, began with the poem, "Spring is Coming", which she read in English and then in Chinese. The students were transfixed, enthralled by the lyrical quality of the poem: They commented that it sounded more like a poem when read in Chinese than in English. Fascinated by the tonal quality of the Mandarin language, the students tried to repeat some of the words and asked what they meant in English. The young reader was overwhelmed by the attention that her classmates showed her and her home language. She also was delighted when her teacher tried to say some of the words in Chinese. It was enheartening for me to witness the sense of safety and trust created in a class where the children are not in any danger of being mocked and where their language and culture are being validated.

The teacher wanted to know what effect these books had on the children so she asked them whether they found these books useful and interesting. Hands shot up in the air. One little Romanian girl's responded: *"I promised my grandmother that I will never forget where I came from and to read and write my home language. I* can't wait to show her how well I can read in Romanian and in English. She will be proud." Many other children also responded enthusiastically about the usefulness of first language books in school, including even one Canadian-born boy from Alberta who exclaimed, "Aren't these books in ALL school libraries? They should be!"

In such classes where value is placed on the students' language and culture and where children are encouraged to write their own cultural stories using the dual track books as models, the results of such specific intervention was highly positive and "enabling." Sylvia Ashton-Warner in her book "Teacher" asks: "How good is any child's book anyway, compared with ones they write themselves? Of course, as I'm always saying, it's not the only reading; it's no more than the first reading. The bridge." (p. 28) I witnessed the enthusiasm and energy with which children organized and wrote their own dual-track stories which later were transformed into professional looking books they proudly brought home to read to their parents. This kind of teaching-learning environment facilitates what Hogan (1988) describes as "empowering relationships which involve feelings of 'connectedness' that are developed in situations of equality, caring and mutual purpose and intention" (p. 12). Schools, therefore, can play a major role in reversing the pattern of ESL children failing at school. By promoting pride in cultural identity via encouraging first language proficiency, as in this specific intervention, children's ambivalence about their culture can be overcome.

"These children do not come to us as blank slates", says ESL teacher Barbara. Rather, *"They have great background knowledge and we can learn from them. I used the books most with the Priority One [students who have just arrived] and are suffering culture shock and are SO pleased to see a book in their own language. And then a little later, they graduate to a bilingual book and can sit together with a few children and have them read the first language and others read the English and they can kind of understand what the English means because they just read the Chinese, for example. All children are interested in fairy tales and they are fascinated to hear the stories in different languages and with slightly different angles. They see the world from a different perspective. They are intrigued by the different sounds. I think there's a value in that. To know that there are many, many different languages in the world and to realize that ours is just one. It's a humbling experience."*

Barbara noted that as the children progress and become more proficient in English, they are less likely to use the dual-track books all the time. But they do return to them after a while and then appreciate them for their story line. Once they are sufficiently confident in their English proficiency, they can return to these books with renewed vigour. It is as if initially, the books act as a security blanket. I myself witnessed how lovingly some of the children would hold onto these books. As time passed and they gradually gained enough confidence in their literacy skills, they could then appreciate these books as a welcome addition to their reading repertoire.

As Barbara explained, "u*sing the bilingual books bridges the gap. Monolingual children react much more positively. It's a whole world they didn't know about. In*

CHAPTER SEVEN

North America, traditionally, we've been very slow to embrace the idea of a second language let alone a third or fourth. I guess geographically, we were able to get away with it, whereas language has been fundamental to education in most other parts of the world. I think more and more children are understanding that – even more and more adults! And the definition of language isn't just 'my' language. And it's also interesting for children to find out that a word in their language is similar to the same word in another person's language."

The dual-track books, in other words, add a wider perspective to what it means to be Canadian. In the past becoming Canadian meant giving up one's ethnicity; now becoming Canadian means weaving one's ethnicity into the fabric of Canadian identity, a work-in-progress. This observation was echoed by a newly-arrived Chinese doctoral student who did some participant-observation in the school as an assignment in one of my graduate seminars. In one class at the school, Halloween was approached as a topic of diversity in that students were asked to write about the superstitions embedded in their own cultures. A multicultural awareness was also cultivated in the mind of this graduate student as she observed the children making use of the bilingual books. In a lengthy journal entry intended for me, she wrote,

When the Chinese girl finished telling a story from her own culture, I heard an Iranian boy saying that he wished that he could read Chinese. As a result, students learn to admire and respect those who come from other backgrounds and languages, rather than to be prejudiced against them. I believe that this is such an important part of multicultural teaching."

These school experiences parallel Corson's (1990) thesis that if schools and teachers are to implement "critical language awareness" they must adopt a more critical approach to their teaching practice, especially as it relates to the use of language and discourse (p.227): they must understand and serve the cultural and linguistic needs of their clientele and allow their students' and parents' voices to be heard in the educational process.

The Student Interviews

In the afternoon of that first research day at Somerset I interviewed Stefan who was eight years old, from Bulgaria, and had been in Canada for about nine months. He was quite fluent in English and was altogether a delightful child. Grinning proudly, he said that he had read a story in Bulgarian to his grade three class and that they had all enjoyed it: *"They asked me all kinds of questions. One boy said he wished he could have the book; another asked whether he could have it. Everyone laughed because it was a funny story. Some of them tried to say the words in Bulgarian but they couldn't."* Pride showed on in his face. The other children were apparently fascinated that he could speak and read another language so well. His self-confidence was transparent as he translated the story for me into English. What makes it possible for a newly-arrived immigrant child in school to feel like a success as opposed to a failure? For Stefan, having the opportunity to access first language books stimulated his literacy development in both his home language as well as in English. He was invited to carry his cultural identity through the school's doors. He can be Stefan – a tapestry of a Bulgarian past and of a Canadian future, all interwoven into the present.

Stefan compared the Bulgarian alphabet with the English (Roman) one, understanding that an object may have several names depending on the language itself. I held up a cup and asked him the word for it in Bulgarian. He shook his head and said definitively that "cup" in Bulgarian is "*tshasha*" but that that particular cup – he pointed to the one I was holding – is not available in Bulgaria. I then realized the error of my question – the cup I was holding was made of styrofoam!

The challenge of the new and strange English language for Stefan was palpable. He referred to his ESL classes as a relief from the difficulties of second language learning and was able to relay the teacher's pedagogic strategies with considerable clarity: *"Every morning, Mrs. B., the ESL teacher, would come into my class and take me to her room with a few other new students. First she taught me the alphabet and then the new words. She would say a word and then I would have to figure out what it meant and then draw it. Then later on she began to teach me how to write the words. I'm pretty good now. I can read all kinds of books."*

It is clear that as a second language learner Stefan was more aware than a monolingual child would be of what is involved in learning language; he was also actively contrasting languages as illustrated by the example of the cup. Stefan was also fully aware of the diverse uses of language in communication: *"I speak Bulgarian and English at home. Normally, I speak Bulgarian but when I don't want my sister (who is three and only speaks Bulgarian) to understand something, then I speak in English with my mother."* Furthermore at school Stefan had taken a newly-arrived Bulgarian child under his wing to help "teach" his older new friend. I sensed that by this teaching experience he was also dignifying his sense of self.

Then there were Nuzhat and her sister Mira born in Canada to Pakistani parents. These two lovely children, with sparkling brown eyes, described their love of being read to in Urdu by their parents. Nuzhat, who is ten years old and bilingual, exclaimed that when she heard her father read Urdu stories *"the words sound more exciting than they do in English."* When I pressed her on this, she said that stories in Urdu trigger feelings about her family and also about her parents' homeland. They were motivated to learn to read and write in Urdu because they wanted their relatives in Pakistan *"to realize that even though we are Canadian, we haven't forgotten where our family comes from and that our relatives will be proud of us. When I speak to them over the telephone, they say `She's really improving.'"* Mira thought that it was great that their classmates responded well to the Urdu books *"because once kids know what your language and culture is like, then they won't make fun of you."* These children articulated clearly the objectives of the multicultural/race relations Board policy in their own childlike but nevertheless intelligent way. They were in tune with the need for cross-cultural education to foster tolerance, respect and understanding among people.

CHAPTER SEVEN

The Parent Interviews

On a subsequent research visit to Somerset I interviewed several parents in addition to the principal of the school. Their stories were powerful in their intensity and honesty; they were hopeful even though full of trauma. Among the priorities emerging from these interviews was the need that newly-arrived parents be given a voice in the educational process. A collaborative home/school literacy program can promote such a sense of voice. In this section, I offer some selected excerpts from my interviews with these parents and highlight some of the discussions with three of them: Ahmed from Afghanistan, Aisha from Eritrea, and Samiya from Iran.

Ahmed

Ahmed grew up in a small village in the northeast of Afghanistan but was educated in Kabul and holds Masters degrees in education and in law. Pain darkens his serious eyes. He was the only one in his village who had received a higher education. As a child, he lived in the mountains and had to walk three and a half hours to school. As an adult he returned to his village to be a teacher. Ahmed started his own school for children in a refugee camp in Pakistan on the border of Afghanistan. He and his family lived in the camp for twelve years subsequent to the invasion of Afghanistan by the Soviets in 1978. In this camp he *"established a committee with people who had a background in education and designed a curriculum."* He went on to add: *"We certainly didn't have enough resources but we did the best we could. I still have that curriculum document. It is dear to me... I came to Canada in 1990 to try and find a better life for my family and I thought that from the outside I would have a better chance to help the refugees in the camp."*

Ahmed liked the multicultural intervention of our project because he saw that it integrated the language of his children into the regular school day as opposed to the heritage language programs that take place outside of it. He told me that *"My children go to heritage (international) language classes on Saturday. It's very hard. They need rest then. I know many parents who just can't send their children then. It would be much better during school time as it is in some schools. The children also should learn about different cultures in school. I like the idea of your books in the library. It helps."* He also saw that our intervention had the potential of teaching *"a way of life for the newcomer."*

Ahmed and I both agree that this issue of heritage language, and whether or not it is integrated in regular school curriculum, is only one piece of a larger picture. Ahmed's philosophy on the importance of heritage language programs to public awareness and community life is echoed in this multicultural intervention within mainstream curriculum as something that is important to the learning of *all* school participants whether newly-arrived or already established. Because Ahmed's words on this are so eloquent I wish to quote him again on his ethnic experience and his reasoning:

This is why, I think, heritage language programs are important – for everybody not just the immigrants. The point is we are all living together and that means that our cultures – we have to bring them into the public – into the mainstream. We have to learn to share what we know. You know, life is a school. You can learn many things that you can't by just reading in a book. Sure, there are many things you can learn in a book but you need the practical, the experience. We want the children of our community to understand their own culture so that they can respect other people's cultures. And I believe that if you respect your neighbour then you will be respected too. That's why heritage language education is so important. But it's a big job and we need money for that. If it is not organized properly, then it's a waste of time. The children need to spend more time and better time at it. We need good teachers who are respected for what they do. It's like sowing the seeds for later fruit. It's valuable. We have to plant for the future. That's education.

Aisha

Aisha's life, too, was full of the war and tragedy in Eritrea. Like Ahmed and myself she has many stories of dislocation and relocation to tell that transcend despair but that cannot be captured in a brief portrait. In terms of the study, Aisha describes how valuable it is for many different cultures to have their voices heard in school. She exemplifies the kind of parent Ahmed had in mind when he had said that *"It is important to teach the parents as well as the children."* She felt that *"to have this multiculturalism is like a dream. All kinds of people, it's interesting. I go to a class to improve my English in the mornings given by the school board. I have made friends with some of the people. From all over the world. We learn about each other. We are all trying to find a better life."*

Although Aisha is an exemplary parent, she does broach the subject of being emotionally challenged by her daughter who is growing up Canadian. She says, *"If you push your children too hard here, they might go completely the other way. You have to find a balance because this is not the country that I come from and the ways are different... After all, they are growing up Canadian. I must remember that... At least here in Canada, things are more in the open and children can talk to their parents. I see it as a good thing. I would like to visit my own country with them and show them the ways there. It would help them to understand why I act the way I do. I hope that will be possible in the future. Then my children will understand their culture and respect it..."*

Samiya

Samiya offers the perspective of an Iranian parent on the value of our multicultural literacy intervention in classrooms and in students' lives: *"The children bring books in Farsi home to read. Such a good idea. We can explain what our world was like to them while we read. It brings us closer together. And I like the heritage language programs but I wish it was during the week. On Saturday, we have shopping to do and all sorts of other things. And the children are tired from a whole week at school..."* Moreover, she provides some insight into the value of the Iranian culture, albeit problematic, to her children's Canadian identity: *" How can we explain what happened in our country [the Islamic Revolution] to our children? We don't even understand it ourselves! We try to teach them about Iranian culture as we knew it. That's what we can do. They should appreciate the great Persian culture and history because there is a lot of good in it."*

Like Ahmed and Aisha, Samiya expressed concern over the growing psychological chasm between many immigrant parents who come from rural, developing nations and their children who are being socialized in post-modern, urban Western society. Consequently, one implication of the study is that first language literacy can help to maintain communication between parent and child, and to foster an awareness of different values.

THE PRINCIPAL'S VIEW

Ron is the quintessential role model of a caring, capable administrator who has faith in and respect for his teachers and students. He was very involved in and supportive of the literacy project right from the start. He is the central force behind the welcoming, homey atmosphere of the school. Co-operative and caring, Ron was sensitive to the children and they responded warmly to him. The teachers too expressed their good fortune in having Ron not only as their team leader but also as a "good father figure." This was his last year of service and the teachers and students were sad about that. Confident and relaxed in his principal's role, he allowed our project team free rein to collect data in the school. Jose, my research assistant, and I visited the school on the last day of classes, corresponding with the last day of Ron's formal career in the elementary school system. In my memory is the image of Ron's final day on the playground being hugged by the children who thanked him and wished him well. My eyes were misty as I watched this remarkable tribute to him.

Ron, witnessing the transformative effects of our literacy project on the children of his school, described the developmental process of our intervention in classrooms. He was open to the positive repercussions of including dual track books in the school library and like the rest of us became still more convinced of its value as he observed its beneficial effects on children and teachers. He told me that:

> At first I saw this project more as a sort of PR thing, but as I have watched the new kids coming in through the door of the library and eyes lighting up when they saw the books for the first time, I realized that they see that here in a Canadian library they have books to read... I've gone into classes and I see these books on the children's desk and I realize the potential... That was the first step. I think the next step is funding books for the collection. It's not as easy as ordering books from a standard catalogue... This has involved a lot of labour on the part of the school librarian. It's been interesting to see how she's

been able to work through this process. And she's been enlisting the help of parents to track down these books. I think even asking the question of where to find the books gives the parent the message that the school cares about where they come from and some of the parents have been available to track down books. One of our parents took a trip to India last summer and she came back with a few books... I think having parents involved is a great second step. But I think that as this moves into a second stage, the big thing that I see is how can we get the classroom teachers to realize the importance of these books as far as their regular daily program is concerned and I think that will be a special challenge...

Like our project team did, Ron perceived many of the teachers as being initially reluctant to get involved in the project. But after several months passed more teachers got on board and Ron suggested that our involvement should continue:

I think the teachers had to see the impact these books had on kids when they first arrived and how it increased their self-confidence and so on. I think the staff might be ready now for a follow-up program. A number of the teachers are starting to use the books in their classes. I think the teachers are now ready to look at practical classroom issues in terms of these books. How could these books be used during the reading process segment of the school day? How could they be used to support their writing program? And I think we're at that stage and I'd like to see that continue and grow.

Ron also felt that there is merit in having the children share bilingual books that open them up to an appreciation for the literature of other cultures. He suggested that this project has implications not only for Somerset School but also for culturally diverse schools throughout greater Metropolitan Toronto and elsewhere:

I think another stage beyond this one is to bring this program to other schools. Our school is far from unique. There are many schools in Toronto with children of different cultural groups with a first language other than English. How can we spread the good feelings that come from these books to other schools in a time of great budget crunch?

I think that one of the things that Judy has been able to do here is to find sources and suppliers and I think that information shared with other librarians and schools would make those folks more receptive to the idea. Because many of them are up to their ears trying to stock their libraries with up-to-date English books and this may seem like a whole new burden on their shoulders. But if some of the groundwork and spadework that Judy has done could be shared with other people, perhaps they would be a little more receptive. Especially if they see the video that you have put together along with a package of addresses and instructions about buying the books... There have to be arrangements, creative ways of purchasing these books because the concept of invoice or purchase orders are foreign to many of these situations – backrooms, grocery store, homes...some willingness on the part of people to venture into something new...

SOME REFLECTIONS

Just as researchers need to listen to teachers, teachers need to listen to the stories of their students and parents. A place needs to be imagined where students and teachers tell stories to one another in order to make sense of their cultural identities. I tried to listen as openly as possible to the stories of these students, their parents and the teachers. What emerged was a shared narrative, a collaborative story about the teaching-learning experience within the context of diversity in the mainstream curriculum. These dual-track language books are a means of sharing our cultural stories which, indeed, are about our humanity. Children who made greater use of first language books had a clearer vision of their ethnicity and a greater feeling of security in their cultural background. However, even for the most culturally confident parents and children, the sense of dislocation, uprootedness and disorientation were apparent. The stories that they shared in their interviews, although laced with anxiety and uncertainty, became a lifeline for the participants just as the first language books became a bridge between parent and child, and school.

Through this project I had explored ways in which to bring children, linguistic/cultural diversity and literature together in an interactive way. The aim was to learn how to take advantage of the cultural backgrounds and interests that children of diverse heritage bring to the classroom and to use folklore so as to understand difference more deeply. My participants and I opened a dialogue on how to empower ESL students to become storytellers and to guide them as they learn how to record the folklore from their own cultures and to create their own stories. We, as educators, must let children know that what they bring from home and from their culture has significance and in order to do that, we have to incorporate their literature within the mainstream classroom. Learning is social – and it is something that happens when we interact with others. We must create interactive spaces where children from all sorts of ethnic backgrounds use written and oral languages in relation to real needs. We need to be the mediators between the children and the text. Storytelling too can be a mediator. The focus is on engaging students in meaningful communication as a result of personal interaction with the text. Through this project, too, teachers have an opportunity to reflect on the educational and personal experiences of their students, and to learn more about the social-psychological struggles of these immigrant students and parents parachuted into a new society and we as educators need to make better sense of what students truly require in terms of academic development.

Teachers, students and parents, as subjects for empirical study, have long felt powerless in the educational research process. There is the all too familiar picture of the researcher who collects data only never to be heard from again. We tried to collect data in the context of open dialogue, school partnerships, and in cultural communities. We focused on the collaborative relationships among researcher, teachers, parents, and students that were promoted by the project and tried to relate these to the interconnected settings of school, home and community. The project became, in fact, a shared experience which validated all participants and empowered them to explore their own participation in the literacy process and offered ESL students an instructional orientation involving active engagement in their first and second languages within the mainstream curriculum.

FROM "FERN HILL" TO SOMERSET

I recently re-read the jewel of a poem "Fern Hill" by Dylan Thomas which is a metaphor not only for the human condition of loss of youth but also more specifically for those who face all manner of life changes. When I saw the last line of the poem again, *"Though I sang in my chains like the sea"*, I couldn't help but think of the newly arrived ESL students at Somerset School and of the transformative dimension of this dual track literacy project with its message of cultural and linguistic coexistence. These books have brought a gentle, perhaps more hopeful, "song" to the work of learning a new language and culture for these children. And with song there is hope in the midst of the chains of upheaval in the uncalm seas of their immigration journey.

This grassroots project can be described as a "reflection-in-action" (see Schon, 1983, 1991) about the assumptions we as teacher/educators consciously and subconsciously make about immigrant children and parents and about how these relate to interaction within the classroom, the school and society in general. It turned out that the experience of sharing their stories with me not only empowered my participants, but also provided me in the role of researcher, with a fresh understanding of the ESL experience. It is a simple but powerful idea, an "aesthetic of pedagogical improvisation" as Tom Barone (2000) would put it. I invite any and all teachers to implement its equivalent in their own classrooms. Behind all the policy statements and curriculum guidelines pertaining to literacy education stands the power of the day-to-day interaction among school participants. A kind word, a warm nudge, an understanding ear, an enthusiastic teacher who respects the identity of each student – this is my vision of what goes on in the kind of classroom wherein the sharing of multicultural and multilingual stories takes place.

NOTES

[1] This chapter has some material from an earlier version of a journal article "A multicultural literacy intervention for minority language students." In *Language and Education*, 8 (3), 123-146, Clevedon, England, 1994).

CHAPTER EIGHT

MY YIDDISH VOICE

Consciously we teach what we know; Unconsciously we teach who we are.
-Source unknown

One reason I wrote this book is to tell what saved me, so that perhaps it may save other children who have experienced deprivation and oppression in their lives. School saved me; some of my teachers saved me; the stolen comforts of someone else's language, culture and identity in the Montreal of my childhood saved me; my students, when I was an elementary school teacher saved me; and now, the teachers whom I teach in my graduate courses as well as the participants in my research projects continue to save me. I was a child with a broken heart who grew up in the shadows of an unspeakable horror. The story of my family being too awful to articulate, silence seemed the better choice. But this was a hysterical silence ready to explode outwards in clusters of inaudible screams. I was never, ever supposed to tell the story. It too was supposed to be buried, along with the corpses of my relatives, in the concentration camps of World War II, in that far-away place of my childhood nightmares called Poland.

At the core of this chapter about my mother tongue is a search for a safe place – for a site of memory and longing and hope – in spite of the certain knowledge that this search will be an everlasting struggle. Intellectually I understand this "homelessness" (see Anzaldua, 1987; Berger, 1984; Minh-ha, 1994; Pinar, 1988). Emotionally however I will forever be wounded in the face of the stark reality. To look back at Yiddish can never be solely a professional pursuit for me. It represents the tortured landscape of my people's exile and ultimate genocide – linked inexorably to the concept of "home" and (im)possibility of return. It is not only an intellectual privation but a psychological, emotional and spiritual one as well[1] (Bar-On, 1991, 1993; Said, 1990, 1996).

Right from the start I had sought to construct a life story that could sustain me. I therefore had to turn my back on my home language and culture because I had been denied even the most basic sense of security within it. How could I ever have believed that the Yiddish language and its culture would be as viable to me as English or French? My Yiddish voice had almost been annihilated along with my relatives, now only shadowy ghosts haunting my day-to-day existence. Could all the suffering in that faraway place where my parents, grandparents, and great-great-great grandparents lived have really happened?

CHAPTER EIGHT

Professionally, I have always focused on minority language learning, cultural maintenance, issues of diversity, intercultural understanding, conflict resolution and peace studies within educational contexts. For me these became a mantle of protection. But, as I write this now, I begin to feel like a participant in one of my own research projects, floating suddenly off the page, a spirit returning from the grave to voice yearning for her first language and her lost home. Why had I never made that connection before? *Language and home.* I have certainly used these words often enough in my research papers: *Home language* ... Other people's homes, and other people's languages, other people's cultures – *but never my own*. "Home is where the heart is", it is said, but I needed to distance myself far away from my heart. And who could blame me?

Unexpectedly, as I sit at my computer writing this, coming into focus is my lost Yiddish, staring wistfully at me, telling me that this is indeed the moment, as T.S. Eliot had put it, to return to the beginning and to see it for the first time. I can sense that my usual research space, filled as it was with a myriad issues of language and cultural has been rendered now – in one fell swoop – less coherent, less powerful, and less articulate than before. Did I accidentally just touch some strange unseen "delete/undelete" key? Suddenly I realize for the first time that although my personal and professional life has been deeply nourished by my many other adopted languages, it is Yiddish that is in fact my soul. Yiddish is my past, my present and my future. Yiddish is my destiny. And so I must write this chapter to recover a story that I thought had been lost forever, one that is intimately connected with why I went into teaching in the first place.

My first language, Yiddish, was the language spoken by millions of Eastern European Jews for nearly 1000 years until the outbreak of World War II, when its native speakers were systematically killed by the Nazis between 1933 and 1945. My *mameloshen*[1] is a language that had been wantonly murdered and I am and always will be in a state of mourning for it. For me, the fate of the Yiddish language stands as a haunting and constant reminder of the devastation of the Jewish people – including many members of my own immediate family. My relationship with Yiddish is simultaneously one of excruciating pain and of precious delight. How can I describe the wounds which are opened every time I hear a Yiddish song or chance to see a Yiddish newspaper? I realize that had I had children I would not have spoken this language with them on a daily basis – except perhaps to convey an occasional delightful phrase or saying dear to me. But I would certainly have passed on my undying love for this fragile language to them. I have never had the luxury of being able to take my mother language for granted, not even for a moment. There now is no ethnic homeland where it thrives. There are only gravesites there, many without even the benefit of proper headstones.

Somewhere in here is the safe place for which I constantly search. Perhaps that is why I have begun to tell this story. Some years ago I dreamt that I was walking through the gates of Auschwitz, not as an inmate but as an observer. It is curious that, as a child of survivors, that was the very first time I had allowed this to emerge from my subconscious. I read somewhere that writing is not therapy, but that it can heal, translating vague, unarticulated pain into narrative. Finally, someone in my family is now going to speak for those who no longer can. I have broken free of the script assigned to me at birth. Keen (1990) claims that storytelling is a communal act; it requires community and it creates community. In the telling, there is a teller and a listener and so removes the isolation and loneliness of the sufferer. By telling stories we remember our past, discover our present and envision our future. In the telling, we exchange our unconscious myths for conscious autobiography. In the telling and the retelling we find meaning and authenticity. This is the task of a life.

YIDDISH IN MEMORY

When I was a small child I spoke to my doll in Yiddish and I told her in hushed tones to be careful not to speak it in public. One never knew where Nazis could be hiding. Yiddish, the small, beautiful bird with a broken wing was irreparable and I had to guard it with my life. Its quiet dignity haunted me in my dreams and in my waking hours. And whenever I became immersed in one of my adopted languages (and that was almost always) there before me would appear my beloved Yiddish like a dying swan. And suddenly I would feel like a traitor. I vowed to myself that I would never abandon my Yiddish and yet it felt like a terrible secret.

I had to run far away from Yiddish all those years ago. I ran into the arms of the French language when I was a child. Then I was schooled in English which offered me (and still does) a sense of power. Still later, at university, I also fell in love with Italian. These languages kept me warm and safe. Yiddish, in contrast, was a drowning man taking others down with him. I understand now that at the tender age of my early life I had to escape the overwhelming clutches of my mother tongue. It was a love that I had to bury and it has taken me more than four decades to begin to retrieve it. Like having to give away a baby because you were too young to handle the responsibility. And yet you never forgot. It stared you always in the face, especially when you were not looking; especially when you thought that you were having a good time for a moment. But I always knew, deep down, that one day I would have to go back and search for this lost child. And try to make my peace with it, finally – to whatever extent might be possible.

YIDDISH IN FANTASY

My first attempt at reconciling with my Yiddish voice was through writing a little story about Alice in Wonderland who becomes a traveler in a Yiddish rather than in an English wonderland. I had dedicated it to all children who have suffered loss through violence, abuse, and war. The piece was published in the "Journal of Curriculum Theorizing" (2000) and also in the book "Difficult Memories: Talk in a Post-Holocaust Era" edited by Marla Morris and John Weaver (2002). Writing this little story offered a space where my childhood self could rest, play, and create and renew her spirit. It came to me as a gift –from where I know not –merging past with present for the first time.

CHAPTER EIGHT

"A YIDDISH KIND OF ALICE"

"Too much pain cannot be good for the soul", she tries to convince herself. Alice in Wonderland – hurtling down an endless, dark tunnel of suffering and – even worse – of doubt. The first words of her memory are mutilated by a Nazi axe. She feels the words through a barbed-wire fence of screaming and terror. Through the gauze-like haze of memory, she barely sees two sad, shadowy figures; their spirits broken. These are her parents; this is her legacy. Her first memory is one of broken glass, and blood. She holds on tightly to a rollercoaster of anxiety and grief. "But my spirit will not be broken!" she cries to the wind. In which language does she utter these words? Yiddish never felt strong. It felt fragile and frightened. It yearned for the protective hands of a gentle mother. Just like the Little Match Girl. Oh, but how beautiful this language was! Those precious sayings chiseled with the wisdom that sometimes arises from deprivation and suffering. Idioms that comforted her in the cold of night. Alice did not play with language as do most other children when they are learning to speak. It was too serious a matter for that.

She read "The Little Match Girl" and cried endlessly. The book did not want to end. Little Yiddish dragged about, in tattered clothes, barefoot. Little Yiddish, an orphan, begging for a home. The Grandmother in that story beckoned to her with pleading arms. Alice had read the story in English. In Yiddish it would have devastated her. The Grandmother she never knew had been killed by those monsters. The Grandmother whose lap she would never sit on. Unlike other children. The Little Match Girl understood. The two girls held onto each other in the freezing night. The Little Match Girl went to heaven and was reunited with her Grandmother. Alice, on the other hand, was stuck in the cruel mire of reality.

"Do other people feel this forlorn about their first language?" Alice never posed that question in those days. It would have been impossible to ponder. (Her subconscious mind was forming pathways out of this dilemma.) She hated the Yiddish language classes she attended after school in the dilapidated basement of a Jewish community center. Alice felt humiliated and angry there. The White Rabbit helped Alice to escape that prison but she knew in her heart that one day she would have to pay a price for this crime.

The White Rabbit beckoned to Alice. He had a spring in his step and a glistening gold watch in his waistcoat pocket. She rubbed her eyes from a drugged-like sleep. Was she still dreaming? It felt real so she started to follow the rabbit. There was something unusual about that watch. It had letters on it instead of numbers. It was telling a different kind of time. Alice was intrigued. She hurried to keep up with the rabbit. She didn't want to lose sight of that watch. It held some magic secret, of that she was sure. She finally caught up with him, totally out-of-breath. They sat down together in a green meadow. A feeling of calm overcame her.

The White Rabbit brought out a picnic basket, brimming with delicacies. They began to eat together and the afternoon ticked lazily by. Alice had not realized how hungry she had been. But the rabbit had known. He understood her needs better than she did. Alice began to feel sleepy but why did the rabbit have a sly little grin on his face? She decided to stay awake. Something was afoot and she did not want to miss it. Suddenly the White Rabbit took out his marvellous watch and placed it in front of her with a flourish. "What an actor," thought Alice. She gingerly picked up the mysterious watch. It felt special. Ornamental. Fancy. Instead of numbers there were letters. Yiddish letters! She peered at the letters of the words. They were the Yiddish letters which she had been trying so desperately to hang onto after she had stopped going to Yiddish classes.

The White Rabbit told her that she could put the letters away for safekeeping. This watch told the time of her future, and in her future she would be reunited with her Yiddish. For the time being, she would find her way through other languages. Alice put the beautiful watch away in a very safe place. Only she and the White Rabbit knew the secret. They walked away hand in hand to meet a new language which would take care of her and nurture her through the long, lonely years of her childhood. This language was called French: "la langue française." Alice was filled with anticipation, excitement...

YIDDISH IN REALITY

Even today, so many years later, I still see that shining gold watch with its Yiddish letters in my mind. Fantasy and reality are beginning to merge. Who would have believed that I *really* would be reunited with my lost Yiddish? A couple of years ago I found a pamphlet while cleaning up my office that I had gotten at the YIVO Institute for Jewish Research in New York City which I had visited during a rainy October a decade earlier. It was a flyer for an exhibit and written in both English and Yiddish: *"Going Home: How American Jews Invent the Old World"; (Zurick Aheim: Vi Americaner Yiddin Klern Oys Di Alte Heim"*). At the time I barely glanced at the Yiddish on the pamphlet, feeling then that it would be just too difficult (both emotionally as well as literally) to read.

Then a strange thing happened one day in the spring of 2003 toward the end of a research visit to Berkeley. I was walking on Telegraph Avenue, the street famous there for its counterculture demonstrations in the sixties, and I noticed a brightly-coloured display of Spanish-English children's books in the window of *Shakespeare & Company*, one of the well-known used bookshops in Berkeley. So I walked in hoping to find more dual-track bilingual children's books to bring back to Toronto for my multicultural literacy research project. I walked to the back of the shop where such books were located. I spent time joyously leafing through a pile of all kinds of beautiful bilingual books in Chinese/English, Arabic/English, Spanish/English (of course!), as well as Asian Cinderella stories, Native-American tales, African-American stories, a book in English about the diversity of the human race, and so on.

And then, hidden under a second pile of books, was a quiet, humble book with the unassuming title "Little Stories for Little Children." I didn't recognize it. I picked it up, completely unprepared for the shock to follow. I opened it. The words that peered out were printed in both Yiddish and English. It was a book that had originally been written in 1922 in St. Petersburg, and in it there were ten short stories for children about Jewish village (shtetl) life in Eastern Europe. The English had been added to the American edition years later. My eyes blurred as I carefully turned the pages of this unexpected treasure. It had been one of the books that I had read as a child in the after-school Yiddish classes that I was forced to attend. I had completely blocked that book out of my consciousness.

Memories came flooding back in a torrent of grief. How I had hated those Yiddish classes which took place twice a week after the regular elementary school day. There was no such thing as "heritage language education" in those days. These classes might as well have taken place on another planet, for how alien and unimportant they seemed. I remember some children making fun of me as I waited for the bus that would take me to the community centre located in a run-down part of the neighbourhood. They knew where I was going and taunted me while I pretended not to hear them. When I would arrive at the centre and enter the class, there was never any sense of community there. It was always winter, or so it felt, dark and cold, and the pipes would hiss and sputter as we recited mindless sentences in Yiddish with our coats and hats on.

The teacher too seemed ancient and exhausted and certainly did not capture our attention as we stared out the window at other children playing in the street. There might as well have been bars on those windows. Nobody wanted to be there. The books were old, torn and grey. At least that is how I remember them. The only fun in class was when the more "creative" boys would sling erasers through the air – a carnival of rubber snowballs. We could then at least imagine that we were playing outside. Once an eraser hit the teacher in the face. Dead silence. She sat down at her desk and began to cry. Poor woman. I remember how sorry I felt for her — but also disgusted. How could anyone allow themselves to be humiliated so? I compared her to the exciting French teacher at my "real" school. I decided not be a party to such a sham! Even then I had more respect for language learning than that and I knew it didn't have to be that way. I had witnessed the dregs of "minority language education" and wanted out. Is it any wonder that my research work focuses on multicultural and multilingual matters in my professional life?

An even more ominous thought took hold of me in those Yiddish classes. Our teacher told us that many children in Russia and Poland before the Holocaust had read this same children's book that we were struggling to read. As if to make it more holy or something. But I knew well what had happened to most of them. This was not discussed in class. I felt I had to get out of that classroom before I too would be suffocated. I kept this anxiety to myself but raised such a tantrum at home that my parents finally took me out. However in the stillness of night I secretly felt guilty for having abandoned my Yiddish schooling. I tried hard to hold onto the spelling as I would drift off to sleep. As the months went by, the letters became fainter and fainter – a slow and miserable death...

So there I stood, four decades later, re-reading this same children's book in the improbable location of a bookstore on Telegraph Avenue in Berkeley. And all I could hear – again – was the screaming of children in Auschwitz. Perhaps some of them were carrying this very book with them when they entered those gates. Suddenly I was transported back to being the lost child in the early years of my life in Montreal searching for some kind of miracle. All these emotions coursed through me as I stood holding that little Yiddish book – a piece of wreckage off the emotional debris of my past. I purchased the book and felt like Atlas with the weight of the world in the plastic bag that I carried out of the store. When I got back to my apartment I immediately packed it away into my valise, as if it were a relic unearthed and meant to be inspected more closely at a later date.

YIDDISH IN DESTINY

Upon returning to Toronto from my stay in Berkeley, as I unpacked, there at the bottom of the valise was the book still enclosed in the plastic bag. I took it out and placed it carefully on my desk. It felt like a monument, a glass one that might break into smithereens in an instant. Several weeks later a new academic year at the University of Toronto began. One afternoon as I was at my computer doing e-mail, I began to steal sidewise glances at the book which was sitting right next to the computer. I finally picked it up and opened it. I ended up sitting there for hours practicing my very rusty Yiddish literacy skills. When I heard my husband come home I finally looked up – I hadn't noticed that it had grown dark outside. The following day I brought the book onto campus for the students in my course "Children's Multicultural Literature Within a Multicultural Context" in order to tell them the story. I now tell it every time I teach that course. As always, my professional space opens to offer me comfort. The book feels a little less heavy and now looks legitimate as it sits on my office bookshelf along with the other children's books in my possession. This little book has taken me on a strange journey back to the beginning of my life and has given me permission to reclaim my past, and to preserve it lovingly for the present.

Recently I came across another jewel of a children's book, this time in a Toronto bookstore: a brand new translation of Dr. Seuss' "The Cat in the Hat" – translated into Yiddish for the first time in 2003! Again I was holding a Yiddish children's book in my hand, but this time the little orphan Yiddish looked pretty and healthy and modern! I was in awe of that transformation and felt the dream-like quality of it. Needless to say, this book is now also in my possession and I bring it too to show my students. Yiddish always has the power to unleash a longing within me for the comfort and nurture of that soft, affectionate mother tongue. This is not sentimentality or nostalgia. It is about facing the evil that tore apart my family, my people, my culture, my language – my home. I cannot ever return to it because it was destroyed, razed to the ground. I will never know "*die alte heim*", my old home. I will always be a border-dweller in search of a safe place in the world.

Why am I writing this? Perhaps because I am on the threshold of a vulnerable although paradoxically liberating narrative. Perhaps I am engaged in a storytelling that enacts what anthropologist Virginia Dominguez (2000) calls "a politics of love and rescue" (as cited in Behar, 2003). It is possible that my personal and professional energy has always derived from a need to invent a new 'home' – on the margins, within the cracks of in-betweeness, in a myriad of languages, just as a bird garnishes its nest with twigs and leaves from wherever she can find them. Perhaps it is not so much that language and culture *per se* saved me but rather it was my yearning, my search to *find life through languages and cultures* that opened the road to recovery, and now leads me back to this bittersweet reunion with my Yiddish. It *is* a homecoming. Of a sort.

Re-reading the words I am writing here empowers me, and provides me with a sense of agency. I feel as if have dominion over every sentence. Writing this may be a means of reclaiming territory, as Maxine Greene might put it – all the while knowing that my personal history will keep me in diaspora, searching for home all the days of my life. And yet that same personal history has also offered me a remarkable gift: the calling to be a teacher, reaching out to students in my classrooms with a desire to share my dream of a better world. Indeed is this not what we are called to do as teachers: to offer a place of shelter in our classrooms for all children who need it, a place where we can listen to their stories of otherness, of difference, of poverty, of war, and any kind of oppression, and help them find hope in the midst of loss – and above all to help them find their way in the world, their way back to 'home' and into the sacred space within their souls where their inner talents can be brought to life.

NOTES

[1] *Mameloshen:* the word for mother tongue in Yiddish also conveying feelings of comfort and home.

CHAPTER NINE

OF WARS AND WONDERLAND

The war occurred half a lifetime ago, and yet the remembering makes it now. And sometimes remembering will lead to a story, which makes it forever. That's what stories are for. Stories are for joining the past to the future. Stories are for those late hours in the night when you can't remember how you got from where you were to where you are. Stories are for eternity, when memory is erased; when there is nothing to remember except the story.

-In "The Things They Carried" by Tim O'Brien[1]

How remarkable it would have been to have a sense of pride in my Yiddish language and in my Jewish culture when I was a child. Instead I had to hide this during the regular school day. It was bad enough to be told by my kindergarten teacher how difficult my surname was to pronounce and how much better it would have been if my parents had changed it when they arrived in Canada. Not all my teachers were like that, but the one who said this to me happened to be my first. It is hard to erase the humiliation and self-hatred that comes from it. I vowed to help erase it for other children whenever I could. As a child of war, I seek to commiserate with other children of war. And what good fortune it was to have been invited to replicate the Somerset School dual-track book project a few years later in Fielding School, my Montreal childhood haven. How remarkably the personal and professional can become intertwined!

During my third research sojourn at Fielding School, two years after my first visit there, I began to spend time in several classrooms and to interview some of the children. My professional "gaze" affords me the luxury of a certain emotional distance and perhaps I, the border-dweller, search for other border-dwellers in an effort to ease their pain – along with my own. We children of war live in a separate universe. It shall never be otherwise. This must be what Eva Hoffman meant when she wrote in her book "Lost In Translation" that it is:

> ...the story of children who came from the war, and who couldn't make sufficient sense of the several worlds they grew up in, and didn't know by what lights to act. I think sometimes that we were children too overshadowed by our parents' stories, and without enough sympathy for ourselves, for the serious dilemmas of our own lives, and who therefore couldn't live up to our parents' desire – amazing in its strength – to create new life and to bestow on us a new world. And who found it hard to learn that in this new world too we must learn all over again, each time from the beginning, the trick of going on (p. 230).

CHAPTER NINE

As a child, I longed to live in a world of harmony and joy and peace. Sometimes, in the darkness of night, I wrote little stories about the end of war. I tried to hide from the suffering of my parents through the medium of my stories, which always featured people of different cultures and different religions living happily together. I was terrified of losing contact with humanity. Nightmares haunted me regularly in which Hitler's henchmen found me in hiding, an orphaned child, and threw my body, splashing it against a barbed wire fence. I see other little children, carrying tattered dolls and teddy bears, being marched to gas chambers. Such scenes haunt me still. For the surviving victims of the Holocaust, "the injury", as Primo Levi (1988, p. 224-235) states it, "cannot be healed; it extends through time... denying peace to the tormented."

But I found a way out by reading and also writing texts of the "other" – those living in other languages and in other cultures. And I especially discovered an escape through my 'professional' world, both in public as well as in higher education. And my teaching, my research, and my writing are fueled by the desire to create a communicative space in which dislocation, marginality, and exile are transcended through compassionate dialogue. Behind this idea of a utopian space in my imagination are the real life experiences of exclusion that haunt immigrants and refugees, and behind it all is the dream of devising a school discourse that embraces all cultures and, finally, even transcends them.

I snapped myself out of this reverie as I sat at a little table in a private alcove off a fifth grade classroom on a snowy December afternoon at Fielding School. I was seated with two little girls from Afghanistan named Fariba and Leila. Their eyes carried haunted expressions which spoke of war and death and I could sense their terror. At first they didn't want to speak with me and I understood. Who was I? Was I part of some trick? You cannot trust others after you have seen one of your own parents shot in front of your eyes. That in fact is what had happened to Fariba. She was only seven years old at the time. She got out with her mother and sisters – a miraculous event – and lived in a refugee camp for fifteen months before being able to emigrate to Montreal.

In the classroom there were Christmas decorations on the wall. It was a cheerful room but Fariba seemed distracted. She was in Montréal but at the same time also in Kabul seeing her father disintegrate. She was polite towards me but not very communicative. I decided to read a story to her instead of talking. I read "A Time for Toys" by Margaret Wild and Julie Vivas, a magnificently sensitive book about children in a Nazi concentration camp and about the older women around them who wanted, in spite of the degradation and loss all around, to create some makeshift toys with any scraps they might find. One older girl in this story remembers the pretty toys that she used to have before the war. She remembers the Friday night Sabbath dinners and Passover seders when her relatives would all gather together to recite the "Haggadah", which in Hebrew simply means the "Telling" – the story about the Exodus of the Jewish People from Egypt.

I then told Fariba and Leila that my cousins and aunts were just like these girls and women in the book and that they did not survive. Only my mother, father and brother survived. And they ended up in Montreal because my father had one sister, his oldest, who had come to Canada long before the war and had sponsored my parents and brother when they were in DP camps.

"What is a DP camp?" I was startled to hear Fariba ask. I had been speaking incessantly, having accepted her and Leila's silence. "It is a refugee camp but they called it a Displaced Persons (DP) camp then." Fariba nodded with understanding. "I was in one of those. There are lots of people and it's hot and sometimes you get sick and lonely. There aren't many nice things there but at least there is something to eat. And nobody is shooting your family or friends. How old was your brother then?" I told her, "He was a little baby and luckily he didn't die." Fariba's big velvet brown eyes became larger still as she stated with much thought, "Yes, he was lucky, and you were lucky that he or your parents didn't die." I wanted to hug this sweet child, but I reminded myself that I was a researcher and that this might overstep boundaries. So I squeezed her tiny hand instead. "War is horrible, isn't it?" "Yes", she answered, "war is awful but it happens because some people hate others and they want to kill them. They killed my father. They killed so many. I wish they would stop. How do you make them stop hating? It's in many places too, not just Afghanistan." The wisdom of this child was illuminating and seemed to come from a place of great authority.

Perhaps Fariba decided to speak to me because she realized that I had not been afraid to stare into the heart of pain. She understood that in some way I was a kindred spirit who also had been witness to evil. My mind wandered back to when I was here in Fielding School at her age, imprisoned in my despair. "Do you like school?" I asked her. "School is really nice", she said with a big smile on her face, "it makes me feel better." I understood exactly what she meant. "Maybe good things will happen to you in school." I also told her that School changed my life – "it gave me a life." "I hope that will happen to me too. I couldn't go to school in Kabul because I was a girl. We were locked up in our house the whole day, " Fariba said. "School is my chance now." For a little girl of ten she was wise beyond her years, an "old soul." A child like this can remind a teacher that education has deep meaning and purpose.

What can I take away from this encounter with Fariba, whose wounds are so much more immediate than mine? There was an intimacy we shared. My tears were something familiar to her. She had often seen them in her mother's eyes. But she herself could not let them flow. At least not yet. I had read her the story "*A Time for Toys*" so as to open a door to hope. The children and women of this (true) story were saved by British soldiers. Theirs was a happy ending, so to speak. They had held onto a thread toward freedom and were lucky. Their brothers, sisters, fathers and mothers were not.

War for Fariba; memories of war for me. Nobody carries these realities without some part remaining in agony forever. This is what sensitized me to the suffering of students in my classrooms, and in the classrooms I visit for my research work. Am I still searching for an end to my own pain? Of course. It is a never-ending battle. As Rachel Naomi Ramen puts it: "Compassion emerges from a sense of belonging: the experience that all suffering is like our suffering and all joy is like our joy. When we know ourselves to be connected to all others, acting compassionately is simply the natural thing to do." Marguerite Duras writes in "La Douleur" (translated into English as "The War: A Memoir"): "If Nazi crime is not seen in world terms, if it isn't understood collectively, then that man who died in the concentration camp ... has been betrayed... The only possible answer to this crime is to turn it into a crime committed by everyone. To share it. Just like the idea of equality and fraternity. In order to bear it, to tolerate the idea of it, we must share the crime." (p.50)

I had read stories about war to Fariba and Leila in order to tell them that they are not quite as alone as they think. I also read them the story of *Rose Blanche* (*White Rose*), a children's book about the compassion of a little German girl who witnessed the Nazi atrocities. She follows the "convoys" and finally comes upon a concentration camp seeing the horrors there. She returns later with some food and secretly hands it to the emaciated people in the striped prisoner uniforms. She continues to do this until one day she is discovered and killed and the prisoners too are all sent away never to return. The last page of this book shows a lovely flower — the white rose which is symbolic of the foliage that blooms eternally in the scorched earth.[2]

Bruno Bettelheim calls this "authentic storytelling" and children respond in authentic ways. It is a 'communion' in Buber's terms, a preparation for constructive dialogue, "working the soil of our hearts" as Kathleen Norris says. Each student takes such a story and uses it in original and extraordinary ways both in the present and for their own future lives. Such stories plant seeds that can take years to grow becoming a force strong enough to change future events. They are messages which evidence a sense of beauty, of life, of feeling love again even after all the loss. They are prayers of resistance: *We shall endure even as we are encircled by our enemies.*

The children in our classrooms remind us that we need to restore our faith in the magic and mystery of our calling as teachers. We must help them to tell us what they have learned from their life stories. In the telling and listening, the teacher and students plant the seeds of compassion, of hope, and of understanding that go forth into the world and transform it – if not today then tomorrow and if not tomorrow then the day after, and if not the day after then the one after that. But we must also understand that it will never be easy.

THE REAL "ALICE IN WONDERLAND"

It was still snowing softly when I left the building of Fielding School. Would Fariba and Leila be saved by school as I had been? I hoped that it would be so. Memories flooded back as I walked out into the crisp air. I needed to take a walk and return, in my mind, to the Fielding School of my childhood. My French classes there will always beckon as candles of hope. But it was another event that happened to me as a child at Fielding that will always warm my heart even though it did not have a happy ending.

When I was in Grade Four I was chosen to play the lead in "Alice in Wonderland." Having no sense of identity, I certainly did not feel that I deserved anything so grand as the leading role in this play! When the women from an amateur drama troupe arrived at our school to audition children for "Alice in Wonderland", all I could think of was what a wonderful story it was – so full of mystery and adventure. Alice had become as lost in the story as I was in life. Nothing in Alice's strange world made sense; and with this at least I could certainly identify. The rabbit hole into which Alice fell was a distortion of reality which to my young mind was a magnificent adventure in which life offered up intriguing new possibilities. I loved the White Rabbit. I felt that he was my friend in spite of his most unusual mannerisms.

We had just finished our Arithmetic lesson when two women from the drama troupe entered our classroom. The teacher announced that they were putting together a play and that they were interested in having us audition for it. I wasn't sure of exactly what that meant. These two well-dressed, well-spoken women explained that they would sit on the stage in the gymnasium and that they would listen to us, one-by-one, read a piece from "Alice in Wonderland." I thought it might be interesting to read a section from this book so I put up my hand to volunteer. Never in my wildest dreams did I imagine that they might like how I would read it.

My turn came to go to the gym to audition. The women were kind, pretending not to notice the patches in my tights. I wasn't even embarrassed by this – it was just another part of the fog that veiled my being. My only escape was through language. When I entered a book, I was "rescued," as Robert Coles described it in "The Call of Stories." And so I shared my readings with those ladies that afternoon.

I read for them about the section of "Pig and Pepper" in "Alice in Wonderland and the peculiar logic of the Duchess who was nursing her child (who was really a little pig).

> Alice went timidly to the door, and knocked. "There's no sort of use in knocking," said the Footman, "and that for two reasons. First because I'm on the same side of the door as you are: secondly, because they're making such a noise inside, no one could possibly hear you," And when Alice later asked the Cheshire Cat "Would you tell me please which way I ought to go from here?" He answered," That depends a good deal on where you want to get to." Alice responded, "I don't much care where –." "Then it doesn't matter which way you go," said the Cat. " – So long as I get somewhere," Alice added as an explanation. "Oh, you're sure to do that," said the Cat, "if you only walk long enough."

Those words were soothing: they offered one a sense of direction! By the time Alice got to the Mad Hatter's tea party, she was starting to gain a sense of confidence:

> Take some more tea," the March Hare said to Alice very earnestly. "I've had nothing yet," Alice replied in an offended tone: "so I can't take more." "You

CHAPTER NINE

mean you can't take less," said the Hatter: "it's very easy to take more than nothing." "Nobody asked your opinion," said Alice.

What sheer FUN in such words and ideas. You never knew where you would be taken next. And yet – odd as these circumstances seemed – there was some sort of underlying logical sequence which allowed you to accept the unexpected conclusions. (Lewis Carroll was a mathematician after all.) The brilliance of this story and its language eclipsed the drabness of my everyday life and turned me into a seeker of truth. The *Jabberwocky* in Alice through the Looking Glass (first published in 1872) opened me to the playful joy with which Lewis Carroll distorted the English language and I succumbed to its charms:

'Twas brillig and the slithy toves
Did gyre and gimble in the wabe:
All mimsy were the borogroves,
And the mome raths outgrabe."...

I also read for them the part of Alice with Humpty Dumpty, one of my favourite sections. I always liked the conversation about names:

My name is Alice, but —" "It's a stupid name enough!" Humpty Dumpty interrupted impatiently. "What does it mean?" "Must a name mean something?" Alice asked doubtfully. "Of course it must," Humpty Dumpty said with a short laugh: "My name means the shape I am – and a good handsome shape it is too. With a name like yours, you might be any shape, almost.

I could identify with Humpty Dumpty's thesis about the importance of a name and with the sense of pride he possessed in his identity. It is as if he spoke to me directly. The two women looked at each other. I guessed they liked that section too. I had no idea what they were thinking.

****

"You have the part of Alice," my teacher said to me the following day. I was startled. How could this be? To play Alice in a really big production? It was to be held at the luxurious Ritz-Carlton Hotel downtown on Sherbrooke Street and was to be televised! It was all as in a dream. The rehearsals were joyful – something I could count on every day for several months. Through those rehearsals a little family of child actors was born. I had never felt the warmth of community before. I never seemed to forget my lines, sailing through the performances with ease.

The sun had finally shone through the clouds for me. I remember the sheer exhilaration of being on stage in front of so many people! There was such intense innocence about the play and the performance. Onstage everything was possible. Our faces shone with such faith that God himself must certainly have been somewhere in the audience that evening. Afterwards, we all had large ice cream sundaes as a reward. I knew I had it in me to perform and had tasted my first success – the beginning of a whole new world!

But then, as I ran towards my mother, I noticed the emptiness in her eyes. I knew she had been in the audience but her expression was as if she hadn't seen me at all. She was with a friend of hers. Words of praise came out of her mouth but they were incongruent with what I had seen in her eyes. A crushing disappointment descended upon me. Had I done something wrong? Guilt enveloped me. How dare I to have had such a good time up there on stage and to have performed so well? Who did I think I was to enjoy myself in that way? It was in any case unseemly for a girl! My mother had never had such opportunities and therefore it was not permitted for me to have them either. I was robbed of my triumph.

Did anyone ever know what happened to the little girl who played Alice so dazzlingly one year and utterly flubbed her audition for a part in another play the following year? Did anyone ever know that she would not be back on stage until an eternity later? Being a child of immigrants and refugees can mean a myriad of things. For some it means having a chance at a better life than the one your parents had – being given wings to fly. For others it means being a betrayer to what your parents had endured, landscapes littered with dead bodies, with broken dreams. I could no longer aspire to be "Alice in Wonderland." I took off the pink chiffon dress with the circle of shimmering white crinoline and felt myself shrink just as Alice had done when she drank one of the potions. But where was the drink that would make her grow again? I disappeared into nothingness and not a word was ever uttered about this turn of events.

For years I used to dream of that dress and the face of a monster shrieking that it had been too beautiful for me. The message was that I was not worthy of it, and it broke my heart. My star burnt out before it had a chance to shine; I became "The Little Match Girl" once again. Years later, in Berkeley – where I fell in love with a young man who became my life partner and where I fell in love with the field of bilingual/multicultural education which later became my life's work – I saw that magical dress again (or at least it looked similar) on a dancer from the New York City Ballet at a performance at Zellerbach auditorium on campus. I cried and cried and when the lights went up after the performance, people in the audience around me wondered what had happened.

I write this not to blame anyone, least of all my wounded parents. I write it in order to bring to light the reality of many children who have endured oppression in any of its myriad forms. Teachers need to look for these forgotten students and be mindful of the lack of abundance in their young lives. They may be children of war or poverty or famine or abuse, or of other types of violence. But one thing is certain: they are wounded and School may be their only ray of hope. I may have lost "Alice in Wonderland" but was saved by my love for languages, and by the safe place that School offered me, which in turn transformed my future. Without a good public education this future would never have happened. School offered me something to hold onto, a lifeboat. I was lucky. I escaped from the abyss. But there are many children who, without care or guidance, are ultimately conquered by a sense of worthlessness. And they are then truly lost. This is why I became a teacher. How else could anyone ever try to set these imprisoned souls (of whom I had been one) free?

NOTES

[1] Cited from Robert E. Gajdusek "Resurrection: A War Journey"(1997).
[2] Between 1942 and 1943 a group of courageous and defiant University of Munich students formed an anti-fascist resistance movement named White Rose. The students wrote and circulated seven leaflets across Germany in protest against Hitler's regime, were found out, jailed, and executed by the Nazis.

CHAPTER TEN

ADOLESCENCE AND TRAUMA

Do not be daunted by the enormity of the world's grief. Do justly, now. Love mercy now. Walk humbly, now. You are not obligated to complete the work, but neither are you free to abandon it.

-The Talmud

It turned out that I was asked to adapt my Somerset elementary dual-track book writing project to the high school level. The vice principal of an inner-city high school in Toronto had heard about the project through one of her teachers and so we met for coffee and chatted about possibilities. It seemed that the ESL teachers and students were very interested in the idea. So we arranged a time for me to visit the school.

I awoke on the morning of my visit to Northlands Collegiate with a sense of clarity. I hadn't felt like this in a long time. The ideas were right there, restless, close to the surface of my mind – like horses chafing at the bit, or greyhounds at the starting gate ready to run. I jumped out of bed ready to begin interviewing some of the immigrant and refugee students at this large, highly diverse, inner-city high school. The research project was entitled "Stories from the Margins: The Immigrant and Refugee Experience in Toronto." I intended to examine their cultural displacement, in-betweeness, border pedagogy, the differential meaning of literacy development, etc. etc. As I rode on the subway to the school, I remembered Maxine Greene's words in her book "Releasing the Imagination: Essays on Education, the Arts and Social Change" (1995):

> This is not romantic or simply a matter of goodwill. We teachers will confront thousands and thousands of newcomers in the years ahead: some from the darkness and dangers of the neglected ghettos, some exhausted from their suffering under dictators, some stunned by lives in refugee camps, some unabashedly in search of economic success. The texts are here, we have to make them accessible, offer the protocols, keep them open. We have to allow opportunities for students to structure their experiences by means of those texts, by means of books men and women have made.

In the spirit of Greene's call that "our obligation today is to find ways for the young to find their voices, to open their spaces, to reclaim their histories in all their variety and discontinuity" (p. 120), I was ready to listen to the stories of these immigrant and refugee students – "those on the margins" – in the safe haven of a little room off the ESL office on the second floor of Northlands Collegiate School.

CHAPTER TEN

The immigrant and refugee experience is first and foremost steeped in trauma. People with trauma live their lives on parallel tracks. Here is an example. You could be taking a break from writing an article for a scholarly journal while sitting on your porch sipping tea on a tranquil summer afternoon. And then –suddenly– an emaciated corpse flies at your face. And not just any corpse. She looks just like you. The one your father always spoke about in whispered anguish. The one in an old photograph that I recently found. That photograph is part of a collection of correspondence that took place over more than a decade between my aunt (my father's oldest sister) – who had left Poland with her husband and baby to settle in Montreal in 1927 – and her family who stayed behind in Poland and were later murdered. My father, the youngest son, was the only member of his family in Poland who had survived. The woman in that picture is one of his sisters, with soft gray eyes and a lovely smile. She has rich chestnut hair done up in the latest fashion (circa 1932) and a long slender neck. She is wearing a dark coloured blouse with a white collar. She is holding her child, my father's nephew, my cousin – a little boy with soulful eyes just like those of his mother. The child, who is about three years old, is dressed impeccably in a winter coat with a thick fur collar. He looks like a little prince. And his mother looks like a queen.

My aunt Anja and her son – I do not know his name –ended up as ashes. They were first gassed and then burned in the death camp of Treblinka in Poland. Nazi technology: the systematic result of well-honed hatred of Jews throughout the centuries in Europe. And then just as suddenly I am here, now sitting on the porch in Toronto, cup of tea in hand watching a young couple walk by with their border collie. They wave at me, and I wave back. I return to my work, reading the transcript of an interview that I had conducted on a December day of that academic year with a young teenage boy from Afghanistan.

I reflect back to that particular afternoon at Northlands Collegiate. I had already visited the school several times and had been able to create a positive rapport with the teachers and students of the ESL program. The first snowfall of the season had fallen. I hadn't been to the high school for a while and it felt good to be back to this neighbourhood brimming with diversity and with people struggling to survive. Don't get me wrong – it is not that I am either a sadist or a masochist. It is simply that I am one of them. These surroundings are so reminiscent of my own childhood: the low-income housing; the little shops with nothing luxurious in them; the longing for a better life, a second chance. Before going into the school, I went into a neighbourhood donut shop for a quick cup of coffee and found out that one of the customers had been robbed just a half hour earlier. He had left his wallet on the counter and had turned his back for only a moment. The police were there writing up a report. The man was very upset and spoke with a thick accent. He could not afford the loss. "It was probably some of the school kids who did it", said the woman behind the counter. I sat with my cup of coffee and felt mournful. I had a premonition that this might be a different kind of afternoon. As I walked over to the school in the cold some kids were hanging around the sidewalk near the rear entrance. They looked tough. You could feel their anger, frustration, and hormones. I wondered if they might have been involved in the theft at the donut shop.

I got to the ESL office on the second floor and was greeted by the ESL coordinator, Ann. I told her what had happened. She said that this was a frequent occurrence in the neighbourhood and seemed suddenly tired. But the librarian was also there and they both wanted to tell me how enthusiastic the ESL students were about the dual track writing project, which I had been implementing in the various ESL classrooms at the school throughout the term. They showed me examples of stories the ESL students had written in their home languages (if they could) and in English (which they were learning).

I had spent my earlier visits to the school introducing this idea to the students in their classrooms. I remember seeing the glow in the eyes of many as they sat at their computers working hard at writing and rewriting their precious stories. They did not complain about how difficult the process was. They asked for help. They seemed happy to be involved in a school project that had meaning for them. It was heart warming to observe these ESL students holding the final products of this writing project: elegantly and professionally bound books, with texts in a rainbow of languages, as well as illustrations. It may not sound like much but they seemed like a handful of jewels to them. I was told that they had been invited to read their "books" to the children of an elementary school nearby. Ann and the librarian were shining with pride.

The stories were filled with the hardscrabble realities of their everyday lives at home and at school – cultural stories about their families, about the lives they left behind, about the new lives they were trying so hard to create. Most of the students tried hard not to dwell on their sense of loss and sadness or, in some cases, rage. When I read some of the stories I was struck by a kind of defiance in their words. To many of their parents their former life is a painful memory but they, the children, located in the no-man's land of uprooted adolescence, were fighting hard against this resignation. Clearly they need more than just such memories. They are young and filled with nature's gifts of abundant energies and must learn to go forward. But to where, and to what? Amidst their dislocation they must find roads toward viable futures in this new country. Can we as educators help them? Perhaps our first step is to listen to their stories when they are ready to tell them. Ann made me a cup of strong black tea and I was ready to meet the boy from Afghanistan. She told me that he would be an interesting participant, that he had quite a story to tell.

Mahmoud and I went into the little room adjacent to the ESL office. I adore that particular small space where private thoughts and fears and hopes find voice. I had already interviewed many other students there. It was a glassed-in alcove with a large table, and file cabinets lined up against the one wall that was not made of glass. There was also a window on that wall which looked out onto the side entrance of the school and the parking lot. The wall also had posters on it of places from all over the world. The juxtaposition of these exciting travel posters and the broken lives of these students was incongruous, to say the least. There were also piles of books on the file cabinets as well as lots of student artwork. The room had a protected feel to it. Mahmoud and I sat down at the desk facing each other. He had sharp black eyes set in a smooth face. Ann told me that he had no parents in Toronto; somehow he had just arrived and was living on his own. No one knew much about him. There was an uncle who was his formal guardian.

I took out my tape recorder and asked him if it was OK to use it. He nodded, looking pleased that someone considered him important enough to be interviewed. I immediately liked him. What was it about him? A fragile yet dignified strength? Surviving without any safety net? The sense of being a psychological orphan? Yes, I could relate. He had gotten out of Afghanistan six years earlier when he was twelve and made it to Iran with his uncle. He had been taking care of a house in Teheran (whose owners supposedly were in the U.S.). "I didn't go to school in Teheran because I was illegal", he told me. Then he said he got to Azerbaidjan and was lucky that a Russian girl offered him private English lessons for free. His uncle had known her family. His uncle and he then made it to a refugee camp in Pakistan and through some agency there (he said the U.N. but may have meant UNHCRA) he succeeded in getting papers to come to Canada.

He had been in Toronto for only six or seven months. He was eighteen years old and worked in an Afghani restaurant after school and on weekends in order to make enough money to live on. His uncle was in Toronto but the boy didn't want to live with his uncle's family. He wanted to be on his own. But not having money, he shared an apartment with a friend of his uncle. I was impressed by his hopes for freedom. He does have youth on his side and maybe he will make it. But that is not guaranteed – he has a great deal of catching up to do. He said that had the Taliban not taken over, he would now be getting ready for university and then medical school at the University of Kabul. But he was certainly not seeking pity:

> I feel really lonely most of the time. My uncle is good to me but he has his own family to worry about. I have to make it on my own. I hope I will see my mother again but I don't know how. The teachers here are kind to me but I have so much catching up to do. It's not easy learning how to read and write a new language well enough to be able to go to university. If it hadn't been for the Taliban and all that, I would have been able to become a doctor. That is what my parents wanted for me. Now I am like an orphan.

I told him about my own parents' situation and my struggles with the war that had devastated them. About the fact that I don't have many relatives – that all were killed, except for one who came to Canada before the war. His eyes widened and real dialogue began. About his being Muslim, about my being Jewish. About the fact that his father and brother had been against the Taliban. That he saw his brother's head sheared by a bullet right in front of his house in Kabul. That his father had disappeared, probably also killed. He was surprised when he realized that my life experience had something to do with the film "Schindler's List," and with "The Diary of Anne Frank," which he knew about because his class had been involved in a unit on World War II that term. He was taken aback and told me: "Your family had it much worse than me."

It is interesting how those of us from lands of war often compare our suffering, measuring carefully to ascertain who was worse or better off: the wounded sharing their war stories. And there is at least some comfort in the sharing. "This is the first time anybody Canadian knows what I'm talking about," he admitted to me. "What does it mean to be Canadian?" I asked him. "To look like you belong," he responded and then asked, "Could I write a story for you about when I was a child in Kabul? I still haven't done one but now I want to."

****

I walked out of the school late that afternoon after classes were over, weighted with the three hour interview I had just completed with Mahmoud. I had set a date with Ann for a return visit to the school and then said good-bye. I felt exhausted as I got to the subway. I considered what Mahmoud had told me during our interview: "You look like you belong." Maybe I do look like I belong. But I don't really feel that I do. Maybe I belong on top of all those corpses. But that is not where I ended up. I wander this planet still searching for the comfort of a home, trying to erase scenes which keep playing over and over again in my mind: about children being marched to gas chambers. Their corpses always follow me always, even as birds sing on a glorious summer afternoon as I sit on a little porch in Toronto.

Living on parallel tracks: one path leads to Auschwitz (or Treblinka or to one of the many other lesser-known camps) and to death; the other to school and to life. I must stay on the second track no matter how much I am being pushed to get back onto the first. In my mind I am a small child again. It is easy to be lost and frightened and alone. It is easy to feel nothing, worthless, hopeless. But I must pick myself up and run. I see myself holding a torn doll and we run together. All the way to my elementary school where I am now able to speak English and read it too. Where everything makes sense and nobody wants to hurt me. I am the only one on my street who goes to this English Protestant school. All the other children go to the French Catholic school which is a lot closer to where I live. I am neither Protestant nor English but kids like me were put in there because they had to put Jews somewhere. I wish I could have gone to the Catholic school but to go there they really wanted you to be Catholic. The Protestant schools took in all the other Christians as well as the non-Christians – which at that time meant only the Jews.

When I first came to kindergarten I felt lonely because I didn't know any of the children and because my teacher disliked my surname. But now I am in Grade One and I have a new teacher who smiles at me. I have a beautiful desk and chair and nice new books this year. My teacher looks lovely – she reminds me of my aunt in the picture. But my teacher will never have to worry about heaps of corpses and smoke curling up the chimneys of the ovens. No, my teacher is lucky. I want to stand near her, to feel safe in her presence.

Does my teacher have any idea what I am feeling? Does she know about the camps and how I feel tainted by them? Does she smell the stench of death? She certainly knows that my parents had come from that war, that they are poor and cannot speak English or French well and that they are not happy. Yet she still likes

CHAPTER TEN

me. She helps me learn to read and to write. I love it when she reads us stories – every day at the end of the day. I am enthralled by her soft, melodious voice. I never heard a voice like hers before. The voices in my family are always intense, shrill, frightened, silent, and bitter. My teacher's voice is like that of the fairy godmother who took Cinderella away from the evil around her. Her voice is like the voice of the nurse who gave us those needles so that we wouldn't get polio. It was scary, but her voice was soothing.

Here in this classroom of my childhood I can forget for a few hours every day. I can pretend to be a normal schoolgirl writing in her exercise book, writing about happy families going about their lives. I am learning to write in English and also in French. I adore French. I wish we could learn it all day instead of only for one hour a day. It reminds me of my best friend, Françoise, who lives next door to me and whose relatives are always coming over to visit her, laughing and having fun.

I am learning how to write and as time goes on I am learning more and more words. With each word I approach closer to the sunshine, closer to the fun that I see in other people's lives. There are other children in my class whose parents also come from that war. They too don't have grandparents or many other relatives. A very few do. My new friend Linka has a grandmother. Her grandmother is always hugging me and I like to peer into her wide face with big blue eyes framed by white hair that is always up in a braided bun. I love to snuggle in her lap although I feel like I should not be allowed to do that. She is always baking delicious cakes and cookies. But Linka's mother is often in her bedroom with her bathrobe on and looks like she cannot stop crying. Linka's father works late at a factory and I sometimes see him on weekends. He looks like he will never be able to give himself permission to cry. Still, Linka is lucky. She has a piano in her apartment. One afternoon I muster the courage to touch the keys. They feel like marble. Their sound is divine. But such luxury was not meant for me.

Then, suddenly, I am back on my porch and it is still a mid-afternoon in summer in Toronto. Birds are still singing and my tea cup sits on the table next to my chair. The pages of transcripts from Mahmoud's interview and from other students at Northlands Collegiate are still in my hands.

There are many other stories. I read the interview I conducted at Northlands Collegiate with Lina, who is from Albania and whose anxiety was tattooed on her clenched jaw when I first met her. She stared at me in a kind of haze during our conversation. Here is an excerpt from the transcript:

> I just don't know if it will ever work out for me. It was bad in Albania but at least I was with my whole family. I miss my mother and my brothers so much. I haven't seen them for over a year and I don't know when we will be together again. It is all legal stuff. In the meantime I am trying to learn English as well as I can because I want to go to university but will I be accepted? I want to be a lawyer but it is only a dream. I want to become Canadian and feel like I belong but that will take a very long time. Most days I wake up in the morning feeling homesick and discouraged. And my father

can't help because he is trying to make enough money to be able to get the rest of the family over here.

At Northlands one morning I also spoke with a seventeen-year-old Tamil boy from Sri Lanka who discussed the gaps in his education due to war:

> Here I had to learn what it is to sit at a desk and listen to the teacher. I am beginning to see how much I missed because I didn't go to school for many years because of war and I am only now learning to read and write in English. I can't read or write much in Tamil. It feels good to be here but also I feel very upset because I missed so much and I don't know how I can catch up.

Then there was Hargan, a boy from Bosnia who told me:

> I realize now that some of my friends here never actually think about the things I'm thinking, that's the difference I realize in myself, it's like, internal. I have seen awful things. I feel old, not like a teenager should feel.

I didn't really know how to console these students, except to nod in silence. I tell them how school became my way of holding on: to a dream, to an idea, to a possibility, to a vision. Some aren't sure if this will work for them but they seemed to like to hear the story, as though we were orphans gathered around a warm stove with good food nearby. In that little ESL interview room we could feel secure. It is the narrow ridge where, as Martin Buber put it, the "I and Thou" meet: the territory of the "in-between" where people can come together in community. The beginning of real human communication. For a moment our wounds disappear and we can lay down our burdens. I think about these adolescents often – about their acute sense of dislocation and rootlessness and the challenges they face: to invent a place and an identity that will become a life-raft through the turbulent waters of their traumatic heritage. There are no magic pills for this, no shortcuts, only blinding loss. But, lest we forget, there is also the quiet benediction of the future – no matter how uncertain it may feel.

You have to escape from Trauma but it is always just around the corner. Trauma robs you of youth, of joy, of hope, of voice. But you have to hold on the best way you can. Perhaps School isn't a salvation for everyone, but it was for me. It gave me a place of rest, of peace, and a sense of future. And I was able to share my story with these teenagers at Northlands. They aren't yet sure about what will happen to them, but this much is true, that for many of them, school is the safest place they have ever known.

In field notes that I kept I recorded my feelings after a particularly trying visit to the school on a mid-December afternoon just before the holidays:

> I feel battle weary but have made it to the end of term. It's a dreary rainy December day. The first snow has melted. Just got back from the high school. Police were all around. Many of the kids seemed dazed and confused, afraid after what had happened last Friday: the stabbing death of one of the students. I was there on the afternoon it happened, interviewing Mahmoud.

CHAPTER TEN

And I was there again today too; this week I interviewed two more students. Their stories are so heavy with the weight of the dilemmas of their lives. They are too heavy for me to carry right now. What to do about a child who had to leave his family at age 12 and roam from Afghanistan to Iran, to Azerbaidjan, to a refugee camp in Pakistan until he got here at age 18?

What to do about another boy who was "illegal" as a Kurd in Syria and then got to Pakistan and then to Cuba but never went to school and didn't even know how to hold a pencil when he arrived at this high school in Toronto? He is trying hard to "catch up." He wants to be a computer programmer. The same litany over and over again: "I want to catch up. Will I be able to catch up?"

And what to do about a seventeen-year-old girl who is here with her father from Albania and trying to get refugee status? Her mother and siblings are still over there. The girl, who has pale skin with soft blue eyes, is depressed. When she speaks of her ambition to become a lawyer, a light goes on in her eyes but then she returns to reality and they grow dull again. She wants to be able to help people as a lawyer. But who will help her now?

What to do about all this misery and injustice, this exile? The stories of these students mingle with the memories of all the broken dreams of my own parents. Their wounds pile onto those of my family and I can hardly breathe. The anger I feel is overwhelming. All that pain, all that deprivation, all that trauma. All my rocking myself back and forth in darkness as a child, hanging on to a thin little thread of hope. Oh God, forgive me for wondering why you let such suffering all just go on. Forgive me for questioning why I and these children, and so many others, have to be robbed of so much. For all that energy wasted just to be able to face the day. For parents who in their brokenness hold their children too tightly or not tightly enough, or simply not at all. Forgive me for wanting to throw something and send it shattering against a wall.

There is another reality that anyone who lives and works in inner-city neighbourhoods must face: that for many of the newly-arrived who have lived under dictatorships, violence, war and so forth, democracy is not a familiar concept. Some students bring the sectarian violence from their home countries into their classrooms and we as educators need to face this new and complex dynamic. For example, in response to that fatal stabbing that took place near the school grounds one student confided to me:

> There are lots of kids in this school who are really crazy, and want to bring the fights of their countries in here. Some Serbian kids hate the Bosnian kids because of the war and because they are Muslim. And some of the Muslim kids from different places think their way is the best way and don't know much about being Christian or anything. And the Christians don't know anything about Islam. I heard some kids saying very bad things about Jews

too. There are lots of fights. It's hard to get along and for everybody to feel OK. How do you make people understand each other? There is no way other than to stare such realities in the eye. Within the context of diversity, issues of cultural difference and conflict resolution no longer can be ignored in schools. Diversity should become a source of genuine learning and we must offer cutting-edge ways to deal with conflict constructively and creatively. As educators we must try to open spaces for dialogue so that such complex issues can be discussed in safe ways and so as to bridge gaps and reconcile difference. This is a daunting task but also a highly necessary one, given the growing frictions in some inner-city high schools both locally and globally.

I have tried here to offer a glimpse into the lives of some newly arrived students in a Toronto inner-city high school, as they confront the process of integration as well as personal and social problems in and out of school. For them it is a time of trauma, upheaval and sometimes despair. It is in fact likely that this is the first time any of these students had been invited to reflect on these difficult and painful personal issues within a school context (or within any other for that matter) and I found it challenging to balance voice and silence in the texts of the participants. Such identity processes are fluid and constantly changing and under construction, like life itself. One can only wonder how they would respond a year from now, what they might say then that they did not dare say to me now during my interviews with them.

Perhaps simply opening the space that allowed these students to consider their "outsiderness" and sense of loss as well as their hopes for the future constitutes an important beginning. If we really care about these students we must rethink and reshape our understanding of teaching and learning that is in a way more fundamentally linked to their lived experiences. These issues are also crucial for nation building and citizenship education in pluralistic Western societies such as Canada – both in and out of school.

On my last visit to the school before the holidays Ann, the ESL coordinator, drove me to the subway after school in the rain and told me how much I mean to these children, how they really look forward to my visits. I told her that I had taken a taxi to the school that day on account of the bad weather, and that when the cab driver realized that he was going into the parking lot of the school (he had heard about the stabbing) he couldn't believe it. He said goodbye to me as though I was heading off to war and treated me like some sort of hero. Ann and I laughed about this. It felt good to laugh a little. Rheinhold Niebuhr said that laughter is the no-man's land between hope and despair. Laughter must surely be the first sign of freedom. We hugged each other and wished each other a happy holiday.

I got back to my office on campus after night had fallen. As I looked out of my window at the torrent of rain I felt somehow as old as those children. I had been immersed in wreckage up to my eyeballs. What does one do with so much mindless suffering? When the girl from Albania learned about what had happened to my parents, she had said that that seemed to have been a much worse a situation. Mahmoud had told me the same thing two weeks earlier. I told the Albanian girl

CHAPTER TEN

that I didn't really know how to help any of the students. She said: *You do your bit, and let others do their part.* Such a caring and such a wise response.

I remembered also what I had told a teacher at Fielding School in Montreal during one of my research visits there, when she told me that dealing with all these children of oppression was getting to be just too much for her: *Just be there and be a witness to their stories. Maybe we can heal each other.* And now I must heed my own advice. I must have faith that opening a space for telling stories has value. Perhaps just showing that one cares really does matter. *Maybe as we tell and listen to such stories, they are being overheard by hidden angels.* I think that one of those angels has been taking care of me forever.

CHAPTER ELEVEN

THE TERM THEY CANCELLED HALLOWEEN

I have come to believe that a great teacher is a great artist and that there are as few as there are any other great artists. Teaching might even be the greatest of the arts since the medium is the human mind and spirit..

-John Steinbeck

CALIFORNIA DREAMIN' – SOME MUSINGS ON PEDAGOGY

During a sabbatical in the winter and spring of 2003, I had been given the opportunity to visit some classrooms in the San Francisco Bay Area. One of the highlights for me was a visit to Rick Ayers' classes at Berkeley High School. I had attended the AERA (American Educational Research Association) conference in Chicago that April and met his brother Bill, who had made statements in one of the sessions that stunned the audience in their grim clarity: "In this gathering darkness that we are living through we must strive to endure. In this period of totalitarian impulse, we are witnessing the beginning of the end of a great progressive experiment: that is public education." It was Bill who urged me to get in touch with his brother Rick in Berkeley to set up a visit to his classes at Berkeley High.

I was grateful to Bill for having facilitated this. He had told Rick about my book "Oasis of Dreams: Teaching and Learning Peace in a Jewish-Palestinian Village in Israel" and Rick invited me to visit and speak to the students in his classes. I was delighted at this and we set a date for the visit. It was the end of May and the weather was unusually hot for the East Bay. The heat seemed almost like a metaphor for what I had been witness to during that particular winter in Northern California: the desperate financial situation of the Oakland and other Bay Area schools, and subsequently the extreme conditions that were facing many teachers. By mid-March the teachers had been told that there would be thousands of pink slips sent out to them. Everything about public education in the Bay Area seemed to be in shambles. On the day of my visit there I walked to Berkeley High School, which was not very far from where I had been staying. It is a large school which takes up an entire block in the downtown core of the city on a boulevard named after Martin Luther King Jr. The motto of the school is carved in stone over its main entrance:

The Truth shall make you strong;

and it shall make you free."

This motto set the tone for my visit. Rick had created there a very special small-scale humanities program entitled "Communication Arts and Science" (CAS), emphasizing media literacy and communications within a context of social justice. Its formal flyer said:

This innovative program will help you to:
- Incorporate real-world experiences into your high school education
- Plan not only for college but for life
- Make Berkeley High smaller and more personal
- Create community among classmates and with teachers
- Explore issues of social justice, social change, and social responsibility

In CAS you will have the opportunity to:
Go to museums, see plays, learn to produce videos, design a magazine, write a journal, work in a TV station, develop strong academic skills, participate in a debate, go on an overnight retreat, learn to think critically, have your opinions be heard, know your classmates well.

Three Essential Objectives of CAS:
- To encourage intellectual and personal growth through communication arts
- To develop a sense of community among students, teachers, and families
- To work for social justice

What Makes CAS Unique
The group stays together
Unlike other students at Berkeley High, CAS students work with same group of 60 to 90 students over the course of their four years of high school.

There is team teaching in English and History
Topics for study are theme-based. Students work on cross-disciplinary projects individually and in groups, involving English, History, video, and other classes.

The student goes to the community and the community comes to the student
Outside speakers visit the program and CAS students and teachers travel to museums, theaters, and Pacific film Archives. Students participate in service learning projects.

Each year there is a special CAS elective
You must take the CAS electives to be in the program. Freshmen take a year-long photo-video-media class, sophomores take Video Production, Juniors take Advanced Writing or Advanced Video.

The senior year includes an internship
CAS Social Justice Senior Seminar leads to a community placement (in a service or social change organization). Each senior produces a major research paper and ties that to community work. Seniors end the year with an exhibition of their work.

During the first period that day, I found myself in a Social Justice Senior Seminar in the portable classroom where Rick teaches all of his classes. I was impressed by how relaxed he was with his students and realized at once that I was in the presence of a master teacher. Perhaps the true mission of teaching is to allow the classroom to become a kind of utopia where there is always room for transformation and liberation in spite of difference and conflict and inequity. I felt that I was in that kind of classroom on that very warm day in May.

My experience as a teacher tells me that a classroom carries the possibility of freedom and can offer a new map, a new vision, a new kind of strength. Rick introduced me as "the professor of education from the University of Toronto who will be talking to them later about her research project in a Jewish-Palestinian village in Israel where people are trying to live in peace." He held up a copy of my book "Oasis of Dreams" and said to them: "Remember I showed this to you last week? We are lucky to be able to meet the author and ask her about this amazing place." I said hello and sat down in a chair that a student placed for me near Rick's desk. The students seemed to stare at me as if I were some winged being who had flown in from a paradise they hadn't known existed on earth. And I was very glad to be there.

There was quite a rainbow of racial and socio-economic diversity in that classroom. Some of these students had the good fortune of being the children of professors (Berkeley is after all a university town) or of other professionals, while others came from homes in which the struggle to keep the wolf at bay pervades. There is nothing fair about it – it simply represents the panorama of human life: ambiguous, complex, evocative. But I noticed also that Rick was *really* listening to each one of his students no matter what neighbourhood they were coming from. And they were listening to him as well as to each other. In that classroom it seemed possible to learn under the tutelage of a teacher whose passion and caring was dedicated to authentic pedagogical process and practice. I could feel boundaries melting away, the multiplicity of ways to "be", the interconnectedness of all things. There was a quality of "community" there and a spirit of "cultural healing" to put it in Theobald's terms. What was being created in that classroom was a cooperative or collective call to moral action in order to, in Maxine Greene's words, "bring about societal repairs" (1995, p. 66).

Rick was very direct and never pretentious with his students. *"This is you standing alone; it's not a group project,"* he said to them about their major research paper assignment that focused on their internship and community work. *"You can't blow it."* This was the afternoon when students were expected to read about their community projects aloud in class. I listened as one strikingly beautiful black female student read aloud from her writing. It was a rap poem filled with pain. *"The face stoked by hate not love..."* etc. She was describing life in her neighbourhood and in her home. Her dignity amidst the violence and poverty struck me. It took a lot of trust for her to read this poem aloud in the classroom. Clearly she felt safe there. There were others too who read and each student shared with the others something of his or her soul. One could feel the weight of the internal luggage in their words. I was in a space that connected with the students' needs and allowed them a possibility of finding meaning through the preciousness of communication. You could do that in Rick Ayers' classroom. You could reflect on the experiences of a fellow classmate in such a way that you could recognize in that dialogue a fragment of your own inner self.

There was so much creativity and energy in the air there that an intimate interchange could occur in body as well as in mind. Students were being encouraged to dig deep to find their own story – a psychological transformation through narrative for changing their world. Story stirs us to action; as Maxine Greene (1995, p. 75) puts it, "The narratives we shape out of the materials of our lived lives must somehow take account of our original landscapes." Or, as Robert Coles (1997) argues, each of us has a story that contains our answers to the old existential questions. Such was the nature of the stories being shared in Rick's classroom. In addition to their written essays, some students offered poetry, paintings, and even a piece of music – art connected to a unifying sense of purpose which, as Jean-Paul Sartre states, "widens our sensitivity, awakens our imagination" (1949, p. 57). I had almost forgotten how engaging such authentic student-teacher and student-student interaction could be. Rick's classes were an oasis amidst an educational climate of "standards," "assessment", "accountability", "programmed learning", and "high stakes test scores."

There was no tension or anxiety in this classroom, just the pleasure students were deriving from their own work. There is a message in this kind of teaching and learning that Maxine Greene conveys in her writing: "We should think of education as opening public spaces in which students, speaking in their own voices and acting on their own initiatives, can identify themselves and choose themselves in relation to such principles as freedom, equality, justice and concern for others" (1998, p. 68). In Rick's classroom, students were finding solace in the common enterprise of their program which offered them the hope of moving forward and of getting out.

But political storms had been gathering for a long time in California. And California has always been a "trend-setter" for a myriad of situations, so it was anxiety-provoking to observe what was happening. Sadly I witnessed there the fragility of the great institution of public education from very close range. In the name of "accountability" and "school effectiveness", more and more innovative school programs were being cut in California. Educational budgets were severely reduced. Ever since Proposition 13 (1978) had passed many years earlier (allowing property owners to stop paying school taxes) the funding base for public education had become severely eroded. Adding to this already critical situation was an ongoing reduction of government spending on education in California – as in many other states throughout the U.S. This placed schools, teachers and students in the poorest districts most at risk. I visited some schools in Oakland, adjacent to Berkeley, and found physical conditions there that were, simply put, unsanitary and even dangerous. And Berkeley High itself was not in the best of physical shape. How can such circumstances not impact upon the lives and morale of teachers and, of their students?

During my study leave there I had an opportunity to speak with many teachers in the Bay Area and saw many of them descend into melancholy or despair. Many who worked in the schools asked: "Will we have to lose everything before we can put it back together again? How many students and teachers will have to be injured or destroyed?" I asked myself about the students in Rick's classes. Will they be among the last to benefit from his creative CAS program? While I found it demoralizing to ponder this, I held on to the belief that there will always be the heroes to work in the in-between places; "border-dwellers" who will keep on going – and who will keep others going – by "subversive" acts of devotion. Rick Ayers is one of these "border dwellers." It was enheartening to learn about the various students from low-income families who made it into the University of California system as a result of the training they had received in Rick's CAS program – a tribute to the value of public education. But are we in fact witnessing the end of an era of progressive education, as Rick's brother Bill had asserted at the AERA meeting? A disturbing question struck me: ***Where would I be now had I not had the blessing of a good public education?***

I was brought back from my reveries in the class on that hot afternoon when Rick finally invited me to speak to his students about my book. I got up from the chair on which I had been sitting for a long time and began to share my experiences with them. I told them how fortunate I felt to have found out about this cooperative Jewish-Palestinian village. I explained to them that what is wonderful about the villagers living there is how they invite us all to become fellow dreamers of peace just as they themselves were seeking to break down barriers of fear and mistrust that have saturated their lives. "But most of all," I told them, "the reason that I kept on going back there over a period of nine years to conduct my research there and to write that book was because these villagers offered me a sense of hope every time I went there and I wanted to share that sense of hope with as many people as possible. To visit that village is to witness a miracle, especially for someone like myself who as a child of Holocaust survivors has been searching all her life for a place of hope and reconciliation."

I also told the students that I was now writing a second book (this one). One student asked a question that caught me off guard: "It's clear why you wrote the first book" he said, "but why are you writing the second book?" I stopped for a moment and thought about it. "Because I want to inspire teachers" was my reply to him. Then the recess bell rang. During the break I left Rick's portable, walked out into the brilliant sunshine and entered the main building of the school. I passed a poster on a wall which said:

> What would happen to music if we didn't support programs that nurtured talent in our young people?

The corridors were untidy but I could hear violin music coming from a classroom – both beautiful and soothing.

CHAPTER ELEVEN

I walked back outside in order to eat an orange. I sat down in the bleachers of the Berkeley High stadium and thought about what I had said to the student in Rick's class. That I was writing this second book *in order to inspire teachers*. I realized that a follow-up to his question could well have been: "But why do you want to inspire teachers?" And I would have answered, "Because some teachers inspired me when I was young and it changed my life." As I sat in the sunshine surveying students wearing red and gold school tracksuits with the busy bee school mascot on their T-shirts and running laps in the stadium, I asked myself: "Who among these students at Berkeley High will become teachers? Who among them will take that risk?" Next to me on the bench where I sat was a book that happened to have been left there by one of the students. As I opened it the words of African-American poet Langston Hughes appeared:

I have almost forgotten my dream

But there it is in front of me

Bright as the sun.

This poem gives voice to those who cannot speak. It issues an admonition: for his people not to abandon their dreams regardless of how battered these may be. I realized that this applies also to teachers whose role is a lifelong one as well. We, who are dedicated to offering an education that promises a future for all students, are in it for the long haul. We must never forget this dream. Perhaps the most important thing a teacher can offer is to bear witness to the ongoing struggle to better the lives of students through the dynamic process of Paulo Freire's (1970) revolutionary perspective of education as a form of social liberation. A meaningful school curriculum should examine what it means to be human. Arnold Berleant views curriculum as, "thought in process, intimately responding to and guiding the actively engaged body... and providing occasions for the emergence of the integrated self" (cited in Greene, 1995, p. 130).

What can be more important than to empathize with fellow human beings and awaken our consciousness to the majesty and frailty of all humanity? Martha Nussbaum muses that "another person, in some ways similar to oneself, has suffered some significant pain or misfortune in a way for which that person is not, or not fully, to blame... Compassion requires one more thing: a sense of one's own vulnerability to misfortune – that this suffering person might be me" (p. 97). In my view, one of the primary goals of teaching is to create a network of relationships through literature and images and art and through all manner of activities. These stir the imagination and make us capable of seeing and hearing the "other," feeling the hurt done to the "other" as a personal wound, thereby making dialogue across difference possible.

ONTARIO: FALL OF 1997

As I sat there in the bleachers of Berkeley High, my mind wandered back to the political climate in the province of Ontario in Canada where I live and work, which had also deteriorated over the years (albeit not as severely as in California). I reflected back to the fall term of 1997 where a collective anxiety and sense of outrage emerged among teachers in reaction to a new piece of legislation (Bill 160) which was being ushered in by a (then) new conservative government that had become obsessed with turning public education into a depersonalized and increasingly bureaucratized business model, and seemed intent on scapegoating teachers as being the source of many of the problems in society. This assault on the self-worth and professional identity of teachers in the province of Ontario resulted in a political strike action by teachers across the entire province.[1] As I taught my graduate course "Multicultural Perspectives in Teacher Development" that fall my students (most of whom were teachers) would congregate in our classroom every Tuesday evening, while the situation for teachers became more and more desperate with each passing week.

As I sat quietly eating my orange in the Berkeley High bleachers, reflecting back to that fall term, I remembered my own attempts at creating spaces for the teachers and for myself as their instructor, to engage in a critical dialogue about our place in the world of education and about our desire for a democratic vision within it – something that seemed sorely lacking in the climate of the time. I offered a space for these graduate students to express what they perceived to be a real injustice. It seemed critical for them to be able to name their anger and to find companionship within it. What could have been more meaningful to my students at the time? Some of the articles we read that term took on greater resonance than they might have in more ordinary times. Maxine Greene's book "Releasing the Imagination: Essays on Education, the Arts and Social Change" (1995) became one of the guiding readings for the course. Indeed Maxine Greene became our de facto "mentor" through the power of her words. One evening, early on in the term, one student, a Grade Ten English teacher, said that she wanted to share an excerpt from Greene's Chapter Four "Discovering a Pedagogy" because that textual experience had changed her sense of being a 'victim' into that of a 'fighter.' Here is the excerpt she chose to discuss:

> They [students and teachers] may, through their coming together, constitute a newly human world, one worthy enough and responsive enough to be both durable and open to continual renewal. Of course this has to begin in local places, in schoolrooms and schoolyards and neighborhood centers; it has to begin where people know each others' names. But it can reach beyond, toward an enlarging public space where more and more common interests are articulated. It can radiate to inform the 'conversation' and to empower individuals to open themselves to what they are making in common...they may be able to identify a better state of things — and go on to transform. Sometimes, I believe it is our only hope.

135

CHAPTER ELEVEN

We became engaged in a "venture, a new beginning, a raid on the inarticulate... There is only the fight to recover what has been lost. And found again and lost again and again; and now, under conditions that seem unpropitious. But perhaps neither gain nor loss. For us there is only the trying." [T.S. Eliot, 1943, p.128 cited in Greene, 1995, p. 59] Our class debated Maxine's call to create change at the grassroots level – not the rigid, top-down approach which the Ontario government of the time was imposing onto schools and teachers. I also introduced my graduate students to Berkeley High School through a videotape called "School Colors," which had been created by students at Berkeley High in 1994 and had ended up on Frontline, a PBS documentary program. A colleague at Cal had given me a copy of the video as a gift and since then I had been using it in my graduate courses. This video turns out to be an effective vehicle for opening discussions on inter-cultural and inter-racial issues and on identity politics in schools from both teacher and student perspectives. It is, however, a controversial piece due to its portrayal of violence and self-segregation at Berkeley High, and many who are connected with that school believe that it offers a skewed and exaggerated portrayal of school life there. Even so this video still provides a very useful tool for addressing the great cultural, linguistic and racial diversity that exists in most schools in the Greater Toronto area, so I find it to be a useful pedagogical tool within curriculum and teacher development courses.

When I showed that video to my fall 1997 class, my graduate students were fascinated as well as shocked by it. They were fascinated by the courage of the Berkeley High adolescents to take a stand on the thorny issue of identity politics and to negotiate and construct connections between the larger national and international identities within the framework of cultural difference. What appealed to my students about "School Colors" was that it offers a portrait of "resistance" and "reinvention", to use Giroux's (1994) terms. But they were also dismayed to see how Berkeley High students congregated into their separate groups on the public areas of the school. The more we pondered such issues throughout the term, the more we began to realize that the Berkeley High adolescents had in fact articulated something that was occurring in many Toronto high schools as well.

We were impressed by the Berkeley High adolescents who vividly and eloquently expressed the tension between longing for the local, familial, and cultural versus their desire to belong to the wider world, to the universal – a tension between local versus global. In a sense, we were being invited to reflect on the complexity of human relations. Self-segregation is indeed disconcerting, but whoever said that diversity in a pluralistic society is necessarily a simple matter? Multicultural education, by its very nature, engenders emotionally intense discussions – situated as it is at cultural crossroads which have been so dramatically altered over the last few decades in all urban centres in North America as well as in other Western countries.

During that fall term of 1997 we found ourselves wishing that these Berkeley high school students might in fact be able somehow to produce a successful model for "cultural bridging" among difference. Such social dilemmas are prevalent in many urban centers around the globe. Giroux (1994) claims that "multiculturalism has become a central discourse in the struggle over issues regarding national identity, the construction of historical memory, the purpose of schooling, and the meaning of democracy." Throughout the term, we considered how multicultural education could provide pedagogical opportunities for students, teachers, and researchers to engage interactively in critical understandings of personal and cultural identity. We also looked closely at the term "multiculturalism" which has been criticized by some as having become entwined with identity politics, especially within the U.S. We reflected on multiculturalism as a space in which students in schools in Toronto can negotiate and re-define their multiple identities – identities that weave and overlap with each other in multi-dimensional ways.

School, as the meeting place, becomes the borderland wherein cultures collide and intersect in complex ways. We focused on how to use our classrooms as safe places to learn, "to become friends with the other" as Julia Kristeva (1991) puts it. Being positioned as the "outsider" or the "other" in the context of school represents a myriad of multi-layered experiences in the immigrant and minority language student's story and puts focus on the need to re-envision the meaning of classroom practice with a new paradigm of intercultural negotiation and understanding in a rapidly changing cultural, linguistic, racial and religious educational landscape. We considered also the ideas of Cornell & Stoddard in their book "Things Fall Together, Liberal Education" (1994) who prefer the term "interculturalism" in contrast to "multiculturalism." Citing from Cornell and Stoddard, Nussbaum states that:

> the latter interculturalism is associated with relativism and identity politics, suggesting a pedagogy "limited to an uncritical recognition or celebration of difference, as if all cultural practices were morally neutral or legitimate. Interculturalism by contrast connotes the sort of comparative searching that they have in mind, which they argue should prominently include the recognition of common human needs across cultures and of dissonance and critical dialogue within cultures. The interculturalist rejects the claim of identity politics that only members of a particular group have the ability to understand the perspective of that group. In fact understanding is achieved in many different ways and being born of a certain group is neither sufficient nor necessary. Knowledge is frequently enhanced by an awareness of difference. (Nussbaum, 1997, p. 82.)

In my graduate course in that fall term we discussed such issues and how at bottom sense of 'home' gives one an identity and a sense of well-being, especially for those uprooted in our world. How important it is to promote the love and care of place that, according to Nell Noddings, in her book "Happiness and Education" "figure so importantly in human flourishing." Indeed any discourse around identity is always about one's perceived and desired location in the world. Are we happy with where we are, or do we wish desperately to be elsewhere? Multicultural education needs to address such fundamental questions in a multiplicity of ways. And that indeed is what we ended up doing during that tumultuous fall term of 1997, but in a totally different way than we had originally intended. Due to the political climate in Ontario that fall, the call for a strike action became, for teachers, a last resort as well as a great unknown. Teachers walked out onto picket lines but would come to my university course every week. And each class for them became an act of faith. We spoke of powerlessness and of being on the defensive – but also of a coming of age, the need to make brave decisions sometimes and live by them.

All of the academic articles we read that term took on new and urgent meanings. *'Marginality', 'exile', 'border crossing', 'living on the edge.'* Yes, we were walking a tightrope, skating on thin ice, but also learning to trust our inner wisdom in the face of an uncaring, and seemingly hostile, provincial government. One evening, a student read out a quote from Martha Nussbaum's book "Cultivating Humanity" which provided another guiding light for the course and suited the reality of our common lived professional experience at the time:

> It is up to us, as educators, to show our students the beauty and interest of a life that is open to the whole world, to show them that there is after all more joy in the kind of citizenship that questions than in the kind that simply applauds, more fascination in the study of human beings in all their real variety and complexity than in the zealous pursuit of superficial stereotypes, more genuine love and friendship in the life of questioning and self-government than in submission to authority. We had better show them this or the future of democracy in this nation and in the world is bleak. (Nussbaum, 1997, p. 84.)

Another student quoted from another section of that same page:

> we need to search for what is good in human life the world over…Becoming a citizen of the world is often a lonely business—a kind of exile from the comfort of assured truths, from the warm nestling feeling of being surrounded by people who share one's convictions and passions… (p. 84.)

The conflictual state between government and teachers in Ontario during that fall term of 1997 was symbolized by what became the BIG issue for elementary school students: the looming reality that, on account of the strike, there would be no Halloween school activities that year. One Grade Two teacher in my course walked into class one evening as the strike action was looming, and told us that one of her pupils had asked her that morning: *"Does this mean that they are cancelling Halloween?"* This became our metaphor for the impasse between teachers and government that had brought all public schooling to a halt in Ontario. My students and I agreed to call it: *"The Term They Cancelled Halloween."* Something profound was happening. One child's question highlighted the loss: that students would be robbed of all the pleasurable activities around Halloween they were so looking forward to: the painting, the costume-making, the singing, the drama skits, the storytelling and story writing. Children know instinctually how important such aesthetic experiences are to pedagogy. They were heartbroken and so were their teachers.

During the weeks that followed, I visited picket lines and honked my car horn in support of the teachers whenever I drove past a school. In my classes it was apparent how much teachers appreciated those who provided such gestures of support during this time of upheaval. I watched with concern from the sidelines, encouraging my students (most of whom were involved in the actions) to construct new meaning for their lived texts. For the teachers this was stuff of uncharted explorations, a delicate balancing act of caring for their pupils as well as of standing up for their professional identity. Their sense of place had been taken away; there had been a lock-out, so their classrooms became out-of-bounds. Their feelings of displacement were palpable as teachers became wanderers in their own educational landscapes, and their ultimate professional survival itself became a kind of triumph.

All of us looked forward to our weekly class gatherings on these Tuesday evenings in that fall 1997. It became 'home'– returning us to "the safest places of our childhood" to use a term from Noddings again. We understood that we needed to commemorate what we were all sharing during this course. Journal writing brought a new kind of professional meaning for my teachers – a desire to record the safety and compassion of our conversations. Our sharing of professional stories through journaling became a bulwark against the external chaos. This writing brought with it its own redemptive quality, a way of constructing professional "selves" and creating a sense of belonging in a world that for teachers had grown suddenly very cold.

Writing about injustice is a moral imperative, says Jean-Paul Sartre:

> And if I am given this world with its injustices, it is not so I might contemplate them coldly, but that I might animate them with my indignation, that I might disclose them and create them with their nature as injustices, that is as abuses to be suppressed. Thus the writer's universe will only reveal itself in all its depth to the examination, the admiration and the indignation of the reader; and the generous love is a promise to maintain, and the generous indignation is a promise to change, and the admiration is a promise to imitate; although literature is one thing and morality a quite different one, at the heart of the aesthetic imperative we discern the moral imperative. For, since the one who writes recognizes, through the very fact that he takes the trouble to write, the freedom of his readers, and since the one who reads, by the mere fact of his opening the book, recognizes the freedom of the writer, the work of art, from whichever side you approach it, is an act of confidence in the freedom of [sic] men (1949, 62-63).

Something spiritual seemed to envelop and protect us on those Tuesday evenings. Our souls were refreshed and uplifted. It made it possible for my students – these harassed teachers – to wrestle some professional sense of worth out of the gathering gloom. How exactly could Bill 160 fit into the framework of an inclusive education that the government was espousing? How needless was all that anxiety, all that hysteria, and all that crisis-making. I watched with respect how these teachers demonstrated a great deal of courage as they faced the uncertainty about the future of their profession.. At bottom it was a matter of social justice. I feel privileged to have spent *"the term they cancelled Halloween"* with these dedicated professionals. As an act of commemorating this difficult moment in the educational history of Ontario, our class decided to collate our reflective journal writings and to publish them in "Among Teachers Community", a local teachers' journal. That provincial government was eventually voted out of power (in 2004) after having wreaked considerable havoc in the education and health care sectors over two successive terms in office.

The final story about the future of public education has of course not yet been written in Ontario, or in California, or anywhere else for that matter. I mulled over such thoughts as I sat in the bleachers on that warm day at Berkeley High. My experience as a teacher and as a researcher suggests that the authentic educational issues are those in which theory and practice are sculpted into a discourse which is situated in the social, political, pedagogical and personal longings for moral compassion and social justice in schools. The hope is that practitioners, theorists, policymakers, parents and students will join in their determination for conflict resolution, moral integrity and a true respect for diversity. An ultimate goal for teachers is to bear witness to the power of their calling and to embrace the sacred opportunity and challenge to teach and learn about how all students must learn to live together peacefully in multicultural, multifaith, multiracial classrooms both locally and throughout the world.

NOTES

[1] The passage of Bill 160 (the 'Education Quality Improvement Act') marked the beginning of a new era in the education of Ontario's students. Despite the massive protests by 126,000 Ontario teachers, Bill 160 passed in December of 1997. The bill represents a major departure from Ontario's educational tradition by transferring control of the most important aspects of education from elected school boards to the provincial government and its representatives. Perhaps the most controversial stipulation within the Bill was to remove critical components of teachers' working conditions from the realm of collective bargaining. Chief among these was the loss of control over preparation time and class sizes.

CHAPTER TWELVE

I [TOO] HAVE A DREAM

I believe that unarmed truth and unconditional love will have the final word.

-Martin Luther King, Jr.

Early September, and the sabbatical stay in Berkeley had ended. Back to the chores and realities of life in Toronto. I hadn't taught for nine months and felt as though I had lead boots on as I walked toward the subway heading to campus to teach my first class of the new academic year. During that summer I had written the syllabus for a graduate course titled "Curriculum Foundations: From Theory to Practice" that I was about to teach for the first time. I remember feeling a sense of nervous energy as I made photocopies of the syllabus at my favourite copy shop downtown near campus over the Labour Day weekend. It had been some years since I had taught an entirely new course, so it felt like a special occasion for me.

"Curriculum Foundations: From Theory to Practice" is a mandatory course for graduate students in my department, and unfortunately, it had gained a reputation for being "dry", "boring" and "a waste of time." I was eager to try my hand at teaching it; to add my 'signature' to the content, so-to-speak. I saw this as an opportunity not only for academic knowledge building but also to engage in a reflective dialogue where we could speak with one another in personal and practical ways about the BIG issues in education. For we are living now in a time when, perhaps more than ever before, young people yearn for meaning and purpose and connectedness in their lives. How can we help them? What, ultimately, is the purpose of education? How can transformative education be made to happen? What kind of curriculum will help open a dialogue in classrooms about justice, and peace, and caring and love? One cannot legislate such a curriculum. To make a curriculum meaningful for students today we need to focus on soul, love and wisdom. Trust is the currency of treasure in complex and troubled times. Examining who young people idealize as their heroes may give indications about how we should teach them. Are their role models only sports figures or celebrities or rap singers? Is the internet becoming the principal source of 'meaningful' social interaction for our students as well as for ourselves?

The sun shone brightly on that Tuesday afternoon of the first class. There wasn't a trace of a cloud in the sky as I walked to the subway station from my house. I was in Toronto but the weather said that this was Berkeley and a wave of nostalgia overcame me. The sabbatical was no more than a memory now. But then a voice within me whispered: *Every time is the first time and that is the mystery of teaching.* I got to campus and passed the assigned classroom on the way to my office. No one had arrived there yet; still several more hours to go. I did some e-mail, spoke with some colleagues and students, and made a cup of tea. At 5:30 pm on the dot I walked into the classroom. And there they were: twenty human souls all wondering what it was that was about to 'go down.' I noticed some looks of apprehension, of uncertainty and fatigue. And then suddenly my lead boots vanished. There was no way I was going to let these students down (all of whom were, as it turned out, teachers in the field). I had planned a dynamite syllabus for them and knew exactly what had to be done, just as I have known ever since I walked into my first classroom as an elementary schoolteacher some three decades ago. **Give them a sense of dignity and meaning and joy**.

My professional life in schools has taught me that at the very end all that truly counts is to share the sanctity of our mission as teachers: to communicate that we have a precious opportunity to make a difference in our students' lives. And, if we are very lucky, we may even change someone's life for the better in a profound way. In fact this message is really all that I need to share with my graduate students. I love teaching teachers and I try to encourage them to go forward, to not give up however difficult the times. I want them to appreciate that teaching will always be a sacred act, no matter how brutalizing any political "policies" of the day may seem. In his book "The Reinvention of Work" Matthew Fox writes that "our work must make way for the heart, i.e., for truth and justice to play an ever-increasing role in our professional lives..." (p. 16, 1996). Now more than ever his words carry urgency: *"People need a spiritual sense of work."*

Referring to the global uncertainties of our times, I told my students on that first evening of the course: "This is a strange moment in history, but we as teachers will endure. In our own way we will not despair nor be defeated. We will soldier on because we are in it for love and for the long haul. And in the final analysis there is no greater gift – and no greater weapon – than love and compassion." And I continued: "This is a tough time and we are being tested. What's new about that? We cannot begin to fathom the kind of power that we as teachers have on our charges. Sometimes we are rewarded, many years later, by finding out that what we did in a classroom saved somebody." I then shared the following quote with them whose origin I am no longer able to recall: *"A teacher affects all of eternity; s/he can never tell where his or her influence stops."* And I said to them: "Don't let anyone rob you of your dreams, of your innocent desire to do good in the world." I also told my students: "It will always be a struggle but can anything possibly be more worthwhile? What choice is there but to keep going on and to fight the good fight?" Such is the sanctity that emanates from the hopes and dreams of true teachers, and indeed from the eternal history of human endurance.

In my version of the course "Curriculum Foundations: From Theory to Practice" the goal is to explore ways in which curriculum forms the basis for creating a spirit of community within the classroom and a vehicle toward intercultural understanding. Here is an excerpt from the syllabus:

This course intends to open a critical and reflective dialogue of curriculum development both locally and internationally. We examine the scholarly literature in order to document the construction and reconstruction of the meaning of teaching and learning from a variety of perspectives for ourselves as educators in our particular settings. As participant-observers in our own everyday classroom activities, we explore the dynamics of power and identity and of cultural and linguistic difference and equality within the context of diversity. We discuss various methods of research in order to focus on how the curriculum and pedagogical strategies in schools can be reconstituted in such a way that they allow students to become critical thinkers in dialogue with their teachers.

One of the aims of this graduate course to give voice to the moral / equitable / creative initiatives that teachers are creating in their respective classrooms / schools. I encourage you to share your personal and professional stories about teaching and learning within the context of the survey of curriculum theory that is the cornerstone of this course. It is very much a 'hands-on' course in which we become reflective theorists and "curriculum planners" as we respond to the scholarly literature both in the form of journal entry writing and oral discussion. This course is exploratory in the sense that it is hoped that we may produce a reflective space around pedagogical, curricular and social issues in education.

Evaluations are based on collaborative oral presentations and of the writing of a final essay. In this regard, I suggest that you respond to the texts you read and create something of a "*pas de deux*" in which you become engaged with the authors of the articles and books that are discussed throughout the term. Your own professional stories become vehicles in which to shape the meaning of these texts that you read. What we try to achieve is an aesthetic piece of inquiry in educational research within a context of curriculum development.

This syllabus attempts to incorporate Freire's notion that all critical educators are also learners – what bell hooks calls the kind of "engaged pedagogy" which empowers both students and teachers. In her book "Teaching to Transgress" bell hooks describes it as the "practice of freedom rooted in a respect for multiculturalism ... with the assumption that we must build 'community' in order to create a climate of openness and intellectual rigor... a feeling of community creates a sense that there is a shared commitment and a common good that binds us."

How do we reconceptualize education so that it responds to the lived realities of today's youth? This BIG question opened a space for us to explore how our actions and lives dwell within a larger context and allowed us to acknowledge that teachers' lives are deeply influenced by what happens to them outside of the classroom. Teachers' personal and cultural stories influence their professional lives all the time, and their perceptions of the world interact with the lived experiences of the students in their classrooms. The construction of curriculum is in fact a relational act, and therefore a discourse of empowerment needs to be created out of the historical, social, linguistic and cultural realities that are the bedrock of the forms of knowledge and meaning that teachers and students bring to school. Reciprocity is important. Reclaiming voice is important. Retelling and comparing stories are important. These activities, however, are in themselves not enough; they need to be positioned within a larger social and intellectual perspective. A curriculum infused with egalitarianism and mutual understanding must be located within both formal and informal school activities.

I witnessed throughout the term the dialectical relationship that was nurtured in class between imagination and social responsibility allowing us to come together and engage in the kind of "significant and impassioned dialogue" which Maxine Greene describes in her book "The Dialectic of Freedom." We as teachers, as human beings, as a community of learners, began to dig deep and to connect to Freire's call for action to create a more nuanced way of seeing the world: "It is a lifetime struggle that requires counter-intuitive insight, honesty, compassion, and a willingness to brush one's personal history against the grain of 'naive consciousness' or commonsense understanding" (as paraphrased in McLaren 1999, p. 53).

Throughout the term, we also reflected on our own educational and personal experiences as these related to the articles we read for the course. We searched for John Dewey's "Great Community" (1954, p. 43) where a common public culture within pluralism can be created, and can thus offer a true culturally responsive curriculum in schools. As educators we uncovered, both theoretically as well as practically, and week by week, the social, psychological and cultural dilemmas and struggles confronting students of diverse backgrounds in an urban, multicultural setting. This combination of intellectual insight and practical knowledge helped my students and myself as the instructor, to make better sense of the pedagogical needs of ALL students in terms of curriculum building and teacher development. And perhaps more importantly, our classroom conversations led us to build a bridge bringing together traditional understandings of curriculum development with emotional and spiritual reinforcements.

TEACHING FOR PEACE, TEACHING FOR JUSTICE, TEACHING FOR LOVE

One the first evening of "Curriculum Foundations" I told my class about a keynote speech I had heard at a conference organized by my colleague Jack Miller on holistic learning and spirituality in education. "We have become slaves of quantifiable measurement," said one of the keynote speakers, Satish Kumar, programme director of Schumacher College in England and author of "Path without Destination." On that first evening of the course, I conveyed to my students Kumar's argument about the need to reconnect with the 'enchantedness' of our world and of our universe – of the cosmos: "Enchanted land is sacred land and we are walking on the land, so then we are enchanted too. When we accept the flow of the universe then we are free spirits and free spirits are not bound by chains."

This is the realm of spiritual practice and therein lies potential for transformation. I also quoted to my students the words of Mahatma Gandhi: *"Be the change you want to see in the world."* To be sure, this certainly was a different way of 'kicking off' this course. I scanned my students' faces. I didn't even know their names yet, but already I could feel that a light had turned on for many of them. We later each introduced ourselves to the rest of the class and then I asked everyone to reflect on the one overarching question that I believe forever guides the professional journey of true educators – a simple question really: *"Why did you go into education in the first place?"* This set the tone. I shared with them a little about my own reasons for having gone into education.

I felt gratified on that first evening of class by the confused and wide-eyed look in the eyes of many of the graduate students in the class, a look which seemed to say *"What is going on? This seems too interesting to be the course "Curriculum Foundations!"* I must repeat here what I wrote in the introduction to this book: that education is about soul and not about ego. I wanted my students to know that I was going to be real and honest with them to the best of my ability because, for me as a teacher, the classroom is first and always a place of possibility and connection – no matter what the level of learning or the subject matter. In "Teaching to Transgress" bell hooks states that "students rightfully expect that professors will not offer them information without addressing the connection between what they are learning and their overall life experiences. When professors bring narratives of their own experiences into classroom discussions it eliminates the possibility that they can function as all-knowing, silent interrogators. It is often productive if professors accept the first risk, linking confessional narratives to academic discussions so as to show how experience can illuminate and enhance the understanding of academic material."

As that first evening of the course progressed, we discussed the syllabus in detail. I also gave out several articles to be read for the following week. And I hoped that the wheels had been set in motion for my version of the "Curriculum Foundations: From Theory to Practice" course. In the ensuing weeks we discussed a vision of the educational enterprise as an exchange, a relationship that involves giving and receiving. We examined conventional ways of knowing and realized that these are not always enough. Our conversations about the teaching-learning experience were situated within the context of collaborative relationships among teachers, students and parents. Dewey's (1938, p. 111) concept of "teaching and learning as a continuous process of reconstruction of experience" epitomizes the quest for meaning and authenticity in curriculum development. We were beginning to build an atmosphere of commitment to a Freirian notion of schooling – as a moral and political project linking the production of meaning to the possibility for human agency, democratic community, language reform and transformative social action.

One evening in early October a student mentioned that she had taped a show which featured excerpts of the speeches given by Dr. Martin Luther King from 1964 to 1968. This student, an English and History teacher, wanted to bring this videotape to class since it seemed relevant to our discussion on meaningful and culturally relevant curriculum. On the day of the class for which the student had promised to bring in the video, I woke up energized by the thought of watching Dr. King again – so many years after I had seen him on television as an adolescent. I had also planned to spend the first half of that class discussing parts of my book "Oasis of Dreams" in order to explore issues of war and violence, social justice and human rights, and their implications for curriculum development in culturally diverse classrooms. The plan was to devote the other half of the class to viewing the Martin Luther King video to be followed by discussion.

I walked into the class that evening a few minutes early. Some students had already arrived and we chatted informally as we waited for the others. You could sense the anticipation as everyone took their seats and our class began. And then something unplanned occurred. One student who was usually a rather quiet individual rushed into class and told of an incident that had occurred that day at her school. She had been sitting in the staff room holding a copy of my book "Oasis of Dreams" and the new Vice-Principal of her school had noticed it and inquired about it. But before my student could respond, the vice-principal asked: "Could this be about *Neve Shalom/Wahat Al-Salam*?" My student looked incredulously at her: "How did you know?"

It turned out that this vice-principal had been to this village when it was still only a dream in the mind of Father Bruno Hussar way back in 1977. Upon graduating from university, this vice-principal had spent six months on an Israeli kibbutz and then had journeyed to this hilltop, having heard about it from another volunteer in the kibbutz. She spent several weeks there with Father Bruno and others – on that barren hilltop overlooking the Ayalon valley, living in tents and dreaming about turning that place into a viable community of Jewish-Arab peaceful coexistence. She subsequently returned to Toronto to resume her "normal life," went to teachers' college, and started her professional life as an elementary schoolteacher, and later as a Vice-Principal. She had lost track of Father Bruno and his dream until that day when she caught sight of the book in my student's hand.

We pondered the serendipity of the situation. Over the past few weeks we had started to discuss the power of the educational dream of the teachers in this cooperative village – their imaginings and longings for a school and a society offering something genuinely different, aesthetically and morally appealing. We had already opened a discussion about these village teachers as artful "curriculum planners" in search for peace in ways that exemplify what Satish Kumar had spoken about in his keynote at the holistic education conference that I had told my students about on the first evening of the course: "We have turned schools into knowledge factories. This is not the way. Every person is a special kind of artist. Real education is when we are walking together on a journey of self-realization: the teacher, the student, the parent. The universe is a communion of subjects not a collection of objects. We are all capable of a great energy which sows the seeds of Divine inspiration."

The educators at *Neve Shalom/Wahat Al-Salam* certainly fit Kumar's outlook and offer an excellent model of a curriculum that is truly transformative:

> These teachers are not afraid to face their relationship to the "other", to their own experience and hence to negotiate the interplay between identity, language and cultural differences. They look within their own village school and within themselves for strategies of negotiation as well as seek conceptual guidance from professional and academic sources from outside. All face the issues of desire and loss as they develop curriculum. It is a question of belonging – to retrieve that which has been expropriated emotionally. Thus they continue to push the limits in their dynamic interaction and to struggle for greater voice as they reach higher and higher and dig deeper and deeper in their community building and social transformation. (Feuerverger, 2001, p. 179)

One student spoke and connected the work in *Neve Shalom/Wahat Al-Salam* with another assigned reading for this course. She said she thought that these teachers in the Israeli village were artists in the same way that Deborah Britzman (1995) describes good teachers as those who:

> still worry about this thing called pedagogy, about what it means to teach and to learn, and about the detours known as history ... artists unafraid to imagine differences within, to address those who may or may not understand, to fashion communities yet to become, and to engage life at its most incomplete. Unlike [other] educators... they are interested in the mistakes, the accidents, the detours, and the unintelligibilities of identities... They gesture to their own constructedness and frailties, troubling the space between representation and the real (p.105).

We discussed how teachers who are artful become cognizant of what I call the "unconscious myths" that shape the emotional and intellectual landscape of their lives and which motivate them in the planning of curriculum and in their choice of interpersonal classroom strategies. Such teachers become "border crossers" in being able to listen critically to the voices of their students. The teachers at *Neve Shalom/Wahat Al-Salam* are an inspiring example of this kind of emancipatory education and its freedom from bondage, its taste of paradise. The *Neve Shalom/Wahat Al-Salam* project thus becomes a global role model of intercultural harmony, of teaching and learning to live together in peace which is applicable anywhere in the world. We adjourned for a ten-minute break energized by the discussions in that first half of the class. It seemed like a perfect segue into the next part of the class: watching Dr. Martin Luther King on videotape.

WATCHING MARTIN LUTHER KING

Wind had swept many leaves off the trees that day; but in spite of the changing weather, the sun was still strong, providing remembrance of softer summer days. The power of the wind was nothing however compared to what lay in store for us in the second half of our class: the intensity of the speeches that Martin Luther King gave so many years ago. The energy in the room was palpable as we all filed back into the classroom after the break. I turned on the VCR that had been set up by the student who had brought in this video treasure. The lights were dimmed. And we listened to Martin Luther King's words – sparks of divine understanding:

"I have a dream …when we will be judged not by the color of our skin but by the content of our character."

… when the children of slaves and the children of slave owners will sit at the table of brotherhood…

I have been to the mountain top, I have seen the promised land… "I may not get there with you"…

Let people remember that I was a drum major for justice"…

And after listening to the intensity of King's words with their love for humanity and for the sanctity of life, and after seeing the clarity in his eyes, the yearning on the faces in the crowds, we heard these final words:

"Free at last, thank God Almighty, we are free at last."

Then we watched the shocking assassination of Martin Luther King Jr. And then the funeral. As a student turned the lights back on, the sense of emotion in the room was high. Everyone looked up to me for what should come next. I then shared with them what it had been like the first time I watched Dr. King speak on television many years ago when I was barely a teenager beginning high school in Montreal. I told them about those days: the Civil Rights Movement, the Free Speech Movement, about efforts to end the Vietnam War, about all the political activism, engagement and ENERGY: we were young then and we believed that we, as the new generation, were on the verge to finally bring justice to the world, that we would truly change the course of history. Dr. King believed that the world would be healed by a creative, redemptive love. And we had believed it too. I still believe it. I told my students that many of my generation, the "baby boomers", feel nostalgia for those days, days which were filled with so much hope for a better tomorrow. (My students seemed surprised to realize I was not as young as they had thought!)

Our class then sat in silence for some moments, transfixed by the enormity of King's vision and by the tragedy of his death. After a time our conversation spontaneously flowed back to my book "Oasis of Dreams." It is remarkable how this book becomes a life raft for my students just as it had been one for me throughout the years of my research journey in that village. I told them that I wrote it in order to share the sense of hope that I was offered by these villagers – those

I [TOO] HAVE A DREAM

same words I had used with the students in Rick Ayers' class at Berkeley High six months earlier. My students became fellow dreamers of peace. One student, in a contemplative moment, said that Dr. Martin Luther King would have been proud of these villagers. We had been given two gifts – one from the villagers at *Neve Shalom/Wahat Al-Salam* and one from Dr. King – to hold on to forever. "An intimate moment of contact with the divine," as Tobin Hart called it.

I read out a quote from Franz Kafka's appearing in my book: "No man's life is long enough to enter Canaan even if he has been on the track of Canaan all his life." We focused on the never-ending journey toward the "promised land" and on how each of us in our own way possesses something unique to offer the tapestry of humanity as we strive toward peace and justice. I explained how in Judaism, the Torah discusses that each and every person – regardless of their religion or background – has their own distinctive contribution to make to help "repair the world." It is termed *Tikkun Haolam* in Hebrew, an empowering idea in its call to action. *Neve Shalom/Wahat Al-Salam* embodies that philosophy allowing every human being to feel that they can and will make a difference on this earth, each according to their own special talents and nature.

Our deliberations that evening pursued a multitude of avenues, including discussions about two other great teachers who **really** made a difference but who never made it to the 'promised land': Moses and Jesus. In spite of all that Moses had accomplished – bringing his people out of slavery and bringing them the Commandments from Mount Sinai – he was not permitted to enter the promised land along with them. And why should Jesus have had to die on the cross? One student reminded us of the resurrection and the promise of renewal. We then returned to issues of how to make education more meaningful for young people today. We were making connections between time and space and the meaning of our lives, past, present and future – science and religion and education coalescing into a new way of knowing that speaks of love and of life.

"When will the violence and hatred amongst people end?" asked a young teacher. "I already see it in some of my Grade Two students and know it comes from their parents." And from their parents' parents, and all the way back through endless generations. A discussion ensued about the inter-generational aspects of such age-old afflictions as racism, anti-Semitism, bigotry, prejudice and hatred, and of how teachers must attempt to overcome it, drawing nourishment from their own lived experiences. One student remarked that we now seem to live in times that are more cynical than what I had described for them about the 1960s. "Maybe these are our years in the wilderness, maybe we are in the desert now, but we are also being given an opportunity and a challenge – to try to offer our students a sense of hope," I replied. I quoted for them an excerpt from the last chapter of Herbert Kohl's (2003) book "Stupidity and Tears" about teaching and learning in troubled times:

> Where is the joy in teaching, and how is that conveyed? To me, these are the essential questions teachers must confront, not the questions of test scores or covering the curriculum. Teachers should be as resistant and resilient as their

students and learn the fine art of defying ignorant authority intelligently. After all, at its best, teaching is a nurturing and militant vocation and a wonderful thing to be doing in cynical times (p. 117).

My students and I recognized the desire of new and veteran teachers to (re)connect with why they had gone into teaching in the first place: to make a difference in the lives of their students. The necessity to recover that passion emerged as an all-important theme in their professional lives. And if that meant becoming *subversive,* then so be it. This *modus operandi* is what Herbert Kohl (pp. 10-11) regards as necessary for teachers who "love children and find teaching magical" and therefore do not want to be "trapped into acting in ways ... that are counter to the work they feel they must do to help their students." It is about being partners with our students in the educational process[1].

It turned quiet in the classroom that windy evening as we came to understand that trying to effect change using theory *without* practice is an illusion. As Albert Schweitzer said, "Example is not the main thing in influencing others, it's the only thing." We all felt as if we had been on this professional path all our lives waiting for a still, small voice to guide us out of the years in the wilderness. Memory, imagination and hope intersected to create images of courage and survival. One student summed it up this way: " I feel uplifted because we discussed the really 'messy stuff' and didn't just spout rhetoric. We wove theory and practice together in an honest way." Then there was silence, the kind that cleanses and heals wounds. My students drifted out of the classroom and into the darkness of the night.

SILENT MUSINGS

That evening I stayed behind for a while and sat in the classroom silently giving thanks to whatever cosmic forces were offering me sustenance, and allowing me to feel that I am doing something that may strengthen these teachers and give them a larger sense of life and purpose in the classroom – perhaps even a sense of adventure and **joy**. This is my understanding of the enterprise that we call education: a process toward recovery and renewal. Inside a good classroom students are always allowed to think – and feel – with impunity. This is what Matthew Fox means when he writes that: "the job of a teacher is not only to be an intellectual guide but a spiritual messenger."

And then, as I sat there musing, a profound realization struck me: **My search for home is over**. The classroom has always been my true home. I had found it long ago as a child of Holocaust survivors in need of safety, and later on as a classroom teacher offering hope to others who needed it. Education was my second chance at life, and in my personal as well as professional worlds I seek out others who want to teach and learn in wholeness and genuine commitment. I choose to reach out to my students because long ago when I was clinging between life and death of spirit, School reached out to me and offered me shelter. Some of my own teachers during my childhood became my witnesses embodying the true meaning of *in loco parentis*. In quiet ways they acknowledged my suffering. When I saw the saying of the great Sufi poet and philosopher Kahlil Gibran on a building plaque during a visit to Boston several years ago: "*It was in my heart to help a little because I was helped much*", I realized that those words embody what I feel about the teaching and learning process.

I believe that good teachers are always ready to share of their souls abundantly with the students in their classrooms. Surely a good education will always be about building trust and safety – and community and confidence –- just as much as it is about building knowledge. And if the gods smile upon us just so, it can even become a road to redemption and salvation: a journey toward freedom and joy. Every so often, after a class, when you are gathering up your books in silence or riding on the subway to go home, an angel appears and says to you, "That was a well-taught lesson. Did you see the looks of wonder in their eyes? Did you see that you gave them something greater than simple knowledge; you gave them your soul. And they *felt* it." And then, no matter what else happens, you know that you have the strength to go on because you have tasted the joy and the ecstasy of teaching for the love of it.

This is a time of global transition and disorientation. Cyclonic forces of economic, ecological and technological change, and of global conflict and terrorism are etched in our psyches. We in the field of education, either as practitioners or administrators or theorists, need to honour and respect the struggle of all students and their parents during such times. We need for them to know that we care. We need absolutely to offer them a meaningful and pluralistic curriculum in a trusting environment. At the centre of my educational universe, I will always see the struggles of a child, of every child, who longs to be rescued, longs to be heard, to speak the truth about his or her lived experience. Every child is waiting for a teacher who seeks to make a genuine difference in the world by giving students permission to acknowledge their inner capacity for greatness. And when such students and teachers come together, miracles happen, and the classroom becomes a nurturing, creative, and safe place that we can call home.

Do we not need to demonstrate that education offers the prospect of hope for the future? Do we not need to teach and to learn that compassion is the holiest among educational pursuits? Surely now is the time when the questions that social philosopher Hannah Arendt (1961, p. 196) posed in the mid-twentieth century, after the atrocities of World War II, are even more urgent than ever before:

> Do we love our children enough to take responsibility for them, in order that we do not expel them from our world and leave them to their own devices, and to strike from their hands their chance of undertaking something new, something unforeseen by us, but to prepare them in advance for the task of renewing a common world? Do we love the world enough to take responsibility for it?

At the end, it will always be about love.

NOTES

[1] I recently came across an article by Riane Eisler (2005) who explains this notion as counter to the old "dominator socialization" with its unconscious valuing of undemocratic, abusive and even violent relations in society. "Through partnership process, teachers can help students experience partnership relations as a viable alternative. Partnership structure provides the learning environment that young people need to develop their unique capacities. But partnership process and structure are not enough without partnership content: narratives that help young people better understand human possibilities." (Eisler, p. 55 in Miller et al.) This indeed is living curriculum and I have recently included Eisler's article in the assigned readings for the course "Curriculum Foundations."

REFERENCES

Anzaldúa, G. (1987). *Borderlands/La Frontera: The new Mestiza.*. San Francisco: Aunt Lute books.
Ashton-Warner, S. (1967). *Teacher.* New York: Simon and Shuster.
Ayers, W. (1993). *To teach: The journey of a teacher.* New York: Teachers College Press.
Bakhtin, M. (1981). *The dialogic imagination.* Austin: University of Texas Press.
Bakhtin, M. (1986). *Speech genres and other late essays.* (V. McGee, Trans.). Austin: University of Texas Press.
Banks, J. (1989). Teacher education and ethnic minorities: Conceptualizing the problem. *Paper presented at the annual conference of the American Educational Research Association*, San Francisco.
Bar-On, D. (1993). First encounter between children of survivors and children of the perpetrators of the Holocaust. *Journal of Humanistic Psychology, 33*(4), 6-14.
Barone, T. (2000). *Aesthetics, politics and educational inquiry.* New York, Berlin: Peter Lang Press.
Bateson, M.C. (1989). *Composing a life.* New York: The Atlantic Monthly Press.
Behar, R. (1996). *The vulnerable observer.* Boston, Beacon Press.
Belenky, M. F., Clinchy, B. M., Goldberger, N. R., & Tarule, J. M. (1986). *Women's ways of knowing: The development of self, voice, and mind.* New York, Basic Books.
Berryman, J. (1988). Ontario's heritage languages program: Advantages and disadvantages of three models of organization, *Multiculturalism/ Multiculturalisme, 11*(3), 18-21.
Bettelheim, B. (1977). *The uses of enchantment: The meaning and importance of fairy tales.* New York, Vintage Books.
Bourdieu, P. (1996). *Democracy, society and education.* Lecture Given at the University of California at Berkeley, Wheeler Auditorium, April 6.
Britzman, D. (1998). On doing something more. In W. Ayers & J. Miller (Eds.), Maxine Greene: A light in the dark times (pp. 97-107). Columbia University, Teachers College Press.
Buber, M. (1958). *I and thou.* New York: C. Scribner's Sons.
Buber, M. (1965). *The knowledge of man.* New York, Harper & Row.
Carter, K. (1993). The place of story in the study of teaching and teacher education. *Educational Researcher, 22*(1), 5-12.
Clandinin, D. J. (1988). *Metaphor and folk model as dimensions of teachers' personal practical knowledge.* Unpublished paper: University of Calgary.
Clandinin, D. J. & Connelly, F. M. (1994). Personal experience methods. In N.K. Denzen and Y.S. Lincoln (Eds.), Handbook of qualitative research (pp. 413-427). Thousand Oaks, CA, Sage.
Cole, A. & Knowles, G. (2000). Researching teaching: Exploring teacher development through reflexive inquiry. Boston, Allyn and Bacon.
Coles, R. (1997). *Doing documentary work.* Oxford, Oxford University Press.
Connelly, F. M., & Clandinin, D. J. (1988). *Teachers as Curriculum Planners: Narratives of Experience.* New York, Teachers College, Columbia University.
Connelly, F. M. & Clandinin, D. J. (1990). Stories of experience and narrative inquiry. *Educational Researcher, 19*(5), 2-14.
Connelly, M. F., & Clandinin, D. J. (1995). *Teachers professional knowledge landscapes.* Teachers College Press, Columbia University.
Corson, D. (1993). *Language, minority education and gender: Linking social justice and power.* Toronto, OISE Press.
Corson, D. (1999). Language policy in schools: A resource for teachers and administrators. Mahwah, New Jersey, Lawrence Erlbaum.
Crites, S. (1971). The narrative quality of experience. *Journal of the American Academy of Religion, 39*(3), 292-311.

REFERENCES

Cummins, J. (1989). *Empowering minority students.* Sacramento, California Association for Bilingual Education.

Cummins, J. (1994). From coercive to collaborative relations of power in the teaching of literacy. In B. M. Ferdman, R. M. Weber & A.G. Ramirez (Eds.), *Literacy Across Languages and Cultures* (pp. 295-331). Albany, SUNY Press.

Cummins, J. & Danesi, M. (1990). *Heritage languages: The development and denial of Canada's linguistic resources.* Toronto, Our Schools/Ourselves Educational Foundation.

Dalley, P. (1989). *Mes Langues, Mes couleurs: Bilingualism in conflict.* Unpublished Masters Thesis, Ontario Institute for Studies in Education/ University of Toronto.

Delgado-Gaitan, C. (1997). Dismantling Borders. In A. Neumann & P. Peterson (Eds.), *Learning from our lives: women, research and autobiography in Education* (pp. 37-51). New York, Teachers College Press.

Delpit, L. (1992). The politics of teaching literate discourse. *Theory Into Practice, 31,* 285-295.

Denzin, N. (1988). *The research act.* (Revised edition) New York: McGraw-Hill.

Dewey, J. (1938). *Experience and Education.* New York, Collier Books.

Duras, M. (1985) *La douleur.* Translated into *The war.* New York: Pantheon Books.

Eisner, E. (1991). *The enlightened eye: Qualitative inquiry and the enhancement of educational practice.* New York, Maxwell MacMillan.

Eisner, E. W. & Peshkin, A. (Eds.). (1990). *Qualitative inquiry in education: The continuing debate.* New York, Teachers College Press.

Feuerverger, G. (1987). *Jewish-Canadian ethnic identity and non-native language learning.* Unpublished doctoral dissertation, University of Toronto, Canada.

Feuerverger, G. (1989). Ethnolinguistic vitality of Italo-Candian students in integrated and on-integrated heritage language programs in Toronto. *The Canadian Modern Language Review, 46,* 50-72.

Feuerverger, G. (1991). University students' perceptions of heritage language learning and ethnic identity maintenance in multicultural Toronto. *Canadian Modern Language Review, 47*(4), Special Issue on Heritage Languages in Canada, 660-677.

Feuerverger, G. (1994). A multicultural literacy intervention for minority language students. *Language and Education, 8*(3), 123-146.

Feuerverger, G. (1995). Oasis of peace: A community of moral education in Israel. *Journal of Moral Education, 24*(2), 113-141.

Feuerverger, G. (1996). Peacemaking through emancipatory discourse: Language awareness in a Jewish-Arab School in Israel. *Curriculum and Teaching 11*(2), 53-61.

Feuerverger, G. (2001). *Oasis of dreams: Teaching and learning peace in a Jewish-Palestinian village in Israel.* New York, RoutledgeFalmer.

Feuerverger, G. (2001). "My Yiddish voice." In Morris, M. & Weaver, J. (eds.) *Difficult memories: Talk in a (post) holocaust era.* New York, Berlin: Peter Lang Press, 12-23.

Feuerverger, G. (2001). Reflections on September 11, *Among Teachers: Experience and Inquiry, 31,* 3-9.

Fine, M. (1993). You can't just say that the only ones who can speak are those who agree with your position: Political discourse in the classroom. *Harvard Educational Review, 63,* 412-433.

Freire, P. (1970). *Pedagogy of the oppressed.* New York, Seabury Press.

Foucault, M. (1984). "What is Enlightenment?" In Rabinow, P. *The Foucault Reader.* New York: Random House, 32-50.

Fox. M. (1995). *The reinvention of work.* San Francisco, HarperCollins.

Gajdusek, R. (1997). *Resurrection: A war journey.* Indiana, University of Notre Dame Press

Geertz, C. (1988). *Works and lives: The anthropologist as author.* Stanford CA, Stanford University Press.

Geertz, C. (1995). *After the fact: Two countries, four decades, one anthropologist.* Cambridge, MA, Harvard University Press.

Gilligan, C. (1982*). In a different voice.* Cambridge: Harvard University Press.

Glesne, C. & Peshkin, A. (1992). *Becoming qualitative researchers: An introduction.* New York, Longman.
Giroux, H. A. (1991). Democracy and the discourse of cultural difference: Towards a politics of border pedagogy. *British Journal of Sociology of Education, 12*(4), 501-519.
Giroux, H. A. (1994). Insurgent multiculturalism and the promise of pedagogy. In D.T. Goldberg (Ed.), *Multiculturalism: A critical reader.* Cambridge, MA, Blackwell.
Greene, M. (1988). *The dialectic of freedom.* New York, Teachers College Press.
Goodson, I. (Ed.). (1991). *Teachers' lives and educational research. Biography, identity and schooling: Episodes in educational research.* London, Falmer.
Grossman, I. (1990). *An ordinary woman in extraordinary times.* Toronto: Multicultural History Society.
Heilbrun, C. (1999). Women's lives: The view from the threshold. Toronto, University of Toronto Press.
Heschel, A.J. (1955). God in search of man. New York: Farrar, Straus & Giroux.
Hopkins, D. (1987). Enhancing validity in action research. Research Paper #16, London, British Library.
hooks, b. (1994). *Teaching to transgress: Education as the practice to freedom.* New York, Routledge.
Hornberger, N. (1990). *Creating successful contexts for bilingual literacy. Teachers College Record, 92*(2), 212-229.
Huberman, A. M. & Miles, M. B. (1984). *Innovation up close.* New York: Plenum.
Hunt, D. (1991). *Beginning with ourselves.* Toronto, Ontario Institute for Studies in Education/University of Toronto Press.
Jackson, S. (1995). Autobiography: Pivot points for engaging lives in multicultural contexts. In J.M. Larkin & C. E. Sleeter (Eds.), *Developing Multicultural Teacher Education Curricula* (pp. 31-44). New York, SUNY Press.
Janesick, V. J. (1979). *Ethnographic inquiry: Understanding culture and experience.* In E. Short (Ed.). *Forms of curriculum inquiry* (pp. 101-119). Albany, SUNY Press.
Kridel, C. (ed.) (1998). *Writing educational biography: Explorations in qualitative research.* New York, Garland.
Kohl, H. (2003). *Stupidity and tears.* New York, The New Press.
Kristeva, J. (1991). *Strangers to ourselves.* (Trans. Leon S. Roudiez). New York, Columbia University Press.
Lopez. B. (1990). Crow and weasel. Portland, North Point Press.
MacLennan, H. (1945/1993). *Two solitudes.* Toronto, Stoddart Publishing.
Michaels, A. (1996). *Fugitive pieces.* Toronto, McLelland and Stewart.
Miller, J. (2000) *The holistic practitioner.* Toronto, OISE Press.
Murphy, M. (2004). Multiculturalism Lecture. *Social Foundations of Education*, (1-9), University of Western Ontario.
Nieto, S. (1992). *Affirming diversity: The sociopolitical context of multicultural education.* White Plains, NY, Longman.
Nhat Hanh, T. (1975). *The miracle of mindfulness.* Boston, Beacon Press.
Nhat Hanh, T. (1991). *Peace is every step.* New York, Bantam Books.
Niebuhr, R. (1960). *Moral man and immoral society.* New York, Charles Scribner.
Noddings, N. (1984). *Caring: A feminine approach to ethics and moral education.* Berkeley, CA, University of California Press.
Noddings, N. (1991). Stories in dialogue: Caring and interpersonal reasoning. In C. Witherell & N. Noddings (Eds.), *Stories Lives Tell: Narrative and Dialogue in Education.* New York, Teachers College Press.
Noddings, N. (2003). *Happiness and Education.* Cambridge University Press.
Nussbaum, M. (1997). *Cultivating humanity: A classical defence of reform in liberal education,* Cambridge, Harvard University Press.
Ogbu, J. (1978). *Minority education and caste.* New York, Academic Press.

REFERENCES

Olesen, V. (1992). Extraordinary events and mundane ailments: The contextual dialectics of the embodied self. In C. Ellis & F. Flaherty (Eds.), *Investigating subjectivity: Research on lived experience.* Newbury Park, CA, Sage.

Palmer, P. (1998). *The courage to teach.* San Francisco, Jossey Bass.

Patterson, D. (1998) *Sun Turned to Darkness: Memory and Recovery in the Holocaust Memoir.* Syracuse University Press.

Pinar, W. F. (1988). Autobiography and the architecture of self. *Journal of Curriculum Theorizing,* 8(1), 7-35.

Pinar, W. F. (1998). *Curriculum: Toward new identities.* New York, Garland.

Polkinghorne, D. E. (1988). *Narrative knowing and the human sciences.* Albany, NY, State University of New York Press.

Ramen, R.N. (2001). The heart of teaching. In Lantieri, L. (Ed.) *Schools with spirit: Nurturing the inner lives of children and teachers.* Boston, Beacon Press.

Said, E. (1990). Reflections on exile. In R. Ferguson, M. Gever, T. Minh-Ha, & C. West, (Eds.) *Out there: Marginalization and contemporary cultures.* Boston, MIT Press.

Sartre, J-P. (1949). *Literature and existentialism* (Trans. By B. Frechtman) Secaucus, NJ, Citadel Press.

Schön, D. (1987). *Educating the reflective practitioner.* San Francisco, Jossey-Bass.

Schön, D. (Ed.) (1991). *The reflective turn: Case studies in and on educational practice.* New York, Teachers College Press.

Sellers, S. (1996). *Helene Cixous : Authorship, autobiography and love.* Cambridge, MA, Blackwell.

Shabatay, V. (1991). The stranger's story: Who calls and who answers? In C. Witherell & N. Noddings (Eds.), *Stories lives tell: Narrative and dialogue in education.* New York, Teachers College Press.

Tabachnick, B. R. & Zeichner, K.M. (1993). Preparing teachers for cultural diversity. In P. Gilroy & M. Smith (Eds.), *International analyses of teacher education* JET Papers One, (pp. 113-124). London: Carfax.

Trueba, H. T. (1989). *Raising silent voices: Educating the linguistic minorities for the twenty-first century.* Cambridge, MA, Newbury House.

Van Manen, M. (1990). *Researching lived experience: Human science for an action sensitive pedagogy.* London, Canada, University of Western Ontario Press.

Vygotsky, L.S. (1962). *Thought and Language.* (Trans. by A.Kozulin). Cambridge, MA, The MIT Press.

Walsh, C.E. (1987). Language, meaning and voice: Puerto Rican students' struggle for a speaking consciousness. *Language Arts, 64,*196-206.

Witherell, C. & Noddings, N. (Eds.). (1991). *Stories lives tell: Narrative and dialogue in education.* New York, Teachers College Press.

Wong-Fillmore, L. (1989). Language and cultural issues in the early education of language minority children. In S. L. Kagan (Ed.), *The care and education of America's young children Obstacles and opportunities.* Chicago, University of Chicago Press.

Yin, R. K. (1984). *Case study research.* London: Sage.

TRANSGRESSIONS: CULTURAL STUDIES AND EDUCATION

Series Editors
Shirley Steinberg, *McGill University, Canada*
Joe Kincheloe, *McGill University, Canada*

Editorial Board
Heinz-Hermann Kruger, *Halle University, Germany*
Norman Denzin, *University of Illinois, Champaign-Urbana, USA*
Roger Slee, *McGill University, Canada*
Rhonda Hammer, *University of California Los Angeles, USA*
Christine Quail, *SUNY, Oneonta*

Scope
Cultural studies provides an analytical toolbox for both making sense of educational practice and extending the insights of educational professionals into their labors. In this context *Transgressions: Cultural Studies and Education* provides a collection of books in the domain that specify this assertion. Crafted for an audience of teachers, teacher educators, scholars and students of cultural studies and others interested in cultural studies and pedagogy, the series documents both the possibilities of and the controversies surrounding the intersection of cultural studies and education. The editors and the authors of this series do not assume that the interaction of cultural studies and education devalues other types of knowledge and analytical forms. Rather the intersection of these knowledge disciplines offers a rejuvenating, optimistic, and positive perspective on education and educational institutions. Some might describe its contribution as democratic, emancipatory, and transformative. The editors and authors maintain that cultural studies helps free educators from sterile, monolithic analyses that have for too long undermined efforts to think of educational practices by providing other words, new languages, and fresh metaphors. Operating in an interdisciplinary cosmos, Transgressions: Cultural Studies and Education is dedicated to exploring the ways cultural studies enhances the study and practice of education. With this in mind the series focuses in a non-exclusive way on popular culture as well as other dimensions of cultural studies including social theory, social justice and positionality, cultural dimensions of technological innovation, new media and media literacy, new forms of oppression emerging in an electronic hyperreality, and postcolonial global concerns. With these concerns in mind cultural studies scholars often argue that the realm of popular culture is the most powerful educational force in contemporary culture. Indeed, in the twenty-first century this pedagogical dynamic is sweeping through the entire world. Educators, they believe, must understand these emerging realities in order to gain an important voice in the pedagogical conversation.

Without an understanding of cultural pedagogy's (education that takes place outside of formal schooling) role in the shaping of individual identity--youth identity in particular--the role educators play in the lives of their students will continue to fade. Why do so many of our students feel that life is incomprehensible and devoid of meaning? What does it mean, teachers wonder, when young people are unable to describe their moods, their affective affiliation to the society around them. Meanings provided young people by mainstream institutions often do little to help them deal with their affective complexity, their difficulty negotiating the rift between meaning and affect. School knowledge and educational expectations seem as anachronistic as a ditto machine, not that learning ways of rational thought and making sense of the world are unimportant.

But school knowledge and educational expectations often have little to offer students about making sense of the way they feel, the way their affective lives are shaped. In no way do we argue that analysis of the production of youth in an electronic mediated world demands some "touchy-feely" educational superficiality. What is needed in this context is a rigorous analysis of the interrelationship between pedagogy, popular culture, meaning making, and youth subjectivity. In an era marked by youth depression, violence, and suicide such insights become extremely important, even life saving. Pessimism about the future is the common sense of many contemporary youth with its concomitant feeling that no one can make a difference.

If affective production can be shaped to reflect these perspectives, then it can be reshaped to lay the groundwork for optimism, passionate commitment, and transformative educational and political activity. In these ways cultural studies adds a dimension to the work of education unfilled by any other sub-discipline. This is what Transgressions: Cultural Studies and Education seeks to produce—literature on these issues that makes a difference. It seeks to publish studies that help those who work with young people, those individuals involved in the disciplines that study children and youth, and young people themselves improve their lives in these bizarre times.

OTHER TITLES OF INTEREST

An Unordinary Death…The Life of a Suicide Bomber

Khalilah Christina Sabra

An Unordinary Death dramatizes social and individual despair in a most detailed way, utilizing fiction to describe facts with grim and vivid authenticity. The book is precise. It is not Al-Aqsa Suicide Brigade that transformed an innocent girl into a human deprecating weapon of destruction. It is not Al-Aqsa, which permitted a Palestinian girl to murder, first, a sense of ethical human recognition in her own heart, and next, her conscience which might have prevented her from directing her devastation outward to those she held in contempt. Basic training did not begin in a terrorist boot camp. It began in childhood and it continued with a vengeance for the duration of Jenna Hayat's life.

> Paperback ISBN:90-77874-36-4 Hardback ISBN:90-77874-37-2
> April 2006, 230 pp
> *SERIES: TRANSGRESSIONS 1*

Self Study and Diversity
Deborah Tidwell and Linda Fitzgerald, *University of Northern Iowa, USA* **(Eds.)**

This is a book about self-study of teaching and teacher education with equity and access as focal issues of practice. Chapters in this book have a shared orientation to diversity grounded in the acknowledgement that educators have a responsibility to address equity and access issues inherent in teaching. To that end, individual chapters address such areas of diversity as race, ethnicity, gender, disability, and power, as well as broader areas of social justice, multiculturalism, and ways of knowing. The dilemmas and responses of a teacher educator, elicited through self-study, can apply well beyond that immediate context. This broadens the appeal of the book beyond the self-study community and beyond specific issues of diversity, to people interested in teaching in general and in the process of improving practice. An additional strength of this book is the inclusion in each chapter of information regarding the use of particular strategies, both for self-study and for teaching for diversity.

> Paperback ISBN: 90-77874-34-8 Hardback ISBN:90-77874-09-7
> April 2006, 314 pp
> *SERIES: PROFESSIONAL LEARNING 2*

Dimensions of Professional Learning
Profesionalism, Practice and Identity
Amanda Berry, Allie Clemans, Alex Kostogriz, Monash University, Clayton, Australia **(eds.)**

The contributors to this volume explore challenges and dilemmas around professional learning that confront educators in Australia. The book is organised around three dimensions of professional learning: professionalism, identity formation and communal sites of professional learning. It addresses important questions. In what ways do policies and practices mediate the construction of 'a professional' among current and future educators? How do communal spaces shape the professional learning of educators? What are the tensions that emerge in the construction of professional identity through professional learning? As a whole, all chapters provide insight into the dynamic nature of 'professional becoming.'

>Paperback ISBN: 90-8790-001-5 Hardback ISBN: 90-8790-002-3
>January 2007, 200 pp
>*SERIES: PROFESSIONAL LEARNING 3*

MY BONDAGE AND MY FREEDOM

Frederick Douglass

TO
HONORABLE GERRIT SMITH,
AS A SLIGHT TOKEN OF
ESTEEM FOR HIS CHARACTER,
ADMIRATION FOR HIS GENIUS AND BENEVOLENCE,
AFFECTION FOR HIS PERSON, AND
GRATITUDE FOR HIS FRIENDSHIP,
AND AS
A Small but most Sincere Acknowledgement of
HIS PRE-EMINENT SERVICES IN BEHALF OF THE RIGHTS AND LIBERTIES
OF AN
AFFLICTED, DESPISED AND DEEPLY OUTRAGED PEOPLE,
BY RANKING SLAVERY WITH PIRACY AND MURDER,
AND BY
DENYING IT EITHER A LEGAL OR CONSTITUTIONAL EXISTENCE,
This Volume is Respectfully Dedicated,
BY HIS FAITHFUL AND FIRMLY ATTACHED FRIEND,

FREDERICK DOUGLAS.
ROCHESTER, N.Y.

CONTENTS

MY BONDAGE AND MY FREEDOM

EDITOR'S PREFACE i
INTRODUCTION iii

MY BONDAGE
I. CHILDHOOD 1
II. REMOVED FROM MY FIRST HOME 5
III. PARENTAGE 8
IV. A GENERAL SURVEY OF THE SLAVE PLANTATION 12
V. GRADUAL INITIATION TO THE MYSTERIES OF SLAVERY 18
VI. TREATMENT OF SLAVES ON LLOYD'S PLANTATION 22
VII. LIFE IN THE GREAT HOUSE 28
VIII. A CHAPTER OF HORRORS 32
IX. PERSONAL TREATMENT 36
X. LIFE IN BALTIMORE 40
XI. "A CHANGE CAME O'ER THE SPIRIT OF MY DREAM" 44
XII. RELIGIOUS NATURE AWAKENED 48
XIII. THE VICISSITUDES OF SLAVE LIFE 52
XIV. EXPERIENCE IN ST. MICHAEL'S 57
XV. COVEY, THE NEGRO BREAKER 64
XVI. ANOTHER PRESSURE OF THE TYRANT'S VICE 70
XVII. THE LAST FLOGGING 74
XVIII. NEW RELATIONS AND DUTIES 80
XIX. THE RUN-AWAY PLOT 87
XX. APPRENTICESHIP LIFE 99
XXI. MY ESCAPE FROM SLAVERY 105

LIFE AS A FREEMAN
XXII. LIBERTY ATTAINED 111
XXIII. INTRODUCED TO THE ABOLITIONISTS 118
XXIV. TWENTY-ONE MONTHS IN GREAT BRITAIN 121
XXV. VARIOUS INCIDENTS 130

APPENDIX 135
RECEPTION SPEECH. 135
LETTER TO HIS OLD MASTER. 143
THE NATURE OF SLAVERY. 147
INHUMANITY OF SLAVERY. 150
WHAT TO THE SLAVE IS THE FOURTH OF JULY? 154
THE INTERNAL SLAVE TRADE. 157
THE SLAVERY PARTY. 160
THE ANTI-SLAVERY MOVEMENT. 163

My Bondage and My Freedom

PREFACE

EDITOR'S PREFACE

If the volume now presented to the public were a mere work of ART, the history of its misfortune might be written in two very simple words—TOO LATE. The nature and character of slavery have been subjects of an almost endless variety of artistic representation; and after the brilliant achievements in that field, and while those achievements are yet fresh in the memory of the million, he who would add another to the legion, must possess the charm of transcendent excellence, or apologize for something worse than rashness. The reader is, therefore, assured, with all due promptitude, that his attention is not invited to a work of ART, but to a work of FACTS—Facts, terrible and almost incredible, it may be yet FACTS, nevertheless.

I am authorized to say that there is not a fictitious name nor place in the whole volume; but that names and places are literally given, and that every transaction therein described actually transpired.

Perhaps the best Preface to this volume is furnished in the following letter of Mr. Douglass, written in answer to my urgent solicitation for such a work:

ROCHESTER, N. Y. July 2, 1855.

DEAR FRIEND: I have long entertained, as you very well know, a somewhat positive repugnance to writing or speaking anything for the public, which could, with any degree of plausibilty, make me liable to the imputation of seeking personal notoriety, for its own sake. Entertaining that feeling very sincerely, and permitting its control, perhaps, quite unreasonably, I have often refused to narrate my personal experience in public anti-slavery meetings, and in sympathizing circles, when urged to do so by friends, with whose views and wishes, ordinarily, it were a pleasure to comply. In my letters and speeches, I have generally aimed to discuss the question of Slavery in the light of fundamental principles, and upon facts, notorious and open to all; making, I trust, no more of the fact of my own former enslavement, than circumstances seemed absolutely to require. I have never placed my opposition to slavery on a basis so narrow as my own enslavement, but rather upon the indestructible and unchangeable laws of human nature, every one of which is perpetually and flagrantly violated by the slave system. I have also felt that it was best for those having histories worth the writing—or supposed to be so—to commit such work to hands other than their own. To write of one's self, in such a manner as not to incur the imputation of weakness, vanity, and egotism, is a work within the ability of but few; and I have little reason to believe that I belong to that fortunate few.

These considerations caused me to hesitate, when first you kindly urged me to prepare for publication a full account of my life as a slave, and my life as a freeman.

Nevertheless, I see, with you, many reasons for regarding my autobiography as exceptional in its character, and as being, in some sense, naturally beyond the reach of those reproaches which honorable and sensitive minds dislike to incur. It is not to illustrate any heroic achievements of a man, but to vindicate a just and beneficent principle, in its application to the whole human family, by letting in the light of truth upon a system, esteemed by some as a blessing, and by others as a curse and a crime. I agree with you, that this system is now at the bar of public opinion—not only of this country, but of the whole civilized world—for judgment. Its friends have made for it the usual plea—"not guilty;" the case must, therefore, proceed. Any facts, either from slaves, slaveholders, or by-standers, calculated to enlighten the public mind, by revealing the true nature, character, and tendency of the slave system, are in order, and can scarcely be innocently withheld.

I see, too, that there are special reasons why I should write my own biography, in preference to employing another to do it. Not only is slavery on trial, but unfortunately, the enslaved people are also on trial. It is alleged, that they are, naturally, inferior; that they are *so low* in the scale of humanity, and so utterly stupid, that they are unconscious of their wrongs, and do not apprehend their rights. Looking, then, at your request, from this stand-point, and wishing everything of which you think

PREFACE

me capable to go to the benefit of my afflicted people, I part with my doubts and hesitation, and proceed to furnish you the desired manuscript; hoping that you may be able to make such arrangements for its publication as shall be best adapted to accomplish that good which you so enthusiastically anticipate.

FREDERICK DOUGLASS

There was little necessity for doubt and hesitation on the part of Mr. Douglass, as to the propriety of his giving to the world a full account of himself. A man who was born and brought up in slavery, a living witness of its horrors; who often himself experienced its cruelties; and who, despite the depressing influences surrounding his birth, youth and manhood, has risen, from a dark and almost absolute obscurity, to the distinguished position which he now occupies, might very well assume the existence of a commendable curiosity, on the part of the public, to know the facts of his remarkable history.

EDITOR

INTRODUCTION

When a man raises himself from the lowest condition in society to the highest, mankind pay him the tribute of their admiration; when he accomplishes this elevation by native energy, guided by prudence and wisdom, their admiration is increased; but when his course, onward and upward, excellent in itself, furthermore proves a possible, what had hitherto been regarded as an impossible, reform, then he becomes a burning and a shining light, on which the aged may look with gladness, the young with hope, and the down-trodden, as a representative of what they may themselves become. To such a man, dear reader, it is my privilege to introduce you.

The life of Frederick Douglass, recorded in the pages which follow, is not merely an example of self-elevation under the most adverse circumstances; it is, moreover, a noble vindication of the highest aims of the American anti-slavery movement. The real object of that movement is not only to disenthrall, it is, also, to bestow upon the Negro the exercise of all those rights, from the possession of which he has been so long debarred.

But this full recognition of the colored man to the right, and the entire admission of the same to the full privileges, political, religious and social, of manhood, requires powerful effort on the part of the enthralled, as well as on the part of those who would disenthrall them. The people at large must feel the conviction, as well as admit the abstract logic, of human equality; the Negro, for the first time in the world's history, brought in full contact with high civilization, must prove his title first to all that is demanded for him; in the teeth of unequal chances, he must prove himself equal to the mass of those who oppress him—therefore, absolutely superior to his apparent fate, and to their relative ability. And it is most cheering to the friends of freedom, today, that evidence of this equality is rapidly accumulating, not from the ranks of the half-freed colored people of the free states, but from the very depths of slavery itself; the indestructible equality of man to man is demonstrated by the ease with which black men, scarce one remove from barbarism—if slavery can be honored with such a distinction—vault into the high places of the most advanced and painfully acquired civilization. Ward and Garnett, Wells Brown and Pennington, Loguen and Douglass, are banners on the outer wall, under which abolition is fighting its most successful battles, because they are living exemplars of the practicability of the most radical abolitionism; for, they were all of them born to the doom of slavery, some of them remained slaves until adult age, yet they all have not only won equality to their white fellow citizens, in civil, religious, political and social rank, but they have also illustrated and adorned our common country by their genius, learning and eloquence.

The characteristics whereby Mr. Douglass has won first rank among these remarkable men, and is still rising toward highest rank among living Americans, are abundantly laid bare in the book before us. Like the autobiography of Hugh Miller, it carries us so far back into early childhood, as to throw light upon the question, "when positive and persistent memory begins in the human being." And, like Hugh Miller, he must have been a shy old-fashioned child, occasionally oppressed by what he could not well account for, peering and poking about among the layers of right and wrong, of tyrant and thrall, and the wonderfulness of that hopeless tide of things which brought power to one race, and unrequited toil to another, until, finally, he stumbled upon his "first-found Ammonite," hidden away down in the depths of his own nature, and which revealed to him the fact that liberty and right, for all men, were anterior to slavery and wrong. When his knowledge of the world was bounded by the visible horizon on Col. Lloyd's plantation, and while every thing around him bore a fixed, iron stamp, as if it had always been so, this was, for one so young, a notable discovery.

To his uncommon memory, then, we must add a keen and accurate insight into men and things; an original breadth of common sense which enabled him to see, and weigh, and compare whatever passed before him, and which kindled a desire to search out and define their relations to other things not so patent, but which never succumbed to the marvelous nor the supernatural; a sacred thirst for liberty and for learning, first as a means of attaining liberty, then as an end in itself most desirable; a will; an unfaltering energy and determination to obtain what his soul pronounced desirable; a majestic

INTRODUCTION

self-hood; determined courage; a deep and agonizing sympathy with his embruted, crushed and bleeding fellow slaves, and an extraordinary depth of passion, together with that rare alliance between passion and intellect, which enables the former, when deeply roused, to excite, develop and sustain the latter.

With these original gifts in view, let us look at his schooling; the fearful discipline through which it pleased God to prepare him for the high calling on which he has since entered—the advocacy of emancipation by the people who are not slaves. And for this special mission, his plantation education was better than any he could have acquired in any lettered school. What he needed, was facts and experiences, welded to acutely wrought up sympathies, and these he could not elsewhere have obtained, in a manner so peculiarly adapted to his nature. His physical being was well trained, also, running wild until advanced into boyhood; hard work and light diet, thereafter, and a skill in handicraft in youth.

For his special mission, then, this was, considered in connection with his natural gifts, a good schooling; and, for his special mission, he doubtless "left school" just at the proper moment. Had he remained longer in slavery—had he fretted under bonds until the ripening of manhood and its passions, until the drear agony of slave-wife and slave-children had been piled upon his already bitter experiences—then, not only would his own history have had another termination, but the drama of American slavery would have been essentially varied; for I cannot resist the belief, that the boy who learned to read and write as he did, who taught his fellow slaves these precious acquirements as he did, who plotted for their mutual escape as he did, would, when a man at bay, strike a blow which would make slavery reel and stagger. Furthermore, blows and insults he bore, at the moment, without resentment; deep but suppressed emotion rendered him insensible to their sting; but it was afterward, when the memory of them went seething through his brain, breeding a fiery indignation at his injured self-hood, that the resolve came to resist, and the time fixed when to resist, and the plot laid, how to resist; and he always kept his self-pledged word. In what he undertook, in this line, he looked fate in the face, and had a cool, keen look at the relation of means to ends. Henry Bibb, to avoid chastisement, strewed his master's bed with charmed leaves and *was whipped*. Frederick Douglass quietly pocketed a like *fetiche*, compared his muscles with those of Covey—and *whipped him*.

In the history of his life in bondage, we find, well developed, that inherent and continuous energy of character which will ever render him distinguished. What his hand found to do, he did with his might; even while conscious that he was wronged out of his daily earnings, he worked, and worked hard. At his daily labor he went with a will; with keen, well set eye, brawny chest, lithe figure, and fair sweep of arm, he would have been king among calkers, had that been his mission.

It must not be overlooked, in this glance at his education, that Mr. Douglass lacked one aid to which so many men of mark have been deeply indebted—he had neither a mother's care, nor a mother's culture, save that which slavery grudgingly meted out to him. Bitter nurse! may not even her features relax with human feeling, when she gazes at such offspring! How susceptible he was to the kindly influences of mother-culture, may be gathered from his own words, on page 57: "It has been a life-long standing grief to me, that I know so little of my mother, and that I was so early separated from her. The counsels of her love must have been beneficial to me. The side view of her face is imaged on my memory, and I take few steps in life, without feeling her presence; but the image is mute, and I have no striking words of hers treasured up."

From the depths of chattel slavery in Maryland, our author escaped into the caste-slavery of the north, in New Bedford, Massachusetts. Here he found oppression assuming another, and hardly less bitter, form; of that very handicraft which the greed of slavery had taught him, his half-freedom denied him the exercise for an honest living; he found himself one of a class—free colored men—whose position he has described in the following words:

"Aliens are we in our native land. The fundamental principles of the republic, to which the humblest white man, whether born here or elsewhere, may appeal with confidence, in the hope of awakening a favorable response, are held to be inapplicable to us. The glorious doctrines of your revolutionary fathers, and the more glorious teachings of the Son of God, are construed and applied against us. We are literally scourged beyond the beneficent range of both authorities, human and

INTRODUCTION

divine. * * * * American humanity hates us, scorns us, disowns and denies, in a thousand ways, our very personality. The outspread wing of American christianity, apparently broad enough to give shelter to a perishing world, refuses to cover us. To us, its bones are brass, and its features iron. In running thither for shelter and succor, we have only fled from the hungry blood-hound to the devouring wolf—from a corrupt and selfish world, to a hollow and hypocritical church."—*Speech before American and Foreign Anti-Slavery Society, May*, 1854.

Four years or more, from 1837 to 1841, he struggled on, in New Bedford, sawing wood, rolling casks, or doing what labor he might, to support himself and young family; four years he brooded over the scars which slavery and semi-slavery had inflicted upon his body and soul; and then, with his wounds yet unhealed, he fell among the Garrisonians—a glorious waif to those most ardent reformers. It happened one day, at Nantucket, that he, diffidently and reluctantly, was led to address an anti-slavery meeting. He was about the age when the younger Pitt entered the House of Commons; like Pitt, too, he stood up a born orator.

William Lloyd Garrison, who was happily present, writes thus of Mr. Douglass' maiden effort; "I shall never forget his first speech at the convention—the extraordinary emotion it excited in my own mind—the powerful impression it created upon a crowded auditory, completely taken by surprise. * * * I think I never hated slavery so intensely as at that moment; certainly, my perception of the enormous outrage which is inflicted by it on the godlike nature of its victims, was rendered far more clear than ever. There stood one in physical proportions and stature commanding and exact—in intellect richly endowed—in natural eloquence a prodigy." [1]

It is of interest to compare Mr. Douglass's account of this meeting with Mr. Garrison's. Of the two, I think the latter the most correct. It must have been a grand burst of eloquence! The pent up agony, indignation and pathos of an abused and harrowed boyhood and youth, bursting out in all their freshness and overwhelming earnestness!

This unique introduction to its great leader, led immediately to the employment of Mr. Douglass as an agent by the American Anti-Slavery Society. So far as his self-relying and independent character would permit, he became, after the strictest sect, a Garrisonian. It is not too much to say, that he formed a complement which they needed, and they were a complement equally necessary to his "make-up." With his deep and keen sensitiveness to wrong, and his wonderful memory, he came from the land of bondage full of its woes and its evils, and painting them in characters of living light; and, on his part, he found, told out in sound Saxon phrase, all those principles of justice and right and liberty, which had dimly brooded over the dreams of his youth, seeking definite forms and verbal expression. It must have been an electric flashing of thought, and a knitting of soul, granted to but few in this life, and will be a life-long memory to those who participated in it. In the society, moreover, of Wendell Phillips, Edmund Quincy, William Lloyd Garrison, and other men of earnest faith and refined culture, Mr. Douglass enjoyed the high advantage of their assistance and counsel in the labor of self-culture, to which he now addressed himself with wonted energy. Yet, these gentlemen, although proud of Frederick Douglass, failed to fathom, and bring out to the light of day, the highest qualities of his mind; the force of their own education stood in their own way: they did not delve into the mind of a colored man for capacities which the pride of race led them to believe to be restricted to their own Saxon blood. Bitter and vindictive sarcasm, irresistible mimicry, and a pathetic narrative of his own experiences of slavery, were the intellectual manifestations which they encouraged him to exhibit on the platform or in the lecture desk.

A visit to England, in 1845, threw Mr. Douglass among men and women of earnest souls and high culture, and who, moreover, had never drank of the bitter waters of American caste. For the first time in his life, he breathed an atmosphere congenial to the longings of his spirit, and felt his manhood free and unrestricted. The cordial and manly greetings of the British and Irish audiences in public, and the refinement and elegance of the social circles in which he mingled, not only as an equal, but as a recognized man of genius, were, doubtless, genial and pleasant resting places in his hitherto thorny and troubled journey through life. There are joys on the earth, and, to the wayfaring fugitive from American slavery or American caste, this is one of them.

INTRODUCTION

But his sojourn in England was more than a joy to Mr. Douglass. Like the platform at Nantucket, it awakened him to the consciousness of new powers that lay in him. From the pupilage of Garrisonism he rose to the dignity of a teacher and a thinker; his opinions on the broader aspects of the great American question were earnestly and incessantly sought, from various points of view, and he must, perforce, bestir himself to give suitable answer. With that prompt and truthful perception which has led their sisters in all ages of the world to gather at the feet and support the hands of reformers, the gentlewomen of England [2] were foremost to encourage and strengthen him to carve out for himself a path fitted to his powers and energies, in the life-battle against slavery and caste to which he was pledged. And one stirring thought, inseparable from the British idea of the evangel of freedom, must have smote his ear from every side—

Hereditary bondmen! know ye not
Who would be free, themselves mast strike the blow?

The result of this visit was, that on his return to the United States, he established a newspaper. This proceeding was sorely against the wishes and the advice of the leaders of the American Anti-Slavery Society, but our author had fully grown up to the conviction of a truth which they had once promulged, but now forgotten, to wit: that in their own elevation—self-elevation—colored men have a blow to strike "on their own hook," against slavery and caste. Differing from his Boston friends in this matter, diffident in his own abilities, reluctant at their dissuadings, how beautiful is the loyalty with which he still clung to their principles in all things else, and even in this.

Now came the trial hour. Without cordial support from any large body of men or party on this side the Atlantic, and too far distant in space and immediate interest to expect much more, after the much already done, on the other side, he stood up, almost alone, to the arduous labor and heavy expenditure of editor and lecturer. The Garrison party, to which he still adhered, did not want a *colored* newspaper—there was an odor of *caste* about it; the Liberty party could hardly be expected to give warm support to a man who smote their principles as with a hammer; and the wide gulf which separated the free colored people from the Garrisonians, also separated them from their brother, Frederick Douglass.

The arduous nature of his labors, from the date of the establishment of his paper, may be estimated by the fact, that anti-slavery papers in the United States, even while organs of, and when supported by, anti-slavery parties, have, with a single exception, failed to pay expenses. Mr. Douglass has maintained, and does maintain, his paper without the support of any party, and even in the teeth of the opposition of those from whom he had reason to expect counsel and encouragement. He has been compelled, at one and the same time, and almost constantly, during the past seven years, to contribute matter to its columns as editor, and to raise funds for its support as lecturer. It is within bounds to say, that he has expended twelve thousand dollars of his own hard earned money, in publishing this paper, a larger sum than has been contributed by any one individual for the general advancement of the colored people. There had been many other papers published and edited by colored men, beginning as far back as 1827, when the Rev. Samuel E. Cornish and John B. Russworm (a graduate of Bowdoin college, and afterward Governor of Cape Palmas) published the *Freedom's Journal*, in New York City; probably not less than one hundred newspaper enterprises have been started in the United States, by free colored men, born free, and some of them of liberal education and fair talents for this work; but, one after another, they have fallen through, although, in several instances, anti-slavery friends contributed to their support. [3] It had almost been given up, as an impracticable thing, to maintain a colored newspaper, when Mr. Douglass, with fewest early advantages of all his competitors, essayed, and has proved the thing perfectly practicable, and, moreover, of great public benefit. This paper, in addition to its power in holding up the hands of those to whom it is especially devoted, also affords irrefutable evidence of the justice, safety and practicability of Immediate Emancipation; it further proves the immense loss which slavery inflicts on the land while it dooms such energies as his to the hereditary degradation of slavery.

It has been said in this Introduction, that Mr. Douglass had raised himself by his own efforts to the highest position in society. As a successful editor, in our land, he occupies this position. Our editors rule the land, and he is one of them. As an orator and thinker, his position is equally high, in the opinion of his countrymen. If a stranger in the United States would seek its most distinguished

INTRODUCTION

men—the movers of public opinion—he will find their names mentioned, and their movements chronicled, under the head of "BY MAGNETIC TELEGRAPH," in the daily papers. The keen caterers for the public attention, set down, in this column, such men only as have won high mark in the public esteem. During the past winter—1854-5—very frequent mention of Frederick Douglass was made under this head in the daily papers; his name glided as often—this week from Chicago, next week from Boston—over the lightning wires, as the name of any other man, of whatever note. To no man did the people more widely nor more earnestly say, *"Tell me thy thought!"* And, somehow or other, revolution seemed to follow in his wake. His were not the mere words of eloquence which Kossuth speaks of, that delight the ear and then pass away. No! They were *work*-able, *do*-able words, that brought forth fruits in the revolution in Illinois, and in the passage of the franchise resolutions by the Assembly of New York.

And the secret of his power, what is it? He is a Representative American man—a type of his countrymen. Naturalists tell us that a full grown man is a resultant or representative of all animated nature on this globe; beginning with the early embryo state, then representing the lowest forms of organic life, [4] and passing through every subordinate grade or type, until he reaches the last and highest—manhood. In like manner, and to the fullest extent, has Frederick Douglass passed through every gradation of rank comprised in our national make-up, and bears upon his person and upon his soul every thing that is American. And he has not only full sympathy with every thing American; his proclivity or bent, to active toil and visible progress, are in the strictly national direction, delighting to outstrip "all creation."

Nor have the natural gifts, already named as his, lost anything by his severe training. When unexcited, his mental processes are probably slow, but singularly clear in perception, and wide in vision, the unfailing memory bringing up all the facts in their every aspect; incongruities he lays hold of incontinently, and holds up on the edge of his keen and telling wit. But this wit never descends to frivolity; it is rigidly in the keeping of his truthful common sense, and always used in illustration or proof of some point which could not so readily be reached any other way. "Beware of a Yankee when he is feeding," is a shaft that strikes home in a matter never so laid bare by satire before. "The Garrisonian views of disunion, if carried to a successful issue, would only place the people of the north in the same relation to American slavery which they now bear to the slavery of Cuba or the Brazils," is a statement, in a few words, which contains the result and the evidence of an argument which might cover pages, but could not carry stronger conviction, nor be stated in less pregnable form. In proof of this, I may say, that having been submitted to the attention of the Garrisonians in print, in March, it was repeated before them at their business meeting in May—the platform, *par excellence*, on which they invite free fight, *a l'outrance*, to all comers. It was given out in the clear, ringing tones, wherewith the hall of shields was wont to resound of old, yet neither Garrison, nor Phillips, nor May, nor Remond, nor Foster, nor Burleigh, with his subtle steel of "the ice brook's temper," ventured to break a lance upon it! The doctrine of the dissolution of the Union, as a means for the abolition of American slavery, was silenced upon the lips that gave it birth, and in the presence of an array of defenders who compose the keenest intellects in the land.

"The man who is right is a majority" is an aphorism struck out by Mr. Douglass in that great gathering of the friends of freedom, at Pittsburgh, in 1852, where he towered among the highest, because, with abilities inferior to none, and moved more deeply than any, there was neither policy nor party to trammel the outpourings of his soul. Thus we find, opposed to all disadvantages which a black man in the United States labors and struggles under, is this one vantage ground—when the chance comes, and the audience where he may have a say, he stands forth the freest, most deeply moved and most earnest of all men.

It has been said of Mr. Douglass, that his descriptive and declamatory powers, admitted to be of the very highest order, take precedence of his logical force. Whilst the schools might have trained him to the exhibition of the formulas of deductive logic, nature and circumstances forced him into the exercise of the higher faculties required by induction. The first ninety pages of this "Life in Bondage," afford specimens of observing, comparing, and careful classifying, of such superior character, that it is difficult to believe them the results of a child's thinking; he questions the earth, and the children and the slaves around him again and again, and finally looks to *"God in the sky"* for

INTRODUCTION

the why and the wherefore of the unnatural thing, slavery. *"Yes, if indeed thou art, wherefore dost thou suffer us to be slain?"* is the only prayer and worship of the God-forsaken Dodos in the heart of Africa. Almost the same was his prayer. One of his earliest observations was that white children should know their ages, while the colored children were ignorant of theirs; and the songs of the slaves grated on his inmost soul, because a something told him that harmony in sound, and music of the spirit, could not consociate with miserable degradation.

To such a mind, the ordinary processes of logical deduction are like proving that two and two make four. Mastering the intermediate steps by an intuitive glance, or recurring to them as Ferguson resorted to geometry, it goes down to the deeper relation of things, and brings out what may seem, to some, mere statements, but which are new and brilliant generalizations, each resting on a broad and stable basis. Thus, Chief Justice Marshall gave his decisions, and then told Brother Story to look up the authorities—and they never differed from him. Thus, also, in his "Lecture on the Anti-Slavery Movement," delivered before the Rochester Ladies' Anti-Slavery Society, Mr. Douglass presents a mass of thought, which, without any showy display of logic on his part, requires an exercise of the reasoning faculties of the reader to keep pace with him. And his "Claims of the Negro Ethnologically Considered," is full of new and fresh thoughts on the dawning science of race-history.

If, as has been stated, his intellection is slow, when unexcited, it is most prompt and rapid when he is thoroughly aroused. Memory, logic, wit, sarcasm, invective pathos and bold imagery of rare structural beauty, well up as from a copious fountain, yet each in its proper place, and contributing to form a whole, grand in itself, yet complete in the minutest proportions. It is most difficult to hedge him in a corner, for his positions are taken so deliberately, that it is rare to find a point in them undefended aforethought. Professor Reason tells me the following: "On a recent visit of a public nature, to Philadelphia, and in a meeting composed mostly of his colored brethren, Mr. Douglass proposed a comparison of views in the matters of the relations and duties of 'our people;' he holding that prejudice was the result of condition, and could be conquered by the efforts of the degraded themselves. A gentleman present, distinguished for logical acumen and subtlety, and who had devoted no small portion of the last twenty-five years to the study and elucidation of this very question, held the opposite view, that prejudice is innate and unconquerable. He terminated a series of well dove-tailed, Socratic questions to Mr. Douglass, with the following: 'If the legislature at Harrisburgh should awaken, to-morrow morning, and find each man's skin turned black and his hair woolly, what could they do to remove prejudice?' 'Immediately pass laws entitling black men to all civil, political and social privileges,' was the instant reply—and the questioning ceased."

The most remarkable mental phenomenon in Mr. Douglass, is his style in writing and speaking. In March, 1855, he delivered an address in the assembly chamber before the members of the legislature of the state of New York. An eye witness [5] describes the crowded and most intelligent audience, and their rapt attention to the speaker, as the grandest scene he ever witnessed in the capitol. Among those whose eyes were riveted on the speaker full two hours and a half, were Thurlow Weed and Lieutenant Governor Raymond; the latter, at the conclusion of the address, exclaimed to a friend, "I would give twenty thousand dollars, if I could deliver that address in that manner." Mr. Raymond is a first class graduate of Dartmouth, a rising politician, ranking foremost in the legislature; of course, his ideal of oratory must be of the most polished and finished description.

The style of Mr. Douglass in writing, is to me an intellectual puzzle. The strength, affluence and terseness may easily be accounted for, because the style of a man is the man; but how are we to account for that rare polish in his style of writing, which, most critically examined, seems the result of careful early culture among the best classics of our language; it equals if it does not surpass the style of Hugh Miller, which was the wonder of the British literary public, until he unraveled the mystery in the most interesting of autobiographies. But Frederick Douglass was still calking the seams of Baltimore clippers, and had only written a "pass," at the age when Miller's style was already formed.

I asked William Whipper, of Pennsylvania, the gentleman alluded to above, whether he thought Mr. Douglass's power inherited from the Negroid, or from what is called the Caucasian side of his make up? After some reflection, he frankly answered, "I must admit, although sorry to do so, that

INTRODUCTION

the Caucasian predominates." At that time, I almost agreed with him; but, facts narrated in the first part of this work, throw a different light on this interesting question.

We are left in the dark as to who was the paternal ancestor of our author; a fact which generally holds good of the Romuluses and Remuses who are to inaugurate the new birth of our republic. In the absence of testimony from the Caucasian side, we must see what evidence is given on the other side of the house.

"My grandmother, though advanced in years, * * * was yet a woman of power and spirit. She was marvelously straight in figure, elastic and muscular." (p. 46.)

After describing her skill in constructing nets, her perseverance in using them, and her widespread fame in the agricultural way he adds, "It happened to her—as it will happen to any careful and thrifty person residing in an ignorant and improvident neighborhood—to enjoy the reputation of being born to good luck." And his grandmother was a black woman.

"My mother was tall, and finely proportioned; of deep black, glossy complexion; had regular features; and among other slaves was remarkably sedate in her manners." "Being a field hand, she was obliged to walk twelve miles and return, between nightfall and daybreak, to see her children" (p. 54.) "I shall never forget the indescribable expression of her countenance when I told her that I had had no food since morning. * * * There was pity in her glance at me, and a fiery indignation at Aunt Katy at the same time; * * * * she read Aunt Katy a lecture which she never forgot." (p. 56.) "I learned after my mother's death, that she could read, and that she was the *only* one of all the slaves and colored people in Tuckahoe who enjoyed that advantage. How she acquired this knowledge, I know not, for Tuckahoe is the last place in the world where she would be apt to find facilities for learning." (p. 57.) "There is, in *Prichard's Natural History of Man*, the head of a figure—on page 157—the features of which so resemble those of my mother, that I often recur to it with something of the feeling which I suppose others experience when looking upon the pictures of dear departed ones." (p. 52.)

The head alluded to is copied from the statue of Ramses the Great, an Egyptian king of the nineteenth dynasty. The authors of the *Types of Mankind* give a side view of the same on page 148, remarking that the profile, "like Napoleon's, is superbly European!" The nearness of its resemblance to Mr. Douglass' mother rests upon the evidence of his memory, and judging from his almost marvelous feats of recollection of forms and outlines recorded in this book, this testimony may be admitted.

These facts show that for his energy, perseverance, eloquence, invective, sagacity, and wide sympathy, he is indebted to his Negro blood. The very marvel of his style would seem to be a development of that other marvel—how his mother learned to read. The versatility of talent which he wields, in common with Dumas, Ira Aldridge, and Miss Greenfield, would seem to be the result of the grafting of the Anglo-Saxon on good, original, Negro stock. If the friends of "Caucasus" choose to claim, for that region, what remains after this analysis—to wit: combination—they are welcome to it. They will forgive me for reminding them that the term "Caucasian" is dropped by recent writers on Ethnology; for the people about Mount Caucasus, are, and have ever been, Mongols. The great "white race" now seek paternity, according to Dr. Pickering, in Arabia—"Arida Nutrix" of the best breed of horses &c. Keep on, gentlemen; you will find yourselves in Africa, by-and-by. The Egyptians, like the Americans, were a *mixed race*, with some Negro blood circling around the throne, as well as in the mud hovels.

This is the proper place to remark of our author, that the same strong self-hood, which led him to measure strength with Mr. Covey, and to wrench himself from the embrace of the Garrisonians, and which has borne him through many resistances to the personal indignities offered him as a colored man, sometimes becomes a hyper-sensitiveness to such assaults as men of his mark will meet with, on paper. Keen and unscrupulous opponents have sought, and not unsuccessfully, to pierce him in this direction; for well they know, that if assailed, he will smite back.

It is not without a feeling of pride, dear reader, that I present you with this book. The son of a self-emancipated bond-woman, I feel joy in introducing to you my brother, who has rent his own bonds, and who, in his every relation—as a public man, as a husband and as a father—is such as does

INTRODUCTION

honor to the land which gave him birth. I shall place this book in the hands of the only child spared me, bidding him to strive and emulate its noble example. You may do likewise. It is an American book, for Americans, in the fullest sense of the idea. It shows that the worst of our institutions, in its worst aspect, cannot keep down energy, truthfulness, and earnest struggle for the right. It proves the justice and practicability of Immediate Emancipation. It shows that any man in our land, "no matter in what battle his liberty may have been cloven down, * * * * no matter what complexion an Indian or an African sun may have burned upon him," not only may "stand forth redeemed and disenthralled," but may also stand up a candidate for the highest suffrage of a great people—the tribute of their honest, hearty admiration. Reader, *Vale! New York*

JAMES M'CUNE SMITH

My Bondage

CHAPTER I.
Childhood

PLACE OF BIRTH—CHARACTER OF THE DISTRICT—TUCKAHOE—ORIGIN OF THE NAME—CHOPTANK RIVER—TIME OF BIRTH—GENEALOGICAL TREES—MODE OF COUNTING TIME—NAMES OF GRANDPARENTS—THEIR POSITION—GRANDMOTHER ESPECIALLY ESTEEMED—"BORN TO GOOD LUCK"—SWEET POTATOES—SUPERSTITION—THE LOG CABIN—ITS CHARMS—SEPARATING CHILDREN—MY AUNTS—THEIR NAMES—FIRST KNOWLEDGE OF BEING A SLAVE—OLD MASTER—GRIEFS AND JOYS OF CHILDHOOD—COMPARATIVE HAPPINESS OF THE SLAVE-BOY AND THE SON OF A SLAVEHOLDER.

In Talbot county, Eastern Shore, Maryland, near Easton, the county town of that county, there is a small district of country, thinly populated, and remarkable for nothing that I know of more than for the worn-out, sandy, desert-like appearance of its soil, the general dilapidation of its farms and fences, the indigent and spiritless character of its inhabitants, and the prevalence of ague and fever.

The name of this singularly unpromising and truly famine stricken district is Tuckahoe, a name well known to all Marylanders, black and white. It was given to this section of country probably, at the first, merely in derision; or it may possibly have been applied to it, as I have heard, because some one of its earlier inhabitants had been guilty of the petty meanness of stealing a hoe—or taking a hoe that did not belong to him. Eastern Shore men usually pronounce the word *took*, as *tuck; Took-a-hoe*, therefore, is, in Maryland parlance, *Tuckahoe*. But, whatever may have been its origin—and about this I will not be positive—that name has stuck to the district in question; and it is seldom mentioned but with contempt and derision, on account of the barrenness of its soil, and the ignorance, indolence, and poverty of its people. Decay and ruin are everywhere visible, and the thin population of the place would have quitted it long ago, but for the Choptank river, which runs through it, from which they take abundance of shad and herring, and plenty of ague and fever.

It was in this dull, flat, and unthrifty district, or neighborhood, surrounded by a white population of the lowest order, indolent and drunken to a proverb, and among slaves, who seemed to ask, *"Oh! what's the use?"* every time they lifted a hoe, that I—without any fault of mine was born, and spent the first years of my childhood.

The reader will pardon so much about the place of my birth, on the score that it is always a fact of some importance to know where a man is born, if, indeed, it be important to know anything about him. In regard to the *time* of my birth, I cannot be as definite as I have been respecting the *place*. Nor, indeed, can I impart much knowledge concerning my parents. Genealogical trees do not flourish among slaves. A person of some consequence here in the north, sometimes designated *father*, is literally abolished in slave law and slave practice. It is only once in a while that an exception is found to this statement. I never met with a slave who could tell me how old he was. Few slave-mothers know anything of the months of the year, nor of the days of the month. They keep no family records, with marriages, births, and deaths. They measure the ages of their children by spring time, winter time, harvest time, planting time, and the like; but these soon become undistinguishable and forgotten. Like other slaves, I cannot tell how old I am. This destitution was among my earliest troubles. I learned when I grew up, that my master—and this is the case with masters generally—allowed no questions to be put to him, by which a slave might learn his age. Such questions deemed evidence of impatience, and even of impudent curiosity. From certain events, however, the dates of which I have since learned, I suppose myself to have been born about the year 1817.

The first experience of life with me that I now remember—and I remember it but hazily—began in the family of my grandmother and grandfather. Betsey and Isaac Baily. They were quite advanced in life, and had long lived on the spot where they then resided. They were considered old settlers in the neighborhood, and, from certain circumstances, I infer that my grandmother, especially, was held in high esteem, far higher than is the lot of most colored persons in the slave states. She was a good nurse, and a capital hand at making nets for catching shad and herring; and these nets were in great demand, not only in Tuckahoe, but at Denton and Hillsboro, neighboring villages. She was not only good at making the nets, but was also somewhat famous for her good fortune in taking the fishes referred to. I have known her to be in the water half the day. Grandmother was likewise more provident than most of her neighbors in the preservation of seedling sweet potatoes, and it happened to her—as it will happen to any careful and thrifty person residing in an ignorant and improvident community—to enjoy the reputation of having been born to "good luck." Her "good luck" was owing to the exceeding care which she took in preventing the succulent root from getting bruised in the digging, and in placing it beyond the reach of frost, by actually burying it under the hearth of her cabin during the winter months. In the time of planting sweet potatoes, "Grandmother Betty," as she was familiarly called, was sent for in all directions, simply to place the seedling potatoes in the hills; for superstition had it, that if "Grandmamma Betty but touches them at planting, they will be sure to grow and flourish." This high reputation was full of advantage to her, and to the children around her. Though Tuckahoe had but few of the good things of life, yet of such as it did possess grandmother got a full share, in the way of presents. If good potato crops came after her planting, she was not forgotten by those for whom she planted; and as she was remembered by others, so she remembered the hungry little ones around her.

The dwelling of my grandmother and grandfather had few pretensions. It was a log hut, or cabin, built of clay, wood, and straw. At a distance it resembled—though it was smaller, less commodious and less substantial—the cabins erected in the western states by the first settlers. To my child's eye, however, it was a noble structure, admirably adapted to promote the comforts and conveniences of its inmates. A few rough, Virginia fence-rails, flung loosely over the rafters above, answered the triple purpose of floors, ceilings, and bedsteads. To be sure, this upper apartment was reached only by a ladder—but what in the world for climbing could be better than a ladder? To me, this ladder was really a high invention, and possessed a sort of charm as I played with delight upon the rounds of it. In this little hut there was a large family of children: I dare not say how many. My grandmother—whether because too old for field service, or because she had so faithfully discharged the duties of her station in early life, I know not—enjoyed the high privilege of living in a cabin, separate from the quarter, with no other burden than her own support, and the necessary care of the little children, imposed. She evidently esteemed it a great fortune to live so. The children were not her own, but her grandchildren—the children of her daughters. She took delight in having them around her, and in attending to their few wants. The practice of separating children from their mother, and hiring the latter out at distances too great to admit of their meeting, except at long intervals, is a marked feature of the cruelty and barbarity of the slave system. But it is in harmony with the grand aim of slavery, which, always and everywhere, is to reduce man to a level with the brute. It is a successful method of obliterating from the mind and heart of the slave, all just ideas of the sacredness of *the family*, as an institution.

Most of the children, however, in this instance, being the children of my grandmother's daughters, the notions of family, and the reciprocal duties and benefits of the relation, had a better chance of being understood than where children are placed—as they often are in the hands of strangers, who have no care for them, apart from the wishes of their masters. The daughters of my grandmother were five in number. Their names were JENNY, ESTHER, MILLY, PRISCILLA, and HARRIET. The daughter last named was my mother, of whom the reader shall learn more by-and-by.

Living here, with my dear old grandmother and grandfather, it was a long time before I knew myself to be *a slave*. I knew many other things before I knew that. Grandmother and grandfather were the greatest people in the world to me; and being with them so snugly in their own little cabin—I supposed it be their own—knowing no higher authority over me or the other children than the authority of grandmamma, for a time there was nothing to disturb me; but, as I grew larger and older, I learned by degrees the sad fact, that the "little hut," and the lot on which it stood, belonged not to my dear old grandparents, but to some person who lived a great distance off, and who was called, by grandmother, "OLD MASTER." I further learned the sadder fact, that not only the house and lot, but that grandmother herself, (grandfather was free,) and all the little children around her, belonged to this mysterious personage, called by grandmother, with every mark of reverence, "Old Master." Thus early did clouds and shadows begin to fall upon my path. Once on the track—troubles never come singly—I was not long in finding out another fact, still more grievous to my childish heart. I was told that this "old master," whose name seemed ever to be mentioned with fear and shuddering, only allowed the children to live with grandmother for a limited time, and that in fact as soon as they were big enough, they were promptly taken away, to live with the said "old master." These were distressing revelations indeed; and though I was quite too young to comprehend the full import of the intelligence, and mostly spent my childhood days in gleesome sports with the other children, a shade of disquiet rested upon me.

The absolute power of this distant "old master" had touched my young spirit with but the point of its cold, cruel iron, and left me something to brood over after the play and in moments of repose. Grandmammy was, indeed, at that time, all the world to me; and the thought of being separated from her, in any considerable time, was more than an unwelcome intruder. It was intolerable.

Children have their sorrows as well as men and women; and it would be well to remember this in our dealings with them. SLAVE-children *are* children, and prove no exceptions to the general rule. The liability to be separated from my grandmother, seldom or never to see her again, haunted me. I dreaded the thought of going to live with that mysterious "old master," whose name I never heard mentioned with affection, but always with fear. I look back to this as among the heaviest of my childhood's sorrows. My grandmother! my grandmother! and the little hut, and the joyous circle under her care, but especially *she*, who made us sorry when she left us but for an hour, and glad on her return,—how could I leave her and the good old home?

But the sorrows of childhood, like the pleasures of after life, are transient. It is not even within the power of slavery to write *indelible* sorrow, at a single dash, over the heart of a child.

> *The tear down childhood's cheek that flows,*
> *Is like the dew-drop on the rose—*
> *When next the summer breeze comes by,*
> *And waves the bush—the flower is dry.*

There is, after all, but little difference in the measure of contentment felt by the slave-child neglected and the slaveholder's child cared for and petted. The spirit of the All Just mercifully holds the balance for the young.

The slaveholder, having nothing to fear from impotent childhood, easily affords to refrain from cruel inflictions; and if cold and hunger do not pierce the tender frame, the first seven or eight years of the slave-boy's life are about as full of sweet content as those of the most favored and petted *white* children of the slaveholder. The slave-boy escapes many troubles which befall and vex his white brother. He seldom has to listen to lectures on propriety of behavior, or on anything else. He is never chided for handling his little knife and fork improperly or awkwardly, for he uses none. He is never reprimanded for soiling the table-cloth, for he takes his meals on the clay floor. He never has the misfortune, in his games or sports, of soiling or tearing his clothes, for he has almost none to soil or tear. He is never expected to act like a nice little gentleman, for he is only a rude little slave. Thus, freed from all restraint, the slave-boy can be, in his life and conduct, a genuine boy, doing whatever his boyish nature suggests; enacting, by turns, all the strange antics and freaks of horses, dogs, pigs, and barn-door fowls, without in any manner compromising his dignity, or incurring reproach of any sort. He literally runs wild; has no pretty little verses to learn in the nursery; no nice little speeches to make for aunts, uncles, or cousins, to show how smart he is; and, if he can only manage to keep out of the way of the heavy feet and fists of the older slave boys, he may trot on, in his joyous and roguish tricks, as happy as any little heathen under the palm trees of Africa. To be sure, he is occasionally reminded, when he stumbles in the path of his master—and this he early learns to avoid—that he is eating his *"white bread,"* and that he will be made to *"see sights"* by-and-by. The threat is soon forgotten; the shadow soon passes, and our sable boy continues to roll in the dust, or play in the mud, as bests suits him, and in the veriest freedom. If he feels uncomfortable, from mud or from dust, the coast is clear; he can plunge into the river or the pond, without the ceremony of undressing, or the fear of wetting his clothes; his little tow-linen shirt—for that is all he has on—is easily dried; and it needed ablution as much as did his skin. His food is of the coarsest kind, consisting for the most part of cornmeal mush, which often finds it way from the wooden tray to his mouth in an oyster shell. His days, when the weather is warm, are spent in the pure, open air, and in the bright sunshine. He always sleeps in airy apartments; he seldom has to take powders, or to be paid to swallow pretty little sugar-coated pills, to cleanse his blood, or to quicken his appetite. He eats no candies; gets no lumps of loaf sugar; always relishes his food; cries but little, for nobody cares for his crying; learns to esteem his bruises but slight, because others so esteem them. In a word, he is, for the most part of the first eight years of his life, a spirited, joyous, uproarious, and happy boy, upon whom troubles fall only like water on a duck's back. And such a boy, so far as I can now remember, was the boy whose life in slavery I am now narrating.

CHAPTER II.
Removed from My First Home

THE NAME "OLD MASTER" A TERROR—COLONEL LLOYD'S PLANTATION—WYE RIVER—WHENCE ITS NAME—POSITION OF THE LLOYDS—HOME ATTRACTION—MEET OFFERING—JOURNEY FROM TUCKAHOE TO WYE RIVER—SCENE ON REACHING OLD MASTER'S—DEPARTURE OF GRANDMOTHER—STRANGE MEETING OF SISTERS AND BROTHERS—REFUSAL TO BE COMFORTED—SWEET SLEEP.

That mysterious individual referred to in the first chapter as an object of terror among the inhabitants of our little cabin, under the ominous title of "old master," was really a man of some consequence. He owned several farms in Tuckahoe; was the chief clerk and butler on the home plantation of Col. Edward Lloyd; had overseers on his own farms; and gave directions to overseers on the farms belonging to Col. Lloyd. This plantation is situated on Wye river—the river receiving its name, doubtless, from Wales, where the Lloyds originated. They (the Lloyds) are an old and honored family in Maryland, exceedingly wealthy. The home plantation, where they have resided, perhaps for a century or more, is one of the largest, most fertile, and best appointed, in the state.

About this plantation, and about that queer old master—who must be something more than a man, and something worse than an angel—the reader will easily imagine that I was not only curious, but eager, to know all that could be known. Unhappily for me, however, all the information I could get concerning him increased my great dread of being carried thither—of being separated from and deprived of the protection of my grandmother and grandfather. It was, evidently, a great thing to go to Col. Lloyd's; and I was not without a little curiosity to see the place; but no amount of coaxing could induce in me the wish to remain there. The fact is, such was my dread of leaving the little cabin, that I wished to remain little forever, for I knew the taller I grew the shorter my stay. The old cabin, with its rail floor and rail bedsteads upstairs, and its clay floor downstairs, and its dirt chimney, and windowless sides, and that most curious piece of workmanship dug in front of the fireplace, beneath which grandmammy placed the sweet potatoes to keep them from the frost, was MY HOME—the only home I ever had; and I loved it, and all connected with it. The old fences around it, and the stumps in the edge of the woods near it, and the squirrels that ran, skipped, and played upon them, were objects of interest and affection. There, too, right at the side of the hut, stood the old well, with its stately and skyward-pointing beam, so aptly placed between the limbs of what had once been a tree, and so nicely balanced that I could move it up and down with only one hand, and could get a drink myself without calling for help. Where else in the world could such a well be found, and where could such another home be met with? Nor were these all the attractions of the place. Down in a little valley, not far from grandmammy's cabin, stood Mr. Lee's mill, where the people came often in large numbers to get their corn ground. It was a watermill; and I never shall be able to tell the many things thought and felt, while I sat on the bank and watched that mill, and the turning of that ponderous wheel. The mill-pond, too, had its charms; and with my pinhook, and thread line, I could get *nibbles*, if I could catch no fish. But, in all my sports and plays, and in spite of them, there would, occasionally, come the painful foreboding that I was not long to remain there, and that I must soon be called away to the home of old master.

I was A SLAVE—born a slave and though the fact was in comprehensible to me, it conveyed to my mind a sense of my entire dependence on the will of *somebody* I had never seen; and, from some cause or other, I had been made to fear this somebody above all else on earth. Born for another's benefit, as the *firstling* of the cabin flock I was soon to be selected as a meet offering to the fearful and inexorable *demigod*, whose huge image on so many occasions haunted my childhood's imagination. When the time of my departure was decided upon, my grandmother, knowing my fears, and in pity for them, kindly kept me ignorant of the dreaded event about to transpire. Up to the morning (a beautiful summer morning) when we were to start, and, indeed, during the whole journey—a journey which, child as I was, I remember as well as if it were yesterday—she kept the sad fact hidden from me. This reserve was necessary; for, could I have known all, I should have given grandmother some trouble in getting me started. As it was, I was helpless, and she—dear woman!—led me along by the hand, resisting, with the reserve and solemnity of a priestess, all my inquiring looks to the last.

The distance from Tuckahoe to Wye river—where my old master lived—was full twelve miles, and the walk was quite a severe test of the endurance of my young legs. The journey would have proved too severe for me, but that my dear old grandmother—blessings on her memory!—afforded occasional relief by "toting" me (as Marylanders have it) on her shoulder. My grandmother, though advanced in years—as was evident from more than one gray hair, which peeped from between the ample and graceful folds of her newly-ironed bandana turban—was yet a woman of power and spirit. She was marvelously straight in figure, elastic, and muscular. I seemed hardly to be a burden to her. She would have "toted" me farther, but that I felt myself too much of a man to allow it, and insisted on walking. Releasing dear grandmamma from carrying me, did not make me altogether independent of her, when we happened to pass through portions of the somber woods which lay between Tuckahoe and Wye river. She often found me increasing the energy of my grip, and holding her clothing, lest something should come out of the woods and eat me up. Several old logs and stumps imposed upon me, and got themselves taken for wild beasts. I could see their legs, eyes, and ears, or I could see something like eyes, legs, and ears, till I got close enough to them to see that the eyes were knots, washed white with rain, and the legs were broken limbs, and the ears, only ears owing to the point from which they were seen. Thus early I learned that the point from which a thing is viewed is of some importance.

As the day advanced the heat increased; and it was not until the afternoon that we reached the much dreaded end of the journey. I found myself in the midst of a group of children of many colors; black, brown, copper colored, and nearly white. I had not seen so many children before. Great houses loomed up in different directions, and a great many men and women were at work in the fields. All this hurry, noise, and singing was very different from the stillness of Tuckahoe. As a new comer, I was an object of special interest; and, after laughing and yelling around me, and playing all sorts of wild tricks, they (the children) asked me to go out and play with them. This I refused to do, preferring to stay with grandmamma. I could not help feeling that our being there boded no good to me. Grandmamma looked sad. She was soon to lose another object of affection, as she had lost many before. I knew she was unhappy, and the shadow fell from her brow on me, though I knew not the cause.

All suspense, however, must have an end; and the end of mine, in this instance, was at hand. Affectionately patting me on the head, and exhorting me to be a good boy, grandmamma told me to go and play with the little children. "They are kin to you," said she; "go and play with them." Among a number of cousins were Phil, Tom, Steve, and Jerry, Nance and Betty.

Grandmother pointed out my brother PERRY, my sister SARAH, and my sister ELIZA, who stood in the group. I had never seen my brother nor my sisters before; and, though I had sometimes heard of them, and felt a curious interest in them, I really did not understand what they were to me, or I to them. We were brothers and sisters, but what of that? Why should they be attached to me, or I to them? Brothers and sisters we were by blood; but *slavery* had made us strangers. I heard the words brother and sisters, and knew they must mean something; but slavery had robbed these terms of their true meaning. The experience through which I was passing, they had passed through before. They had already been initiated into the mysteries of old master's domicile, and they seemed to look upon me with a certain degree of compassion; but my heart clave to my grandmother. Think it not strange, dear reader, that so little sympathy of feeling existed between us. The conditions of brotherly and sisterly feeling were wanting—we had never nestled and played together. My poor mother, like many other slave-women, had many *children*, but NO FAMILY! The domestic hearth, with its holy lessons and precious endearments, is abolished in the case of a slave-mother and her children. "Little children, love one another," are words seldom heard in a slave cabin.

I really wanted to play with my brother and sisters, but they were strangers to me, and I was full of fear that grandmother might leave without taking me with her. Entreated to do so, however, and that, too, by my dear grandmother, I went to the back part of the house, to play with them and the other children. *Play*, however, I did not, but stood with my back against the wall, witnessing the playing of the others. At last, while standing there, one of the children, who had been in the kitchen, ran up to me, in a sort of roguish glee, exclaiming, "Fed, Fed! grandmammy gone! grandmammy gone!" I could not believe it; yet, fearing the worst, I ran into the kitchen, to see for myself, and found it even so. Grandmammy had indeed gone, and was now far away, "clean" out of sight. I need not tell all that happened now. Almost heart-broken at the discovery, I fell upon the ground, and wept a boy's bitter tears, refusing to be comforted. My brother and sisters came around me, and said, "Don't cry," and gave me peaches and pears, but I flung them away, and refused all their kindly advances. I had never been deceived before; and I felt not only grieved at parting—as I supposed forever—with my grandmother, but indignant that a trick had been played upon me in a matter so serious.

It was now late in the afternoon. The day had been an exciting and wearisome one, and I knew not how or where, but I suppose I sobbed myself to sleep. There is a healing in the angel wing of sleep, even for the slave-boy; and its balm was never more welcome to any wounded soul than it was to mine, the first night I spent at the domicile of old master. The reader may be surprised that I narrate so minutely an incident apparently so trivial, and which must have occurred when I was not more than seven years old; but as I wish to give a faithful history of my experience in slavery, I cannot withhold a circumstance which, at the time, affected me so deeply. Besides, this was, in fact, my first introduction to the realities of slavery.

CHAPTER III.
PARENTAGE

MY FATHER SHROUDED IN MYSTERY—MY MOTHER—HER PERSONAL APPEARANCE—INTERFERENCE OF SLAVERY WITH THE NATURAL AFFECTIONS OF MOTHER AND CHILDREN—SITUATION OF MY MOTHER—HER NIGHTLY VISITS TO HER BOY—STRIKING INCIDENT—HER DEATH—HER PLACE OF BURIAL.

If the reader will now be kind enough to allow me time to grow bigger, and afford me an opportunity for my experience to become greater, I will tell him something, by-and-by, of slave life, as I saw, felt, and heard it, on Col. Edward Lloyd's plantation, and at the house of old master, where I had now, despite of myself, most suddenly, but not unexpectedly, been dropped. Meanwhile, I will redeem my promise to say something more of my dear mother.

I say nothing of *father*, for he is shrouded in a mystery I have never been able to penetrate. Slavery does away with fathers, as it does away with families. Slavery has no use for either fathers or families, and its laws do not recognize their existence in the social arrangements of the plantation. When they *do* exist, they are not the outgrowths of slavery, but are antagonistic to that system. The order of civilization is reversed here. The name of the child is not expected to be that of its father, and his condition does not necessarily affect that of the child. He may be the slave of Mr. Tilgman; and his child, when born, may be the slave of Mr. Gross. He may be a *freeman;* and yet his child may be a *chattel.* He may be white, glorying in the purity of his Anglo-Saxon blood; and his child may be ranked with the blackest slaves. Indeed, he *may* be, and often *is*, master and father to the same child. He can be father without being a husband, and may sell his child without incurring reproach, if the child be by a woman in whose veins courses one thirty-second part of African blood. My father was a white man, or nearly white. It was sometimes whispered that my master was my father.

But to return, or rather, to begin. My knowledge of my mother is very scanty, but very distinct. Her personal appearance and bearing are ineffaceably stamped upon my memory. She was tall, and finely proportioned; of deep black, glossy complexion; had regular features, and, among the other slaves, was remarkably sedate in her manners. There is in *Prichard's Natural History of Man*, the head of a figure—on page 157—the features of which so resemble those of my mother, that I often recur to it with something of the feeling which I suppose others experience when looking upon the pictures of dear departed ones.

Yet I cannot say that I was very deeply attached to my mother; certainly not so deeply as I should have been had our relations in childhood been different. We were separated, according to the common custom, when I was but an infant, and, of course, before I knew my mother from any one else.

The germs of affection with which the Almighty, in his wisdom and mercy, arms the hopeless infant against the ills and vicissitudes of his lot, had been directed in their growth toward that loving old grandmother, whose gentle hand and kind deportment it was in the first effort of my infantile understanding to comprehend and appreciate. Accordingly, the tenderest affection which a beneficent Father allows, as a partial compensation to the mother for the pains and lacerations of her heart, incident to the maternal relation, was, in my case, diverted from its true and natural object, by the envious, greedy, and treacherous hand of slavery. The slave-mother can be spared long enough from the field to endure all the bitterness of a mother's anguish, when it adds another name to a master's ledger, but *not* long enough to receive the joyous reward afforded by the intelligent smiles of her child. I never think of this terrible interference of slavery with my infantile affections, and its diverting them from their natural course, without feelings to which I can give no adequate expression.

I do not remember to have seen my mother at my grandmother's at any time. I remember her only in her visits to me at Col. Lloyd's plantation, and in the kitchen of my old master. Her visits to me there were few in number, brief in duration, and mostly made in the night. The pains she took, and the toil she endured, to see me, tells me that a true mother's heart was hers, and that slavery had difficulty in paralyzing it with unmotherly indifference.

My mother was hired out to a Mr. Stewart, who lived about twelve miles from old master's, and, being a field hand, she seldom had leisure, by day, for the performance of the journey. The nights and the distance were both obstacles to her visits. She was obliged to walk, unless chance flung into her way an opportunity to ride; and the latter was sometimes her good luck. But she always had to walk one way or the other. It was a greater luxury than slavery could afford, to allow a black slave-mother a horse or a mule, upon which to travel twenty-four miles, when she could walk the distance. Besides, it is deemed a foolish whim for a slave-mother to manifest concern to see her children, and, in one point of view, the case is made out—she can do nothing for them. She has no control over them; the master is even more than the mother, in all matters touching the fate of her child. Why, then, should she give herself any concern? She has no responsibility. Such is the reasoning, and such the practice. The iron rule of the plantation, always passionately and violently enforced in that neighborhood, makes flogging the penalty of failing to be in the field before sunrise in the morning, unless special permission be given to the absenting slave. "I went to see my child," is no excuse to the ear or heart of the overseer.

One of the visits of my mother to me, while at Col. Lloyd's, I remember very vividly, as affording a bright gleam of a mother's love, and the earnestness of a mother's care.

"I had on that day offended "Aunt Katy," (called "Aunt" by way of respect,) the cook of old master's establishment. I do not now remember the nature of my offense in this instance, for my offenses were numerous in that quarter, greatly depending, however, upon the mood of Aunt Katy, as to their heinousness; but she had adopted, that day, her favorite mode of punishing me, namely, making me go without food all day—that is, from after breakfast. The first hour or two after dinner, I succeeded pretty well in keeping up my spirits; but though I made an excellent stand against the foe, and fought bravely during the afternoon, I knew I must be conquered at last, unless I got the accustomed reenforcement of a slice of corn bread, at sundown. Sundown came, but *no bread*, and, in its stead, their came the threat, with a scowl well suited to its terrible import, that she "meant to *starve the life out of me!*" Brandishing her knife, she chopped off the heavy slices for the other children, and put the loaf away, muttering, all the while, her savage designs upon myself. Against this disappointment, for I was expecting that her heart would relent at last, I made an extra effort to maintain my dignity; but when I saw all the other children around me with merry and satisfied faces, I could stand it no longer. I went out behind the house, and cried like a fine fellow! When tired of this, I returned to the kitchen, sat by the fire, and brooded over my hard lot. I was too hungry to sleep. While I sat in the corner, I caught sight of an ear of Indian corn on an upper shelf of the kitchen. I watched my chance, and got it, and, shelling off a few grains, I put it back again. The grains in my hand, I quickly put in some ashes, and covered them with embers, to roast them. All this I did at the risk of getting a brutal thumping, for Aunt Katy could beat, as well as starve me. My corn was not long in roasting, and, with my keen appetite, it did not matter even if the grains were not exactly done. I eagerly pulled them out, and placed them on my stool, in a clever little pile. Just as I began to help myself to my very dry meal, in came my dear mother. And now, dear reader, a scene occurred which was altogether worth beholding, and to me it was instructive as well as interesting. The friendless and hungry boy, in his extremest need—and when he did not dare to look for succor—found himself in the strong, protecting arms of a mother; a mother who was, at the moment (being endowed with high powers of manner as well as matter) more than a match for all his enemies. I shall never forget the indescribable expression of her countenance, when I told her that I had had no food since morning; and that Aunt Katy said she "meant to starve the life out of me." There was pity in her glance at me, and a fiery indignation at Aunt Katy at the same time; and, while she took the corn from me, and gave me a large ginger cake, in its stead, she read Aunt Katy a lecture which she never forgot. My mother threatened her with complaining to old master in my behalf; for the latter, though harsh and cruel himself, at times, did not sanction the meanness, injustice, partiality and oppressions enacted by Aunt Katy in the kitchen. That night I learned the fact, that I was, not only a child, but *somebody's* child. The "sweet cake" my mother gave me was in the shape of a heart, with a rich, dark ring glazed upon the edge of it. I was victorious, and well off for the moment; prouder, on my mother's knee, than a king upon his throne. But my triumph was short. I dropped off to sleep, and waked in the morning only to find my mother gone, and myself left at the mercy of the sable virago, dominant in my old master's kitchen, whose fiery wrath was my constant dread.

I do not remember to have seen my mother after this occurrence. Death soon ended the little communication that had existed between us; and with it, I believe, a life judging from her weary, sad, down-cast countenance and mute demeanor—full of heartfelt sorrow. I was not allowed to visit her during any part of her long illness; nor did I see her for a long time before she was taken ill and died. The heartless and ghastly form of *slavery* rises between mother and child, even at the bed of death. The mother, at the verge of the grave, may not gather her children, to impart to them her holy admonitions, and invoke for them her dying benediction. The bond-woman lives as a slave, and is left to die as a beast; often with fewer attentions than are paid to a favorite horse. Scenes of sacred tenderness, around the death-bed, never forgotten, and which often arrest the vicious and confirm the virtuous during life, must be looked for among the free, though they sometimes occur among the slaves. It has been a life-long, standing grief to me, that I knew so little of my mother; and that I was so early separated from her. The counsels of her love must have been beneficial to me. The side view of her face is imaged on my memory, and I take few steps in life, without feeling her presence; but the image is mute, and I have no striking words of her's treasured up.

I learned, after my mother's death, that she could read, and that she was the *only* one of all the slaves and colored people in Tuckahoe who enjoyed that advantage. How she acquired this knowledge, I know not, for Tuckahoe is the last place in the world where she would be apt to find facilities for learning. I can, therefore, fondly and proudly ascribe to her an earnest love of knowledge. That a "field hand" should learn to read, in any slave state, is remarkable; but the achievement of my mother, considering the place, was very extraordinary; and, in view of that fact, I am quite willing, and even happy, to attribute any love of letters I possess, and for which I have got—despite of prejudices only too much credit, *not* to my admitted Anglo-Saxon paternity, but to the native genius of my sable, unprotected, and uncultivated *mother*—a woman, who belonged to a race whose mental endowments it is, at present, fashionable to hold in disparagement and contempt.

Summoned away to her account, with the impassable gulf of slavery between us during her entire illness, my mother died without leaving me a single intimation of *who* my father was. There was a whisper, that my master was my father; yet it was only a whisper, and I cannot say that I ever gave it credence. Indeed, I now have reason to think he was not; nevertheless, the fact remains, in all its glaring odiousness, that, by the laws of slavery, children, in all cases, are reduced to the condition of their mothers. This arrangement admits of the greatest license to brutal slaveholders, and their profligate sons, brothers, relations and friends, and gives to the pleasure of sin, the additional attraction of profit. A whole volume might be written on this single feature of slavery, as I have observed it.

One might imagine, that the children of such connections, would fare better, in the hands of their masters, than other slaves. The rule is quite the other way; and a very little reflection will satisfy the reader that such is the case. A man who will enslave his own blood, may not be safely relied on for magnanimity. Men do not love those who remind them of their sins unless they have a mind to repent—and the mulatto child's face is a standing accusation against him who is master and father to the child. What is still worse, perhaps, such a child is a constant offense to the wife. She hates its very presence, and when a slaveholding woman hates, she wants not means to give that hate telling effect. Women—white women, I mean—are IDOLS at the south, not WIVES, for the slave women are preferred in many instances; and if these *idols* but nod, or lift a finger, woe to the poor victim: kicks, cuffs and stripes are sure to follow. Masters are frequently compelled to sell this class of their slaves, out of deference to the feelings of their white wives; and shocking and scandalous as it may seem for a man to sell his own blood to the traffickers in human flesh, it is often an act of humanity toward the slave-child to be thus removed from his merciless tormentors.

It is not within the scope of the design of my simple story, to comment upon every phase of slavery not within my experience as a slave.

But, I may remark, that, if the lineal descendants of Ham are only to be enslaved, according to the scriptures, slavery in this country will soon become an unscriptural institution; for thousands are ushered into the world, annually, who—like myself—owe their existence to white fathers, and, most frequently, to their masters, and master's sons. The slave-woman is at the mercy of the fathers, sons or brothers of her master. The thoughtful know the rest.

After what I have now said of the circumstances of my mother, and my relations to her, the reader will not be surprised, nor be disposed to censure me, when I tell but the simple truth, viz: that I received the tidings of her death with no strong emotions of sorrow for her, and with very little regret for myself on account of her loss. I had to learn the value of my mother long after her death, and by witnessing the devotion of other mothers to their children.

There is not, beneath the sky, an enemy to filial affection so destructive as slavery. It had made my brothers and sisters strangers to me; it converted the mother that bore me, into a myth; it shrouded my father in mystery, and left me without an intelligible beginning in the world.

My mother died when I could not have been more than eight or nine years old, on one of old master's farms in Tuckahoe, in the neighborhood of Hillsborough. Her grave is, as the grave of the dead at sea, unmarked, and without stone or stake.

CHAPTER IV.
A General Survey of the Slave Plantation

ISOLATION OF LLOYD S PLANTATION—PUBLIC OPINION THERE NO PROTECTION TO THE SLAVE—ABSOLUTE POWER OF THE OVERSEER—NATURAL AND ARTIFICIAL CHARMS OF THE PLACE—ITS BUSINESS-LIKE APPEARANCE—SUPERSTITION ABOUT THE BURIAL GROUND—GREAT IDEAS OF COL. LLOYD—ETIQUETTE AMONG SLAVES—THE COMIC SLAVE DOCTOR—PRAYING AND FLOGGING—OLD MASTER LOSING ITS TERRORS—HIS BUSINESS—CHARACTER OF AUNT KATY—SUFFERINGS FROM HUNGER—OLD MASTER'S HOME—JARGON OF THE PLANTATION—GUINEA SLAVES—MASTER DANIEL—FAMILY OF COL. LLOYD—FAMILY OF CAPT. ANTHONY—HIS SOCIAL POSITION—NOTIONS OF RANK AND STATION.

It is generally supposed that slavery, in the state of Maryland, exists in its mildest form, and that it is totally divested of those harsh and terrible peculiarities, which mark and characterize the slave system, in the southern and south-western states of the American union. The argument in favor of this opinion, is the contiguity of the free states, and the exposed condition of slavery in Maryland to the moral, religious and humane sentiment of the free states.

I am not about to refute this argument, so far as it relates to slavery in that state, generally; on the contrary, I am willing to admit that, to this general point, the arguments is well grounded. Public opinion is, indeed, an unfailing restraint upon the cruelty and barbarity of masters, overseers, and slave-drivers, whenever and wherever it can reach them; but there are certain secluded and out-of-the-way places, even in the state of Maryland, seldom visited by a single ray of healthy public sentiment—where slavery, wrapt in its own congenial, midnight darkness, *can*, and *does*, develop all its malign and shocking characteristics; where it can be indecent without shame, cruel without shuddering, and murderous without apprehension or fear of exposure.

Just such a secluded, dark, and out-of-the-way place, is the "home plantation" of Col. Edward Lloyd, on the Eastern Shore, Maryland. It is far away from all the great thoroughfares, and is proximate to no town or village. There is neither school-house, nor town-house in its neighborhood. The school-house is unnecessary, for there are no children to go to school. The children and grand-children of Col. Lloyd were taught in the house, by a private tutor—a Mr. Page a tall, gaunt sapling of a man, who did not speak a dozen words to a slave in a whole year. The overseers' children go off somewhere to school; and they, therefore, bring no foreign or dangerous influence from abroad, to embarrass the natural operation of the slave system of the place. Not even the mechanics—through whom there is an occasional out-burst of honest and telling indignation, at cruelty and wrong on other plantations—are white men, on this plantation. Its whole public is made up of, and divided into, three classes—SLAVEHOLDERS, SLAVES and OVERSEERS. Its blacksmiths, wheelwrights, shoemakers, weavers, and coopers, are slaves. Not even commerce, selfish and iron-hearted at it is, and ready, as it ever is, to side with the strong against the weak—the rich against the poor—is trusted or permitted within its secluded precincts. Whether with a view of guarding against the escape of its secrets, I know not, but it is a fact, the every leaf and grain of the produce of this plantation, and those of the neighboring farms belonging to Col. Lloyd, are transported to Baltimore in Col. Lloyd's own vessels; every man and boy on board of which—except the captain—are owned by him. In return, everything brought to the plantation, comes through the same channel. Thus, even the glimmering and unsteady light of trade, which sometimes exerts a civilizing influence, is excluded from this "tabooed" spot.

Nearly all the plantations or farms in the vicinity of the "home plantation" of Col. Lloyd, belong to him; and those which do not, are owned by personal friends of his, as deeply interested in maintaining the slave system, in all its rigor, as Col. Lloyd himself. Some of his neighbors are said to be even more stringent than he. The Skinners, the Peakers, the Tilgmans, the Lockermans, and the Gipsons, are in the same boat; being slaveholding neighbors, they may have strengthened each other in their iron rule. They are on intimate terms, and their interests and tastes are identical.

Public opinion in such a quarter, the reader will see, is not likely to very efficient in protecting the slave from cruelty. On the contrary, it must increase and intensify his wrongs. Public opinion seldom differs very widely from public practice. To be a restraint upon cruelty and vice, public opinion must emanate from a humane and virtuous community. To no such humane and virtuous community, is Col. Lloyd's plantation exposed. That plantation is a little nation of its own, having its own language, its own rules, regulations and customs. The laws and institutions of the state, apparently touch it nowhere. The troubles arising here, are not settled by the civil power of the state. The overseer is generally accuser, judge, jury, advocate and executioner. The criminal is always dumb. The overseer attends to all sides of a case.

There are no conflicting rights of property, for all the people are owned by one man; and they can themselves own no property. Religion and politics are alike excluded. One class of the population is too high to be reached by the preacher; and the other class is too low to be cared for by the preacher. The poor have the gospel preached to them, in this neighborhood, only when they are able to pay for it. The slaves, having no money, get no gospel. The politician keeps away, because the people have no votes, and the preacher keeps away, because the people have no money. The rich planter can afford to learn politics in the parlor, and to dispense with religion altogether.

In its isolation, seclusion, and self-reliant independence, Col. Lloyd's plantation resembles what the baronial domains were during the middle ages in Europe. Grim, cold, and unapproachable by all genial influences from communities without, *there it stands;* full three hundred years behind the age, in all that relates to humanity and morals.

This, however, is not the only view that the place presents. Civilization is shut out, but nature cannot be. Though separated from the rest of the world; though public opinion, as I have said, seldom gets a chance to penetrate its dark domain; though the whole place is stamped with its own peculiar, ironlike individuality; and though crimes, high-handed and atrocious, may there be committed, with almost as much impunity as upon the deck of a pirate ship—it is, nevertheless, altogether, to outward seeming, a most strikingly interesting place, full of life, activity, and spirit; and presents a very favorable contrast to the indolent monotony and languor of Tuckahoe. Keen as was my regret and great as was my sorrow at leaving the latter, I was not long in adapting myself to this, my new home. A man's troubles are always half disposed of, when he finds endurance his only remedy. I found myself here; there was no getting away; and what remained for me, but to make the best of it? Here were plenty of children to play with, and plenty of places of pleasant resort for boys of my age, and boys older. The little tendrils of affection, so rudely and treacherously broken from around the darling objects of my grandmother's hut, gradually began to extend, and to entwine about the new objects by which I now found myself surrounded.

There was a windmill (always a commanding object to a child's eye) on Long Point—a tract of land dividing Miles river from the Wye a mile or more from my old master's house. There was a creek to swim in, at the bottom of an open flat space, of twenty acres or more, called "the Long Green"—a very beautiful play-ground for the children.

In the river, a short distance from the shore, lying quietly at anchor, with her small boat dancing at her stern, was a large sloop—the Sally Lloyd; called by that name in honor of a favorite daughter of the colonel. The sloop and the mill were wondrous things, full of thoughts and ideas. A child cannot well look at such objects without *thinking*.

Then here were a great many houses; human habitations, full of the mysteries of life at every stage of it. There was the little red house, up the road, occupied by Mr. Sevier, the overseer. A little nearer to my old master's, stood a very long, rough, low building, literally alive with slaves, of all ages, conditions and sizes. This was called "the Longe Quarter." Perched upon a hill, across the Long

Green, was a very tall, dilapidated, old brick building—the architectural dimensions of which proclaimed its erection for a different purpose—now occupied by slaves, in a similar manner to the Long Quarter. Besides these, there were numerous other slave houses and huts, scattered around in the neighborhood, every nook and corner of which was completely occupied. Old master's house, a long, brick building, plain, but substantial, stood in the center of the plantation life, and constituted one independent establishment on the premises of Col. Lloyd.

Besides these dwellings, there were barns, stables, store-houses, and tobacco-houses; blacksmiths' shops, wheelwrights' shops, coopers' shops—all objects of interest; but, above all, there stood the grandest building my eyes had then ever beheld, called, by every one on the plantation, the "Great House." This was occupied by Col. Lloyd and his family. They occupied it; *I* enjoyed it. The great house was surrounded by numerous and variously shaped out-buildings. There were kitchens, wash-houses, dairies, summer-house, green-houses, hen-houses, turkey-houses, pigeon-houses, and arbors, of many sizes and devices, all neatly painted, and altogether interspersed with grand old trees, ornamental and primitive, which afforded delightful shade in summer, and imparted to the scene a high degree of stately beauty. The great house itself was a large, white, wooden building, with wings on three sides of it. In front, a large portico, extending the entire length of the building, and supported by a long range of columns, gave to the whole establishment an air of solemn grandeur. It was a treat to my young and gradually opening mind, to behold this elaborate exhibition of wealth, power, and vanity. The carriage entrance to the house was a large gate, more than a quarter of a mile distant from it; the intermediate space was a beautiful lawn, very neatly trimmed, and watched with the greatest care. It was dotted thickly over with delightful trees, shrubbery, and flowers. The road, or lane, from the gate to the great house, was richly paved with white pebbles from the beach, and, in its course, formed a complete circle around the beautiful lawn. Carriages going in and retiring from the great house, made the circuit of the lawn, and their passengers were permitted to behold a scene of almost Eden-like beauty. Outside this select inclosure, were parks, where as about the residences of the English nobility—rabbits, deer, and other wild game, might be seen, peering and playing about, with none to molest them or make them afraid. The tops of the stately poplars were often covered with the red-winged black-birds, making all nature vocal with the joyous life and beauty of their wild, warbling notes. These all belonged to me, as well as to Col. Edward Lloyd, and for a time I greatly enjoyed them.

A short distance from the great house, were the stately mansions of the dead, a place of somber aspect. Vast tombs, embowered beneath the weeping willow and the fir tree, told of the antiquities of the Lloyd family, as well as of their wealth. Superstition was rife among the slaves about this family burying ground. Strange sights had been seen there by some of the older slaves. Shrouded ghosts, riding on great black horses, had been seen to enter; balls of fire had been seen to fly there at midnight, and horrid sounds had been repeatedly heard. Slaves know enough of the rudiments of theology to believe that those go to hell who die slaveholders; and they often fancy such persons wishing themselves back again, to wield the lash. Tales of sights and sounds, strange and terrible, connected with the huge black tombs, were a very great security to the grounds about them, for few of the slaves felt like approaching them even in the day time. It was a dark, gloomy and forbidding place, and it was difficult to feel that the spirits of the sleeping dust there deposited, reigned with the blest in the realms of eternal peace.

The business of twenty or thirty farms was transacted at this, called, by way of eminence, "great house farm." These farms all belonged to Col. Lloyd, as did, also, the slaves upon them. Each farm was under the management of an overseer. As I have said of the overseer of the home plantation, so I may say of the overseers on the smaller ones; they stand between the slave and all civil constitutions—their word is law, and is implicitly obeyed.

The colonel, at this time, was reputed to be, and he apparently was, very rich. His slaves, alone, were an immense fortune. These, small and great, could not have been fewer than one thousand in number, and though scarcely a month passed without the sale of one or more lots to the Georgia traders, there was no apparent diminution in the number of his human stock: the home plantation merely groaned at a removal of the young increase, or human crop, then proceeded as lively as ever. Horse-shoeing, cart-mending, plow-repairing, coopering, grinding, and weaving, for all the neighboring farms, were performed here, and slaves were employed in all these branches. "Uncle Tony" was the blacksmith; "Uncle Harry" was the cartwright; "Uncle Abel" was the shoemaker; and all these had hands to assist them in their several departments.

These mechanics were called "uncles" by all the younger slaves, not because they really sustained that relationship to any, but according to plantation *etiquette*, as a mark of respect, due from the younger to the older slaves. Strange, and even ridiculous as it may seem, among a people so uncultivated, and with so many stern trials to look in the face, there is not to be found, among any people, a more rigid enforcement of the law of respect to elders, than they maintain. I set this down as partly constitutional with my race, and partly conventional. There is no better material in the world for making a gentleman, than is furnished in the African. He shows to others, and exacts for himself, all the tokens of respect which he is compelled to manifest toward his master. A young slave must approach the company of the older with hat in hand, and woe betide him, if he fails to acknowledge a favor, of any sort, with the accustomed *"tank'ee,"* &c. So uniformly are good manners enforced among slaves, I can easily detect a "bogus" fugitive by his manners.

Among other slave notabilities of the plantation, was one called by everybody Uncle Isaac Copper. It is seldom that a slave gets a surname from anybody in Maryland; and so completely has the south shaped the manners of the north, in this respect, that even abolitionists make very little of the surname of a Negro. The only improvement on the "Bills," "Jacks," "Jims," and "Neds" of the south, observable here is, that "William," "John," "James," "Edward," are substituted. It goes against the grain to treat and address a Negro precisely as they would treat and address a white man. But, once in a while, in slavery as in the free states, by some extraordinary circumstance, the Negro has a surname fastened to him, and holds it against all conventionalities. This was the case with Uncle Isaac Copper. When the "uncle" was dropped, he generally had the prefix "doctor," in its stead. He was our doctor of medicine, and doctor of divinity as well. Where he took his degree I am unable to say, for he was not very communicative to inferiors, and I was emphatically such, being but a boy seven or eight years old. He was too well established in his profession to permit questions as to his native skill, or his attainments. One qualification he undoubtedly had—he was a confirmed *cripple*; and he could neither work, nor would he bring anything if offered for sale in the market. The old man, though lame, was no sluggard. He was a man that made his crutches do him good service. He was always on the alert, looking up the sick, and all such as were supposed to need his counsel. His remedial prescriptions embraced four articles. For diseases of the body, *Epsom salts and castor oil;* for those of the soul, *the Lord's Prayer,* and *hickory switches*!

I was not long at Col. Lloyd's before I was placed under the care of Doctor Issac Copper. I was sent to him with twenty or thirty other children, to learn the "Lord's Prayer." I found the old gentleman seated on a huge three-legged oaken stool, armed with several large hickory switches; and, from his position, he could reach—lame as he was—any boy in the room. After standing awhile to learn what was expected of us, the old gentleman, in any other than a devotional tone, commanded us to kneel down. This done, he commenced telling us to say everything he said. "Our Father"—this was repeated after him with promptness and uniformity; "Who art in heaven"—was less promptly and uniformly repeated; and the old gentleman paused in the prayer, to give us a short lecture upon the consequences of inattention, both immediate and future, and especially those more immediate. About these he was absolutely certain, for he held in his right hand the means of bringing all his predictions and warnings to pass. On he proceeded with the prayer; and we with our thick tongues and unskilled ears, followed him to the best of our ability. This, however, was not sufficient to please the old gentleman. Everybody, in the south, wants the privilege of whipping somebody else. Uncle Isaac shared the common passion of his country, and, therefore, seldom found any means of keeping his disciples in order short of flogging. "Say everything I say;" and bang would come the switch on some poor boy's undevotional head. *"What you looking at there"*—*"Stop that pushing"*—and down again would come the lash.

The whip is all in all. It is supposed to secure obedience to the slaveholder, and is held as a sovereign remedy among the slaves themselves, for every form of disobedience, temporal or spiritual. Slaves, as well as slaveholders, use it with an unsparing hand. Our devotions at Uncle Isaac's combined too much of the tragic and comic, to make them very salutary in a spiritual point of view;

and it is due to truth to say, I was often a truant when the time for attending the praying and flogging of Doctor Isaac Copper came on.

The windmill under the care of Mr. Kinney, a kind hearted old Englishman, was to me a source of infinite interest and pleasure. The old man always seemed pleased when he saw a troop of darkey little urchins, with their tow-linen shirts fluttering in the breeze, approaching to view and admire the whirling wings of his wondrous machine. From the mill we could see other objects of deep interest. These were, the vessels from St. Michael's, on their way to Baltimore. It was a source of much amusement to view the flowing sails and complicated rigging, as the little crafts dashed by, and to speculate upon Baltimore, as to the kind and quality of the place. With so many sources of interest around me, the reader may be prepared to learn that I began to think very highly of Col. L.'s plantation. It was just a place to my boyish taste. There were fish to be caught in the creek, if one only had a hook and line; and crabs, clams and oysters were to be caught by wading, digging and raking for them. Here was a field for industry and enterprise, strongly inviting; and the reader may be assured that I entered upon it with spirit.

Even the much dreaded old master, whose merciless fiat had brought me from Tuckahoe, gradually, to my mind, parted with his terrors. Strange enough, his reverence seemed to take no particular notice of me, nor of my coming. Instead of leaping out and devouring me, he scarcely seemed conscious of my presence. The fact is, he was occupied with matters more weighty and important than either looking after or vexing me. He probably thought as little of my advent, as he would have thought of the addition of a single pig to his stock!

As the chief butler on Col. Lloyd's plantation, his duties were numerous and perplexing. In almost all important matters he answered in Col. Lloyd's stead. The overseers of all the farms were in some sort under him, and received the law from his mouth. The colonel himself seldom addressed an overseer, or allowed an overseer to address him. Old master carried the keys of all store houses; measured out the allowance for each slave at the end of every month; superintended the storing of all goods brought to the plantation; dealt out the raw material to all the handicraftsmen; shipped the grain, tobacco, and all saleable produce of the plantation to market, and had the general oversight of the coopers' shop, wheelwrights' shop, blacksmiths' shop, and shoemakers' shop. Besides the care of these, he often had business for the plantation which required him to be absent two and three days.

Thus largely employed, he had little time, and perhaps as little disposition, to interfere with the children individually. What he was to Col. Lloyd, he made Aunt Katy to him. When he had anything to say or do about us, it was said or done in a wholesale manner; disposing of us in classes or sizes, leaving all minor details to Aunt Katy, a person of whom the reader has already received no very favorable impression. Aunt Katy was a woman who never allowed herself to act greatly within the margin of power granted to her, no matter how broad that authority might be. Ambitious, ill-tempered and cruel, she found in her present position an ample field for the exercise of her ill-omened qualities. She had a strong hold on old master she was considered a first rate cook, and she really was very industrious. She was, therefore, greatly favored by old master, and as one mark of his favor, she was the only mother who was permitted to retain her children around her. Even to these children she was often fiendish in her brutality. She pursued her son Phil, one day, in my presence, with a huge butcher knife, and dealt a blow with its edge which left a shocking gash on his arm, near the wrist. For this, old master did sharply rebuke her, and threatened that if she ever should do the like again, he would take the skin off her back. Cruel, however, as Aunt Katy was to her own children, at times she was not destitute of maternal feeling, as I often had occasion to know, in the bitter pinches of hunger I had to endure. Differing from the practice of Col. Lloyd, old master, instead of allowing so much for each slave, committed the allowance for all to the care of Aunt Katy, to be divided after cooking it, amongst us. The allowance, consisting of coarse corn-meal, was not very abundant—indeed, it was very slender; and in passing through Aunt Katy's hands, it was made more slender still, for some of us. William, Phil and Jerry were her children, and it is not to accuse her too severely, to allege that she was often guilty of starving myself and the other children, while she was literally cramming her own. Want of food was my chief trouble the first summer at my old master's. Oysters and clams would do very well, with an occasional supply of bread, but they soon failed in the absence of bread. I speak but the simple truth, when I say, I have often been so pinched with hunger, that I have fought with the dog—"Old Nep"—for the smallest crumbs that fell from the kitchen table, and have been glad when I won a single crumb in the combat. Many times have I followed, with eager step, the waiting-girl when she went out to shake the table cloth, to get the crumbs and small bones flung out for the cats. The water, in which meat had been boiled, was as eagerly sought for by me. It was a great thing to get the privilege of dipping a piece of bread in such water; and the skin taken from rusty bacon, was a positive luxury. Nevertheless, I sometimes got full meals and kind words from sympathizing old slaves, who knew my sufferings, and received the comforting assurance that I should be a man some day. "Never mind, honey—better day comin'," was even then a solace, a cheering consolation to me in my troubles. Nor were all the kind words I received from slaves. I had a friend in the parlor, as well, and one to whom I shall be glad to do justice, before I have finished this part of my story.

I was not long at old master's, before I learned that his surname was Anthony, and that he was generally called "Captain Anthony"—a title which he probably acquired by sailing a craft in the Chesapeake Bay. Col. Lloyd's slaves never called Capt. Anthony "old master," but always Capt. Anthony; and *me* they called "Captain Anthony Fred." There is not, probably, in the whole south, a plantation where the English language is more imperfectly spoken than on Col. Lloyd's. It is a mixture of Guinea and everything else you please. At the time of which I am now writing, there were slaves there who had been brought from the coast of Africa. They never used the "s" in indication of the possessive case. "Cap'n Ant'ney Tom," "Lloyd Bill," "Aunt Rose Harry," means "Captain Anthony's Tom," "Lloyd's Bill," &c. *"Oo you dem long to?"* means, "Whom do you belong to?" *"Oo dem got any peachy?"* means, "Have you got any peaches?" I could scarcely understand them when I first went among them, so broken was their speech; and I am persuaded that I could not have been dropped anywhere on the globe, where I could reap less, in the way of knowledge, from my immediate associates, than on this plantation. Even "MAS' DANIEL," by his association with his father's slaves, had measurably adopted their dialect and their ideas, so far as they had ideas to be adopted. The equality of nature is strongly asserted in childhood, and childhood requires children for associates. *Color* makes no difference with a child. Are you a child with wants, tastes and pursuits common to children, not put on, but natural? then, were you black as ebony you would be welcome to the child of alabaster whiteness. The law of compensation holds here, as well as elsewhere. Mas' Daniel could not associate with ignorance without sharing its shade; and he could not give his black playmates his company, without giving them his intelligence, as well. Without knowing this, or caring about it, at the time, I, for some cause or other, spent much of my time with Mas' Daniel, in preference to spending it with most of the other boys.

Mas' Daniel was the youngest son of Col. Lloyd; his older brothers were Edward and Murray—both grown up, and fine looking men. Edward was especially esteemed by the children, and by me among the rest; not that he ever said anything to us or for us, which could be called especially kind; it was enough for us, that he never looked nor acted scornfully toward us. There were also three sisters, all married; one to Edward Winder; a second to Edward Nicholson; a third to Mr. Lownes.

The family of old master consisted of two sons, Andrew and Richard; his daughter, Lucretia, and her newly married husband, Capt. Auld. This was the house family. The kitchen family consisted of Aunt Katy, Aunt Esther, and ten or a dozen children, most of them older than myself. Capt. Anthony was not considered a rich slaveholder, but was pretty well off in the world. He owned about thirty *"head"* of slaves, and three farms in Tuckahoe. The most valuable part of his property was his slaves, of whom he could afford to sell one every year. This crop, therefore, brought him seven or eight hundred dollars a year, besides his yearly salary, and other revenue from his farms.

The idea of rank and station was rigidly maintained on Col. Lloyd's plantation. Our family never visited the great house, and the Lloyds never came to our home. Equal non-intercourse was observed between Capt. Anthony's family and that of Mr. Sevier, the overseer.

Such, kind reader, was the community, and such the place, in which my earliest and most lasting impressions of slavery, and of slave-life, were received; of which impressions you will learn more in the coming chapters of this book.

CHAPTER V.
Gradual Initiation to the Mysteries of Slavery

GROWING ACQUAINTANCE WITH OLD MASTER—HIS CHARACTER—EVILS OF UNRESTRAINED PASSION—APPARENT TENDERNESS—OLD MASTER A MAN OF TROUBLE—CUSTOM OF MUTTERING TO HIMSELF—NECESSITY OF BEING AWARE OF HIS WORDS—THE SUPPOSED OBTUSENESS OF SLAVE-CHILDREN—BRUTAL OUTRAGE—DRUNKEN OVERSEER—SLAVEHOLDER'S IMPATIENCE—WISDOM OF APPEALING TO SUPERIORS—THE SLAVEHOLDER S WRATH BAD AS THAT OF THE OVERSEER—A BASE AND SELFISH ATTEMPT TO BREAK UP A COURTSHIP—A HARROWING SCENE.

Although my old master—Capt. Anthony—gave me at first, (as the reader will have already seen) very little attention, and although that little was of a remarkably mild and gentle description, a few months only were sufficient to convince me that mildness and gentleness were not the prevailing or governing traits of his character. These excellent qualities were displayed only occasionally. He could, when it suited him, appear to be literally insensible to the claims of humanity, when appealed to by the helpless against an aggressor, and he could himself commit outrages, deep, dark and nameless. Yet he was not by nature worse than other men. Had he been brought up in a free state, surrounded by the just restraints of free society—restraints which are necessary to the freedom of all its members, alike and equally—Capt. Anthony might have been as humane a man, and every way as respectable, as many who now oppose the slave system; certainly as humane and respectable as are members of society generally. The slaveholder, as well as the slave, is the victim of the slave system. A man's character greatly takes its hue and shape from the form and color of things about him. Under the whole heavens there is no relation more unfavorable to the development of honorable character, than that sustained by the slaveholder to the slave. Reason is imprisoned here, and passions run wild. Like the fires of the prairie, once lighted, they are at the mercy of every wind, and must burn, till they have consumed all that is combustible within their remorseless grasp. Capt. Anthony could be kind, and, at times, he even showed an affectionate disposition. Could the reader have seen him gently leading me by the hand—as he sometimes did—patting me on the head, speaking to me in soft, caressing tones and calling me his "little Indian boy," he would have deemed him a kind old man, and really, almost fatherly. But the pleasant moods of a slaveholder are remarkably brittle; they are easily snapped; they neither come often, nor remain long. His temper is subjected to perpetual trials; but, since these trials are never borne patiently, they add nothing to his natural stock of patience.

Old master very early impressed me with the idea that he was an unhappy man. Even to my child's eye, he wore a troubled, and at times, a haggard aspect. His strange movements excited my curiosity, and awakened my compassion. He seldom walked alone without muttering to himself; and he occasionally stormed about, as if defying an army of invisible foes. "He would do this, that, and the other; he'd be d—d if he did not,"—was the usual form of his threats. Most of his leisure was spent in walking, cursing and gesticulating, like one possessed by a demon. Most evidently, he was a wretched man, at war with his own soul, and with all the world around him. To be overheard by the children, disturbed him very little. He made no more of our presence, than of that of the ducks and geese which he met on the green. He little thought that the little black urchins around him, could see, through those vocal crevices, the very secrets of his heart. Slaveholders ever underrate the intelligence with which they have to grapple. I really understood the old man's mutterings, attitudes and gestures, about as well as he did himself. But slaveholders never encourage that kind of communication, with the slaves, by which they might learn to measure the depths of his knowledge. Ignorance is a high virtue in a human chattel; and as the master studies to keep the slave ignorant, the slave is cunning enough to make the master think he succeeds. The slave fully appreciates the saying, "where ignorance is bliss, 'tis folly to be wise." When old master's gestures were violent, ending with a threatening shake of the head, and a sharp snap of his middle finger and thumb, I deemed it wise to keep at a respectable distance from him; for, at such times, trifling faults stood, in his eyes, as momentous offenses; and, having both the power and the disposition, the victim had only to be near him to catch the punishment, deserved or undeserved.

One of the first circumstances that opened my eyes to the cruelty and wickedness of slavery, and the heartlessness of my old master, was the refusal of the latter to interpose his authority, to protect and shield a young woman, who had been most cruelly abused and beaten by his overseer in Tuckahoe. This overseer—a Mr. Plummer—was a man like most of his class, little better than a human brute; and, in addition to his general profligacy and repulsive coarseness, the creature was a miserable drunkard. He was, probably, employed by my old master, less on account of the excellence of his services, than for the cheap rate at which they could be obtained. He was not fit to have the management of a drove of mules. In a fit of drunken madness, he committed the outrage which brought the young woman in question down to my old master's for protection. This young woman was the daughter of Milly, an own aunt of mine. The poor girl, on arriving at our house, presented a pitiable appearance. She had left in haste, and without preparation; and, probably, without the knowledge of Mr. Plummer. She had traveled twelve miles, bare-footed, bare-necked and bare-headed. Her neck and shoulders were covered with scars, newly made; and not content with marring her neck and shoulders, with the cowhide, the cowardly brute had dealt her a blow on the head with a hickory club, which cut a horrible gash, and left her face literally covered with blood. In this condition, the poor young woman came down, to implore protection at the hands of my old master. I expected to see him boil over with rage at the revolting deed, and to hear him fill the air with curses upon the brutal Plummer; but I was disappointed. He sternly told her, in an angry tone, he "believed she deserved every bit of it," and, if she did not go home instantly, he would himself take the remaining skin from her neck and back. Thus was the poor girl compelled to return, without redress, and perhaps to receive an additional flogging for daring to appeal to old master against the overseer.

Old master seemed furious at the thought of being troubled by such complaints. I did not, at that time, understand the philosophy of his treatment of my cousin. It was stern, unnatural, violent. Had the man no bowels of compassion? Was he dead to all sense of humanity? No. I think I now understand it. This treatment is a part of the system, rather than a part of the man. Were slaveholders to listen to complaints of this sort against the overseers, the luxury of owning large numbers of slaves, would be impossible. It would do away with the office of overseer, entirely; or, in other words, it would convert the master himself into an overseer. It would occasion great loss of time and labor, leaving the overseer in fetters, and without the necessary power to secure obedience to his orders. A privilege so dangerous as that of appeal, is, therefore, strictly prohibited; and any one exercising it, runs a fearful hazard. Nevertheless, when a slave has nerve enough to exercise it, and boldly approaches his master, with a well-founded complaint against an overseer, though he may be repulsed, and may even have that of which he complains repeated at the time, and, though he may be beaten by his master, as well as by the overseer, for his temerity, in the end the policy of complaining is, generally, vindicated by the relaxed rigor of the overseer's treatment. The latter becomes more careful, and less disposed to use the lash upon such slaves thereafter. It is with this final result in view, rather than with any expectation of immediate good, that the outraged slave is induced to meet his master with a complaint. The overseer very naturally dislikes to have the ear of the master disturbed by complaints; and, either upon this consideration, or upon advice and warning privately given him by his employers, he generally modifies the rigor of his rule, after an outbreak of the kind to which I have been referring.

Howsoever the slaveholder may allow himself to act toward his slave, and, whatever cruelty he may deem it wise, for example's sake, or for the gratification of his humor, to inflict, he cannot, in the absence of all provocation, look with pleasure upon the bleeding wounds of a defenseless slave-woman. When he drives her from his presence without redress, or the hope of redress, he acts, generally, from motives of policy, rather than from a hardened nature, or from innate brutality. Yet, let but his own temper be stirred, his own passions get loose, and the slave-owner will go *far beyond* the overseer in cruelty. He will convince the slave that his wrath is far more terrible and boundless, and vastly more to be dreaded, than that of the underling overseer. What may have been mechanically and heartlessly done by the overseer, is now done with a will. The man who now wields the lash is irresponsible. He may, if he pleases, cripple or kill, without fear of consequences; except in so far as it may concern profit or loss. To a man of violent temper—as my old master was—this was but a very slender and inefficient restraint. I have seen him in a tempest of passion, such as I have just described—a passion into which entered all the bitter ingredients of pride, hatred, envy, jealousy, and the thrist(sic) for revenge.

The circumstances which I am about to narrate, and which gave rise to this fearful tempest of passion, are not singular nor isolated in slave life, but are common in every slaveholding community in which I have lived. They are incidental to the relation of master and slave, and exist in all sections of slave-holding countries.

The reader will have noticed that, in enumerating the names of the slaves who lived with my old master, *Esther* is mentioned. This was a young woman who possessed that which is ever a curse to the slave-girl; namely—personal beauty. She was tall, well formed, and made a fine appearance. The daughters of Col. Lloyd could scarcely surpass her in personal charms. Esther was courted by Ned Roberts, and he was as fine looking a young man, as she was a woman. He was the son of a favorite slave of Col. Lloyd. Some slaveholders would have been glad to promote the marriage of two such persons; but, for some reason or other, my old master took it upon him to break up the growing intimacy between Esther and Edward. He strictly ordered her to quit the company of said Roberts, telling her that he would punish her severely if he ever found her again in Edward's company. This unnatural and heartless order was, of course, broken. A woman's love is not to be annihilated by the peremptory command of any one, whose breath is in his nostrils. It was impossible to keep Edward and Esther apart. Meet they would, and meet they did. Had old master been a man of honor and purity, his motives, in this matter, might have been viewed more favorably. As it was, his motives were as abhorrent, as his methods were foolish and contemptible. It was too evident that he was not concerned for the girl's welfare. It is one of the damning characteristics of the slave system, that it robs its victims of every earthly incentive to a holy life. The fear of God, and the hope of heaven, are found sufficient to sustain many slave-women, amidst the snares and dangers of their strange lot; but, this side of God and heaven, a slave-woman is at the mercy of the power, caprice and passion of her owner. Slavery provides no means for the honorable continuance of the race. Marriage as imposing obligations on the parties to it—has no existence here, except in such hearts as are purer and higher than the standard morality around them. It is one of the consolations of my life, that I know of many honorable instances of persons who maintained their honor, where all around was corrupt.

Esther was evidently much attached to Edward, and abhorred—as she had reason to do—the tyrannical and base behavior of old master. Edward was young, and fine looking, and he loved and courted her. He might have been her husband, in the high sense just alluded to; but WHO and *what* was this old master? His attentions were plainly brutal and selfish, and it was as natural that Esther should loathe him, as that she should love Edward. Abhorred and circumvented as he was, old master, having the power, very easily took revenge. I happened to see this exhibition of his rage and cruelty toward Esther. The time selected was singular. It was early in the morning, when all besides was still, and before any of the family, in the house or kitchen, had left their beds. I saw but few of the shocking preliminaries, for the cruel work had begun before I awoke. I was probably awakened by the shrieks and piteous cries of poor Esther. My sleeping place was on the floor of a little, rough closet, which opened into the kitchen; and through the cracks of its unplaned boards, I could distinctly see and hear what was going on, without being seen by old master. Esther's wrists were firmly tied, and the twisted rope was fastened to a strong staple in a heavy wooden joist above, near the fireplace. Here she stood, on a bench, her arms tightly drawn over her breast. Her back and shoulders were bare to the waist. Behind her stood old master, with cowskin in hand, preparing his barbarous work with all manner of harsh, coarse, and tantalizing epithets. The screams of his victim were most piercing. He was cruelly deliberate, and protracted the torture, as one who was delighted with the scene. Again and again he drew the hateful whip through his hand, adjusting it with a view of dealing the most pain-giving blow. Poor Esther had never yet been severely whipped, and her shoulders were plump and tender. Each blow, vigorously laid on, brought screams as well as blood. *"Have mercy; Oh! have mercy"* she cried; *"I won't do so no more;"* but her piercing cries seemed only to increase his fury. His answers to them are too coarse and blasphemous to be produced here. The whole scene, with all its attendants, was revolting and shocking, to the last degree; and when the motives of this brutal castigation are considered,—language has no power to convey a just sense of its awful criminality. After laying on some thirty or forty stripes, old master untied his suffering victim, and let her get down. She could scarcely stand, when untied. From my heart I pitied her, and—child though I was—the outrage kindled in me a feeling far from peaceful; but I was hushed, terrified, stunned, and could do nothing, and the fate of Esther might be mine next. The scene here described was often repeated in the case of poor Esther, and her life, as I knew it, was one of wretchedness.

CHAPTER VI.
TREATMENT OF SLAVES ON LLOYD'S PLANTATION

EARLY REFLECTIONS ON SLAVERY—PRESENTIMENT OF ONE DAY BEING A FREEMAN—COMBAT BETWEEN AN OVERSEER AND A SLAVEWOMAN—THE ADVANTAGES OF RESISTANCE—ALLOWANCE DAY ON THE HOME PLANTATION—THE SINGING OF SLAVES—AN EXPLANATION—THE SLAVES FOOD AND CLOTHING—NAKED CHILDREN—LIFE IN THE QUARTER—DEPRIVATION OF SLEEP—NURSING CHILDREN CARRIED TO THE FIELD—DESCRIPTION OF THE COWSKIN—THE ASH-CAKE—MANNER OF MAKING IT—THE DINNER HOUR—THE CONTRAST.

The heart-rending incidents, related in the foregoing chapter, led me, thus early, to inquire into the nature and history of slavery. *Why am I a slave? Why are some people slaves, and others masters? Was there ever a time this was not so? How did the relation commence?* These were the perplexing questions which began now to claim my thoughts, and to exercise the weak powers of my mind, for I was still but a child, and knew less than children of the same age in the free states. As my questions concerning these things were only put to children a little older, and little better informed than myself, I was not rapid in reaching a solid footing. By some means I learned from these inquiries that *"God, up in the sky,"* made every body; and that he made *white* people to be masters and mistresses, and *black* people to be slaves. This did not satisfy me, nor lessen my interest in the subject. I was told, too, that God was good, and that He knew what was best for me, and best for everybody. This was less satisfactory than the first statement; because it came, point blank, against all my notions of goodness. It was not good to let old master cut the flesh off Esther, and make her cry so. Besides, how did people know that God made black people to be slaves? Did they go up in the sky and learn it? or, did He come down and tell them so? All was dark here. It was some relief to my hard notions of the goodness of God, that, although he made white men to be slaveholders, he did not make them to be *bad* slaveholders, and that, in due time, he would punish the bad slaveholders; that he would, when they died, send them to the bad place, where they would be "burnt up." Nevertheless, I could not reconcile the relation of slavery with my crude notions of goodness.

Then, too, I found that there were puzzling exceptions to this theory of slavery on both sides, and in the middle. I knew of blacks who were *not* slaves; I knew of whites who were *not* slaveholders; and I knew of persons who were *nearly* white, who were slaves. *Color*, therefore, was a very unsatisfactory basis for slavery.

Once, however, engaged in the inquiry, I was not very long in finding out the true solution of the matter. It was not *color*, but *crime*, not *God*, but *man*, that afforded the true explanation of the existence of slavery; nor was I long in finding out another important truth, viz: what man can make, man can unmake. The appalling darkness faded away, and I was master of the subject. There were slaves here, direct from Guinea; and there were many who could say that their fathers and mothers were stolen from Africa—forced from their homes, and compelled to serve as slaves. This, to me, was knowledge; but it was a kind of knowledge which filled me with a burning hatred of slavery, increased my suffering, and left me without the means of breaking away from my bondage. Yet it was knowledge quite worth possessing. I could not have been more than seven or eight years old, when I began to make this subject my study. It was with me in the woods and fields; along the shore of the river, and wherever my boyish wanderings led me; and though I was, at that time, quite ignorant of the existence of the free states, I distinctly remember being, *even then*, most strongly impressed with the idea of being a freeman some day. This cheering assurance was an inborn dream of my human nature a constant menace to slavery—and one which all the powers of slavery were unable to silence or extinguish.

Up to the time of the brutal flogging of my Aunt Esther—for she was my own aunt—and the horrid plight in which I had seen my cousin from Tuckahoe, who had been so badly beaten by the cruel Mr. Plummer, my attention had not been called, especially, to the gross features of slavery. I had, of course, heard of whippings and of savage *rencontres* between overseers and slaves, but I had always been out of the way at the times and places of their occurrence. My plays and sports, most of the time, took me from the corn and tobacco fields, where the great body of the hands were at work, and where scenes of cruelty were enacted and witnessed. But, after the whipping of Aunt Esther, I saw many cases of the same shocking nature, not only in my master's house, but on Col. Lloyd's plantation. One of the first which I saw, and which greatly agitated me, was the whipping of a woman belonging to Col. Lloyd, named Nelly. The offense alleged against Nelly, was one of the commonest and most indefinite in the whole catalogue of offenses usually laid to the charge of slaves, viz: "impudence." This may mean almost anything, or nothing at all, just according to the caprice of the master or overseer, at the moment. But, whatever it is, or is not, if it gets the name of "impudence," the party charged with it is sure of a flogging. This offense may be committed in various ways; in the tone of an answer; in answering at all; in not answering; in the expression of countenance; in the motion of the head; in the gait, manner and bearing of the slave. In the case under consideration, I can easily believe that, according to all slaveholding standards, here was a genuine instance of impudence. In Nelly there were all the necessary conditions for committing the offense. She was a bright mulatto, the recognized wife of a favorite "hand" on board Col. Lloyd's sloop, and the mother of five sprightly children. She was a vigorous and spirited woman, and one of the most likely, on the plantation, to be guilty of impudence. My attention was called to the scene, by the noise, curses and screams that proceeded from it; and, on going a little in that direction, I came upon the parties engaged in the skirmish. Mr. Siever, the overseer, had hold of Nelly, when I caught sight of them; he was endeavoring to drag her toward a tree, which endeavor Nelly was sternly resisting; but to no purpose, except to retard the progress of the overseer's plans. Nelly—as I have said—was the mother of five children; three of them were present, and though quite small (from seven to ten years old, I should think) they gallantly came to their mother's defense, and gave the overseer an excellent pelting with stones. One of the little fellows ran up, seized the overseer by the leg and bit him; but the monster was too busily engaged with Nelly, to pay any attention to the assaults of the children. There were numerous bloody marks on Mr. Sevier's face, when I first saw him, and they increased as the struggle went on. The imprints of Nelly's fingers were visible, and I was glad to see them. Amidst the wild screams of the children—"*Let my mammy go*"—"*let my mammy go*"—there escaped, from between the teeth of the bullet-headed overseer, a few bitter curses, mingled with threats, that "he would teach the d—d b—h how to give a white man impudence." There is no doubt that Nelly felt herself superior, in some respects, to the slaves around her. She was a wife and a mother; her husband was a valued and favorite slave. Besides, he was one of the first hands on board of the sloop, and the sloop hands—since they had to represent the plantation abroad—were generally treated tenderly. The overseer never was allowed to whip Harry; why then should he be allowed to whip Harry's wife? Thoughts of this kind, no doubt, influenced her; but, for whatever reason, she nobly resisted, and, unlike most of the slaves, seemed determined to make her whipping cost Mr. Sevier as much as possible. The blood on his (and her) face, attested her skill, as well as her courage and dexterity in using her nails. Maddened by her resistance, I expected to see Mr. Sevier level her to the ground by a stunning blow; but no; like a savage bull-dog—which he resembled both in temper and appearance—he maintained his grip, and steadily dragged his victim toward the tree, disregarding alike her blows, and the cries of the children for their mother's release. He would, doubtless, have knocked her down with his hickory stick, but that such act might have cost him his place. It is often deemed advisable to knock a *man* slave down, in order to tie him, but it is considered cowardly and inexcusable, in an overseer, thus to deal with a *woman*. He is expected to tie her up, and to give her what is called, in southern parlance, a "genteel flogging," without any very great outlay of strength or skill. I watched, with palpitating interest, the course of the preliminary struggle, and was saddened by every new advantage gained over her by the ruffian. There were times when she seemed likely to get the better of the brute, but he finally overpowered her, and succeeded in getting his rope around her arms, and in firmly tying her to the tree, at which he had been aiming. This done, and Nelly was at the mercy of his merciless lash; and now, what followed, I have no heart to describe. The cowardly creature made good his every threat; and wielded the lash with all the hot zest of furious revenge. The cries of the woman, while undergoing the terrible infliction, were mingled with those of the children, sounds which I hope the reader may never be called upon to hear. When Nelly was untied, her back was covered with blood. The red stripes were all over her shoulders. She was whipped—severely whipped; but she was not subdued, for she continued to denounce the overseer, and to call him every vile name. He had bruised her flesh, but had left her invincible spirit undaunted. Such floggings are seldom repeated by the same overseer. They prefer to whip those who are most easily whipped. The old doctrine that submission is the very best cure for outrage and wrong, does not hold good on the slave plantation. He is whipped oftenest, who is whipped easiest; and that slave who has the courage to stand up for himself against the overseer, although he may have many hard stripes at the first, becomes, in the end, a freeman, even though he sustain the formal relation of a slave. "You can shoot me but you can't whip me," said a slave to Rigby Hopkins; and the result was that he was neither whipped nor shot. If the latter had been his fate, it would have been less deplorable than the living and lingering death to which cowardly and slavish souls are subjected. I do not know that Mr. Sevier ever undertook to whip Nelly again. He probably never did, for it was not long after his attempt to subdue her, that he was taken sick, and died. The wretched man died as he had lived, unrepentant; and it was said—with how much truth I know not—that in the very last hours of his life, his ruling passion showed itself, and that when wrestling with death, he was uttering horrid oaths, and flourishing the cowskin, as though he was tearing the flesh off some helpless slave. One thing is certain, that when he was in health, it was enough to chill the blood, and to stiffen the hair of an ordinary man, to hear Mr. Sevier talk. Nature, or his cruel habits, had given to his face an expression of unusual savageness, even for a slave-driver. Tobacco and rage had worn his teeth short, and nearly every sentence that escaped their compressed grating, was commenced or concluded with some outburst of profanity. His presence made the field alike the field of blood, and of blasphemy. Hated for his cruelty, despised for his cowardice, his death was deplored by no one outside his own house—if indeed it was deplored there; it was regarded by the slaves as a merciful interposition of Providence. Never went there a man to the grave loaded with heavier curses. Mr. Sevier's place was promptly taken by a Mr. Hopkins, and the change was quite a relief, he being a very different man. He was, in all respects, a better man than his predecessor; as good as any man can be, and yet be an overseer. His course was characterized by no extraordinary cruelty; and when he whipped a slave, as he sometimes did, he seemed to take no especial pleasure in it, but, on the contrary, acted as though he felt it to be a mean business. Mr. Hopkins stayed but a short time; his place much to the regret of the slaves generally—was taken by a Mr. Gore, of whom more will be said hereafter. It is enough, for the present, to say, that he was no improvement on Mr. Sevier, except that he was less noisy and less profane.

I have already referred to the business-like aspect of Col. Lloyd's plantation. This business-like appearance was much increased on the two days at the end of each month, when the slaves from the different farms came to get their monthly allowance of meal and meat. These were gala days for the slaves, and there was much rivalry among them as to *who* should be elected to go up to the great house farm for the allowance, and, indeed, to attend to any business at this (for them) the capital. The beauty and grandeur of the place, its numerous slave population, and the fact that Harry, Peter and Jake the sailors of the sloop—almost always kept, privately, little trinkets which they bought at Baltimore, to sell, made it a privilege to come to the great house farm. Being selected, too, for this office, was deemed a high honor. It was taken as a proof of confidence and favor; but, probably, the chief motive of the competitors for the place, was, a desire to break the dull monotony of the field, and to get beyond the overseer's eye and lash. Once on the road with an ox team, and seated on the tongue of his cart, with no overseer to look after him, the slave was comparatively free; and, if thoughtful, he had time to think. Slaves are generally expected to sing as well as to work. A silent slave is not liked by masters or overseers. *"Make a noise," "make a noise,"* and *"bear a hand,"* are the words usually addressed to the slaves when there is silence amongst them. This may account for the almost constant singing heard in the southern states. There was, generally, more or less singing among the teamsters, as it was one means of letting the overseer know where they were, and that they were moving on with the work. But, on allowance day, those who visited the great house farm were peculiarly excited and noisy. While on their way, they would make the dense old woods, for miles around, reverberate with their wild notes. These were not always merry because they were wild. On the contrary, they were mostly of a plaintive cast, and told a tale of grief and sorrow. In the most boisterous outbursts of rapturous sentiment, there was ever a tinge of deep melancholy. I have never heard any songs like those anywhere since I left slavery, except when in Ireland. There I heard the same *wailing notes*, and was much affected by them. It was during the famine of 1845-6. In all the songs of the slaves, there was ever some expression in praise of the great house farm; something which would flatter the pride of the owner, and, possibly, draw a favorable glance from him.

> *I am going away to the great house farm,*
> *O yea! O yea! O yea!*
> *My old master is a good old master,*
> *O yea! O yea! O yea!*

This they would sing, with other words of their own improvising—jargon to others, but full of meaning to themselves. I have sometimes thought, that the mere hearing of those songs would do more to impress truly spiritual-minded men and women with the soul-crushing and death-dealing character of slavery, than the reading of whole volumes of its mere physical cruelties. They speak to the heart and to the soul of the thoughtful. I cannot better express my sense of them now, than ten years ago, when, in sketching my life, I thus spoke of this feature of my plantation experience:

I did not, when a slave, understand the deep meanings of those rude, and apparently incoherent songs. I was myself within the circle, so that I neither saw or heard as those without might see and hear. They told a tale which was then altogether beyond my feeble comprehension; they were tones, loud, long and deep, breathing the prayer and complaint of souls boiling over with the bitterest anguish. Every tone was a testimony against slavery, and a prayer to God for deliverance from chains. The hearing of those wild notes always depressed my spirits, and filled my heart with ineffable sadness. The mere recurrence, even now, afflicts my spirit, and while I am writing these lines, my tears are falling. To those songs I trace my first glimmering conceptions of the dehumanizing character of slavery. I can never get rid of that conception. Those songs still follow me, to deepen my hatred of slavery, and quicken my sympathies for my brethren in bonds. If any one wishes to be impressed with a sense of the soul-killing power of slavery, let him go to Col. Lloyd's plantation, and, on allowance day, place himself in the deep, pine woods, and there let him, in silence, thoughtfully analyze the sounds that shall pass through the chambers of his soul, and if he is not thus impressed, it will only be because "there is no flesh in his obdurate heart."

The remark is not unfrequently made, that slaves are the most contended and happy laborers in the world. They dance and sing, and make all manner of joyful noises—so they do; but it is a great mistake to suppose them happy because they sing. The songs of the slave represent the sorrows, rather than the joys, of his heart; and he is relieved by them, only as an aching heart is relieved by its tears. Such is the constitution of the human mind, that, when pressed to extremes, it often avails itself of the most opposite methods. Extremes meet in mind as in matter. When the slaves on board of the "Pearl" were overtaken, arrested, and carried to prison—their hopes for freedom blasted—as they marched in chains they sang, and found (as Emily Edmunson tells us) a melancholy relief in singing. The singing of a man cast away on a desolate island, might be as appropriately considered an evidence of his contentment and happiness, as the singing of a slave. Sorrow and desolation have their songs, as well as joy and peace. Slaves sing more to *make* themselves happy, than to express their happiness.

It is the boast of slaveholders, that their slaves enjoy more of the physical comforts of life than the peasantry of any country in the world. My experience contradicts this. The men and the women slaves on Col. Lloyd's farm, received, as their monthly allowance of food, eight pounds of pickled pork, or their equivalent in fish. The pork was often tainted, and the fish was of the poorest quality—herrings, which would bring very little if offered for sale in any northern market. With their pork or fish, they had one bushel of Indian meal—unbolted—of which quite fifteen per cent was fit only to feed pigs. With this, one pint of salt was given; and this was the entire monthly allowance of a full grown slave, working constantly in the open field, from morning until night, every day in the month except Sunday, and living on a fraction more than a quarter of a pound of meat per day, and less than a peck of corn-meal per week. There is no kind of work that a man can do which requires a better supply of food to prevent physical exhaustion, than the field-work of a slave. So much for the slave's allowance of food; now for his raiment. The yearly allowance of clothing for the slaves on this plantation, consisted of two tow-linen shirts—such linen as the coarsest crash towels are made of; one pair of trowsers of the same material, for summer, and a pair of trowsers and a jacket of woolen, most slazily put together, for winter; one pair of yarn stockings, and one pair of shoes of the coarsest description. The slave's entire apparel could not have cost more than eight dollars per year. The allowance of food and clothing for the little children, was committed to their mothers, or to the older slavewomen having the care of them. Children who were unable to work in the field, had neither shoes, stockings, jackets nor trowsers given them. Their clothing consisted of two coarse tow-linen shirts—already described—per year; and when these failed them, as they often did, they went naked until the next allowance day. Flocks of little children from five to ten years old, might be seen on Col. Lloyd's plantation, as destitute of clothing as any little heathen on the west coast of Africa; and this, not merely during the summer months, but during the frosty weather of March. The little girls were no better off than the boys; all were nearly in a state of nudity.

As to beds to sleep on, they were known to none of the field hands; nothing but a coarse blanket—not so good as those used in the north to cover horses—was given them, and this only to the men and women. The children stuck themselves in holes and corners, about the quarters; often in the corner of the huge chimneys, with their feet in the ashes to keep them warm. The want of beds, however, was not considered a very great privation. Time to sleep was of far greater importance, for, when the day's work is done, most of the slaves have their washing, mending and cooking to do; and, having few or none of the ordinary facilities for doing such things, very many of their sleeping hours are consumed in necessary preparations for the duties of the coming day.

The sleeping apartments—if they may be called such—have little regard to comfort or decency. Old and young, male and female, married and single, drop down upon the common clay floor, each covering up with his or her blanket,—the only protection they have from cold or exposure. The night, however, is shortened at both ends. The slaves work often as long as they can see, and are late in cooking and mending for the coming day; and, at the first gray streak of morning, they are summoned to the field by the driver's horn.

More slaves are whipped for oversleeping than for any other fault. Neither age nor sex finds any favor. The overseer stands at the quarter door, armed with stick and cowskin, ready to whip any who may be a few minutes behind time. When the horn is blown, there is a rush for the door, and the hindermost one is sure to get a blow from the overseer. Young mothers who worked in the field, were allowed an hour, about ten o'clock in the morning, to go home to nurse their children. Sometimes they were compelled to take their children with them, and to leave them in the corner of the fences, to prevent loss of time in nursing them. The overseer generally rides about the field on horseback. A cowskin and a hickory stick are his constant companions. The cowskin is a kind of whip seldom seen in the northern states. It is made entirely of untanned, but dried, ox hide, and is about as hard as a piece of well-seasoned live oak. It is made of various sizes, but the usual length is about three feet. The part held in the hand is nearly an inch in thickness; and, from the extreme end of the butt or handle, the cowskin tapers its whole length to a point. This makes it quite elastic and springy. A blow with it, on the hardest back, will gash the flesh, and make the blood start. Cowskins are painted red, blue and green, and are the favorite slave whip. I think this whip worse than the "cat-o'nine-tails." It condenses the whole strength of the arm to a single point, and comes with a spring that makes the air whistle. It is a terrible instrument, and is so handy, that the overseer can always have it on his person, and ready for use. The temptation to use it is ever strong; and an overseer can, if disposed, always have cause for using it. With him, it is literally a word and a blow, and, in most cases, the blow comes first.

As a general rule, slaves do not come to the quarters for either breakfast or dinner, but take their "ash cake" with them, and eat it in the field. This was so on the home plantation; probably, because the distance from the quarter to the field, was sometimes two, and even three miles.

The dinner of the slaves consisted of a huge piece of ash cake, and a small piece of pork, or two salt herrings. Not having ovens, nor any suitable cooking utensils, the slaves mixed their meal with a little water, to such thickness that a spoon would stand erect in it; and, after the wood had burned away to coals and ashes, they would place the dough between oak leaves and lay it carefully in the ashes, completely covering it; hence, the bread is called ash cake. The surface of this peculiar bread is covered with ashes, to the depth of a sixteenth part of an inch, and the ashes, certainly, do not make it very grateful to the teeth, nor render it very palatable. The bran, or coarse part of the meal, is baked with the fine, and bright scales run through the bread. This bread, with its ashes and bran, would disgust and choke a northern man, but it is quite liked by the slaves. They eat it with avidity, and are more concerned about the quantity than about the quality. They are far too scantily provided for, and are worked too steadily, to be much concerned for the quality of their food. The few minutes allowed them at dinner time, after partaking of their coarse repast, are variously spent. Some lie down on the "turning row," and go to sleep; others draw together, and talk; and others are at work with needle and thread, mending their tattered garments. Sometimes you may hear a wild, hoarse laugh arise from a circle, and often a song. Soon, however, the overseer comes dashing through the field. *"Tumble up! Tumble up*, and to *work, work,"* is the cry; and, now, from twelve o'clock (mid-day) till dark, the human cattle are in motion, wielding their clumsy hoes; hurried on by no hope of reward, no sense of gratitude, no love of children, no prospect of bettering their condition; nothing, save the dread and terror of the slave-driver's lash. So goes one day, and so comes and goes another.

But, let us now leave the rough usage of the field, where vulgar coarseness and brutal cruelty spread themselves and flourish, rank as weeds in the tropics; where a vile wretch, in the shape of a man, rides, walks, or struts about, dealing blows, and leaving gashes on broken-spirited men and helpless women, for thirty dollars per month—a business so horrible, hardening and disgraceful, that, rather, than engage in it, a decent man would blow his own brains out—and let the reader view with me the equally wicked, but less repulsive aspects of slave life; where pride and pomp roll luxuriously at ease; where the toil of a thousand men supports a single family in easy idleness and sin. This is the great house; it is the home of the LLOYDS! Some idea of its splendor has already been given—and, it is here that we shall find that height of luxury which is the opposite of that depth of poverty and physical wretchedness that we have just now been contemplating. But, there is this difference in the two extremes; viz: that in the case of the slave, the miseries and hardships of his lot are imposed by others, and, in the master's case, they are imposed by himself. The slave is a subject, subjected by others; the slaveholder is a subject, but he is the author of his own subjection. There is more truth in the saying, that slavery is a greater evil to the master than to the slave, than many, who utter it, suppose. The self-executing laws of eternal justice follow close on the heels of the evil-doer here, as well as elsewhere; making escape from all its penalties impossible. But, let others philosophize; it is my province here to relate and describe; only allowing myself a word or two, occasionally, to assist the reader in the proper understanding of the facts narrated.

FREDERICK DOUGLASS

CHAPTER VII.
LIFE IN THE GREAT HOUSE

COMFORTS AND LUXURIES—ELABORATE EXPENDITURE—HOUSE SERVANTS—MEN SERVANTS AND MAID SERVANTS—APPEARANCES—SLAVE ARISTOCRACY—STABLE AND CARRIAGE HOUSE—BOUNDLESS HOSPITALITY—FRAGRANCE OF RICH DISHES—THE DECEPTIVE CHARACTER OF SLAVERY—SLAVES SEEM HAPPY—SLAVES AND SLAVEHOLDERS ALIKE WRETCHED—FRETFUL DISCONTENT OF SLAVEHOLDERS—FAULT-FINDING—OLD BARNEY—HIS PROFESSION—WHIPPING—HUMILIATING SPECTACLE—CASE EXCEPTIONAL—WILLIAM WILKS—SUPPOSED SON OF COL. LLOYD—CURIOUS INCIDENT—SLAVES PREFER RICH MASTERS TO POOR ONES.

The close-fisted stinginess that fed the poor slave on coarse corn-meal and tainted meat; that clothed him in crashy tow-linen, and hurried him to toil through the field, in all weathers, with wind and rain beating through his tattered garments; that scarcely gave even the young slave-mother time to nurse her hungry infant in the fence corner; wholly vanishes on approaching the sacred precincts of the great house, the home of the Lloyds. There the scriptural phrase finds an exact illustration; the highly favored inmates of this mansion are literally arrayed "in purple and fine linen," and fare sumptuously every day! The table groans under the heavy and blood-bought luxuries gathered with painstaking care, at home and abroad. Fields, forests, rivers and seas, are made tributary here. Immense wealth, and its lavish expenditure, fill the great house with all that can please the eye, or tempt the taste. Here, appetite, not food, is the great *desideratum*. Fish, flesh and fowl, are here in profusion. Chickens, of all breeds; ducks, of all kinds, wild and tame, the common, and the huge Muscovite; Guinea fowls, turkeys, geese, and pea fowls, are in their several pens, fat and fatting for the destined vortex. The graceful swan, the mongrels, the black-necked wild goose; partridges, quails, pheasants and pigeons; choice water fowl, with all their strange varieties, are caught in this huge family net. Beef, veal, mutton and venison, of the most select kinds and quality, roll bounteously to this grand consumer. The teeming riches of the Chesapeake bay, its rock, perch, drums, crocus, trout, oysters, crabs, and terrapin, are drawn hither to adorn the glittering table of the great house. The dairy, too, probably the finest on the Eastern Shore of Maryland—supplied by cattle of the best English stock, imported for the purpose, pours its rich donations of fragrant cheese, golden butter, and delicious cream, to heighten the attraction of the gorgeous, unending round of feasting. Nor are the fruits of the earth forgotten or neglected. The fertile garden, many acres in size, constituting a separate establishment, distinct from the common farm—with its scientific gardener, imported from Scotland (a Mr. McDermott) with four men under his direction, was not behind, either in the abundance or in the delicacy of its contributions to the same full board. The tender asparagus, the succulent celery, and the delicate cauliflower; egg plants, beets, lettuce, parsnips, peas, and French beans, early and late; radishes, cantelopes, melons of all kinds; the fruits and flowers of all climes and of all descriptions, from the hardy apple of the north, to the lemon and orange of the south, culminated at this point. Baltimore gathered figs, raisins, almonds and juicy grapes from Spain. Wines and brandies from France; teas of various flavor, from China; and rich, aromatic coffee from Java, all conspired to swell the tide of high life, where pride and indolence rolled and lounged in magnificence and satiety.

Behind the tall-backed and elaborately wrought chairs, stand the servants, men and maidens—fifteen in number—discriminately selected, not only with a view to their industry and faithfulness, but with special regard to their personal appearance, their graceful agility and captivating address. Some of these are armed with fans, and are fanning reviving breezes toward the over-heated brows of the alabaster ladies; others watch with eager eye, and with fawn-like step anticipate and supply wants before they are sufficiently formed to be announced by word or sign.

These servants constituted a sort of black aristocracy on Col. Lloyd's plantation. They resembled the field hands in nothing, except in color, and in this they held the advantage of a velvet-like glossiness, rich and beautiful. The hair, too, showed the same advantage. The delicate colored maid rustled in the scarcely worn silk of her young mistress, while the servant men were equally well attired from the over-flowing wardrobe of their young masters; so that, in dress, as well as in form and feature, in manner and speech, in tastes and habits, the distance between these favored few, and the sorrow and hunger-smitten multitudes of the quarter and the field, was immense; and this is seldom passed over.

Let us now glance at the stables and the carriage house, and we shall find the same evidences of pride and luxurious extravagance. Here are three splendid coaches, soft within and lustrous without. Here, too, are gigs, phaetons, barouches, sulkeys and sleighs. Here are saddles and harnesses—beautifully wrought and silver mounted—kept with every care. In the stable you will find, kept only for pleasure, full thirty-five horses, of the most approved blood for speed and beauty. There are two men here constantly employed in taking care of these horses. One of these men must be always in the stable, to answer every call from the great house. Over the way from the stable, is a house built expressly for the hounds—a pack of twenty-five or thirty—whose fare would have made glad the heart of a dozen slaves. Horses and hounds are not the only consumers of the slave's toil. There was practiced, at the Lloyd's, a hospitality which would have astonished and charmed any health-seeking northern divine or merchant, who might have chanced to share it. Viewed from his own table, and *not* from the field, the colonel was a model of generous hospitality. His house was, literally, a hotel, for weeks during the summer months. At these times, especially, the air was freighted with the rich fumes of baking, boiling, roasting and broiling. The odors I shared with the winds; but the meats were under a more stringent monopoly except that, occasionally, I got a cake from Mas' Daniel. In Mas' Daniel I had a friend at court, from whom I learned many things which my eager curiosity was excited to know. I always knew when company was expected, and who they were, although I was an outsider, being the property, not of Col. Lloyd, but of a servant of the wealthy colonel. On these occasions, all that pride, taste and money could do, to dazzle and charm, was done.

Who could say that the servants of Col. Lloyd were not well clad and cared for, after witnessing one of his magnificent entertainments? Who could say that they did not seem to glory in being the slaves of such a master? Who, but a fanatic, could get up any sympathy for persons whose every movement was agile, easy and graceful, and who evinced a consciousness of high superiority? And who would ever venture to suspect that Col. Lloyd was subject to the troubles of ordinary mortals? Master and slave seem alike in their glory here? Can it all be seeming? Alas! it may only be a sham at last! This immense wealth; this gilded splendor; this profusion of luxury; this exemption from toil; this life of ease; this sea of plenty; aye, what of it all? Are the pearly gates of happiness and sweet content flung open to such suitors? *far from it!* The poor slave, on his hard, pine plank, but scantily covered with his thin blanket, sleeps more soundly than the feverish voluptuary who reclines upon his feather bed and downy pillow. Food, to the indolent lounger, is poison, not sustenance. Lurking beneath all their dishes, are invisible spirits of evil, ready to feed the self-deluded gormandizers which aches, pains, fierce temper, uncontrolled passions, dyspepsia, rheumatism, lumbago and gout; and of these the Lloyds got their full share. To the pampered love of ease, there is no resting place. What is pleasant today, is repulsive tomorrow; what is soft now, is hard at another time; what is sweet in the morning, is bitter in the evening. Neither to the wicked, nor to the idler, is there any solid peace: *"Troubled, like the restless sea."*

I had excellent opportunities of witnessing the restless discontent and the capricious irritation of the Lloyds. My fondness for horses—not peculiar to me more than to other boys attracted me, much of the time, to the stables. This establishment was especially under the care of "old" and "young" Barney—father and son. Old Barney was a fine looking old man, of a brownish complexion, who was quite portly, and wore a dignified aspect for a slave. He was, evidently, much devoted to his profession, and held his office an honorable one. He was a farrier as well as an ostler; he could bleed, remove lampers from the mouths of the horses, and was well instructed in horse medicines. No one on the farm knew, so well as Old Barney, what to do with a sick horse. But his gifts and acquirements were of little advantage to him. His office was by no means an enviable one. He often got presents, but he got stripes as well; for in nothing was Col. Lloyd more unreasonable and exacting, than in respect to the management of his pleasure horses. Any supposed inattention to these animals were sure to be visited with degrading punishment. His horses and dogs fared better than his men. Their beds must be softer and cleaner than those of his human cattle. No excuse could shield Old Barney, if the colonel only suspected something wrong about his horses; and, consequently, he was often punished when faultless. It was absolutely painful to listen to the many unreasonable and fretful scoldings, poured out at the stable, by Col. Lloyd, his sons and sons-in-law. Of the latter, he had three—Messrs. Nicholson, Winder and Lownes. These all lived at the great house a portion of the year, and enjoyed the luxury of whipping the servants when they pleased, which was by no means unfrequently. A horse was seldom brought out of the stable to which no objection could be raised. "There was dust in his hair;" "there was a twist in his reins;" "his mane did not lie straight;" "he had not been properly grained;" "his head did not look well;" "his fore-top was not combed out;" "his fetlocks had not been properly trimmed;" something was always wrong. Listening to complaints, however groundless, Barney must stand, hat in hand, lips sealed, never answering a word. He must make no reply, no explanation; the judgment of the master must be deemed infallible, for his power is absolute and irresponsible. In a free state, a master, thus complaining without cause, of his ostler, might be told—"Sir, I am sorry I cannot please you, but, since I have done the best I can, your remedy is to dismiss me." Here, however, the ostler must stand, listen and tremble. One of the most heart-saddening and humiliating scenes I ever witnessed, was the whipping of Old Barney, by Col. Lloyd himself. Here were two men, both advanced in years; there were the silvery locks of Col. L., and there was the bald and toil-worn brow of Old Barney; master and slave; superior and inferior here, but *equals* at the bar of God; and, in the common course of events, they must both soon meet in another world, in a world where all distinctions, except those based on obedience and disobedience, are blotted out forever. "Uncover your head!" said the imperious master; he was obeyed. "Take off your jacket, you old rascal!" and off came Barney's jacket. "Down on your knees!" down knelt the old man, his shoulders bare, his bald head glistening in the sun, and his aged knees on the cold, damp ground. In his humble and debasing attitude, the master—that master to whom he had given the best years and the best strength of his life—came forward, and laid on thirty lashes, with his horse whip. The old man bore it patiently, to the last, answering each blow with a slight shrug of the shoulders, and a groan. I cannot think that Col. Lloyd succeeded in marring the flesh of Old Barney very seriously, for the whip was a light, riding whip; but the spectacle of an aged man—a husband and a father—humbly kneeling before a worm of the dust, surprised and shocked me at the time; and since I have grown old enough to think on the wickedness of slavery, few facts have been of more value to me than this, to which I was a witness. It reveals slavery in its true color, and in its maturity of repulsive hatefulness. I owe it to truth, however, to say, that this was the first and the last time I ever saw Old Barney, or any other slave, compelled to kneel to receive a whipping.

I saw, at the stable, another incident, which I will relate, as it is illustrative of a phase of slavery to which I have already referred in another connection. Besides two other coachmen, Col. Lloyd owned one named William, who, strangely enough, was often called by his surname, Wilks, by white and colored people on the home plantation. Wilks was a very fine looking man. He was about as white as anybody on the plantation; and in manliness of form, and comeliness of features, he bore a very striking resemblance to Mr. Murray Lloyd. It was whispered, and pretty generally admitted as a fact, that William Wilks was a son of Col. Lloyd, by a highly favored slave-woman, who was still on the plantation. There were many reasons for believing this whisper, not only in William's appearance, but in the undeniable freedom which he enjoyed over all others, and his apparent consciousness of being something more than a slave to his master. It was notorious, too, that William had a deadly enemy in Murray Lloyd, whom he so much resembled, and that the latter greatly worried his father with importunities to sell William. Indeed, he gave his father no rest until he did sell him, to Austin Woldfolk, the great slave-trader at that time. Before selling him, however, Mr. L. tried what giving William a whipping would do, toward making things smooth; but this was a failure. It was a compromise, and defeated itself; for, immediately after the infliction, the heart-sickened colonel atoned to William for the abuse, by giving him a gold watch and chain. Another fact, somewhat curious, is, that though sold to the remorseless *Woldfolk*, taken in irons to Baltimore and cast into prison, with a view to being driven to the south, William, by *some* means—always a mystery to me—outbid all his purchasers, paid for himself, *and now resides in Baltimore, a* FREEMAN.

Is there not room to suspect, that, as the gold watch was presented to atone for the whipping, a purse of gold was given him by the same hand, with which to effect his purchase, as an atonement for the indignity involved in selling his own flesh and blood. All the circumstances of William, on the great house farm, show him to have occupied a different position from the other slaves, and, certainly, there is nothing in the supposed hostility of slaveholders to amalgamation, to forbid the supposition that William Wilks was the son of Edward Lloyd. *Practical* amalgamation is common in every neighborhood where I have been in slavery.

Col. Lloyd was not in the way of knowing much of the real opinions and feelings of his slaves respecting him. The distance between him and them was far too great to admit of such knowledge. His slaves were so numerous, that he did not know them when he saw them. Nor, indeed, did all his slaves know him. In this respect, he was inconveniently rich. It is reported of him, that, while riding along the road one day, he met a colored man, and addressed him in the usual way of speaking to colored people on the public highways of the south: "Well, boy, who do you belong to?" "To Col. Lloyd," replied the slave. "Well, does the colonel treat you well?" "No, sir," was the ready reply. "What? does he work you too hard?" "Yes, sir." "Well, don't he give enough to eat?" "Yes, sir, he gives me enough, such as it is." The colonel, after ascertaining where the slave belonged, rode on; the slave also went on about his business, not dreaming that he had been conversing with his master. He thought, said and heard nothing more of the matter, until two or three weeks afterwards. The poor man was then informed by his overseer, that, for having found fault with his master, he was now to be sold to a Georgia trader. He was immediately chained and handcuffed; and thus, without a moment's warning he was snatched away, and forever sundered from his family and friends, by a hand more unrelenting than that of death. *This* is the penalty of telling the simple truth, in answer to a series of plain questions. It is partly in consequence of such facts, that slaves, when inquired of as to their condition and the character of their masters, almost invariably say they are contented, and that their masters are kind. Slaveholders have been known to send spies among their slaves, to ascertain, if possible, their views and feelings in regard to their condition. The frequency of this had the effect to establish among the slaves the maxim, that a still tongue makes a wise head. They suppress the truth rather than take the consequence of telling it, and, in so doing, they prove themselves a part of the human family. If they have anything to say of their master, it is, generally, something in his favor, especially when speaking to strangers. I was frequently asked, while a slave, if I had a kind master, and I do not remember ever to have given a negative reply. Nor did I, when pursuing this course, consider myself as uttering what was utterly false; for I always measured the kindness of my master by the standard of kindness set up by slaveholders around us. However, slaves are like other people, and imbibe similar prejudices. They are apt to think *their condition* better than that of others. Many, under the influence of this prejudice, think their own masters are better than the masters of other slaves; and this, too, in some cases, when the very reverse is true. Indeed, it is not uncommon for slaves even to fall out and quarrel among themselves about the relative kindness of their masters, contending for the superior goodness of his own over that of others. At the very same time, they mutually execrate their masters, when viewed separately. It was so on our plantation. When Col. Lloyd's slaves met those of Jacob Jepson, they seldom parted without a quarrel about their masters; Col. Lloyd's slaves contending that he was the richest, and Mr. Jepson's slaves that he was the smartest, man of the two. Col. Lloyd's slaves would boost his ability to buy and sell Jacob Jepson; Mr. Jepson's slaves would boast his ability to whip Col. Lloyd. These quarrels would almost always end in a fight between the parties; those that beat were supposed to have gained the point at issue. They seemed to think that the greatness of their masters was transferable to themselves. To be a SLAVE, was thought to be bad enough; but to be a *poor man's* slave, was deemed a disgrace, indeed.

FREDERICK DOUGLASS

CHAPTER VIII.
A CHAPTER OF HORRORS

AUSTIN GORE—A SKETCH OF HIS CHARACTER—OVERSEERS AS A CLASS—THEIR PECULIAR CHARACTERISTICS—THE MARKED INDIVIDUALITY OF AUSTIN GORE—HIS SENSE OF DUTY—HOW HE WHIPPED—MURDER OF POOR DENBY—HOW IT OCCURRED—SENSATION—HOW GORE MADE PEACE WITH COL. LLOYD—THE MURDER UNPUNISHED—ANOTHER DREADFUL MURDER NARRATED—NO LAWS FOR THE PROTECTION OF SLAVES CAN BE ENFORCED IN THE SOUTHERN STATES.

As I have already intimated elsewhere, the slaves on Col. Lloyd's plantation, whose hard lot, under Mr. Sevier, the reader has already noticed and deplored, were not permitted to enjoy the comparatively moderate rule of Mr. Hopkins. The latter was succeeded by a very different man. The name of the new overseer was Austin Gore. Upon this individual I would fix particular attention; for under his rule there was more suffering from violence and bloodshed than had—according to the older slaves ever been experienced before on this plantation. I confess, I hardly know how to bring this man fitly before the reader. He was, it is true, an overseer, and possessed, to a large extent, the peculiar characteristics of his class; yet, to call him merely an overseer, would not give the reader a fair notion of the man. I speak of overseers as a class. They are such. They are as distinct from the slaveholding gentry of the south, as are the fishwomen of Paris, and the coal-heavers of London, distinct from other members of society. They constitute a separate fraternity at the south, not less marked than is the fraternity of Park Lane bullies in New York. They have been arranged and classified by that great law of attraction, which determines the spheres and affinities of men; which ordains, that men, whose malign and brutal propensities predominate over their moral and intellectual endowments, shall, naturally, fall into those employments which promise the largest gratification to those predominating instincts or propensities. The office of overseer takes this raw material of vulgarity and brutality, and stamps it as a distinct class of southern society. But, in this class, as in all other classes, there are characters of marked individuality, even while they bear a general resemblance to the mass. Mr. Gore was one of those, to whom a general characterization would do no manner of justice. He was an overseer; but he was something more. With the malign and tyrannical qualities of an overseer, he combined something of the lawful master. He had the artfulness and the mean ambition of his class; but he was wholly free from the disgusting swagger and noisy bravado of his fraternity. There was an easy air of independence about him; a calm self-possession, and a sternness of glance, which might well daunt hearts less timid than those of poor slaves, accustomed from childhood and through life to cower before a driver's lash. The home plantation of Col. Lloyd afforded an ample field for the exercise of the qualifications for overseership, which he possessed in such an eminent degree.

Mr. Gore was one of those overseers, who could torture the slightest word or look into impudence; he had the nerve, not only to resent, but to punish, promptly and severely. He never allowed himself to be answered back, by a slave. In this, he was as lordly and as imperious as Col. Edward Lloyd, himself; acting always up to the maxim, practically maintained by slaveholders, that it is better that a dozen slaves suffer under the lash, without fault, than that the master or the overseer should *seem* to have been wrong in the presence of the slave. *Everything must be absolute here.* Guilty or not guilty, it is enough to be accused, to be sure of a flogging. The very presence of this man Gore was painful, and I shunned him as I would have shunned a rattlesnake. His piercing, black eyes, and sharp, shrill voice, ever awakened sensations of terror among the slaves. For so young a man (I describe him as he was, twenty-five or thirty years ago) Mr. Gore was singularly reserved and grave in the presence of slaves. He indulged in no jokes, said no funny things, and kept his own counsels. Other overseers, how brutal soever they might be, were, at times, inclined to gain favor with the slaves, by indulging a little pleasantry; but Gore was never known to be guilty of any such weakness. He was always the cold, distant, unapproachable *overseer* of Col. Edward Lloyd's plantation, and needed no higher pleasure than was involved in a faithful discharge of the duties of his office. When he whipped, he seemed to do so from a sense of duty, and feared no consequences. What Hopkins did reluctantly, Gore did with alacrity. There was a stern will, an iron-like reality, about this Gore, which would have easily made him the chief of a band of pirates, had his environments been favorable to such a course of life. All the coolness, savage barbarity and freedom from moral restraint, which are necessary in the character of a pirate-chief, centered, I think, in this man Gore. Among many other deeds of shocking cruelty which he perpetrated, while I was at Mr. Lloyd's, was the murder of a young colored man, named Denby. He was sometimes called Bill Denby, or Demby; (I write from sound, and the sounds on Lloyd's plantation are not very certain.) I knew him well. He was a powerful young man, full of animal spirits, and, so far as I know, he was among the most valuable of Col. Lloyd's slaves. In something—I know not what—he offended this Mr. Austin Gore, and, in accordance with the custom of the latter, he under took to flog him. He gave Denby but few stripes; the latter broke away from him and plunged into the creek, and, standing there to the depth of his neck in water, he refused to come out at the order of the overseer; whereupon, for this refusal, *Gore shot him dead!* It is said that Gore gave Denby three calls, telling him that if he did not obey the last call, he would shoot him. When the third call was given, Denby stood his ground firmly; and this raised the question, in the minds of the by-standing slaves—"Will he dare to shoot?" Mr. Gore, without further parley, and without making any further effort to induce Denby to come out of the water, raised his gun deliberately to his face, took deadly aim at his standing victim, and, in an instant, poor Denby was numbered with the dead. His mangled body sank out of sight, and only his warm, red blood marked the place where he had stood.

This devilish outrage, this fiendish murder, produced, as it was well calculated to do, a tremendous sensation. A thrill of horror flashed through every soul on the plantation, if I may except the guilty wretch who had committed the hell-black deed. While the slaves generally were panic-struck, and howling with alarm, the murderer himself was calm and collected, and appeared as though nothing unusual had happened. The atrocity roused my old master, and he spoke out, in reprobation of it; but the whole thing proved to be less than a nine days' wonder. Both Col. Lloyd and my old master arraigned Gore for his cruelty in the matter, but this amounted to nothing. His reply, or explanation—as I remember to have heard it at the time was, that the extraordinary expedient was demanded by necessity; that Denby had become unmanageable; that he had set a dangerous example to the other slaves; and that, without some such prompt measure as that to which he had resorted, were adopted, there would be an end to all rule and order on the plantation. That very convenient covert for all manner of cruelty and outrage that cowardly alarm-cry, that the slaves would *"take the place,"* was pleaded, in extenuation of this revolting crime, just as it had been cited in defense of a thousand similar ones. He argued, that if one slave refused to be corrected, and was allowed to escape with his life, when he had been told that he should lose it if he persisted in his course, the other slaves would soon copy his example; the result of which would be, the freedom of the slaves, and the enslavement of the whites. I have every reason to believe that Mr. Gore's defense, or explanation, was deemed satisfactory—at least to Col. Lloyd. He was continued in his office on the plantation. His fame as an overseer went abroad, and his horrid crime was not even submitted to judicial investigation. The murder was committed in the presence of slaves, and they, of course, could neither institute a suit, nor testify against the murderer. His bare word would go further in a court of law, than the united testimony of ten thousand black witnesses.

All that Mr. Gore had to do, was to make his peace with Col. Lloyd. This done, and the guilty perpetrator of one of the most foul murders goes unwhipped of justice, and uncensured by the community in which he lives. Mr. Gore lived in St. Michael's, Talbot county, when I left Maryland; if he is still alive he probably yet resides there; and I have no reason to doubt that he is now as highly esteemed, and as greatly respected, as though his guilty soul had never been stained with innocent blood. I am well aware that what I have now written will by some be branded as false and malicious. It will be denied, not only that such a thing ever did transpire, as I have now narrated, but that such a thing could happen in *Maryland*. I can only say—believe it or not—that I have said nothing but the literal truth, gainsay it who may.

I speak advisedly when I say this,—that killing a slave, or any colored person, in Talbot county, Maryland, is not treated as a crime, either by the courts or the community. Mr. Thomas Lanman, ship carpenter, of St. Michael's, killed two slaves, one of whom he butchered with a hatchet, by knocking his brains out. He used to boast of the commission of the awful and bloody deed. I have heard him do so, laughingly, saying, among other things, that he was the only benefactor of his country in the company, and that when "others would do as much as he had done, we should be relieved of the d——d niggers."

As an evidence of the reckless disregard of human life where the life is that of a slave I may state the notorious fact, that the wife of Mr. Giles Hicks, who lived but a short distance from Col. Lloyd's, with her own hands murdered my wife's cousin, a young girl between fifteen and sixteen years of age—mutilating her person in a most shocking manner. The atrocious woman, in the paroxysm of her wrath, not content with murdering her victim, literally mangled her face, and broke her breast bone. Wild, however, and infuriated as she was, she took the precaution to cause the slave-girl to be buried; but the facts of the case coming abroad, very speedily led to the disinterment of the remains of the murdered slave-girl. A coroner's jury was assembled, who decided that the girl had come to her death by severe beating. It was ascertained that the offense for which this girl was thus hurried out of the world, was this: she had been set that night, and several preceding nights, to mind Mrs. Hicks's baby, and having fallen into a sound sleep, the baby cried, waking Mrs. Hicks, but not the slave-girl. Mrs. Hicks, becoming infuriated at the girl's tardiness, after calling several times, jumped from her bed and seized a piece of fire-wood from the fireplace; and then, as she lay fast asleep, she deliberately pounded in her skull and breast-bone, and thus ended her life. I will not say that this most horrid murder produced no sensation in the community. It *did* produce a sensation; but, incredible to tell, the moral sense of the community was blunted too entirely by the ordinary nature of slavery horrors, to bring the murderess to punishment. A warrant was issued for her arrest, but, for some reason or other, that warrant was never served. Thus did Mrs. Hicks not only escape condign punishment, but even the pain and mortification of being arraigned before a court of justice.

Whilst I am detailing the bloody deeds that took place during my stay on Col. Lloyd's plantation, I will briefly narrate another dark transaction, which occurred about the same time as the murder of Denby by Mr. Gore.

On the side of the river Wye, opposite from Col. Lloyd's, there lived a Mr. Beal Bondley, a wealthy slaveholder. In the direction of his land, and near the shore, there was an excellent oyster fishing ground, and to this, some of the slaves of Col. Lloyd occasionally resorted in their little canoes, at night, with a view to make up the deficiency of their scanty allowance of food, by the oysters that they could easily get there. This, Mr. Bondley took it into his head to regard as a trespass, and while an old man belonging to Col. Lloyd was engaged in catching a few of the many millions of oysters that lined the bottom of that creek, to satisfy his hunger, the villainous Mr. Bondley, lying in ambush, without the slightest ceremony, discharged the contents of his musket into the back and shoulders of the poor old man. As good fortune would have it, the shot did not prove mortal, and Mr. Bondley came over, the next day, to see Col. Lloyd—whether to pay him for his property, or to justify himself for what he had done, I know not; but this I *can* say, the cruel and dastardly transaction was speedily hushed up; there was very little said about it at all, and nothing was publicly done which looked like the application of the principle of justice to the man whom *chance*, only, saved from being an actual murderer. One of the commonest sayings to which my ears early became accustomed, on Col. Lloyd's plantation and elsewhere in Maryland, was, that it was *"worth but half a cent to kill a nigger, and a half a cent to bury him;"* and the facts of my experience go far to justify the practical truth of this strange proverb. Laws for the protection of the lives of the slaves, are, as they must needs be, utterly incapable of being enforced, where the very parties who are nominally protected, are not permitted to give evidence, in courts of law, against the only class of persons from whom abuse, outrage and murder might be reasonably apprehended. While I heard of numerous murders committed by slaveholders on the Eastern Shores of Maryland, I never knew a solitary instance in which a slaveholder was either hung or imprisoned for having murdered a slave. The usual pretext for killing a slave is, that the slave has offered resistance. Should a slave, when assaulted, but raise his hand in self defense, the white assaulting party is fully justified by southern, or Maryland, public opinion, in shooting the slave down. Sometimes this is done, simply because it is alleged that the slave has been saucy. But here I leave this phase of the society of my early childhood, and will relieve the kind reader of these heart-sickening details.

CHAPTER IX.
Personal Treatment

MISS LUCRETIA—HER KINDNESS—HOW IT WAS MANIFESTED—"IKE"—A BATTLE WITH HIM—THE CONSEQUENCES THEREOF—MISS LUCRETIA'S BALSAM—BREAD—HOW I OBTAINED IT—BEAMS OF SUNLIGHT AMIDST THE GENERAL DARKNESS—SUFFERING FROM COLD—HOW WE TOOK OUR MEALS—ORDERS TO PREPARE FOR BALTIMORE—OVERJOYED AT THE THOUGHT OF QUITTING THE PLANTATION—EXTRAORDINARY CLEANSING—COUSIN TOM'S VERSION OF BALTIMORE—ARRIVAL THERE—KIND RECEPTION GIVEN ME BY MRS. SOPHIA AULD—LITTLE TOMMY—MY NEW POSITION—MY NEW DUTIES—A TURNING POINT IN MY HISTORY.

I have nothing cruel or shocking to relate of my own personal experience, while I remained on Col. Lloyd's plantation, at the home of my old master. An occasional cuff from Aunt Katy, and a regular whipping from old master, such as any heedless and mischievous boy might get from his father, is all that I can mention of this sort. I was not old enough to work in the field, and, there being little else than field work to perform, I had much leisure. The most I had to do, was, to drive up the cows in the evening, to keep the front yard clean, and to perform small errands for my young mistress, Lucretia Auld. I have reasons for thinking this lady was very kindly disposed toward me, and, although I was not often the object of her attention, I constantly regarded her as my friend, and was always glad when it was my privilege to do her a service. In a family where there was so much that was harsh, cold and indifferent, the slightest word or look of kindness passed, with me, for its full value. Miss Lucretia—as we all continued to call her long after her marriage—had bestowed upon me such words and looks as taught me that she pitied me, if she did not love me. In addition to words and looks, she sometimes gave me a piece of bread and butter; a thing not set down in the bill of fare, and which must have been an extra ration, planned aside from either Aunt Katy or old master, solely out of the tender regard and friendship she had for me. Then, too, I one day got into the wars with Uncle Able's son, "Ike," and had got sadly worsted; in fact, the little rascal had struck me directly in the forehead with a sharp piece of cinder, fused with iron, from the old blacksmith's forge, which made a cross in my forehead very plainly to be seen now. The gash bled very freely, and I roared very loudly and betook myself home. The coldhearted Aunt Katy paid no attention either to my wound or my roaring, except to tell me it served me right; I had no business with Ike; it was good for me; I would now keep away *"from dem Lloyd niggers."* Miss Lucretia, in this state of the case, came forward; and, in quite a different spirit from that manifested by Aunt Katy, she called me into the parlor (an extra privilege of itself) and, without using toward me any of the hard-hearted and reproachful epithets of my kitchen tormentor, she quietly acted the good Samaritan. With her own soft hand she washed the blood from my head and face, fetched her own balsam bottle, and with the balsam wetted a nice piece of white linen, and bound up my head. The balsam was not more healing to the wound in my head, than her kindness was healing to the wounds in my spirit, made by the unfeeling words of Aunt Katy. After this, Miss Lucretia was my friend. I felt her to be such; and I have no doubt that the simple act of binding up my head, did much to awaken in her mind an interest in my welfare. It is quite true, that this interest was never very marked, and it seldom showed itself in anything more than in giving me a piece of bread when I was hungry; but this was a great favor on a slave plantation, and I was the only one of the children to whom such attention was paid. When very hungry, I would go into the back yard and play under Miss Lucretia's window. When pretty severely pinched by hunger, I had a habit of singing, which the good lady very soon came to understand as a petition for a piece of bread. When I sung under Miss Lucretia's window, I was very apt to get well paid for my music. The reader will see that I now had two friends, both at important points—Mas' Daniel at the great house, and Miss Lucretia at home. From Mas' Daniel I got protection from the bigger boys; and from Miss Lucretia I got bread, by singing when I was hungry, and sympathy when I was abused by that termagant, who had the reins of government in the kitchen. For such friendship I felt deeply grateful, and bitter as are my recollections of slavery, I love to recall any instances of kindness, any sunbeams of humane treatment, which found way to my soul through the iron grating of my house of bondage. Such beams seem all the brighter from the general darkness into which they penetrate, and the impression they make is vividly distinct and beautiful.

As I have before intimated, I was seldom whipped—and never severely—by my old master. I suffered little from the treatment I received, except from hunger and cold. These were my two great physical troubles. I could neither get a sufficiency of food nor of clothing; but I suffered less from hunger than from cold. In hottest summer and coldest winter, I was kept almost in a state of nudity; no shoes, no stockings, no jacket, no trowsers; nothing but coarse sackcloth or tow-linen, made into a sort of shirt, reaching down to my knees. This I wore night and day, changing it once a week. In the day time I could protect myself pretty well, by keeping on the sunny side of the house; and in bad weather, in the corner of the kitchen chimney. The great difficulty was, to keep warm during the night. I had no bed. The pigs in the pen had leaves, and the horses in the stable had straw, but the children had no beds. They lodged anywhere in the ample kitchen. I slept, generally, in a little closet, without even a blanket to cover me. In very cold weather. I sometimes got down the bag in which corn meal was usually carried to the mill, and crawled into that. Sleeping there, with my head in and feet out, I was partly protected, though not comfortable. My feet have been so cracked with the frost, that the pen with which I am writing might be laid in the gashes. The manner of taking our meals at old master's, indicated but little refinement. Our corn-meal mush, when sufficiently cooled, was placed in a large wooden tray, or trough, like those used in making maple sugar here in the north. This tray was set down, either on the floor of the kitchen, or out of doors on the ground; and the children were called, like so many pigs; and like so many pigs they would come, and literally devour the mush—some with oyster shells, some with pieces of shingles, and none with spoons. He that eat fastest got most, and he that was strongest got the best place; and few left the trough really satisfied. I was the most unlucky of any, for Aunt Katy had no good feeling for me; and if I pushed any of the other children, or if they told her anything unfavorable of me, she always believed the worst, and was sure to whip me.

As I grew older and more thoughtful, I was more and more filled with a sense of my wretchedness. The cruelty of Aunt Katy, the hunger and cold I suffered, and the terrible reports of wrong and outrage which came to my ear, together with what I almost daily witnessed, led me, when yet but eight or nine years old, to wish I had never been born. I used to contrast my condition with the black-birds, in whose wild and sweet songs I fancied them so happy! Their apparent joy only deepened the shades of my sorrow. There are thoughtful days in the lives of children—at least there were in mine when they grapple with all the great, primary subjects of knowledge, and reach, in a moment, conclusions which no subsequent experience can shake. I was just as well aware of the unjust, unnatural and murderous character of slavery, when nine years old, as I am now. Without any appeal to books, to laws, or to authorities of any kind, it was enough to accept God as a father, to regard slavery as a crime.

I was not ten years old when I left Col. Lloyd's plantation for Balitmore(sic). I left that plantation with inexpressible joy. I never shall forget the ecstacy with which I received the intelligence from my friend, Miss Lucretia, that my old master had determined to let me go to Baltimore to live with Mr. Hugh Auld, a brother to Mr. Thomas Auld, my old master's son-in-law. I received this information about three days before my departure. They were three of the happiest days of my childhood. I spent the largest part of these three days in the creek, washing off the plantation scurf, and preparing for my new home. Mrs. Lucretia took a lively interest in getting me ready. She told me I must get all the dead skin off my feet and knees, before I could go to Baltimore, for the people there were very cleanly, and would laugh at me if I looked dirty; and, besides, she was intending to give me a pair of trowsers, which I should not put on unless I got all the dirt off. This was a warning to which I was bound to take heed; for the thought of owning a pair of trowsers, was great, indeed. It was almost a sufficient motive, not only to induce me to scrub off the *mange* (as pig drovers would call it) but the skin as well. So I went at it in good earnest, working for the first time in the hope of reward. I was greatly excited, and could hardly consent to sleep, lest I should be left. The ties that, ordinarily, bind children to their homes, were all severed, or they never had any existence in my case, at least so far as the home plantation of Col. L. was concerned. I therefore found no severe trail at the moment of my departure, such as I had experienced when separated from my home in Tuckahoe. My home at my old master's was charmless to me; it was not home, but a prison to me; on parting from it, I could not feel that I was leaving anything which I could have enjoyed by staying. My mother was now long dead; my grandmother was far away, so that I seldom saw her; Aunt Katy was my unrelenting tormentor; and my two sisters and brothers, owing to our early separation in life, and the family-destroying power of slavery, were, comparatively, strangers to me. The fact of our relationship was almost blotted out. I looked for *home* elsewhere, and was confident of finding none which I should relish less than the one I was leaving. If, however, I found in my new home to which I was going with such blissful anticipations—hardship, whipping and nakedness, I had the questionable consolation that I should not have escaped any one of these evils by remaining under the management of Aunt Katy. Then, too, I thought, since I had endured much in this line on Lloyd's plantation, I could endure as much elsewhere, and especially at Baltimore; for I had something of the feeling about that city which is expressed in the saying, that being "hanged in England, is better than dying a natural death in Ireland." I had the strongest desire to see Baltimore. My cousin Tom—a boy two or three years older than I—had been there, and though not fluent (he stuttered immoderately) in speech, he had inspired me with that desire, by his eloquent description of the place. Tom was, sometimes, Capt. Auld's cabin boy; and when he came from Baltimore, he was always a sort of hero amongst us, at least till his Baltimore trip was forgotten. I could never tell him of anything, or point out anything that struck me as beautiful or powerful, but that he had seen something in Baltimore far surpassing it. Even the great house itself, with all its pictures within, and pillars without, he had the hardihood to say "was nothing to Baltimore." He bought a trumpet (worth six pence) and brought it home; told what he had seen in the windows of stores; that he had heard shooting crackers, and seen soldiers; that he had seen a steamboat; that there were ships in Baltimore that could carry four such sloops as the "Sally Lloyd." He said a great deal about the market-house; he spoke of the bells ringing; and of many other things which roused my curiosity very much; and, indeed, which heightened my hopes of happiness in my new home.

We sailed out of Miles river for Baltimore early on a Saturday morning. I remember only the day of the week; for, at that time, I had no knowledge of the days of the month, nor, indeed, of the months of the year. On setting sail, I walked aft, and gave to Col. Lloyd's plantation what I hoped would be the last look I should ever give to it, or to any place like it. My strong aversion to the great farm, was not owing to my own personal suffering, but the daily suffering of others, and to the certainty that I must, sooner or later, be placed under the barbarous rule of an overseer, such as the accomplished Gore, or the brutal and drunken Plummer. After taking this last view, I quitted the quarter deck, made my way to the bow of the sloop, and spent the remainder of the day in looking ahead; interesting myself in what was in the distance, rather than what was near by or behind. The vessels, sweeping along the bay, were very interesting objects. The broad bay opened like a shoreless ocean on my boyish vision, filling me with wonder and admiration.

Late in the afternoon, we reached Annapolis, the capital of the state, stopping there not long enough to admit of my going ashore. It was the first large town I had ever seen; and though it was inferior to many a factory village in New England, my feelings, on seeing it, were excited to a pitch very little below that reached by travelers at the first view of Rome. The dome of the state house was especially imposing, and surpassed in grandeur the appearance of the great house. The great world was opening upon me very rapidly, and I was eagerly acquainting myself with its multifarious lessons.

We arrived in Baltimore on Sunday morning, and landed at Smith's wharf, not far from Bowly's wharf. We had on board the sloop a large flock of sheep, for the Baltimore market; and, after assisting in driving them to the slaughter house of Mr. Curtis, on Loudon Slater's Hill, I was speedily conducted by Rich—one of the hands belonging to the sloop—to my new home in Alliciana street, near Gardiner's ship-yard, on Fell's Point. Mr. and Mrs. Hugh Auld, my new mistress and master, were both at home, and met me at the door with their rosy cheeked little son, Thomas, to take care of whom was to constitute my future occupation. In fact, it was to "little Tommy," rather than to his parents, that old master made a present of me; and though there was no *legal* form or arrangement entered into, I have no doubt that Mr. and Mrs. Auld felt that, in due time, I should be the legal property of their bright-eyed and beloved boy, Tommy. I was struck with the appearance, especially, of my new mistress. Her face was lighted with the kindliest emotions; and the reflex influence of her countenance, as well as the tenderness with which she seemed to regard me, while asking me sundry little questions, greatly delighted me, and lit up, to my fancy, the pathway of my future. Miss Lucretia was kind; but my new mistress, "Miss Sophy," surpassed her in kindness of manner. Little Thomas was affectionately told by his mother, that *"there was his Freddy,"* and that "Freddy would take care of him;" and I was told to "be kind to little Tommy"—an injunction I scarcely needed, for I had already fallen in love with the dear boy; and with these little ceremonies I was initiated into my new home, and entered upon my peculiar duties, with not a cloud above the horizon.

I may say here, that I regard my removal from Col. Lloyd's plantation as one of the most interesting and fortunate events of my life. Viewing it in the light of human likelihoods, it is quite probable that, but for the mere circumstance of being thus removed before the rigors of slavery had fastened upon me; before my young spirit had been crushed under the iron control of the slave-driver, instead of being, today, a FREEMAN, I might have been wearing the galling chains of slavery. I have sometimes felt, however, that there was something more intelligent than *chance*, and something more certain than *luck*, to be seen in the circumstance. If I have made any progress in knowledge; if I have cherished any honorable aspirations, or have, in any manner, worthily discharged the duties of a member of an oppressed people; this little circumstance must be allowed its due weight in giving my life that direction. I have ever regarded it as the first plain manifestation of that

> *Divinity that shapes our ends,*
> *Rough hew them as we will.*

I was not the only boy on the plantation that might have been sent to live in Baltimore. There was a wide margin from which to select. There were boys younger, boys older, and boys of the same age, belonging to my old master some at his own house, and some at his farm—but the high privilege fell to my lot.

I may be deemed superstitious and egotistical, in regarding this event as a special interposition of Divine Providence in my favor; but the thought is a part of my history, and I should be false to the earliest and most cherished sentiments of my soul, if I suppressed, or hesitated to avow that opinion, although it may be characterized as irrational by the wise, and ridiculous by the scoffer. From my earliest recollections of serious matters, I date the entertainment of something like an ineffaceable conviction, that slavery would not always be able to hold me within its foul embrace; and this conviction, like a word of living faith, strengthened me through the darkest trials of my lot. This good spirit was from God; and to him I offer thanksgiving and praise.

CHAPTER X.
Life in Baltimore

CITY ANNOYANCES—PLANTATION REGRETS—MY MISTRESS, MISS SOPHA—HER HISTORY—HER KINDNESS TO ME—MY MASTER, HUGH AULD—HIS SOURNESS—MY INCREASED SENSITIVENESS—MY COMFORTS—MY OCCUPATION—THE BANEFUL EFFECTS OF SLAVEHOLDING ON MY DEAR AND GOOD MISTRESS—HOW SHE COMMENCED TEACHING ME TO READ—WHY SHE CEASED TEACHING ME—CLOUDS GATHERING OVER MY BRIGHT PROSPECTS—MASTER AULD'S EXPOSITION OF THE TRUE PHILOSOPHY OF SLAVERY—CITY SLAVES—PLANTATION SLAVES—THE CONTRAST—EXCEPTIONS—MR. HAMILTON'S TWO SLAVES, HENRIETTA AND MARY—MRS. HAMILTON'S CRUEL TREATMENT OF THEM—THE PITEOUS ASPECT THEY PRESENTED— NO POWER MUST COME BETWEEN THE SLAVE AND THE SLAVEHOLDER.

Once in Baltimore, with hard brick pavements under my feet, which almost raised blisters, by their very heat, for it was in the height of summer; walled in on all sides by towering brick buildings; with troops of hostile boys ready to pounce upon me at every street corner; with new and strange objects glaring upon me at every step, and with startling sounds reaching my ears from all directions, I for a time thought that, after all, the home plantation was a more desirable place of residence than my home on Alliciana street, in Baltimore. My country eyes and ears were confused and bewildered here; but the boys were my chief trouble. They chased me, and called me *"Eastern Shore man,"* till really I almost wished myself back on the Eastern Shore. I had to undergo a sort of moral acclimation, and when that was over, I did much better. My new mistress happily proved to be all she *seemed* to be, when, with her husband, she met me at the door, with a most beaming, benignant countenance. She was, naturally, of an excellent disposition, kind, gentle and cheerful. The supercilious contempt for the rights and feelings of the slave, and the petulance and bad humor which generally characterize slaveholding ladies, were all quite absent from kind "Miss" Sophia's manner and bearing toward me. She had, in truth, never been a slaveholder, but had—a thing quite unusual in the south—depended almost entirely upon her own industry for a living. To this fact the dear lady, no doubt, owed the excellent preservation of her natural goodness of heart, for slavery can change a saint into a sinner, and an angel into a demon. I hardly knew how to behave toward "Miss Sopha," as I used to call Mrs. Hugh Auld. I had been treated as a *pig* on the plantation; I was treated as a *child* now. I could not even approach her as I had formerly approached Mrs. Thomas Auld. How could I hang down my head, and speak with bated breath, when there was no pride to scorn me, no coldness to repel me, and no hatred to inspire me with fear? I therefore soon learned to regard her as something more akin to a mother, than a slaveholding mistress. The crouching servility of a slave, usually so acceptable a quality to the haughty slaveholder, was not understood nor desired by this gentle woman. So far from deeming it impudent in a slave to look her straight in the face, as some slaveholding ladies do, she seemed ever to say, "look up, child; don't be afraid; see, I am full of kindness and good will toward you." The hands belonging to Col. Lloyd's sloop, esteemed it a great privilege to be the bearers of parcels or messages to my new mistress; for whenever they came, they were sure of a most kind and pleasant reception. If little Thomas was her son, and her most dearly beloved child, she, for a time, at least, made me something like his half-brother in her affections. If dear Tommy was exalted to a place on his mother's knee, "Feddy" was honored by a place at his mother's side. Nor did he lack the caressing strokes of her gentle hand, to convince him that, though *motherless*, he was not *friendless*. Mrs. Auld was not only a kind-hearted woman, but she was remarkably pious; frequent in her attendance of public worship, much given to reading the bible, and to chanting hymns of praise, when alone. Mr. Hugh Auld was altogether a different character. He cared very little about religion, knew more of the world, and was more of the world, than his wife. He set out, doubtless to be—as the world goes—a respectable man, and to get on by becoming a successful ship builder, in that city of ship building. This was his ambition, and it fully occupied him. I was, of course, of very little consequence to him, compared with what I was to good Mrs. Auld; and, when he smiled upon me, as he sometimes did, the smile was borrowed from his lovely wife, and, like all borrowed light, was transient, and vanished with the source whence it was derived. While I must characterize Master Hugh as being a very sour man, and of forbidding appearance, it is due to him to acknowledge, that he was never very cruel to me, according to the notion of cruelty in Maryland. The first year or two which I spent in his house, he left me almost exclusively to the management of his wife. She was my law-giver. In hands so tender as hers, and in the absence of the cruelties of the plantation, I became, both physically and mentally, much more sensitive to good and ill treatment; and, perhaps, suffered more from a frown from my mistress, than I formerly did from a cuff at the hands of Aunt Katy. Instead of the cold, damp floor of my old master's kitchen, I found myself on carpets; for the corn bag in winter, I now had a good straw bed, well furnished with covers; for the coarse corn-meal in the morning, I now had good bread, and mush occasionally; for my poor tow-lien shirt, reaching to my knees, I had good, clean clothes. I was really well off. My employment was to run errands, and to take care of Tommy; to prevent his getting in the way of carriages, and to keep him out of harm's way generally. Tommy, and I, and his mother, got on swimmingly together, for a time. I say *for a time*, because the fatal poison of irresponsible power, and the natural influence of slavery customs, were not long in making a suitable impression on the gentle and loving disposition of my excellent mistress. At first, Mrs. Auld evidently regarded me simply as a child, like any other child; she had not come to regard me as *property*. This latter thought was a thing of conventional growth. The first was natural and spontaneous. A noble nature, like hers, could not, instantly, be wholly perverted; and it took several years to change the natural sweetness of her temper into fretful bitterness. In her worst estate, however, there were, during the first seven years I lived with her, occasional returns of her former kindly disposition.

The frequent hearing of my mistress reading the bible for she often read aloud when her husband was absent soon awakened my curiosity in respect to this *mystery* of reading, and roused in me the desire to learn. Having no fear of my kind mistress before my eyes, (she had then given me no reason to fear,) I frankly asked her to teach me to read; and, without hesitation, the dear woman began the task, and very soon, by her assistance, I was master of the alphabet, and could spell words of three or four letters. My mistress seemed almost as proud of my progress, as if I had been her own child; and, supposing that her husband would be as well pleased, she made no secret of what she was doing for me. Indeed, she exultingly told him of the aptness of her pupil, of her intention to persevere in teaching me, and of the duty which she felt it to teach me, at least to read *the bible*. Here arose the first cloud over my Baltimore prospects, the precursor of drenching rains and chilling blasts.

Master Hugh was amazed at the simplicity of his spouse, and, probably for the first time, he unfolded to her the true philosophy of slavery, and the peculiar rules necessary to be observed by masters and mistresses, in the management of their human chattels. Mr. Auld promptly forbade continuance of her instruction; telling her, in the first place, that the thing itself was unlawful; that it was also unsafe, and could only lead to mischief. To use his own words, further, he said, "if you give a nigger an inch, he will take an ell;" "he should know nothing but the will of his master, and learn to obey it." "if you teach that nigger—speaking of myself—how to read the bible, there will be no keeping him;" "it would forever unfit him for the duties of a slave;" and "as to himself, learning would do him no good, but probably, a great deal of harm—making him disconsolate and unhappy." "If you learn him now to read, he'll want to know how to write; and, this accomplished, he'll be running away with himself." Such was the tenor of Master Hugh's oracular exposition of the true philosophy of training a human chattel; and it must be confessed that he very clearly comprehended the nature and the requirements of the relation of master and slave. His discourse was the first decidedly anti-slavery lecture to which it had been my lot to listen. Mrs. Auld evidently felt the force of his remarks; and, like an obedient wife, began to shape her course in the direction indicated by her husband. The effect of his words, *on me*, was neither slight nor transitory. His iron sentences—cold and harsh—sunk deep into my heart, and stirred up not only my feelings into a sort of rebellion, but awakened within me a slumbering train of vital thought. It was a new and special revelation, dispelling a painful mystery, against which my youthful understanding had struggled, and struggled in vain, to wit: the *white* man's power to perpetuate the enslavement of the *black* man. "Very well," thought I; "knowledge unfits a child to be a slave." I instinctively assented to the proposition; and from that moment I understood the direct pathway from slavery to freedom. This was just what I needed; and I got it at a time, and from a source, whence I least expected it. I was saddened at the thought of losing the assistance of my kind mistress; but the information, so instantly derived, to some extent compensated me for the loss I had sustained in this direction. Wise as Mr. Auld was, he evidently underrated my comprehension, and had little idea of the use to which I was capable of putting the impressive lesson he was giving to his wife. *He* wanted me to be *a slave;* I had already voted against that on the home plantation of Col. Lloyd. That which he most loved I most hated; and the very determination which he expressed to keep me in ignorance, only rendered me the more resolute in seeking intelligence. In learning to read, therefore, I am not sure that I do not owe quite as much to the opposition of my master, as to the kindly assistance of my amiable mistress. I acknowledge the benefit rendered me by the one, and by the other; believing, that but for my mistress, I might have grown up in ignorance.

I had resided but a short time in Baltimore, before I observed a marked difference in the manner of treating slaves, generally, from which I had witnessed in that isolated and out-of-the-way part of the country where I began life. A city slave is almost a free citizen, in Baltimore, compared with a slave on Col. Lloyd's plantation. He is much better fed and clothed, is less dejected in his appearance, and enjoys privileges altogether unknown to the whip-driven slave on the plantation. Slavery dislikes a dense population, in which there is a majority of non-slaveholders. The general sense of decency that must pervade such a population, does much to check and prevent those outbreaks of atrocious cruelty, and those dark crimes without a name, almost openly perpetrated on the plantation. He is a desperate slaveholder who will shock the humanity of his non-slaveholding neighbors, by the cries of the lacerated slaves; and very few in the city are willing to incur the odium of being cruel masters. I found, in Baltimore, that no man was more odious to the white, as well as to the colored people, than he, who had the reputation of starving his slaves. Work them, flog them, if need be, but don't starve them. These are, however, some painful exceptions to this rule. While it is quite true that most of the slaveholders in Baltimore feed and clothe their slaves well, there are others who keep up their country cruelties in the city.

An instance of this sort is furnished in the case of a family who lived directly opposite to our house, and were named Hamilton. Mrs. Hamilton owned two slaves. Their names were Henrietta and Mary. They had always been house slaves. One was aged about twenty-two, and the other about fourteen. They were a fragile couple by nature, and the treatment they received was enough to break down the constitution of a horse. Of all the dejected, emaciated, mangled and excoriated creatures I ever saw, those two girls—in the refined, church going and Christian city of Baltimore were the most deplorable. Of stone must that heart be made, that could look upon Henrietta and Mary, without being sickened to the core with sadness. Especially was Mary a heart-sickening object. Her head, neck and shoulders, were literally cut to pieces. I have frequently felt her head, and found it nearly covered over with festering sores, caused by the lash of her cruel mistress. I do not know that her master ever whipped her, but I have often been an eye witness of the revolting and brutal inflictions by Mrs. Hamilton; and what lends a deeper shade to this woman's conduct, is the fact, that, almost in the very moments of her shocking outrages of humanity and decency, she would charm you by the sweetness of her voice and her seeming piety. She used to sit in a large rocking chair, near the middle of the room, with a heavy cowskin, such as I have elsewhere described; and I speak within the truth when I say, that these girls seldom passed that chair, during the day, without a blow from that cowskin, either upon their bare arms, or upon their shoulders. As they passed her, she would draw her cowskin and give them a blow, saying, *"move faster, you black jip!"* and, again, *"take that, you black jip!"* continuing, *"if you don't move faster, I will give you more."* Then the lady would go on, singing her sweet hymns, as though her *righteous* soul were sighing for the holy realms of paradise.

Added to the cruel lashings to which these poor slave-girls were subjected—enough in themselves to crush the spirit of men—they were, really, kept nearly half starved; they seldom knew what it was to eat a full meal, except when they got it in the kitchens of neighbors, less mean and stingy than the psalm-singing Mrs. Hamilton. I have seen poor Mary contending for the offal, with the pigs in the street. So much was the poor girl pinched, kicked, cut and pecked to pieces, that the boys in the street knew her only by the name of *"pecked,"* a name derived from the scars and blotches on her neck, head and shoulders.

It is some relief to this picture of slavery in Baltimore, to say—what is but the simple truth—that Mrs. Hamilton's treatment of her slaves was generally condemned, as disgraceful and shocking; but while I say this, it must also be remembered, that the very parties who censured the cruelty of Mrs. Hamilton, would have condemned and promptly punished any attempt to interfere with Mrs. Hamilton's *right* to cut and slash her slaves to pieces. There must be no force between the slave and the slaveholder, to restrain the power of the one, and protect the weakness of the other; and the cruelty of Mrs. Hamilton is as justly chargeable to the upholders of the slave system, as drunkenness is chargeable on those who, by precept and example, or by indifference, uphold the drinking system.

FREDERICK DOUGLASS

CHAPTER XI.
"A Change Came O'er the Spirit of My Dream"

HOW I LEARNED TO READ—MY MISTRESS—HER SLAVEHOLDING DUTIES—THEIR DEPLORABLE EFFECTS UPON HER ORIGINALLY NOBLE NATURE—THE CONFLICT IN HER MIND—HER FINAL OPPOSITION TO MY LEARNING TO READ—TOO LATE—SHE HAD GIVEN ME THE INCH, I WAS RESOLVED TO TAKE THE ELL—HOW I PURSUED MY EDUCATION—MY TUTORS—HOW I COMPENSATED THEM—WHAT PROGRESS I MADE—SLAVERY—WHAT I HEARD SAID ABOUT IT—THIRTEEN YEARS OLD—THE Columbian Orator—A RICH SCENE—A DIALOGUE—SPEECHES OF CHATHAM, SHERIDAN, PITT AND FOX—KNOWLEDGE EVER INCREASING—MY EYES OPENED—LIBERTY—HOW I PINED FOR IT—MY SADNESS—THE DISSATISFACTION OF MY POOR MISTRESS—MY HATRED OF SLAVERY—ONE UPAS TREE OVERSHADOWED US BOTH.

I lived in the family of Master Hugh, at Baltimore, seven years, during which time—as the almanac makers say of the weather—my condition was variable. The most interesting feature of my history here, was my learning to read and write, under somewhat marked disadvantages. In attaining this knowledge, I was compelled to resort to indirections by no means congenial to my nature, and which were really humiliating to me. My mistress—who, as the reader has already seen, had begun to teach me was suddenly checked in her benevolent design, by the strong advice of her husband. In faithful compliance with this advice, the good lady had not only ceased to instruct me, herself, but had set her face as a flint against my learning to read by any means. It is due, however, to my mistress to say, that she did not adopt this course in all its stringency at the first. She either thought it unnecessary, or she lacked the depravity indispensable to shutting me up in mental darkness. It was, at least, necessary for her to have some training, and some hardening, in the exercise of the slaveholder's prerogative, to make her equal to forgetting my human nature and character, and to treating me as a thing destitute of a moral or an intellectual nature. Mrs. Auld—my mistress—was, as I have said, a most kind and tender-hearted woman; and, in the humanity of her heart, and the simplicity of her mind, she set out, when I first went to live with her, to treat me as she supposed one human being ought to treat another.

It is easy to see, that, in entering upon the duties of a slaveholder, some little experience is needed. Nature has done almost nothing to prepare men and women to be either slaves or slaveholders. Nothing but rigid training, long persisted in, can perfect the character of the one or the other. One cannot easily forget to love freedom; and it is as hard to cease to respect that natural love in our fellow creatures. On entering upon the career of a slaveholding mistress, Mrs. Auld was singularly deficient; nature, which fits nobody for such an office, had done less for her than any lady I had known. It was no easy matter to induce her to think and to feel that the curly-headed boy, who stood by her side, and even leaned on her lap; who was loved by little Tommy, and who loved little Tommy in turn; sustained to her only the relation of a chattel. I was *more* than that, and she felt me to be more than that. I could talk and sing; I could laugh and weep; I could reason and remember; I could love and hate. I was human, and she, dear lady, knew and felt me to be so. How could she, then, treat me as a brute, without a mighty struggle with all the noble powers of her own soul. That struggle came, and the will and power of the husband was victorious. Her noble soul was overthrown; but, he that overthrew it did not, himself, escape the consequences. He, not less than the other parties, was injured in his domestic peace by the fall.

When I went into their family, it was the abode of happiness and contentment. The mistress of the house was a model of affection and tenderness. Her fervent piety and watchful uprightness made it impossible to see her without thinking and feeling—"*that woman is a Christian.*" There was no sorrow nor suffering for which she had not a tear, and there was no innocent joy for which she did not a smile. She had bread for the hungry, clothes for the naked, and comfort for every mourner that came within her reach. Slavery soon proved its ability to divest her of these excellent qualities, and her home of its early happiness. Conscience cannot stand much violence. Once thoroughly broken down, *who* is he that can repair the damage? It may be broken toward the slave, on Sunday, and toward the master on Monday. It cannot endure such shocks. It must stand entire, or it does not stand at all. If my condition waxed bad, that of the family waxed not better. The first step, in the wrong direction, was the violence done to nature and to conscience, in arresting the benevolence that would have enlightened my young mind. In ceasing to instruct me, she must begin to justify herself *to* herself; and, once consenting to take sides in such a debate, she was riveted to her position. One needs very little knowledge of moral philosophy, to see *where* my mistress now landed. She finally became even more violent in her opposition to my learning to read, than was her husband himself. She was not satisfied with simply doing as *well* as her husband had commanded her, but seemed resolved to better his instruction. Nothing appeared to make my poor mistress—after her turning toward the downward path—more angry, than seeing me, seated in some nook or corner, quietly reading a book or a newspaper. I have had her rush at me, with the utmost fury, and snatch from my hand such newspaper or book, with something of the wrath and consternation which a traitor might be supposed to feel on being discovered in a plot by some dangerous spy.

Mrs. Auld was an apt woman, and the advice of her husband, and her own experience, soon demonstrated, to her entire satisfaction, that education and slavery are incompatible with each other. When this conviction was thoroughly established, I was most narrowly watched in all my movements. If I remained in a separate room from the family for any considerable length of time, I was sure to be suspected of having a book, and was at once called upon to give an account of myself. All this, however, was entirely *too late*. The first, and never to be retraced, step had been taken. In teaching me the alphabet, in the days of her simplicity and kindness, my mistress had given me the *"inch,"* and now, no ordinary precaution could prevent me from taking the *"ell."*

Seized with a determination to learn to read, at any cost, I hit upon many expedients to accomplish the desired end. The plea which I mainly adopted, and the one by which I was most successful, was that of using my young white playmates, with whom I met in the streets as teachers. I used to carry, almost constantly, a copy of Webster's spelling book in my pocket; and, when sent of errands, or when play time was allowed me, I would step, with my young friends, aside, and take a lesson in spelling. I generally paid my *tuition fee* to the boys, with bread, which I also carried in my pocket. For a single biscuit, any of my hungry little comrades would give me a lesson more valuable to me than bread. Not every one, however, demanded this consideration, for there were those who took pleasure in teaching me, whenever I had a chance to be taught by them. I am strongly tempted to give the names of two or three of those little boys, as a slight testimonial of the gratitude and affection I bear them, but prudence forbids; not that it would injure me, but it might, possibly, embarrass them; for it is almost an unpardonable offense to do any thing, directly or indirectly, to promote a slave's freedom, in a slave state. It is enough to say, of my warm-hearted little play fellows, that they lived on Philpot street, very near Durgin & Bailey's shipyard.

Although slavery was a delicate subject, and very cautiously talked about among grown up people in Maryland, I frequently talked about it—and that very freely—with the white boys. I would, sometimes, say to them, while seated on a curb stone or a cellar door, "I wish I could be free, as you will be when you get to be men." "You will be free, you know, as soon as you are twenty-one, and can go where you like, but I am a slave for life. Have I not as good a right to be free as you have?" Words like these, I observed, always troubled them; and I had no small satisfaction in wringing from the boys, occasionally, that fresh and bitter condemnation of slavery, that springs from nature, unseared and unperverted. Of all consciences let me have those to deal with which have not been bewildered by the cares of life. I do not remember ever to have met with a *boy*, while I was in slavery, who defended the slave system; but I have often had boys to console me, with the hope that something would yet occur, by which I might be made free. Over and over again, they have told me, that "they believed I had as good a right to be free as *they* had;" and that "they did not believe God ever made any one to be a slave." The reader will easily see, that such little conversations with my play fellows, had no tendency to weaken my love of liberty, nor to render me contented with my condition as a slave.

When I was about thirteen years old, and had succeeded in learning to read, every increase of knowledge, especially respecting the FREE STATES, added something to the almost intolerable burden of the thought—I AM A SLAVE FOR LIFE. To my bondage I saw no end. It was a terrible reality, and I shall never be able to tell how sadly that thought chafed my young spirit. Fortunately, or unfortunately, about this time in my life, I had made enough money to buy what was then a very popular school book, viz: the *Columbian Orator*. I bought this addition to my library, of Mr. Knight, on Thames street, Fell's Point, Baltimore, and paid him fifty cents for it. I was first led to buy this book, by hearing some little boys say they were going to learn some little pieces out of it for the Exhibition. This volume was, indeed, a rich treasure, and every opportunity afforded me, for a time, was spent in diligently perusing it. Among much other interesting matter, that which I had perused and reperused with unflagging satisfaction, was a short dialogue between a master and his slave. The slave is represented as having been recaptured, in a second attempt to run away; and the master opens the dialogue with an upbraiding speech, charging the slave with ingratitude, and demanding to know what he has to say in his own defense. Thus upbraided, and thus called upon to reply, the slave rejoins, that he knows how little anything that he can say will avail, seeing that he is completely in the hands of his owner; and with noble resolution, calmly says, "I submit to my fate." Touched by the slave's answer, the master insists upon his further speaking, and recapitulates the many acts of kindness which he has performed toward the slave, and tells him he is permitted to speak for himself. Thus invited to the debate, the quondam slave made a spirited defense of himself, and thereafter the whole argument, for and against slavery, was brought out. The master was vanquished at every turn in the argument; and seeing himself to be thus vanquished, he generously and meekly emancipates the slave, with his best wishes for his prosperity. It is scarcely neccessary(sic) to say, that a dialogue, with such an origin, and such an ending—read when the fact of my being a slave was a constant burden of grief—powerfully affected me; and I could not help feeling that the day might come, when the well-directed answers made by the slave to the master, in this instance, would find their counterpart in myself.

This, however, was not all the fanaticism which I found in this *Columbian Orator*. I met there one of Sheridan's mighty speeches, on the subject of Catholic Emancipation, Lord Chatham's speech on the American war, and speeches by the great William Pitt and by Fox. These were all choice documents to me, and I read them, over and over again, with an interest that was ever increasing, because it was ever gaining in intelligence; for the more I read them, the better I understood them. The reading of these speeches added much to my limited stock of language, and enabled me to give tongue to many interesting thoughts, which had frequently flashed through my soul, and died away for want of utterance. The mighty power and heart-searching directness of truth, penetrating even the heart of a slaveholder, compelling him to yield up his earthly interests to the claims of eternal justice, were finely illustrated in the dialogue, just referred to; and from the speeches of Sheridan, I got a bold and powerful denunciation of oppression, and a most brilliant vindication of the rights of man. Here was, indeed, a noble acquisition. If I ever wavered under the consideration, that the Almighty, in some way, ordained slavery, and willed my enslavement for his own glory, I wavered no longer. I had now penetrated the secret of all slavery and oppression, and had ascertained their true foundation to be in the pride, the power and the avarice of man. The dialogue and the speeches were all redolent of the principles of liberty, and poured floods of light on the nature and character of slavery. With a book of this kind in my hand, my own human nature, and the facts of my experience, to help me, I was equal to a contest with the religious advocates of slavery, whether among the whites or among the colored people, for blindness, in this matter, is not confined to the former. I have met many religious colored people, at the south, who are under the delusion that God requires them to submit to slavery, and to wear their chains with meekness and humility. I could entertain no such nonsense as this; and I almost lost my patience when I found any colored man weak enough to believe such stuff. Nevertheless, the increase of knowledge was attended with bitter, as well as sweet results. The more I read, the more I was led to abhor and detest slavery, and my enslavers. "Slaveholders," thought I, "are only a band of successful robbers, who left their homes and went into Africa for the purpose of stealing and reducing my people to slavery." I loathed them as the meanest and the most wicked of men. As I read, behold! the very discontent so graphically pre dicted by Master Hugh, had already come upon me. I was no longer the light-hearted, gleesome boy, full of mirth and play, as when I landed first at Baltimore. Knowledge had come; light had penetrated the moral dungeon where I dwelt; and, behold! there lay the bloody whip, for my back, and here was the iron chain; and my good, *kind master*, he was the author of my situation. The revelation haunted me, stung me, and made me gloomy and miserable. As I writhed under the sting and torment of this knowledge, I almost envied my fellow slaves their stupid contentment. This knowledge opened my eyes to the horrible pit, and revealed the teeth of the frightful dragon that was ready to pounce upon me, but it opened no way for my escape. I have often wished myself a beast, or a bird—anything, rather than a slave. I was wretched and gloomy, beyond my ability to describe. I was too thoughtful to be happy. It was this everlasting thinking which distressed and tormented me; and yet there was no getting rid of the subject of my thoughts. All nature was redolent of it. Once awakened by the silver trump of knowledge, my spirit was roused to eternal wakefulness. Liberty! the inestimable birthright of every man, had, for me, converted every object into an asserter of this great right. It was heard in every sound, and beheld in every object. It was ever present, to torment me with a sense of my wretched condition. The more beautiful and charming were the smiles of nature, the more horrible and desolate was my condition. I saw nothing without seeing it, and I heard nothing without hearing it. I do not exaggerate, when I say, that it looked from every star, smiled in every calm, breathed in every wind, and moved in every storm.

    I have no doubt that my state of mind had something to do with the change in the treatment adopted, by my once kind mistress toward me. I can easily believe, that my leaden, downcast, and discontented look, was very offensive to her. Poor lady! She did not know my trouble, and I dared not tell her. Could I have freely made her acquainted with the real state of my mind, and given her the reasons therefor, it might have been well for both of us. Her abuse of me fell upon me like the blows of the false prophet upon his ass; she did not know that an *angel* stood in the way; and—such is the relation of master and slave I could not tell her. Nature had made us *friends;* slavery made us *enemies*. My interests were in a direction opposite to hers, and we both had our private thoughts and plans. She aimed to keep me ignorant; and I resolved to know, although knowledge only increased my discontent. My feelings were not the result of any marked cruelty in the treatment I received; they sprung from the consideration of my being a slave at all. It was *slavery*—not its mere *incidents*—that I hated. I had been cheated. I saw through the attempt to keep me in ignorance; I saw that slaveholders would have gladly made me believe that they were merely acting under the authority of God, in making a slave of me, and in making slaves of others; and I treated them as robbers and deceivers. The feeding and clothing me well, could not atone for taking my liberty from me. The smiles of my mistress could not remove the deep sorrow that dwelt in my young bosom. Indeed, these, in time, came only to deepen my sorrow. She had changed; and the reader will see that I had changed, too. We were both victims to the same overshadowing evil—*she*, as mistress, I, as slave. I will not censure her harshly; she cannot censure me, for she knows I speak but the truth, and have acted in my opposition to slavery, just as she herself would have acted, in a reverse of circumstances.

CHAPTER XII.
Religious Nature Awakened

ABOLITIONISTS SPOKEN OF—MY EAGERNESS TO KNOW WHAT THIS WORD MEANT—MY CONSULTATION OF THE DICTIONARY—INCENDIARY INFORMATION—HOW AND WHERE DERIVED—THE ENIGMA SOLVED—NATHANIEL TURNER'S INSURRECTION—THE CHOLERA—RELIGION—FIRST AWAKENED BY A METHODIST MINISTER NAMED HANSON—MY DEAR AND GOOD OLD COLORED FRIEND, LAWSON—HIS CHARACTER AND OCCUPATION—HIS INFLUENCE OVER ME—OUR MUTUAL ATTACHMENT—THE COMFORT I DERIVED FROM HIS TEACHING—NEW HOPES AND ASPIRATIONS—HEAVENLY LIGHT AMIDST EARTHLY DARKNESS—THE TWO IRISHMEN ON THE WHARF—THEIR CONVERSATION—HOW I LEARNED TO WRITE—WHAT WERE MY AIMS.

Whilst in the painful state of mind described in the foregoing chapter, almost regretting my very existence, because doomed to a life of bondage, so goaded and so wretched, at times, that I was even tempted to destroy my own life, I was keenly sensitive and eager to know any, and every thing that transpired, having any relation to the subject of slavery. I was all ears, all eyes, whenever the words *slave, slavery*, dropped from the lips of any white person, and the occasions were not unfrequent when these words became leading ones, in high, social debate, at our house. Every little while, I could hear Master Hugh, or some of his company, speaking with much warmth and excitement about *"abolitionists."* Of *who* or *what* these were, I was totally ignorant. I found, however, that whatever they might be, they were most cordially hated and soundly abused by slaveholders, of every grade. I very soon discovered, too, that slavery was, in some sort, under consideration, whenever the abolitionists were alluded to. This made the term a very interesting one to me. If a slave, for instance, had made good his escape from slavery, it was generally alleged, that he had been persuaded and assisted by the abolitionists. If, also, a slave killed his master—as was sometimes the case—or struck down his overseer, or set fire to his master's dwelling, or committed any violence or crime, out of the common way, it was certain to be said, that such a crime was the legitimate fruits of the abolition movement. Hearing such charges often repeated, I, naturally enough, received the impression that abolition—whatever else it might be—could not be unfriendly to the slave, nor very friendly to the slaveholder. I therefore set about finding out, if possible, *who* and *what* the abolitionists were, and *why* they were so obnoxious to the slaveholders. The dictionary afforded me very little help. It taught me that abolition was the "act of abolishing;" but it left me in ignorance at the very point where I most wanted information—and that was, as to the *thing* to be abolished. A city newspaper, the *Baltimore American*, gave me the incendiary information denied me by the dictionary. In its columns I found, that, on a certain day, a vast number of petitions and memorials had been presented to congress, praying for the abolition of slavery in the District of Columbia, and for the abolition of the slave trade between the states of the Union. This was enough. The vindictive bitterness, the marked caution, the studied reverse, and the cumbrous ambiguity, practiced by our white folks, when alluding to this subject, was now fully explained. Ever, after that, when I heard the words "abolition," or "abolition movement," mentioned, I felt the matter one of a personal concern; and I drew near to listen, when I could do so, without seeming too solicitous and prying. There was HOPE in those words. Ever and anon, too, I could see some terrible denunciation of slavery, in our papers—copied from abolition papers at the north—and the injustice of such denunciation commented on. These I read with avidity. I had a deep satisfaction in the thought, that the rascality of slaveholders was not concealed from the eyes of the world, and that I was not alone in abhorring the cruelty and brutality of slavery. A still deeper train of thought was stirred. I saw that there was *fear*, as well as *rage*, in the manner of speaking of the abolitionists. The latter, therefore, I was compelled to regard as having some power in the country; and I felt that they might, possibly, succeed in their designs. When I met with a slave to whom I deemed it safe to talk on the subject, I would impart to him so much of the mystery as I had been able to penetrate. Thus, the light of this grand movement broke in upon my mind, by degrees; and I must say, that, ignorant as I then was of the philosophy of that movement, I believe in it from the first—and I believed in it, partly, because I saw that it alarmed the consciences of slaveholders. The insurrection of Nathaniel Turner had been quelled, but the alarm and terror had not subsided. The cholera was on its way, and the thought was present, that God was angry with the white people because of their slaveholding wickedness, and, therefore, his judgments were abroad in the land. It was impossible for me not to hope much from the abolition movement, when I saw it supported by the Almighty, and armed with DEATH!

Previous to my contemplation of the anti-slavery movement, and its probable results, my mind had been seriously awakened to the subject of religion. I was not more than thirteen years old, when I felt the need of God, as a father and protector. My religious nature was awakened by the preaching of a white Methodist minister, named Hanson. He thought that all men, great and small, bond and free, were sinners in the sight of God; that they were, by nature, rebels against His government; and that they must repent of their sins, and be reconciled to God, through Christ. I cannot say that I had a very distinct notion of what was required of me; but one thing I knew very well—I was wretched, and had no means of making myself otherwise. Moreover, I knew that I could pray for light. I consulted a good colored man, named Charles Johnson; and, in tones of holy affection, he told me to pray, and what to pray for. I was, for weeks, a poor, brokenhearted mourner, traveling through the darkness and misery of doubts and fears. I finally found that change of heart which comes by "casting all one's care" upon God, and by having faith in Jesus Christ, as the Redeemer, Friend, and Savior of those who diligently seek Him.

After this, I saw the world in a new light. I seemed to live in a new world, surrounded by new objects, and to be animated by new hopes and desires. I loved all mankind—slaveholders not excepted; though I abhorred slavery more than ever. My great concern was, now, to have the world converted. The desire for knowledge increased, and especially did I want a thorough acquaintance with the contents of the bible. I have gathered scattered pages from this holy book, from the filthy street gutters of Baltimore, and washed and dried them, that in the moments of my leisure, I might get a word or two of wisdom from them. While thus religiously seeking knowledge, I became acquainted with a good old colored man, named Lawson. A more devout man than he, I never saw. He drove a dray for Mr. James Ramsey, the owner of a rope-walk on Fell's Point, Baltimore. This man not only prayed three time a day, but he prayed as he walked through the streets, at his work—on his dray everywhere. His life was a life of prayer, and his words (when he spoke to his friends,) were about a better world. Uncle Lawson lived near Master Hugh's house; and, becoming deeply attached to the old man, I went often with him to prayer-meeting, and spent much of my leisure time with him on Sunday. The old man could read a little, and I was a great help to him, in making out the hard words, for I was a better reader than he. I could teach him *"the letter,"* but he could teach me *"the spirit;"* and high, refreshing times we had together, in singing, praying and glorifying God. These meetings with Uncle Lawson went on for a long time, without the knowledge of Master Hugh or my mistress. Both knew, how ever, that I had become religious, and they seemed to respect my conscientious piety. My mistress was still a professor of religion, and belonged to class. Her leader was no less a person than the Rev. Beverly Waugh, the presiding elder, and now one of the bishops of the Methodist Episcopal church. Mr. Waugh was then stationed over Wilk street church. I am careful to state these facts, that the reader may be able to form an idea of the precise influences which had to do with shaping and directing my mind.

In view of the cares and anxieties incident to the life she was then leading, and, especially, in view of the separation from religious associations to which she was subjected, my mistress had, as I have before stated, become lukewarm, and needed to be looked up by her leader. This brought Mr. Waugh to our house, and gave me an opportunity to hear him exhort and pray. But my chief instructor, in matters of religion, was Uncle Lawson. He was my spiritual father; and I loved him intensely, and was at his house every chance I got.

This pleasure was not long allowed me. Master Hugh became averse to my going to Father Lawson's, and threatened to whip me if I ever went there again. I now felt myself persecuted by a wicked man; and I *would* go to Father Lawson's, notwithstanding the threat. The good old man had told me, that the "Lord had a great work for me to do;" and I must prepare to do it; and that he had been shown that I must preach the gospel. His words made a deep impression on my mind, and I verily felt that some such work was before me, though I could not see *how* I should ever engage in its performance. "The good Lord," he said, "would bring it to pass in his own good time," and that I must go on reading and studying the scriptures. The advice and the suggestions of Uncle Lawson, were not without their influence upon my character and destiny. He threw my thoughts into a channel from which they have never entirely diverged. He fanned my already intense love of knowledge into a flame, by assuring me that I was to be a useful man in the world. When I would say to him, "How can these things be and what can *I* do?" his simple reply was, *"Trust in the Lord."* When I told him that "I was a slave, and a slave FOR LIFE," he said, "the Lord can make you free, my dear. All things are possible with him, only *have faith in God."* "Ask, and it shall be given." "If you want liberty," said the good old man, "ask the Lord for it, *in faith*, AND HE WILL GIVE IT TO YOU."

Thus assured, and cheered on, under the inspiration of hope, I worked and prayed with a light heart, believing that my life was under the guidance of a wisdom higher than my own. With all other blessings sought at the mercy seat, I always prayed that God would, of His great mercy, and in His own good time, deliver me from my bondage.

I went, one day, on the wharf of Mr. Waters; and seeing two Irishmen unloading a large scow of stone, or ballast I went on board, unasked, and helped them. When we had finished the work, one of the men came to me, aside, and asked me a number of questions, and among them, if I were a slave. I told him "I was a slave, and a slave for life." The good Irishman gave his shoulders a shrug, and seemed deeply affected by the statement. He said, "it was a pity so fine a little fellow as myself should be a slave for life." They both had much to say about the matter, and expressed the deepest sympathy with me, and the most decided hatred of slavery. They went so far as to tell me that I ought to run away, and go to the north; that I should find friends there, and that I would be as free as anybody. I, however, pretended not to be interested in what they said, for I feared they might be treacherous. White men have been known to encourage slaves to escape, and then—to get the reward—they have kidnapped them, and returned them to their masters. And while I mainly inclined to the notion that these men were honest and meant me no ill, I feared it might be otherwise. I nevertheless remembered their words and their advice, and looked forward to an escape to the north, as a possible means of gaining the liberty for which my heart panted. It was not my enslavement, at the then present time, that most affected me; the being a slave *for life*, was the saddest thought. I was too young to think of running away immediately; besides, I wished to learn how to write, before going, as I might have occasion to write my own pass. I now not only had the hope of freedom, but a foreshadowing of the means by which I might, some day, gain that inestimable boon. Meanwhile, I resolved to add to my educational attainments the art of writing.

After this manner I began to learn to write: I was much in the ship yard—Master Hugh's, and that of Durgan & Bailey—and I observed that the carpenters, after hewing and getting a piece of timber ready for use, wrote on it the initials of the name of that part of the ship for which it was intended. When, for instance, a piece of timber was ready for the starboard side, it was marked with a capital "S." A piece for the larboard side was marked "L;" larboard forward, "L. F.;" larboard aft, was marked "L. A.;" starboard aft, "S. A.;" and starboard forward "S. F." I soon learned these letters, and for what they were placed on the timbers.

My work was now, to keep fire under the steam box, and to watch the ship yard while the carpenters had gone to dinner. This interval gave me a fine opportunity for copying the letters named. I soon astonished myself with the ease with which I made the letters; and the thought was soon present, "if I can make four, I can make more." But having made these easily, when I met boys about Bethel church, or any of our play-grounds, I entered the lists with them in the art of writing, and would make the letters which I had been so fortunate as to learn, and ask them to "beat that if they could." With playmates for my teachers, fences and pavements for my copy books, and chalk for my pen and ink, I learned the art of writing. I, however, afterward adopted various methods of improving my hand. The most successful, was copying the *italics* in Webster's spelling book, until I could make them all without looking on the book. By this time, my little "Master Tommy" had grown to be a big boy, and had written over a number of copy books, and brought them home. They had been shown to the neighbors, had elicited due praise, and were now laid carefully away. Spending my time between the ship yard and house, I was as often the lone keeper of the latter as of the former. When my mistress left me in charge of the house, I had a grand time; I got Master Tommy's copy books and a pen and ink, and, in the ample spaces between the lines, I wrote other lines, as nearly like his as possible. The process was a tedious one, and I ran the risk of getting a flogging for marring the highly prized copy books of the oldest son. In addition to those opportunities, sleeping, as I did, in the kitchen loft—a room seldom visited by any of the family—I got a flour barrel up there, and a chair; and upon the head of that barrel I have written (or endeavored to write) copying from the bible and the Methodist hymn book, and other books which had accumulated on my hands, till late at night, and when all the family were in bed and asleep. I was supported in my endeavors by renewed advice, and by holy promises from the good Father Lawson, with whom I continued to meet, and pray, and read the scriptures. Although Master Hugh was aware of my going there, I must say, for his credit, that he never executed his threat to whip me, for having thus, innocently, employed-my leisure time.

CHAPTER XIII.
THE VICISSITUDES OF SLAVE LIFE

DEATH OF OLD MASTER'S SON RICHARD, SPEEDILY FOLLOWED BY THAT OF OLD MASTER—VALUATION AND DIVISION OF ALL THE PROPERTY, INCLUDING THE SLAVES—MY PRESENCE REQUIRED AT HILLSBOROUGH TO BE APPRAISED AND ALLOTTED TO A NEW OWNER—MY SAD PROSPECTS AND GRIEF—PARTING—THE UTTER POWERLESSNESS OF THE SLAVES TO DECIDE THEIR OWN DESTINY—A GENERAL DREAD OF MASTER ANDREW—HIS WICKEDNESS AND CRUELTY—MISS LUCRETIA MY NEW OWNER—MY RETURN TO BALTIMORE—JOY UNDER THE ROOF OF MASTER HUGH—DEATH OF MRS. LUCRETIA—MY POOR OLD GRANDMOTHER—HER SAD FATE—THE LONE COT IN THE WOODS—MASTER THOMAS AULD'S SECOND MARRIAGE—AGAIN REMOVED FROM MASTER HUGH'S—REASONS FOR REGRETTING THE CHANGE—A PLAN OF ESCAPE ENTERTAINED.

I must now ask the reader to go with me a little back in point of time, in my humble story, and to notice another circumstance that entered into my slavery experience, and which, doubtless, has had a share in deepening my horror of slavery, and increasing my hostility toward those men and measures that practically uphold the slave system.

It has already been observed, that though I was, after my removal from Col. Lloyd's plantation, in *form* the slave of Master Hugh, I was, in *fact*, and in *law*, the slave of my old master, Capt. Anthony. Very well.

In a very short time after I went to Baltimore, my old master's youngest son, Richard, died; and, in three years and six months after his death, my old master himself died, leaving only his son, Andrew, and his daughter, Lucretia, to share his estate. The old man died while on a visit to his daughter, in Hillsborough, where Capt. Auld and Mrs. Lucretia now lived. The former, having given up the command of Col. Lloyd's sloop, was now keeping a store in that town.

Cut off, thus unexpectedly, Capt. Anthony died intestate; and his property must now be equally divided between his two children, Andrew and Lucretia.

The valuation and the division of slaves, among contending heirs, is an important incident in slave life. The character and tendencies of the heirs, are generally well understood among the slaves who are to be divided, and all have their aversions and preferences. But, neither their aversions nor their preferences avail them anything.

On the death of old master, I was immediately sent for, to be valued and divided with the other property. Personally, my concern was, mainly, about my possible removal from the home of Master Hugh, which, after that of my grandmother, was the most endeared to me. But, the whole thing, as a feature of slavery, shocked me. It furnished me anew insight into the unnatural power to which I was subjected. My detestation of slavery, already great, rose with this new conception of its enormity.

That was a sad day for me, a sad day for little Tommy, and a sad day for my dear Baltimore mistress and teacher, when I left for the Eastern Shore, to be valued and divided. We, all three, wept bitterly that day; for we might be parting, and we feared we were parting, forever. No one could tell among which pile of chattels I should be flung. Thus early, I got a foretaste of that painful uncertainty which slavery brings to the ordinary lot of mortals. Sickness, adversity and death may interfere with the plans and purposes of all; but the slave has the added danger of changing homes, changing hands, and of having separations unknown to other men. Then, too, there was the intensified degradation of the spectacle. What an assemblage! Men and women, young and old, married and single; moral and intellectual beings, in open contempt of their humanity, level at a blow with horses, sheep, horned cattle and swine! Horses and men—cattle and women—pigs and children—all holding the same rank in the scale of social existence; and all subjected to the same narrow inspection, to ascertain their value in gold and silver—the only standard of worth applied by slaveholders to slaves! How vividly, at that moment, did the brutalizing power of slavery flash before me! Personality swallowed up in the sordid idea of property! Manhood lost in chattelhood!

After the valuation, then came the division. This was an hour of high excitement and distressing anxiety. Our destiny was now to be *fixed for life*, and we had no more voice in the decision of the question, than the oxen and cows that stood chewing at the haymow. One word from the appraisers, against all preferences or prayers, was enough to sunder all the ties of friendship and affection, and even to separate husbands and wives, parents and children. We were all appalled before that power, which, to human seeming, could bless or blast us in a moment. Added to the dread of separation, most painful to the majority of the slaves, we all had a decided horror of the thought of falling into the hands of Master Andrew. He was distinguished for cruelty and intemperance.

Slaves generally dread to fall into the hands of drunken owners. Master Andrew was almost a confirmed sot, and had already, by his reckless mismanagement and profligate dissipation, wasted a large portion of old master's property. To fall into his hands, was, therefore, considered merely as the first step toward being sold away to the far south. He would spend his fortune in a few years, and his farms and slaves would be sold, we thought, at public outcry; and we should be hurried away to the cotton fields, and rice swamps, of the sunny south. This was the cause of deep consternation.

The people of the north, and free people generally, I think, have less attachment to the places where they are born and brought up, than have the slaves. Their freedom to go and come, to be here and there, as they list, prevents any extravagant attachment to any one particular place, in their case. On the other hand, the slave is a fixture; he has no choice, no goal, no destination; but is pegged down to a single spot, and must take root here, or nowhere. The idea of removal elsewhere, comes, generally, in the shape of a threat, and in punishment of crime. It is, therefore, attended with fear and dread. A slave seldom thinks of bettering his condition by being sold, and hence he looks upon separation from his native place, with none of the enthusiasm which animates the bosoms of young freemen, when they contemplate a life in the far west, or in some distant country where they intend to rise to wealth and distinction. Nor can those from whom they separate, give them up with that cheerfulness with which friends and relations yield each other up, when they feel that it is for the good of the departing one that he is removed from his native place. Then, too, there is correspondence, and there is, at least, the hope of reunion, because reunion is *possible*. But, with the slave, all these mitigating circumstances are wanting. There is no improvement in his condition *probable*,—no correspondence *possible*,—no reunion attainable. His going out into the world, is like a living man going into the tomb, who, with open eyes, sees himself buried out of sight and hearing of wife, children and friends of kindred tie.

In contemplating the likelihoods and possibilities of our circumstances, I probably suffered more than most of my fellow servants. I had known what it was to experience kind, and even tender treatment; they had known nothing of the sort. Life, to them, had been rough and thorny, as well as dark. They had—most of them—lived on my old master's farm in Tuckahoe, and had felt the reign of Mr. Plummer's rule. The overseer had written his character on the living parchment of most of their backs, and left them callous; my back (thanks to my early removal from the plantation to Baltimore) was yet tender. I had left a kind mistress at Baltimore, who was almost a mother to me. She was in tears when we parted, and the probabilities of ever seeing her again, trembling in the balance as they did, could not be viewed without alarm and agony. The thought of leaving that kind mistress forever, and, worse still, of being the slave of Andrew Anthony—a man who, but a few days before the division of the property, had, in my presence, seized my brother Perry by the throat, dashed him on the ground, and with the heel of his boot stamped him on the head, until the blood gushed from his nose and ears—was terrible! This fiendish proceeding had no better apology than the fact, that Perry had gone to play, when Master Andrew wanted him for some trifling service. This cruelty, too, was of a piece with his general character. After inflicting his heavy blows on my brother, on observing me looking at him with intense astonishment, he said, "*That* is the way I will serve you, one of these days;" meaning, no doubt, when I should come into his possession. This threat, the reader may well suppose, was not very tranquilizing to my feelings. I could see that he really thirsted to get hold of me. But I was there only for a few days. I had not received any orders, and had violated none, and there was, therefore, no excuse for flogging me.

At last, the anxiety and suspense were ended; and they ended, thanks to a kind Providence, in accordance with my wishes. I fell to the portion of Mrs. Lucretia—the dear lady who bound up my head, when the savage Aunt Katy was adding to my sufferings her bitterest maledictions.

Capt. Thomas Auld and Mrs. Lucretia at once decided on my return to Baltimore. They knew how sincerely and warmly Mrs. Hugh Auld was attached to me, and how delighted Mr. Hugh's son would be to have me back; and, withal, having no immediate use for one so young, they willingly let me off to Baltimore.

I need not stop here to narrate my joy on returning to Baltimore, nor that of little Tommy; nor the tearful joy of his mother; nor the evident saticfaction(sic) of Master Hugh. I was just one month absent from Baltimore, before the matter was decided; and the time really seemed full six months.

One trouble over, and on comes another. The slave's life is full of uncertainty. I had returned to Baltimore but a short time, when the tidings reached me, that my friend, Mrs. Lucretia, who was only second in my regard to Mrs. Hugh Auld, was dead, leaving her husband and only one child—a daughter, named Amanda.

Shortly after the death of Mrs. Lucretia, strange to say, Master Andrew died, leaving his wife and one child. Thus, the whole family of Anthonys was swept away; only two children remained. All this happened within five years of my leaving Col. Lloyd's.

No alteration took place in the condition of the slaves, in consequence of these deaths, yet I could not help feeling less secure, after the death of my friend, Mrs. Lucretia, than I had done during her life. While she lived, I felt that I had a strong friend to plead for me in any emergency. Ten years ago, while speaking of the state of things in our family, after the events just named, I used this language:

Now all the property of my old master, slaves included, was in the hands of strangers—strangers who had nothing to do in accumulating it. Not a slave was left free. All remained slaves, from youngest to oldest. If any one thing in my experience, more than another, served to deepen my conviction of the infernal character of slavery, and to fill me with unutterable loathing of slaveholders, it was their base ingratitude to my poor old grandmother. She had served my old master faithfully from youth to old age. She had been the source of all his wealth; she had peopled his plantation with slaves; she had become a great-grandmother in his service. She had rocked him in infancy, attended him in childhood, served him through life, and at his death wiped from his icy brow the cold death-sweat, and closed his eyes forever. She was nevertheless left a slave—a slave for life—a slave in the hands of strangers; and in their hands she saw her children, her grandchildren, and her great-grandchildren, divided, like so many sheep, without being gratified with the small privilege of a single word, as to their or her own destiny. And, to cap the climax of their base ingratitude and fiendish barbarity, my grandmother, who was now very old, having outlived my old master and all his children, having seen the beginning and end of all of them, and her present owners finding she was of but little value, her frame already racked with the pains of old age, and complete helplessness fast stealing over her once active limbs, they took her to the woods, built her a little hut, put up a little mud-chimney, and then made her welcome to the privilege of supporting herself there in perfect loneliness; thus virtually turning her out to die! If my poor old grandmother now lives, she lives to suffer in utter loneliness; she lives to remember and mourn over the loss of children, the loss of grandchildren, and the loss of great-grandchildren. They are, in the language of the slave's poet, Whittier—

> *Gone, gone, sold and gone,*
> *To the rice swamp dank and lone,*
> *Where the slave-whip ceaseless swings,*
> *Where the noisome insect stings,*
> *Where the fever-demon strews*
> *Poison with the falling dews,*

> *Where the sickly sunbeams glare*
> *Through the hot and misty air:—*
>   *Gone, gone, sold and gone*
>   *To the rice swamp dank and lone,*
>   *From Virginia hills and waters—*
>   *Woe is me, my stolen daughters!*

The hearth is desolate. The children, the unconscious children, who once sang and danced in her presence, are gone. She gropes her way, in the darkness of age, for a drink of water. Instead of the voices of her children, she hears by day the moans of the dove, and by night the screams of the hideous owl. All is gloom. The grave is at the door. And now, when weighed down by the pains and aches of old age, when the head inclines to the feet, when the beginning and ending of human existence meet, and helpless infancy and painful old age combine together—at this time, this most needful time, the time for the exercise of that tenderness and affection which children only can exercise toward a declining parent—my poor old grandmother, the devoted mother of twelve children, is left all alone, in yonder little hut, before a few dim embers.

Two years after the death of Mrs. Lucretia, Master Thomas married his second wife. Her name was Rowena Hamilton, the eldest daughter of Mr. William Hamilton, a rich slaveholder on the Eastern Shore of Maryland, who lived about five miles from St. Michael's, the then place of my master's residence.

Not long after his marriage, Master Thomas had a misunderstanding with Master Hugh, and, as a means of punishing his brother, he ordered him to send me home.

As the ground of misunderstanding will serve to illustrate the character of southern chivalry, and humanity, I will relate it.

Among the children of my Aunt Milly, was a daughter, named Henny. When quite a child, Henny had fallen into the fire, and burnt her hands so bad that they were of very little use to her. Her fingers were drawn almost into the palms of her hands. She could make out to do something, but she was considered hardly worth the having—of little more value than a horse with a broken leg. This unprofitable piece of human property, ill shapen, and disfigured, Capt. Auld sent off to Baltimore, making his brother Hugh welcome to her services.

After giving poor Henny a fair trial, Master Hugh and his wife came to the conclusion, that they had no use for the crippled servant, and they sent her back to Master Thomas. Thus, the latter took as an act of ingratitude, on the part of his brother; and, as a mark of his displeasure, he required him to send me immediately to St. Michael's, saying, if he cannot keep *"Hen,"* he shall not have *"Fred."*

Here was another shock to my nerves, another breaking up of my plans, and another severance of my religious and social alliances. I was now a big boy. I had become quite useful to several young colored men, who had made me their teacher. I had taught some of them to read, and was accustomed to spend many of my leisure hours with them. Our attachment was strong, and I greatly dreaded the separation. But regrets, especially in a slave, are unavailing. I was only a slave; my wishes were nothing, and my happiness was the sport of my masters.

My regrets at now leaving Baltimore, were not for the same reasons as when I before left that city, to be valued and handed over to my proper owner. My home was not now the pleasant place it had formerly been. A change had taken place, both in Master Hugh, and in his once pious and affectionate wife. The influence of brandy and bad company on him, and the influence of slavery and social isolation upon her, had wrought disastrously upon the characters of both. Thomas was no longer "little Tommy," but was a big boy, and had learned to assume the airs of his class toward me. My condition, therefore, in the house of Master Hugh, was not, by any means, so comfortable as in former years. My attachments were now outside of our family. They were felt to those to whom I *imparted* instruction, and to those little white boys from whom I *received* instruction. There, too, was my dear old father, the pious Lawson, who was, in christian graces, the very counterpart of "Uncle" Tom. The resemblance is so perfect, that he might have been the original of Mrs. Stowe's christian hero. The thought of leaving these dear friends, greatly troubled me, for I was going without the hope of ever returning to Baltimore again; the feud between Master Hugh and his brother being bitter and irreconcilable, or, at least, supposed to be so.

In addition to thoughts of friends from whom I was parting, as I supposed, *forever*, I had the grief of neglected chances of escape to brood over. I had put off running away, until now I was to be placed where the opportunities for escaping were much fewer than in a large city like Baltimore.

On my way from Baltimore to St. Michael's, down the Chesapeake bay, our sloop—the "Amanda"—was passed by the steamers plying between that city and Philadelphia, and I watched the course of those steamers, and, while going to St. Michael's, I formed a plan to escape from slavery; of which plan, and matters connected therewith the kind reader shall learn more hereafter.

CHAPTER XIV.
Experience in St. Michael's

THE VILLAGE—ITS INHABITANTS—THEIR OCCUPATION AND LOW PROPENSITIES CAPTAN(sic) THOMAS AULD—HIS CHARACTER—HIS SECOND WIFE, ROWENA—WELL MATCHED—SUFFERINGS FROM HUNGER—OBLIGED TO TAKE FOOD—MODE OF ARGUMENT IN VINDICATION THEREOF—NO MORAL CODE OF FREE SOCIETY CAN APPLY TO SLAVE SOCIETY—SOUTHERN CAMP MEETING—WHAT MASTER THOMAS DID THERE—HOPES—SUSPICIONS ABOUT HIS CONVERSION—THE RESULT—FAITH AND WORKS ENTIRELY AT VARIANCE—HIS RISE AND PROGRESS IN THE CHURCH—POOR COUSIN "HENNY"—HIS TREATMENT OF HER—THE METHODIST PREACHERS—THEIR UTTER DISREGARD OF US—ONE EXCELLENT EXCEPTION—REV. GEORGE COOKMAN—SABBATH SCHOOL—HOW BROKEN UP AND BY WHOM—A FUNERAL PALL CAST OVER ALL MY PROSPECTS—COVEY THE NEGRO-BREAKER.

St. Michael's, the village in which was now my new home, compared favorably with villages in slave states, generally. There were a few comfortable dwellings in it, but the place, as a whole, wore a dull, slovenly, enterprise-forsaken aspect. The mass of the buildings were wood; they had never enjoyed the artificial adornment of paint, and time and storms had worn off the bright color of the wood, leaving them almost as black as buildings charred by a conflagration.

St. Michael's had, in former years, (previous to 1833, for that was the year I went to reside there,) enjoyed some reputation as a ship building community, but that business had almost entirely given place to oyster fishing, for the Baltimore and Philadelphia markets—a course of life highly unfavorable to morals, industry, and manners. Miles river was broad, and its oyster fishing grounds were extensive; and the fishermen were out, often, all day, and a part of the night, during autumn, winter and spring. This exposure was an excuse for carrying with them, in considerable quanties(sic), spirituous liquors, the then supposed best antidote for cold. Each canoe was supplied with its jug of rum; and tippling, among this class of the citizens of St. Michael's, became general. This drinking habit, in an ignorant population, fostered coarseness, vulgarity and an indolent disregard for the social improvement of the place, so that it was admitted, by the few sober, thinking people who remained there, that St. Michael's had become a very *unsaintly*, as well as unsightly place, before I went there to reside.

I left Baltimore for St. Michael's in the month of March, 1833. I know the year, because it was the one succeeding the first cholera in Baltimore, and was the year, also, of that strange phenomenon, when the heavens seemed about to part with its starry train. I witnessed this gorgeous spectacle, and was awe-struck. The air seemed filled with bright, descending messengers from the sky. It was about daybreak when I saw this sublime scene. I was not without the suggestion, at the moment, that it might be the harbinger of the coming of the Son of Man; and, in my then state of mind, I was prepared to hail Him as my friend and deliverer. I had read, that the "stars shall fall from heaven"; and they were now falling. I was suffering much in my mind. It did seem that every time the young tendrils of my affection became attached, they were rudely broken by some unnatural outside power; and I was beginning to look away to heaven for the rest denied me on earth.

But, to my story. It was now more than seven years since I had lived with Master Thomas Auld, in the family of my old master, on Col. Lloyd's plantation. We were almost entire strangers to each other; for, when I knew him at the house of my old master, it was not as a *master*, but simply as "Captain Auld," who had married old master's daughter. All my lessons concerning his temper and disposition, and the best methods of pleasing him, were yet to be learnt. Slaveholders, however, are not very ceremonious in approaching a slave; and my ignorance of the new material in shape of a master was but transient. Nor was my mistress long in making known her animus. She was not a "Miss Lucretia," traces of whom I yet remembered, and the more especially, as I saw them shining in the face of little Amanda, her daughter, now living under a step-mother's government. I had not forgotten the soft hand, guided by a tender heart, that bound up with healing balsam the gash made in my head by Ike, the son of Abel. Thomas and Rowena, I found to be a well-matched pair. *He* was stingy, and *she* was cruel; and—what was quite natural in such cases—she possessed the ability to make him as cruel as herself, while she could easily descend to the level of his meanness. In the house of Master Thomas, I was made—for the first time in seven years to feel the pinchings of hunger, and this was not very easy to bear.

For, in all the changes of Master Hugh's family, there was no change in the bountifulness with which they supplied me with food. Not to give a slave enough to eat, is meanness intensified, and it is so recognized among slaveholders generally, in Maryland. The rule is, no matter how coarse the food, only let there be enough of it. This is the theory, and—in the part of Maryland I came from—the general practice accords with this theory. Lloyd's plantation was an exception, as was, also, the house of Master Thomas Auld.

All know the lightness of Indian corn-meal, as an article of food, and can easily judge from the following facts whether the statements I have made of the stinginess of Master Thomas, are borne out. There were four slaves of us in the kitchen, and four whites in the great house Thomas Auld, Mrs. Auld, Hadaway Auld (brother of Thomas Auld) and little Amanda. The names of the slaves in the kitchen, were Eliza, my sister; Priscilla, my aunt; Henny, my cousin; and myself. There were eight persons in the family. There was, each week, one half bushel of corn-meal brought from the mill; and in the kitchen, corn-meal was almost our exclusive food, for very little else was allowed us. Out of this bushel of corn-meal, the family in the great house had a small loaf every morning; thus leaving us, in the kitchen, with not quite a half a peck per week, apiece. This allowance was less than half the allowance of food on Lloyd's plantation. It was not enough to subsist upon; and we were, therefore, reduced to the wretched necessity of living at the expense of our neighbors. We were compelled either to beg, or to steal, and we did both. I frankly confess, that while I hated everything like stealing, *as such*, I nevertheless did not hesitate to take food, when I was hungry, wherever I could find it. Nor was this practice the mere result of an unreasoning instinct; it was, in my case, the result of a clear apprehension of the claims of morality. I weighed and considered the matter closely, before I ventured to satisfy my hunger by such means. Considering that my labor and person were the property of Master Thomas, and that I was by him deprived of the necessaries of life necessaries obtained by my own labor—it was easy to deduce the right to supply myself with what was my own. It was simply appropriating what was my own to the use of my master, since the health and strength derived from such food were exerted in *his* service. To be sure, this was stealing, according to the law and gospel I heard from St. Michael's pulpit; but I had already begun to attach less importance to what dropped from that quarter, on that point, while, as yet, I retained my reverence for religion. It was not always convenient to steal from master, and the same reason why I might, innocently, steal from him, did not seem to justify me in stealing from others. In the case of my master, it was only a question of *removal*—the taking his meat out of one tub, and putting it into another; the ownership of the meat was not affected by the transaction. At first, he owned it in the *tub*, and last, he owned it in *me*. His meat house was not always open. There was a strict watch kept on that point, and the key was on a large bunch in Rowena's pocket. A great many times have we, poor creatures, been severely pinched with hunger, when meat and bread have been moulding under the lock, while the key was in the pocket of our mistress. This had been so when she *knew* we were nearly half starved; and yet, that mistress, with saintly air, would kneel with her husband, and pray each morning that a merciful God would bless them in basket and in store, and save them, at last, in his kingdom. But I proceed with the argument.

It was necessary that right to steal from *others* should be established; and this could only rest upon a wider range of generalization than that which supposed the right to steal from my master.

It was sometime before I arrived at this clear right. The reader will get some idea of my train of reasoning, by a brief statement of the case. "I am," thought I, "not only the slave of Thomas, but I am the slave of society at large. Society at large has bound itself, in form and in fact, to assist Master

Thomas in robbing me of my rightful liberty, and of the just reward of my labor; therefore, whatever rights I have against Master Thomas, I have, equally, against those confederated with him in robbing me of liberty. As society has marked me out as privileged plunder, on the principle of self-preservation I am justified in plundering in turn. Since each slave belongs to all; all must, therefore, belong to each."

I shall here make a profession of faith which may shock some, offend others, and be dissented from by all. It is this: Within the bounds of his just earnings, I hold that the slave is fully justified in helping himself to the *gold and silver, and the best apparel of his master, or that of any other slaveholder; and that such taking is not stealing in any just sense of that word.*

The morality of *free* society can have no application to *slave* society. Slaveholders have made it almost impossible for the slave to commit any crime, known either to the laws of God or to the laws of man. If he steals, he takes his own; if he kills his master, he imitates only the heroes of the revolution. Slaveholders I hold to be individually and collectively responsible for all the evils which grow out of the horrid relation, and I believe they will be so held at the judgment, in the sight of a just God. Make a man a slave, and you rob him of moral responsibility. Freedom of choice is the essence of all accountability. But my kind readers are, probably, less concerned about my opinions, than about that which more nearly touches my personal experience; albeit, my opinions have, in some sort, been formed by that experience.

Bad as slaveholders are, I have seldom met with one so entirely destitute of every element of character capable of inspiring respect, as was my present master, Capt. Thomas Auld.

When I lived with him, I thought him incapable of a noble action. The leading trait in his character was intense selfishness. I think he was fully aware of this fact himself, and often tried to conceal it. Capt. Auld was not a *born* slaveholder—not a birthright member of the slaveholding oligarchy. He was only a slaveholder by *marriage-right;* and, of all slaveholders, these latter are, *by far,* the most exacting. There was in him all the love of domination, the pride of mastery, and the swagger of authority, but his rule lacked the vital element of consistency. He could be cruel; but his methods of showing it were cowardly, and evinced his meanness rather than his spirit. His commands were strong, his enforcement weak.

Slaves are not insensible to the whole-souled characteristics of a generous, dashing slaveholder, who is fearless of consequences; and they prefer a master of this bold and daring kind—even with the risk of being shot down for impudence to the fretful, little soul, who never uses the lash but at the suggestion of a love of gain.

Slaves, too, readily distinguish between the birthright bearing of the original slaveholder and the assumed attitudes of the accidental slaveholder; and while they cannot respect either, they certainly despise the latter more than the former.

The luxury of having slaves wait upon him was something new to Master Thomas; and for it he was wholly unprepared. He was a slaveholder, without the ability to hold or manage his slaves. We seldom called him "master," but generally addressed him by his "bay craft" title—"*Capt. Auld.*" It is easy to see that such conduct might do much to make him appear awkward, and, consequently, fretful. His wife was especially solicitous to have us call her husband "master." Is your *master* at the store?"—"Where is your *master*?"—"Go and tell your *master*"—"I will make your *master* acquainted with your conduct"—she would say; but we were inapt scholars. Especially were I and my sister Eliza inapt in this particular. Aunt Priscilla was less stubborn and defiant in her spirit than Eliza and myself; and, I think, her road was less rough than ours.

In the month of August, 1833, when I had almost become desperate under the treatment of Master Thomas, and when I entertained more strongly than ever the oft-repeated determination to run away, a circumstance occurred which seemed to promise brighter and better days for us all. At a Methodist camp-meeting, held in the Bay Side (a famous place for campmeetings) about eight miles from St. Michael's, Master Thomas came out with a profession of religion. He had long been an object of interest to the church, and to the ministers, as I had seen by the repeated visits and lengthy exhortations of the latter. He was a fish quite worth catching, for he had money and standing. In the community of St. Michael's he was equal to the best citizen. He was strictly temperate; *perhaps,* from principle, but most likely, from interest. There was very little to do for him, to give him the appearance of piety, and to make him a pillar in the church. Well, the camp-meeting continued a week; people gathered from all parts of the county, and two steamboat loads came from Baltimore. The ground was happily chosen; seats were arranged; a stand erected; a rude altar fenced in, fronting the preachers' stand, with straw in it for the accommodation of mourners. This latter would hold at least one hundred persons. In front, and on the sides of the preachers' stand, and outside the long rows of seats, rose the first class of stately tents, each vieing with the other in strength, neatness, and capacity for accommodating its inmates. Behind this first circle of tents was another, less imposing, which reached round the camp-ground to the speakers' stand. Outside this second class of tents were covered wagons, ox carts, and vehicles of every shape and size. These served as tents to their owners. Outside of these, huge fires were burning, in all directions, where roasting, and boiling, and frying, were going on, for the benefit of those who were attending to their own spiritual welfare within the circle. *Behind* the preachers' stand, a narrow space was marked out for the use of the colored people. There were no seats provided for this class of persons; the preachers addressed them, *"over the left,"* if they addressed them at all. After the preaching was over, at every service, an invitation was given to mourners to come into the pen; and, in some cases, ministers went out to persuade men and women to come in. By one of these ministers, Master Thomas Auld was persuaded to go inside the pen. I was deeply interested in that matter, and followed; and, though colored people were not allowed either in the pen or in front of the preachers' stand, I ventured to take my stand at a sort of half-way place between the blacks and whites, where I could distinctly see the movements of mourners, and especially the progress of Master Thomas.

"If he has got religion," thought I, "he will emancipate his slaves; and if he should not do so much as this, he will, at any rate, behave toward us more kindly, and feed us more generously than he has heretofore done." Appealing to my own religious experience, and judging my master by what was true in my own case, I could not regard him as soundly converted, unless some such good results followed his profession of religion.

But in my expectations I was doubly disappointed; Master Thomas was *Master Thomas* still. The fruits of his righteousness were to show themselves in no such way as I had anticipated. His conversion was not to change his relation toward men—at any rate not toward BLACK men—but toward God. My faith, I confess, was not great. There was something in his appearance that, in my mind, cast a doubt over his conversion. Standing where I did, I could see his every movement. I watched narrowly while he remained in the little pen; and although I saw that his face was extremely red, and his hair disheveled, and though I heard him groan, and saw a stray tear halting on his cheek, as if inquiring "which way shall I go?"—I could not wholly confide in the genuineness of his conversion. The hesitating behavior of that tear-drop and its loneliness, distressed me, and cast a doubt upon the whole transaction, of which it was a part. But people said, "Capt. Auld had come through," and it was for me to hope for the best. I was bound to do this, in charity, for I, too, was religious, and had been in the church full three years, although now I was not more than sixteen years old. Slaveholders may, sometimes, have confidence in the piety of some of their slaves; but the slaves seldom have confidence in the piety of their masters. *"He cant go to heaven with our blood in his skirts,"* is a settled point in the creed of every slave; rising superior to all teaching to the contrary, and standing forever as a fixed fact. The highest evidence the slaveholder can give the slave of his acceptance with God, is the emancipation of his slaves. This is proof that he is willing to give up all to God, and for the sake of God. Not to do this, was, in my estimation, and in the opinion of all the slaves, an evidence of half-heartedness, and wholly inconsistent with the idea of genuine conversion. I had read, also, somewhere in the Methodist Discipline, the following question and answer:

"*Question.* What shall be done for the extirpation of slavery?

"*Answer.* We declare that we are much as ever convinced of the great evil of slavery; therefore, no slaveholder shall be eligible to any official station in our church."

These words sounded in my ears for a long time, and encouraged me to hope. But, as I have before said, I was doomed to disappointment. Master Thomas seemed to be aware of my hopes and expectations concerning him. I have thought, before now, that he looked at me in answer to my glances, as much as to say, "I will teach you, young man, that, though I have parted with my sins, I have not parted with my sense. I shall hold my slaves, and go to heaven too."

Possibly, to convince us that we must not presume *too much* upon his recent conversion, he became rather more rigid and stringent in his exactions. There always was a scarcity of good nature about the man; but now his whole countenance was *soured* over with the seemings of piety. His religion, therefore, neither made him emancipate his slaves, nor caused him to treat them with greater humanity. If religion had any effect on his character at all, it made him more cruel and hateful in all his ways. The natural wickedness of his heart had not been removed, but only reinforced, by the profession of religion. Do I judge him harshly? God forbid. Facts *are* facts. Capt. Auld made the greatest profession of piety. His house was, literally, a house of prayer. In the morning, and in the evening, loud prayers and hymns were heard there, in which both himself and his wife joined; yet, *no more meal* was brought from the mill, *no more attention* was paid to the moral welfare of the kitchen; and nothing was done to make us feel that the heart of Master Thomas was one whit better than it was before he went into the little pen, opposite to the preachers' stand, on the camp ground.

Our hopes (founded on the discipline) soon vanished; for the authorities let him into the church *at once*, and before he was out of his term of *probation*, I heard of his leading class! He distinguished himself greatly among the brethren, and was soon an exhorter. His progress was almost as rapid as the growth of the fabled vine of Jack's bean. No man was more active than he, in revivals. He would go many miles to assist in carrying them on, and in getting outsiders interested in religion. His house being one of the holiest, if not the happiest in St. Michael's, became the "preachers' home." These preachers evidently liked to share Master Thomas's hospitality; for while he *starved us*, he *stuffed* them. Three or four of these ambassadors of the gospel—according to slavery—have been there at a time; all living on the fat of the land, while we, in the kitchen, were nearly starving. Not often did we get a smile of recognition from these holy men. They seemed almost as unconcerned about our getting to heaven, as they were about our getting out of slavery. To this general charge there was one exception—the Rev. GEORGE COOKMAN. Unlike Rev. Messrs. Storks, Ewry, Hickey, Humphrey and Cooper (all whom were on the St. Michael's circuit) he kindly took an interest in our temporal and spiritual welfare. Our souls and our bodies were all alike sacred in his sight; and he really had a good deal of genuine anti-slavery feeling mingled with his colonization ideas. There was not a slave in our neighborhood that did not love, and almost venerate, Mr. Cookman. It was pretty generally believed that he had been chiefly instrumental in bringing one of the largest slaveholders—Mr. Samuel Harrison—in that neighborhood, to emancipate all his slaves, and, indeed, the general impression was, that Mr. Cookman had labored faithfully with slaveholders, whenever he met them, to induce them to emancipate their bondmen, and that he did this as a religious duty. When this good man was at our house, we were all sure to be called in to prayers in the morning; and he was not slow in making inquiries as to the state of our minds, nor in giving us a word of exhortation and of encouragement. Great was the sorrow of all the slaves, when this faithful preacher of the gospel was removed from the Talbot county circuit. He was an eloquent preacher, and possessed what few ministers, south of Mason Dixon's line, possess, or *dare* to show, viz: a warm and philanthropic heart. The Mr. Cookman, of whom I speak, was an Englishman by birth, and perished while on his way to England, on board the ill-fated "President". Could the thousands of slaves in Maryland know the fate of the good man, to whose words of comfort they were so largely indebted, they would thank me for dropping a tear on this page, in memory of their favorite preacher, friend and benefactor.

But, let me return to Master Thomas, and to my experience, after his conversion. In Baltimore, I could, occasionally, get into a Sabbath school, among the free children, and receive lessons, with the rest; but, having already learned both to read and to write, I was more of a teacher than a pupil, even there. When, however, I went back to the Eastern Shore, and was at the house of Master Thomas, I was neither allowed to teach, nor to be taught. The whole community—with but a single exception, among the whites—frowned upon everything like imparting instruction either to slaves or to free colored persons. That single exception, a pious young man, named Wilson, asked me, one day, if I would like to assist him in teaching a little Sabbath school, at the house of a free colored man in St. Michael's, named James Mitchell. The idea was to me a delightful one, and I told him I would gladly devote as much of my Sabbath as I could command, to that most laudable work. Mr.

Wilson soon mustered up a dozen old spelling books, and a few testaments; and we commenced operations, with some twenty scholars, in our Sunday school. Here, thought I, is something worth living for; here is an excellent chance for usefulness; and I shall soon have a company of young friends, lovers of knowledge, like some of my Baltimore friends, from whom I now felt parted forever.

Our first Sabbath passed delightfully, and I spent the week after very joyously. I could not go to Baltimore, but I could make a little Baltimore here. At our second meeting, I learned that there was some objection to the existence of the Sabbath school; and, sure enough, we had scarcely got at work—*good work*, simply teaching a few colored children how to read the gospel of the Son of God—when in rushed a mob, headed by Mr. Wright Fairbanks and Mr. Garrison West—two class-leaders—and Master Thomas; who, armed with sticks and other missiles, drove us off, and commanded us never to meet for such a purpose again. One of this pious crew told me, that as for my part, I wanted to be another Nat Turner; and if I did not look out, I should get as many balls into me, as Nat did into him. Thus ended the infant Sabbath school, in the town of St. Michael's. The reader will not be surprised when I say, that the breaking up of my Sabbath school, by these class-leaders, and professedly holy men, did not serve to strengthen my religious convictions. The cloud over my St. Michael's home grew heavier and blacker than ever.

It was not merely the agency of Master Thomas, in breaking up and destroying my Sabbath school, that shook my confidence in the power of southern religion to make men wiser or better; but I saw in him all the cruelty and meanness, *after* his conversion, which he had exhibited before he made a profession of religion. His cruelty and meanness were especially displayed in his treatment of my unfortunate cousin, Henny, whose lameness made her a burden to him. I have no extraordinary personal hard usage toward myself to complain of, against him, but I have seen him tie up the lame and maimed woman, and whip her in a manner most brutal, and shocking; and then, with blood-chilling blasphemy, he would quote the passage of scripture, "That servant which knew his lord's will, and prepared not himself, neither did according to his will, shall be beaten with many stripes." Master would keep this lacerated woman tied up by her wrists, to a bolt in the joist, three, four and five hours at a time. He would tie her up early in the morning, whip her with a cowskin before breakfast; leave her tied up; go to his store, and, returning to his dinner, repeat the castigation; laying on the rugged lash, on flesh already made raw by repeated blows. He seemed desirous to get the poor girl out of existence, or, at any rate, off his hands. In proof of this, he afterwards gave her away to his sister Sarah (Mrs. Cline) but, as in the case of Master Hugh, Henny was soon returned on his hands. Finally, upon a pretense that he could do nothing with her (I use his own words) he "set her adrift, to take care of herself." Here was a recently converted man, holding, with tight grasp, the well-framed, and able bodied slaves left him by old master—the persons, who, in freedom, could have taken care of themselves; yet, turning loose the only cripple among them, virtually to starve and die.

No doubt, had Master Thomas been asked, by some pious northern brother, *why* he continued to sustain the relation of a slaveholder, to those whom he retained, his answer would have been precisely the same as many other religious slaveholders have returned to that inquiry, viz: "I hold my slaves for their own good."

Bad as my condition was when I lived with Master Thomas, I was soon to experience a life far more goading and bitter. The many differences springing up between myself and Master Thomas, owing to the clear perception I had of his character, and the boldness with which I defended myself against his capricious complaints, led him to declare that I was unsuited to his wants; that my city life had affected me perniciously; that, in fact, it had almost ruined me for every good purpose, and had fitted me for everything that was bad. One of my greatest faults, or offenses, was that of letting his horse get away, and go down to the farm belonging to his father-in-law. The animal had a liking for that farm, with which I fully sympathized. Whenever I let it out, it would go dashing down the road to Mr. Hamilton's, as if going on a grand frolic. My horse gone, of course I must go after it. The explanation of our mutual attachment to the place is the same; the horse found there good pasturage, and I found there plenty of bread. Mr. Hamilton had his faults, but starving his slaves was not among them. He gave food, in abundance, and that, too, of an excellent quality. In Mr.

Hamilton's cook—Aunt Mary—I found a most generous and considerate friend. She never allowed me to go there without giving me bread enough to make good the deficiencies of a day or two. Master Thomas at last resolved to endure my behavior no longer; he could neither keep me, nor his horse, we liked so well to be at his father-in-law's farm. I had now lived with him nearly nine months, and he had given me a number of severe whippings, without any visible improvement in my character, or my conduct; and now he was resolved to put me out—as he said—"*to be broken.*"

There was, in the Bay Side, very near the camp ground, where my master got his religious impressions, a man named Edward Covey, who enjoyed the execrated reputation, of being a first rate hand at breaking young Negroes. This Covey was a poor man, a farm renter; and this reputation (hateful as it was to the slaves and to all good men) was, at the same time, of immense advantage to him. It enabled him to get his farm tilled with very little expense, compared with what it would have cost him without this most extraordinary reputation. Some slaveholders thought it an advantage to let Mr. Covey have the government of their slaves a year or two, almost free of charge, for the sake of the excellent training such slaves got under his happy management! Like some horse breakers, noted for their skill, who ride the best horses in the country without expense, Mr. Covey could have under him, the most fiery bloods of the neighborhood, for the simple reward of returning them to their owners, *well broken*. Added to the natural fitness of Mr. Covey for the duties of his profession, he was said to "enjoy religion," and was as strict in the cultivation of piety, as he was in the cultivation of his farm. I was made aware of his character by some who had been under his hand; and while I could not look forward to going to him with any pleasure, I was glad to get away from St. Michael's. I was sure of getting enough to eat at Covey's, even if I suffered in other respects. *This*, to a hungry man, is not a prospect to be regarded with indifference.

CHAPTER XV.
COVEY, THE NEGRO BREAKER

JOURNEY TO MY NEW MASTER'S—MEDITATIONS BY THE WAY—VIEW OF COVEY'S RESIDENCE—THE FAMILY—MY AWKWARDNESS AS A FIELD HAND—A CRUEL BEATING—WHY IT WAS GIVEN—DESCRIPTION OF COVEY—FIRST ADVENTURE AT OX DRIVING—HAIR BREADTH ESCAPES—OX AND MAN ALIKE PROPERTY—COVEY'S MANNER OF PROCEEDING TO WHIP—HARD LABOR BETTER THAN THE WHIP FOR BREAKING DOWN THE SPIRIT—CUNNING AND TRICKERY OF COVEY—FAMILY WORSHIP—SHOCKING CONTEMPT FOR CHASTITY—I AM BROKEN DOWN—GREAT MENTAL AGITATION IN CONTRASTING THE FREEDOM OF THE SHIPS WITH HIS OWN SLAVERY—ANGUISH BEYOND DESCRIPTION.

The morning of the first of January, 1834, with its chilling wind and pinching frost, quite in harmony with the winter in my own mind, found me, with my little bundle of clothing on the end of a stick, swung across my shoulder, on the main road, bending my way toward Covey's, whither I had been imperiously ordered by Master Thomas. The latter had been as good as his word, and had committed me, without reserve, to the mastery of Mr. Edward Covey. Eight or ten years had now passed since I had been taken from my grandmother's cabin, in Tuckahoe; and these years, for the most part, I had spent in Baltimore, where—as the reader has already seen—I was treated with comparative tenderness. I was now about to sound profounder depths in slave life. The rigors of a field, less tolerable than the field of battle, awaited me. My new master was notorious for his fierce and savage disposition, and my only consolation in going to live with him was, the certainty of finding him precisely as represented by common fame. There was neither joy in my heart, nor elasticity in my step, as I started in search of the tyrant's home. Starvation made me glad to leave Thomas Auld's, and the cruel lash made me dread to go to Covey's. Escape was impossible; so, heavy and sad, I paced the seven miles, which separated Covey's house from St. Michael's—thinking much by the solitary way—averse to my condition; but *thinking* was all I could do. Like a fish in a net, allowed to play for a time, I was now drawn rapidly to the shore, secured at all points. "I am," thought I, "but the sport of a power which makes no account, either of my welfare or of my happiness. By a law which I can clearly comprehend, but cannot evade nor resist, I am ruthlessly snatched from the hearth of a fond grandmother, and hurried away to the home of a mysterious 'old master;' again I am removed from there, to a master in Baltimore; thence am I snatched away to the Eastern Shore, to be valued with the beasts of the field, and, with them, divided and set apart for a possessor; then I am sent back to Baltimore; and by the time I have formed new attachments, and have begun to hope that no more rude shocks shall touch me, a difference arises between brothers, and I am again broken up, and sent to St. Michael's; and now, from the latter place, I am footing my way to the home of a new master, where, I am given to understand, that, like a wild young working animal, I am to be broken to the yoke of a bitter and life-long bondage."

With thoughts and reflections like these, I came in sight of a small wood-colored building, about a mile from the main road, which, from the description I had received, at starting, I easily recognized as my new home. The Chesapeake bay—upon the jutting banks of which the little wood-colored house was standing—white with foam, raised by the heavy north-west wind; Poplar Island, covered with a thick, black pine forest, standing out amid this half ocean; and Kent Point, stretching its sandy, desert-like shores out into the foam-cested bay—were all in sight, and deepened the wild and desolate aspect of my new home.

The good clothes I had brought with me from Baltimore were now worn thin, and had not been replaced; for Master Thomas was as little careful to provide us against cold, as against hunger. Met here by a north wind, sweeping through an open space of forty miles, I was glad to make any port; and, therefore, I speedily pressed on to the little wood-colored house. The family consisted of

Mr. and Mrs. Covey; Miss Kemp (a broken-backed woman) a sister of Mrs. Covey; William Hughes, cousin to Edward Covey; Caroline, the cook; Bill Smith, a hired man; and myself. Bill Smith, Bill Hughes, and myself, were the working force of the farm, which consisted of three or four hundred acres. I was now, for the first time in my life, to be a field hand; and in my new employment I found myself even more awkward than a green country boy may be supposed to be, upon his first entrance into the bewildering scenes of city life; and my awkwardness gave me much trouble. Strange and unnatural as it may seem, I had been at my new home but three days, before Mr. Covey (my brother in the Methodist church) gave me a bitter foretaste of what was in reserve for me. I presume he thought, that since he had but a single year in which to complete his work, the sooner he began, the better. Perhaps he thought that by coming to blows at once, we should mutually better understand our relations. But to whatever motive, direct or indirect, the cause may be referred, I had not been in his possession three whole days, before he subjected me to a most brutal chastisement. Under his heavy blows, blood flowed freely, and wales were left on my back as large as my little finger. The sores on my back, from this flogging, continued for weeks, for they were kept open by the rough and coarse cloth which I wore for shirting. The occasion and details of this first chapter of my experience as a field hand, must be told, that the reader may see how unreasonable, as well as how cruel, my new master, Covey, was. The whole thing I found to be characteristic of the man; and I was probably treated no worse by him than scores of lads who had previously been committed to him, for reasons similar to those which induced my master to place me with him. But, here are the facts connected with the affair, precisely as they occurred.

On one of the coldest days of the whole month of January, 1834, I was ordered, at day break, to get a load of wood, from a forest about two miles from the house. In order to perform this work, Mr. Covey gave me a pair of unbroken oxen, for, it seems, his breaking abilities had not been turned in this direction; and I may remark, in passing, that working animals in the south, are seldom so well trained as in the north. In due form, and with all proper ceremony, I was introduced to this huge yoke of unbroken oxen, and was carefully told which was "Buck," and which was "Darby"—which was the "in hand," and which was the "off hand" ox. The master of this important ceremony was no less a person than Mr. Covey, himself; and the introduction was the first of the kind I had ever had. My life, hitherto, had led me away from horned cattle, and I had no knowledge of the art of managing them. What was meant by the "in ox," as against the "off ox," when both were equally fastened to one cart, and under one yoke, I could not very easily divine; and the difference, implied by the names, and the peculiar duties of each, were alike *Greek* to me. Why was not the "off ox" called the "in ox?" Where and what is the reason for this distinction in names, when there is none in the things themselves? After initiating me into the *"woa," "back" "gee," "hither"*—the entire spoken language between oxen and driver—Mr. Covey took a rope, about ten feet long and one inch thick, and placed one end of it around the horns of the "in hand ox," and gave the other end to me, telling me that if the oxen started to run away, as the scamp knew they would, I must hold on to the rope and stop them. I need not tell any one who is acquainted with either the strength of the disposition of an untamed ox, that this order was about as unreasonable as a command to shoulder a mad bull! I had never driven oxen before, and I was as awkward, as a driver, as it is possible to conceive. It did not answer for me to plead ignorance, to Mr. Covey; there was something in his manner that quite forbade that. He was a man to whom a slave seldom felt any disposition to speak. Cold, distant, morose, with a face wearing all the marks of captious pride and malicious sternness, he repelled all advances. Covey was not a large man; he was only about five feet ten inches in height, I should think; short necked, round shoulders; of quick and wiry motion, of thin and wolfish visage; with a pair of small, greenish-gray eyes, set well back under a forehead without dignity, and constantly in motion, and floating his passions, rather than his thoughts, in sight, but denying them utterance in words. The creature presented an appearance altogether ferocious and sinister, disagreeable and forbidding, in the extreme. When he spoke, it was from the corner of his mouth, and in a sort of light growl, like a dog, when an attempt is made to take a bone from him. The fellow had already made me believe him even *worse* than he had been presented. With his directions, and without stopping to question, I started for the woods, quite anxious to perform my first exploit in driving, in a creditable manner. The distance from the house to the woods gate a full mile, I should think—was passed over with very little difficulty; for although the animals ran, I was fleet enough, in the open field, to keep pace with them; especially as they pulled me along at the end of the rope; but, on reaching the woods, I was speedily thrown into a distressing plight. The animals took fright, and started off ferociously into the woods, carrying the cart, full tilt, against trees, over stumps, and dashing from side to side, in a manner altogether frightful. As I held the rope, I expected every moment to be crushed between the cart and the huge trees, among which they were so furiously dashing. After running thus for several minutes, my oxen were, finally, brought to a stand, by a tree, against which they dashed themselves with great violence, upsetting the cart, and entangling themselves among sundry young saplings. By the shock, the body of the cart was flung in one direction, and the wheels and tongue in another, and all in the greatest confusion. There I was, all alone, in a thick wood, to which I was a stranger; my cart upset and shattered; my oxen entangled, wild, and enraged; and I, poor soul! but a green hand, to set all this disorder right. I knew no more of oxen than the ox driver is supposed to know of wisdom. After standing a few moments surveying the damage and disorder, and not without a presentiment that this trouble would draw after it others, even more distressing, I took one end of the cart body, and, by an extra outlay of strength, I lifted it toward the axle-tree, from which it had been violently flung; and after much pulling and straining, I succeeded in getting the body of the cart in its place. This was an important step out of the difficulty, and its performance increased my courage for the work which remained to be done. The cart was provided with an ax, a tool with which I had become pretty well acquainted in the ship yard at Baltimore. With this, I cut down the saplings by which my oxen were entangled, and again pursued my journey, with my heart in my mouth, lest the oxen should again take it into their senseless heads to cut up a caper. My fears were groundless. Their spree was over for the present, and the rascals now moved off as soberly as though their behavior had been natural and exemplary. On reaching the part of the forest where I had been, the day before, chopping wood, I filled the cart with a heavy load, as a security against another running away. But, the neck of an ox is equal in strength to iron. It defies all ordinary burdens, when excited. Tame and docile to a proverb, when *well* trained, the ox is the most sullen and intractable of animals when but half broken to the yoke.

I now saw, in my situation, several points of similarity with that of the oxen. They were property, so was I; they were to be broken, so was I. Covey was to break me, I was to break them; break and be broken—such is life.

Half the day already gone, and my face not yet homeward! It required only two day's experience and observation to teach me, that such apparent waste of time would not be lightly overlooked by Covey. I therefore hurried toward home; but, on reaching the lane gate, I met with the crowning disaster for the day. This gate was a fair specimen of southern handicraft. There were two huge posts, eighteen inches in diameter, rough hewed and square, and the heavy gate was so hung on one of these, that it opened only about half the proper distance. On arriving here, it was necessary for me to let go the end of the rope on the horns of the "in hand ox;" and now as soon as the gate was open, and I let go of it to get the rope, again, off went my oxen—making nothing of their load—full tilt; and in doing so they caught the huge gate between the wheel and the cart body, literally crushing it to splinters, and coming only within a few inches of subjecting me to a similar crushing, for I was just in advance of the wheel when it struck the left gate post. With these two hair-breadth escape, I thought I could sucessfully(sic) explain to Mr. Covey the delay, and avert apprehended punishment. I was not without a faint hope of being commended for the stern resolution which I had displayed in accomplishing the difficult task—a task which, I afterwards learned, even Covey himself would not have undertaken, without first driving the oxen for some time in the open field, preparatory to their going into the woods. But, in this I was disappointed. On coming to him, his countenance assumed an aspect of rigid displeasure, and, as I gave him a history of the casualties of my trip, his wolfish face, with his greenish eyes, became intensely ferocious. "Go back to the woods again," he said, muttering something else about wasting time. I hastily obeyed; but I had not gone far on my way, when I saw him coming after me. My oxen now behaved themselves with singular propriety, opposing their present conduct to my representation of their former antics. I almost wished, now that Covey was coming, they would do something in keeping with the character I had given them; but no, they had already had their spree, and they could afford now to be extra good, readily obeying my orders, and seeming to understand them quite as well as I did myself. On reaching the woods, my tormentor—who seemed all the way to be remarking upon the good behavior of his oxen—came up to me, and ordered me to stop the cart, accompanying the same with the threat that he would now teach me how to break gates, and idle away my time, when he sent me to the woods. Suiting the action to the word, Covey paced off, in his own wiry fashion, to a large, black gum tree, the young shoots of which are generally used for ox *goads*, they being exceedingly tough. Three of these *goads*, from four to six feet long, he cut off, and trimmed up, with his large jack-knife. This done, he ordered me to take off my clothes. To this unreasonable order I made no reply, but sternly refused to take off my clothing. "If you will beat me," thought I, "you shall do so over my clothes." After many threats, which made no impression on me, he rushed at me with something of the savage fierceness of a wolf, tore off the few and thinly worn clothes I had on, and proceeded to wear out, on my back, the heavy goads which he had cut from the gum tree. This flogging was the first of a series of floggings; and though very severe, it was less so than many which came after it, and these, for offenses far lighter than the gate breaking.

    I remained with Mr. Covey one year (I cannot say I *lived* with him) and during the first six months that I was there, I was whipped, either with sticks or cowskins, every week. Aching bones and a sore back were my constant companions. Frequent as the lash was used, Mr. Covey thought less of it, as a means of breaking down my spirit, than that of hard and long continued labor. He worked me steadily, up to the point of my powers of endurance. From the dawn of day in the morning, till the darkness was complete in the evening, I was kept at hard work, in the field or the woods. At certain seasons of the year, we were all kept in the field till eleven and twelve o'clock at night. At these times, Covey would attend us in the field, and urge us on with words or blows, as it seemed best to him. He had, in his life, been an overseer, and he well understood the business of slave driving. There was no deceiving him. He knew just what a man or boy could do, and he held both to strict account. When he pleased, he would work himself, like a very Turk, making everything fly before him. It was, however, scarcely necessary for Mr. Covey to be really present in the field, to have his work go on industriously. He had the faculty of making us feel that he was always present. By a series of adroitly managed surprises, which he practiced, I was prepared to expect him at any moment. His plan was, never to approach the spot where his hands were at work, in an open, manly and direct manner. No thief was ever more artful in his devices than this man Covey. He would creep and crawl, in ditches and gullies; hide behind stumps and bushes, and practice so much of the cunning of the serpent, that Bill Smith and I—between ourselves—never called him by any other name than *"the snake."* We fancied that in his eyes and his gait we could see a snakish resemblance. One half of his proficiency in the art of Negro breaking, consisted, I should think, in this species of cunning. We were never secure. He could see or hear us nearly all the time. He was, to us, behind every stump, tree, bush and fence on the plantation. He carried this kind of trickery so far, that he would sometimes mount his horse, and make believe he was going to St. Michael's; and, in thirty minutes afterward, you might find his horse tied in the woods, and the snake-like Covey lying flat in the ditch, with his head lifted above its edge, or in a fence corner, watching every movement of the slaves! I have known him walk up to us and give us special orders, as to our work, in advance, as if he were leaving home with a view to being absent several days; and before he got half way to the house, he would avail himself of our inattention to his movements, to turn short on his heels, conceal himself behind a fence corner or a tree, and watch us until the going down of the sun. Mean and contemptible as is all this, it is in keeping with the character which the life of a slaveholder is calculated to produce. There is no earthly inducement, in the slave's condition, to incite him to labor faithfully. The fear of punishment is the sole motive for any sort of industry, with him. Knowing this fact, as the slaveholder does, and judging the slave by himself, he naturally concludes the slave will be idle whenever the cause for this fear is absent. Hence, all sorts of petty deceptions are practiced, to inspire this fear.

    But, with Mr. Covey, trickery was natural. Everything in the shape of learning or religion, which he possessed, was made to conform to this semi-lying propensity. He did not seem conscious that the practice had anything unmanly, base or contemptible about it. It was a part of an important system, with him, essential to the relation of master and slave. I thought I saw, in his very religious devotions, this controlling element of his character. A long prayer at night made up for the short prayer in the morning; and few men could seem more devotional than he, when he had nothing else to do.

Mr. Covey was not content with the cold style of family worship, adopted in these cold latitudes, which begin and end with a simple prayer. No! the voice of praise, as well as of prayer, must be heard in his house, night and morning. At first, I was called upon to bear some part in these exercises; but the repeated flogging given me by Covey, turned the whole thing into mockery. He was a poor singer, and mainly relied on me for raising the hymn for the family, and when I failed to do so, he was thrown into much confusion. I do not think that he ever abused me on account of these vexations. His religion was a thing altogether apart from his worldly concerns. He knew nothing of it as a holy principle, directing and controlling his daily life, making the latter conform to the requirements of the gospel. One or two facts will illustrate his character better than a volume of generalties(sic).

I have already said, or implied, that Mr. Edward Covey was a poor man. He was, in fact, just commencing to lay the foundation of his fortune, as fortune is regarded in a slave state. The first condition of wealth and respectability there, being the ownership of human property, every nerve is strained, by the poor man, to obtain it, and very little regard is had to the manner of obtaining it. In pursuit of this object, pious as Mr. Covey was, he proved himself to be as unscrupulous and base as the worst of his neighbors. In the beginning, he was only able—as he said—"to buy one slave;" and, scandalous and shocking as is the fact, he boasted that he bought her simply "*as a breeder.*" But the worst is not told in this naked statement. This young woman (Caroline was her name) was virtually compelled by Mr. Covey to abandon herself to the object for which he had purchased her; and the result was, the birth of twins at the end of the year. At this addition to his human stock, both Edward Covey and his wife, Susan, were ecstatic with joy. No one dreamed of reproaching the woman, or of finding fault with the hired man—Bill Smith—the father of the children, for Mr. Covey himself had locked the two up together every night, thus inviting the result.

But I will pursue this revolting subject no further. No better illustration of the unchaste and demoralizing character of slavery can be found, than is furnished in the fact that this professedly Christian slaveholder, amidst all his prayers and hymns, was shamelessly and boastfully encouraging, and actually compelling, in his own house, undisguised and unmitigated fornication, as a means of increasing his human stock. I may remark here, that, while this fact will be read with disgust and shame at the north, it will be *laughed at*, as smart and praiseworthy in Mr. Covey, at the south; for a man is no more condemned there for buying a woman and devoting her to this life of dishonor, than for buying a cow, and raising stock from her. The same rules are observed, with a view to increasing the number and quality of the former, as of the latter.

I will here reproduce what I said of my own experience in this wretched place, more than ten years ago:

If at any one time of my life, more than another, I was made to drink the bitterest dregs of slavery, that time was during the first six months of my stay with Mr. Covey. We were worked all weathers. It was never too hot or too cold; it could never rain, blow, snow, or hail too hard for us to work in the field. Work, work, work, was scarcely more the order of the day than the night. The longest days were too short for him, and the shortest nights were too long for him. I was somewhat unmanageable when I first went there; but a few months of his discipline tamed me. Mr. Covey succeeded in breaking me. I was broken in body, soul and spirit. My natural elasticity was crushed; my intellect languished; the disposition to read departed; the cheerful spark that lingered about my eye died; the dark night of slavery closed in upon me; and behold a man transformed into a brute!

Sunday was my only leisure time. I spent this in a sort of beast-like stupor, between sleep and wake, under some large tree. At times, I would rise up, a flash of energetic freedom would dart through my soul, accompanied with a faint beam of hope, flickered for a moment, and then vanished. I sank down again, mourning over my wretched condition. I was sometimes prompted to take my life, and that of Covey, but was prevented by a combination of hope and fear. My sufferings on this plantation seem now like a dream rather than a stern reality.

Our house stood within a few rods of the Chesapeake bay, whose broad bosom was ever white with sails from every quarter of the habitable globe. Those beautiful vessels, robed in purest white, so delightful to the eye of freemen, were to me so many shrouded ghosts, to terrify and torment me with thoughts of my wretched condition. I have often, in the deep stillness of a summer's Sabbath, stood all alone upon the banks of that noble bay, and traced, with saddened heart and tearful eye, the countless number of sails moving off to the mighty ocean. The sight of these always affected me powerfully. My thoughts would compel utterance; and there, with no audience but the Almighty, I would pour out my soul's complaint in my rude way, with an apostrophe to the moving multitude of ships:

"You are loosed from your moorings, and free; I am fast in my chains, and am a slave! You move merrily before the gentle gale, and I sadly before the bloody whip! You are freedom's swift-winged angels, that fly around the world; I am confined in bands of iron! O, that I were free! O, that I were on one of your gallant decks, and under your protecting wing! Alas! betwixt me and you the turbid waters roll. Go on, go on. O that I could also go! Could I but swim! If I could fly! O, why was I born a man, of whom to make a brute! The glad ship is gone; she hides in the dim distance. I am left in the hottest hell of unending slavery. O God, save me! God, deliver me! Let me be free! Is there any God? Why am I a slave? I will run away. I will not stand it. Get caught, or get clear, I'll try it. I had as well die with ague as with fever. I have only one life to lose. I had as well be killed running as die standing. Only think of it; one hundred miles straight north, and I am free! Try it? Yes! God helping me, I will. It cannot be that I shall live and die a slave. I will take to the water. This very bay shall yet bear me into freedom. The steamboats steered in a north-east coast from North Point. I will do the same; and when I get to the head of the bay, I will turn my canoe adrift, and walk straight through Delaware into Pennsylvania. When I get there, I shall not be required to have a pass; I will travel without being disturbed. Let but the first opportunity offer, and come what will, I am off. Meanwhile, I will try to bear up under the yoke. I am not the only slave in the world. Why should I fret? I can bear as much as any of them. Besides, I am but a boy, and all boys are bound to some one. It may be that my misery in slavery will only increase my happiness when I get free. There is a better day coming."

I shall never be able to narrate the mental experience through which it was my lot to pass during my stay at Covey's. I was completely wrecked, changed and bewildered; goaded almost to madness at one time, and at another reconciling myself to my wretched condition. Everything in the way of kindness, which I had experienced at Baltimore; all my former hopes and aspirations for usefulness in the world, and the happy moments spent in the exercises of religion, contrasted with my then present lot, but increased my anguish.

I suffered bodily as well as mentally. I had neither sufficient time in which to eat or to sleep, except on Sundays. The overwork, and the brutal chastisements of which I was the victim, combined with that ever-gnawing and soul-devouring thought—"*I am a slave—a slave for life—a slave with no rational ground to hope for freedom*"—rendered me a living embodiment of mental and physical wretchedness.

CHAPTER XVI.
Another Pressure of the Tyrant's Vice

EXPERIENCE AT COVEY'S SUMMED UP—FIRST SIX MONTHS SEVERER THAN THE SECOND—PRELIMINARIES TO THE CHANCE—REASONS FOR NARRATING THE CIRCUMSTANCES—SCENE IN TREADING YARD—TAKEN ILL—UNUSUAL BRUTALITY OF COVEY—ESCAPE TO ST. MICHAEL'S—THE PURSUIT—SUFFERING IN THE WOODS—DRIVEN BACK AGAIN TO COVEY'S—BEARING OF MASTER THOMAS—THE SLAVE IS NEVER SICK—NATURAL TO EXPECT SLAVES TO FEIGN SICKNESS—LAZINESS OF SLAVEHOLDERS.

The foregoing chapter, with all its horrid incidents and shocking features, may be taken as a fair representation of the first six months of my life at Covey's. The reader has but to repeat, in his own mind, once a week, the scene in the woods, where Covey subjected me to his merciless lash, to have a true idea of my bitter experience there, during the first period of the breaking process through which Mr. Covey carried me. I have no heart to repeat each separate transaction, in which I was victim of his violence and brutality. Such a narration would fill a volume much larger than the present one. I aim only to give the reader a truthful impression of my slave life, without unnecessarily affecting him with harrowing details.

As I have elsewhere intimated that my hardships were much greater during the first six months of my stay at Covey's, than during the remainder of the year, and as the change in my condition was owing to causes which may help the reader to a better understanding of human nature, when subjected to the terrible extremities of slavery, I will narrate the circumstances of this change, although I may seem thereby to applaud my own courage. You have, dear reader, seen me humbled, degraded, broken down, enslaved, and brutalized, and you understand how it was done; now let us see the converse of all this, and how it was brought about; and this will take us through the year 1834.

On one of the hottest days of the month of August, of the year just mentioned, had the reader been passing through Covey's farm, he might have seen me at work, in what is there called the "treading yard"—a yard upon which wheat is trodden out from the straw, by the horses' feet. I was there, at work, feeding the "fan," or rather bringing wheat to the fan, while Bill Smith was feeding. Our force consisted of Bill Hughes, Bill Smith, and a slave by the name of Eli; the latter having been hired for this occasion. The work was simple, and required strength and activity, rather than any skill or intelligence, and yet, to one entirely unused to such work, it came very hard. The heat was intense and overpowering, and there was much hurry to get the wheat, trodden out that day, through the fan; since, if that work was done an hour before sundown, the hands would have, according to a promise of Covey, that hour added to their night's rest. I was not behind any of them in the wish to complete the day's work before sundown, and, hence, I struggled with all my might to get the work forward. The promise of one hour's repose on a week day, was sufficient to quicken my pace, and to spur me on to extra endeavor. Besides, we had all planned to go fishing, and I certainly wished to have a hand in that. But I was disappointed, and the day turned out to be one of the bitterest I ever experienced. About three o'clock, while the sun was pouring down his burning rays, and not a breeze was stirring, I broke down; my strength failed me; I was seized with a violent aching of the head, attended with extreme dizziness, and trembling in every limb. Finding what was coming, and feeling it would never do to stop work, I nerved myself up, and staggered on until I fell by the side of the wheat fan, feeling that the earth had fallen upon me. This brought the entire work to a dead stand. There was work for four; each one had his part to perform, and each part depended on the other, so that when one stopped, all were compelled to stop. Covey, who had now become my dread, as well as my tormentor, was at the house, about a hundred yards from where I was fanning, and instantly, upon hearing the fan stop, he came down to the treading yard, to inquire into the cause of our stopping. Bill Smith told him I was sick, and that I was unable longer to bring wheat to the fan.

I had, by this time, crawled away, under the side of a post-and-rail fence, in the shade, and was exceeding ill. The intense heat of the sun, the heavy dust rising from the fan, the stooping, to take up the wheat from the yard, together with the hurrying, to get through, had caused a rush of blood to my head. In this condition, Covey finding out where I was, came to me; and, after standing over me a while, he asked me what the matter was. I told him as well as I could, for it was with difficulty that I could speak. He then gave me a savage kick in the side, which jarred my whole frame, and commanded me to get up. The man had obtained complete control over me; and if he had commanded me to do any possible thing, I should, in my then state of mind, have endeavored to comply. I made an effort to rise, but fell back in the attempt, before gaining my feet. The brute now gave me another heavy kick, and again told me to rise. I again tried to rise, and succeeded in gaining my feet; but upon stooping to get the tub with which I was feeding the fan, I again staggered and fell to the ground; and I must have so fallen, had I been sure that a hundred bullets would have pierced me, as the consequence. While down, in this sad condition, and perfectly helpless, the merciless Negro breaker took up the hickory slab, with which Hughes had been striking off the wheat to a level with the sides of the half bushel measure (a very hard weapon) and with the sharp edge of it, he dealt me a heavy blow on my head which made a large gash, and caused the blood to run freely, saying, at the same time, "If *you have got the headache, I'll cure you.*" This done, he ordered me again to rise, but I made no effort to do so; for I had made up my mind that it was useless, and that the heartless monster might now do his worst; he could but kill me, and that might put me out of my misery. Finding me unable to rise, or rather despairing of my doing so, Covey left me, with a view to getting on with the work without me. I was bleeding very freely, and my face was soon covered with my warm blood. Cruel and merciless as was the motive that dealt that blow, dear reader, the wound was fortunate for me. Bleeding was never more efficacious. The pain in my head speedily abated, and I was soon able to rise. Covey had, as I have said, now left me to my fate; and the question was, shall I return to my work, or shall I find my way to St. Michael's, and make Capt. Auld acquainted with the atrocious cruelty of his brother Covey, and beseech him to get me another master? Remembering the object he had in view, in placing me under the management of Covey, and further, his cruel treatment of my poor crippled cousin, Henny, and his meanness in the matter of feeding and clothing his slaves, there was little ground to hope for a favorable reception at the hands of Capt. Thomas Auld. Nevertheless, I resolved to go straight to Capt. Auld, thinking that, if not animated by motives of humanity, he might be induced to interfere on my behalf from selfish considerations. "He cannot," thought I, "allow his property to be thus bruised and battered, marred and defaced; and I will go to him, and tell him the simple truth about the matter." In order to get to St. Michael's, by the most favorable and direct road, I must walk seven miles; and this, in my sad condition, was no easy performance. I had already lost much blood; I was exhausted by over exertion; my sides were sore from the heavy blows planted there by the stout boots of Mr. Covey; and I was, in every way, in an unfavorable plight for the journey. I however watched my chance, while the cruel and cunning Covey was looking in an opposite direction, and started off, across the field, for St. Michael's. This was a daring step; if it failed, it would only exasperate Covey, and increase the rigors of my bondage, during the remainder of my term of service under him; but the step was taken, and I must go forward. I succeeded in getting nearly half way across the broad field, toward the woods, before Mr. Covey observed me. I was still bleeding, and the exertion of running had started the blood afresh. *"Come back! Come back!"* vociferated Covey, with threats of what he would do if I did not return instantly. But, disregarding his calls and his threats, I pressed on toward the woods as fast as my feeble state would allow. Seeing no signs of my stopping, Covey caused his horse to be brought out and saddled, as if he intended to pursue me. The race was now to be an unequal one; and, thinking I might be overhauled by him, if I kept the main road, I walked nearly the whole distance in the woods, keeping far enough from the road to avoid detection and pursuit. But, I had not gone far, before my little strength again failed me, and I laid down. The blood was still oozing from the wound in my head; and, for a time, I suffered more than I can describe. There I was, in the deep woods, sick and emaciated, pursued by a wretch whose character for revolting cruelty beggars all opprobrious speech—bleeding, and almost bloodless. I was not without the fear of bleeding to death. The thought of dying in the woods, all alone, and of being torn to pieces by the buzzards, had not yet been rendered tolerable by my many troubles and hardships, and I was glad when the shade of the trees, and the cool evening breeze, combined with my matted hair to stop the flow of blood. After lying there about three quarters of an hour, brooding over the singular and mournful lot to which I was doomed, my mind passing over the whole scale or circle of belief and unbelief, from faith in the overruling providence of God, to the blackest atheism, I again took up my journey toward St. Michael's, more weary and sad than in the morning when I left Thomas Auld's for the home of Mr. Covey. I was bare-footed and bare-headed, and in my shirt sleeves. The way was through bogs and briers, and I tore my feet often during the journey. I was full five hours in going the seven or eight miles; partly, because of the difficulties of the way, and partly, because of the feebleness induced by my illness, bruises and loss of blood. On gaining my master's store, I presented an appearance of wretchedness and woe, fitted to move any but a heart of stone. From the crown of my head to the sole of my feet, there were marks of blood. My hair was all clotted with dust and blood, and the back of my shirt was literally stiff with the same. Briers and thorns had scarred and torn my feet and legs, leaving blood marks there. Had I escaped from a den of tigers, I could not have looked worse than I did on reaching St. Michael's. In this unhappy plight, I appeared before my professedly *Christian* master, humbly to invoke the interposition of his power and authority, to protect me from further abuse and violence. I had begun to hope, during the latter part of my tedious journey toward St. Michael's, that Capt. Auld would now show himself in a nobler light than I had ever before seen him. I was disappointed. I had jumped from a sinking ship into the sea; I had fled from the tiger to something worse. I told him all the circumstances, as well as I could; how I was endeavoring to please Covey; how hard I was at work in the present instance; how unwilling I sunk down under the heat, toil and pain; the brutal manner in which Covey had kicked me in the side; the gash cut in my head; my hesitation about troubling him (Capt. Auld) with complaints; but, that now I felt it would not be best longer to conceal from him the outrages committed on me from time to time by Covey. At first, master Thomas seemed somewhat affected by the story of my wrongs, but he soon repressed his feelings and became cold as iron. It was impossible—as I stood before him at the first—for him to seem indifferent. I distinctly saw his human nature asserting its conviction against the slave system, which made cases like mine *possible;* but, as I have said, humanity fell before the systematic tyranny of slavery. He first walked the floor, apparently much agitated by my story, and the sad spectacle I presented; but, presently, it was *his* turn to talk. He began moderately, by finding excuses for Covey, and ending with a full justification of him, and a passionate condemnation of me. "He had no doubt I deserved the flogging. He did not believe I was sick; I was only endeavoring to get rid of work. My dizziness was laziness, and Covey did right to flog me, as he had done." After thus fairly annihilating me, and rousing himself by his own eloquence, he fiercely demanded what I wished *him* to do in the case!

With such a complete knock-down to all my hopes, as he had given me, and feeling, as I did, my entire subjection to his power, I had very little heart to reply. I must not affirm my innocence of the allegations which he had piled up against me; for that would be impudence, and would probably call down fresh violence as well as wrath upon me. The guilt of a slave is always, and everywhere, presumed; and the innocence of the slaveholder or the slave employer, is always asserted. The word of the slave, against this presumption, is generally treated as impudence, worthy of punishment. "Do you contradict me, you rascal?" is a final silencer of counter statements from the lips of a slave.

Calming down a little in view of my silence and hesitation, and, perhaps, from a rapid glance at the picture of misery I presented, he inquired again, "what I would have him do?" Thus invited a second time, I told Master Thomas I wished him to allow me to get a new home and to find a new master; that, as sure as I went back to live with Mr. Covey again, I should be killed by him; that he would never forgive my coming to him (Capt. Auld) with a complaint against him (Covey); that, since I had lived with him, he almost crushed my spirit, and I believed that he would ruin me for future service; that my life was not safe in his hands. This, Master Thomas *(my brother in the church)* regarded as "nonsence(sic)." "There was no danger of Mr. Covey's killing me; he was a good man, industrious and religious, and he would not think of removing me from that home; besides," said he and this I found was the most distressing thought of all to him—"if you should leave Covey now, that your year has but half expired, I should lose your wages for the entire year. You belong to Mr. Covey for one year, and you *must go back* to him, come what will. You must not trouble me with any more stories about Mr. Covey; and if you do not go immediately home, I will get hold of you myself." This was just what I expected, when I found he had *prejudged* the case against me. "But, Sir," I said, "I am sick and tired, and I cannot get home to-night." At this, he again relented, and finally he allowed me to remain all night at St. Michael's; but said I must be off early in the morning, and concluded his directions by making me swallow a huge dose of *epsom salts*—about the only medicine ever administered to slaves.

It was quite natural for Master Thomas to presume I was feigning sickness to escape work, for he probably thought that were *he* in the place of a slave with no wages for his work, no praise for well doing, no motive for toil but the lash—he would try every possible scheme by which to escape labor. I say I have no doubt of this; the reason is, that there are not, under the whole heavens, a set of men who cultivate such an intense dread of labor as do the slaveholders. The charge of laziness against the slave is ever on their lips, and is the standing apology for every species of cruelty and brutality. These men literally "bind heavy burdens, grievous to be borne, and lay them on men's shoulders; but they, themselves, will not move them with one of their fingers."

My kind readers shall have, in the next chapter—what they were led, perhaps, to expect to find in this—namely: an account of my partial disenthrallment from the tyranny of Covey, and the marked change which it brought about.

CHAPTER XVII.
THE LAST FLOGGING

A SLEEPLESS NIGHT—RETURN TO COVEY'S—PURSUED BY COVEY—THE CHASE DEFEATED—VENGEANCE POSTPONED—MUSINGS IN THE WOODS—THE ALTERNATIVE—DEPLORABLE SPECTACLE—NIGHT IN THE WOODS—EXPECTED ATTACK—ACCOSTED BY SANDY, A FRIEND, NOT A HUNTER—SANDY'S HOSPITALITY—THE "ASH CAKE" SUPPER—THE INTERVIEW WITH SANDY—HIS ADVICE—SANDY A CONJURER AS WELL AS A CHRISTIAN—THE MAGIC ROOT—STRANGE MEETING WITH COVEY—HIS MANNER—COVEY'S SUNDAY FACE—MY DEFENSIVE RESOLVE—THE FIGHT—THE VICTORY, AND ITS RESULTS.

Sleep itself does not always come to the relief of the weary in body, and the broken in spirit; especially when past troubles only foreshadow coming disasters. The last hope had been extinguished. My master, who I did not venture to hope would protect me as *a man*, had even now refused to protect me as *his property;* and had cast me back, covered with reproaches and bruises, into the hands of a stranger to that mercy which was the soul of the religion he professed. May the reader never spend such a night as that allotted to me, previous to the morning which was to herald my return to the den of horrors from which I had made a temporary escape.

I remained all night—sleep I did not—at St. Michael's; and in the morning (Saturday) I started off, according to the order of Master Thomas, feeling that I had no friend on earth, and doubting if I had one in heaven. I reached Covey's about nine o'clock; and just as I stepped into the field, before I had reached the house, Covey, true to his snakish habits, darted out at me from a fence corner, in which he had secreted himself, for the purpose of securing me. He was amply provided with a cowskin and a rope; and he evidently intended to *tie me up*, and to wreak his vengeance on me to the fullest extent. I should have been an easy prey, had he succeeded in getting his hands upon me, for I had taken no refreshment since noon on Friday; and this, together with the pelting, excitement, and the loss of blood, had reduced my strength. I, however, darted back into the woods, before the ferocious hound could get hold of me, and buried myself in a thicket, where he lost sight of me. The corn-field afforded me cover, in getting to the woods. But for the tall corn, Covey would have overtaken me, and made me his captive. He seemed very much chagrined that he did not catch me, and gave up the chase, very reluctantly; for I could see his angry movements, toward the house from which he had sallied, on his foray.

Well, now I am clear of Covey, and of his wrathful lash, for present. I am in the wood, buried in its somber gloom, and hushed in its solemn silence; hid from all human eyes; shut in with nature and nature's God, and absent from all human contrivances. Here was a good place to pray; to pray for help for deliverance—a prayer I had often made before. But how could I pray? Covey could pray—Capt. Auld could pray—I would fain pray; but doubts (arising partly from my own neglect of the means of grace, and partly from the sham religion which everywhere prevailed, cast in my mind a doubt upon all religion, and led me to the conviction that prayers were unavailing and delusive) prevented my embracing the opportunity, as a religious one. Life, in itself, had almost become burdensome to me. All my outward relations were against me; I must stay here and starve (I was already hungry) or go home to Covey's, and have my flesh torn to pieces, and my spirit humbled under the cruel lash of Covey. This was the painful alternative presented to me. The day was long and irksome. My physical condition was deplorable. I was weak, from the toils of the previous day, and from the want of food and rest; and had been so little concerned about my appearance, that I had not yet washed the blood from my garments. I was an object of horror, even to myself. Life, in Baltimore, when most oppressive, was a paradise to this. What had I done, what had my parents done, that such a life as this should be mine? That day, in the woods, I would have exchanged my manhood for the brutehood of an ox.

Night came. I was still in the woods, unresolved what to do. Hunger had not yet pinched me to the point of going home, and I laid myself down in the leaves to rest; for I had been watching for hunters all day, but not being molested during the day, I expected no disturbance during the night. I had come to the conclusion that Covey relied upon hunger to drive me home; and in this I was quite correct—the facts showed that he had made no effort to catch me, since morning.

During the night, I heard the step of a man in the woods. He was coming toward the place where I lay. A person lying still has the advantage over one walking in the woods, in the day time, and this advantage is much greater at night. I was not able to engage in a physical struggle, and I had recourse to the common resort of the weak. I hid myself in the leaves to prevent discovery. But, as the night rambler in the woods drew nearer, I found him to be a *friend*, not an enemy; it was a slave of Mr. William Groomes, of Easton, a kind hearted fellow, named "Sandy." Sandy lived with Mr. Kemp that year, about four miles from St. Michael's. He, like myself had been hired out by the year; but, unlike myself, had not been hired out to be broken. Sandy was the husband of a free woman, who lived in the lower part of *"Potpie Neck,"* and he was now on his way through the woods, to see her, and to spend the Sabbath with her.

As soon as I had ascertained that the disturber of my solitude was not an enemy, but the good-hearted Sandy—a man as famous among the slaves of the neighborhood for his good nature, as for his good sense I came out from my hiding place, and made myself known to him. I explained the circumstances of the past two days, which had driven me to the woods, and he deeply compassionated my distress. It was a bold thing for him to shelter me, and I could not ask him to do so; for, had I been found in his hut, he would have suffered the penalty of thirty-nine lashes on his bare back, if not something worse. But Sandy was too generous to permit the fear of punishment to prevent his relieving a brother bondman from hunger and exposure; and, therefore, on his own motion, I accompanied him to his home, or rather to the home of his wife—for the house and lot were hers. His wife was called up—for it was now about midnight—a fire was made, some Indian meal was soon mixed with salt and water, and an ash cake was baked in a hurry to relieve my hunger. Sandy's wife was not behind him in kindness—both seemed to esteem it a privilege to succor me; for, although I was hated by Covey and by my master, I was loved by the colored people, because *they* thought I was hated for my knowledge, and persecuted because I was feared. I was the *only* slave *now* in that region who could read and write. There had been one other man, belonging to Mr. Hugh Hamilton, who could read (his name was "Jim"), but he, poor fellow, had, shortly after my coming into the neighborhood, been sold off to the far south. I saw Jim ironed, in the cart, to be carried to Easton for sale—pinioned like a yearling for the slaughter. My knowledge was now the pride of my brother slaves; and, no doubt, Sandy felt something of the general interest in me on that account. The supper was soon ready, and though I have feasted since, with honorables, lord mayors and aldermen, over the sea, my supper on ash cake and cold water, with Sandy, was the meal, of all my life, most sweet to my taste, and now most vivid in my memory.

Supper over, Sandy and I went into a discussion of what was *possible* for me, under the perils and hardships which now overshadowed my path. The question was, must I go back to Covey, or must I now tempt to run away? Upon a careful survey, the latter was found to be impossible; for I was on a narrow neck of land, every avenue from which would bring me in sight of pursuers. There was the Chesapeake bay to the right, and "Pot-pie" river to the left, and St. Michael's and its neighborhood occupying the only space through which there was any retreat.

I found Sandy an old advisor. He was not only a religious man, but he professed to believe in a system for which I have no name. He was a genuine African, and had inherited some of the so-called magical powers, said to be possessed by African and eastern nations. He told me that he could help me; that, in those very woods, there was an herb, which in the morning might be found, possessing all the powers required for my protection (I put his thoughts in my own language); and that, if I would take his advice, he would procure me the root of the herb of which he spoke. He told me further, that if I would take that root and wear it on my right side, it would be impossible for Covey to strike me a blow; that with this root about my person, no white man could whip me. He said he had carried it for years, and that he had fully tested its virtues. He had never received a blow from a slaveholder since he carried it; and he never expected to receive one, for he always meant to carry that root as a protection. He knew Covey well, for Mrs. Covey was the daughter of Mr. Kemp; and he (Sandy) had heard of the barbarous treatment to which I was subjected, and he wanted to do something for me.

Now all this talk about the root, was to me, very absurd and ridiculous, if not positively sinful. I at first rejected the idea that the simple carrying a root on my right side (a root, by the way, over which I walked every time I went into the woods) could possess any such magic power as he ascribed to it, and I was, therefore, not disposed to cumber my pocket with it. I had a positive aversion to all pretenders to *"divination."* It was beneath one of my intelligence to countenance such dealings with the devil, as this power implied. But, with all my learning—it was really precious little—Sandy was more than a match for me. "My book learning," he said, "had not kept Covey off me" (a powerful argument just then) and he entreated me, with flashing eyes, to try this. If it did me no good, it could do me no harm, and it would cost me nothing, any way. Sandy was so earnest, and so confident of the good qualities of this weed, that, to please him, rather than from any conviction of its excellence, I was induced to take it. He had been to me the good Samaritan, and had, almost providentially, found me, and helped me when I could not help myself; how did I know but that the hand of the Lord was in it? With thoughts of this sort, I took the roots from Sandy, and put them in my right hand pocket.

This was, of course, Sunday morning. Sandy now urged me to go home, with all speed, and to walk up bravely to the house, as though nothing had happened. I saw in Sandy too deep an insight into human nature, with all his superstition, not to have some respect for his advice; and perhaps, too, a slight gleam or shadow of his superstition had fallen upon me. At any rate, I started off toward Covey's, as directed by Sandy. Having, the previous night, poured my griefs into Sandy's ears, and got him enlisted in my behalf, having made his wife a sharer in my sorrows, and having, also, become well refreshed by sleep and food, I moved off, quite courageously, toward the much dreaded Covey's. Singularly enough, just as I entered his yard gate, I met him and his wife, dressed in their Sunday best—looking as smiling as angels—on their way to church. The manner of Covey astonished me. There was something really benignant in his countenance. He spoke to me as never before; told me that the pigs had got into the lot, and he wished me to drive them out; inquired how I was, and seemed an altered man. This extraordinary conduct of Covey, really made me begin to think that Sandy's herb had more virtue in it than I, in my pride, had been willing to allow; and, had the day been other than Sunday, I should have attributed Covey's altered manner solely to the magic power of the root. I suspected, however, that the *Sabbath*, and not the *root*, was the real explanation of Covey's manner. His religion hindered him from breaking the Sabbath, but not from breaking my skin. He had more respect for the *day* than for the *man*, for whom the day was mercifully given; for while he would cut and slash my body during the week, he would not hesitate, on Sunday, to teach me the value of my soul, or the way of life and salvation by Jesus Christ.

All went well with me till Monday morning; and then, whether the root had lost its virtue, or whether my tormentor had gone deeper into the black art than myself (as was sometimes said of him), or whether he had obtained a special indulgence, for his faithful Sabbath day's worship, it is not necessary for me to know, or to inform the reader; but, this I *may* say—the pious and benignant smile which graced Covey's face on *Sunday*, wholly disappeared on *Monday*. Long before daylight, I was called up to go and feed, rub, and curry the horses. I obeyed the call, and would have so obeyed it, had it been made at an earilier(sic) hour, for I had brought my mind to a firm resolve, during that Sunday's reflection, viz: to obey every order, however unreasonable, if it were possible, and, if Mr. Covey should then undertake to beat me, to defend and protect myself to the best of my ability. My religious views on the subject of resisting my master, had suffered a serious shock, by the savage persecution to which I had been subjected, and my hands were no longer tied by my religion. Master Thomas's indifference had served the last link. I had now to this extent "backslidden" from this point in the slave's religious creed; and I soon had occasion to make my fallen state known to my Sunday-pious brother, Covey.

Whilst I was obeying his order to feed and get the horses ready for the field, and when in the act of going up the stable loft for the purpose of throwing down some blades, Covey sneaked into the stable, in his peculiar snake-like way, and seizing me suddenly by the leg, he brought me to the stable floor, giving my newly mended body a fearful jar. I now forgot my roots, and remembered my pledge to *stand up in my own defense*. The brute was endeavoring skillfully to get a slip-knot on my legs, before I could draw up my feet. As soon as I found what he was up to, I gave a sudden spring (my two day's rest had been of much service to me,) and by that means, no doubt, he was able to bring me to the floor so heavily. He was defeated in his plan of tying me. While down, he seemed to think he had me very securely in his power. He little thought he was—as the rowdies say—"in" for a "rough and tumble" fight; but such was the fact. Whence came the daring spirit necessary to grapple with a man who, eight-and-forty hours before, could, with his slightest word have made me tremble like a leaf in a storm, I do not know; at any rate, *I was resolved to fight*, and, what was better still, I was actually hard at it. The fighting madness had come upon me, and I found my strong fingers firmly attached to the throat of my cowardly tormentor; as heedless of consequences, at the moment, as though we stood as equals before the law. The very color of the man was forgotten. I felt as supple as a cat, and was ready for the snakish creature at every turn. Every blow of his was parried, though I dealt no blows in turn. I was strictly on the *defensive*, preventing him from injuring me, rather than trying to injure him. I flung him on the ground several times, when he meant to have hurled me there. I held him so firmly by the throat, that his blood followed my nails. He held me, and I held him.

All was fair, thus far, and the contest was about equal. My resistance was entirely unexpected, and Covey was taken all aback by it, for he trembled in every limb. *"Are you going to resist*, you scoundrel?" said he. To which, I returned a polite *"Yes sir;"* steadily gazing my interrogator in the eye, to meet the first approach or dawning of the blow, which I expected my answer would call forth. But, the conflict did not long remain thus equal. Covey soon cried out lustily for help; not that I was obtaining any marked advantage over him, or was injuring him, but because he was gaining none over me, and was not able, single handed, to conquer me. He called for his cousin Hughs, to come to his assistance, and now the scene was changed. I was compelled to give blows, as well as to parry them; and, since I was, in any case, to suffer for resistance, I felt (as the musty proverb goes) that "I might as well be hanged for an old sheep as a lamb." I was still *defensive* toward Covey, but *aggressive* toward Hughs; and, at the first approach of the latter, I dealt a blow, in my desperation, which fairly sickened my youthful assailant. He went off, bending over with pain, and manifesting no disposition to come within my reach again. The poor fellow was in the act of trying to catch and tie my right hand, and while flattering himself with success, I gave him the kick which sent him staggering away in pain, at the same time that I held Covey with a firm hand.

Taken completely by surprise, Covey seemed to have lost his usual strength and coolness. He was frightened, and stood puffing and blowing, seemingly unable to command words or blows. When he saw that poor Hughs was standing half bent with pain—his courage quite gone the cowardly tyrant asked if I "meant to persist in my resistance." I told him "*I did mean to resist, come what might;*" that I had been by him treated like a *brute*, during the last six months; and that I should stand it *no longer*. With that, he gave me a shake, and attempted to drag me toward a stick of wood, that was lying just outside the stable door. He meant to knock me down with it; but, just as he leaned over to get the stick, I seized him with both hands by the collar, and, with a vigorous and sudden snatch, I brought my assailant harmlessly, his full length, on the *not* overclean ground—for we were now in the cow yard. He had selected the place for the fight, and it was but right that he should have all the advantges(sic) of his own selection.

By this time, Bill, the hiredman, came home. He had been to Mr. Hemsley's, to spend the Sunday with his nominal wife, and was coming home on Monday morning, to go to work. Covey and I had been skirmishing from before daybreak, till now, that the sun was almost shooting his beams over the eastern woods, and we were still at it. I could not see where the matter was to terminate. He evidently was afraid to let me go, lest I should again make off to the woods; otherwise, he would probably have obtained arms from the house, to frighten me. Holding me, Covey called upon Bill for assistance. The scene here, had something comic about it. "Bill," who knew *precisely* what Covey wished him to do, affected ignorance, and pretended he did not know what to do. "What shall I do, Mr. Covey," said Bill. "Take hold of him—take hold of him!" said Covey. With a toss of his head, peculiar to Bill, he said, "indeed, Mr. Covey I want to go to work." *"This is* your work," said Covey; "take hold of him." Bill replied, with spirit, "My master hired me here, to work, and *not* to help you whip Frederick." It was now my turn to speak. "Bill," said I, "don't put your hands on me." To which he replied, "My GOD! Frederick, I ain't goin' to tech ye," and Bill walked off, leaving Covey and myself to settle our matters as best we might.

But, my present advantage was threatened when I saw Caroline (the slave-woman of Covey) coming to the cow yard to milk, for she was a powerful woman, and could have mastered me very easily, exhausted as I now was. As soon as she came into the yard, Covey attempted to rally her to his aid. Strangely—and, I may add, fortunately—Caroline was in no humor to take a hand in any such sport. We were all in open rebellion, that morning. Caroline answered the command of her master to *"take hold of me,"* precisely as Bill had answered, but in *her*, it was at greater peril so to answer; she was the slave of Covey, and he could do what he pleased with her. It was *not* so with Bill, and Bill knew it. Samuel Harris, to whom Bill belonged, did not allow his slaves to be beaten, unless they were guilty of some crime which the law would punish. But, poor Caroline, like myself, was at the mercy of the merciless Covey; nor did she escape the dire effects of her refusal. He gave her several sharp blows.

Covey at length (two hours had elapsed) gave up the contest. Letting me go, he said—puffing and blowing at a great rate—"Now, you scoundrel, go to your work; I would not have whipped you half so much as I have had you not resisted." The fact was, *he had not whipped me at all*. He had not, in all the scuffle, drawn a single drop of blood from me. I had drawn blood from him; and, even without this satisfaction, I should have been victorious, because my aim had not been to injure him, but to prevent his injuring me.

During the whole six months that I lived with Covey, after this transaction, he never laid on me the weight of his finger in anger. He would, occasionally, say he did not want to have to get hold of me again—a declaration which I had no difficulty in believing; and I had a secret feeling, which answered, "You need not wish to get hold of me again, for you will be likely to come off worse in a second fight than you did in the first."

Well, my dear reader, this battle with Mr. Covey—undignified as it was, and as I fear my narration of it is—was the turning point in my *"life as a slave."* It rekindled in my breast the smouldering embers of liberty; it brought up my Baltimore dreams, and revived a sense of my own manhood. I was a changed being after that fight. I was *nothing* before; I WAS A MAN NOW. It recalled to life my crushed self-respect and my self-confidence, and inspired me with a renewed determination to be A FREEMAN. A man, without force, is without the essential dignity of humanity. Human nature is so constituted, that it cannot *honor* a helpless man, although it can *pity* him; and even this it cannot do long, if the signs of power do not arise.

He can only understand the effect of this combat on my spirit, who has himself incurred something, hazarded something, in repelling the unjust and cruel aggressions of a tyrant. Covey was a tyrant, and a cowardly one, withal. After resisting him, I felt as I had never felt before. It was a resurrection from the dark and pestiferous tomb of slavery, to the heaven of comparative freedom. I was no longer a servile coward, trembling under the frown of a brother worm of the dust, but, my long-cowed spirit was roused to an attitude of manly independence. I had reached the point, at which I was *not afraid to die*. This spirit made me a freeman in *fact*, while I remained a slave in *form*. When a slave cannot be flogged he is more than half free. He has a domain as broad as his own manly heart to defend, and he is really *"a power on earth."* While slaves prefer their lives, with flogging, to instant death, they will always find Christians enough, like unto Covey, to accommodate that preference. From this time, until that of my escape from slavery, I was never fairly whipped. Several attempts were made to whip me, but they were always unsuccessful. Bruises I did get, as I shall hereafter inform the reader; but the case I have been describing, was the end of the brutification to which slavery had subjected me.

The reader will be glad to know why, after I had so grievously offended Mr. Covey, he did not have me taken in hand by the authorities; indeed, why the law of Maryland, which assigns hanging to the slave who resists his master, was not put in force against me; at any rate, why I was not taken up, as is usual in such cases, and publicly whipped, for an example to other slaves, and as a means of deterring me from committing the same offense again. I confess, that the easy manner in which I got off, for a long time, a surprise to me, and I cannot, even now, fully explain the cause.

MY BONDAGE

The only explanation I can venture to suggest, is the fact, that Covey was, probably, ashamed to have it known and confessed that he had been mastered by a boy of sixteen. Mr. Covey enjoyed the unbounded and very valuable reputation, of being a first rate overseer and *Negro breaker*. By means of this reputation, he was able to procure his hands for *very trifling* compensation, and with very great ease. His interest and his pride mutually suggested the wisdom of passing the matter by, in silence. The story that he had undertaken to whip a lad, and had been resisted, was, of itself, sufficient to damage him; for his bearing should, in the estimation of slaveholders, be of that imperial order that should make such an occurrence *impossible*. I judge from these circumstances, that Covey deemed it best to give me the go-by. It is, perhaps, not altogether creditable to my natural temper, that, after this conflict with Mr. Covey, I did, at times, purposely aim to provoke him to an attack, by refusing to keep with the other hands in the field, but I could never bully him to another battle. I had made up my mind to do him serious damage, if he ever again attempted to lay violent hands on me.

Hereditary bondmen, know ye not
Who would be free, themselves must strike the blow?

CHAPTER XVIII.
New Relations and Duties

CHANGE OF MASTERS—BENEFITS DERIVED BY THE CHANGE—FAME OF THE FIGHT WITH COVEY—RECKLESS UNCONCERN—MY ABHORRENCE OF SLAVERY—ABILITY TO READ A CAUSE OF PREJUDICE—THE HOLIDAYS—HOW SPENT—SHARP HIT AT SLAVERY—EFFECTS OF HOLIDAYS—A DEVICE OF SLAVERY—DIFFERENCE BETWEEN COVEY AND FREELAND—AN IRRELIGIOUS MASTER PREFERRED TO A RELIGIOUS ONE—CATALOGUE OF FLOGGABLE OFFENSES—HARD LIFE AT COVEY'S USEFUL—IMPROVED CONDITION NOT FOLLOWED BY CONTENTMENT—CONGENIAL SOCIETY AT FREELAND'S—SABBATH SCHOOL INSTITUTED—SECRECY NECESSARY—AFFECTIONATE RELATIONS OF TUTOR AND PUPILS—CONFIDENCE AND FRIENDSHIP AMONG SLAVES—I DECLINE PUBLISHING PARTICULARS OF CONVERSATIONS WITH MY FRIENDS—SLAVERY THE INVITER OF VENGEANCE.

My term of actual service to Mr. Edward Covey ended on Christmas day, 1834. I gladly left the snakish Covey, although he was now as gentle as a lamb. My home for the year 1835 was already secured—my next master was already selected. There is always more or less excitement about the matter of changing hands, but I had become somewhat reckless. I cared very little into whose hands I fell—I meant to fight my way. Despite of Covey, too, the report got abroad, that I was hard to whip; that I was guilty of kicking back; that though generally a good tempered Negro, I sometimes "*got the devil in me.*" These sayings were rife in Talbot county, and they distinguished me among my servile brethren. Slaves, generally, will fight each other, and die at each other's hands; but there are few who are not held in awe by a white man. Trained from the cradle up, to think and feel that their masters are superior, and invested with a sort of sacredness, there are few who can outgrow or rise above the control which that sentiment exercises. I had now got free from it, and the thing was known. One bad sheep will spoil a whole flock. Among the slaves, I was a bad sheep. I hated slavery, slaveholders, and all pertaining to them; and I did not fail to inspire others with the same feeling, wherever and whenever opportunity was presented. This made me a marked lad among the slaves, and a suspected one among the slaveholders. A knowledge of my ability to read and write, got pretty widely spread, which was very much against me.

The days between Christmas day and New Year's, are allowed the slaves as holidays. During these days, all regular work was suspended, and there was nothing to do but to keep fires, and look after the stock. This time was regarded as our own, by the grace of our masters, and we, therefore used it, or abused it, as we pleased. Those who had families at a distance, were now expected to visit them, and to spend with them the entire week. The younger slaves, or the unmarried ones, were expected to see to the cattle, and attend to incidental duties at home. The holidays were variously spent. The sober, thinking and industrious ones of our number, would employ themselves in manufacturing corn brooms, mats, horse collars and baskets, and some of these were very well made. Another class spent their time in hunting opossums, coons, rabbits, and other game. But the majority spent the holidays in sports, ball playing, wrestling, boxing, running foot races, dancing, and drinking whisky; and this latter mode of spending the time was generally most agreeable to their masters. A slave who would work during the holidays, was thought, by his master, undeserving of holidays. Such an one had rejected the favor of his master. There was, in this simple act of continued work, an accusation against slaves; and a slave could not help thinking, that if he made three dollars during the holidays, he might make three hundred during the year. Not to be drunk during the holidays, was disgraceful; and he was esteemed a lazy and improvident man, who could not afford to drink whisky during Christmas.

The fiddling, dancing and *"jubilee beating,"* was going on in all directions. This latter performance is strictly southern. It supplies the place of a violin, or of other musical instruments, and is played so easily, that almost every farm has its "Juba" beater. The performer improvises as he beats, and sings his merry songs, so ordering the words as to have them fall pat with the movement of his hands. Among a mass of nonsense and wild frolic, once in a while a sharp hit is given to the meanness of slaveholders. Take the following, for an example:

> *We raise de wheat,*
> *Dey gib us de corn;*
> *We bake de bread,*
> *Dey gib us de cruss;*
> *We sif de meal,*
> *Dey gib us de huss;*
> *We peal de meat,*
> *Dey gib us de skin,*
> *And dat's de way*
> *Dey takes us in.*
> *We skim de pot,*
> *Dey gib us the liquor,*
> *And say dat's good enough for nigger.*
>   *Walk over! walk over!*
> *Tom butter and de fat;*
>   *Poor nigger you can't get over dat;*
>   *Walk over!*

This is not a bad summary of the palpable injustice and fraud of slavery, giving—as it does—to the lazy and idle, the comforts which God designed should be given solely to the honest laborer. But to the holiday's.

Judging from my own observation and experience, I believe these holidays to be among the most effective means, in the hands of slaveholders, of keeping down the spirit of insurrection among the slaves.

To enslave men, successfully and safely, it is necessary to have their minds occupied with thoughts and aspirations short of the liberty of which they are deprived. A certain degree of attainable good must be kept before them. These holidays serve the purpose of keeping the minds of the slaves occupied with prospective pleasure, within the limits of slavery. The young man can go wooing; the married man can visit his wife; the father and mother can see their children; the industrious and money loving can make a few dollars; the great wrestler can win laurels; the young people can meet, and enjoy each other's society; the drunken man can get plenty of whisky; and the religious man can hold prayer meetings, preach, pray and exhort during the holidays. Before the holidays, these are pleasures in prospect; after the holidays, they become pleasures of memory, and they serve to keep out thoughts and wishes of a more dangerous character. Were slaveholders at once to abandon the practice of allowing their slaves these liberties, periodically, and to keep them, the year round, closely confined to the narrow circle of their homes, I doubt not that the south would blaze with insurrections. These holidays are conductors or safety valves to carry off the explosive elements inseparable from the human mind, when reduced to the condition of slavery. But for these, the rigors of bondage would become too severe for endurance, and the slave would be forced up to dangerous desperation. Woe to the slaveholder when he undertakes to hinder or to prevent the operation of these electric conductors. A succession of earthquakes would be less destructive, than the insurrectionary fires which would be sure to burst forth in different parts of the south, from such interference.

Thus, the holidays, became part and parcel of the gross fraud, wrongs and inhumanity of slavery. Ostensibly, they are institutions of benevolence, designed to mitigate the rigors of slave life, but, practically, they are a fraud, instituted by human selfishness, the better to secure the ends of injustice and oppression. The slave's happiness is not the end sought, but, rather, the master's safety. It is not from a generous unconcern for the slave's labor that this cessation from labor is allowed, but from a prudent regard to the safety of the slave system. I am strengthened in this opinion, by the fact, that most slaveholders like to have their slaves spend the holidays in such a manner as to be of no real benefit to the slaves. It is plain, that everything like rational enjoyment among the slaves, is frowned upon; and only those wild and low sports, peculiar to semi-civilized people, are encouraged. All the license allowed, appears to have no other object than to disgust the slaves with their temporary freedom, and to make them as glad to return to their work, as they were to leave it. By plunging them into exhausting depths of drunkenness and dissipation, this effect is almost certain to follow. I have known slaveholders resort to cunning tricks, with a view of getting their slaves deplorably drunk. A usual plan is, to make bets on a slave, that he can drink more whisky than any other; and so to induce a rivalry among them, for the mastery in this degradation. The scenes, brought about in this way, were often scandalous and loathsome in the extreme. Whole multitudes might be found stretched out in brutal drunkenness, at once helpless and disgusting. Thus, when the slave asks for a few hours of virtuous freedom, his cunning master takes advantage of his ignorance, and cheers him with a dose of vicious and revolting dissipation, artfully labeled with the name of LIBERTY. We were induced to drink, I among the rest, and when the holidays were over, we all staggered up from our filth and wallowing, took a long breath, and went away to our various fields of work; feeling, upon the whole, rather glad to go from that which our masters artfully deceived us into the belief was freedom, back again to the arms of slavery. It was not what we had taken it to be, nor what it might have been, had it not been abused by us. It was about as well to be a slave to *master*, as to be a slave to *rum* and *whisky*.

I am the more induced to take this view of the holiday system, adopted by slaveholders, from what I know of their treatment of slaves, in regard to other things. It is the commonest thing for them to try to disgust their slaves with what they do not want them to have, or to enjoy. A slave, for instance, likes molasses; he steals some; to cure him of the taste for it, his master, in many cases, will go away to town, and buy a large quantity of the *poorest* quality, and set it before his slave, and, with whip in hand, compel him to eat it, until the poor fellow is made to sicken at the very thought of molasses. The same course is often adopted to cure slaves of the disagreeable and inconvenient practice of asking for more food, when their allowance has failed them. The same disgusting process works well, too, in other things, but I need not cite them. When a slave is drunk, the slaveholder has no fear that he will plan an insurrection; no fear that he will escape to the north. It is the sober, thinking slave who is dangerous, and needs the vigilance of his master, to keep him a slave. But, to proceed with my narrative.

On the first of January, 1835, I proceeded from St. Michael's to Mr. William Freeland's, my new home. Mr. Freeland lived only three miles from St. Michael's, on an old worn out farm, which required much labor to restore it to anything like a self-supporting establishment.

I was not long in finding Mr. Freeland to be a very different man from Mr. Covey. Though not rich, Mr. Freeland was what may be called a well-bred southern gentleman, as different from Covey, as a well-trained and hardened Negro breaker is from the best specimen of the first families of the south. Though Freeland was a slaveholder, and shared many of the vices of his class, he seemed alive to the sentiment of honor. He had some sense of justice, and some feelings of humanity. He was fretful, impulsive and passionate, but I must do him the justice to say, he was free from the mean and selfish characteristics which distinguished the creature from which I had now, happily, escaped. He was open, frank, imperative, and practiced no concealments, disdaining to play the spy. In all this, he was the opposite of the crafty Covey.

Among the many advantages gained in my change from Covey's to Freeland's—startling as the statement may be—was the fact that the latter gentleman made no profession of religion. I assert *most unhesitatingly*, that the religion of the south—as I have observed it and proved it—is a mere covering for the most horrid crimes; the justifier of the most appalling barbarity; a sanctifier of the most hateful frauds; and a secure shelter, under which the darkest, foulest, grossest, and most infernal abominations fester and flourish. Were I again to be reduced to the condition of a slave, *next* to that calamity, I should regard the fact of being the slave of a religious slaveholder, the greatest that could befall me. For all slaveholders with whom I have ever met, religious slaveholders are the worst. I have found them, almost invariably, the vilest, meanest and basest of their class. Exceptions there may be, but this is true of religious slaveholders, *as a class*. It is not for me to explain the fact. Others may do that; I simply state it as a fact, and leave the theological, and psychological inquiry, which it raises, to be decided by others more competent than myself. Religious slaveholders, like religious persecutors, are ever extreme in their malice and violence. Very near my new home, on an adjoining farm, there lived the Rev. Daniel Weeden, who was both pious and cruel after the real Covey pattern. Mr. Weeden was a local preacher of the Protestant Methodist persuasion, and a most zealous supporter of the ordinances of religion, generally. This Weeden owned a woman called "Ceal," who was a standing proof of his mercilessness. Poor Ceal's back, always scantily clothed, was kept literally raw, by the lash of this religious man and gospel minister. The most notoriously wicked man—so called in distinction from church members—could hire hands more easily than this brute. When sent out to find a home, a slave would never enter the gates of the preacher Weeden, while a sinful sinner needed a hand. Be have ill, or behave well, it was the known maxim of Weeden, that it is the duty of a master to use the lash. If, for no other reason, he contended that this was essential to remind a slave of his condition, and of his master's authority. The good slave must be whipped, to be *kept* good, and the bad slave must be whipped, to be *made* good. Such was Weeden's theory, and such was his practice. The back of his slave-woman will, in the judgment, be the swiftest witness against him.

While I am stating particular cases, I might as well immortalize another of my neighbors, by calling him by name, and putting him in print. He did not think that a "chiel" was near, "taking notes," and will, doubtless, feel quite angry at having his character touched off in the ragged style of a slave's pen. I beg to introduce the reader to REV. RIGBY HOPKINS. Mr. Hopkins resides between Easton and St. Michael's, in Talbot county, Maryland. The severity of this man made him a perfect terror to the slaves of his neighborhood. The peculiar feature of his government, was, his system of whipping slaves, as he said, *in advance* of deserving it. He always managed to have one or two slaves to whip on Monday morning, so as to start his hands to their work, under the inspiration of a new assurance on Monday, that his preaching about kindness, mercy, brotherly love, and the like, on Sunday, did not interfere with, or prevent him from establishing his authority, by the cowskin. He seemed to wish to assure them, that his tears over poor, lost and ruined sinners, and his pity for them, did not reach to the blacks who tilled his fields. This saintly Hopkins used to boast, that he was the best hand to manage a Negro in the county. He whipped for the smallest offenses, by way of preventing the commission of large ones.

The reader might imagine a difficulty in finding faults enough for such frequent whipping. But this is because you have no idea how easy a matter it is to offend a man who is on the look-out for offenses. The man, unaccustomed to slaveholding, would be astonished to observe how many *foggable* offenses there are in the slaveholder's catalogue of crimes; and how easy it is to commit any one of them, even when the slave least intends it. A slaveholder, bent on finding fault, will hatch up a dozen a day, if he chooses to do so, and each one of these shall be of a punishable description. A mere look, word, or motion, a mistake, accident, or want of power, are all matters for which a slave may be whipped at any time. Does a slave look dissatisfied with his condition? It is said, that he has the devil in him, and it must be whipped out. Does he answer *loudly*, when spoken to by his master, with an air of self-consciousness? Then, must he be taken down a button-hole lower, by the lash, well laid on. Does he forget, and omit to pull off his hat, when approaching a white person? Then, he must, or may be, whipped for his bad manners. Does he ever venture to vindicate his conduct, when harshly and unjustly accused? Then, he is guilty of impudence, one of the greatest crimes in the social catalogue of southern society. To allow a slave to escape punishment, who has impudently attempted to exculpate himself from unjust charges, preferred against him by some white person, is to be guilty of great dereliction of duty. Does a slave ever venture to suggest a better way of doing a thing, no matter what? He is, altogether, too officious—wise above what is written—and he deserves, even if he does not get, a flogging for his presumption. Does he, while plowing, break a plow, or while hoeing, break a hoe, or while chopping, break an ax? No matter what were the imperfections of the implement broken, or the natural liabilities for breaking, the slave can be whipped for carelessness. The *reverend* slaveholder could always find something of this sort, to justify him in using the lash several times during the week. Hopkins—like Covey and Weeden—were shunned by slaves who had the privilege (as many had) of finding their own masters at the end of each year; and yet, there was not a man in all that section of country, who made a louder profession of religion, than did MR. RIGBY HOPKINS.

But, to continue the thread of my story, through my experience when at Mr. William Freeland's.

My poor, weather-beaten bark now reached smoother water, and gentler breezes. My stormy life at Covey's had been of service to me. The things that would have seemed very hard, had I gone direct to Mr. Freeland's, from the home of Master Thomas, were now (after the hardships at Covey's) "trifles light as air." I was still a field hand, and had come to prefer the severe labor of the field, to the enervating duties of a house servant. I had become large and strong; and had begun to take pride in the fact, that I could do as much hard work as some of the older men. There is much rivalry among slaves, at times, as to which can do the most work, and masters generally seek to promote such rivalry. But some of us were too wise to race with each other very long. Such racing, we had the sagacity to see, was not likely to pay. We had our times for measuring each other's strength, but we knew too much to keep up the competition so long as to produce an extraordinary day's work. We knew that if, by extraordinary exertion, a large quantity of work was done in one day, the fact, becoming known to the master, might lead him to require the same amount every day. This thought was enough to bring us to a dead halt when over so much excited for the race.

At Mr. Freeland's, my condition was every way improved. I was no longer the poor scape-goat that I was when at Covey's, where every wrong thing done was saddled upon me, and where other slaves were whipped over my shoulders. Mr. Freeland was too just a man thus to impose upon me, or upon any one else.

It is quite usual to make one slave the object of especial abuse, and to beat him often, with a view to its effect upon others, rather than with any expectation that the slave whipped will be improved by it, but the man with whom I now was, could descend to no such meanness and wickedness. Every man here was held individually responsible for his own conduct.

This was a vast improvement on the rule at Covey's. There, I was the general pack horse. Bill Smith was protected, by a positive prohibition made by his rich master, and the command of the rich slaveholder is LAW to the poor one; Hughes was favored, because of his relationship to Covey; and the hands hired temporarily, escaped flogging, except as they got it over my poor shoulders. Of course, this comparison refers to the time when Covey *could* whip me.

Mr. Freeland, like Mr. Covey, gave his hands enough to eat, but, unlike Mr. Covey, he gave them time to take their meals; he worked us hard during the day, but gave us the night for rest—another advantage to be set to the credit of the sinner, as against that of the saint. We were seldom in the field after dark in the evening, or before sunrise in the morning. Our implements of husbandry were of the most improved pattern, and much superior to those used at Covey's.

Nothwithstanding the improved condition which was now mine, and the many advantages I had gained by my new home, and my new master, I was still restless and discontented. I was about as hard to please by a master, as a master is by slave. The freedom from bodily torture and unceasing labor, had given my mind an increased sensibility, and imparted to it greater activity. I was not yet exactly in right relations. "How be it, that was not first which is spiritual, but that which is natural, and afterward that which is spiritual." When entombed at Covey's, shrouded in darkness and physical wretchedness, temporal wellbeing was the grand *desideratum;* but, temporal wants supplied, the spirit puts in its claims. Beat and cuff your slave, keep him hungry and spiritless, and he will follow the chain of his master like a dog; but, feed and clothe him well—work him moderately—surround him with physical comfort—and dreams of freedom intrude. Give him a *bad* master, and he aspires to a *good* master; give him a good master, and he wishes to become his *own* master. Such is human nature. You may hurl a man so low, beneath the level of his kind, that he loses all just ideas of his natural position; but elevate him a little, and the clear conception of rights arises to life and power, and leads him onward. Thus elevated, a little, at Freeland's, the dreams called into being by that good man, Father Lawson, when in Baltimore, began to visit me; and shoots from the tree of liberty began to put forth tender buds, and dim hopes of the future began to dawn.

I found myself in congenial society, at Mr. Freeland's. There were Henry Harris, John Harris, Handy Caldwell, and Sandy Jenkins. [6]

Henry and John were brothers, and belonged to Mr. Freeland. They were both remarkably bright and intelligent, though neither of them could read. Now for mischief! I had not been long at Freeland's before I was up to my old tricks. I early began to address my companions on the subject of education, and the advantages of intelligence over ignorance, and, as far as I dared, I tried to show the agency of ignorance in keeping men in slavery. Webster's spelling book and the *Columbian Orator* were looked into again. As summer came on, and the long Sabbath days stretched themselves over our idleness, I became uneasy, and wanted a Sabbath school, in which to exercise my gifts, and to impart the little knowledge of letters which I possessed, to my brother slaves. A house was hardly necessary in the summer time; I could hold my school under the shade of an old oak tree, as well as any where else. The thing was, to get the scholars, and to have them thoroughly imbued with the desire to learn. Two such boys were quickly secured, in Henry and John, and from them the contagion spread. I was not long bringing around me twenty or thirty young men, who enrolled themselves, gladly, in my Sabbath school, and were willing to meet me regularly, under the trees or elsewhere, for the purpose of learning to read. It was surprising with what ease they provided themselves with spelling books. These were mostly the cast off books of their young masters or mistresses. I taught, at first, on our own farm. All were impressed with the necessity of keeping the matter as private as possible, for the fate of the St. Michael's attempt was notorious, and fresh in the minds of all. Our pious masters, at St. Michael's, must not know that a few of their dusky brothers were learning to read the word of God, lest they should come down upon us with the lash and chain. We might have met to drink whisky, to wrestle, fight, and to do other unseemly things, with no fear of interruption from the saints or sinners of St. Michael's.

But, to meet for the purpose of improving the mind and heart, by learning to read the sacred scriptures, was esteemed a most dangerous nuisance, to be instantly stopped. The slaveholders of St. Michael's, like slaveholders elsewhere, would always prefer to see the slaves engaged in degrading sports, rather than to see them acting like moral and accountable beings.

Had any one asked a religious white man, in St. Michael's, twenty years ago, the names of three men in that town, whose lives were most after the pattern of our Lord and Master, Jesus Christ, the first three would have been as follows:

GARRISON WEST, *Class Leader.*
WRIGHT FAIRBANKS, *Class Leader.*
THOMAS AULD, *Class Leader.*

And yet, these were men who ferociously rushed in upon my Sabbath school, at St. Michael's, armed with mob-like missiles, and I must say, I thought him a Christian, until he took part in bloody by the lash. This same Garrison West was my class leader, and I must say, I thought him a Christian, until he took part in breaking up my school. He led me no more after that. The plea for this outrage was then, as it is now and at all times—the danger to good order. If the slaves learnt to read, they would learn something else, and something worse. The peace of slavery would be disturbed; slave rule would be endangered. I leave the reader to characterize a system which is endangered by such causes. I do not dispute the soundness of the reasoning. It is perfectly sound; and, if slavery be *right*, Sabbath schools for teaching slaves to read the bible are *wrong*, and ought to be put down. These Christian class leaders were, to this extent, consistent. They had settled the question, that slavery is *right*, and, by that standard, they determined that Sabbath schools are wrong. To be sure, they were Protestant, and held to the great Protestant right of every man to *"search the scriptures"* for himself; but, then, to all general rules, there are *exceptions*. How convenient! What crimes may not be committed under the doctrine of the last remark. But, my dear, class leading Methodist brethren, did not condescend to give me a reason for breaking up the Sabbath school at St. Michael's; it was enough that they had determined upon its destruction. I am, however, digressing.

After getting the school cleverly into operation, the second time holding it in the woods, behind the barn, and in the shade of trees—I succeeded in inducing a free colored man, who lived several miles from our house, to permit me to hold my school in a room at his house. He, very kindly, gave me this liberty; but he incurred much peril in doing so, for the assemblage was an unlawful one. I shall not mention, here, the name of this man; for it might, even now, subject him to persecution, although the offenses were committed more than twenty years ago. I had, at one time, more than forty scholars, all of the right sort; and many of them succeeded in learning to read. I have met several slaves from Maryland, who were once my scholars; and who obtained their freedom, I doubt not, partly in consequence of the ideas imparted to them in that school. I have had various employments during my short life; but I look back to *none* with more satisfaction, than to that afforded by my Sunday school. An attachment, deep and lasting, sprung up between me and my persecuted pupils, which made parting from them intensely grievous; and, when I think that most of these dear souls are yet shut up in this abject thralldom, I am overwhelmed with grief.

Besides my Sunday school, I devoted three evenings a week to my fellow slaves, during the winter. Let the reader reflect upon the fact, that, in this christian country, men and women are hiding from professors of religion, in barns, in the woods and fields, in order to learn to read the *holy bible*. Those dear souls, who came to my Sabbath school, came *not* because it was popular or reputable to attend such a place, for they came under the liability of having forty stripes laid on their naked backs. Every moment they spend in my school, they were under this terrible liability; and, in this respect, I was sharer with them. Their minds had been cramped and starved by their cruel masters; the light of education had been completely excluded; and their hard earnings had been taken to educate their master's children. I felt a delight in circumventing the tyrants, and in blessing the victims of their curses.

The year at Mr. Freeland's passed off very smoothly, to outward seeming. Not a blow was given me during the whole year. To the credit of Mr. Freeland—irreligious though he was—it must be stated, that he was the best master I ever had, until I became my own master, and assumed for myself, as I had a right to do, the responsibility of my own existence and the exercise of my own powers. For much of the happiness—or absence of misery—with which I passed this year with Mr. Freeland, I am indebted to the genial temper and ardent friendship of my brother slaves. They were, every one of them, manly, generous and brave, yes; I say they were brave, and I will add, fine looking. It is seldom the lot of mortals to have truer and better friends than were the slaves on this farm. It is not uncommon to charge slaves with great treachery toward each other, and to believe them incapable of confiding in each other; but I must say, that I never loved, esteemed, or confided in men, more than I did in these. They were as true as steel, and no band of brothers could have been more loving. There were no mean advantages taken of each other, as is sometimes the case where slaves are situated as we were; no tattling; no giving each other bad names to Mr. Freeland; and no elevating one at the expense of the other. We never undertook to do any thing, of any importance, which was likely to affect each other, without mutual consultation. We were generally a unit, and moved together. Thoughts and sentiments were exchanged between us, which might well be called very incendiary, by oppressors and tyrants; and perhaps the time has not even now come, when it is safe to unfold all the flying suggestions which arise in the minds of intelligent slaves. Several of my friends and brothers, if yet alive, are still in some part of the house of bondage; and though twenty years have passed away, the suspicious malice of slavery might punish them for even listening to my thoughts.

The slaveholder, kind or cruel, is a slaveholder still—the every hour violator of the just and inalienable rights of man; and he is, therefore, every hour silently whetting the knife of vengeance for his own throat. He never lisps a syllable in commendation of the fathers of this republic, nor denounces any attempted oppression of himself, without inviting the knife to his own throat, and asserting the rights of rebellion for his own slaves.

The year is ended, and we are now in the midst of the Christmas holidays, which are kept this year as last, according to the general description previously given.

CHAPTER XIX.
The Run-Away Plot

NEW YEAR'S THOUGHTS AND MEDITATIONS—AGAIN BOUGHT BY FREELAND—NO AMBITION TO BE A SLAVE—KINDNESS NO COMPENSATION FOR SLAVERY—INCIPIENT STEPS TOWARD ESCAPE—CONSIDERATIONS LEADING THERETO—IRRECONCILABLE HOSTILITY TO SLAVERY—SOLEMN VOW TAKEN—PLAN DIVULGED TO THE SLAVES—*Columbian Orator*—SCHEME GAINS FAVOR, DESPITE PRO-SLAVERY PREACHING—DANGER OF DISCOVERY—SKILL OF SLAVEHOLDERS IN READING THE MINDS OF THEIR SLAVES—SUSPICION AND COERCION—HYMNS WITH DOUBLE MEANING—VALUE, IN DOLLARS, OF OUR COMPANY—PRELIMINARY CONSULTATION—PASS-WORD—CONFLICTS OF HOPE AND FEAR—DIFFICULTIES TO BE OVERCOME—IGNORANCE OF GEOGRAPHY—SURVEY OF IMAGINARY DIFFICULTIES—EFFECT ON OUR MINDS—PATRICK HENRY—SANDY BECOMES A DREAMER—ROUTE TO THE NORTH LAID OUT—OBJECTIONS CONSIDERED—FRAUDS PRACTICED ON FREEMEN—PASSES WRITTEN—ANXIETIES AS THE TIME DREW NEAR—DREAD OF FAILURE—APPEALS TO COMRADES—STRANGE PRESENTIMENT—COINCIDENCE—THE BETRAYAL DISCOVERED—THE MANNER OF ARRESTING US—RESISTANCE MADE BY HENRY HARRIS—ITS EFFECT—THE UNIQUE SPEECH OF MRS. FREELAND—OUR SAD PROCESSION TO PRISON—BRUTAL JEERS BY THE MULTITUDE ALONG THE ROAD—PASSES EATEN—THE DENIAL—SANDY TOO WELL LOVED TO BE SUSPECTED—DRAGGED BEHIND HORSES—THE JAIL A RELIEF—A NEW SET OF TORMENTORS—SLAVE-TRADERS—JOHN, CHARLES AND HENRY RELEASED—ALONE IN PRISON—I AM TAKEN OUT, AND SENT TO BALTIMORE.

I am now at the beginning of the year 1836, a time favorable for serious thoughts. The mind naturally occupies itself with the mysteries of life in all its phases—the ideal, the real and the actual. Sober people look both ways at the beginning of the year, surveying the errors of the past, and providing against possible errors of the future. I, too, was thus exercised. I had little pleasure in retrospect, and the prospect was not very brilliant. "Notwithstanding," thought I, "the many resolutions and prayers I have made, in behalf of freedom, I am, this first day of the year 1836, still a slave, still wandering in the depths of spirit-devouring thralldom. My faculties and powers of body and soul are not my own, but are the property of a fellow mortal, in no sense superior to me, except that he has the physical power to compel me to be owned and controlled by him. By the combined physical force of the community, I am his slave—a slave for life." With thoughts like these, I was perplexed and chafed; they rendered me gloomy and disconsolate. The anguish of my mind may not be written.

At the close of the year 1835, Mr. Freeland, my temporary master, had bought me of Capt. Thomas Auld, for the year 1836. His promptness in securing my services, would have been flattering to my vanity, had I been ambitious to win the reputation of being a valuable slave. Even as it was, I felt a slight degree of complacency at the circumstance. It showed he was as well pleased with me as a slave, as I was with him as a master. I have already intimated my regard for Mr. Freeland, and I may say here, in addressing northern readers—where is no selfish motive for speaking in praise of a slaveholder—that Mr. Freeland was a man of many excellent qualities, and to me quite preferable to any master I ever had.

But the kindness of the slavemaster only gilds the chain of slavery, and detracts nothing from its weight or power. The thought that men are made for other and better uses than slavery, thrives best under the gentle treatment of a kind master. But the grim visage of slavery can assume no smiles which can fascinate the partially enlightened slave, into a forgetfulness of his bondage, nor of the desirableness of liberty.

I was not through the first month of this, my second year with the kind and gentlemanly Mr. Freeland, before I was earnestly considering and advising plans for gaining that freedom, which, when I was but a mere child, I had ascertained to be the natural and inborn right of every member of the human family. The desire for this freedom had been benumbed, while I was under the brutalizing dominion of Covey; and it had been postponed, and rendered inoperative, by my truly pleasant Sunday school engagements with my friends, during the year 1835, at Mr. Freeland's. It had, however, never entirely subsided. I hated slavery, always, and the desire for freedom only needed a favorable breeze, to fan it into a blaze, at any moment. The thought of only being a creature of the *present* and the *past*, troubled me, and I longed to have a *future*—a future with hope in it. To be shut up entirely to the past and present, is abhorrent to the human mind; it is to the soul—whose life and happiness is unceasing progress—what the prison is to the body; a blight and mildew, a hell of horrors. The dawning of this, another year, awakened me from my temporary slumber, and roused into life my latent, but long cherished aspirations for freedom. I was now not only ashamed to be contented in slavery, but ashamed to *seem* to be contented, and in my present favorable condition, under the mild rule of Mr. F., I am not sure that some kind reader will not condemn me for being over ambitious, and greatly wanting in proper humility, when I say the truth, that I now drove from me all thoughts of making the best of my lot, and welcomed only such thoughts as led me away from the house of bondage. The intense desires, now felt, *to be free*, quickened by my present favorable circumstances, brought me to the determination to act, as well as to think and speak. Accordingly, at the beginning of this year 1836, I took upon me a solemn vow, that the year which had now dawned upon me should not close, without witnessing an earnest attempt, on my part, to gain my liberty. This vow only bound me to make my escape individually; but the year spent with Mr. Freeland had attached me, as with "hooks of steel," to my brother slaves. The most affectionate and confiding friendship existed between us; and I felt it my duty to give them an opportunity to share in my virtuous determination by frankly disclosing to them my plans and purposes. Toward Henry and John Harris, I felt a friendship as strong as one man can feel for another; for I could have died with and for them. To them, therefore, with a suitable degree of caution, I began to disclose my sentiments and plans; sounding them, the while on the subject of running away, provided a good chance should offer. I scarcely need tell the reader, that I did my *very best* to imbue the minds of my dear friends with my own views and feelings. Thoroughly awakened, now, and with a definite vow upon me, all my little reading, which had any bearing on the subject of human rights, was rendered available in my communications with my friends. That (to me) gem of a book, the *Columbian Orator*, with its eloquent orations and spicy dialogues, denouncing oppression and slavery—telling of what had been dared, done and suffered by men, to obtain the inestimable boon of liberty—was still fresh in my memory, and whirled into the ranks of my speech with the aptitude of well trained soldiers, going through the drill. The fact is, I here began my public speaking. I canvassed, with Henry and John, the subject of slavery, and dashed against it the condemning brand of God's eternal justice, which it every hour violates. My fellow servants were neither indifferent, dull, nor inapt. Our feelings were more alike than our opinions. All, however, were ready to act, when a feasible plan should be proposed. "Show us *how* the thing is to be done," said they, "and all is clear."

We were all, except Sandy, quite free from slaveholding priestcraft. It was in vain that we had been taught from the pulpit at St. Michael's, the duty of obedience to our masters; to recognize God as the author of our enslavement; to regard running away an offense, alike against God and man; to deem our enslavement a merciful and beneficial arrangement; to esteem our condition, in this country, a paradise to that from which we had been snatched in Africa; to consider our hard hands and dark color as God's mark of displeasure, and as pointing us out as the proper subjects of slavery; that the relation of master and slave was one of reciprocal benefits; that our work was not more serviceable to our masters, than our master's thinking was serviceable to us. I say, it was in vain that the pulpit of St. Michael's had constantly inculcated these plausible doctrine. Nature laughed them to scorn. For my own part, I had now become altogether too big for my chains. Father Lawson's solemn words, of what I ought to be, and might be, in the providence of God, had not fallen dead on my soul. I was fast verging toward manhood, and the prophecies of my childhood were still unfulfilled. The thought, that year after year had passed away, and my resolutions to run away had failed and faded—that I was *still a slave*, and a slave, too, with chances for gaining my freedom diminished and still diminishing—was not a matter to be slept over easily; nor did I easily sleep over it.

But here came a new trouble. Thoughts and purposes so incendiary as those I now cherished, could not agitate the mind long, without danger of making themselves manifest to scrutinizing and unfriendly beholders. I had reason to fear that my sable face might prove altogether too transparent for the safe concealment of my hazardous enterprise. Plans of greater moment have leaked through stone walls, and revealed their projectors. But, here was no stone wall to hide my purpose. I would have given my poor, tell tale face for the immoveable countenance of an Indian, for it was far from being proof against the daily, searching glances of those with whom I met.

It is the interest and business of slaveholders to study human nature, with a view to practical results, and many of them attain astonishing proficiency in discerning the thoughts and emotions of slaves. They have to deal not with earth, wood, or stone, but with *men;* and, by every regard they have for their safety and prosperity, they must study to know the material on which they are at work. So much intellect as the slaveholder has around him, requires watching. Their safety depends upon their vigilance. Conscious of the injustice and wrong they are every hour perpetrating, and knowing what they themselves would do if made the victims of such wrongs, they are looking out for the first signs of the dread retribution of justice. They watch, therefore, with skilled and practiced eyes, and have learned to read, with great accuracy, the state of mind and heart of the slaves, through his sable face. These uneasy sinners are quick to inquire into the matter, where the slave is concerned. Unusual sobriety, apparent abstraction, sullenness and indifference—indeed, any mood out of the common way—afford ground for suspicion and inquiry. Often relying on their superior position and wisdom, they hector and torture the slave into a confession, by affecting to know the truth of their accusations. "You have got the devil in you," say they, "and we will whip him out of you." I have often been put thus to the torture, on bare suspicion. This system has its disadvantages as well as their opposite. The slave is sometimes whipped into the confession of offenses which he never committed. The reader will see that the good old rule—"a man is to be held innocent until proved to be guilty"—does not hold good on the slave plantation. Suspicion and torture are the approved methods of getting at the truth, here. It was necessary for me, therefore, to keep a watch over my deportment, lest the enemy should get the better of me.

But with all our caution and studied reserve, I am not sure that Mr. Freeland did not suspect that all was not right with us. It *did* seem that he watched us more narrowly, after the plan of escape had been conceived and discussed amongst us. Men seldom see themselves as others see them; and while, to ourselves, everything connected with our contemplated escape appeared concealed, Mr. Freeland may have, with the peculiar prescience of a slaveholder, mastered the huge thought which was disturbing our peace in slavery.

I am the more inclined to think that he suspected us, because, prudent as we were, as I now look back, I can see that we did many silly things, very well calculated to awaken suspicion. We were, at times, remarkably buoyant, singing hymns and making joyous exclamations, almost as triumphant in their tone as if we reached a land of freedom and safety. A keen observer might have detected in our repeated singing of

> *O Canaan, sweet Canaan,*
> *I am bound for the land of Canaan,*

something more than a hope of reaching heaven. We meant to reach the *north*—and the north was our Canaan.

> *I thought I heard them say,*
> *There were lions in the way,*
> *I don't expect to Star*
>   *Much longer here.*

FREDERICK DOUGLASS

Run to Jesus—shun the danger—
I don't expect to stay
Much longer here.

was a favorite air, and had a double meaning. In the lips of some, it meant the expectation of a speedy summons to a world of spirits; but, in the lips of *our* company, it simply meant, a speedy pilgrimage toward a free state, and deliverance from all the evils and dangers of slavery.

I had succeeded in winning to my (what slaveholders would call wicked) scheme, a company of five young men, the very flower of the neighborhood, each one of whom would have commanded one thousand dollars in the home market. At New Orleans, they would have brought fifteen hundred dollars a piece, and, perhaps, more. The names of our party were as follows: Henry Harris; John Harris, brother to Henry; Sandy Jenkins, of root memory; Charles Roberts, and Henry Bailey. I was the youngest, but one, of the party. I had, however, the advantage of them all, in experience, and in a knowledge of letters. This gave me great influence over them. Perhaps not one of them, left to himself, would have dreamed of escape as a possible thing. Not one of them was self-moved in the matter. They all wanted to be free; but the serious thought of running away, had not entered into their minds, until I won them to the undertaking. They all were tolerably well off—for slaves—and had dim hopes of being set free, some day, by their masters. If any one is to blame for disturbing the quiet of the slaves and slave-masters of the neighborhood of St. Michael's, *I am the man*. I claim to be the instigator of the high crime (as the slaveholders regard it) and I kept life in it, until life could be kept in it no longer.

Pending the time of our contemplated departure out of our Egypt, we met often by night, and on every Sunday. At these meetings we talked the matter over; told our hopes and fears, and the difficulties discovered or imagined; and, like men of sense, we counted the cost of the enterprise to which we were committing ourselves.

These meetings must have resembled, on a small scale, the meetings of revolutionary conspirators, in their primary condition. We were plotting against our (so called) lawful rulers; with this difference that we sought our own good, and not the harm of our enemies. We did not seek to overthrow them, but to escape from them. As for Mr. Freeland, we all liked him, and would have gladly remained with him, *as freeman*. LIBERTY was our aim; and we had now come to think that we had a right to liberty, against every obstacle even against the lives of our enslavers.

We had several words, expressive of things, important to us, which we understood, but which, even if distinctly heard by an outsider, would convey no certain meaning. I have reasons for suppressing these *pass-words*, which the reader will easily divine. I hated the secrecy; but where slavery is powerful, and liberty is weak, the latter is driven to concealment or to destruction.

The prospect was not always a bright one. At times, we were almost tempted to abandon the enterprise, and to get back to that comparative peace of mind, which even a man under the gallows might feel, when all hope of escape had vanished. Quiet bondage was felt to be better than the doubts, fears and uncertainties, which now so sadly perplexed and disturbed us.

The infirmities of humanity, generally, were represented in our little band. We were confident, bold and determined, at times; and, again, doubting, timid and wavering; whistling, like the boy in the graveyard, to keep away the spirits.

To look at the map, and observe the proximity of Eastern Shore, Maryland, to Delaware and Pennsylvania, it may seem to the reader quite absurd, to regard the proposed escape as a formidable undertaking. But to *understand*, some one has said a man must *stand under*. The real distance was great enough, but the imagined distance was, to our ignorance, even greater. Every slaveholder seeks to impress his slave with a belief in the boundlessness of slave territory, and of his own almost illimitable power. We all had vague and indistinct notions of the geography of the country.

The distance, however, is not the chief trouble. The nearer are the lines of a slave state and the borders of a free one, the greater the peril. Hired kidnappers infest these borders. Then, too, we knew that merely reaching a free state did not free us; that, wherever caught, we could be returned to slavery. We could see no spot on this side the ocean, where we could be free. We had heard of

Canada, the real Canaan of the American bondmen, simply as a country to which the wild goose and the swan repaired at the end of winter, to escape the heat of summer, but not as the home of man. I knew something of theology, but nothing of geography. I really did not, at that time, know that there was a state of New York, or a state of Massachusetts. I had heard of Pennsylvania, Delaware and New Jersey, and all the southern states, but was ignorant of the free states, generally. New York city was our northern limit, and to go there, and be forever harassed with the liability of being hunted down and returned to slavery—with the certainty of being treated ten times worse than we had ever been treated before was a prospect far from delightful, and it might well cause some hesitation about engaging in the enterprise. The case, sometimes, to our excited visions, stood thus: At every gate through which we had to pass, we saw a watchman; at every ferry, a guard; on every bridge, a sentinel; and in every wood, a patrol or slave-hunter. We were hemmed in on every side. The good to be sought, and the evil to be shunned, were flung in the balance, and weighed against each other. On the one hand, there stood slavery; a stern reality, glaring frightfully upon us, with the blood of millions in his polluted skirts—terrible to behold—greedily devouring our hard earnings and feeding himself upon our flesh. Here was the evil from which to escape. On the other hand, far away, back in the hazy distance, where all forms seemed but shadows, under the flickering light of the north star—behind some craggy hill or snow-covered mountain—stood a doubtful freedom, half frozen, beckoning us to her icy domain. This was the good to be sought. The inequality was as great as that between certainty and uncertainty. This, in itself, was enough to stagger us; but when we came to survey the untrodden road, and conjecture the many possible difficulties, we were appalled, and at times, as I have said, were upon the point of giving over the struggle altogether.

The reader can have little idea of the phantoms of trouble which flit, in such circumstances, before the uneducated mind of the slave. Upon either side, we saw grim death assuming a variety of horrid shapes. Now, it was starvation, causing us, in a strange and friendless land, to eat our own flesh. Now, we were contending with the waves (for our journey was in part by water) and were drowned. Now, we were hunted by dogs, and overtaken and torn to pieces by their merciless fangs. We were stung by scorpions—chased by wild beasts—bitten by snakes; and, worst of all, after having succeeded in swimming rivers—encountering wild beasts—sleeping in the woods—suffering hunger, cold, heat and nakedness—we supposed ourselves to be overtaken by hired kidnappers, who, in the name of the law, and for their thrice accursed reward, would, perchance, fire upon us—kill some, wound others, and capture all. This dark picture, drawn by ignorance and fear, at times greatly shook our determination, and not unfrequently caused us to

> *Rather bear those ills we had*
> *Than fly to others which we knew not of.*

I am not disposed to magnify this circumstance in my experience, and yet I think I shall seem to be so disposed, to the reader. No man can tell the intense agony which is felt by the slave, when wavering on the point of making his escape. All that he has is at stake; and even that which he has not, is at stake, also. The life which he has, may be lost, and the liberty which he seeks, may not be gained.

Patrick Henry, to a listening senate, thrilled by his magic eloquence, and ready to stand by him in his boldest flights, could say, GIVE ME LIBERTY OR GIVE ME DEATH, and this saying was a sublime one, even for a freeman; but, incomparably more sublime, is the same sentiment, when *practically* asserted by men accustomed to the lash and chain—men whose sensibilities must have become more or less deadened by their bondage. With us it was a *doubtful* liberty, at best, that we sought; and a certain, lingering death in the rice swamps and sugar fields, if we failed. Life is not lightly regarded by men of sane minds. It is precious, alike to the pauper and to the prince—to the slave, and to his master; and yet, I believe there was not one among us, who would not rather have been shot down, than pass away life in hopeless bondage.

In the progress of our preparations, Sandy, the root man, became troubled. He began to have dreams, and some of them were very distressing. One of these, which happened on a Friday night, was, to him, of great significance; and I am quite ready to confess, that I felt somewhat damped by it myself. He said, "I dreamed, last night, that I was roused from sleep, by strange noises, like the voices of a swarm of angry birds, that caused a roar as they passed, which fell upon my ear like a coming gale over the tops of the trees. Looking up to see what it could mean," said Sandy, "I saw you, Frederick, in the claws of a huge bird, surrounded by a large number of birds, of all colors and sizes. These were all picking at you, while you, with your arms, seemed to be trying to protect your eyes. Passing over me, the birds flew in a south-westerly direction, and I watched them until they were clean out of sight. Now, I saw this as plainly as I now see you; and furder, honey, watch de Friday night dream; dare is sumpon in it, shose you born; dare is, indeed, honey."

I confess I did not like this dream; but I threw off concern about it, by attributing it to the general excitement and perturbation consequent upon our contemplated plan of escape. I could not, however, shake off its effect at once. I felt that it boded me no good. Sandy was unusually emphatic and oracular, and his manner had much to do with the impression made upon me.

The plan of escape which I recommended, and to which my comrades assented, was to take a large canoe, owned by Mr. Hamilton, and, on the Saturday night previous to the Easter holidays, launch out into the Chesapeake bay, and paddle for its head—a distance of seventy miles with all our might. Our course, on reaching this point, was, to turn the canoe adrift, and bend our steps toward the north star, till we reached a free state.

There were several objections to this plan. One was, the danger from gales on the bay. In rough weather, the waters of the Chesapeake are much agitated, and there is danger, in a canoe, of being swamped by the waves. Another objection was, that the canoe would soon be missed; the absent persons would, at once, be suspected of having taken it; and we should be pursued by some of the fast sailing bay craft out of St. Michael's. Then, again, if we reached the head of the bay, and turned the canoe adrift, she might prove a guide to our track, and bring the land hunters after us.

These and other objections were set aside, by the stronger ones which could be urged against every other plan that could then be suggested. On the water, we had a chance of being regarded as fishermen, in the service of a master. On the other hand, by taking the land route, through the counties adjoining Delaware, we should be subjected to all manner of interruptions, and many very disagreeable questions, which might give us serious trouble. Any white man is authorized to stop a man of color, on any road, and examine him, and arrest him, if he so desires.

By this arrangement, many abuses (considered such even by slaveholders) occur. Cases have been known, where freemen have been called upon to show their free papers, by a pack of ruffians—and, on the presentation of the papers, the ruffians have torn them up, and seized their victim, and sold him to a life of endless bondage.

The week before our intended start, I wrote a pass for each of our party, giving them permission to visit Baltimore, during the Easter holidays. The pass ran after this manner:

> *This is to certify, that I, the undersigned, have given the bearer, my servant, John, full liberty to go to Baltimore, to spend the Easter holidays.*
> W.H.
Near St. Michael's, Talbot county, Maryland

Although we were not going to Baltimore, and were intending to land east of North Point, in the direction where I had seen the Philadelphia steamers go, these passes might be made useful to us in the lower part of the bay, while steering toward Baltimore. These were not, however, to be shown by us, until all other answers failed to satisfy the inquirer. We were all fully alive to the importance of being calm and self-possessed, when accosted, if accosted we should be; and we more times than one rehearsed to each other how we should behave in the hour of trial.

These were long, tedious days and nights. The suspense was painful, in the extreme. To balance probabilities, where life and liberty hang on the result, requires steady nerves. I panted for action, and was glad when the day, at the close of which we were to start, dawned upon us. Sleeping, the night before, was out of the question. I probably felt more deeply than any of my companions, because I was the instigator of the movement. The responsibility of the whole enterprise rested on my shoulders. The glory of success, and the shame and confusion of failure, could not be matters of indifference to me. Our food was prepared; our clothes were packed up; we were all ready to go, and impatient for Saturday morning—considering that the last morning of our bondage.

I cannot describe the tempest and tumult of my brain, that morning. The reader will please to bear in mind, that, in a slave state, an unsuccessful runaway is not only subjected to cruel torture, and sold away to the far south, but he is frequently execrated by the other slaves. He is charged with making the condition of the other slaves intolerable, by laying them all under the suspicion of their masters—subjecting them to greater vigilance, and imposing greater limitations on their privileges. I dreaded murmurs from this quarter. It is difficult, too, for a slavemaster to believe that slaves escaping have not been aided in their flight by some one of their fellow slaves. When, therefore, a slave is missing, every slave on the place is closely examined as to his knowledge of the undertaking; and they are sometimes even tortured, to make them disclose what they are suspected of knowing of such escape.

Our anxiety grew more and more intense, as the time of our intended departure for the north drew nigh. It was truly felt to be a matter of life and death with us; and we fully intended to *fight* as well as *run*, if necessity should occur for that extremity. But the trial hour was not yet to come. It was easy to resolve, but not so easy to act. I expected there might be some drawing back, at the last. It was natural that there should be; therefore, during the intervening time, I lost no opportunity to explain away difficulties, to remove doubts, to dispel fears, and to inspire all with firmness. It was too late to look back; and *now* was the time to go forward. Like most other men, we had done the talking part of our work, long and well; and the time had come to *act* as if we were in earnest, and meant to be as true in action as in words. I did not forget to appeal to the pride of my comrades, by telling them that, if after having solemnly promised to go, as they had done, they now failed to make the attempt, they would, in effect, brand themselves with cowardice, and might as well sit down, fold their arms, and acknowledge themselves as fit only to be *slaves*. This detestable character, all were unwilling to assume. Every man except Sandy (he, much to our regret, withdrew) stood firm; and at our last meeting we pledged ourselves afresh, and in the most solemn manner, that, at the time appointed, we *would* certainly start on our long journey for a free country. This meeting was in the middle of the week, at the end of which we were to start.

Early that morning we went, as usual, to the field, but with hearts that beat quickly and anxiously. Any one intimately acquainted with us, might have seen that all was not well with us, and that some monster lingered in our thoughts. Our work that morning was the same as it had been for several days past—drawing out and spreading manure. While thus engaged, I had a sudden presentiment, which flashed upon me like lightning in a dark night, revealing to the lonely traveler the gulf before, and the enemy behind. I instantly turned to Sandy Jenkins, who was near me, and said to him, *"Sandy, we are betrayed;* something has just told me so."* I felt as sure of it, as if the officers were there in sight. Sandy said, "Man, dat is strange; but I feel just as you do." If my mother—then long in her grave—had appeared before me, and told me that we were betrayed, I could not, at that moment, have felt more certain of the fact.

In a few minutes after this, the long, low and distant notes of the horn summoned us from the field to breakfast. I felt as one may be supposed to feel before being led forth to be executed for some great offense. I wanted no breakfast; but I went with the other slaves toward the house, for form's sake. My feelings were not disturbed as to the right of running away; on that point I had no trouble, whatever. My anxiety arose from a sense of the consequences of failure.

In thirty minutes after that vivid presentiment came the apprehended crash. On reaching the house, for breakfast, and glancing my eye toward the lane gate, the worst was at once made known. The lane gate off Mr. Freeland's house, is nearly a half mile from the door, and shaded by the heavy wood which bordered the main road. I was, however, able to descry four white men, and two colored men, approaching. The white men were on horseback, and the colored men were walking behind, and seemed to be tied. *"It is all over with us,"* thought I, *"we are surely betrayed."* I now became composed, or at least comparatively so, and calmly awaited the result. I watched the ill-omened company, till I saw them enter the gate. Successful flight was impossible, and I made up my mind to stand, and meet the evil, whatever it might be; for I was not without a slight hope that things might turn differently from what I at first expected. In a few moments, in came Mr. William Hamilton, riding very rapidly, and evidently much excited. He was in the habit of riding very slowly, and was seldom known to gallop his horse. This time, his horse was nearly at full speed, causing the dust to roll thick behind him. Mr. Hamilton, though one of the most resolute men in the whole neighborhood, was, nevertheless, a remarkably mild spoken man; and, even when greatly excited, his language was cool and circumspect. He came to the door, and inquired if Mr. Freeland was in. I told him that Mr. Freeland was at the barn. Off the old gentleman rode, toward the barn, with unwonted speed. Mary, the cook, was at a loss to know what was the matter, and I did not profess any skill in making her understand. I knew she would have united, as readily as any one, in cursing me for bringing trouble into the family; so I held my peace, leaving matters to develop themselves, without my assistance. In a few moments, Mr. Hamilton and Mr. Freeland came down from the barn to the house; and, just as they made their appearance in the front yard, three men (who proved to be constables) came dashing into the lane, on horseback, as if summoned by a sign requiring quick work. A few seconds brought them into the front yard, where they hastily dismounted, and tied their horses. This done, they joined Mr. Freeland and Mr. Hamilton, who were standing a short distance from the kitchen. A few moments were spent, as if in consulting how to proceed, and then the whole party walked up to the kitchen door. There was now no one in the kitchen but myself and John Harris. Henry and Sandy were yet at the barn. Mr. Freeland came inside the kitchen door, and with an agitated voice, called me by name, and told me to come forward; that there was some gentlemen who wished to see me. I stepped toward them, at the door, and asked what they wanted, when the constables grabbed me, and told me that I had better not resist; that I had been in a scrape, or was said to have been in one; that they were merely going to take me where I could be examined; that they were going to carry me to St. Michael's, to have me brought before my master. They further said, that, in case the evidence against me was not true, I should be acquitted. I was now firmly tied, and completely at the mercy of my captors. Resistance was idle. They were five in number, armed to the very teeth. When they had secured me, they next turned to John Harris, and, in a few moments, succeeded in tying him as firmly as they had already tied me. They next turned toward Henry Harris, who had now returned from the barn. "Cross your hands," said the constables, to Henry. "I won't" said Henry, in a voice so firm and clear, and in a manner so determined, as for a moment to arrest all proceedings. "Won't you cross your hands?" said Tom Graham, the constable. "*No I won't*," said Henry, with increasing emphasis. Mr. Hamilton, Mr. Freeland, and the officers, now came near to Henry. Two of the constables drew out their shining pistols, and swore by the name of God, that he should cross his hands, or they would shoot him down. Each of these hired ruffians now cocked their pistols, and, with fingers apparently on the triggers, presented their deadly weapons to the breast of the unarmed slave, saying, at the same time, if he did not cross his hands, they would "blow his d——d heart out of him."

"*Shoot! shoot me!*" said Henry. "*You can't kill me but once.* Shoot!—shoot! and be d——d. *I won't be tied.*" This, the brave fellow said in a voice as defiant and heroic in its tone, as was the language itself; and, at the moment of saying this, with the pistols at his very breast, he quickly raised his arms, and dashed them from the puny hands of his assassins, the weapons flying in opposite directions. Now came the struggle. All hands was now rushed upon the brave fellow, and, after beating him for some time, they succeeded in overpowering and tying him. Henry put me to shame; he fought, and fought bravely. John and I had made no resistance. The fact is, I never see much use in fighting, unless there is a reasonable probability of whipping somebody. Yet there was something almost providential in the resistance made by the gallant Henry. But for that resistance, every soul of us would have been hurried off to the far south. Just a moment previous to the trouble with Henry, Mr. Hamilton *mildly* said—and this gave me the unmistakable clue to the cause of our arrest—"Perhaps we had now better make a search for those protections, which we understand Frederick has written for himself and the rest." Had these passes been found, they would have been point blank proof against us, and would have confirmed all the statements of our betrayer. Thanks to the resistance of Henry, the excitement produced by the scuffle drew all attention in that direction, and I succeeded in flinging my pass, unobserved, into the fire. The confusion attendant upon the scuffle, and the apprehension of further trouble, perhaps, led our captors to forego, for the present, any search for *"those protections" which Frederick was said to have written for his companions*; so we were not yet convicted of the purpose to run away; and it was evident that there was some doubt, on the part of all, whether we had been guilty of such a purpose.

Just as we were all completely tied, and about ready to start toward St. Michael's, and thence to jail, Mrs. Betsey Freeland (mother to William, who was very much attached—after the southern fashion—to Henry and John, they having been reared from childhood in her house) came to the kitchen door, with her hands full of biscuits—for we had not had time to take our breakfast that morning—and divided them between Henry and John. This done, the lady made the following parting address to me, looking and pointing her bony finger at me. "You devil! you yellow devil! It was you that put it into the heads of Henry and John to run away. But for *you*, you *long legged yellow devil*, Henry and John would never have thought of running away." I gave the lady a look, which called forth a scream of mingled wrath and terror, as she slammed the kitchen door, and went in, leaving me, with the rest, in hands as harsh as her own broken voice.

Could the kind reader have been quietly riding along the main road to or from Easton, that morning, his eye would have met a painful sight. He would have seen five young men, guilty of no crime, save that of preferring *liberty* to a life of *bondage*, drawn along the public highway—firmly bound together—tramping through dust and heat, bare-footed and bare-headed—fastened to three strong horses, whose riders were armed to the teeth, with pistols and daggers—on their way to prison, like felons, and suffering every possible insult from the crowds of idle, vulgar people, who clustered around, and heartlessly made their failure the occasion for all manner of ribaldry and sport. As I looked upon this crowd of vile persons, and saw myself and friends thus assailed and persecuted, I could not help seeing the fulfillment of Sandy's dream. I was in the hands of moral vultures, and firmly held in their sharp talons, and was hurried away toward Easton, in a south-easterly direction, amid the jeers of new birds of the same feather, through every neighborhood we passed. It seemed to me (and this shows the good understanding between the slaveholders and their allies) that every body we met knew the cause of our arrest, and were out, awaiting our passing by, to feast their vindictive eyes on our misery and to gloat over our ruin. Some said, *I ought to be hanged*, and others, *I ought to be burnt*, others, I ought to have the *"hide"* taken from my back; while no one gave us a kind word or sympathizing look, except the poor slaves, who were lifting their heavy hoes, and who cautiously glanced at us through the post-and-rail fences, behind which they were at work. Our sufferings, that morning, can be more easily imagined than described. Our hopes were all blasted, at a blow. The cruel injustice, the victorious crime, and the helplessness of innocence, led me to ask, in my ignorance and weakness "Where now is the God of justice and mercy? And why have these wicked men the power thus to trample upon our rights, and to insult our feelings?" And yet, in the next moment, came the consoling thought, *"The day of oppressor will come at last."* Of one thing I could be glad—not one of my dear friends, upon whom I had brought this great calamity, either by word or look, reproached me for having led them into it. We were a band of brothers, and never dearer to each other than now. The thought which gave us the most pain, was the probable separation which would now take place, in case we were sold off to the far south, as we were likely to be. While the constables were looking forward, Henry and I, being fastened together, could occasionally exchange a word, without being observed by the kidnappers who had us in charge. "What shall I do with my pass?" said Henry. "Eat it with your biscuit," said I; "it won't do to tear it up." We were now near St. Michael's. The direction concerning the passes was passed around, and executed. *"Own nothing!"* said I. *"Own nothing!"* was passed around and enjoined, and assented to. Our confidence in each other was unshaken; and we were quite resolved to succeed or fail together—as much after the calamity which had befallen us, as before.

On reaching St. Michael's, we underwent a sort of examination at my master's store, and it was evident to my mind, that Master Thomas suspected the truthfulness of the evidence upon which they had acted in arresting us; and that he only affected, to some extent, the positiveness with which he asserted our guilt. There was nothing said by any of our company, which could, in any manner, prejudice our cause; and there was hope, yet, that we should be able to return to our homes—if for nothing else, at least to find out the guilty man or woman who had betrayed us.

To this end, we all denied that we had been guilty of intended flight. Master Thomas said that the evidence he had of our intention to run away, was strong enough to hang us, in a case of murder.

"But," said I, "the cases are not equal. If murder were committed, some one must have committed it—the thing is done! In our case, nothing has been done! We have not run away. Where is the evidence against us? We were quietly at our work." I talked thus, with unusual freedom, to bring out the evidence against us, for we all wanted, above all things, to know the guilty wretch who had betrayed us, that we might have something tangible upon which to pour the execrations. From something which dropped, in the course of the talk, it appeared that there was but one witness against us—and that that witness could not be produced. Master Thomas would not tell us *who* his informant was; but we suspected, and suspected *one* person *only*. Several circumstances seemed to point SANDY out, as our betrayer. His entire knowledge of our plans his participation in them—his withdrawal from us—his dream, and his simultaneous presentiment that we were betrayed—the taking us, and the leaving him—were calculated to turn suspicion toward him; and yet, we could not suspect him. We all loved him too well to think it *possible* that he could have betrayed us. So we rolled the guilt on other shoulders.

We were literally dragged, that morning, behind horses, a distance of fifteen miles, and placed in the Easton jail. We were glad to reach the end of our journey, for our pathway had been the scene of insult and mortification. Such is the power of public opinion, that it is hard, even for the innocent, to feel the happy consolations of innocence, when they fall under the maledictions of this power. How could we regard ourselves as in the right, when all about us denounced us as criminals, and had the power and the disposition to treat us as such.

In jail, we were placed under the care of Mr. Joseph Graham, the sheriff of the county. Henry, and John, and myself, were placed in one room, and Henry Baily and Charles Roberts, in another, by themselves. This separation was intended to deprive us of the advantage of concert, and to prevent trouble in jail.

Once shut up, a new set of tormentors came upon us. A swarm of imps, in human shape the slave-traders, deputy slave-traders, and agents of slave-traders—that gather in every country town of the state, watching for chances to buy human flesh (as buzzards to eat carrion) flocked in upon us, to ascertain if our masters had placed us in jail to be sold. Such a set of debased and villainous creatures, I never saw before, and hope never to see again. I felt myself surrounded as by a pack of *fiends*, fresh from *perdition*. They laughed, leered, and grinned at us; saying, "Ah! boys, we've got you, havn't we? So you were about to make your escape? Where were you going to?" After taunting us, and peering at us, as long as they liked, they one by one subjected us to an examination, with a view to ascertain our value; feeling our arms and legs, and shaking us by the shoulders to see if we were sound and healthy; impudently asking us, "how we would like to have them for masters?" To such questions, we were, very much to their annoyance, quite dumb, disdaining to answer them. For one, I detested the whisky-bloated gamblers in human flesh; and I believe I was as much detested by them in turn. One fellow told me, "if he had me, he would cut the devil out of me pretty quick."

These Negro buyers are very offensive to the genteel southern Christian public. They are looked upon, in respectable Maryland society, as necessary, but detestable characters. As a class, they are hardened ruffians, made such by nature and by occupation. Their ears are made quite familiar with the agonizing cry of outraged and woe-smitten humanity. Their eyes are forever open to human misery. They walk amid desecrated affections, insulted virtue, and blasted hopes. They have grown intimate with vice and blood; they gloat over the wildest illustrations of their soul-damning and earth-polluting business, and are moral pests. Yes; they are a legitimate fruit of slavery; and it is a puzzle to make out a case of greater villainy for them, than for the slaveholders, who make such a class *possible*. They are mere hucksters of the surplus slave produce of Maryland and Virginia coarse, cruel, and swaggering bullies, whose very breathing is of blasphemy and blood.

Aside from these slave-buyers, who infested the prison, from time to time, our quarters were much more comfortable than we had any right to expect they would be. Our allowance of food was small and coarse, but our room was the best in the jail—neat and spacious, and with nothing about it necessarily reminding us of being in prison, but its heavy locks and bolts and the black, iron lattice-work at the windows. We were prisoners of state, compared with most slaves who are put into that Easton jail. But the place was not one of contentment. Bolts, bars and grated windows are not acceptable to freedom-loving people of any color. The suspense, too, was painful. Every step on the stairway was listened to, in the hope that the comer would cast a ray of light on our fate. We would have given the hair off our heads for half a dozen words with one of the waiters in Sol. Lowe's hotel. Such waiters were in the way of hearing, at the table, the probable course of things. We could see them flitting about in their white jackets in front of this hotel, but could speak to none of them.

Soon after the holidays were over, contrary to all our expectations, Messrs. Hamilton and Freeland came up to Easton; not to make a bargain with the "Georgia traders," nor to send us up to Austin Woldfolk, as is usual in the case of run-away salves, but to release Charles, Henry Harris, Henry Baily and John Harris, from prison, and this, too, without the infliction of a single blow. I was now left entirely alone in prison. The innocent had been taken, and the guilty left. My friends were separated from me, and apparently forever. This circumstance caused me more pain than any other incident connected with our capture and imprisonment. Thirty-nine lashes on my naked and bleeding back, would have been joyfully borne, in preference to this separation from these, the friends of my youth. And yet, I could not but feel that I was the victim of something like justice. Why should these young men, who were led into this scheme by me, suffer as much as the instigator? I felt glad that they were leased from prison, and from the dread prospect of a life (or death I should rather say) in the rice swamps. It is due to the noble Henry, to say, that he seemed almost as reluctant to leave the prison with me in it, as he was to be tied and dragged to prison. But he and the rest knew that we should, in all the likelihoods of the case, be separated, in the event of being sold; and since we were now completely in the hands of our owners, we all concluded it would be best to go peaceably home.

Not until this last separation, dear reader, had I touched those profounder depths of desolation, which it is the lot of slaves often to reach. I was solitary in the world, and alone within the walls of a stone prison, left to a fate of life-long misery. I had hoped and expected much, for months before, but my hopes and expectations were now withered and blasted. The ever dreaded slave life in Georgia, Louisiana and Alabama—from which escape is next to impossible now, in my loneliness, stared me in the face. The possibility of ever becoming anything but an abject slave, a mere machine in the hands of an owner, had now fled, and it seemed to me it had fled forever. A life of living death, beset with the innumerable horrors of the cotton field, and the sugar plantation, seemed to be my doom. The fiends, who rushed into the prison when we were first put there, continued to visit me, and to ply me with questions and with their tantalizing remarks. I was insulted, but helpless; keenly alive to the demands of justice and liberty, but with no means of asserting them. To talk to those imps about justice and mercy, would have been as absurd as to reason with bears and tigers. Lead and steel are the only arguments that they understand.

After remaining in this life of misery and despair about a week, which, by the way, seemed a month, Master Thomas, very much to my surprise, and greatly to my relief, came to the prison, and took me out, for the purpose, as he said, of sending me to Alabama, with a friend of his, who would emancipate me at the end of eight years. I was glad enough to get out of prison; but I had no faith in the story that this friend of Capt. Auld would emancipate me, at the end of the time indicated. Besides, I never had heard of his having a friend in Alabama, and I took the announcement, simply as an easy and comfortable method of shipping me off to the far south. There was a little scandal, too, connected with the idea of one Christian selling another to the Georgia traders, while it was deemed every way proper for them to sell to others. I thought this friend in Alabama was an invention, to meet this difficulty, for Master Thomas was quite jealous of his Christian reputation, however unconcerned he might be about his real Christian character. In these remarks, however, it is possible that I do Master Thomas Auld injustice. He certainly did not exhaust his power upon me, in the case, but acted, upon the whole, very generously, considering the nature of my offense. He had the power and the provocation to send me, without reserve, into the very everglades of Florida, beyond the remotest hope of emancipation; and his refusal to exercise that power, must be set down to his credit.

After lingering about St. Michael's a few days, and no friend from Alabama making his appearance, to take me there, Master Thomas decided to send me back again to Baltimore, to live with his brother Hugh, with whom he was now at peace; possibly he became so by his profession of religion, at the camp-meeting in the Bay Side. Master Thomas told me that he wished me to go to

Baltimore, and learn a trade; and that, if I behaved myself properly, he would *emancipate me at twenty-five!* Thanks for this one beam of hope in the future. The promise had but one fault; it seemed too good to be true.

CHAPTER XX.
Apprenticeship Life

NOTHING LOST BY THE ATTEMPT TO RUN AWAY—COMRADES IN THEIR OLD HOMES—REASONS FOR SENDING ME AWAY—RETURN TO BALTIMORE—CONTRAST BETWEEN TOMMY AND THAT OF HIS COLORED COMPANION—TRIALS IN GARDINER'S SHIP YARD—DESPERATE FIGHT—ITS CAUSES—CONFLICT BETWEEN WHITE AND BLACK LABOR—DESCRIPTION OF THE OUTRAGE—COLORED TESTIMONY NOTHING—CONDUCT OF MASTER HUGH—SPIRIT OF SLAVERY IN BALTIMORE—MY CONDITION IMPROVES—NEW ASSOCIATIONS—SLAVEHOLDER'S RIGHT TO TAKE HIS WAGES—HOW TO MAKE A CONTENTED SLAVE.

Well! dear reader, I am not, as you may have already inferred, a loser by the general upstir, described in the foregoing chapter. The little domestic revolution, notwithstanding the sudden snub it got by the treachery of somebody—I dare not say or think who—did not, after all, end so disastrously, as when in the iron cage at Easton, I conceived it would. The prospect, from that point, did look about as dark as any that ever cast its gloom over the vision of the anxious, out-looking, human spirit. "All is well that ends well." My affectionate comrades, Henry and John Harris, are still with Mr. William Freeland. Charles Roberts and Henry Baily are safe at their homes. I have not, therefore, any thing to regret on their account. Their masters have mercifully forgiven them, probably on the ground suggested in the spirited little speech of Mrs. Freeland, made to me just before leaving for the jail—namely: that they had been allured into the wicked scheme of making their escape, by me; and that, but for me, they would never have dreamed of a thing so shocking! My friends had nothing to regret, either; for while they were watched more closely on account of what had happened, they were, doubtless, treated more kindly than before, and got new assurances that they would be legally emancipated, some day, provided their behavior should make them deserving, from that time forward. Not a blow, as I learned, was struck any one of them. As for Master William Freeland, good, unsuspecting soul, he did not believe that we were intending to run away at all. Having given—as he thought—no occasion to his boys to leave him, he could not think it probable that they had entertained a design so grievous. This, however, was not the view taken of the matter by "Mas' Billy," as we used to call the soft spoken, but crafty and resolute Mr. William Hamilton. He had no doubt that the crime had been meditated; and regarding me as the instigator of it, he frankly told Master Thomas that he must remove me from that neighborhood, or he would shoot me down. He would not have one so dangerous as "Frederick" tampering with his slaves. William Hamilton was not a man whose threat might be safely disregarded. I have no doubt that he would have proved as good as his word, had the warning given not been promptly taken. He was furious at the thought of such a piece of high-handed *theft*, as we were about to perpetrate the stealing of our own bodies and souls! The feasibility of the plan, too, could the first steps have been taken, was marvelously plain. Besides, this was a *new* idea, this use of the bay. Slaves escaping, until now, had taken to the woods; they had never dreamed of profaning and abusing the waters of the noble Chesapeake, by making them the highway from slavery to freedom. Here was a broad road of destruction to slavery, which, before, had been looked upon as a wall of security by slaveholders. But Master Billy could not get Mr. Freeland to see matters precisely as he did; nor could he get Master Thomas so excited as he was himself. The latter—I must say it to his credit—showed much humane feeling in his part of the transaction, and atoned for much that had been harsh, cruel and unreasonable in his former treatment of me and others. His clemency was quite unusual and unlooked for. "Cousin Tom" told me that while I was in jail, Master Thomas was very unhappy; and that the night before his going up to release me, he had walked the floor nearly all night, evincing great distress; that very tempting offers had been made to him, by the Negro-traders, but he had rejected them all, saying that *money could not tempt him to sell me to the far south*. All this I can easily believe, for he seemed quite reluctant to send me away, at all. He told me that he only consented to do so, because of the very strong prejudice against me in the neighborhood, and that he feared for my safety if I remained there.

Thus, after three years spent in the country, roughing it in the field, and experiencing all sorts of hardships, I was again permitted to return to Baltimore, the very place, of all others, short of a free state, where I most desired to live. The three years spent in the country, had made some difference in me, and in the household of Master Hugh. "Little Tommy" was no longer *little* Tommy; and I was not the slender lad who had left for the Eastern Shore just three years before. The loving relations between me and Mas' Tommy were broken up. He was no longer dependent on me for protection, but felt himself a *man*, with other and more suitable associates. In childhood, he scarcely considered me inferior to himself certainly, as good as any other boy with whom he played; but the time had come when his *friend* must become his *slave*. So we were cold, and we parted. It was a sad thing to me, that, loving each other as we had done, we must now take different roads. To him, a thousand avenues were open. Education had made him acquainted with all the treasures of the world, and liberty had flung open the gates thereunto; but I, who had attended him seven years, and had watched over him with the care of a big brother, fighting his battles in the street, and shielding him from harm, to an extent which had induced his mother to say, "Oh! Tommy is always safe, when he is with Freddy," must be confined to a single condition. He could grow, and become a MAN; I could grow, though I could *not* become a man, but must remain, all my life, a minor—a mere boy. Thomas Auld, Junior, obtained a situation on board the brig "Tweed," and went to sea. I know not what has become of him; he certainly has my good wishes for his welfare and prosperity. There were few persons to whom I was more sincerely attached than to him, and there are few in the world I would be more pleased to meet.

Very soon after I went to Baltimore to live, Master Hugh succeeded in getting me hired to Mr. William Gardiner, an extensive ship builder on Fell's Point. I was placed here to learn to calk, a trade of which I already had some knowledge, gained while in Mr. Hugh Auld's ship-yard, when he was a master builder. Gardiner's, however, proved a very unfavorable place for the accomplishment of that object. Mr. Gardiner was, that season, engaged in building two large man-of-war vessels, professedly for the Mexican government. These vessels were to be launched in the month of July, of that year, and, in failure thereof, Mr. G. would forfeit a very considerable sum of money. So, when I entered the ship-yard, all was hurry and driving. There were in the yard about one hundred men; of these about seventy or eighty were regular carpenters—privileged men. Speaking of my condition here I wrote, years ago—and I have now no reason to vary the picture as follows:

There was no time to learn any thing. Every man had to do that which he knew how to do. In entering the ship-yard, my orders from Mr. Gardiner were, to do whatever the carpenters commanded me to do. This was placing me at the beck and call of about seventy-five men. I was to regard all these as masters. Their word was to be my law. My situation was a most trying one. At times I needed a dozen pair of hands. I was called a dozen ways in the space of a single minute. Three or four voices would strike my ear at the same moment. It was—"Fred., come help me to cant this timber here." "Fred., come carry this timber yonder."—"Fred., bring that roller here."—"Fred., go get a fresh can of water."—"Fred., come help saw off the end of this timber."—"Fred., go quick and get the crow bar."—"Fred., hold on the end of this fall."—"Fred., go to the blacksmith's shop, and get a new punch."—

"Hurra, Fred.! run and bring me a cold chisel."—"I say, Fred., bear a hand, and get up a fire as quick as lightning under that steam-box."—"Halloo, nigger! come, turn this grindstone."—"Come, come! move, move! and *bowse* this timber forward."—"I say, darkey, blast your eyes, why don't you heat up some pitch?"—"Halloo! halloo! halloo!" (Three voices at the same time.) "Come here!—Go there!—Hold on where you are! D—n you, if you move, I'll knock your brains out!"

Such, dear reader, is a glance at the school which was mine, during, the first eight months of my stay at Baltimore. At the end of the eight months, Master Hugh refused longer to allow me to remain with Mr. Gardiner. The circumstance which led to his taking me away, was a brutal outrage, committed upon me by the white apprentices of the ship-yard. The fight was a desperate one, and I came out of it most shockingly mangled. I was cut and bruised in sundry places, and my left eye was nearly knocked out of its socket. The facts, leading to this barbarous outrage upon me, illustrate a phase of slavery destined to become an important element in the overthrow of the slave system, and I may, therefore state them with some minuteness. That phase is this: *the conflict of slavery with the interests of the white mechanics and laborers of the south.* In the country, this conflict is not so apparent; but, in cities, such as Baltimore, Richmond, New Orleans, Mobile, &c., it is seen pretty clearly. The slaveholders, with a craftiness peculiar to themselves, by encouraging the enmity of the poor, laboring white man against the blacks, succeeds in making the said white man almost as much a slave as the black slave himself. The difference between the white slave, and the black slave, is this: the latter belongs to *one* slaveholder, and the former belongs to *all* the slaveholders, collectively. The white slave has taken from him, by indirection, what the black slave has taken from him, directly, and without ceremony. Both are plundered, and by the same plunderers. The slave is robbed, by his master, of all his earnings, above what is required for his bare physical necessities; and the white man is robbed by the slave system, of the just results of his labor, because he is flung into competition with a class of laborers who work without wages. The competition, and its injurious consequences, will, one day, array the nonslaveholding white people of the slave states, against the slave system, and make them the most effective workers against the great evil. At present, the slaveholders blind them to this competition, by keeping alive their prejudice against the slaves, *as men*—not against them *as slaves.* They appeal to their pride, often denouncing emancipation, as tending to place the white man, on an equality with Negroes, and, by this means, they succeed in drawing off the minds of the poor whites from the real fact, that, by the rich slave-master, they are already regarded as but a single remove from equality with the slave. The impression is cunningly made, that slavery is the only power that can prevent the laboring white man from falling to the level of the slave's poverty and degradation. To make this enmity deep and broad, between the slave and the poor white man, the latter is allowed to abuse and whip the former, without hinderance. But—as I have suggested—this state of facts prevails *mostly* in the country. In the city of Baltimore, there are not unfrequent murmurs, that educating the slaves to be mechanics may, in the end, give slavemasters power to dispense with the services of the poor white man altogether. But, with characteristic dread of offending the slaveholders, these poor, white mechanics in Mr. Gardiner's ship-yard—instead of applying the natural, honest remedy for the apprehended evil, and objecting at once to work there by the side of slaves—made a cowardly attack upon the free colored mechanics, saying *they* were eating the bread which should be eaten by American freemen, and swearing that they would not work with them. The feeling was, *really*, against having their labor brought into competition with that of the colored people at all; but it was too much to strike directly at the interest of the slaveholders; and, therefore proving their servility and cowardice they dealt their blows on the poor, colored freeman, and aimed to prevent *him* from serving himself, in the evening of life, with the trade with which he had served his master, during the more vigorous portion of his days. Had they succeeded in driving the black freemen out of the ship-yard, they would have determined also upon the removal of the black slaves. The feeling was very bitter toward all colored people in Baltimore, about this time (1836), and they—free and slave suffered all manner of insult and wrong.

Until a very little before I went there, white and black ship carpenters worked side by side, in the ship yards of Mr. Gardiner, Mr. Duncan, Mr. Walter Price, and Mr. Robb. Nobody seemed to see any impropriety in it. To outward seeming, all hands were well satisfied. Some of the blacks were first rate workmen, and were given jobs requiring highest skill. All at once, however, the white carpenters knocked off, and swore that they would no longer work on the same stage with free Negroes. Taking advantage of the heavy contract resting upon Mr. Gardiner, to have the war vessels for Mexico ready to launch in July, and of the difficulty of getting other hands at that season of the year, they swore they would not strike another blow for him, unless he would discharge his free colored workmen.

Now, although this movement did not extend to me, *in form*, it did reach me, *in fact.* The spirit which it awakened was one of malice and bitterness, toward colored people *generally*, and I suffered with the rest, and suffered severely. My fellow apprentices very soon began to feel it to be degrading to work with me. They began to put on high looks, and to talk contemptuously and maliciously of *"the Niggers;"* saying, that "they would take the country," that "they ought to be killed." Encouraged by the cowardly workmen, who, knowing me to be a slave, made no issue with Mr.

Gardiner about my being there, these young men did their utmost to make it impossible for me to stay. They seldom called me to do any thing, without coupling the call with a curse, and Edward North, the biggest in every thing, rascality included, ventured to strike me, whereupon I picked him up, and threw him into the dock. Whenever any of them struck me, I struck back again, regardless of consequences. I could manage any of them *singly*, and, while I could keep them from combining, I succeeded very well. In the conflict which ended my stay at Mr. Gardiner's, I was beset by four of them at once—Ned North, Ned Hays, Bill Stewart, and Tom Humphreys. Two of them were as large as myself, and they came near killing me, in broad day light. The attack was made suddenly, and simultaneously. One came in front, armed with a brick; there was one at each side, and one behind, and they closed up around me. I was struck on all sides; and, while I was attending to those in front, I received a blow on my head, from behind, dealt with a heavy hand-spike. I was completely stunned by the blow, and fell, heavily, on the ground, among the timbers. Taking advantage of my fall, they rushed upon me, and began to pound me with their fists. I let them lay on, for a while, after I came to myself, with a view of gaining strength. They did me little damage, so far; but, finally, getting tired of that sport, I gave a sudden surge, and, despite their weight, I rose to my hands and knees. Just as I did this, one of their number (I know not which) planted a blow with his boot in my left eye, which, for a time, seemed to have burst my eyeball. When they saw my eye completely closed, my face covered with blood, and I staggering under the stunning blows they had given me, they left me. As soon as I gathered sufficient strength, I picked up the hand-spike, and, madly enough, attempted to pursue them; but here the carpenters interfered, and compelled me to give up my frenzied pursuit. It was impossible to stand against so many.

Dear reader, you can hardly believe the statement, but it is true, and, therefore, I write it down: not fewer than fifty white men stood by, and saw this brutal and shameless outrage committed, and not a man of them all interposed a single word of mercy. There were four against one, and that one's face was beaten and battered most horribly, and no one said, "that is enough;" but some cried out, "Kill him—kill him—kill the d——d nigger! knock his brains out—he struck a white person." I mention this inhuman outcry, to show the character of the men, and the spirit of the times, at Gardiner's ship yard, and, indeed, in Baltimore generally, in 1836. As I look back to this period, I am almost amazed that I was not murdered outright, in that ship yard, so murderous was the spirit which prevailed there. On two occasions, while there, I came near losing my life. I was driving bolts in the hold, through the keelson, with Hays. In its course, the bolt bent. Hays cursed me, and said that it was my blow which bent the bolt. I denied this, and charged it upon him. In a fit of rage he seized an adze, and darted toward me. I met him with a maul, and parried his blow, or I should have then lost my life. A son of old Tom Lanman (the latter's double murder I have elsewhere charged upon him), in the spirit of his miserable father, made an assault upon me, but the blow with his maul missed me. After the united assault of North, Stewart, Hays and Humphreys, finding that the carpenters were as bitter toward me as the apprentices, and that the latter were probably set on by the former, I found my only chances for life was in flight. I succeeded in getting away, without an additional blow. To strike a white man, was death, by Lynch law, in Gardiner's ship yard; nor was there much of any other law toward colored people, at that time, in any other part of Maryland. The whole sentiment of Baltimore was murderous.

After making my escape from the ship yard, I went straight home, and related the story of the outrage to Master Hugh Auld; and it is due to him to say, that his conduct—though he was not a religious man—was every way more humane than that of his brother, Thomas, when I went to the latter in a somewhat similar plight, from the hands of *"Brother Edward Covey."* He listened attentively to my narration of the circumstances leading to the ruffianly outrage, and gave many proofs of his strong indignation at what was done. Hugh was a rough, but manly-hearted fellow, and, at this time, his best nature showed itself.

The heart of my once almost over-kind mistress, Sophia, was again melted in pity toward me. My puffed-out eye, and my scarred and blood-covered face, moved the dear lady to tears. She kindly drew a chair by me, and with friendly, consoling words, she took water, and washed the blood from my face. No mother's hand could have been more tender than hers. She bound up my head, and covered my wounded eye with a lean piece of fresh beef. It was almost compensation for the murderous assault, and my suffering, that it furnished and occasion for the manifestation, once more, of the orignally(sic) characteristic kindness of my mistress. Her affectionate heart was not yet dead, though much hardened by time and by circumstances.

As for Master Hugh's part, as I have said, he was furious about it; and he gave expression to his fury in the usual forms of speech in that locality. He poured curses on the heads of the whole ship yard company, and swore that he would have satisfaction for the outrage. His indignation was really strong and healthy; but, unfortunately, it resulted from the thought that his rights of property, in my person, had not been respected, more than from any sense of the outrage committed on me *as a man*. I inferred as much as this, from the fact that he could, himself, beat and mangle when it suited him to do so. Bent on having satisfaction, as he said, just as soon as I got a little the better of my bruises, Master Hugh took me to Esquire Watson's office, on Bond street, Fell's Point, with a view to procuring the arrest of those who had assaulted me. He related the outrage to the magistrate, as I had related it to him, and seemed to expect that a warrant would, at once, be issued for the arrest of the lawless ruffians.

Mr. Watson heard it all, and instead of drawing up his warrant, he inquired.—

"Mr. Auld, who saw this assault of which you speak?"

"It was done, sir, in the presence of a ship yard full of hands."

"Sir," said Watson, "I am sorry, but I cannot move in this matter except upon the oath of white witnesses."

"But here's the boy; look at his head and face," said the excited Master Hugh; *"they* show *what* has been done."

But Watson insisted that he was not authorized to do anything, unless *white* witnesses of the transaction would come forward, and testify to what had taken place. He could issue no warrant on my word, against white persons; and, if I had been killed in the presence of a *thousand blacks*, their testimony, combined would have been insufficient to arrest a single murderer. Master Hugh, for once, was compelled to say, that this state of things was *too bad;* and he left the office of the magistrate, disgusted.

Of course, it was impossible to get any white man to testify against my assailants. The carpenters saw what was done; but the actors were but the agents of their malice, and only what the carpenters sanctioned. They had cried, with one accord, *"Kill the nigger!" "Kill the nigger!"* Even those who may have pitied me, if any such were among them, lacked the moral courage to come and volunteer their evidence. The slightest manifestation of sympathy or justice toward a person of color, was denounced as abolitionism; and the name of abolitionist, subjected its bearer to frightful liabilities. "D—n *abolitionists,"* and *"Kill the niggers,"* were the watch-words of the foul-mouthed ruffians of those days. Nothing was done, and probably there would not have been any thing done, had I been killed in the affray. The laws and the morals of the Christian city of Baltimore, afforded no protection to the sable denizens of that city.

Master Hugh, on finding he could get no redress for the cruel wrong, withdrew me from the employment of Mr. Gardiner, and took me into his own family, Mrs. Auld kindly taking care of me, and dressing my wounds, until they were healed, and I was ready to go again to work.

While I was on the Eastern Shore, Master Hugh had met with reverses, which overthrew his business; and he had given up ship building in his own yard, on the City Block, and was now acting as foreman of Mr. Walter Price. The best he could now do for me, was to take me into Mr. Price's yard, and afford me the facilities there, for completing the trade which I had began to learn at Gardiner's. Here I rapidly became expert in the use of my calking tools; and, in the course of a single year, I was able to command the highest wages paid to journeymen calkers in Baltimore.

The reader will observe that I was now of some pecuniary value to my master. During the busy season, I was bringing six and seven dollars per week. I have, sometimes, brought him as much as nine dollars a week, for the wages were a dollar and a half per day.

After learning to calk, I sought my own employment, made my own contracts, and collected my own earnings; giving Master Hugh no trouble in any part of the transactions to which I was a party.

Here, then, were better days for the Eastern Shore *slave*. I was now free from the vexatious assalts(sic) of the apprentices at Mr. Gardiner's; and free from the perils of plantation life, and once more in a favorable condition to increase my little stock of education, which had been at a dead stand since my removal from Baltimore. I had, on the Eastern Shore, been only a teacher, when in company with other slaves, but now there were colored persons who could instruct me. Many of the young calkers could read, write and cipher. Some of them had high notions about mental improvement; and the free ones, on Fell's Point, organized what they called the *"East Baltimore Mental Improvement Society."* To this society, notwithstanding it was intended that only free persons should attach themselves, I was admitted, and was, several times, assigned a prominent part in its debates. I owe much to the society of these young men.

The reader already knows enough of the *ill* effects of good treatment on a slave, to anticipate what was now the case in my improved condition. It was not long before I began to show signs of disquiet with slavery, and to look around for means to get out of that condition by the shortest route. I was living among *free men;* and was, in all respects, equal to them by nature and by attainments. *Why should I be a slave?* There was *no* reason why I should be the thrall of any man.

Besides, I was now getting—as I have said—a dollar and fifty cents per day. I contracted for it, worked for it, earned it, collected it; it was paid to me, and it was *rightfully* my own; and yet, upon every returning Saturday night, this money—my own hard earnings, every cent of it—was demanded of me, and taken from me by Master Hugh. He did not earn it; he had no hand in earning it; why, then, should he have it? I owed him nothing. He had given me no schooling, and I had received from him only my food and raiment; and for these, my services were supposed to pay, from the first. The right to take my earnings, was the right of the robber. He had the power to compel me to give him the fruits of my labor, and this power was his only right in the case. I became more and more dissatisfied with this state of things; and, in so becoming, I only gave proof of the same human nature which every reader of this chapter in my life—slaveholder, or nonslaveholder—is conscious of possessing.

To make a contented slave, you must make a thoughtless one. It is necessary to darken his moral and mental vision, and, as far as possible, to annihilate his power of reason. He must be able to detect no inconsistencies in slavery. The man that takes his earnings, must be able to convince him that he has a perfect right to do so. It must not depend upon mere force; the slave must know no Higher Law than his master's will. The whole relationship must not only demonstrate, to his mind, its necessity, but its absolute rightfulness. If there be one crevice through which a single drop can fall, it will certainly rust off the slave's chain.

CHAPTER XXI.
My Escape from Slavery

CLOSING INCIDENTS OF "MY LIFE AS A SLAVE"—REASONS WHY FULL PARTICULARS OF THE MANNER OF MY ESCAPE WILL NOT BE GIVEN—CRAFTINESS AND MALICE OF SLAVEHOLDERS—SUSPICION OF AIDING A SLAVE'S ESCAPE ABOUT AS DANGEROUS AS POSITIVE EVIDENCE—WANT OF WISDOM SHOWN IN PUBLISHING DETAILS OF THE ESCAPE OF THE FUGITIVES—PUBLISHED ACCOUNTS REACH THE MASTERS, NOT THE SLAVES—SLAVEHOLDERS STIMULATED TO GREATER WATCHFULNESS—MY CONDITION—DISCONTENT—SUSPICIONS IMPLIED BY MASTER HUGH'S MANNER, WHEN RECEIVING MY WAGES—HIS OCCASIONAL GENEROSITY!—DIFFICULTIES IN THE WAY OF ESCAPE—EVERY AVENUE GUARDED—PLAN TO OBTAIN MONEY—I AM ALLOWED TO HIRE MY TIME—A GLEAM OF HOPE—ATTENDS CAMP-MEETING, WITHOUT PERMISSION—ANGER OF MASTER HUGH THEREAT—THE RESULT—MY PLANS OF ESCAPE ACCELERATED THERBY—THE DAY FOR MY DEPARTURE FIXED—HARASSED BY DOUBTS AND FEARS—PAINFUL THOUGHTS OF SEPARATION FROM FRIENDS—THE ATTEMPT MADE—ITS SUCCESS.

I will now make the kind reader acquainted with the closing incidents of my "Life as a Slave," having already trenched upon the limit allotted to my "Life as a Freeman." Before, however, proceeding with this narration, it is, perhaps, proper that I should frankly state, in advance, my intention to withhold a part of the(sic) connected with my escape from slavery. There are reasons for this suppression, which I trust the reader will deem altogether valid. It may be easily conceived, that a full and complete statement of all facts pertaining to the flight of a bondman, might implicate and embarrass some who may have, wittingly or unwittingly, assisted him; and no one can wish me to involve any man or woman who has befriended me, even in the liability of embarrassment or trouble.

Keen is the scent of the slaveholder; like the fangs of the rattlesnake, his malice retains its poison long; and, although it is now nearly seventeen years since I made my escape, it is well to be careful, in dealing with the circumstances relating to it. Were I to give but a shadowy outline of the process adopted, with characteristic aptitude, the crafty and malicious among the slaveholders might, possibly, hit upon the track I pursued, and involve some one in suspicion which, in a slave state, is about as bad as positive evidence. The colored man, there, must not only shun evil, but shun the very *appearance* of evil, or be condemned as a criminal. A slaveholding community has a peculiar taste for ferreting out offenses against the slave system, justice there being more sensitive in its regard for the peculiar rights of this system, than for any other interest or institution. By stringing together a train of events and circumstances, even if I were not very explicit, the means of escape might be ascertained, and, possibly, those means be rendered, thereafter, no longer available to the liberty-seeking children of bondage I have left behind me. No antislavery man can wish me to do anything favoring such results, and no slaveholding reader has any right to expect the impartment of such information.

While, therefore, it would afford me pleasure, and perhaps would materially add to the interest of my story, were I at liberty to gratify a curiosity which I know to exist in the minds of many, as to the manner of my escape, I must deprive myself of this pleasure, and the curious of the gratification, which such a statement of facts would afford. I would allow myself to suffer under the greatest imputations that evil minded men might suggest, rather than exculpate myself by explanation, and thereby run the hazards of closing the slightest avenue by which a brother in suffering might clear himself of the chains and fetters of slavery.

FREDERICK DOUGLASS

The practice of publishing every new invention by which a slave is known to have escaped from slavery, has neither wisdom nor necessity to sustain it. Had not Henry Box Brown and his friends attracted slaveholding attention to the manner of his escape, we might have had a thousand *Box Browns* per annum. The singularly original plan adopted by William and Ellen Crafts, perished with the first using, because every slaveholder in the land was apprised of it. The *salt water slave* who hung in the guards of a steamer, being washed three days and three nights—like another Jonah—by the waves of the sea, has, by the publicity given to the circumstance, set a spy on the guards of every steamer departing from southern ports.

I have never approved of the very public manner, in which some of our western friends have conducted what *they* call the *"Under-ground Railroad,"* but which, I think, by their open declarations, has been made, most emphatically, the *"Upper-*ground Railroad." Its stations are far better known to the slaveholders than to the slaves. I honor those good men and women for their noble daring, in willingly subjecting themselves to persecution, by openly avowing their participation in the escape of slaves; nevertheless, the good resulting from such avowals, is of a very questionable character. It may kindle an enthusiasm, very pleasant to inhale; but that is of no practical benefit to themselves, nor to the slaves escaping. Nothing is more evident, than that such disclosures are a positive evil to the slaves remaining, and seeking to escape. In publishing such accounts, the anti-slavery man addresses the slaveholder, *not the slave;* he stimulates the former to greater watchfulness, and adds to his facilities for capturing his slave. We owe something to the slaves, south of Mason and Dixon's line, as well as to those north of it; and, in discharging the duty of aiding the latter, on their way to freedom, we should be careful to do nothing which would be likely to hinder the former, in making their escape from slavery. Such is my detestation of slavery, that I would keep the merciless slaveholder profoundly ignorant of the means of flight adopted by the slave. He should be left to imagine himself surrounded by myriads of invisible tormentors, ever ready to snatch, from his infernal grasp, his trembling prey. In pursuing his victim, let him be left to feel his way in the dark; let shades of darkness, commensurate with his crime, shut every ray of light from his pathway; and let him be made to feel, that, at every step he takes, with the hellish purpose of reducing a brother man to slavery, he is running the frightful risk of having his hot brains dashed out by an invisible hand.

But, enough of this. I will now proceed to the statement of those facts, connected with my escape, for which I am alone responsible, and for which no one can be made to suffer but myself.

My condition in the year (1838) of my escape, was, comparatively, a free and easy one, so far, at least, as the wants of the physical man were concerned; but the reader will bear in mind, that my troubles from the beginning, have been less physical than mental, and he will thus be prepared to find, after what is narrated in the previous chapters, that slave life was adding nothing to its charms for me, as I grew older, and became better acquainted with it. The practice, from week to week, of openly robbing me of all my earnings, kept the nature and character of slavery constantly before me. I could be robbed by *indirection*, but this was *too* open and barefaced to be endured. I could see no reason why I should, at the end of each week, pour the reward of my honest toil into the purse of any man. The thought itself vexed me, and the manner in which Master Hugh received my wages, vexed me more than the original wrong. Carefully counting the money and rolling it out, dollar by dollar, he would look me in the face, as if he would search my heart as well as my pocket, and reproachfully ask me, *"Is that all?"*—implying that I had, perhaps, kept back part of my wages; or, if not so, the demand was made, possibly, to make me feel, that, after all, I was an "unprofitable servant." Draining me of the last cent of my hard earnings, he would, however, occasionally—when I brought home an extra large sum—dole out to me a sixpence or a shilling, with a view, perhaps, of kindling up my gratitude; but this practice had the opposite effect—it was an admission of *my right to the whole sum.* The fact, that he gave me any part of my wages, was proof that he suspected that I had a right *to the whole of them.* I always felt uncomfortable, after having received anything in this way, for I feared that the giving me a few cents, might, possibly, ease his conscience, and make him feel himself a pretty honorable robber, after all!

Held to a strict account, and kept under a close watch—the old suspicion of my running away not having been entirely removed—escape from slavery, even in Baltimore, was very difficult. The railroad from Baltimore to Philadelphia was under regulations so stringent, that even *free* colored travelers were almost excluded. They must have *free* papers; they must be measured and carefully examined, before they were allowed to enter the cars; they only went in the day time, even when so examined. The steamboats were under regulations equally stringent. All the great turnpikes, leading northward, were beset with kidnappers, a class of men who watched the newspapers for advertisements for runaway slaves, making their living by the accursed reward of slave hunting.

My discontent grew upon me, and I was on the look-out for means of escape. With money, I could easily have managed the matter, and, therefore, I hit upon the plan of soliciting the privilege of hiring my time. It is quite common, in Baltimore, to allow slaves this privilege, and it is the practice, also, in New Orleans. A slave who is considered trustworthy, can, by paying his master a definite sum regularly, at the end of each week, dispose of his time as he likes. It so happened that I was not in very good odor, and I was far from being a trustworthy slave. Nevertheless, I watched my opportunity when Master Thomas came to Baltimore (for I was still his property, Hugh only acted as his agent) in the spring of 1838, to purchase his spring supply of goods, and applied to him, directly, for the much-coveted privilege of hiring my time. This request Master Thomas unhesitatingly refused to grant; and he charged me, with some sternness, with inventing this stratagem to make my escape. He told me, "I could go *nowhere* but he could catch me; and, in the event of my running away, I might be assured he should spare no pains in his efforts to recapture me." He recounted, with a good deal of eloquence, the many kind offices he had done me, and exhorted me to be contented and obedient. "Lay out no plans for the future," said he. "If you behave yourself properly, I will take care of you." Now, kind and considerate as this offer was, it failed to soothe me into repose. In spite of Master Thomas, and, I may say, in spite of myself, also, I continued to think, and worse still, to think almost exclusively about the injustice and wickedness of slavery. No effort of mine or of his could silence this trouble-giving thought, or change my purpose to run away.

About two months after applying to Master Thomas for the privilege of hiring my time, I applied to Master Hugh for the same liberty, supposing him to be unacquainted with the fact that I had made a similar application to Master Thomas, and had been refused. My boldness in making this request, fairly astounded him at the first. He gazed at me in amazement. But I had many good reasons for pressing the matter; and, after listening to them awhile, he did not absolutely refuse, but told me he would think of it. Here, then, was a gleam of hope. Once master of my own time, I felt sure that I could make, over and above my obligation to him, a dollar or two every week. Some slaves have made enough, in this way, to purchase their freedom. It is a sharp spur to industry; and some of the most enterprising colored men in Baltimore hire themselves in this way. After mature reflection—as I must suppose it was Master Hugh granted me the privilege in question, on the following terms: I was to be allowed all my time; to make all bargains for work; to find my own employment, and to collect my own wages; and, in return for this liberty, I was required, or obliged, to pay him three dollars at the end of each week, and to board and clothe myself, and buy my own calking tools. A failure in any of these particulars would put an end to my privilege. This was a hard bargain. The wear and tear of clothing, the losing and breaking of tools, and the expense of board, made it necessary for me to earn at least six dollars per week, to keep even with the world. All who are acquainted with calking, know how uncertain and irregular that employment is. It can be done to advantage only in dry weather, for it is useless to put wet oakum into a seam. Rain or shine, however, work or no work, at the end of each week the money must be forthcoming.

Master Hugh seemed to be very much pleased, for a time, with this arrangement; and well he might be, for it was decidedly in his favor. It relieved him of all anxiety concerning me. His money was sure. He had armed my love of liberty with a lash and a driver, far more efficient than any I had before known; and, while he derived all the benefits of slaveholding by the arrangement, without its evils, I endured all the evils of being a slave, and yet suffered all the care and anxiety of a responsible freeman. "Nevertheless," thought I, "it is a valuable privilege another step in my career toward freedom." It was something even to be permitted to stagger under the disadvantages of liberty, and I was determined to hold on to the newly gained footing, by all proper industry. I was ready to work by night as well as by day; and being in the enjoyment of excellent health, I was able not only to meet my current expenses, but also to lay by a small sum at the end of each week. All went on thus, from the month of May till August; then—for reasons which will become apparent as I proceed—my much valued liberty was wrested from me.

During the week previous to this (to me) calamitous event, I had made arrangements with a few young friends, to accompany them, on Saturday night, to a camp-meeting, held about twelve miles from Baltimore. On the evening of our intended start for the camp-ground, something occurred in the ship yard where I was at work, which detained me unusually late, and compelled me either to disappoint my young friends, or to neglect carrying my weekly dues to Master Hugh. Knowing that I had the money, and could hand it to him on another day, I decided to go to camp-meeting, and to pay him the three dollars, for the past week, on my return. Once on the camp-ground, I was induced to remain one day longer than I had intended, when I left home. But, as soon as I returned, I went straight to his house on Fell street, to hand him his (my) money. Unhappily, the fatal mistake had been committed. I found him exceedingly angry. He exhibited all the signs of apprehension and wrath, which a slaveholder may be surmised to exhibit on the supposed escape of a favorite slave. "You rascal! I have a great mind to give you a severe whipping. How dare you go out of the city without first asking and obtaining my permission?" "Sir," said I, "I hired my time and paid you the price you asked for it. I did not know that it was any part of the bargain that I should ask you when or where I should go."

"You did not know, you rascal! You are bound to show yourself here every Saturday night." After reflecting, a few moments, he became somewhat cooled down; but, evidently greatly troubled, he said, "Now, you scoundrel! you have done for yourself; you shall hire your time no longer. The next thing I shall hear of, will be your running away. Bring home your tools and your clothes, at once. I'll teach you how to go off in this way."

Thus ended my partial freedom. I could hire my time no longer; and I obeyed my master's orders at once. The little taste of liberty which I had had—although as the reader will have seen, it was far from being unalloyed—by no means enhanced my contentment with slavery. Punished thus by Master Hugh, it was now my turn to punish him. "Since," thought I, "you *will* make a slave of me, I will await your orders in all things;" and, instead of going to look for work on Monday morning, as I had formerly done, I remained at home during the entire week, without the performance of a single stroke of work. Saturday night came, and he called upon me, as usual, for my wages. I, of course, told him I had done no work, and had no wages. Here we were at the point of coming to blows. His wrath had been accumulating during the whole week; for he evidently saw that I was making no effort to get work, but was most aggravatingly awaiting his orders, in all things. As I look back to this behavior of mine, I scarcely know what possessed me, thus to trifle with those who had such unlimited power to bless or to blast me. Master Hugh raved and swore his determination to *"get hold of me;"* but, wisely for *him*, and happily for *me*, his wrath only employed those very harmless, impalpable missiles, which roll from a limber tongue. In my desperation, I had fully made up my mind to measure strength with Master Hugh, in case he should undertake to execute his threats. I am glad there was no necessity for this; for resistance to him could not have ended so happily for me, as it did in the case of Covey. He was not a man to be safely resisted by a slave; and I freely own, that in my conduct toward him, in this instance, there was more folly than wisdom. Master Hugh closed his reproofs, by telling me that, hereafter, I need give myself no uneasiness about getting work; that he "would, himself, see to getting work for me, and enough of it, at that." This threat I confess had some terror in it; and, on thinking the matter over, during the Sunday, I resolved, not only to save him the trouble of getting me work, but that, upon the third day of September, I would attempt to make my escape from slavery. The refusal to allow me to hire my time, therefore, hastened the period of flight. I had three weeks, now, in which to prepare for my journey.

Once resolved, I felt a certain degree of repose, and on Monday, instead of waiting for Master Hugh to seek employment for me, I was up by break of day, and off to the ship yard of Mr. Butler, on the City Block, near the draw-bridge. I was a favorite with Mr. B., and, young as I was, I had served as his foreman on the float stage, at calking. Of course, I easily obtained work, and, at the end of the week—which by the way was exceedingly fine I brought Master Hugh nearly nine dollars. The effect of this mark of returning good sense, on my part, was excellent. He was very much pleased; he took the money, commended me, and told me I might have done the same thing the week before. It is a blessed thing that the tyrant may not always know the thoughts and purposes of his victim. Master Hugh little knew what my plans were. The going to camp-meeting without asking his permission—the insolent answers made to his reproaches—the sulky deportment the week after being deprived of the privilege of hiring my time—had awakened in him the suspicion that I might be cherishing disloyal purposes. My object, therefore, in working steadily, was to remove suspicion, and in this I succeeded admirably. He probably thought I was never better satisfied with my condition, than at the very time I was planning my escape. The second week passed, and again I carried him my full week's wages—*nine dollars;* and so well pleased was he, that he gave me TWENTY-FIVE CENTS! and "bade me make good use of it!" I told him I would, for one of the uses to which I meant to put it, was to pay my fare on the underground railroad.

Things without went on as usual; but I was passing through the same internal excitement and anxiety which I had experienced two years and a half before. The failure, in that instance, was not calculated to increase my confidence in the success of this, my second attempt; and I knew that a second failure could not leave me where my first did—I must either get to the *far north*, or be sent to the *far south*. Besides the exercise of mind from this state of facts, I had the painful sensation of being about to separate from a circle of honest and warm hearted friends, in Baltimore. The thought of such a separation, where the hope of ever meeting again is excluded, and where there can be no correspondence, is very painful. It is my opinion, that thousands would escape from slavery who now remain there, but for the strong cords of affection that bind them to their families, relatives and friends. The daughter is hindered from escaping, by the love she bears her mother, and the father, by the love he bears his children; and so, to the end of the chapter. I had no relations in Baltimore, and I saw no probability of ever living in the neighborhood of sisters and brothers; but the thought of leaving my friends, was among the strongest obstacles to my running away. The last two days of the week—Friday and Saturday—were spent mostly in collecting my things together, for my journey. Having worked four days that week, for my master, I handed him six dollars, on Saturday night. I seldom spent my Sundays at home; and, for fear that something might be discovered in my conduct, I kept up my custom, and absented myself all day. On Monday, the third day of September, 1838, in accordance with my resolution, I bade farewell to the city of Baltimore, and to that slavery which had been my abhorrence from childhood.

How I got away—in what direction I traveled—whether by land or by water; whether with or without assistance—must, for reasons already mentioned, remain unexplained.

LIFE as a FREEMAN

CHAPTER XXII.
Liberty Attained

TRANSITION FROM SLAVERY TO FREEDOM—A WANDERER IN NEW YORK—FEELINGS ON REACHING THAT CITY—AN OLD ACQUAINTANCE MET—UNFAVORABLE IMPRESSIONS—LONELINESS AND INSECURITY—APOLOGY FOR SLAVES WHO RETURN TO THEIR MASTERS—COMPELLED TO TELL MY CONDITION—SUCCORED BY A SAILOR—DAVID RUGGLES—THE UNDERGROUND RAILROAD—MARRIAGE—BAGGAGE TAKEN FROM ME—KINDNESS OF NATHAN JOHNSON—MY CHANGE OF NAME—DARK NOTIONS OF NORTHERN CIVILIZATION—THE CONTRAST—COLORED PEOPLE IN NEW BEDFORD—AN INCIDENT ILLUSTRATING THEIR SPIRIT—A COMMON LABORER—DENIED WORK AT MY TRADE—THE FIRST WINTER AT THE NORTH—REPULSE AT THE DOORS OF THE CHURCH—SANCTIFIED HATE—THE Liberator AND ITS EDITOR.

There is no necessity for any extended notice of the incidents of this part of my life. There is nothing very striking or peculiar about my career as a freeman, when viewed apart from my life as a slave. The relation subsisting between my early experience and that which I am now about to narrate, is, perhaps, my best apology for adding another chapter to this book.

Disappearing from the kind reader, in a flying cloud or balloon (pardon the figure), driven by the wind, and knowing not where I should land—whether in slavery or in freedom—it is proper that I should remove, at once, all anxiety, by frankly making known where I alighted. The flight was a bold and perilous one; but here I am, in the great city of New York, safe and sound, without loss of blood or bone. In less than a week after leaving Baltimore, I was walking amid the hurrying throng, and gazing upon the dazzling wonders of Broadway. The dreams of my childhood and the purposes of my manhood were now fulfilled. A free state around me, and a free earth under my feet! What a moment was this to me! A whole year was pressed into a single day. A new world burst upon my agitated vision. I have often been asked, by kind friends to whom I have told my story, how I felt when first I found myself beyond the limits of slavery; and I must say here, as I have often said to them, there is scarcely anything about which I could not give a more satisfactory answer. It was a moment of joyous excitement, which no words can describe. In a letter to a friend, written soon after reaching New York. I said I felt as one might be supposed to feel, on escaping from a den of hungry lions. But, in a moment like that, sensations are too intense and too rapid for words. Anguish and grief, like darkness and rain, may be described, but joy and gladness, like the rainbow of promise, defy alike the pen and pencil.

For ten or fifteen years I had been dragging a heavy chain, with a huge block attached to it, cumbering my every motion. I had felt myself doomed to drag this chain and this block through life. All efforts, before, to separate myself from the hateful encumbrance, had only seemed to rivet me the more firmly to it. Baffled and discouraged at times, I had asked myself the question, May not this, after all, be God's work? May He not, for wise ends, have doomed me to this lot? A contest had been going on in my mind for years, between the clear consciousness of right and the plausible errors of superstition; between the wisdom of manly courage, and the foolish weakness of timidity. The contest was now ended; the chain was severed; God and right stood vindicated. I was A FREEMAN, and the voice of peace and joy thrilled my heart.

Free and joyous, however, as I was, joy was not the only sensation I experienced. It was like the quick blaze, beautiful at the first, but which subsiding, leaves the building charred and desolate. I was soon taught that I was still in an enemy's land. A sense of loneliness and insecurity oppressed me sadly. I had been but a few hours in New York, before I was met in the streets by a fugitive slave, well known to me, and the information I got from him respecting New York, did nothing to lessen my apprehension of danger. The fugitive in question was "Allender's Jake," in Baltimore; but, said he, I am "WILLIAM DIXON," in New York! I knew Jake well, and knew when Tolly Allender and Mr. Price (for the latter employed Master Hugh as his foreman, in his shipyard on Fell's Point) made an attempt to recapture Jake, and failed. Jake told me all about his circumstances, and how narrowly he escaped being taken back to slavery; that the city was now full of southerners, returning from the springs; that the black people in New York were not to be trusted; that there were hired men on the lookout for fugitives from slavery, and who, for a few dollars, would betray me into the hands of the slave-catchers; that I must trust no man with my secret; that I must not think of going either on the wharves to work, or to a boarding-house to board; and, worse still, this same Jake told me it was not in his power to help me. He seemed, even while cautioning me, to be fearing lest, after all, I might be a party to a second attempt to recapture him. Under the inspiration of this thought, I must suppose it was, he gave signs of a wish to get rid of me, and soon left me his whitewash brush in hand—as he said, for his work. He was soon lost to sight among the throng, and I was alone again, an easy prey to the kidnappers, if any should happen to be on my track.

New York, seventeen years ago, was less a place of safety for a runaway slave than now, and all know how unsafe it now is, under the new fugitive slave bill. I was much troubled. I had very little money enough to buy me a few loaves of bread, but not enough to pay board, outside a lumber yard. I saw the wisdom of keeping away from the ship yards, for if Master Hugh pursued me, he would naturally expect to find me looking for work among the calkers. For a time, every door seemed closed against me. A sense of my loneliness and helplessness crept over me, and covered me with something bordering on despair. In the midst of thousands of my fellowmen, and yet a perfect stranger! In the midst of human brothers, and yet more fearful of them than of hungry wolves! I was without home, without friends, without work, without money, and without any definite knowledge of which way to go, or where to look for succor.

Some apology can easily be made for the few slaves who have, after making good their escape, turned back to slavery, preferring the actual rule of their masters, to the life of loneliness, apprehension, hunger, and anxiety, which meets them on their first arrival in a free state. It is difficult for a freeman to enter into the feelings of such fugitives. He cannot see things in the same light with the slave, because he does not, and cannot, look from the same point from which the slave does. "Why do you tremble," he says to the slave "you are in a free state;" but the difficulty is, in realizing that he is in a free state, the slave might reply. A freeman cannot understand why the slave-master's shadow is bigger, to the slave, than the might and majesty of a free state; but when he reflects that the slave knows more about the slavery of his master than he does of the might and majesty of the free state, he has the explanation. The slave has been all his life learning the power of his master—being trained to dread his approach—and only a few hours learning the power of the state. The master is to him a stern and flinty reality, but the state is little more than a dream. He has been accustomed to regard every white man as the friend of his master, and every colored man as more or less under the control of his master's friends—the white people. It takes stout nerves to stand up, in such circumstances. A man, homeless, shelterless, breadless, friendless, and moneyless, is not in a condition to assume a very proud or joyous tone; and in just this condition was I, while wandering about the streets of New York city and lodging, at least one night, among the barrels on one of its wharves. I was not only free from slavery, but I was free from home, as well. The reader will easily see that I had something more than the simple fact of being free to think of, in this extremity.

I kept my secret as long as I could, and at last was forced to go in search of an honest man—a man sufficiently *human* not to betray me into the hands of slave-catchers. I was not a bad reader of the human face, nor long in selecting the right man, when once compelled to disclose the facts of my condition to some one.

I found my man in the person of one who said his name was Stewart. He was a sailor, warm-hearted and generous, and he listened to my story with a brother's interest. I told him I was running for my freedom—knew not where to go—money almost gone—was hungry—thought it unsafe to go the shipyards for work, and needed a friend. Stewart promptly put me in the way of getting out of my trouble. He took me to his house, and went in search of the late David Ruggles, who was then the secretary of the New York Vigilance Committee, and a very active man in all anti-slavery works. Once in the hands of Mr. Ruggles, I was comparatively safe. I was hidden with Mr. Ruggles several days. In the meantime, my intended wife, Anna, came on from Baltimore—to whom I had written, informing her of my safe arrival at New York—and, in the presence of Mrs. Mitchell and Mr. Ruggles, we were married, by Rev. James W. C. Pennington.

Mr. Ruggles [7] was the first officer on the under-ground railroad with whom I met after reaching the north, and, indeed, the first of whom I ever heard anything. Learning that I was a calker by trade, he promptly decided that New Bedford was the proper place to send me. "Many ships," said he, "are there fitted out for the whaling business, and you may there find work at your trade, and make a good living." Thus, in one fortnight after my flight from Maryland, I was safe in New Bedford, regularly entered upon the exercise of the rights, responsibilities, and duties of a freeman.

I may mention a little circumstance which annoyed me on reaching New Bedford. I had not a cent of money, and lacked two dollars toward paying our fare from Newport, and our baggage not very costly—was taken by the stage driver, and held until I could raise the money to redeem it. This difficulty was soon surmounted. Mr. Nathan Johnson, to whom we had a line from Mr. Ruggles, not only received us kindly and hospitably, but, on being informed about our baggage, promptly loaned me two dollars with which to redeem my little property. I shall ever be deeply grateful, both to Mr. and Mrs. Nathan Johnson, for the lively interest they were pleased to take in me, in this hour of my extremest need. They not only gave myself and wife bread and shelter, but taught us how to begin to secure those benefits for ourselves. Long may they live, and may blessings attend them in this life and in that which is to come!

Once initiated into the new life of freedom, and assured by Mr. Johnson that New Bedford was a safe place, the comparatively unimportant matter, as to what should be my name, came up for considertion(sic). It was necessary to have a name in my new relations. The name given me by my beloved mother was no less pretentious than "Frederick Augustus Washington Bailey." I had, however, before leaving Maryland, dispensed with the *Augustus Washington*, and retained the name *Frederick Bailey*. Between Baltimore and New Bedford, however, I had several different names, the better to avoid being overhauled by the hunters, which I had good reason to believe would be put on my track. Among honest men an honest man may well be content with one name, and to acknowledge it at all times and in all places; but toward fugitives, Americans are not honest. When I arrived at New Bedford, my name was Johnson; and finding that the Johnson family in New Bedford were already quite numerous—sufficiently so to produce some confusion in attempts to distinguish one from another—there was the more reason for making another change in my name. In fact, "Johnson" had been assumed by nearly every slave who had arrived in New Bedford from Maryland, and this, much to the annoyance of the original "Johnsons" (of whom there were many) in that place. Mine host, unwilling to have another of his own name added to the community in this unauthorized way, after I spent a night and a day at his house, gave me my present name. He had been reading the "Lady of the Lake," and was pleased to regard me as a suitable person to wear this, one of Scotland's many famous names. Considering the noble hospitality and manly character of Nathan Johnson, I have felt that he, better than I, illustrated the virtues of the great Scottish chief. Sure I am, that had any slave-catcher entered his domicile, with a view to molest any one of his household, he would have shown himself like him of the "stalwart hand."

The reader will be amused at my ignorance, when I tell the notions I had of the state of northern wealth, enterprise, and civilization. Of wealth and refinement, I supposed the north had none. My *Columbian Orator*, which was almost my only book, had not done much to enlighten me concerning northern society. The impressions I had received were all wide of the truth. New Bedford, especially, took me by surprise, in the solid wealth and grandeur there exhibited. I had formed my notions respecting the social condition of the free states, by what I had seen and known of free, white, non-slaveholding people in the slave states. Regarding slavery as the basis of wealth, I fancied that no people could become very wealthy without slavery. A free white man, holding no slaves, in the country, I had known to be the most ignorant and poverty-stricken of men, and the laugh ing stock even of slaves themselves—called generally by them, in derision, *"poor white trash."* Like the non-slaveholders at the south, in holding no slaves, I suppose the northern people like them, also, in poverty and degradation. Judge, then, of my amazement and joy, when I found—as I did find—the very laboring population of New Bedford living in better houses, more elegantly furnished—surrounded by more comfort and refinement—than a majority of the slaveholders on the Eastern Shore of Maryland. There was my friend, Mr. Johnson, himself a colored man (who at the south would have been regarded as a proper marketable commodity), who lived in a better house—dined at a richer board—was the owner of more books—the reader of more newspapers—was more conversant with the political and social condition of this nation and the world—than nine-tenths of all the slaveholders of Talbot county, Maryland. Yet Mr. Johnson was a working man, and his hands were hardened by honest toil. Here, then, was something for observation and study. Whence the difference? The explanation was soon furnished, in the superiority of mind over simple brute force. Many pages might be given to the contrast, and in explanation of its causes. But an incident or two will suffice to show the reader as to how the mystery gradually vanished before me.

My first afternoon, on reaching New Bedford, was spent in visiting the wharves and viewing the shipping. The sight of the broad brim and the plain, Quaker dress, which met me at every turn, greatly increased my sense of freedom and security. "I am among the Quakers," thought I, "and am safe." Lying at the wharves and riding in the stream, were full-rigged ships of finest model, ready to start on whaling voyages. Upon the right and the left, I was walled in by large granite-fronted warehouses, crowded with the good things of this world. On the wharves, I saw industry without bustle, labor without noise, and heavy toil without the whip. There was no loud singing, as in southern ports, where ships are loading or unloading—no loud cursing or swearing—but everything went on as smoothly as the works of a well adjusted machine. How different was all this from the nosily fierce and clumsily absurd manner of labor-life in Baltimore and St. Michael's! One of the first incidents which illustrated the superior mental character of northern labor over that of the south, was the manner of unloading a ship's cargo of oil. In a southern port, twenty or thirty hands would have been employed to do what five or six did here, with the aid of a single ox attached to the end of a fall. Main strength, unassisted by skill, is slavery's method of labor. An old ox, worth eighty dollars, was doing, in New Bedford, what would have required fifteen thousand dollars worth of human bones and muscles to have performed in a southern port. I found that everything was done here with a scrupulous regard to economy, both in regard to men and things, time and strength. The maid servant, instead of spending at least a tenth part of her time in bringing and carrying water, as in Baltimore, had the pump at her elbow. The wood was dry, and snugly piled away for winter. Woodhouses, in-door pumps, sinks, drains, self-shutting gates, washing machines, pounding barrels, were all new things, and told me that I was among a thoughtful and sensible people. To the ship-repairing dock I went, and saw the same wise prudence. The carpenters struck where they aimed, and the calkers wasted no blows in idle flourishes of the mallet. I learned that men went from New Bedford to Baltimore, and bought old ships, and brought them here to repair, and made them better and more valuable than they ever were before. Men talked here of going whaling on a four *years'* voyage with more coolness than sailors where I came from talked of going a four *months'* voyage.

I now find that I could have landed in no part of the United States, where I should have found a more striking and gratifying contrast to the condition of the free people of color in Baltimore, than I found here in New Bedford. No colored man is really free in a slaveholding state. He wears the badge of bondage while nominally free, and is often subjected to hardships to which the slave is a stranger; but here in New Bedford, it was my good fortune to see a pretty near approach to freedom on the part of the colored people. I was taken all aback when Mr. Johnson—who lost no time in making me acquainted with the fact—told me that there was nothing in the constitution of Massachusetts to prevent a colored man from holding any office in the state. There, in New Bedford, the black man's children—although anti-slavery was then far from popular—went to school side by side with the white children, and apparently without objection from any quarter. To make me at home, Mr. Johnson assured me that no slaveholder could take a slave from New Bedford; that there were men there who would lay down their lives, before such an outrage could be perpetrated. The colored people themselves were of the best metal, and would fight for liberty to the death.

Soon after my arrival in New Bedford, I was told the following story, which was said to illustrate the spirit of the colored people in that goodly town: A colored man and a fugitive slave happened to have a little quarrel, and the former was heard to threaten the latter with informing his master of his whereabouts. As soon as this threat became known, a notice was read from the desk of what was then the only colored church in the place, stating that business of importance was to be then and there transacted. Special measures had been taken to secure the attendance of the would-be Judas, and had proved successful. Accordingly, at the hour appointed, the people came, and the betrayer also. All the usual formalities of public meetings were scrupulously gone through, even to the offering prayer for Divine direction in the duties of the occasion. The president himself performed this part of the ceremony, and I was told that he was unusually fervent. Yet, at the close of his prayer, the old man (one of the numerous family of Johnsons) rose from his knees, deliberately surveyed his audience, and then said, in a tone of solemn resolution, *"Well, friends, we have got him here, and I would now recommend that you young men should just take him outside the door and kill him."* With this, a large body of the congregation, who well understood the business they had come there to transact, made a rush at the villain, and doubtless would have killed him, had he not availed himself of an open sash, and made good his escape. He has never shown his head in New Bedford since that time. This little incident is perfectly characteristic of the spirit of the colored people in New Bedford. A slave could not be taken from that town seventeen years ago, any more than he could be so taken away now. The reason is, that the colored people in that city are educated up to the point of fighting for their freedom, as well as speaking for it.

Once assured of my safety in New Bedford, I put on the habiliments of a common laborer, and went on the wharf in search of work. I had no notion of living on the honest and generous sympathy of my colored brother, Johnson, or that of the abolitionists. My cry was like that of Hood's laborer, "Oh! only give me work." Happily for me, I was not long in searching. I found employment, the third day after my arrival in New Bedford, in stowing a sloop with a load of oil for the New York market. It was new, hard, and dirty work, even for a calker, but I went at it with a glad heart and a willing hand. I was now my own master—a tremendous fact—and the rapturous excitement with which I seized the job, may not easily be understood, except by some one with an experience like mine. The thoughts—"I can work! I can work for a living; I am not afraid of work; I have no Master Hugh to rob me of my earnings"—placed me in a state of independence, beyond seeking friendship or support of any man. That day's work I considered the real starting point of something like a new existence. Having finished this job and got my pay for the same, I went next in pursuit of a job at calking. It so happened that Mr. Rodney French, late mayor of the city of New Bedford, had a ship fitting out for sea, and to which there was a large job of calking and coppering to be done. I applied to that noblehearted man for employment, and he promptly told me to go to work; but going on the float-stage for the purpose, I was informed that every white man would leave the ship if I struck a blow upon her. "Well, well," thought I, "this is a hardship, but yet not a very serious one for me." The difference between the wages of a calker and that of a common day laborer, was an hundred per cent in favor of the former; but then I was free, and free to work, though not at my trade. I now prepared myself to do anything which came to hand in the way of turning an honest penny; sawed wood—dug cellars—shoveled coal—swept chimneys with Uncle Lucas Debuty—rolled oil casks on the wharves—helped to load and unload vessels—worked in Ricketson's candle works—in Richmond's brass foundery, and elsewhere; and thus supported myself and family for three years.

The first winter was unusually severe, in consequence of the high prices of food; but even during that winter we probably suffered less than many who had been free all their lives. During the hardest of the winter, I hired out for nine dolars(sic) a month; and out of this rented two rooms for nine dollars per quarter, and supplied my wife—who was unable to work—with food and some necessary articles of furniture. We were closely pinched to bring our wants within our means; but the jail stood over the way, and I had a wholesome dread of the consequences of running in debt. This winter past, and I was up with the times—got plenty of work—got well paid for it—and felt that I had not done a foolish thing to leave Master Hugh and Master Thomas. I was now living in a new world, and was wide awake to its advantages. I early began to attend the meetings of the colored people of New Bedford, and to take part in them. I was somewhat amazed to see colored men drawing up resolutions and offering them for consideration. Several colored young men of New Bedford, at that period, gave promise of great usefulness. They were educated, and possessed what seemed to me, at the time, very superior talents. Some of them have been cut down by death, and others have removed to different parts of the world, and some remain there now, and justify, in their present activities, my early impressions of them.

Among my first concerns on reaching New Bedford, was to become united with the church, for I had never given up, in reality, my religious faith. I had become lukewarm and in a backslidden state, but I was still convinced that it was my duty to join the Methodist church. I was not then aware of the powerful influence of that religious body in favor of the enslavement of my race, nor did I see how the northern churches could be responsible for the conduct of southern churches; neither did I fully understand how it could be my duty to remain separate from the church, because bad men were connected with it. The slaveholding church, with its Coveys, Weedens, Aulds, and Hopkins, I could see through at once, but I could not see how Elm Street church, in New Bedford, could be regarded as sanctioning the Christianity of these characters in the church at St. Michael's. I therefore resolved to join the Methodist church in New Bedford, and to enjoy the spiritual advantage of public worship. The minister of the Elm Street Methodist church, was the Rev. Mr. Bonney; and although I was not allowed a seat in the body of the house, and was proscribed on account of my color, regarding this proscription simply as an accommodation of the unconverted congregation who had not yet been won to Christ and his brotherhood, I was willing thus to be proscribed, lest sinners should be driven away form the saving power of the gospel. Once converted, I thought they would be sure to treat me as a man and a brother. "Surely," thought I, "these Christian people have none of this feeling against color. They, at least, have renounced this unholy feeling." Judge, then, dear reader, of my astonishment and mortification, when I found, as soon I did find, all my charitable assumptions at fault.

An opportunity was soon afforded me for ascertaining the exact position of Elm Street church on that subject. I had a chance of seeing the religious part of the congregation by themselves; and although they disowned, in effect, their black brothers and sisters, before the world, I did think that where none but the saints were assembled, and no offense could be given to the wicked, and the gospel could not be "blamed," they would certainly recognize us as children of the same Father, and heirs of the same salvation, on equal terms with themselves.

The occasion to which I refer, was the sacrament of the Lord's Supper, that most sacred and most solemn of all the ordinances of the Christian church. Mr. Bonney had preached a very solemn and searching discourse, which really proved him to be acquainted with the inmost secerts(sic) of the human heart. At the close of his discourse, the congregation was dismissed, and the church remained to partake of the sacrament. I remained to see, as I thought, this holy sacrament celebrated in the spirit of its great Founder.

There were only about a half dozen colored members attached to the Elm Street church, at this time. After the congregation was dismissed, these descended from the gallery, and took a seat against the wall most distant from the altar. Brother Bonney was very animated, and sung very sweetly, "Salvation 'tis a joyful sound," and soon began to administer the sacrament. I was anxious to observe the bearing of the colored members, and the result was most humiliating. During the whole ceremony, they looked like sheep without a shepherd. The white members went forward to the altar by the bench full; and when it was evident that all the whites had been served with the bread and wine, Brother Bonney—pious Brother Bonney—after a long pause, as if inquiring whether all the whites members had been served, and fully assuring himself on that important point, then raised his voice to an unnatural pitch, and looking to the corner where his black sheep seemed penned, beckoned with his hand, exclaiming, "Come forward, colored friends! come forward! You, too, have an interest in the blood of Christ. God is no respecter of persons. Come forward, and take this holy sacrament to your comfort." The colored members poor, slavish souls went forward, as invited. I went out, and have never been in that church since, although I honestly went there with a view to joining that body. I found it impossible to respect the religious profession of any who were under the dominion of this wicked prejudice, and I could not, therefore, feel that in joining them, I was joining a Christian church, at all. I tried other churches in New Bedford, with the same result, and finally, I attached myself to a small body of colored Methodists, known as the Zion Methodists. Favored with the affection and confidence of the members of this humble communion, I was soon made a classleader and a local preacher among them. Many seasons of peace and joy I experienced among them, the remembrance of which is still precious, although I could not see it to be my duty to remain with that body, when I found that it consented to the same spirit which held my brethren in chains.

In four or five months after reaching New Bedford, there came a young man to me, with a copy of the *Liberator*, the paper edited by WILLIAM LLOYD GARRISON, and published by ISAAC KNAPP, and asked me to subscribe for it. I told him I had but just escaped from slavery, and was of course very poor, and remarked further, that I was unable to pay for it then; the agent, however, very willingly took me as a subscriber, and appeared to be much pleased with securing my name to his list. From this time I was brought in contact with the mind of William Lloyd Garrison. His paper took its place with me next to the bible.

The *Liberator* was a paper after my own heart. It detested slavery exposed hypocrisy and wickedness in high places—made no truce with the traffickers in the bodies and souls of men; it preached human brotherhood, denounced oppression, and, with all the solemnity of God's word, demanded the complete emancipation of my race. I not only liked—I *loved* this paper, and its editor. He seemed a match for all the oponents(sic) of emancipation, whether they spoke in the name of the law, or the gospel. His words were few, full of holy fire, and straight to the point. Learning to love him, through his paper, I was prepared to be pleased with his presence. Something of a hero worshiper, by nature, here was one, on first sight, to excite my love and reverence.

Seventeen years ago, few men possessed a more heavenly countenance than William Lloyd Garrison, and few men evinced a more genuine or a more exalted piety. The bible was his text book—held sacred, as the word of the Eternal Father—sinless perfection—complete submission to insults and injuries—literal obedience to the injunction, if smitten on one side to turn the other also. Not only was Sunday a Sabbath, but all days were Sabbaths, and to be kept holy. All sectarism false and mischievous—the regenerated, throughout the world, members of one body, and the HEAD Christ Jesus. Prejudice against color was rebellion against God. Of all men beneath the sky, the slaves, because most neglected and despised, were nearest and dearest to his great heart. Those ministers who defended slavery from the bible, were of their "father the devil"; and those churches which fellowshiped slaveholders as Christians, were synagogues of Satan, and our nation was a nation of liars. Never loud or noisy—calm and serene as a summer sky, and as pure. "You are the man, the Moses, raised up by God, to deliver his modern Israel from bondage," was the spontaneous feeling of my heart, as I sat away back in the hall and listened to his mighty words; mighty in truth—mighty in their simple earnestness.

I had not long been a reader of the *Liberator*, and listener to its editor, before I got a clear apprehension of the principles of the anti-slavery movement. I had already the spirit of the movement, and only needed to understand its principles and measures. These I got from the *Liberator*, and from those who believed in that paper. My acquaintance with the movement increased my hope for the ultimate freedom of my race, and I united with it from a sense of delight, as well as duty.

Every week the *Liberator* came, and every week I made myself master of its contents. All the anti-slavery meetings held in New Bedford I promptly attended, my heart burning at every true utterance against the slave system, and every rebuke of its friends and supporters. Thus passed the first three years of my residence in New Bedford. I had not then dreamed of the posibility(sic) of my becoming a public advocate of the cause so deeply imbedded in my heart. It was enough for me to listen—to receive and applaud the great words of others, and only whisper in private, among the white laborers on the wharves, and elsewhere, the truths which burned in my breast.

CHAPTER XXIII.
INTRODUCED TO THE ABOLITIONISTS

FIRST SPEECH AT NANTUCKET—MUCH SENSATION—EXTRAORDINARY SPEECH OF MR. GARRISON—AUTHOR BECOMES A PUBLIC LECTURER—FOURTEEN YEARS EXPERIENCE—YOUTHFUL ENTHUSIASM—A BRAND NEW FACT—MATTER OF MY AUTHOR'S SPEECH—COULD NOT FOLLOW THE PROGRAMME—FUGITIVE SLAVESHIP DOUBTED—TO SETTLE ALL DOUBT I WRITE MY EXPERIENCE OF SLAVERY—DANGER OF RECAPTURE INCREASED.

In the summer of 1841, a grand anti-slavery convention was held in Nantucket, under the auspices of Mr. Garrison and his friends. Until now, I had taken no holiday since my escape from slavery. Having worked very hard that spring and summer, in Richmond's brass foundery—sometimes working all night as well as all day—and needing a day or two of rest, I attended this convention, never supposing that I should take part in the proceedings. Indeed, I was not aware that any one connected with the convention even so much as knew my name. I was, however, quite mistaken. Mr. William C. Coffin, a prominent abolitionst(sic) in those days of trial, had heard me speaking to my colored friends, in the little school house on Second street, New Bedford, where we worshiped. He sought me out in the crowd, and invited me to say a few words to the convention. Thus sought out, and thus invited, I was induced to speak out the feelings inspired by the occasion, and the fresh recollection of the scenes through which I had passed as a slave. My speech on this occasion is about the only one I ever made, of which I do not remember a single connected sentence. It was with the utmost difficulty that I could stand erect, or that I could command and articulate two words without hesitation and stammering. I trembled in every limb. I am not sure that my embarrassment was not the most effective part of my speech, if speech it could be called. At any rate, this is about the only part of my performance that I now distinctly remember. But excited and convulsed as I was, the audience, though remarkably quiet before, became as much excited as myself. Mr. Garrison followed me, taking me as his text; and now, whether I had made an eloquent speech in behalf of freedom or not, his was one never to be forgotten by those who heard it. Those who had heard Mr. Garrison oftenest, and had known him longest, were astonished. It was an effort of unequaled power, sweeping down, like a very tornado, every opposing barrier, whether of sentiment or opinion. For a moment, he possessed that almost fabulous inspiration, often referred to but seldom attained, in which a public meeting is transformed, as it were, into a single individuality—the orator wielding a thousand heads and hearts at once, and by the simple majesty of his all controlling thought, converting his hearers into the express image of his own soul. That night there were at least one thousand Garrisonians in Nantucket! A(sic) the close of this great meeting, I was duly waited on by Mr. John A. Collins—then the general agent of the Massachusetts anti-slavery society—and urgently solicited by him to become an agent of that society, and to publicly advocate its anti-slavery principles. I was reluctant to take the proffered position. I had not been quite three years from slavery—was honestly distrustful of my ability—wished to be excused; publicity exposed me to discovery and arrest by my master; and other objections came up, but Mr. Collins was not to be put off, and I finally consented to go out for three months, for I supposed that I should have got to the end of my story and my usefulness, in that length of time.

Here opened upon me a new life a life for which I had had no preparation. I was a "graduate from the peculiar institution," Mr. Collins used to say, when introducing me, *"with my diploma written on my back!"* The three years of my freedom had been spent in the hard school of adversity. My hands had been furnished by nature with something like a solid leather coating, and I had bravely marked out for myself a life of rough labor, suited to the hardness of my hands, as a means of supporting myself and rearing my children.

MY FREEDOM

Now what shall I say of this fourteen years' experience as a public advocate of the cause of my enslaved brothers and sisters? The time is but as a speck, yet large enough to justify a pause for retrospection—and a pause it must only be.

Young, ardent, and hopeful, I entered upon this new life in the full gush of unsuspecting enthusiasm. The cause was good; the men engaged in it were good; the means to attain its triumph, good; Heaven's blessing must attend all, and freedom must soon be given to the pining millions under a ruthless bondage. My whole heart went with the holy cause, and my most fervent prayer to the Almighty Disposer of the hearts of men, were continually offered for its early triumph. "Who or what," thought I, "can withstand a cause so good, so holy, so indescribably glorious. The God of Israel is with us. The might of the Eternal is on our side. Now let but the truth be spoken, and a nation will start forth at the sound!" In this enthusiastic spirit, I dropped into the ranks of freedom's friends, and went forth to the battle. For a time I was made to forget that my skin was dark and my hair crisped. For a time I regretted that I could not have shared the hardships and dangers endured by the earlier workers for the slave's release. I soon, however, found that my enthusiasm had been extravagant; that hardships and dangers were not yet passed; and that the life now before me, had shadows as well as sunbeams.

Among the first duties assigned me, on entering the ranks, was to travel, in company with Mr. George Foster, to secure subscribers to the *Anti-slavery Standard* and the *Liberator*. With him I traveled and lectured through the eastern counties of Massachusetts. Much interest was awakened—large meetings assembled. Many came, no doubt, from curiosity to hear what a Negro could say in his own cause. I was generally introduced as a *"chattel"*—a *"thing"*—a piece of southern *"property"*—the chairman assuring the audience that *it* could speak. Fugitive slaves, at that time, were not so plentiful as now; and as a fugitive slave lecturer, I had the advantage of being a *"brand new fact"*—the first one out. Up to that time, a colored man was deemed a fool who confessed himself a runaway slave, not only because of the danger to which he exposed himself of being retaken, but because it was a confession of a very *low* origin! Some of my colored friends in New Bedford thought very badly of my wisdom for thus exposing and degrading myself. The only precaution I took, at the beginning, to prevent Master Thomas from knowing where I was, and what I was about, was the withholding my former name, my master's name, and the name of the state and county from which I came. During the first three or four months, my speeches were almost exclusively made up of narrations of my own personal experience as a slave. "Let us have the facts," said the people. So also said Friend George Foster, who always wished to pin me down to my simple narrative. "Give us the facts," said Collins, "we will take care of the philosophy." Just here arose some embarrassment. It was impossible for me to repeat the same old story month after month, and to keep up my interest in it. It was new to the people, it is true, but it was an old story to me; and to go through with it night after night, was a task altogether too mechanical for my nature. "Tell your story, Frederick," would whisper my then revered friend, William Lloyd Garrison, as I stepped upon the platform. I could not always obey, for I was now reading and thinking. New views of the subject were presented to my mind. It did not entirely satisfy me to *narrate* wrongs; I felt like *denouncing* them. I could not always curb my moral indignation for the perpetrators of slaveholding villainy, long enough for a circumstantial statement of the facts which I felt almost everybody must know. Besides, I was growing, and needed room. "People won't believe you ever was a slave, Frederick, if you keep on this way," said Friend Foster. "Be yourself," said Collins, "and tell your story." It was said to me, "Better have a *little* of the plantation manner of speech than not; 'tis not best that you seem too learned." These excellent friends were actuated by the best of motives, and were not altogether wrong in their advice; and still I must speak just the word that seemed to *me* the word to be spoken *by* me.

At last the apprehended trouble came. People doubted if I had ever been a slave. They said I did not talk like a slave, look like a slave, nor act like a slave, and that they believed I had never been south of Mason and Dixon's line. "He don't tell us where he came from—what his master's name was—how he got away—nor the story of his experience. Besides, he is educated, and is, in this, a contradiction of all the facts we have concerning the ignorance of the slaves." Thus, I was in a pretty fair way to be denounced as an impostor. The committee of the Massachusetts anti-slavery society knew all the facts in my case, and agreed with me in the prudence of keeping them private. They, therefore, never doubted my being a genuine fugitive; but going down the aisles of the churches in which I spoke, and hearing the free spoken Yankees saying, repeatedly, *"He's never been a slave, I'll warrant ye,"* I resolved to dispel all doubt, at no distant day, by such a revelation of facts as could not be made by any other than a genuine fugitive.

In a little less than four years, therefore, after becoming a public lecturer, I was induced to write out the leading facts connected with my experience in slavery, giving names of persons, places, and dates—thus putting it in the power of any who doubted, to ascertain the truth or falsehood of my story of being a fugitive slave. This statement soon became known in Maryland, and I had reason to believe that an effort would be made to recapture me.

It is not probable that any open attempt to secure me as a slave could have succeeded, further than the obtainment, by my master, of the money value of my bones and sinews. Fortunately for me, in the four years of my labors in the abolition cause, I had gained many friends, who would have suffered themselves to be taxed to almost any extent to save me from slavery. It was felt that I had committed the double offense of running away, and exposing the secrets and crimes of slavery and slaveholders. There was a double motive for seeking my reenslavement—avarice and vengeance; and while, as I have said, there was little probability of successful recapture, if attempted openly, I was constantly in danger of being spirited away, at a moment when my friends could render me no assistance. In traveling about from place to place—often alone I was much exposed to this sort of attack. Any one cherishing the design to betray me, could easily do so, by simply tracing my whereabouts through the anti-slavery journals, for my meetings and movements were promptly made known in advance. My true friends, Mr. Garrison and Mr. Phillips, had no faith in the power of Massachusetts to protect me in my right to liberty. Public sentiment and the law, in their opinion, would hand me over to the tormentors. Mr. Phillips, especially, considered me in danger, and said, when I showed him the manuscript of my story, if in my place, he would throw it into the fire. Thus, the reader will observe, the settling of one difficulty only opened the way for another; and that though I had reached a free state, and had attained position for public usefulness, I ws(sic) still tormented with the liability of losing my liberty. How this liability was dispelled, will be related, with other incidents, in the next chapter.

CHAPTER XXIV.
Twenty-One Months in Great Britain

GOOD ARISING OUT OF UNPROPITIOUS EVENTS—DENIED CABIN PASSAGE—PROSCRIPTION TURNED TO GOOD ACCOUNT—THE HUTCHINSON FAMILY—THE MOB ON BOARD THE "CAMBRIA"—HAPPY INTRODUCTION TO THE BRITISH PUBLIC—LETTER ADDRESSED TO WILLIAM LLOYD GARRISON—TIME AND LABORS WHILE ABROAD—FREEDOM PURCHASED—MRS. HENRY RICHARDSON—FREE PAPERS—ABOLITIONISTS DISPLEASED WITH THE RANSOM—HOW MY ENERGIES WERE DIRECTED—RECEPTION SPEECH IN LONDON—CHARACTER OF THE SPEECH DEFENDED—CIRCUMSTANCES EXPLAINED—CAUSES CONTRIBUTING TO THE SUCCESS OF MY MISSION—FREE CHURCH OF SCOTLAND—TESTIMONIAL.

The allotments of Providence, when coupled with trouble and anxiety, often conceal from finite vision the wisdom and goodness in which they are sent; and, frequently, what seemed a harsh and invidious dispensation, is converted by after experience into a happy and beneficial arrangement. Thus, the painful liability to be returned again to slavery, which haunted me by day, and troubled my dreams by night, proved to be a necessary step in the path of knowledge and usefulness. The writing of my pamphlet, in the spring of 1845, endangered my liberty, and led me to seek a refuge from republican slavery in monarchical England. A rude, uncultivated fugitive slave was driven, by stern necessity, to that country to which young American gentlemen go to increase their stock of knowledge, to seek pleasure, to have their rough, democratic manners softened by contact with English aristocratic refinement. On applying for a passage to England, on board the "Cambria", of the Cunard line, my friend, James N. Buffum, of Lynn, Massachusetts, was informed that I could not be received on board as a cabin passenger. American prejudice against color triumphed over British liberality and civilization, and erected a color test and condition for crossing the sea in the cabin of a British vessel. The insult was keenly felt by my white friends, but to me, it was common, expected, and therefore, a thing of no great consequence, whether I went in the cabin or in the steerage. Moreover, I felt that if I could not go into the first cabin, first-cabin passengers could come into the second cabin, and the result justified my anticipations to the fullest extent. Indeed, I soon found myself an object of more general interest than I wished to be; and so far from being degraded by being placed in the second cabin, that part of the ship became the scene of as much pleasure and refinement, during the voyage, as the cabin itself. The Hutchinson Family, celebrated vocalists—fellow-passengers—often came to my rude forecastle deck, and sung their sweetest songs, enlivening the place with eloquent music, as well as spirited conversation, during the voyage. In two days after leaving Boston, one part of the ship was about as free to me as another. My fellow-passengers not only visited me, but invited me to visit them, on the saloon deck. My visits there, however, were but seldom. I preferred to live within my privileges, and keep upon my own premises. I found this quite as much in accordance with good policy, as with my own feelings. The effect was, that with the majority of the passengers, all color distinctions were flung to the winds, and I found myself treated with every mark of respect, from the beginning to the end of the voyage, except in a single instance; and in that, I came near being mobbed, for complying with an invitation given me by the passengers, and the captain of the "Cambria," to deliver a lecture on slavery. Our New Orleans and Georgia passengers were pleased to regard my lecture as an insult offered to them, and swore I should not speak. They went so far as to threaten to throw me overboard, and but for the firmness of Captain Judkins, probably would have (under the inspiration of *slavery* and *brandy*) attempted to put their threats into execution. I have no space to describe this scene, although its tragic and comic peculiarities are well worth describing. An end was put to the *melee*, by the captain's calling the ship's company to put the salt water mobocrats in irons. At this determined order, the gentlemen of the lash scampered, and for the rest of the voyage conducted themselves very decorously.

This incident of the voyage, in two days after landing at Liverpool, brought me at once before the British public, and that by no act of my own. The gentlemen so promptly snubbed in their meditated violence, flew to the press to justify their conduct, and to denounce me as a worthless and insolent Negro. This course was even less wise than the conduct it was intended to sustain; for, besides awakening something like a national interest in me, and securing me an audience, it brought out counter statements, and threw the blame upon themselves, which they had sought to fasten upon me and the gallant captain of the ship.

Some notion may be formed of the difference in my feelings and circumstances, while abroad, from the following extract from one of a series of letters addressed by me to Mr. Garrison, and published in the *Liberator*. It was written on the first day of January, 1846:

MY DEAR FRIEND GARRISON: Up to this time, I have given no direct expression of the views, feelings, and opinions which I have formed, respecting the character and condition of the people of this land. I have refrained thus, purposely. I wish to speak advisedly, and in order to do this, I have waited till, I trust, experience has brought my opinions to an intelligent maturity. I have been thus careful, not because I think what I say will have much effect in shaping the opinions of the world, but because whatever of influence I may possess, whether little or much, I wish it to go in the right direction, and according to truth. I hardly need say that, in speaking of Ireland, I shall be influenced by no prejudices in favor of America. I think my circumstances all forbid that. I have no end to serve, no creed to uphold, no government to defend; and as to nation, I belong to none. I have no protection at home, or resting-place abroad. The land of my birth welcomes me to her shores only as a slave, and spurns with contempt the idea of treating me differently; so that I am an outcast from the society of my childhood, and an outlaw in the land of my birth. "I am a stranger with thee, and a sojourner, as all my fathers were." That men should be patriotic, is to me perfectly natural; and as a philosophical fact, I am able to give it an *intellectual* recognition. But no further can I go. If ever I had any patriotism, or any capacity for the feeling, it was whipped out of me long since, by the lash of the American soul-drivers.

In thinking of America, I sometimes find myself admiring her bright blue sky, her grand old woods, her fertile fields, her beautiful rivers, her mighty lakes, and star-crowned mountains. But my rapture is soon checked, my joy is soon turned to mourning. When I remember that all is cursed with the infernal spirit of slaveholding, robbery, and wrong; when I remember that with the waters of her noblest rivers, the tears of my brethren are borne to the ocean, disregarded and forgotten, and that her most fertile fields drink daily of the warm blood of my outraged sisters; I am filled with unutterable loathing, and led to reproach myself that anything could fall from my lips in praise of such a land. America will not allow her children to love her. She seems bent on compelling those who would be her warmest friends, to be her worst enemies. May God give her repentance, before it is too late, is the ardent prayer of my heart. I will continue to pray, labor, and wait, believing that she cannot always be insensible to the dictates of justice, or deaf to the voice of humanity.

My opportunities for learning the character and condition of the people of this land have been very great. I have traveled almost from the Hill of Howth to the Giant's Causeway, and from the Giant's Causway, to Cape Clear. During these travels, I have met with much in the character and condition of the people to approve, and much to condemn; much that has thrilled me with pleasure, and very much that has filled me with pain. I will not, in this letter, attempt to give any description of those scenes which have given me pain. This I will do hereafter. I have enough, and more than your subscribers will be disposed to read at one time, of the bright side of the picture. I can truly say, I have spent some of the happiest moments of my life since landing in this country. I seem to have undergone a transformation. I live a new life. The warm and generous cooperation extended to me by the friends of my despised race; the prompt and liberal manner with which the press has rendered me its aid; the glorious enthusiasm with which thousands have flocked to hear the cruel wrongs of my down-trodden and long-enslaved fellow-countrymen portrayed; the deep sympathy for the slave, and the strong abhorrence of the slaveholder, everywhere evinced; the cordiality with which members and ministers of various religious bodies, and of various shades of religious opinion, have embraced me, and lent me their aid; the kind of hospitality constantly proffered to me by persons of the highest rank in society; the spirit of freedom that seems to animate all with whom I come in contact, and the entire absence of everything that looked like prejudice against me, on account of the color of my skin—contrasted so strongly with my long and bitter experience in the United States, that I look with wonder and amazement on the transition. In the southern part of the United States, I was a slave, thought of and spoken of as property; in the language of the LAW, "*held, taken, reputed, and adjudged to be a chattel in the hands of my owners and possessors, and their executors, administrators, and assigns, to all intents, constructions, and purposes whatsoever.*" (Brev. Digest, 224). In the northern states, a fugitive slave, liable to be hunted at any moment, like a felon, and to be hurled into the terrible jaws of slavery—doomed by an inveterate prejudice against color to insult and outrage on every hand (Massachusetts out of the question)—denied the privileges and courtesies common to others in the use of the most humble means of conveyance—shut out from the cabins on steamboats—refused admission to respectable hotels—caricatured, scorned, scoffed, mocked, and maltreated with impunity by any one (no matter how black his heart), so he has a white skin. But now behold the change! Eleven days and a half gone, and I have crossed three thousand miles of the perilous deep. Instead of a democratic government, I am under a monarchical government. Instead of the bright, blue sky of America, I am covered with the soft, grey fog of the Emerald Isle. I breathe, and lo! the chattel becomes a man. I gaze around in vain for one who will question my equal humanity, claim me as his slave, or offer me an insult. I employ a cab—I am seated beside white people—I reach the hotel—I enter the same door—I am shown into the same parlor—I dine at the same table and no one is offended. No delicate nose grows deformed in my presence. I find no difficulty here in obtaining admission into any place of worship, instruction, or amusement, on equal terms with people as white as any I ever saw in the United States. I meet nothing to remind me of my complexion. I find myself regarded and treated at every turn with the kindness and deference paid to white people. When I go to church, I am met by no upturned nose and scornful lip to tell me, "*We don't allow niggers in here!*"

I remember, about two years ago, there was in Boston, near the south-west corner of Boston Common, a menagerie. I had long desired to see such a collection as I understood was being exhibited there. Never having had an opportunity while a slave, I resolved to seize this, my first, since my escape. I went, and as I approached the entrance to gain admission, I was met and told by the door-keeper, in a harsh and contemptuous tone, "*We don't allow niggers in here.*" I also remember attending a revival meeting in the Rev. Henry Jackson's meeting-house, at New Bedford, and going up the broad aisle to find a seat, I was met by a good deacon, who told me, in a pious tone, "*We don't allow niggers in here!*" Soon after my arrival in New Bedford, from the south, I had a strong desire to attend the Lyceum, but was told, "*They don't allow niggers in here!*" While passing from New York to Boston, on the steamer Massachusetts, on the night of the 9th of December, 1843, when chilled almost through with the cold, I went into the cabin to get a little warm. I was soon touched upon the shoulder, and told, "*We don't allow niggers in here!*" On arriving in Boston, from an anti-slavery tour, hungry and tired, I went into an eating-house, near my friend, Mr. Campbell's to get some refreshments. I was met by a lad in a white apron, "*We don't allow niggers in here!*" A week or two before leaving the United States, I had a meeting appointed at Weymouth, the home of that glorious band of true abolitionists, the Weston family, and others. On attempting to take a seat in the omnibus to that place, I was told by the driver (and I never shall forget his fiendish hate). "*I don't allow niggers in here!*" Thank heaven for the respite I now enjoy! I had been in Dublin but a few days, when a gentleman of great respectability kindly offered to conduct me through all the public buildings of that beautiful city; and a little afterward, I found myself dining with the lord mayor of Dublin. What a pity there was not some American democratic Christian at the door of his splendid mansion, to bark out at my approach, "*They don't allow niggers in here!*" The truth is, the people here know nothing of the republican Negro hate prevalent in our glorious land. They measure and esteem men according to their moral and intellectual worth, and not according to the color of their skin. Whatever may be said of the aristocracies here, there is none based on the color of a man's skin. This species of aristocracy belongs preeminently to "the land of the free, and the home of the brave." I have never found it abroad, in any but Americans. It sticks to them wherever they go. They find it almost as hard to get rid of, as to get rid of their skins.

FREDERICK DOUGLASS

The second day after my arrival at Liverpool, in company with my friend, Buffum, and several other friends, I went to Eaton Hall, the residence of the Marquis of Westminster, one of the most splendid buildings in England. On approaching the door, I found several of our American passengers, who came out with us in the "Cambria," waiting for admission, as but one party was allowed in the house at a time. We all had to wait till the company within came out. And of all the faces, expressive of chagrin, those of the Americans were preeminent. They looked as sour as vinegar, and as bitter as gall, when they found I was to be admitted on equal terms with themselves. When the door was opened, I walked in, on an equal footing with my white fellow-citizens, and from all I could see, I had as much attention paid me by the servants that showed us through the house, as any with a paler skin. As I walked through the building, the statuary did not fall down, the pictures did not leap from their places, the doors did not refuse to open, and the servants did not say, "*We don't allow niggers in here!*"

A happy new-year to you, and all the friends of freedom.

My time and labors, while abroad were divided between England, Ireland, Scotland, and Wales. Upon this experience alone, I might write a book twice the size of this, *My Bondage and My Freedom*. I visited and lectured in nearly all the large towns and cities in the United Kingdom, and enjoyed many favorable opportunities for observation and information. But books on England are abundant, and the public may, therefore, dismiss any fear that I am meditating another infliction in that line; though, in truth, I should like much to write a book on those countries, if for nothing else, to make grateful mention of the many dear friends, whose benevolent actions toward me are ineffaceably stamped upon my memory, and warmly treasured in my heart. To these friends I owe my freedom in the United States. On their own motion, without any solicitation from me (Mrs. Henry Richardson, a clever lady, remarkable for her devotion to every good work, taking the lead), they raised a fund sufficient to purchase my freedom, and actually paid it over, and placed the papers [8] of my manumission in my hands, before they would tolerate the idea of my returning to this, my native country. To this commercial transaction I owe my exemption from the democratic operation of the Fugitive Slave Bill of 1850. But for this, I might at any time become a victim of this most cruel and scandalous enactment, and be doomed to end my life, as I began it, a slave. The sum paid for my freedom was one hundred and fifty pounds sterling.

Some of my uncompromising anti-slavery friends in this country failed to see the wisdom of this arrangement, and were not pleased that I consented to it, even by my silence. They thought it a violation of anti-slavery principles—conceding a right of property in man—and a wasteful expenditure of money. On the other hand, viewing it simply in the light of a ransom, or as money extorted by a robber, and my liberty of more value than one hundred and fifty pounds sterling, I could not see either a violation of the laws of morality, or those of economy, in the transaction.

It is true, I was not in the possession of my claimants, and could have easily remained in England, for the same friends who had so generously purchased my freedom, would have assisted me in establishing myself in that country. To this, however, I could not consent. I felt that I had a duty to perform—and that was, to labor and suffer with the oppressed in my native land. Considering, therefore, all the circumstances—the fugitive slave bill included—I think the very best thing was done in letting Master Hugh have the hundred and fifty pounds sterling, and leaving me free to return to my appropriate field of labor. Had I been a private person, having no other relations or duties than those of a personal and family nature, I should never have consented to the payment of so large a sum for the privilege of living securely under our glorious republican form of government. I could have remained in England, or have gone to some other country; and perhaps I could even have lived unobserved in this. But to this I could not consent. I had already become some what notorious, and withal quite as unpopular as notorious; and I was, therefore, much exposed to arrest and recapture.

The main object to which my labors in Great Britain were directed, was the concentration of the moral and religious sentiment of its people against American slavery. England is often charged with having established slavery in the United States, and if there were no other justification than this, for appealing to her people to lend their moral aid for the abolition of slavery, I should be justified. My speeches in Great Britain were wholly extemporaneous, and I may not always have been so guarded in my expressions, as I otherwise should have been. I was ten years younger then than now, and only seven years from slavery. I cannot give the reader a better idea of the nature of my discourses, than by republishing one of them, delivered in Finsbury chapel, London, to an audience of about two thousand persons, and which was published in the *London Universe*, at the time. [9]

Those in the United States who may regard this speech as being harsh in its spirit and unjust in its statements, because delivered before an audience supposed to be anti-republican in their principles and feelings, may view the matter differently, when they learn that the case supposed did not exist. It so happened that the great mass of the people in England who attended and patronized my anti-slavery meetings, were, in truth, about as good republicans as the mass of Americans, and with this decided advantage over the latter—they are lovers of republicanism for all men, for black men as well as for white men. They are the people who sympathize with Louis Kossuth and Mazzini, and with the oppressed and enslaved, of every color and nation, the world over. They constitute the democratic element in British politics, and are as much opposed to the union of church and state as we, in America, are to such an union. At the meeting where this speech was delivered, Joseph Sturge—a world-wide philanthropist, and a member of the society of Friends—presided, and addressed the meeting. George William Alexander, another Friend, who has spent more than an Ameriacn(sic) fortune in promoting the anti-slavery cause in different sections of the world, was on the platform; and also Dr. Campbell (now of the *British Banner*) who combines all the humane tenderness of Melanchthon, with the directness and boldness of Luther. He is in the very front ranks of non-conformists, and looks with no unfriendly eye upon America. George Thompson, too, was there; and America will yet own that he did a true man's work in relighting the rapidly dying-out fire of true republicanism in the American heart, and be ashamed of the treatment he met at her hands. Coming generations in this country will applaud the spirit of this much abused republican friend of freedom. There were others of note seated on the platform, who would gladly ingraft upon English institutions all that is purely republican in the institutions of America. Nothing, therefore, must be set down against this speech on the score that it was delivered in the presence of those who cannot appreciate the many excellent things belonging to our system of government, and with a view to stir up prejudice against republican institutions.

Again, let it also be remembered—for it is the simple truth—that neither in this speech, nor in any other which I delivered in England, did I ever allow myself to address Englishmen as against Americans. I took my stand on the high ground of human brotherhood, and spoke to Englishmen as men, in behalf of men. Slavery is a crime, not against Englishmen, but against God, and all the members of the human family; and it belongs to the whole human family to seek its suppression. In a letter to Mr. Greeley, of the New York Tribune, written while abroad, I said:

I am, nevertheless aware that the wisdom of exposing the sins of one nation in the ear of another, has been seriously questioned by good and clear-sighted people, both on this and on your side of the Atlantic. And the thought is not without weight on my own mind. I am satisfied that there are many evils which can be best removed by confining our efforts to the immediate locality where such evils exist. This, however, is by no means the case with the system of slavery. It is such a giant sin—such a monstrous aggregation of iniquity—so hardening to the human heart—so destructive to the moral sense, and so well calculated to beget a character, in every one around it, favorable to its own continuance,—that I feel not only at liberty, but abundantly justified, in appealing to the whole world to aid in its removal.

But, even if I had—as has been often charged—labored to bring American institutions generally into disrepute, and had not confined my labors strictly within the limits of humanity and morality, I should not have been without illustrious examples to support me. Driven into semi-exile by civil and barbarous laws, and by a system which cannot be thought of without a shudder, I was fully justified in turning, if possible, the tide of the moral universe against the heaven-daring outrage.

Four circumstances greatly assisted me in getting the question of American slavery before the British public. First, the mob on board the "Cambria," already referred to, which was a sort of national announcement of my arrival in England. Secondly, the highly reprehensible course pursued by the Free Church of Scotland, in soliciting, receiving, and retaining money in its sustentation fund for supporting the gospel in Scotland, which was evidently the ill-gotten gain of slaveholders and slave-traders. Third, the great Evangelical Alliance—or rather the attempt to form such an alliance, which should include slaveholders of a certain description—added immensely to the interest felt in the slavery question. About the same time, there was the World's Temperance Convention, where I had the misfortune to come in collision with sundry American doctors of divinity—Dr. Cox among the number—with whom I had a small controversy.

It has happened to me—as it has happened to most other men engaged in a good cause—often to be more indebted to my enemies than to my own skill or to the assistance of my friends, for whatever success has attended my labors. Great surprise was expressed by American newspapers, north and south, during my stay in Great Britain, that a person so illiterate and insignificant as myself could awaken an interest so marked in England. These papers were not the only parties surprised. I was myself not far behind them in surprise. But the very contempt and scorn, the systematic and extravagant disparagement of which I was the object, served, perhaps, to magnify my few merits, and to render me of some account, whether deserving or not. A man is sometimes made great, by the greatness of the abuse a portion of mankind may think proper to heap upon him. Whether I was of as much consequence as the English papers made me out to be, or not, it was easily seen, in England, that I could not be the ignorant and worthless creature, some of the American papers would have them believe I was. Men, in their senses, do not take bowie-knives to kill mosquitoes, nor pistols to shoot flies; and the American passengers who thought proper to get up a mob to silence me, on board the "Cambria," took the most effective method of telling the British public that I had something to say.

But to the second circumstance, namely, the position of the Free Church of Scotland, with the great Doctors Chalmers, Cunningham, and Candlish at its head. That church, with its leaders, put it out of the power of the Scotch people to ask the old question, which we in the north have often most wickedly asked—"*What have we to do with slavery?*" That church had taken the price of blood into its treasury, with which to build *free* churches, and to pay *free* church ministers for preaching the gospel; and, worse still, when honest John Murray, of Bowlien Bay—now gone to his reward in heaven—with William Smeal, Andrew Paton, Frederick Card, and other sterling anti-slavery men in Glasgow, denounced the transaction as disgraceful and shocking to the religious sentiment of Scotland, this church, through its leading divines, instead of repenting and seeking to mend the mistake into which it had fallen, made it a flagrant sin, by undertaking to defend, in the name of God and the bible, the principle not only of taking the money of slave-dealers to build churches, but of holding fellowship with the holders and traffickers in human flesh. This, the reader will see, brought up the whole question of slavery, and opened the way to its full discussion, without any agency of mine. I have never seen a people more deeply moved than were the people of Scotland, on this very question. Public meeting succeeded public meeting. Speech after speech, pamphlet after pamphlet, editorial after editorial, sermon after sermon, soon lashed the conscientious Scotch people into a perfect *furore*. "SEND BACK THE MONEY!" was indignantly cried out, from Greenock to Edinburgh, and from Edinburgh to Aberdeen. George Thompson, of London, Henry C. Wright, of the United States, James N. Buffum, of Lynn, Massachusetts, and myself were on the anti-slavery side; and Doctors Chalmers, Cunningham, and Candlish on the other. In a conflict where the latter could have had even the show of right, the truth, in our hands as against them, must have been driven to the wall; and while I believe we were able to carry the conscience of the country against the action of the Free Church, the battle, it must be confessed, was a hard-fought one. Abler defenders of the doctrine of fellowshiping slaveholders as christians, have not been met with. In defending this doctrine, it was necessary to deny that slavery is a sin. If driven from this position, they were compelled to deny that slaveholders were responsible for the sin; and if driven from both these positions, they must deny that it is a sin in such a sense, and that slaveholders are sinners in such a sense, as to make it wrong, in the circumstances in which they were placed, to recognize them as Christians. Dr. Cunningham was the most powerful debater on the slavery side of the question; Mr. Thompson was the ablest on the anti-slavery side. A scene occurred between these two men, a parallel to which I think I never witnessed before, and I know I never have since. The scene was caused by a single exclamation on the part of Mr. Thompson.

The general assembly of the Free Church was in progress at Cannon Mills, Edinburgh. The building would hold about twenty-five hundred persons; and on this occasion it was densely packed, notice having been given that Doctors Cunningham and Candlish would speak, that day, in defense of the relations of the Free Church of Scotland to slavery in America. Messrs. Thompson, Buffum, myself, and a few anti-slavery friends, attended, but sat at such a distance, and in such a position, that, perhaps we were not observed from the platform. The excitement was intense, having been greatly increased by a series of meetings held by Messrs. Thompson, Wright, Buffum, and myself, in the most splendid hall in that most beautiful city, just previous to the meetings of the general assembly. "SEND BACK THE MONEY!" stared at us from every street corner; "SEND BACK THE MONEY!" in large capitals, adorned the broad flags of the pavement; "SEND BACK THE MONEY!" was the chorus of the popular street songs; "SEND BACK THE MONEY!" was the heading of leading editorials in the daily newspapers. This day, at Cannon Mills, the great doctors of the church were to give an answer to this loud and stern demand. Men of all parties and all sects were most eager to hear. Something great was expected. The occasion was great, the men great, and great speeches were expected from them.

In addition to the outside pressure upon Doctors Cunningham and Candlish, there was wavering in their own ranks. The conscience of the church itself was not at ease. A dissatisfaction with the position of the church touching slavery, was sensibly manifest among the members, and something must be done to counteract this untoward influence. The great Dr. Chalmers was in feeble health, at the time. His most potent eloquence could not now be summoned to Cannon Mills, as formerly. He whose voice was able to rend asunder and dash down the granite walls of the established church of Scotland, and to lead a host in solemn procession from it, as from a doomed city, was now old and enfeebled. Besides, he had said his word on this very question; and his word had not silenced the clamor without, nor stilled the anxious heavings within. The occasion was momentous, and felt to be so. The church was in a perilous condition. A change of some sort must take place in her condition, or she must go to pieces. To stand where she did, was impossible. The whole weight of the matter fell on Cunningham and Candlish. No shoulders in the church were broader than theirs; and I must say, badly as I detest the principles laid down and defended by them, I was compelled to acknowledge the vast mental endowments of the men. Cunningham rose; and his rising was the signal for almost tumultous applause. You will say this was scarcely in keeping with the solemnity of the occasion, but to me it served to increase its grandeur and gravity. The applause, though tumultuous, was not joyous. It seemed to me, as it thundered up from the vast audience, like the fall of an immense shaft, flung from shoulders already galled by its crushing weight. It was like saying, "Doctor, we have borne this burden long enough, and willingly fling it upon you. Since it was you who brought it upon us, take it now, and do what you will with it, for we are too weary to bear it. ["no close"].

Doctor Cunningham proceeded with his speech, abounding in logic, learning, and eloquence, and apparently bearing down all opposition; but at the moment—the fatal moment—when he was just bringing all his arguments to a point, and that point being, that neither Jesus Christ nor his holy apostles regarded slaveholding as a sin, George Thompson, in a clear, sonorous, but rebuking voice, broke the deep stillness of the audience, exclaiming, HEAR! HEAR! HEAR! The effect of this simple and common exclamation is almost incredible. It was as if a granite wall had been suddenly flung up against the advancing current of a mighty river. For a moment, speaker and audience were brought to a dead silence. Both the doctor and his hearers seemed appalled by the audacity, as well as the fitness of the rebuke. At length a shout went up to the cry of "*Put him out!*" Happily, no one attempted to execute this cowardly order, and the doctor proceeded with his discourse. Not, however, as before, did the learned doctor proceed. The exclamation of Thompson must have reechoed itself a thousand times in his memory, during the remainder of his speech, for the doctor never recovered from the blow.

The deed was done, however; the pillars of the church—*the proud, Free Church of Scotland*—were committed and the humility of repentance was absent. The Free Church held on to the blood-stained money, and continued to justify itself in its position—and of course to apologize for slavery—and does so till this day. She lost a glorious opportunity for giving her voice, her vote, and her example to the cause of humanity; and to-day she is staggering under the curse of the enslaved, whose blood is in her skirts. The people of Scotland are, to this day, deeply grieved at the course pursued by the Free Church, and would hail, as a relief from a deep and blighting shame, the "sending back the money" to the slaveholders from whom it was gathered.

One good result followed the conduct of the Free Church; it furnished an occasion for making the people of Scotland thoroughly acquainted with the character of slavery, and for arraying against the system the moral and religious sentiment of that country. Therefore, while we did not succeed in accomplishing the specific object of our mission, namely—procure the sending back of the money—we were amply justified by the good which really did result from our labors.

Next comes the Evangelical Alliance. This was an attempt to form a union of all evangelical Christians throughout the world. Sixty or seventy American divines attended, and some of them went there merely to weave a world-wide garment with which to clothe evangelical slaveholders. Foremost among these divines, was the Rev. Samuel Hanson Cox, moderator of the New School Presbyterian General Assembly. He and his friends spared no pains to secure a platform broad enough to hold American slaveholders, and in this partly succeeded. But the question of slavery is too large a question to be finally disposed of, even by the Evangelical Alliance. We appealed from the judgment of the Alliance, to the judgment of the people of Great Britain, and with the happiest effect. This controversy with the Alliance might be made the subject of extended remark, but I must forbear, except to say, that this effort to shield the Christian character of slaveholders greatly served to open a way to the British ear for anti-slavery discussion, and that it was well improved.

The fourth and last circumstance that assisted me in getting before the British public, was an attempt on the part of certain doctors of divinity to silence me on the platform of the World's Temperance Convention. Here I was brought into point blank collison with Rev. Dr. Cox, who made me the subject not only of bitter remark in the convention, but also of a long denunciatory letter published in the New York Evangelist and other American papers. I replied to the doctor as well as I could, and was successful in getting a respectful hearing before the British public, who are by nature and practice ardent lovers of fair play, especially in a conflict between the weak and the strong.

Thus did circumstances favor me, and favor the cause of which I strove to be the advocate. After such distinguished notice, the public in both countries was compelled to attach some importance to my labors. By the very ill usage I received at the hands of Dr. Cox and his party, by the mob on board the "Cambria," by the attacks made upon me in the American newspapers, and by the aspersions cast upon me through the organs of the Free Church of Scotland, I became one of that class of men, who, for the moment, at least, "have greatness forced upon them." People became the more anxious to hear for themselves, and to judge for themselves, of the truth which I had to unfold. While, therefore, it is by no means easy for a stranger to get fairly before the British public, it was my lot to accomplish it in the easiest manner possible.

Having continued in Great Britain and Ireland nearly two years, and being about to return to America—not as I left it, a slave, but a freeman—leading friends of the cause of emancipation in that country intimated their intention to make me a testimonial, not only on grounds of personal regard to myself, but also to the cause to which they were so ardently devoted. How far any such thing could have succeeded, I do not know; but many reasons led me to prefer that my friends should simply give me the means of obtaining a printing press and printing materials, to enable me to start a paper, devoted to the interests of my enslaved and oppressed people. I told them that perhaps the greatest hinderance to the adoption of abolition principles by the people of the United States, was the low estimate, everywhere in that country, placed upon the Negro, as a man; that because of his assumed natural inferiority, people reconciled themselves to his enslavement and oppression, as things inevitable, if not desirable. The grand thing to be done, therefore, was to change the estimation in which the colored people of the United States were held; to remove the prejudice which depreciated and depressed them; to prove them worthy of a higher consideration; to disprove their alleged inferiority, and demonstrate their capacity for a more exalted civilization than slavery and prejudice had assigned to them. I further stated, that, in my judgment, a tolerably well conducted press, in the hands of persons of the despised race, by calling out the mental energies of the race itself; by making them acquainted with their own latent powers; by enkindling among them the hope that for them there is a future; by developing their moral power; by combining and reflecting their talents—would prove a most powerful means of removing prejudice, and of awakening an interest in them. I further informed them—and at that time the statement was true—that there was not, in the United States, a single newspaper regularly published by the colored people; that many attempts had been made to establish such papers; but that, up to that time, they had all failed. These views I laid before my friends. The result was, nearly two thousand five hundred dollars were speedily raised toward starting my paper. For this prompt and generous assistance, rendered upon my bare suggestion, without any personal efforts on my part, I shall never cease to feel deeply grateful; and the thought of fulfilling the noble expectations of the dear friends who gave me this evidence of their confidence, will never cease to be a motive for persevering exertion.

Proposing to leave England, and turning my face toward America, in the spring of 1847, I was met, on the threshold, with something which painfully reminded me of the kind of life which awaited me in my native land. For the first time in the many months spent abroad, I was met with proscription on account of my color. A few weeks before departing from England, while in London, I was careful to purchase a ticket, and secure a berth for returning home, in the "Cambria"—the steamer in which I left the United States—paying therefor the round sum of forty pounds and nineteen shillings sterling. This was first cabin fare. But on going aboard the Cambria, I found that the Liverpool agent had ordered my berth to be given to another, and had forbidden my entering the saloon! This contemptible conduct met with stern rebuke from the British press. For, upon the point of leaving England, I took occasion to expose the disgusting tyranny, in the columns of the London *Times*. That journal, and other leading journals throughout the United Kingdom, held up the outrage to unmitigated condemnation. So good an opportunity for calling out a full expression of British sentiment on the subject, had not before occurred, and it was most fully embraced. The result was, that Mr. Cunard came out in a letter to the public journals, assuring them of his regret at the outrage, and promising that the like should never occur again on board his steamers; and the like, we believe, has never since occurred on board the steamships of the Cunard line.

It is not very pleasant to be made the subject of such insults; but if all such necessarily resulted as this one did, I should be very happy to bear, patiently, many more than I have borne, of the same sort. Albeit, the lash of proscription, to a man accustomed to equal social position, even for a time, as I was, has a sting for the soul hardly less severe than that which bites the flesh and draws the blood from the back of the plantation slave. It was rather hard, after having enjoyed nearly two years of equal social privileges in England, often dining with gentlemen of great literary, social, political, and religious eminence never, during the whole time, having met with a single word, look, or gesture, which gave me the slightest reason to think my color was an offense to anybody—now to be cooped up in the stern of the "Cambria," and denied the right to enter the saloon, lest my dark presence should be deemed an offense to some of my democratic fellow-passengers. The reader will easily imagine what must have been my feelings.

CHAPTER XXV.
Various Incidents

NEWSPAPER ENTERPRISE—UNEXPECTED OPPOSITION—THE OBJECTIONS TO IT—THEIR PLAUSIBILITY ADMITTED—MOTIVES FOR COMING TO ROCHESTER—DISCIPLE OF MR. GARRISON—CHANGE OF OPINION—CAUSES LEADING TO IT—THE CONSEQUENCES OF THE CHANGE—PREJUDICE AGAINST COLOR—AMUSING CONDESCENSION—"JIM CROW CARS"—COLLISIONS WITH CONDUCTORS AND BRAKEMEN—TRAINS ORDERED NOT TO STOP AT LYNN—AMUSING DOMESTIC SCENE—SEPARATE TABLES FOR MASTER AND MAN—PREJUDICE UNNATURAL—ILLUSTRATIONS—IN HIGH COMPANY—ELEVATION OF THE FREE PEOPLE OF COLOR—PLEDGE FOR THE FUTURE.

I have now given the reader an imperfect sketch of nine years' experience in freedom—three years as a common laborer on the wharves of New Bedford, four years as a lecturer in New England, and two years of semi-exile in Great Britain and Ireland. A single ray of light remains to be flung upon my life during the last eight years, and my story will be done.

A trial awaited me on my return from England to the United States, for which I was but very imperfectly prepared. My plans for my then future usefulness as an anti-slavery advocate were all settled. My friends in England had resolved to raise a given sum to purchase for me a press and printing materials; and I already saw myself wielding my pen, as well as my voice, in the great work of renovating the public mind, and building up a public sentiment which should, at least, send slavery and oppression to the grave, and restore to "liberty and the pursuit of happiness" the people with whom I had suffered, both as a slave and as a freeman. Intimation had reached my friends in Boston of what I intended to do, before my arrival, and I was prepared to find them favorably disposed toward my much cherished enterprise. In this I was mistaken. I found them very earnestly opposed to the idea of my starting a paper, and for several reasons. First, the paper was not needed; secondly, it would interfere with my usefulness as a lecturer; thirdly, I was better fitted to speak than to write; fourthly, the paper could not succeed. This opposition, from a quarter so highly esteemed, and to which I had been accustomed to look for advice and direction, caused me not only to hesitate, but inclined me to abandon the enterprise. All previous attempts to establish such a journal having failed, I felt that probably I should but add another to the list of failures, and thus contribute another proof of the mental and moral deficiencies of my race. Very much that was said to me in respect to my imperfect literary acquirements, I felt to be most painfully true. The unsuccessful projectors of all the previous colored newspapers were my superiors in point of education, and if they failed, how could I hope for success? Yet I did hope for success, and persisted in the undertaking. Some of my English friends greatly encouraged me to go forward, and I shall never cease to be grateful for their words of cheer and generous deeds.

I can easily pardon those who have denounced me as ambitious and presumptuous, in view of my persistence in this enterprise. I was but nine years from slavery. In point of mental experience, I was but nine years old. That one, in such circumstances, should aspire to establish a printing press, among an educated people, might well be considered, if not ambitious, quite silly. My American friends looked at me with astonishment! "A wood-sawyer" offering himself to the public as an editor! A slave, brought up in the very depths of ignorance, assuming to instruct the highly civilized people of the north in the principles of liberty, justice, and humanity! The thing looked absurd. Nevertheless, I persevered. I felt that the want of education, great as it was, could be overcome by study, and that knowledge would come by experience; and further (which was perhaps the most controlling consideration). I thought that an intelligent public, knowing my early history, would easily pardon a large share of the deficiencies which I was sure that my paper would exhibit. The most distressing thing, however, was the offense which I was about to give my Boston friends, by what seemed to them a reckless disregard of their sage advice. I am not sure that I was not under the influence of something like a slavish adoration of my Boston friends, and I labored hard to convince them of the wisdom of my undertaking, but without success. Indeed, I never expect to succeed, although time has answered all their original objections. The paper has been successful. It is a large sheet, costing eighty dollars per week—has three thousand subscribers—has been published regularly nearly eight years—and bids fair to stand eight years longer. At any rate, the eight years to come are as full of promise as were the eight that are past.

It is not to be concealed, however, that the maintenance of such a journal, under the circumstances, has been a work of much difficulty; and could all the perplexity, anxiety, and trouble attending it, have been clearly foreseen, I might have shrunk from the undertaking. As it is, I rejoice in having engaged in the enterprise, and count it joy to have been able to suffer, in many ways, for its success, and for the success of the cause to which it has been faithfully devoted. I look upon the time, money, and labor bestowed upon it, as being amply rewarded, in the development of my own mental and moral energies, and in the corresponding development of my deeply injured and oppressed people.

From motives of peace, instead of issuing my paper in Boston, among my New England friends, I came to Rochester, western New York, among strangers, where the circulation of my paper could not interfere with the local circulation of the *Liberator* and the *Standard;* for at that time I was, on the anti-slavery question, a faithful disciple of William Lloyd Garrison, and fully committed to his doctrine touching the pro-slavery character of the constitution of the United States, and the *non-voting principle*, of which he is the known and distinguished advocate. With Mr. Garrison, I held it to be the first duty of the non-slaveholding states to dissolve the union with the slaveholding states; and hence my cry, like his, was, "No union with slaveholders." With these views, I came into western New York; and during the first four years of my labor here, I advocated them with pen and tongue, according to the best of my ability.

About four years ago, upon a reconsideration of the whole subject, I became convinced that there was no necessity for dissolving the "union between the northern and southern states;" that to seek this dissolution was no part of my duty as an abolitionist; that to abstain from voting, was to refuse to exercise a legitimate and powerful means for abolishing slavery; and that the constitution of the United States not only contained no guarantees in favor of slavery, but, on the contrary, it is, in its letter and spirit, an anti-slavery instrument, demanding the abolition of slavery as a condition of its own existence, as the supreme law of the land.

Here was a radical change in my opinions, and in the action logically resulting from that change. To those with whom I had been in agreement and in sympathy, I was now in opposition. What they held to be a great and important truth, I now looked upon as a dangerous error. A very painful, and yet a very natural, thing now happened. Those who could not see any honest reasons for changing their views, as I had done, could not easily see any such reasons for my change, and the common punishment of apostates was mine.

The opinions first entertained were naturally derived and honestly entertained, and I trust that my present opinions have the same claims to respect. Brought directly, when I escaped from slavery, into contact with a class of abolitionists regarding the constitution as a slaveholding instrument, and finding their views supported by the united and entire history of every department of the government, it is not strange that I assumed the constitution to be just what their interpretation made it. I was bound, not only by their superior knowledge, to take their opinions as the true ones, in respect to the subject, but also because I had no means of showing their unsoundness. But for the responsibility of conducting a public journal, and the necessity imposed upon me of meeting opposite views from abolitionists in this state, I should in all probability have remained as firm in my disunion views as any other disciple of William Lloyd Garrison.

My new circumstances compelled me to re-think the whole subject, and to study, with some care, not only the just and proper rules of legal interpretation, but the origin, design, nature, rights, powers, and duties of civil government, and also the relations which human beings sustain to it. By such a course of thought and reading, I was conducted to the conclusion that the constitution of the United States—inaugurated "to form a more perfect union, establish justice, insure domestic tranquillity, provide for the common defense, promote the general welfare, and secure the blessing of liberty"—could not well have been designed at the same time to maintain and perpetuate a system of rapine and murder, like slavery; especially, as not one word can be found in the constitution to authorize such a belief. Then, again, if the declared purposes of an instrument are to govern the meaning of all its parts and details, as they clearly should, the constitution of our country is our warrant for the abolition of slavery in every state in the American Union. I mean, however, not to argue, but simply to state my views. It would require very many pages of a volume like this, to set forth the arguments demonstrating the unconstitutionality and the complete illegality of slavery in our land; and as my experience, and not my arguments, is within the scope and contemplation of this volume, I omit the latter and proceed with the former.

I will now ask the kind reader to go back a little in my story, while I bring up a thread left behind for convenience sake, but which, small as it is, cannot be properly omitted altogether; and that thread is American prejudice against color, and its varied illustrations in my own experience.

When I first went among the abolitionists of New England, and began to travel, I found this prejudice very strong and very annoying. The abolitionists themselves were not entirely free from it, and I could see that they were nobly struggling against it. In their eagerness, sometimes, to show their contempt for the feeling, they proved that they had not entirely recovered from it; often illustrating the saying, in their conduct, that a man may "stand up so straight as to lean backward." When it was said to me, "Mr. Douglass, I will walk to meeting with you; I am not afraid of a black man," I could not help thinking—seeing nothing very frightful in my appearance—"And why should you be?" The children at the north had all been educated to believe that if they were bad, the old *black* man—not the old *devil*—would get them; and it was evidence of some courage, for any so educated to get the better of their fears.

The custom of providing separate cars for the accommodation of colored travelers, was established on nearly all the railroads of New England, a dozen years ago. Regarding this custom as fostering the spirit of caste, I made it a rule to seat myself in the cars for the accommodation of passengers generally. Thus seated, I was sure to be called upon to betake myself to the "*Jim Crow car.*" Refusing to obey, I was often dragged out of my seat, beaten, and severely bruised, by conductors and brakemen. Attempting to start from Lynn, one day, for Newburyport, on the Eastern railroad, I went, as my custom was, into one of the best railroad carriages on the road. The seats were very luxuriant and beautiful. I was soon waited upon by the conductor, and ordered out; whereupon I demanded the reason for my invidious removal. After a good deal of parleying, I was told that it was because I was black. This I denied, and appealed to the company to sustain my denial; but they were evidently unwilling to commit themselves, on a point so delicate, and requiring such nice powers of discrimination, for they remained as dumb as death. I was soon waited on by half a dozen fellows of the baser sort (just such as would volunteer to take a bull-dog out of a meeting-house in time of public worship), and told that I must move out of that seat, and if I did not, they would drag me out. I refused to move, and they clutched me, head, neck, and shoulders. But, in anticipation of the stretching to which I was about to be subjected, I had interwoven myself among the seats. In dragging me out, on this occasion, it must have cost the company twenty-five or thirty dollars, for I tore up seats and all. So great was the excitement in Lynn, on the subject, that the superintendent, Mr. Stephen A. Chase, ordered the trains to run through Lynn without stopping, while I remained in that town; and this ridiculous farce was enacted. For several days the trains went dashing through Lynn without stopping. At the same time that they excluded a free colored man from their cars, this same company allowed slaves, in company with their masters and mistresses, to ride unmolested.

After many battles with the railroad conductors, and being roughly handled in not a few instances, proscription was at last abandoned; and the "Jim Crow car"—set up for the degradation of colored people—is nowhere found in New England. This result was not brought about without the intervention of the people, and the threatened enactment of a law compelling railroad companies to respect the rights of travelers. Hon. Charles Francis Adams performed signal service in the Massachusetts legislature, in bringing this reformation; and to him the colored citizens of that state are deeply indebted.

MY FREEDOM

Although often annoyed, and sometimes outraged, by this prejudice against color, I am indebted to it for many passages of quiet amusement. A half-cured subject of it is sometimes driven into awkward straits, especially if he happens to get a genuine specimen of the race into his house.

In the summer of 1843, I was traveling and lecturing, in company with William A. White, Esq., through the state of Indiana. Anti-slavery friends were not very abundant in Indiana, at that time, and beds were not more plentiful than friends. We often slept out, in preference to sleeping in the houses, at some points. At the close of one of our meetings, we were invited home with a kindly-disposed old farmer, who, in the generous enthusiasm of the moment, seemed to have forgotten that he had but one spare bed, and that his guests were an ill-matched pair. All went on pretty well, till near bed time, when signs of uneasiness began to show themselves, among the unsophisticated sons and daughters. White is remarkably fine looking, and very evidently a born gentleman; the idea of putting us in the same bed was hardly to be tolerated; and yet, there we were, and but the one bed for us, and that, by the way, was in the same room occupied by the other members of the family. White, as well as I, perceived the difficulty, for yonder slept the old folks, there the sons, and a little farther along slept the daughters; and but one other bed remained. Who should have this bed, was the puzzling question. There was some whispering between the old folks, some confused looks among the young, as the time for going to bed approached. After witnessing the confusion as long as I liked, I relieved the kindly-disposed family by playfully saying, "Friend White, having got entirely rid of my prejudice against color, I think, as a proof of it, I must allow you to sleep with me to-night." White kept up the joke, by seeming to esteem himself the favored party, and thus the difficulty was removed. If we went to a hotel, and called for dinner, the landlord was sure to set one table for White and another for me, always taking him to be master, and me the servant. Large eyes were generally made when the order was given to remove the dishes from my table to that of White's. In those days, it was thought strange that a white man and a colored man could dine peaceably at the same table, and in some parts the strangeness of such a sight has not entirely subsided.

Some people will have it that there is a natural, an inherent, and an invincible repugnance in the breast of the white race toward dark-colored people; and some very intelligent colored men think that their proscription is owing solely to the color which nature has given them. They hold that they are rated according to their color, and that it is impossible for white people ever to look upon dark races of men, or men belonging to the African race, with other than feelings of aversion. My experience, both serious and mirthful, combats this conclusion. Leaving out of sight, for a moment, grave facts, to this point, I will state one or two, which illustrate a very interesting feature of American character as well as American prejudice. Riding from Boston to Albany, a few years ago, I found myself in a large car, well filled with passengers. The seat next to me was about the only vacant one. At every stopping place we took in new passengers, all of whom, on reaching the seat next to me, cast a disdainful glance upon it, and passed to another car, leaving me in the full enjoyment of a hole form. For a time, I did not know but that my riding there was prejudicial to the interest of the railroad company. A circumstance occurred, however, which gave me an elevated position at once. Among the passengers on this train was Gov. George N. Briggs. I was not acquainted with him, and had no idea that I was known to him, however, I was, for upon observing me, the governor left his place, and making his way toward me, respectfully asked the privilege of a seat by my side; and upon introducing himself, we entered into a conversation very pleasant and instructive to me. The despised seat now became honored. His excellency had removed all the prejudice against sitting by the side of a Negro; and upon his leaving it, as he did, on reaching Pittsfield, there were at least one dozen applicants for the place. The governor had, without changing my skin a single shade, made the place respectable which before was despicable.

A similar incident happened to me once on the Boston and New Bedford railroad, and the leading party to it has since been governor of the state of Massachusetts. I allude to Col. John Henry Clifford. Lest the reader may fancy I am aiming to elevate myself, by claiming too much intimacy with great men, I must state that my only acquaintance with Col. Clifford was formed while I was *his hired servant*, during the first winter of my escape from slavery. I owe it him to say, that in that relation I found him always kind and gentlemanly. But to the incident. I entered a car at Boston, for New Bedford, which, with the exception of a single seat was full, and found I must occupy this, or stand up, during the journey. Having no mind to do this, I stepped up to the man having the next seat, and who had a few parcels on the seat, and gently asked leave to take a seat by his side. My fellow-passenger gave me a look made up of reproach and indignation, and asked me why I should come to that particular seat. I assured him, in the gentlest manner, that of all others this was the seat for me. Finding that I was actually about to sit down, he sang out, "O! stop, stop! and let me get out!" Suiting the action to the word, up the agitated man got, and sauntered to the other end of the car, and was compelled to stand for most of the way thereafter. Halfway to New Bedford, or more, Col. Clifford, recognizing me, left his seat, and not having seen me before since I had ceased to wait on him (in everything except hard arguments against his pro-slavery position), apparently forgetful of his rank, manifested, in greeting me, something of the feeling of an old friend. This demonstration was not lost on the gentleman whose dignity I had, an hour before, most seriously offended. Col. Clifford was known to be about the most aristocratic gentleman in Bristol county; and it was evidently thought that I must be somebody, else I should not have been thus noticed, by a person so distinguished. Sure enough, after Col. Clifford left me, I found myself surrounded with friends; and among the number, my offended friend stood nearest, and with an apology for his rudeness, which I could not resist, although it was one of the lamest ever offered. With such facts as these before me—and I have many of them—I am inclined to think that pride and fashion have much to do with the treatment commonly extended to colored people in the United States. I once heard a very plain man say (and he was cross-eyed, and awkwardly flung together in other respects) that he should be a handsome man when public opinion shall be changed.

Since I have been editing and publishing a journal devoted to the cause of liberty and progress, I have had my mind more directed to the condition and circumstances of the free colored people than when I was the agent of an abolition society. The result has been a corresponding change in the disposition of my time and labors. I have felt it to be a part of my mission—under a gracious Providence to impress my sable brothers in this country with the conviction that, notwithstanding the ten thousand discouragements and the powerful hinderances, which beset their existence in this country—notwithstanding the blood-written history of Africa, and her children, from whom we have descended, or the clouds and darkness (whose stillness and gloom are made only more awful by wrathful thunder and lightning) now overshadowing them—progress is yet possible, and bright skies shall yet shine upon their pathway; and that "Ethiopia shall yet reach forth her hand unto God."

Believing that one of the best means of emancipating the slaves of the south is to improve and elevate the character of the free colored people of the north I shall labor in the future, as I have labored in the past, to promote the moral, social, religious, and intellectual elevation of the free colored people; never forgetting my own humble orgin(sic), nor refusing, while Heaven lends me ability, to use my voice, my pen, or my vote, to advocate the great and primary work of the universal and unconditional emancipation of my entire race.

APPENDIX

RECEPTION SPEECH[10].

AT FINSBURY CHAPEL, MOORFIELDS, ENGLAND, MAY 12, 1846.

Mr. Douglass rose amid loud cheers, and said: I feel exceedingly glad of the opportunity now afforded me of presenting the claims of my brethren in bonds in the United States, to so many in London and from various parts of Britain, who have assembled here on the present occasion. I have nothing to commend me to your consideration in the way of learning, nothing in the way of education, to entitle me to your attention; and you are aware that slavery is a very bad school for rearing teachers of morality and religion. Twenty-one years of my life have been spent in slavery—personal slavery—surrounded by degrading influences, such as can exist nowhere beyond the pale of slavery; and it will not be strange, if under such circumstances, I should betray, in what I have to say to you, a deficiency of that refinement which is seldom or ever found, except among persons that have experienced superior advantages to those which I have enjoyed. But I will take it for granted that you know something about the degrading influences of slavery, and that you will not expect great things from me this evening, but simply such facts as I may be able to advance immediately in connection with my own experience of slavery.

Now, what is this system of slavery? This is the subject of my lecture this evening—what is the character of this institution? I am about to answer the inquiry, what is American slavery? I do this the more readily, since I have found persons in this country who have identified the term slavery with that which I think it is not, and in some instances, I have feared, in so doing, have rather (unwittingly, I know) detracted much from the horror with which the term slavery is contemplated. It is common in this country to distinguish every bad thing by the name of slavery. Intemperance is slavery; to be deprived of the right to vote is slavery, says one; to have to work hard is slavery, says another; and I do not know but that if we should let them go on, they would say that to eat when we are hungry, to walk when we desire to have exercise, or to minister to our necessities, or have necessities at all, is slavery. I do not wish for a moment to detract from the horror with which the evil of intemperance is contemplated—not at all; nor do I wish to throw the slightest obstruction in the way of any political freedom that any class of persons in this country may desire to obtain. But I am here to say that I think the term slavery is sometimes abused by identifying it with that which it is not. Slavery in the United States is the granting of that power by which one man exercises and enforces a right of property in the body and soul of another. The condition of a slave is simply that of the brute beast. He is a piece of property—a marketable commodity, in the language of the law, to be bought or sold at the will and caprice of the master who claims him to be his property; he is spoken of, thought of, and treated as property. His own good, his conscience, his intellect, his affections, are all set aside by the master. The will and the wishes of the master are the law of the slave. He is as much a piece of property as a horse. If he is fed, he is fed because he is property. If he is clothed, it is with a view to the increase of his value as property. Whatever of comfort is necessary to him for his body or soul that is inconsistent with his being property, is carefully wrested from him, not only by public opinion, but by the law of the country. He is carefully deprived of everything that tends in the slightest degree to detract from his value as property. He is deprived of education. God has given him an intellect; the slaveholder declares it shall not be cultivated. If his moral perception leads him in a course contrary to his value as property, the slaveholder declares he shall not exercise it. The marriage institution cannot exist among slaves, and one-sixth of the population of democratic America is denied its privileges by the law of the land. What is to be thought of a nation boasting of its liberty, boasting of its humanity, boasting of its Christianity, boasting of its love of justice and purity, and yet having within its own borders three millions of persons denied by law the right of marriage?—what must be the condition of that people? I need not lift up the veil by giving you any experience of my own. Every one that can put two ideas together, must see the most fearful results from such a state of things as I have just mentioned. If any of these three millions find for themselves companions, and prove themselves honest, upright, virtuous persons to each other, yet in these cases—few as I am bound to confess they are—the virtuous live in constant apprehension of being torn asunder by the merciless men-stealers that claim them as their property. This is American slavery; no marriage—no education—the light of the gospel shut out from the dark mind of the bondman—and he forbidden by law to learn to read. If a mother shall teach her children to read, the law in Louisiana proclaims that she may be hanged by the neck. If the father attempt to give his son a knowledge of letters, he may be punished by the whip in one instance, and in another be killed, at the discretion of the court. Three millions of people shut out from the light of knowledge! It is easy for you to conceive the evil that must result from such a state of things.

I now come to the physical evils of slavery. I do not wish to dwell at length upon these, but it seems right to speak of them, not so much to influence your minds on this question, as to let the slaveholders of America know that the curtain which conceals their crimes is being lifted abroad; that we are opening the dark cell, and leading the people into the horrible recesses of what they are pleased to call their domestic institution. We want them to know that a knowledge of their whippings, their scourgings, their brandings, their chainings, is not confined to their plantations, but that some Negro of theirs has broken loose from his chains—has burst through the dark incrustation of slavery, and is now exposing their deeds of deep damnation to the gaze of the christian people of England.

The slaveholders resort to all kinds of cruelty. If I were disposed, I have matter enough to interest you on this question for five or six evenings, but I will not dwell at length upon these cruelties. Suffice it to say, that all of the peculiar modes of torture that were resorted to in the West India islands, are resorted to, I believe, even more frequently, in the United States of America. Starvation, the bloody whip, the chain, the gag, the thumb-screw, cat-hauling, the cat-o'-nine-tails, the dungeon, the blood-hound, are all in requisition to keep the slave in his condition as a slave in the United States. If any one has a doubt upon this point, I would ask him to read the chapter on slavery in Dickens's *Notes on America*. If any man has a doubt upon it, I have here the "testimony of a thousand witnesses," which I can give at any length, all going to prove the truth of my statement. The blood-hound is regularly trained in the United States, and advertisements are to be found in the southern papers of the Union, from persons advertising themselves as blood-hound trainers, and offering to hunt down slaves at fifteen dollars a piece, recommending their hounds as the fleetest in the neighborhood, never known to fail. Advertisements are from time to time inserted, stating that slaves have escaped with iron collars about their necks, with bands of iron about their feet, marked with the lash, branded with red-hot irons, the initials of their master's name burned into their flesh; and the masters advertise the fact of their being thus branded with their own signature, thereby proving to the world, that, however damning it may appear to non-slavers, such practices are not regarded discreditable among the slaveholders themselves. Why, I believe if a man should brand his horse in this country—burn the initials of his name into any of his cattle, and publish the ferocious deed here—that the united execrations of Christians in Britain would descend upon him. Yet in the United States, human beings are thus branded. As Whittier says—

> ... *Our countrymen in chains,*
> *The whip on woman's shrinking flesh,*
> *Our soil yet reddening with the stains*
> *Caught from her scourgings warm and fresh.*

The slave-dealer boldly publishes his infamous acts to the world. Of all things that have been said of slavery to which exception has been taken by slaveholders, this, the charge of cruelty, stands foremost, and yet there is no charge capable of clearer demonstration, than that of the most barbarous inhumanity on the part of the slaveholders toward their slaves. And all this is necessary; it is necessary to resort to these cruelties, in order to *make the slave a slave*, and to *keep him a slave*. Why, my experience all goes to prove the truth of what you will call a marvelous proposition, that the better you treat a slave, the more you destroy his value *as a slave*, and enhance the probability of his eluding

APPENDIX

the grasp of the slaveholder; the more kindly you treat him, the more wretched you make him, while you keep him in the condition of a slave. My experience, I say, confirms the truth of this proposition. When I was treated exceedingly ill; when my back was being scourged daily; when I was whipped within an inch of my life—*life* was all I cared for. "Spare my life," was my continual prayer. When I was looking for the blow about to be inflicted upon my head, I was not thinking of my liberty; it was my life. But, as soon as the blow was not to be feared, then came the longing for liberty. If a slave has a bad master, his ambition is to get a better; when he gets a better, he aspires to have the best; and when he gets the best, he aspires to be his own master. But the slave must be brutalized to keep him as a slave. The slaveholder feels this necessity. I admit this necessity. If it be right to hold slaves at all, it is right to hold them in the only way in which they can be held; and this can be done only by shutting out the light of education from their minds, and brutalizing their persons. The whip, the chain, the gag, the thumb-screw, the blood-hound, the stocks, and all the other bloody paraphernalia of the slave system, are indispensably necessary to the relation of master and slave. The slave must be subjected to these, or he ceases to be a slave. Let him know that the whip is burned; that the fetters have been turned to some useful and profitable employment; that the chain is no longer for his limbs; that the blood-hound is no longer to be put upon his track; that his master's authority over him is no longer to be enforced by taking his life—and immediately he walks out from the house of bondage and asserts his freedom as a man. The slaveholder finds it necessary to have these implements to keep the slave in bondage; finds it necessary to be able to say, "Unless you do so and so; unless you do as I bid you—I will take away your life!"

Some of the most awful scenes of cruelty are constantly taking place in the middle states of the Union. We have in those states what are called the slave-breeding states. Allow me to speak plainly. Although it is harrowing to your feelings, it is necessary that the facts of the case should be stated. We have in the United States slave-breeding states. The very state from which the minister from our court to yours comes, is one of these states—Maryland, where men, women, and children are reared for the market, just as horses, sheep, and swine are raised for the market. Slave-rearing is there looked upon as a legitimate trade; the law sanctions it, public opinion upholds it, the church does not condemn it. It goes on in all its bloody horrors, sustained by the auctioneer's block. If you would see the cruelties of this system, hear the following narrative. Not long since the following scene occurred. A slave-woman and a slaveman had united themselves as man and wife in the absence of any law to protect them as man and wife. They had lived together by the permission, not by right, of their master, and they had reared a family. The master found it expedient, and for his interest, to sell them. He did not ask them their wishes in regard to the matter at all; they were not consulted. The man and woman were brought to the auctioneer's block, under the sound of the hammer. The cry was raised, "Here goes; who bids cash?" Think of it—a man and wife to be sold! The woman was placed on the auctioneer's block; her limbs, as is customary, were brutally exposed to the purchasers, who examined her with all the freedom with which they would examine a horse. There stood the husband, powerless; no right to his wife; the master's right preeminent. She was sold. He was next brought to the auctioneer's block. His eyes followed his wife in the distance; and he looked beseechingly, imploringly, to the man that had bought his wife, to buy him also. But he was at length bid off to another person. He was about to be separated forever from her he loved. No word of his, no work of his, could save him from this separation. He asked permission of his new master to go and take the hand of his wife at parting. It was denied him. In the agony of his soul he rushed from the man who had just bought him, that he might take a farewell of his wife; but his way was obstructed, he was struck over the head with a loaded whip, and was held for a moment; but his agony was too great. When he was let go, he fell a corpse at the feet of his master. His heart was broken. Such scenes are the everyday fruits of American slavery. Some two years since, the Hon. Seth. M. Gates, an anti-slavery gentleman of the state of New York, a representative in the congress of the United States, told me he saw with his own eyes the following circumstances. In the national District of Columbia, over which the star-spangled emblem is constantly waving, where orators are ever holding forth on the subject of American liberty, American democracy, American republicanism, there are two slave prisons. When going across a bridge, leading to one of these prisons, he saw a young woman run out, bare-footed and bare-headed, and with very little clothing on. She was running with all speed to the bridge he was approaching. His eye was fixed upon her, and he stopped to see what was the matter. He had not paused long before he saw three men run out after her. He now knew what the nature of the case was; a slave escaping from her chains—a young woman, a sister—escaping from the bondage in which she had been held. She made her way to the bridge, but had not reached, ere from the Virginia side there came two slaveholders. As soon as they saw them, her pursuers called out, "Stop her!" True to their Virginian instincts, they came to the rescue of their brother kidnappers, across the bridge. The poor girl now saw that there was no chance for her. It was a trying time. She knew if she went back, she must be a slave forever—she must be dragged down to the scenes of pollution which the slaveholders continually provide for most of the poor, sinking, wretched young women, whom they call their property. She formed her resolution; and just as those who were about to take her, were going to put hands upon her, to drag her back, she leaped over the balustrades of the bridge, and down she went to rise no more. She chose death, rather than to go back into the hands of those christian slaveholders from whom she had escaped.

Can it be possible that such things as these exist in the United States? Are not these the exceptions? Are any such scenes as this general? Are not such deeds condemned by the law and denounced by public opinion? Let me read to you a few of the laws of the slaveholding states of America. I think no better exposure of slavery can be made than is made by the laws of the states in which slavery exists. I prefer reading the laws to making any statement in confirmation of what I have said myself; for the slaveholders cannot object to this testimony, since it is the calm, the cool, the deliberate enactment of their wisest heads, of their most clear-sighted, their own constituted representatives. "If more than seven slaves together are found in any road without a white person, twenty lashes a piece; for visiting a plantation without a written pass, ten lashes; for letting loose a boat from where it is made fast, thirty-nine lashes for the first offense; and for the second, shall have cut off from his head one ear; for keeping or carrying a club, thirty-nine lashes; for having any article for sale, without a ticket from his master, ten lashes; for traveling in any other than the most usual and accustomed road, when going alone to any place, forty lashes; for traveling in the night without a pass, forty lashes." I am afraid you do not understand the awful character of these lashes. You must bring it before your mind. A human being in a perfect state of nudity, tied hand and foot to a stake, and a strong man standing behind with a heavy whip, knotted at the end, each blow cutting into the flesh, and leaving the warm blood dripping to the feet; and for these trifles. "For being found in another person's negro-quarters, forty lashes; for hunting with dogs in the woods, thirty lashes; for being on horseback without the written permission of his master, twenty-five lashes; for riding or going abroad in the night, or riding horses in the day time, without leave, a slave may be whipped, cropped, or branded in the cheek with the letter R. or otherwise punished, such punishment not extending to life, or so as to render him unfit for labor." The laws referred to, may be found by consulting *Brevard's Digest; Haywood's Manual; Virginia Revised Code; Prince's Digest; Missouri Laws; Mississippi Revised Code.* A man, for going to visit his brethren, without the permission of his master—and in many instances he may not have that permission; his master, from caprice or other reasons, may not be willing to allow it—may be caught on his way, dragged to a post, the branding-iron heated, and the name of his master or the letter R branded into his cheek or on his forehead. They treat slaves thus, on the principle that they must punish for light offenses, in order to prevent the commission of larger ones. I wish you to mark that in the single state of Virginia there are seventy-one crimes for which a colored man may be executed; while there are only three of these crimes, which, when committed by a white man, will subject him to that punishment. There are many of these crimes which if the white man did not commit, he would be regarded as a scoundrel and a coward. In the state of Maryland, there is a law to this effect: that if a slave shall strike his master, he may be hanged, his head severed from his body, his body quartered, and his head and quarters set up in the most prominent places in the neighborhood. If a colored woman, in the defense of her own virtue, in defense of her own person, should shield herself from the brutal attacks of her tyrannical master, or make the slightest resistance, she may be killed on the spot. No law whatever will bring the guilty man to justice for the crime.

But you will ask me, can these things be possible in a land professing Christianity? Yes, they are so; and this is not the worst. No; a darker feature is yet to be presented than the mere existence of these facts. I have to inform you that the religion of the southern states, at this time, is the great supporter, the great sanctioner of the bloody atrocities to which I have referred. While America is

APPENDIX

printing tracts and bibles; sending missionaries abroad to convert the heathen; expending her money in various ways for the promotion of the gospel in foreign lands—the slave not only lies forgotten, uncared for, but is trampled under foot by the very churches of the land. What have we in America? Why, we have slavery made part of the religion of the land. Yes, the pulpit there stands up as the great defender of this cursed *institution*, as it is called. Ministers of religion come forward and torture the hallowed pages of inspired wisdom to sanction the bloody deed. They stand forth as the foremost, the strongest defenders of this "institution." As a proof of this, I need not do more than state the general fact, that slavery has existed under the droppings of the sanctuary of the south for the last two hundred years, and there has not been any war between the *religion* and the *slavery* of the south. Whips, chains, gags, and thumb-screws have all lain under the droppings of the sanctuary, and instead of rusting from off the limbs of the bondman, those droppings have served to preserve them in all their strength. Instead of preaching the gospel against this tyranny, rebuke, and wrong, ministers of religion have sought, by all and every means, to throw in the back-ground whatever in the bible could be construed into opposition to slavery, and to bring forward that which they could torture into its support. This I conceive to be the darkest feature of slavery, and the most difficult to attack, because it is identified with religion, and exposes those who denounce it to the charge of infidelity. Yes, those with whom I have been laboring, namely, the old organization anti-slavery society of America, have been again and again stigmatized as infidels, and for what reason? Why, solely in consequence of the faithfulness of their attacks upon the slaveholding religion of the southern states, and the northern religion that sympathizes with it. I have found it difficult to speak on this matter without persons coming forward and saying, "Douglass, are you not afraid of injuring the cause of Christ? You do not desire to do so, we know; but are you not undermining religion?" This has been said to me again and again, even since I came to this country, but I cannot be induced to leave off these exposures. I love the religion of our blessed Savior. I love that religion that comes from above, in the "wisdom of God," which is first pure, then peaceable, gentle, and easy to be entreated, full of mercy and good fruits, without partiality and without hypocrisy. I love that religion that sends its votaries to bind up the wounds of him that has fallen among thieves. I love that religion that makes it the duty of its disciples to visit the father less and the widow in their affliction. I love that religion that is based upon the glorious principle, of love to God and love to man; which makes its followers do unto others as they themselves would be done by. If you demand liberty to yourself, it says, grant it to your neighbors. If you claim a right to think for yourself, it says, allow your neighbors the same right. If you claim to act for yourself, it says, allow your neighbors the same right. It is because I love this religion that I hate the slaveholding, the woman-whipping, the mind-darkening, the soul-destroying religion that exists in the southern states of America. It is because I regard the one as good, and pure, and holy, that I cannot but regard the other as bad, corrupt, and wicked. Loving the one I must hate the other; holding to the one I must reject the other.

I may be asked, why I am so anxious to bring this subject before the British public—why I do not confine my efforts to the United States? My answer is, first, that slavery is the common enemy of mankind, and all mankind should be made acquainted with its abominable character. My next answer is, that the slave is a man, and, as such, is entitled to your sympathy as a brother. All the feelings, all the susceptibilities, all the capacities, which you have, he has. He is a part of the human family. He has been the prey—the common prey—of Christendom for the last three hundred years, and it is but right, it is but just, it is but proper, that his wrongs should be known throughout the world. I have another reason for bringing this matter before the British public, and it is this: slavery is a system of wrong, so blinding to all around, so hardening to the heart, so corrupting to the morals, so deleterious to religion, so sapping to all the principles of justice in its immediate vicinity, that the community surrounding it lack the moral stamina necessary to its removal. It is a system of such gigantic evil, so strong, so overwhelming in its power, that no one nation is equal to its removal. It requires the humanity of Christianity, the morality of the world to remove it. Hence, I call upon the people of Britain to look at this matter, and to exert the influence I am about to show they possess, for the removal of slavery from America. I can appeal to them, as strongly by their regard for the slaveholder as for the slave, to labor in this cause. I am here, because you have an influence on America that no other nation can have. You have been drawn together by the power of steam to a marvelous extent; the distance between London and Boston is now reduced to some twelve or fourteen days, so that the denunciations against slavery, uttered in London this week, may be heard in a fortnight in the streets of Boston, and reverberating amidst the hills of Massachusetts. There is nothing said here against slavery that will not be recorded in the United States. I am here, also, because the slaveholders do not want me to be here; they would rather that I were not here. I have adopted a maxim laid down by Napoleon, never to occupy ground which the enemy would like me to occupy. The slaveholders would much rather have me, if I will denounce slavery, denounce it in the northern states, where their friends and supporters are, who will stand by and mob me for denouncing it. They feel something as the man felt, when he uttered his prayer, in which he made out a most horrible case for himself, and one of his neighbors touched him and said, "My friend, I always had the opinion of you that you have now expressed for yourself—that you are a very great sinner." Coming from himself, it was all very well, but coming from a stranger it was rather cutting. The slaveholders felt that when slavery was denounced among themselves, it was not so bad; but let one of the slaves get loose, let him summon the people of Britain, and make known to them the conduct of the slaveholders toward their slaves, and it cuts them to the quick, and produces a sensation such as would be produced by nothing else. The power I exert now is something like the power that is exerted by the man at the end of the lever; my influence now is just in proportion to the distance that I am from the United States. My exposure of slavery abroad will tell more upon the hearts and consciences of slaveholders, than if I was attacking them in America; for almost every paper that I now receive from the United States, comes teeming with statements about this fugitive Negro, calling him a "glib-tongued scoundrel," and saying that he is running out against the institutions and people of America. I deny the charge that I am saying a word against the institutions of America, or the people, as such. What I have to say is against slavery and slaveholders. I feel at liberty to speak on this subject. I have on my back the marks of the lash; I have four sisters and one brother now under the galling chain. I feel it my duty to cry aloud and spare not. I am not averse to having the good opinion of my fellow creatures. I am not averse to being kindly regarded by all men; but I am bound, even at the hazard of making a large class of religionists in this country hate me, oppose me, and malign me as they have done—I am bound by the prayers, and tears, and entreaties of three millions of kneeling bondsmen, to have no compromise with men who are in any shape or form connected with the slaveholders of America. I expose slavery in this country, because to expose it is to kill it. Slavery is one of those monsters of darkness to whom the light of truth is death. Expose slavery, and it dies. Light is to slavery what the heat of the sun is to the root of a tree; it must die under it. All the slaveholder asks of me is silence. He does not ask me to go abroad and preach *in favor* of slavery; he does not ask any one to do that. He would not say that slavery is a good thing, but the best under the circumstances. The slaveholders want total darkness on the subject. They want the hatchway shut down, that the monster may crawl in his den of darkness, crushing human hopes and happiness, destroying the bondman at will, and having no one to reprove or rebuke him. Slavery shrinks from the light; it hateth the light, neither cometh to the light, lest its deeds should be reproved. To tear off the mask from this abominable system, to expose it to the light of heaven, aye, to the heat of the sun, that it may burn and wither it out of existence, is my object in coming to this country. I want the slaveholder surrounded, as by a wall of anti-slavery fire, so that he may see the condemnation of himself and his system glaring down in letters of light. I want him to feel that he has no sympathy in England, Scotland, or Ireland; that he has none in Canada, none in Mexico, none among the poor wild Indians; that the voice of the civilized, aye, and savage world is against him. I would have condemnation blaze down upon him in every direction, till, stunned and overwhelmed with shame and confusion, he is compelled to let go the grasp he holds upon the persons of his victims, and restore them to their long-lost rights.

APPENDIX

Dr. Campbell's Reply

From Rev. Dr. Campbell's brilliant reply we extract the following: FREDERICK DOUGLASS, "the beast of burden," the portion of "goods and chattels," the representative of three millions of men, has been raised up! Shall I say the *man*? If there is a man on earth, he is a man. My blood boiled within me when I heard his address tonight, and thought that he had left behind him three millions of such men.

We must see more of this man; we must have more of this man. One would have taken a voyage round the globe some forty years back—especially since the introduction of steam—to have heard such an exposure of slavery from the lips of a slave. It will be an era in the individual history of the present assembly. Our children—our boys and girls—I have tonight seen the delightful sympathy of their hearts evinced by their heaving breasts, while their eyes sparkled with wonder and admiration, that this black man—this slave—had so much logic, so much wit, so much fancy, so much eloquence. He was something more than a man, according to their little notions. Then, I say, we must hear him again. We have got a purpose to accomplish. He has appealed to the pulpit of England. The English pulpit is with him. He has appealed to the press of England; the press of England is conducted by English hearts, and that press will do him justice. About ten days hence, and his second master, who may well prize "such a piece of goods," will have the pleasure of reading his burning words, and his first master will bless himself that he has got quit of him. We have to create public opinion, or rather, not to create it, for it is created already; but we have to foster it; and when tonight I heard those magnificent words—the words of Curran, by which my heart, from boyhood, has ofttimes been deeply moved—I rejoice to think that they embody an instinct of an Englishman's nature. I heard, with inexpressible delight, how they told on this mighty mass of the citizens of the metropolis.

Britain has now no slaves; we can therefore talk to the other nations now, as we could not have talked a dozen years ago. I want the whole of the London ministry to meet Douglass. For as his appeal is to England, and throughout England, I should rejoice in the idea of churchmen and dissenters merging all sectional distinctions in this cause. Let us have a public breakfast. Let the ministers meet him; let them hear him; let them grasp his hand; and let him enlist their sympathies on behalf of the slave. Let him inspire them with abhorrence of the man-stealer—the slaveholder. No slaveholding American shall ever my cross my door. No slaveholding or slavery-supporting minister shall ever pollute my pulpit. While I have a tongue to speak, or a hand to write, I will, to the utmost of my power, oppose these slaveholding men. We must have Douglass amongst us to aid in fostering public opinion.

The great conflict with slavery must now take place in America; and while they are adding other slave states to the Union, our business is to step forward and help the abolitionists there. It is a pleasing circumstance that such a body of men has risen in America, and whilst we hurl our thunders against her slavers, let us make a distinction between those who advocate slavery and those who oppose it. George Thompson has been there. This man, Frederick Douglass, has been there, and has been compelled to flee. I wish, when he first set foot on our shores, he had made a solemn vow, and said, "Now that I am free, and in the sanctuary of freedom, I will never return till I have seen the emancipation of my country completed." He wants to surround these men, the slaveholders, as by a wall of fire; and he himself may do much toward kindling it. Let him travel over the island—east, west, north, and south—everywhere diffusing knowledge and awakening principle, till the whole nation become a body of petitioners to America. He will, he must, do it. He must for a season make England his home. He must send for his wife. He must send for his children. I want to see the sons and daughters of such a sire. We, too, must do something for him and them worthy of the English name. I do not like the idea of a man of such mental dimensions, such moral courage, and all but incomparable talent, having his own small wants, and the wants of a distant wife and children, supplied by the poor profits of his publication, the sketch of his life. Let the pamphlet be bought by tens of thousands. But we will do something more for him, shall we not?

FREDERICK DOUGLASS

It only remains that we pass a resolution of thanks to Frederick Douglass, the slave that was, the man that is! He that was covered with chains, and that is now being covered with glory, and whom we will send back a gentleman.

APPENDIX

LETTER TO HIS OLD MASTER.[11]
TO MY OLD MASTER, THOMAS AULD

SIR—The long and intimate, though by no means friendly, relation which unhappily subsisted between you and myself, leads me to hope that you will easily account for the great liberty which I now take in addressing you in this open and public manner. The same fact may remove any disagreeable surprise which you may experience on again finding your name coupled with mine, in any other way than in an advertisement, accurately describing my person, and offering a large sum for my arrest. In thus dragging you again before the public, I am aware that I shall subject myself to no inconsiderable amount of censure. I shall probably be charged with an unwarrantable, if not a wanton and reckless disregard of the rights and properties of private life. There are those north as well as south who entertain a much higher respect for rights which are merely conventional, than they do for rights which are personal and essential. Not a few there are in our country, who, while they have no scruples against robbing the laborer of the hard earned results of his patient industry, will be shocked by the extremely indelicate manner of bringing your name before the public. Believing this to be the case, and wishing to meet every reasonable or plausible objection to my conduct, I will frankly state the ground upon which I justfy(sic) myself in this instance, as well as on former occasions when I have thought proper to mention your name in public. All will agree that a man guilty of theft, robbery, or murder, has forfeited the right to concealment and private life; that the community have a right to subject such persons to the most complete exposure. However much they may desire retirement, and aim to conceal themselves and their movements from the popular gaze, the public have a right to ferret them out, and bring their conduct before the proper tribunals of the country for investigation. Sir, you will undoubtedly make the proper application of these generally admitted principles, and will easily see the light in which you are regarded by me; I will not therefore manifest ill temper, by calling you hard names. I know you to be a man of some intelligence, and can readily determine the precise estimate which I entertain of your character. I may therefore indulge in language which may seem to others indirect and ambiguous, and yet be quite well understood by yourself.

I have selected this day on which to address you, because it is the anniversary of my emancipation; and knowing no better way, I am led to this as the best mode of celebrating that truly important events. Just ten years ago this beautiful September morning, yon bright sun beheld me a slave—a poor degraded chattel—trembling at the sound of your voice, lamenting that I was a man, and wishing myself a brute. The hopes which I had treasured up for weeks of a safe and successful escape from your grasp, were powerfully confronted at this last hour by dark clouds of doubt and fear, making my person shake and my bosom to heave with the heavy contest between hope and fear. I have no words to describe to you the deep agony of soul which I experienced on that never-to-be-forgotten morning—for I left by daylight. I was making a leap in the dark. The probabilities, so far as I could by reason determine them, were stoutly against the undertaking. The preliminaries and precautions I had adopted previously, all worked badly. I was like one going to war without weapons—ten chances of defeat to one of victory. One in whom I had confided, and one who had promised me assistance, appalled by fear at the trial hour, deserted me, thus leaving the responsibility of success or failure solely with myself. You, sir, can never know my feelings. As I look back to them, I can scarcely realize that I have passed through a scene so trying. Trying, however, as they were, and gloomy as was the prospect, thanks be to the Most High, who is ever the God of the oppressed, at the moment which was to determine my whole earthly career, His grace was sufficient; my mind was made up. I embraced the golden opportunity, took the morning tide at the flood, and a free man, young, active, and strong, is the result.

I have often thought I should like to explain to you the grounds upon which I have justified myself in running away from you. I am almost ashamed to do so now, for by this time you may have discovered them yourself. I will, however, glance at them. When yet but a child about six years old, I imbibed the determination to run away. The very first mental effort that I now remember on my part, was an attempt to solve the mystery—why am I a slave? and with this question my youthful mind was troubled for many days, pressing upon me more heavily at times than others. When I saw the slave-driver whip a slave-woman, cut the blood out of her neck, and heard her piteous cries, I went away into the corner of the fence, wept and pondered over the mystery. I had, through some medium, I know not what, got some idea of God, the Creator of all mankind, the black and the white, and that he had made the blacks to serve the whites as slaves. How he could do this and be *good*, I could not tell. I was not satisfied with this theory, which made God responsible for slavery, for it pained me greatly, and I have wept over it long and often. At one time, your first wife, Mrs. Lucretia, heard me sighing and saw me shedding tears, and asked of me the matter, but I was afraid to tell her. I was puzzled with this question, till one night while sitting in the kitchen, I heard some of the old slaves talking of their parents having been stolen from Africa by white men, and were sold here as slaves. The whole mystery was solved at once. Very soon after this, my Aunt Jinny and Uncle Noah ran away, and the great noise made about it by your father-in-law, made me for the first time acquainted with the fact, that there were free states as well as slave states. From that time, I resolved that I would some day run away. The morality of the act I dispose of as follows: I am myself; you are yourself; we are two distinct persons, equal persons. What you are, I am. You are a man, and so am I. God created both, and made us separate beings. I am not by nature bond to you, or you to me. Nature does not make your existence depend upon me, or mine to depend upon yours. I cannot walk upon your legs, or you upon mine. I cannot breathe for you, or you for me; I must breathe for myself, and you for yourself. We are distinct persons, and are each equally provided with faculties necessary to our individual existence. In leaving you, I took nothing but what belonged to me, and in no way lessened your means for obtaining an *honest* living. Your faculties remained yours, and mine became useful to their rightful owner. I therefore see no wrong in any part of the transaction. It is true, I went off secretly; but that was more your fault than mine. Had I let you into the secret, you would have defeated the enterprise entirely; but for this, I should have been really glad to have made you acquainted with my intentions to leave.

You may perhaps want to know how I like my present condition. I am free to say, I greatly prefer it to that which I occupied in Maryland. I am, however, by no means prejudiced against the state as such. Its geography, climate, fertility, and products, are such as to make it a very desirable abode for any man; and but for the existence of slavery there, it is not impossible that I might again take up my abode in that state. It is not that I love Maryland less, but freedom more. You will be surprised to learn that people at the north labor under the strange delusion that if the slaves were emancipated at the south, they would flock to the north. So far from this being the case, in that event, you would see many old and familiar faces back again to the south. The fact is, there are few here who would not return to the south in the event of emancipation. We want to live in the land of our birth, and to lay our bones by the side of our fathers; and nothing short of an intense love of personal freedom keeps us from the south. For the sake of this, most of us would live on a crust of bread and a cup of cold water.

Since I left you, I have had a rich experience. I have occupied stations which I never dreamed of when a slave. Three out of the ten years since I left you, I spent as a common laborer on the wharves of New Bedford, Massachusetts. It was there I earned my first free dollar. It was mine. I could spend it as I pleased. I could buy hams or herring with it, without asking any odds of anybody. That was a precious dollar to me. You remember when I used to make seven, or eight, or even nine dollars a week in Baltimore, you would take every cent of it from me every Saturday night, saying that I belonged to you, and my earnings also. I never liked this conduct on your part—to say the best, I thought it a little mean. I would not have served you so. But let that pass. I was a little awkward about counting money in New England fashion when I first landed in New Bedford. I came near betraying myself several times. I caught myself saying phip, for fourpence; and at one time a man actually charged me with being a runaway, whereupon I was silly enough to become one by running away from him, for I was greatly afraid he might adopt measures to get me again into slavery, a condition I then dreaded more than death.

I soon learned, however, to count money, as well as to make it, and got on swimmingly. I married soon after leaving you; in fact, I was engaged to be married before I left you; and instead of finding my companion a burden, she was truly a helpmate. She went to live at service, and I to work on the wharf, and though we toiled hard the first winter, we never lived more happily. After

APPENDIX

remaining in New Bedford for three years, I met with William Lloyd Garrison, a person of whom you have *possibly* heard, as he is pretty generally known among slaveholders. He put it into my head that I might make myself serviceable to the cause of the slave, by devoting a portion of my time to telling my own sorrows, and those of other slaves, which had come under my observation. This was the commencement of a higher state of existence than any to which I had ever aspired. I was thrown into society the most pure, enlightened, and benevolent, that the country affords. Among these I have never forgotten you, but have invariably made you the topic of conversation—thus giving you all the notoriety I could do. I need not tell you that the opinion formed of you in these circles is far from being favorable. They have little respect for your honesty, and less for your religion.

But I was going on to relate to you something of my interesting experience. I had not long enjoyed the excellent society to which I have referred, before the light of its excellence exerted a beneficial influence on my mind and heart. Much of my early dislike of white persons was removed, and their manners, habits, and customs, so entirely unlike what I had been used to in the kitchen-quarters on the plantations of the south, fairly charmed me, and gave me a strong disrelish for the coarse and degrading customs of my former condition. I therefore made an effort so to improve my mind and deportment, as to be somewhat fitted to the station to which I seemed almost providentially called. The transition from degradation to respectability was indeed great, and to get from one to the other without carrying some marks of one's former condition, is truly a difficult matter. I would not have you think that I am now entirely clear of all plantation peculiarities, but my friends here, while they entertain the strongest dislike to them, regard me with that charity to which my past life somewhat entitles me, so that my condition in this respect is exceedingly pleasant. So far as my domestic affairs are concerned, I can boast of as comfortable a dwelling as your own. I have an industrious and neat companion, and four dear children—the oldest a girl of nine years, and three fine boys, the oldest eight, the next six, and the youngest four years old. The three oldest are now going regularly to school—two can read and write, and the other can spell, with tolerable correctness, words of two syllables. Dear fellows! they are all in comfortable beds, and are sound asleep, perfectly secure under my own roof. There are no slaveholders here to rend my heart by snatching them from my arms, or blast a mother's dearest hopes by tearing them from her bosom. These dear children are ours—not to work up into rice, sugar, and tobacco, but to watch over, regard, and protect, and to rear them up in the nurture and admonition of the gospel—to train them up in the paths of wisdom and virtue, and, as far as we can, to make them useful to the world and to themselves. Oh! sir, a slaveholder never appears to me so completely an agent of hell, as when I think of and look upon my dear children. It is then that my feelings rise above my control. I meant to have said more with respect to my own prosperity and happiness, but thoughts and feelings which this recital has quickened, unfit me to proceed further in that direction. The grim horrors of slavery rise in all their ghastly terror before me; the wails of millions pierce my heart and chill my blood. I remember the chain, the gag, the bloody whip; the death-like gloom overshadowing the broken spirit of the fettered bondman; the appalling liability of his being torn away from wife and children, and sold like a beast in the market. Say not that this is a picture of fancy. You well know that I wear stripes on my back, inflicted by your direction; and that you, while we were brothers in the same church, caused this right hand, with which I am now penning this letter, to be closely tied to my left, and my person dragged, at the pistol's mouth, fifteen miles, from the Bay Side to Easton, to be sold like a beast in the market, for the alleged crime of intending to escape from your possession. All this, and more, you remember, and know to be perfectly true, not only of yourself, but of nearly all of the slaveholders around you.

At this moment, you are probably the guilty holder of at least three of my own dear sisters, and my only brother, in bondage. These you regard as your property. They are recorded on your ledger, or perhaps have been sold to human flesh-mongers, with a view to filling our own ever-hungry purse. Sir, I desire to know how and where these dear sisters are. Have you sold them? or are they still in your possession? What has become of them? are they living or dead? And my dear old grandmother, whom you turned out like an old horse to die in the woods—is she still alive? Write and let me know all about them. If my grandmother be still alive, she is of no service to you, for by this time she must be nearly eighty years old—too old to be cared for by one to whom she has ceased to be of service; send her to me at Rochester, or bring her to Philadelphia, and it shall be the crowning happiness of my life to take care of her in her old age. Oh! she was to me a mother and a father, so far as hard toil for my comfort could make her such. Send me my grandmother! that I may watch over and take care of her in her old age. And my sisters—let me know all about them. I would write to them, and learn all I want to know of them, without disturbing you in any way, but that, through your unrighteous conduct, they have been entirely deprived of the power to read and write. You have kept them in utter ignorance, and have therefore robbed them of the sweet enjoyments of writing or receiving letters from absent friends and relatives. Your wickedness and cruelty, committed in this respect on your fellow-creatures, are greater than all the stripes you have laid upon my back or theirs. It is an outrage upon the soul, a war upon the immortal spirit, and one for which you must give account at the bar of our common Father and Creator.

The responsibility which you have assumed in this regard is truly awful, and how you could stagger under it these many years is marvelous. Your mind must have become darkened, your heart hardened, your conscience seared and petrified, or you would have long since thrown off the accursed load, and sought relief at the hands of a sin-forgiving God. How, let me ask, would you look upon me, were I, some dark night, in company with a band of hardened villains, to enter the precincts of your elegant dwelling, and seize the person of your own lovely daughter, Amanda, and carry her off from your family, friends, and all the loved ones of her youth—make her my slave—compel her to work, and I take her wages—place her name on my ledger as property—disregard her personal rights—fetter the powers of her immortal soul by denying her the right and privilege of learning to read and write—feed her coarsely—clothe her scantily, and whip her on the naked back occasionally; more, and still more horrible, leave her unprotected—a degraded victim to the brutal lust of fiendish overseers, who would pollute, blight, and blast her fair soul—rob her of all dignity—destroy her virtue, and annihilate in her person all the graces that adorn the character of virtuous womanhood? I ask, how would you regard me, if such were my conduct? Oh! the vocabulary of the damned would not afford a word sufficiently infernal to express your idea of my God-provoking wickedness. Yet, sir, your treatment of my beloved sisters is in all essential points precisely like the case I have now supposed. Damning as would be such a deed on my part, it would be no more so than that which you have committed against me and my sisters.

I will now bring this letter to a close; you shall hear from me again unless you let me hear from you. I intend to make use of you as a weapon with which to assail the system of slavery—as a means of concentrating public attention on the system, and deepening the horror of trafficking in the souls and bodies of men. I shall make use of you as a means of exposing the character of the American church and clergy—and as a means of bringing this guilty nation, with yourself, to repentance. In doing this, I entertain no malice toward you personally. There is no roof under which you would be more safe than mine, and there is nothing in my house which you might need for your comfort, which I would not readily grant. Indeed, I should esteem it a privilege to set you an example as to how mankind ought to treat each other.

I am your fellow-man, but not your slave.

APPENDIX

THE NATURE OF SLAVERY.
EXTRACT FROM A LECTURE ON SLAVERY, AT ROCHESTER, DECEMBER 1, 1850

More than twenty years of my life were consumed in a state of slavery. My childhood was environed by the baneful peculiarities of the slave system. I grew up to manhood in the presence of this hydra headed monster—not as a master—not as an idle spectator—not as the guest of the slaveholder—but as A SLAVE, eating the bread and drinking the cup of slavery with the most degraded of my brother-bondmen, and sharing with them all the painful conditions of their wretched lot. In consideration of these facts, I feel that I have a right to speak, and to speak *strongly*. Yet, my friends, I feel bound to speak truly.

Goading as have been the cruelties to which I have been subjected—bitter as have been the trials through which I have passed—exasperating as have been, and still are, the indignities offered to my manhood—I find in them no excuse for the slightest departure from truth in dealing with any branch of this subject.

First of all, I will state, as well as I can, the legal and social relation of master and slave. A master is one—to speak in the vocabulary of the southern states—who claims and exercises a right of property in the person of a fellow-man. This he does with the force of the law and the sanction of southern religion. The law gives the master absolute power over the slave. He may work him, flog him, hire him out, sell him, and, in certain contingencies, *kill* him, with perfect impunity. The slave is a human being, divested of all rights—reduced to the level of a brute—a mere "chattel" in the eye of the law—placed beyond the circle of human brotherhood—cut off from his kind—his name, which the "recording angel" may have enrolled in heaven, among the blest, is impiously inserted in a *master's ledger*, with horses, sheep, and swine. In law, the slave has no wife, no children, no country, and no home. He can own nothing, possess nothing, acquire nothing, but what must belong to another. To eat the fruit of his own toil, to clothe his person with the work of his own hands, is considered stealing. He toils that another may reap the fruit; he is industrious that another may live in idleness; he eats unbolted meal that another may eat the bread of fine flour; he labors in chains at home, under a burning sun and biting lash, that another may ride in ease and splendor abroad; he lives in ignorance that another may be educated; he is abused that another may be exalted; he rests his toil-worn limbs on the cold, damp ground that another may repose on the softest pillow; he is clad in coarse and tattered raiment that another may be arrayed in purple and fine linen; he is sheltered only by the wretched hovel that a master may dwell in a magnificent mansion; and to this condition he is bound down as by an arm of iron.

From this monstrous relation there springs an unceasing stream of most revolting cruelties. The very accompaniments of the slave system stamp it as the offspring of hell itself. To ensure good behavior, the slaveholder relies on the whip; to induce proper humility, he relies on the whip; to rebuke what he is pleased to term insolence, he relies on the whip; to supply the place of wages as an incentive to toil, he relies on the whip; to bind down the spirit of the slave, to imbrute and destroy his manhood, he relies on the whip, the chain, the gag, the thumb-screw, the pillory, the bowie knife the pistol, and the blood-hound. These are the necessary and unvarying accompaniments of the system. Wherever slavery is found, these horrid instruments are also found. Whether on the coast of Africa, among the savage tribes, or in South Carolina, among the refined and civilized, slavery is the same, and its accompaniments one and the same. It makes no difference whether the slaveholder worships the God of the Christians, or is a follower of Mahomet, he is the minister of the same cruelty, and the author of the same misery. *Slavery* is always *slavery;* always the same foul, haggard, and damning scourge, whether found in the eastern or in the western hemisphere.

There is a still deeper shade to be given to this picture. The physical cruelties are indeed sufficiently harassing and revolting; but they are as a few grains of sand on the sea shore, or a few drops of water in the great ocean, compared with the stupendous wrongs which it inflicts upon the mental, moral, and religious nature of its hapless victims. It is only when we contemplate the slave as a moral and intellectual being, that we can adequately comprehend the unparalleled enormity of slavery, and the intense criminality of the slaveholder. I have said that the slave was a man. "What a piece of work is man! How noble in reason! How infinite in faculties! In form and moving how express and admirable! In action how like an angel! In apprehension how like a God! The beauty of the world! The paragon of animals!"

The slave is a man, "the image of God," but "a little lower than the angels;" possessing a soul, eternal and indestructible; capable of endless happiness, or immeasurable woe; a creature of hopes and fears, of affections and passions, of joys and sorrows, and he is endowed with those mysterious powers by which man soars above the things of time and sense, and grasps, with undying tenacity, the elevating and sublimely glorious idea of a God. It is *such* a being that is smitten and blasted. The first work of slavery is to mar and deface those characteristics of its victims which distinguish *men* from *things*, and *persons* from *property*. Its first aim is to destroy all sense of high moral and religious responsibility. It reduces man to a mere machine. It cuts him off from his Maker, it hides from him the laws of God, and leaves him to grope his way from time to eternity in the dark, under the arbitrary and despotic control of a frail, depraved, and sinful fellow-man. As the serpent-charmer of India is compelled to extract the deadly teeth of his venomous prey before he is able to handle him with impunity, so the slaveholder must strike down the conscience of the slave before he can obtain the entire mastery over his victim.

It is, then, the first business of the enslaver of men to blunt, deaden, and destroy the central principle of human responsibility. Conscience is, to the individual soul, and to society, what the law of gravitation is to the universe. It holds society together; it is the basis of all trust and confidence; it is the pillar of all moral rectitude. Without it, suspicion would take the place of trust; vice would be more than a match for virtue; men would prey upon each other, like the wild beasts of the desert; and earth would become a *hell*.

Nor is slavery more adverse to the conscience than it is to the mind. This is shown by the fact, that in every state of the American Union, where slavery exists, except the state of Kentucky, there are laws absolutely prohibitory of education among the slaves. The crime of teaching a slave to read is punishable with severe fines and imprisonment, and, in some instances, with *death itself*.

Nor are the laws respecting this matter a dead letter. Cases may occur in which they are disregarded, and a few instances may be found where slaves may have learned to read; but such are isolated cases, and only prove the rule. The great mass of slaveholders look upon education among the slaves as utterly subversive of the slave system. I well remember when my mistress first announced to my master that she had dis covered that I could read. His face colored at once with surprise and chagrin. He said that "I was ruined, and my value as a slave destroyed; that a slave should know nothing but to obey his master; that to give a negro an inch would lead him to take an ell; that having learned how to read, I would soon want to know how to write; and that by-and-by I would be running away." I think my audience will bear witness to the correctness of this philosophy, and to the literal fulfillment of this prophecy.

It is perfectly well understood at the south, that to educate a slave is to make him discontened(sic) with slavery, and to invest him with a power which shall open to him the treasures of freedom; and since the object of the slaveholder is to maintain complete authority over his slave, his constant vigilance is exercised to prevent everything which militates against, or endangers, the stability of his authority. Education being among the menacing influences, and, perhaps, the most dangerous, is, therefore, the most cautiously guarded against.

It is true that we do not often hear of the enforcement of the law, punishing as a crime the teaching of slaves to read, but this is not because of a want of disposition to enforce it. The true reason or explanation of the matter is this: there is the greatest unanimity of opinion among the white population in the south in favor of the policy of keeping the slave in ignorance. There is, perhaps, another reason why the law against education is so seldom violated. The slave is too poor to be able to offer a temptation sufficiently strong to induce a white man to violate it; and it is not to be supposed that in a community where the moral and religious sentiment is in favor of slavery, many martyrs will be found sacrificing their liberty and lives by violating those prohibitory enactments.

APPENDIX

As a general rule, then, darkness reigns over the abodes of the enslaved, and "how great is that darkness!"

We are sometimes told of the contentment of the slaves, and are entertained with vivid pictures of their happiness. We are told that they often dance and sing; that their masters frequently give them wherewith to make merry; in fine, that they have little of which to complain. I admit that the slave does sometimes sing, dance, and appear to be merry. But what does this prove? It only proves to my mind, that though slavery is armed with a thousand stings, it is not able entirely to kill the elastic spirit of the bondman. That spirit will rise and walk abroad, despite of whips and chains, and extract from the cup of nature occasional drops of joy and gladness. No thanks to the slaveholder, nor to slavery, that the vivacious captive may sometimes dance in his chains; his very mirth in such circumstances stands before God as an accusing angel against his enslaver.

It is often said, by the opponents of the anti-slavery cause, that the condition of the people of Ireland is more deplorable than that of the American slaves. Far be it from me to underrate the sufferings of the Irish people. They have been long oppressed; and the same heart that prompts me to plead the cause of the American bondman, makes it impossible for me not to sympathize with the oppressed of all lands. Yet I must say that there is no analogy between the two cases. The Irishman is poor, but he is not a slave. He may be in rags, but he is not a slave. He is still the master of his own body, and can say with the poet, "The hand of Douglass is his own." "The world is all before him, where to choose;" and poor as may be my opinion of the British parliament, I cannot believe that it will ever sink to such a depth of infamy as to pass a law for the recapture of fugitive Irishmen! The shame and scandal of kidnapping will long remain wholly monopolized by the American congress. The Irishman has not only the liberty to emigrate from his country, but he has liberty at home. He can write, and speak, and cooperate for the attainment of his rights and the redress of his wrongs.

The multitude can assemble upon all the green hills and fertile plains of the Emerald Isle; they can pour out their grievances, and proclaim their wants without molestation; and the press, that "swift-winged messenger," can bear the tidings of their doings to the extreme bounds of the civilized world. They have their "Conciliation Hall," on the banks of the Liffey, their reform clubs, and their newspapers; they pass resolutions, send forth addresses, and enjoy the right of petition. But how is it with the American slave? Where may he assemble? Where is his Conciliation Hall? Where are his newspapers? Where is his right of petition? Where is his freedom of speech? his liberty of the press? and his right of locomotion? He is said to be happy; happy men can speak. But ask the slave what is his condition—what his state of mind—what he thinks of enslavement? and you had as well address your inquiries to the *silent dead*. There comes no *voice* from the enslaved. We are left to gather his feelings by imagining what ours would be, were our souls in his soul's stead.

If there were no other fact descriptive of slavery, than that the slave is dumb, this alone would be sufficient to mark the slave system as a grand aggregation of human horrors.

Most who are present, will have observed that leading men in this country have been putting forth their skill to secure quiet to the nation. A system of measures to promote this object was adopted a few months ago in congress. The result of those measures is known. Instead of quiet, they have produced alarm; instead of peace, they have brought us war; and so it must ever be.

While this nation is guilty of the enslavement of three millions of innocent men and women, it is as idle to think of having a sound and lasting peace, as it is to think there is no God to take cognizance of the affairs of men. There can be no peace to the wicked while slavery continues in the land. It will be condemned; and while it is condemned there will be agitation. Nature must cease to be nature; men must become monsters; humanity must be transformed; Christianity must be exterminated; all ideas of justice and the laws of eternal goodness must be utterly blotted out from the human soul—ere a system so foul and infernal can escape condemnation, or this guilty republic can have a sound, enduring peace.

FREDERICK DOUGLASS

INHUMANITY OF SLAVERY.
EXTRACT FROM A LECTURE ON SLAVERY, AT ROCHESTER, DECEMBER 8, 1850

The relation of master and slave has been called patriarchal, and only second in benignity and tenderness to that of the parent and child. This representation is doubtless believed by many northern people; and this may account, in part, for the lack of interest which we find among persons whom we are bound to believe to be honest and humane. What, then, are the facts? Here I will not quote my own experience in slavery; for this you might call one-sided testimony. I will not cite the declarations of abolitionists; for these you might pronounce exaggerations. I will not rely upon advertisements cut from newspapers; for these you might call isolated cases. But I will refer you to the laws adopted by the legislatures of the slave states. I give you such evidence, because it cannot be invalidated nor denied. I hold in my hand sundry extracts from the slave codes of our country, from which I will quote. * * *

Now, if the foregoing be an indication of kindness, *what is cruelty*? If this be parental affection, *what is bitter malignity*? A more atrocious and blood-thirsty string of laws could not well be conceived of. And yet I am bound to say that they fall short of indicating the horrible cruelties constantly practiced in the slave states.

I admit that there are individual slaveholders less cruel and barbarous than is allowed by law; but these form the exception. The majority of slaveholders find it necessary, to insure obedience, at times, to avail themselves of the utmost extent of the law, and many go beyond it. If kindness were the rule, we should not see advertisements filling the columns of almost every southern newspaper, offering large rewards for fugitive slaves, and describing them as being branded with irons, loaded with chains, and scarred by the whip. One of the most telling testimonies against the pretended kindness of slaveholders, is the fact that uncounted numbers of fugitives are now inhabiting the Dismal Swamp, preferring the untamed wilderness to their cultivated homes—choosing rather to encounter hunger and thirst, and to roam with the wild beasts of the forest, running the hazard of being hunted and shot down, than to submit to the authority of *kind* masters.

I tell you, my friends, humanity is never driven to such an unnatural course of life, without great wrong. The slave finds more of the milk of human kindness in the bosom of the savage Indian, than in the heart of his *Christian* master. He leaves the man of the *bible*, and takes refuge with the man of the *tomahawk*. He rushes from the praying slaveholder into the paws of the bear. He quits the homes of men for the haunts of wolves. He prefers to encounter a life of trial, however bitter, or death, however terrible, to dragging out his existence under the dominion of these *kind* masters.

The apologists for slavery often speak of the abuses of slavery; and they tell us that they are as much opposed to those abuses as we are; and that they would go as far to correct those abuses and to ameliorate the condition of the slave as anybody. The answer to that view is, that slavery is itself an abuse; that it lives by abuse; and dies by the absence of abuse. Grant that slavery is right; grant that the relations of master and slave may innocently exist; and there is not a single outrage which was ever committed against the slave but what finds an apology in the very necessity of the case. As we said by a slaveholder (the Rev. A. G. Few) to the Methodist conference, "If the relation be right, the means to maintain it are also right;" for without those means slavery could not exist. Remove the dreadful scourge—the plaited thong—the galling fetter—the accursed chain—and let the slaveholder rely solely upon moral and religious power, by which to secure obedience to his orders, and how long do you suppose a slave would remain on his plantation? The case only needs to be stated; it carries its own refutation with it.

Absolute and arbitrary power can never be maintained by one man over the body and soul of another man, without brutal chastisement and enormous cruelty.

To talk of *kindness* entering into a relation in which one party is robbed of wife, of children, of his hard earnings, of home, of friends, of society, of knowledge, and of all that makes this life desirable, is most absurd, wicked, and preposterous.

APPENDIX

I have shown that slavery is wicked—wicked, in that it violates the great law of liberty, written on every human heart—wicked, in that it violates the first command of the decalogue—wicked, in that it fosters the most disgusting licentiousness—wicked, in that it mars and defaces the image of God by cruel and barbarous inflictions—wicked, in that it contravenes the laws of eternal justice, and tramples in the dust all the humane and heavenly precepts of the New Testament.

The evils resulting from this huge system of iniquity are not confined to the states south of Mason and Dixon's line. Its noxious influence can easily be traced throughout our northern borders. It comes even as far north as the state of New York. Traces of it may be seen even in Rochester; and travelers have told me it casts its gloomy shadows across the lake, approaching the very shores of Queen Victoria's dominions.

The presence of slavery may be explained by—as it is the explanation of—the mobocratic violence which lately disgraced New York, and which still more recently disgraced the city of Boston. These violent demonstrations, these outrageous invasions of human rights, faintly indicate the presence and power of slavery here. It is a significant fact, that while meetings for almost any purpose under heaven may be held unmolested in the city of Boston, that in the same city, a meeting cannot be peaceably held for the purpose of preaching the doctrine of the American Declaration of Independence, "that all men are created equal." The pestiferous breath of slavery taints the whole moral atmosphere of the north, and enervates the moral energies of the whole people.

The moment a foreigner ventures upon our soil, and utters a natural repugnance to oppression, that moment he is made to feel that there is little sympathy in this land for him. If he were greeted with smiles before, he meets with frowns now; and it shall go well with him if he be not subjected to that peculiarly fining method of showing fealty to slavery, the assaults of a mob.

Now, will any man tell me that such a state of things is natural, and that such conduct on the part of the people of the north, springs from a consciousness of rectitude? No! every fibre of the human heart unites in detestation of tyranny, and it is only when the human mind has become familiarized with slavery, is accustomed to its injustice, and corrupted by its selfishness, that it fails to record its abhorrence of slavery, and does not exult in the triumphs of liberty.

The northern people have been long connected with slavery; they have been linked to a decaying corpse, which has destroyed the moral health. The union of the government; the union of the north and south, in the political parties; the union in the religious organizations of the land, have all served to deaden the moral sense of the northern people, and to impregnate them with sentiments and ideas forever in conflict with what as a nation we call *genius of American institutions*. Rightly viewed, this is an alarming fact, and ought to rally all that is pure, just, and holy in one determined effort to crush the monster of corruption, and to scatter "its guilty profits" to the winds. In a high moral sense, as well as in a national sense, the whole American people are responsible for slavery, and must share, in its guilt and shame, with the most obdurate men-stealers of the south.

While slavery exists, and the union of these states endures, every American citizen must bear the chagrin of hearing his country branded before the world as a nation of liars and hypocrites; and behold his cherished flag pointed at with the utmost scorn and derision. Even now an American *abroad* is pointed out in the crowd, as coming from a land where men gain their fortunes by "the blood of souls," from a land of slave markets, of blood-hounds, and slave-hunters; and, in some circles, such a man is shunned altogether, as a moral pest. Is it not time, then, for every American to awake, and inquire into his duty with respect to this subject?

Wendell Phillips—the eloquent New England orator—on his return from Europe, in 1842, said, "As I stood upon the shores of Genoa, and saw floating on the placid waters of the Mediterranean, the beautiful American war ship Ohio, with her masts tapering proportionately aloft, and an eastern sun reflecting her noble form upon the sparkling waters, attracting the gaze of the multitude, my first impulse was of pride, to think myself an American; but when I thought that the first time that gallant ship would gird on her gorgeous apparel, and wake from beneath her sides her dormant thunders, it would be in defense of the African slave trade, I blushed in utter *shame* for my country."

Let me say again, *slavery is alike the sin and the shame of the American people;* it is a blot upon the American name, and the only national reproach which need make an American hang his head in shame, in the presence of monarchical governments.

With this gigantic evil in the land, we are constantly told to look *at home;* if we say ought against crowned heads, we are pointed to our enslaved millions; if we talk of sending missionaries and bibles abroad, we are pointed to three millions now lying in worse than heathen darkness; if we express a word of sympathy for Kossuth and his Hungarian fugitive brethren, we are pointed to that horrible and hell-black enactment, "the fugitive slave bill."

Slavery blunts the edge of all our rebukes of tyranny abroad—the criticisms that we make upon other nations, only call forth ridicule, contempt, and scorn. In a word, we are made a reproach and a by-word to a mocking earth, and we must continue to be so made, so long as slavery continues to pollute our soil.

We have heard much of late of the virtue of patriotism, the love of country, &c., and this sentiment, so natural and so strong, has been impiously appealed to, by all the powers of human selfishness, to cherish the viper which is stinging our national life away. In its name, we have been called upon to deepen our infamy before the world, to rivet the fetter more firmly on the limbs of the enslaved, and to become utterly insensible to the voice of human woe that is wafted to us on every southern gale. We have been called upon, in its name, to desecrate our whole land by the footprints of slave-hunters, and even to engage ourselves in the horrible business of kidnapping.

I, too, would invoke the spirit of patriotism; not in a narrow and restricted sense, but, I trust, with a broad and manly signification; not to cover up our national sins, but to inspire us with sincere repentance; not to hide our shame from the the(sic) world's gaze, but utterly to abolish the cause of that shame; not to explain away our gross inconsistencies as a nation, but to remove the hateful, jarring, and incongruous elements from the land; not to sustain an egregious wrong, but to unite all our energies in the grand effort to remedy that wrong.

I would invoke the spirit of patriotism, in the name of the law of the living God, natural and revealed, and in the full belief that "righteousness exalteth a nation, while sin is a reproach to any people." "He that walketh righteously, and speaketh uprightly; he that despiseth the gain of oppressions, that shaketh his hands from the holding of bribes, he shall dwell on high, his place of defense shall be the munitions of rocks, bread shall be given him, his water shall be sure."

We have not only heard much lately of patriotism, and of its aid being invoked on the side of slavery and injustice, but the very prosperity of this people has been called in to deafen them to the voice of duty, and to lead them onward in the pathway of sin. Thus has the blessing of God been converted into a curse. In the spirit of genuine patriotism, I warn the American people, by all that is just and honorable, to BEWARE!

I warn them that, strong, proud, and prosperous though we be, there is a power above us that can "bring down high looks; at the breath of whose mouth our wealth may take wings; and before whom every knee shall bow;" and who can tell how soon the avenging angel may pass over our land, and the sable bondmen now in chains, may become the instruments of our nation's chastisement! Without appealing to any higher feeling, I would warn the American people, and the American government, to be wise in their day and generation. I exhort them to remember the history of other nations; and I remind them that America cannot always sit "as a queen," in peace and repose; that prouder and stronger governments than this have been shattered by the bolts of a just God; that the time may come when those they now despise and hate, may be needed; when those whom they now compel by oppression to be enemies, may be wanted as friends. What has been, may be again. There is a point beyond which human endurance cannot go. The crushed worm may yet turn under the heel of the oppressor. I warn them, then, with all solemnity, and in the name of retributive justice, *to look to their ways;* for in an evil hour, those sable arms that have, for the last two centuries, been engaged in cultivating and adorning the fair fields of our country, may yet become the instruments of terror, desolation, and death, throughout our borders.

It was the sage of the Old Dominion that said—while speaking of the possibility of a conflict between the slaves and the slaveholders—"God has no attribute that could take sides with the

APPENDIX

oppressor in such a contest. I tremble for my country when I reflect that God *is just*, and that his justice cannot sleep forever." Such is the warning voice of Thomas Jefferson; and every day's experience since its utterance until now, confirms its wisdom, and commends its truth.

FREDERICK DOUGLASS

WHAT TO THE SLAVE IS THE FOURTH OF JULY?

EXTRACT FROM AN ORATION, AT ROCHESTER, JULY 5, 1852

Fellow-Citizens—Pardon me, and allow me to ask, why am I called upon to speak here to-day? What have I, or those I represent, to do with your national independence? Are the great principles of political freedom and of natural justice, embodied in that Declaration of Independence, extended to us? and am I, therefore, called upon to bring our humble offering to the national altar, and to confess the benefits, and express devout gratitude for the blessings, resulting from your independence to us?

Would to God, both for your sakes and ours, that an affirmative answer could be truthfully returned to these questions! Then would my task be light, and my burden easy and delightful. For who is there so cold that a nation's sympathy could not warm him? Who so obdurate and dead to the claims of gratitude, that would not thankfully acknowledge such priceless benefits? Who so stolid and selfish, that would not give his voice to swell the hallelujahs of a nation's jubilee, when the chains of servitude had been torn from his limbs? I am not that man. In a case like that, the dumb might eloquently speak, and the "lame man leap as an hart."

But, such is not the state of the case. I say it with a sad sense of the disparity between us. I am not included within the pale of this glorious anniversary! Your high independence only reveals the immeasurable distance between us. The blessings in which you this day rejoice, are not enjoyed in common. The rich inheritance of justice, liberty, prosperity, and independence, bequeathed by your fathers, is shared by you, not by me. The sunlight that brought life and healing to you, has brought stripes and death to me. This Fourth of July is *yours*, not mine. You may rejoice, I must mourn. To drag a man in fetters into the grand illuminated temple of liberty, and call upon him to join you in joyous anthems, were inhuman mockery and sacrilegious irony. Do you mean, citizens, to mock me, by asking me to speak to-day? If so, there is a parallel to your conduct. And let me warn you that it is dangerous to copy the example of a nation whose crimes, towering up to heaven, were thrown down by the breath of the Almighty, burying that nation in irrecoverable ruin! I can to-day take up the plaintive lament of a peeled and woe-smitten people.

"By the rivers of Babylon, there we sat down. Yea! we wept when we remembered Zion. We hanged our harps upon the willows in the midst thereof. For there, they that carried us away captive, required of us a song; and they who wasted us required of us mirth, saying, Sing us one of the songs of Zion. How can we sing the Lord's song in a strange land? If I forget thee, O Jerusalem, let my right hand forget her cunning. If I do not remember thee, let my tongue cleave to the roof of my mouth."

Fellow-citizens, above your national, tumultous joy, I hear the mournful wail of millions, whose chains, heavy and grievous yesterday, are to-day rendered more intolerable by the jubilant shouts that reach them. If I do forget, if I do not faithfully remember those bleeding children of sorrow this day, "may my right hand forget her cunning, and may my tongue cleave to the roof of my mouth!" To forget them, to pass lightly over their wrongs, and to chime in with the popular theme, would be treason most scandalous and shocking, and would make me a reproach before God and the world. My subject, then, fellow-citizens, is AMERICAN SLAVERY. I shall see this day and its popular characteristics from the slave's point of view. Standing there, identified with the American bondman, making his wrongs mine, I do not hesitate to declare, with all my soul, that the character and conduct of this nation never looked blacker to me than on this Fourth of July. Whether we turn to the declarations of the past, or to the professions of the present, the conduct of the nation seems equally hideous and revolting. America is false to the past, false to the present, and solemnly binds herself to be false to the future. Standing with God and the crushed and bleeding slave on this occasion, I will, in the name of humanity which is outraged, in the name of liberty which is fettered, in the name of the constitution and the bible, which are disregarded and trampled upon, dare to call in question and

APPENDIX

to denounce, with all the emphasis I can command, everything that serves to perpetuate slavery—the great sin and shame of America! "I will not equivocate; I will not excuse;" I will use the severest language I can command; and yet not one word shall escape me that any man, whose judgment is not blinded by prejudice, or who is not at heart a slaveholder, shall not confess to be right and just.

But I fancy I hear some one of my audience say, it is just in this circumstance that you and your brother abolitionists fail to make a favorable impression on the public mind. Would you argue more, and denounce less, would you persuade more and rebuke less, your cause would be much more likely to succeed. But, I submit, where all is plain there is nothing to be argued. What point in the anti-slavery creed would you have me argue? On what branch of the subject do the people of this country need light? Must I undertake to prove that the slave is a man? That point is conceded already. Nobody doubts it. The slaveholders themselves acknowledge it in the enactment of laws for their government. They acknowledge it when they punish disobedience on the part of the slave. There are seventy-two crimes in the state of Virginia, which, if committed by a black man (no matter how ignorant he be), subject him to the punishment of death; while only two of these same crimes will subject a white man to the like punishment. What is this but the acknowledgement that the slave is a moral, intellectual, and responsible being. The manhood of the slave is conceded. It is admitted in the fact that southern statute books are covered with enactments forbidding, under severe fines and penalties, the teaching of the slave to read or write. When you can point to any such laws, in reference to the beasts of the field, then I may consent to argue the manhood of the slave. When the dogs in your streets, when the fowls of the air, when the cattle on your hills, when the fish of the sea, and the reptiles that crawl, shall be unable to distinguish the slave from a brute, then will I argue with you that the slave is a man!

For the present, it is enough to affirm the equal manhood of the Negro race. Is it not astonishing that, while we are plowing, planting, and reaping, using all kinds of mechanical tools, erecting houses, constructing bridges, building ships, working in metals of brass, iron, copper, silver, and gold; that, while we are reading, writing, and cyphering, acting as clerks, merchants, and secretaries, having among us lawyers, doctors, ministers, poets, authors, editors, orators, and teachers; that, while we are engaged in all manner of enterprises common to other men—digging gold in California, capturing the whale in the Pacific, feeding sheep and cattle on the hillside, living, moving, acting, thinking, planning, living in families as husbands, wives, and children, and, above all, confessing and worshiping the Christian's God, and looking hopefully for life and immortality beyond the grave—we are called upon to prove that we are men!

Would you have me argue that man is entitled to liberty? that he is the rightful owner of his own body? You have already declared it. Must I argue the wrongfulness of slavery? Is that a question for republicans? Is it to be settled by the rules of logic and argumentation, as a matter beset with great difficulty, involving a doubtful application of the principle of justice, hard to be understood? How should I look to-day in the presence of Americans, dividing and subdividing a discourse, to show that men have a natural right to freedom, speaking of it relatively and positively, negatively and affirmatively? To do so, would be to make myself ridiculous, and to offer an insult to your understanding. There is not a man beneath the canopy of heaven that does not know that slavery is wrong for *him*.

What! am I to argue that it is wrong to make men brutes, to rob them of their liberty, to work them without wages, to keep them ignorant of their relations to their fellow-men, to beat them with sticks, to flay their flesh with the lash, to load their limbs with irons, to hunt them with dogs, to sell them at auction, to sunder their families, to knock out their teeth, to burn their flesh, to starve them into obedience and submission to their masters? Must I argue that a system, thus marked with blood and stained with pollution, is wrong? No; I will not. I have better employment for my time and strength than such arguments would imply.

What, then, remains to be argued? Is it that slavery is not divine; that God did not establish it; that our doctors of divinity are mistaken? There is blasphemy in the thought. That which is inhuman cannot be divine. Who can reason on such a proposition! They that can, may! I cannot. The time for such argument is past.

FREDERICK DOUGLASS

At a time like this, scorching irony, not convincing argument, is needed. Oh! had I the ability, and could I reach the nation's ear, I would to-day pour out a fiery stream of biting ridicule, blasting reproach, withering sarcasm, and stern rebuke. For it is not light that is needed, but fire; it is not the gentle shower, but thunder. We need the storm, the whirlwind, and the earthquake. The feeling of the nation must be quickened; the conscience of the nation must be roused; the propriety of the nation must be startled; the hypocrisy of the nation must be exposed; and its crimes against God and man must be proclaimed and denounced.

What to the American slave is your Fourth of July? I answer, a day that reveals to him, more than all other days in the year, the gross injustice and cruelty to which he is the constant victim. To him, your celebration is a sham; your boasted liberty, an unholy license; your national greatness, swelling vanity; your sounds of rejoicing are empty and heartless; your denunciations of tyrants, brass-fronted impudence; your shouts of liberty and equality, hollow mockery; your prayers and hymns, your sermons and thanksgivings, with all your religious parade and solemnity, are to him mere bombast, fraud, deception, impiety, and hypocrisy—a thin veil to cover up crimes which would disgrace a nation of savages. There is not a nation on the earth guilty of practices more shocking and bloody, than are the people of these United States, at this very hour.

Go where you may, search where you will, roam through all the monarchies and despotisms of the old world, travel through South America, search out every abuse, and when you have found the last, lay your facts by the side of the every-day practices of this nation, and you will say with me, that, for revolting barbarity and shameless hypocrisy, America reigns without a rival.

APPENDIX

The Internal Slave Trade.
Extract from an Oration, at Rochester, July 5, 1852

Take the American slave trade, which, we are told by the papers, is especially prosperous just now. Ex-senator Benton tells us that the price of men was never higher than now. He mentions the fact to show that slavery is in no danger. This trade is one of the peculiarities of American institutions. It is carried on in all the large towns and cities in one-half of this confederacy; and millions are pocketed every year by dealers in this horrid traffic. In several states this trade is a chief source of wealth. It is called (in contradistinction to the foreign slave trade) *"the internal slave trade."* It is, probably, called so, too, in order to divert from it the horror with which the foreign slave trade is contemplated. That trade has long since been denounced by this government as piracy. It has been denounced with burning words, from the high places of the nation, as an execrable traffic. To arrest it, to put an end to it, this nation keeps a squadron, at immense cost, on the coast of Africa. Everywhere in this country, it is safe to speak of this foreign slave trade as a most inhuman traffic, opposed alike to the laws of God and of man. The duty to extirpate and destroy it is admitted even by our *doctors of divinity*. In order to put an end to it, some of these last have consented that their colored brethren (nominally free) should leave this country, and establish themselves on the western coast of Africa. It is, however, a notable fact, that, while so much execration is poured out by Americans, upon those engaged in the foreign slave trade, the men engaged in the slave trade between the states pass without condemnation, and their business is deemed honorable.

Behold the practical operation of this internal slave trade—the American slave trade sustained by American politics and American religion! Here you will see men and women reared like swine for the market. You know what is a swine-drover? I will show you a man-drover. They inhabit all our southern states. They perambulate the country, and crowd the highways of the nation with droves of human stock. You will see one of these human-flesh-jobbers, armed with pistol, whip, and bowie-knife, driving a company of a hundred men, women, and children, from the Potomac to the slave market at New Orleans. These wretched people are to be sold singly, or in lots, to suit purchasers. They are food for the cotton-field and the deadly sugar-mill. Mark the sad procession as it moves wearily along, and the inhuman wretch who drives them. Hear his savage yells and his blood-chilling oaths, as he hurries on his affrighted captives. There, see the old man, with locks thinned and gray. Cast one glance, if you please, upon that young mother, whose shoulders are bare to the scorching sun, her briny tears falling on the brow of the babe in her arms. See, too, that girl of thirteen, weeping, yes, weeping, as she thinks of the mother from whom she has been torn. The drove moves tardily. Heat and sorrow have nearly consumed their strength. Suddenly you hear a quick snap, like the discharge of a rifle; the fetters clank, and the chain rattles simultaneously; your ears are saluted with a scream that seems to have torn its way to the center of your soul. The crack you heard was the sound of the slave whip; the scream you heard was from the woman you saw with the babe. Her speed had faltered under the weight of her child and her chains; that gash on her shoulder tells her to move on. Follow this drove to New Orleans. Attend the auction; see men examined like horses; see the forms of women rudely and brutally exposed to the shocking gaze of American slave-buyers. See this drove sold and separated forever; and never forget the deep, sad sobs that arose from that scattered multitude. Tell me, citizens, where, under the sun, can you witness a spectacle more fiendish and shocking. Yet this is but a glance at the American slave trade, as it exists at this moment, in the ruling part of the United States.

I was born amid such sights and scenes. To me the American slave trade is a terrible reality. When a child, my soul was often pierced with a sense of its horrors. I lived on Philpot street, Fell's Point, Baltimore, and have watched from the wharves the slave ships in the basin, anchored from the shore, with their cargoes of human flesh, waiting for favorable winds to waft them down the Chesapeake. There was, at that time, a grand slave mart kept at the head of Pratt street, by Austin Woldfolk. His agents were sent into every town and county in Maryland, announcing their arrival through the papers, and on flaming hand-bills, headed, "cash for negroes." These men were generally well dressed, and very captivating in their manners; ever ready to drink, to treat, and to gamble. The fate of many a slave has depended upon the turn of a single card; and many a child has been snatched from the arms of its mothers by bargains arranged in a state of brutal drunkenness.

The flesh-mongers gather up their victims by dozens, and drive them, chained, to the general depot at Baltimore. When a sufficient number have been collected here, a ship is chartered, for the purpose of conveying the forlorn crew to Mobile or to New Orleans. From the slave-prison to the ship, they are usually driven in the darkness of night; for since the anti-slavery agitation a certain caution is observed.

In the deep, still darkness of midnight, I have been often aroused by the dead, heavy footsteps and the piteous cries of the chained gangs that passed our door. The anguish of my boyish heart was intense; and I was often consoled, when speaking to my mistress in the morning, to hear her say that the custom was very wicked; that she hated to hear the rattle of the chains, and the heart-rending cries. I was glad to find one who sympathized with me in my horror.

Fellow citizens, this murderous traffic is to-day in active operation in this boasted republic. In the solitude of my spirit, I see clouds of dust raised on the highways of the south; I see the bleeding footsteps; I hear the doleful wail of fettered humanity, on the way to the slave markets, where the victims are to be sold like horses, sheep, and swine, knocked off to the highest bidder. There I see the tenderest ties ruthlessly broken, to gratify the lust, caprice, and rapacity of the buyers and sellers of men. My soul sickens at the sight.

> *Is this the land your fathers loved?*
> *The freedom which they toiled to win?*
> *Is this the earth whereon they moved?*
> *Are these the graves they slumber in?*

But a still more inhuman, disgraceful, and scandalous state of things remains to be presented. By an act of the American congress, not yet two years old, slavery has been nationalized in its most horrible and revolting form. By that act, Mason and Dixon's line has been obliterated; New York has become as Virginia; and the power to hold, hunt, and sell men, women, and children as slaves, remains no longer a mere state institution, but is now an institution of the whole United States. The power is coextensive with the star-spangled banner and American christianity. Where these go, may also go the merciless slave-hunter. Where these are, man is not sacred. He is a bird for the sportsman's gun. By that most foul and fiendish of all human decrees, the liberty and person of every man are put in peril. Your broad republican domain is a hunting-ground for *men*. Not for thieves and robbers, enemies of society, merely, but for men guilty of no crime. Your law-makers have commanded all good citizens to engage in this hellish sport. Your president, your secretary of state, your lords, nobles, and ecclesiastics, enforce as a duty you owe to your free and glorious country and to your God, that you do this accursed thing. Not fewer than forty Americans have within the past two years been hunted down, and without a moment's warning, hurried away in chains, and consigned to slavery and excruciating torture. Some of these have had wives and children dependent on them for bread; but of this no account was made. The right of the hunter to his prey, stands superior to the right of marriage, and to *all* rights in this republic, the rights of God included! For black men there are neither law, justice, humanity, nor religion. The fugitive slave law makes MERCY TO THEM A CRIME; and bribes the judge who tries them. An American judge GETS TEN DOLLARS FOR EVERY VICTIM HE CONSIGNS to slavery, and five, when he fails to do so. The oath of an(sic) two villains is sufficient, under this hell-black enactment, to send the most pious and exemplary black man into the remorseless jaws of slavery! His own testimony is nothing. He can bring no witnesses for himself. The minister of American justice is bound by the law to hear but *one side*, and that side is the side of the oppressor. Let this damning fact be perpetually told. Let it be thundered around the world, that, in tyrant-killing, king hating, people-loving, democratic, Christian America, the seats of justice are filled with judges, who hold their office under an open and palpable *bribe*, and are bound, in deciding in the case of a man's liberty, *to hear only his accusers!*

In glaring violation of justice, in shameless disregard of the forms of administering law, in cunning arrangement to entrap the defenseless, and in diabolical intent, this fugitive slave law stands

APPENDIX

alone in the annals of tyrannical legislation. I doubt if there be another nation on the globe having the brass and the baseness to put such a law on the statute-book. If any man in this assembly thinks differently from me in this matter, and feels able to disprove my statements, I will gladly confront him at any suitable time and place he may select.

FREDERICK DOUGLASS

The Slavery Party.
Extract from a Speech Delivered before the A. A. S. Society, in New York, May, 1853.

Sir, it is evident that there is in this country a purely slavery party—a party which exists for no other earthly purpose but to promote the interests of slavery. The presence of this party is felt everywhere in the republic. It is known by no particular name, and has assumed no definite shape; but its branches reach far and wide in the church and in the state. This shapeless and nameless party is not intangible in other and more important respects. That party, sir, has determined upon a fixed, definite, and comprehensive policy toward the whole colored population of the United States. What that policy is, it becomes us as abolitionists, and especially does it become the colored people themselves, to consider and to understand fully. We ought to know who our enemies are, where they are, and what are their objects and measures. Well, sir, here is my version of it—not original with me—but mine because I hold it to be true.

I understand this policy to comprehend five cardinal objects. They are these: 1st. The complete suppression of all anti-slavery discussion. 2d. The expatriation of the entire free people of color from the United States. 3d. The unending perpetuation of slavery in this republic. 4th. The nationalization of slavery to the extent of making slavery respected in every state of the Union. 5th. The extension of slavery over Mexico and the entire South American states.

Sir, these objects are forcibly presented to us in the stern logic of passing events; in the facts which are and have been passing around us during the last three years. The country has been and is now dividing on these grand issues. In their magnitude, these issues cast all others into the shade, depriving them of all life and vitality. Old party ties are broken. Like is finding its like on either side of these great issues, and the great battle is at hand. For the present, the best representative of the slavery party in politics is the democratic party. Its great head for the present is President Pierce, whose boast it was, before his election, that his whole life had been consistent with the interests of slavery, that he is above reproach on that score. In his inaugural address, he reassures the south on this point. Well, the head of the slave power being in power, it is natural that the pro slavery elements should cluster around the administration, and this is rapidly being done. A fraternization is going on. The stringent protectionists and the free-traders strike hands. The supporters of Fillmore are becoming the supporters of Pierce. The silver-gray whig shakes hands with the hunker democrat; the former only differing from the latter in name. They are of one heart, one mind, and the union is natural and perhaps inevitable. Both hate Negroes; both hate progress; both hate the "higher law;" both hate William H. Seward; both hate the free democratic party; and upon this hateful basis they are forming a union of hatred. "Pilate and Herod are thus made friends." Even the central organ of the whig party is extending its beggar hand for a morsel from the table of slavery democracy, and when spurned from the feast by the more deserving, it pockets the insult; when kicked on one side it turns the other, and preseveres in its importunities. The fact is, that paper comprehends the demands of the times; it understands the age and its issues; it wisely sees that slavery and freedom are the great antagonistic forces in the country, and it goes to its own side. Silver grays and hunkers all understand this. They are, therefore, rapidly sinking all other questions to nothing, compared with the increasing demands of slavery. They are collecting, arranging, and consolidating their forces for the accomplishment of their appointed work.

The keystone to the arch of this grand union of the slavery party of the United States, is the compromise of 1850. In that compromise we have all the objects of our slaveholding policy specified. It is, sir, favorable to this view of the designs of the slave power, that both the whig and the democratic party bent lower, sunk deeper, and strained harder, in their conventions, preparatory to the late presidential election, to meet the demands of the slavery party than at any previous time in their history. Never did parties come before the northern people with propositions of such undisguised contempt for the moral sentiment and the religious ideas of that people. They virtually asked them to unite in a war upon free speech, and upon conscience, and to drive the Almighty presence from the councils of the nation. Resting their platforms upon the fugitive slave bill, they

APPENDIX

boldly asked the people for political power to execute the horrible and hell-black provisions of that bill. The history of that election reveals, with great clearness, the extent to which slavery has shot its leprous distillment through the life-blood of the nation. The party most thoroughly opposed to the cause of justice and humanity, triumphed; while the party suspected of a leaning toward liberty, was overwhelmingly defeated, some say annihilated.

But here is a still more important fact, illustrating the designs of the slave power. It is a fact full of meaning, that no sooner did the democratic slavery party come into power, than a system of legislation was presented to the legislatures of the northern states, designed to put the states in harmony with the fugitive slave law, and the malignant bearing of the national government toward the colored inhabitants of the country. This whole movement on the part of the states, bears the evidence of having one origin, emanating from one head, and urged forward by one power. It was simultaneous, uniform, and general, and looked to one end. It was intended to put thorns under feet already bleeding; to crush a people already bowed down; to enslave a people already but half free; in a word, it was intended to discourage, dishearten, and drive the free colored people out of the country. In looking at the recent black law of Illinois, one is struck dumb with its enormity. It would seem that the men who enacted that law, had not only banished from their minds all sense of justice, but all sense of shame. It coolly proposes to sell the bodies and souls of the blacks to increase the intelligence and refinement of the whites; to rob every black stranger who ventures among them, to increase their literary fund.

While this is going on in the states, a pro-slavery, political board of health is established at Washington. Senators Hale, Chase, and Sumner are robbed of a part of their senatorial dignity and consequence as representing sovereign states, because they have refused to be inoculated with the slavery virus. Among the services which a senator is expected by his state to perform, are many that can only be done efficiently on committees; and, in saying to these honorable senators, you shall not serve on the committees of this body, the slavery party took the responsibility of robbing and insulting the states that sent them. It is an attempt at Washington to decide for the states who shall be sent to the senate. Sir, it strikes me that this aggression on the part of the slave power did not meet at the hands of the proscribed senators the rebuke which we had a right to expect would be administered. It seems to me that an opportunity was lost, that the great principle of senatorial equality was left undefended, at a time when its vindication was sternly demanded. But it is not to the purpose of my present statement to criticise the conduct of our friends. I am persuaded that much ought to be left to the discretion of anti slavery men in congress, and charges of recreancy should never be made but on the most sufficient grounds. For, of all the places in the world where an anti-slavery man needs the confidence and encouragement of friends, I take Washington to be that place.

Let me now call attention to the social influences which are operating and cooperating with the slavery party of the country, designed to contribute to one or all of the grand objects aimed at by that party. We see here the black man attacked in his vital interests; prejudice and hate are excited against him; enmity is stirred up between him and other laborers. The Irish people, warm-hearted, generous, and sympathizing with the oppressed everywhere, when they stand upon their own green island, are instantly taught, on arriving in this Christian country, to hate and despise the colored people. They are taught to believe that we eat the bread which of right belongs to them. The cruel lie is told the Irish, that our adversity is essential to their prosperity. Sir, the Irish-American will find out his mistake one day. He will find that in assuming our avocation he also has assumed our degradation. But for the present we are sufferers. The old employments by which we have heretofore gained our livelihood, are gradually, and it may be inevitably, passing into other hands. Every hour sees us elbowed out of some employment to make room perhaps for some newly-arrived emigrants, whose hunger and color are thought to give them a title to especial favor. White men are becoming house-servants, cooks, and stewards, common laborers, and flunkeys to our gentry, and, for aught I see, they adjust themselves to their stations with all becoming obsequiousness. This fact proves that if we cannot rise to the whites, the whites can fall to us. Now, sir, look once more. While the colored people are thus elbowed out of employment; while the enmity of emigrants is being excited against us; while state after state enacts laws against us; while we are hunted down, like wild game, and oppressed with a general feeling of insecurity—the American colonization society—that old offender against the best interests and slanderer of the colored people—awakens to new life, and vigorously presses its scheme upon the consideration of the people and the government. New papers are started—some for the north and some for the south—and each in its tone adapting itself to its latitude. Government, state and national, is called upon for appropriations to enable the society to send us out of the country by steam! They want steamers to carry letters and Negroes to Africa. Evidently, this society looks upon our "extremity as its opportunity," and we may expect that it will use the occasion well. They do not deplore, but glory, in our misfortunes.

But, sir, I must hasten. I have thus briefly given my view of one aspect of the present condition and future prospects of the colored people of the United States. And what I have said is far from encouraging to my afflicted people. I have seen the cloud gather upon the sable brows of some who hear me. I confess the case looks black enough. Sir, I am not a hopeful man. I think I am apt even to undercalculate the benefits of the future. Yet, sir, in this seemingly desperate case, I do not despair for my people. There is a bright side to almost every picture of this kind; and ours is no exception to the general rule. If the influences against us are strong, those for us are also strong. To the inquiry, will our enemies prevail in the execution of their designs. In my God and in my soul, I believe they *will not*. Let us look at the first object sought for by the slavery party of the country, viz: the suppression of anti slavery discussion. They desire to suppress discussion on this subject, with a view to the peace of the slaveholder and the security of slavery. Now, sir, neither the principle nor the subordinate objects here declared, can be at all gained by the slave power, and for this reason: It involves the proposition to padlock the lips of the whites, in order to secure the fetters on the limbs of the blacks. The right of speech, precious and priceless, *cannot, will not*, be surrendered to slavery. Its suppression is asked for, as I have said, to give peace and security to slaveholders. Sir, that thing cannot be done. God has interposed an insuperable obstacle to any such result. "There can be *no peace*, saith my God, to the wicked." Suppose it were possible to put down this discussion, what would it avail the guilty slaveholder, pillowed as he is upon heaving bosoms of ruined souls? He could not have a peaceful spirit. If every anti-slavery tongue in the nation were silent—every anti-slavery organization dissolved—every anti-slavery press demolished—every anti slavery periodical, paper, book, pamphlet, or what not, were searched out, gathered, deliberately burned to ashes, and their ashes given to the four winds of heaven, still, still the slaveholder could have *"no peace."* In every pulsation of his heart, in every throb of his life, in every glance of his eye, in the breeze that soothes, and in the thunder that startles, would be waked up an accuser, whose cause is, "Thou art, verily, guilty concerning thy brother."

APPENDIX

THE ANTI-SLAVERY MOVEMENT.
EXTRACTS FROM A LECTURE BEFORE VARIOUS ANTI-SLAVERY BODIES, IN THE WINTER OF 1855.

A grand movement on the part of mankind, in any direction, or for any purpose, moral or political, is an interesting fact, fit and proper to be studied. It is such, not only for those who eagerly participate in it, but also for those who stand aloof from it—even for those by whom it is opposed. I take the anti-slavery movement to be such an one, and a movement as sublime and glorious in its character, as it is holy and beneficent in the ends it aims to accomplish. At this moment, I deem it safe to say, it is properly engrossing more minds in this country than any other subject now before the American people. The late John C. Calhoun—one of the mightiest men that ever stood up in the American senate—did not deem it beneath him; and he probably studied it as deeply, though not as honestly, as Gerrit Smith, or William Lloyd Garrison. He evinced the greatest familiarity with the subject; and the greatest efforts of his last years in the senate had direct reference to this movement. His eagle eye watched every new development connected with it; and he was ever prompt to inform the south of every important step in its progress. He never allowed himself to make light of it; but always spoke of it and treated it as a matter of grave import; and in this he showed himself a master of the mental, moral, and religious constitution of human society. Daniel Webster, too, in the better days of his life, before he gave his assent to the fugitive slave bill, and trampled upon all his earlier and better convictions—when his eye was yet single—he clearly comprehended the nature of the elements involved in this movement; and in his own majestic eloquence, warned the south, and the country, to have a care how they attempted to put it down. He is an illustration that it is easier to give, than to take, good advice. To these two men—the greatest men to whom the nation has yet given birth—may be traced the two great facts of the present—the south triumphant, and the north humbled. Their names may stand thus—Calhoun and domination—Webster and degradation. Yet again. If to the enemies of liberty this subject is one of engrossing interest, vastly more so should it be such to freedom's friends. The latter, it leads to the gates of all valuable knowledge—philanthropic, ethical, and religious; for it brings them to the study of man, wonderfully and fearfully made—the proper study of man through all time—the open book, in which are the records of time and eternity.

Of the existence and power of the anti-slavery movement, as a fact, you need no evidence. The nation has seen its face, and felt the controlling pressure of its hand. You have seen it moving in all directions, and in all weathers, and in all places, appearing most where desired least, and pressing hardest where most resisted. No place is exempt. The quiet prayer meeting, and the stormy halls of national debate, share its presence alike. It is a common intruder, and of course has the name of being ungentlemanly. Brethren who had long sung, in the most affectionate fervor, and with the greatest sense of security,

Together let us sweetly live—together let us die,

have been suddenly and violently separated by it, and ranged in hostile attitude toward each other. The Methodist, one of the most powerful religious organizations of this country, has been rent asunder, and its strongest bolts of denominational brotherhood started at a single surge. It has changed the tone of the northern pulpit, and modified that of the press. A celebrated divine, who, four years ago, was for flinging his own mother, or brother, into the remorseless jaws of the monster slavery, lest he should swallow up the Union, now recognizes anti-slavery as a characteristic of future civilization. Signs and wonders follow this movement; and the fact just stated is one of them. Party ties are loosened by it; and men are compelled to take sides for or against it, whether they will or not. Come from where he may, or come for what he may, he is compelled to show his hand. What is this mighty force? What is its history? and what is its destiny? Is it ancient or modern, transient or permanent? Has it turned aside, like a stranger and a sojourner, to tarry for a night? or has it come to rest with us forever? Excellent chances are here for speculation; and some of them are quite profound. We might, for instance, proceed to inquire not only into the philosophy of the anti-slavery movement, but into the philosophy of the law, in obedience to which that movement started into existence. We might demand to know what is that law or power, which, at different times, disposes the minds of men to this or that particular object—now for peace, and now for war—now for free dom, and now for slavery; but this profound question I leave to the abolitionists of the superior class to answer. The speculations which must precede such answer, would afford, perhaps, about the same satisfaction as the learned theories which have rained down upon the world, from time to time, as to the origin of evil. I shall, therefore, avoid water in which I cannot swim, and deal with anti-slavery as a fact, like any other fact in the history of mankind, capable of being described and understood, both as to its internal forces, and its external phases and relations.

[After an eloquent, a full, and highly interesting exposition of the nature, character, and history of the anti-slavery movement, from the insertion of which want of space precludes us, he concluded in the following happy manner.]

Present organizations may perish, but the cause will go on. That cause has a life, distinct and independent of the organizations patched up from time to time to carry it forward. Looked at, apart from the bones and sinews and body, it is a thing immortal. It is the very essence of justice, liberty, and love. The moral life of human society, it cannot die while conscience, honor, and humanity remain. If but one be filled with it, the cause lives. Its incarnation in any one individual man, leaves the whole world a priesthood, occupying the highest moral eminence even that of disinterested benevolence. Whoso has ascended his height, and has the grace to stand there, has the world at his feet, and is the world's teacher, as of divine right. He may set in judgment on the age, upon the civilization of the age, and upon the religion of the age; for he has a test, a sure and certain test, by which to try all institutions, and to measure all men. I say, he may do this, but this is not the chief business for which he is qualified. The great work to which he is called is not that of judgment. Like the Prince of Peace, he may say, if I judge, I judge righteous judgment; still mainly, like him, he may say, this is not his work. The man who has thoroughly embraced the principles of justice, love, and liberty, like the true preacher of Christianity, is less anxious to reproach the world of its sins, than to win it to repentance. His great work on earth is to exemplify, and to illustrate, and to ingraft those principles upon the living and practical understandings of all men within the reach of his influence. This is his work; long or short his years, many or few his adherents, powerful or weak his instrumentalities, through good report, or through bad report, this is his work. It is to snatch from the bosom of nature the latent facts of each individual man's experience, and with steady hand to hold them up fresh and glowing, enforcing, with all his power, their acknowledgment and practical adoption. If there be but *one* such man in the land, no matter what becomes of abolition societies and parties, there will be an anti-slavery cause, and an anti-slavery movement. Fortunately for that cause, and fortunately for him by whom it is espoused, it requires no extraordinary amount of talent to preach it or to receive it when preached. The grand secret of its power is, that each of its principles is easily rendered appreciable to the faculty of reason in man, and that the most unenlightened conscience has no difficulty in deciding on which side to register its testimony. It can call its preachers from among the fishermen, and raise them to power. In every human breast, it has an advocate which can be silent only when the heart is dead. It comes home to every man's understanding, and appeals directly to every man's conscience. A man that does not recognize and approve for himself the rights and privileges contended for, in behalf of the American slave, has not yet been found. In whatever else men may differ, they are alike in the apprehension of their natural and personal rights. The difference between abolitionists and those by whom they are opposed, is not as to principles. All are agreed in respect to these. The manner of applying them is the point of difference.

The slaveholder himself, the daily robber of his equal brother, discourses eloquently as to the excellency of justice, and the man who employs a brutal driver to flay the flesh of his negroes, is not offended when kindness and humanity are commended. Every time the abolitionist speaks of justice, the anti-abolitionist assents says, yes, I wish the world were filled with a disposition to render to every man what is rightfully due him; I should then get what is due me. That's right; let us have justice. By all means, let us have justice. Every time the abolitionist speaks in honor of human liberty, he touches a chord in the heart of the anti-abolitionist, which responds in harmonious vibrations. Liberty—yes, that is evidently my right, and let him beware who attempts to invade or abridge that right. Every time he speaks of love, of human brotherhood, and the reciprocal duties of man and man, the anti-abolitionist assents—says, yes, all right—all true—we cannot have such ideas too often, or too fully expressed. So he says, and so he feels, and only shows thereby that he is a man as well as

APPENDIX

an anti-abolitionist. You have only to keep out of sight the manner of applying your principles, to get them endorsed every time. Contemplating himself, he sees truth with absolute clearness and distinctness. He only blunders when asked to lose sight of himself. In his own cause he can beat a Boston lawyer, but he is dumb when asked to plead the cause of others. He knows very well whatsoever he would have done unto himself, but is quite in doubt as to having the same thing done unto others. It is just here, that lions spring up in the path of duty, and the battle once fought in heaven is refought on the earth. So it is, so hath it ever been, and so must it ever be, when the claims of justice and mercy make their demand at the door of human selfishness. Nevertheless, there is that within which ever pleads for the right and the just.

In conclusion, I have taken a sober view of the present anti-slavery movement. I am sober, but not hopeless. There is no denying, for it is everywhere admitted, that the anti-slavery question is the great moral and social question now before the American people. A state of things has gradually been developed, by which that question has become the first thing in order. It must be met. Herein is my hope. The great idea of impartial liberty is now fairly before the American people. Anti-slavery is no longer a thing to be prevented. The time for prevention is past. This is great gain. When the movement was younger and weaker—when it wrought in a Boston garret to human apprehension, it might have been silently put out of the way. Things are different now. It has grown too large—its friends are too numerous—its facilities too abundant—its ramifications too extended—its power too omnipotent, to be snuffed out by the contingencies of infancy. A thousand strong men might be struck down, and its ranks still be invincible. One flash from the heart-supplied intellect of Harriet Beecher Stowe could light a million camp fires in front of the embattled host of slavery, which not all the waters of the Mississippi, mingled as they are with blood, could extinguish. The present will be looked to by after coming generations, as the age of anti-slavery literature—when supply on the gallop could not keep pace with the ever growing demand—when a picture of a Negro on the cover was a help to the sale of a book—when conservative lyceums and other American literary associations began first to select their orators for distinguished occasions from the ranks of the previously despised abolitionists. If the anti-slavery movement shall fail now, it will not be from outward opposition, but from inward decay. Its auxiliaries are everywhere. Scholars, authors, orators, poets, and statesmen give it their aid. The most brilliant of American poets volunteer in its service. Whittier speaks in burning verse to more than thirty thousand, in the National Era. Your own Longfellow whispers, in every hour of trial and disappointment, "labor and wait." James Russell Lowell is reminding us that "men are more than institutions." Pierpont cheers the heart of the pilgrim in search of liberty, by singing the praises of "the north star." Bryant, too, is with us; and though chained to the car of party, and dragged on amidst a whirl of political excitement, he snatches a moment for letting drop a smiling verse of sympathy for the man in chains. The poets are with us. It would seem almost absurd to say it, considering the use that has been made of them, that we have allies in the Ethiopian songs; those songs that constitute our national music, and without which we have no national music. They are heart songs, and the finest feelings of human nature are expressed in them. "Lucy Neal," "Old Kentucky Home," and "Uncle Ned," can make the heart sad as well as merry, and can call forth a tear as well as a smile. They awaken the sympathies for the slave, in which antislavery principles take root, grow, and flourish. In addition to authors, poets, and scholars at home, the moral sense of the civilized world is with us. England, France, and Germany, the three great lights of modern civilization, are with us, and every American traveler learns to regret the existence of slavery in his country. The growth of intelligence, the influence of commerce, steam, wind, and lightning are our allies. It would be easy to amplify this summary, and to swell the vast conglomeration of our material forces; but there is a deeper and truer method of measuring the power of our cause, and of comprehending its vitality. This is to be found in its accordance with the best elements of human nature. It is beyond the power of slavery to annihilate affinities recognized and established by the Almighty. The slave is bound to mankind by the powerful and inextricable net-work of human brotherhood. His voice is the voice of a man, and his cry is the cry of a man in distress, and man must cease to be man before he can become insensible to that cry. It is the righteous of the cause—the humanity of the cause—which constitutes its potency. As one genuine bankbill is worth more than a thousand counterfeits, so is one man, with right on his side, worth more than a thousand in the wrong. "One may chase a thousand, and put ten thousand to flight." It is, therefore, upon the goodness of our cause, more than upon all other auxiliaries, that we depend for its final triumph.

Another source of congratulations is the fact that, amid all the efforts made by the church, the government, and the people at large, to stay the onward progress of this movement, its course has been onward, steady, straight, unshaken, and unchecked from the beginning. Slavery has gained victories large and numerous; but never as against this movement—against a temporizing policy, and against northern timidity, the slave power has been victorious; but against the spread and prevalence in the country, of a spirit of resistance to its aggression, and of sentiments favorable to its entire overthrow, it has yet accomplished nothing. Every measure, yet devised and executed, having for its object the suppression of anti-slavery, has been as idle and fruitless as pouring oil to extinguish fire. A general rejoicing took place on the passage of "the compromise measures" of 1850. Those measures were called peace measures, and were afterward termed by both the great parties of the country, as well as by leading statesmen, a final settlement of the whole question of slavery; but experience has laughed to scorn the wisdom of pro-slavery statesmen; and their final settlement of agitation seems to be the final revival, on a broader and grander scale than ever before, of the question which they vainly attempted to suppress forever. The fugitive slave bill has especially been of positive service to the anti-slavery movement. It has illustrated before all the people the horrible character of slavery toward the slave, in hunting him down in a free state, and tearing him away from wife and children, thus setting its claims higher than marriage or parental claims. It has revealed the arrogant and overbearing spirit of the slave states toward the free states; despising their principles—shocking their feelings of humanity, not only by bringing before them the abominations of slavery, but by attempting to make them parties to the crime. It has called into exercise among the colored people, the hunted ones, a spirit of manly resistance well calculated to surround them with a bulwark of sympathy and respect hitherto unknown. For men are always disposed to respect and defend rights, when the victims of oppression stand up manfully for themselves.

There is another element of power added to the anti-slavery movement, of great importance; it is the conviction, becoming every day more general and universal, that slavery must be abolished at the south, or it will demoralize and destroy liberty at the north. It is the nature of slavery to beget a state of things all around it favorable to its own continuance. This fact, connected with the system of bondage, is beginning to be more fully realized. The slave-holder is not satisfied to associate with men in the church or in the state, unless he can thereby stain them with the blood of his slaves. To be a slave-holder is to be a propagandist from necessity; for slavery can only live by keeping down the under-growth morality which nature supplies. Every new-born white babe comes armed from the Eternal presence, to make war on slavery. The heart of pity, which would melt in due time over the brutal chastisements it sees inflicted on the helpless, must be hardened. And this work goes on every day in the year, and every hour in the day.

What is done at home is being done also abroad here in the north. And even now the question may be asked, have we at this moment a single free state in the Union? The alarm at this point will become more general. The slave power must go on in its career of exactions. Give, give, will be its cry, till the timidity which concedes shall give place to courage, which shall resist. Such is the voice of experience, such has been the past, such is the present, and such will be that future, which, so sure as man is man, will come. Here I leave the subject; and I leave off where I began, consoling myself and congratulating the friends of freedom upon the fact that the anti-slavery cause is not a new thing under the sun; not some moral delusion which a few years' experience may dispel. It has appeared among men in all ages, and summoned its advocates from all ranks. Its foundations are laid in the deepest and holiest convictions, and from whatever soul the demon, selfishness, is expelled, there will this cause take up its abode. Old as the everlasting hills; immovable as the throne of God; and certain as the purposes of eternal power, against all hinderances, and against all delays, and despite all the mutations of human instrumentalities, it is the faith of my soul, that this anti-slavery cause will triumph.

APPENDIX

FOOTNOTES

1. Letter, Introduction to Life of Frederick Douglass, Boston, 1841.
2. One of these ladies, impelled by the same noble spirit which carried Miss Nightingale to Scutari, has devoted her time, her untiring energies, to a great extent her means, and her high literary abilities, to the advancement and support of Frederick Douglass' Paper, the only organ of the downtrodden, edited and published by one of themselves, in the United States.
3. Mr. Stephen Myers, of Albany, deserves mention as one of the most persevering among the colored editorial fraternity.
4. The German physiologists have even discovered vegetable matter—starch—in the human body. See Med. Chirurgical Rev., Oct., 1854, p. 339.
5. Mr. Wm. H. Topp, of Albany.
6. This is the same man who gave me the roots to prevent my being whipped by Mr. Covey. He was "a clever soul." We used frequently to talk about the fight with Covey, and as often as we did so, he would claim my success as the result of the roots which he gave me. This superstition is very common among the more ignorant slaves. A slave seldom dies, but that his death is attributed to trickery.
7. He was a whole-souled man, fully imbued with a love of his afflicted and hunted people, and took pleasure in being to me, as was his wont, "Eyes to the blind, and legs to the lame." This brave and devoted man suffered much from the persecutions common to all who have been prominent benefactors. He at last became blind, and needed a friend to guide him, even as he had been a guide to others. Even in his blindness, he exhibited his manly character. In search of health, he became a physician. When hope of gaining is(sic) own was gone, he had hope for others. Believing in hydropathy, he established, at Northampton, Massachusetts, a large "Water Cure," and became one of the most successful of all engaged in that mode of treatment.
8. The following is a copy of these curious papers, both of my transfer from Thomas to Hugh Auld, and from Hugh to myself:

    "Know all men by these Presents, That I, Thomas Auld, of Talbot county, and state of Maryland, for and in consideration of the sum of one hundred dollars, current money, to me paid by Hugh Auld, of the city of Baltimore, in the said state, at and before the sealing and delivery of these presents, the receipt whereof, I, the said Thomas Auld, do hereby acknowledge, have granted, bargained, and sold, and by these presents do grant, bargain, and sell unto the said Hugh Auld, his executors, administrators, and assigns, ONE NEGRO MAN, by the name of FREDERICK BAILY, or DOUGLASS, as he callls(sic) himself—he is now about twenty-eight years of age—to have and to hold the said negro man for life. And I, the said Thomas Auld, for myself my heirs, executors, and administrators, all and singular, the said FREDERICK BAILY alias DOUGLASS, unto the said Hugh Auld, his executors, administrators, and assigns against me, the said Thomas Auld, my executors, and administrators, and against ali and every other person or persons whatsoever, shall and will warrant and forever defend by these presents. In witness whereof, I set my hand and seal, this thirteenth day of November, eighteen hundred and forty-six.

    THOMAS AULD
    "Signed, sealed, and delivered in presence of Wrightson Jones.
    "JOHN C. LEAS.
    The authenticity of this bill of sale is attested by N. Harrington, a justice of the peace of the state of Maryland, and for the county of Talbot, dated same day as above.

    "To all whom it may concern: Be it known, that I, Hugh Auld, of the city of Baltimore, in Baltimore county, in the state of Maryland, for divers good causes and considerations, me thereunto moving, have released from slavery, liberated, manumitted, and set free, and by these presents do hereby release from slavery, liberate, manumit, and set free, MY NEGRO MAN, named FREDERICK BAILY, otherwise called DOUGLASS, being of the age of twenty-eight years, or thereabouts, and able to work and gain a sufficient livelihood and maintenance; and him the said negro man named FREDERICK BAILY, otherwise called FREDERICK DOUGLASS, I do declare to be henceforth free, manumitted, and discharged from all manner of servitude to me, my executors, and administrators forever.

"In witness whereof, I, the said Hugh Auld, have hereunto set my hand and seal the fifth of December, in the year one thousand eight hundred and forty-six.
Hugh Auld
"Sealed and delivered in presence of T. Hanson Belt.
"JAMES N. S. T. WRIGHT"

9   See Appendix to this volume, page 317.
10 Mr. Douglass' published speeches alone, would fill two volumes of the size of this. Our space will only permit the insertion of the extracts which follow; and which, for originality of thought, beauty and force of expression, and for impassioned, indignatory eloquence, have seldom been equaled.
11 It is not often that chattels address their owners. The following letter is unique; and probably the only specimen of the kind extant. It was written while in England.

Printed in Great Britain
by Amazon

The 2006 Go-Ahead Bus Handbook

British Bus Publishing

Body codes used in the Bus Handbook series:

Type:
A	Articulated vehicle
B	Bus, either single-deck or double-deck
BC	Interurban - high-back seated buses and high-capacity school transport 3+2 seated vehicles.
C	Coach
M	Minibus with design capacity of sixteen seats or less
N	Low-floor bus (*Niederflur*), either single-deck or double-deck
O	Open-top bus (CO = convertible; PO = partial open-top)

Seating capacity is then shown. For double-decks the upper deck capacity is followed by the lower deck.

Door position:
C	Centre entrance/exit
D	Dual doorway.
F	Front entrance/exit
R	Rear entrance/exit (no distinction between doored and open)
T	Three or more access points

Equipment:
L	Lift for wheelchair	TV	Training vehicle.
M	Mail compartment	RV	Used as tow bus or engineer's vehicle.
T	Toilet	w	Vehicle is withdrawn and awaiting disposal.

e.g. - B32/28F is a double-deck bus with thirty-two seats upstairs, twenty-eight down and a front entrance/exit.
N43D is a low-floor bus with two or more doorways.

Re-registrations:
Where a vehicle has gained new index marks, the details are listed at the end of each fleet showing the current mark, followed in sequence by those previously carried starting with the original mark. Marks carried more than once are not always repeated.

Regional books in the series:
The Scottish Bus Handbook
The Ireland & Islands Bus Handbook
The North East Bus Handbook
The Yorkshire Bus Handbook
The North West Bus Handbook
The East Midlands Bus Handbook
The West Midlands Bus Handbook
The Welsh Bus Handbook
The Eastern Bus Handbook
The London Bus Handbook
The South East Bus Handbook
The South West Bus Handbook

Annual books are produced for the major groups:
The Stagecoach Bus Handbook
The Go-Ahead Bus Handbook
The First Bus Handbook
The Arriva Bus Handbook
The National Express Handbook (bi-annual)
Most editions for earlier years are available direct from the publisher.

Associated series:
The Hong Kong Bus Handbook
The Malta Bus Handbook
The Leyland Lynx Handbook
The Postbus Handbook
The Mailvan Handbook
The Overall Advertisement Bus Handbook - Volume 1
The Toy & Model Bus Handbook - Volume 1 - Early Diecasts
The Fire Brigade Handbook (fleet list of each local authority fire brigade)
The Police Range Rover Handbook

Some earlier editions of these books are still available. Please contact the publisher on 01952 255669.

The 2006-07 Go-Ahead Bus Handbook

The 2006-07 Go-Ahead Bus Handbook is the third edition of this volume dedicated to the bus operations of the group. The Bus Handbook series is published by *British Bus Publishing*, an independent publisher of quality books for the industry and bus enthusiasts. Further information on these may be obtained from the address below.

Although this book has been produced with the encouragement of, and in co-operation with, Go-Ahead management, it is not an official fleet list and the vehicles included are subject to variation, particularly as the vehicle investment programme continues. Some vehicles listed are no longer in regular use on services but are retained for special purposes. Also, out of use vehicles awaiting disposal are not all listed. The services operated and the allocation of vehicles to subsidiary companies are subject to variation at any time, although accurate at the time of going to print. The contents are correct to 1st September 2006.

To keep the fleet information up-to-date we recommend the Ian Allan publication, *Buses*, published monthly, or for more detailed information, the PSV Circle monthly news sheets.

Principal Editors: Bill Potter and David Donati.

Acknowledgments:
We are grateful to Keith Grimes, Mark Jameson, Tom Johnson, Malcolm Jones, Keith Lee, Stuart Martin, the PSV Circle and the management and officials of Go-Ahead Group and their operating companies for their kind assistance and co-operation in the compilation of this book.

The cover photographs are by Mark Lyons while the frontispiece is by Keith Lee.

ISBN 1 904875 36 X
Published by British Bus Publishing Ltd, 16 St Margaret's Drive, Wellington, Telford, TF1 3PH

Telephone: 01952 255669 - Web: www.britishbuspublishing.co.uk - e-mail: sales@britishbuspublishing.co.uk
© British Bus Publishing Ltd, September 2006

Contents

History	5
Go North East	9
Diamond	23
Oxford Bus Company	29
Go-Ahead London	34
Metrobus	52
Brighton & Hove	60
Go South Coast	66
Meteor	81
Aviance	84
Vehicle Index	85

Pictured in Effra Road, Brixton, is PDL50, PN03UMK, a TransBus President-bodied Trident and one of the last of this body type to be built. London Central was purchased by the Go-Ahead Group upon privatisation in the autumn of 1994. *Mark Lyons*

A brief history of "Northern"

At the outset of the third millennium, the Go-Ahead Group buses that run out of the garages at Chester-le-Street are branded Go Northern. In an era of rapid change, this is a small touch of respect to the antecedents of the group. Those antecedents were in their time just as capable of responding to change as today's business. For that reason, the Northern name continues to carry, within the public transport industry, the resonance of enterprise and quality.

Northern's origins however, lie in nineteenth century tramcars. A group founded in 1896, known as British Electric Traction (BET), had established operations nationwide. Pre-existing concerns at Tynemouth and Gateshead, both dating back to 1883, were purchased and BET interests in the North East then grew further. In November 1913, the Northern General Transport Co. Ltd. was created to oversee all these operations.

The first stage in the process of evolution was the transition from tram to bus. A start was made soon after Northern's foundation, when Gateshead's first bus route which ran from Low Fell to Chester-le-Street and had also started in 1913 was transferred to Northern. After the First World War, Northern's activities boomed. It would take until 1951 before the last tram in Gateshead ran, but all the while it was buses that represented the future. So the balance swung to innovation and Northern went further than many of its competitors between the wars.

Northern had a works in Bensham and had been building its own bus bodies, then in 1933, started building its own buses. With low railway bridges in the area, the company wanted the best engineering and the largest capacity a single deck vehicle could deliver, which resulted in Northern undertaking the job itself. These vehicles, which existed in some number, marked Northern out for the next two decades and an example is now in safekeeping with the Northern Omnibus Trust. Vehicle innovation would continue to be a tradition at Northern, but in the meantime a threat appeared.

Around the late 1940s, it looked as if the company would be nationalized. The company and its BET parent ran an aggressive campaign to remain private and that threat receded, although, ultimately the company would be nationalized, but not until 1968. In the meantime, in order to obtain the best vehicles for its passengers, the company notched up another first. In London, the AEC Routemaster was being built for London Transport and Northern, determined to have what was best, bought 51 examples, one of which is still retained by a former Go-Ahead director. Until recently, many of the remaining Routemasters in London were operated by Go-Ahead's London Central and London General companies, although across the capital these have been replaced with modern low-floor vehicles.

At first, nationalization in 1968 did not seem to have much effect, although that changed in the 1970s. The Gateshead, Tyneside, Tynemouth, Sunderland District and Venture subsidiaries were eventually to disappear from the road, but in a prescient move, not wound up. Many of the vehicles were painted in National Bus Company red, while some carried yellow, because they operated in the area of the Tyne and Wear Passenger Transport Executive. This important planning authority remains a valued partner in the provision under its Nexus public face.

In the late 1970s, the pace of the industry might have appeared to have become staid, with passenger numbers falling, the private car seeming to be well in the ascendancy and innovation in public transport was centred on the North East's new Tyne and Wear Metro. Despite this, Northern continued to be profitable and it was soon to face the need for further evolution. The National Bus Company was to be dismembered and Northern's own management had great confidence that from this trauma, they could create a very healthy business. On the 7th May 1987, Northern re-entered the private sector, owned by its own senior management. The company had already branded itself Go-Ahead Northern and that become the motto.

The list of changes and innovations since privatization could fill a book in itself. The public noted that the dormant subsidiaries reappeared in one shape or another. Private ownership brought in many new buses and at the same time, the Gateshead MetroCentre was opened.

The company was asked to manage the new bus station there and a totally new bus service was created, including a special service to Gateshead that was known as the X66 Supershuttle. This one service deserves its place in the story, not just because the best buses were used on it, with stylish DAF Optare Deltas appearing in 1989, but also because its existence influenced the latest stage in the Northern saga - the group expanding away from North East England. What had twice been the child of a national parent in the BET and NBC groups was becoming a national group in its own right. One consequence was that the Northern brand was restricted to a company based at the two original garages of Northern at Chester-le-Street and Stanley. Another result was to re-name Go-Ahead Northern as the Go-Ahead Group for stock market flotation in 1994.

In a further move, one of the North East's oldest, largest and most respected independent bus company's was purchased in March 1995, adding 225 vehicles. This was OK Motor Services of Bishop Auckland, which had roots dating back to 1912. A development in 1997 addressed the issue of image, with the successful blue, red and yellow colours of the MetroCentre Supershuttle operation being taken as the basis of the new livery for the North Eastern operations. What was the powerful Northern General member of the National Bus Company twenty years ago, is now the more powerful Go-Ahead Group, with, in the North East, the strongly and similarly branded Go Northern, Go Gateshead and Go Wear Buses local operations.

It is the bus and its livery that the passenger sees and in recent times, a move to increase comfort levels has become apparent too. The new trend in design is the low floor bus, which offers vastly improved access for elderly passengers and parents shepherding children. Once again, with links that re-invent the past, the group has been quick to embrace new technology. London put the first of the new low-floor buses into service in 1993 and Go North East followed suit in 1994 with five Wright Pathfinder bodied Dennis Lance SLF single-deckers on dedicated routes on North Tyneside and it now runs one of the UK's largest low-floor bus fleets.

The tale started at the Northern heartlands of Chester-le-Street and Stanley, but needs to end far from the North East. Of the twelve key bus-operating companies in 2006, nine are based in London and the south of England, while there is also a substantial presence in the West Midlands. Privatization of London Transport Buses brought London Central and London General into the fold. Seven more bus companies are in the group: Brighton and Hove, the Oxford Bus Company, Metrobus, Southern Vectis, Solent Blue Line, Wilts & Dorset and more recently, the Birmingham Coach Company. All play a leading role in their

Metrobus introduced *Fastway* services in 2003 following a prestigious Gatwick Direct service that started in May 2000. The new network covers the Gatwick and Crawley areas. Integral Scania OmniCity 535, YN03WPR, carries the *Fastway* livery. *Mark Lyons*

areas and are able to demonstrate the group's technical prowess. The Oxford Bus Company, under Go-Ahead ownership, was the first in Britain to fit buses with particulate traps and other equipment that have reduced certain emissions by ninety per cent and the whole of Go-Ahead's bus fleet now runs on ultra-low sulphur diesel.

Rail privatization presented another opportunity to the group, with two franchises, Thameslink and Thames Trains being gained in 1996/1997 and both benefited from modern rolling stock. Thameslink, running between Bedford and Brighton was strategically placed to benefit from the one national rail connection available across the centre of London, with a fleet of over seventy trains consisting of approximately three hundred carriages, carrying over 110,000 passengers on a normal weekday. Around eleven million train kilometres are covered each year and over forty million passenger journeys made. The Thames Trains franchise expired in April 2004 and a short-term two-year franchise was awarded to First Group pending the merger of Thames and the Great Western franchises in 2006.

In 2001, Go-Ahead took over the operation of the remainder of the South Central rail franchise from Connex. A new franchise was signed in 2003, to run until 2009, and the company was rebranded as 'Southern' in 2004. Southern operates a passenger rail service connecting London, Surrey, Sussex and parts of Kent and Hampshire. Southern operates 160 stations, as well as serving many more owned by other train-operating companies. Carrying nearly 120 million passengers each year, Southern's trains travel twenty-seven million kilometres annually and the company has headquarters in Croydon, employing nearly 3,500 people.

Through the acquisition of the Southern franchise, Go-Ahead has been able to strengthen its position within its key marketplace, the South East commuter network. The partnership with French operator Keolis, under the name GOVIA, has enabled the Group to combine technical, commercial and financial skills. Pictured in Southern colours is one of the class 170 units.

Development of the group has not stopped at bus and rail services and in 1998 the aviation services company GHI joined the group. Now merged with other Go-Ahead aviation acquisitions, the rebranded 'Aviance' operates at seventeen airports in Britain and Ireland and handles forty-five million passenger journeys per annum. Providing a wide range of ground support services to airlines, Aviance is also a member of an international trade alliance of the same name. In addition, 2004 saw Go-Ahead expand its interests in aviation by acquiring the remaining fifty per cent of Plane Handling, an aviation cargo handling company operating at Heathrow, Manchester and Glasgow airports. Plane Handling was previously under the joint ownership of Go-Ahead and Virgin Aviation.

Go-Ahead has also expanded into the parking services sector with the acquisition of Meteor Parking in 2002. Meteor is now the UK's second largest off-street parking operator by turnover, with clients including BAA, retail centres and hospitals, as well as managing station parking for Go-Ahead's rail franchises. Meteor also incorporates a sub-division called Meteor Security, which offers services including security guarding, rail supervision and remote monitoring. The acquisition of Meteor affords Go-Ahead the opportunity to truly integrate public transport services with the private car.

This very abbreviated narrative only summarizes a fascinating tale. Therein, the themes of evolution in the face of new circumstances and a commitment to technological excellence in the cause of customer satisfaction have consistently marked the old and the new 'Northern' in a tradition lasting well over a lifetime.

GO NORTH EAST

Go Northern - Go Wear Buses - Go Gateshead

Go North East, 117 Queen Street, Bensham, Gateshead, NE8 2UA

Go North East's history can be traced back to 1883 with steam trams in Gateshead, through to a management buyout of Go-Ahead Northern in 1987, that became the birthplace of what has become the Go-Ahead Group plc. Now the largest bus operator in the North East of England and largest public transport provider in Tyne & Wear, Go North East's focus is firmly on the future.

Since pioneering the introduction of low-floor buses on North Tyneside in 1994, with the introduction of five Wright Pathfinder bodied Dennis Lance SLF single-deckers, that were the first to be used outside of London, Go North East's commitment to providing modern, accessible services has led to the point where 75% of the local bus service vehicle requirements is provided by high specification kneeling buses, with powered ramps.

In 2001, the company introduced the first, high specification, Scania articulated buses to the X66 MetroCentre Shuttle and in 2005, a batch of Wright Gemini bodied Volvo B7TL low-floor double-deckers were bought for exclusive use on the Tyne-Tees express X10 between Newcastle and Middlesbrough.

Go North East has remained committed to combining integration and choice for its customers, by helping to maintain the fully integrated Network Ticketing scheme, supporting further integration through the concessionary fares schemes in Tyne & Wear and County Durham, while also introducing bus to bus transfer tickets. At the same time, it has grown its own brand *Go 'n 'Save* tickets and developed a travel club with membership of over 10,000.

Bus services serving Metro stations are greater in number than before 1986 and Go North East is a member of the North East Travel Information Service partnership (NETIS), which provides the Traveline integrated information service. Go North East's unique Easy Access Guarantee and its commitment to customer service, involvement of passengers and

Optare's double-deck design is the Spectra, built on the DAF, later VDL Bus, DB250 chassis. Pictured in Newcastle while en route to Whitley Bay is 3848, K316FYG.
Keith Lee

In 2001 four Scania L94UA articulated buses joined the Go North East fleet for use on route X66 that links the Metro Centre with Gateshead. These feature the Wrightbus Solar Fusion body as shown by 4952, NK51OLU.
Phillip Stephenson

the community, have all been recognized through awards such as the first Bus Industry Award for Accessibility, a Daily Telegraph/Energis Customer Service Award, being 'highly commended' in the Bus Operator of the Year and the Innovation categories of the Bus Industry Awards, also nominations from partners Nexus and Gateshead Council for Local Authority Public Transport Awards.

Changes in 2006 saw the closure of Bishop Auckland depot that had been acquired with the OK Motor Services business in 1995 and the transfer of most local routes to Arriva, although some routes, including the prestigious service 724 between Bishop Auckland and Newcastle was retained and received an allocation of four brand new, low-floor Wright Gemini bodied Volvo B7TL double-deckers.

The Go North East brand is supported by the instantly recognisable blue, red and yellow livery on the buses of its three operating divisions: Go Gateshead, Go Northern and Go Wear Buses, providing services mostly in Tyne and Wear and County Durham, but with some services extending to Hartlepool, Bishop Auckland and Middlesborough in the south, also Blyth and Cramlington in the north. New marketing initiatives, introduced during the summer of 2006, have seen the introduction of improved services, bespoke route branding and buses carrying dedicated liveries for the services being operated.

A major order for new buses has just been placed and Go North East aims to be 100% low-floor on all mainstream services before the end of 2007.

448-469			Optare Solo M850		Optare		N25F	1998	
448	NT	S248KNL	454	SY	S254KNL	460	NT	T460BCN	465	NT	T465BCN
449	NT	S249KNL	455	SY	S255KNL	461	SY	T461BCN	466	NT	T466BCN
450	NT	S250KNL	456	NT	T456BCN	462	SY	T462BCN	467	NT	T467BCN
451	NT	S251KNL	457	NT	T457BCN	463	NT	T463BCN	468	NT	T468BCN
452	SY	S252KNL	458	NT	T458BCN	464	NT	T464BCN	469	NT	T469BCN
453	SY	S253KNL	459	NT	T459BCN						

Seventy-four Mini Pointer Darts are operated by Go North East. Pictured in the recently introduced *Black Cats* branding is 550, NK53TKE, seen at Sunderland Interchange. Pictured with the *Black Cats* operate services 26 and 36 between Pennywell, Sunderland city centre and Town End Farm. *Keith Lee*

501-522   Dennis Dart SLF 8.8m   Plaxton Pointer MPD   N25F   2000-01

501	SD	X501WRG	507	WN	X507WRG	513	SD	X513WRG	518	WA	NK51MJY
502	SD	X502WRG	508	WN	X508WRG	514	NT	X514WRG	519	SD	NK51MKA
503	SD	X503WRG	509	SD	X509WRG	515	SD	NK51MJU	520	WA	NK51MKC
504	WN	X504WRG	510	SD	X551FBB	516	SD	NK51MJV	521	WA	NK51MKD
505	WN	X595FBB	511	SD	X511WRG	517	WA	NK51MJX	522	SD	NK51MKE
506	WN	X506WRG	512	SD	X512WRG						

523-548   TransBus Dart 8.8m   TransBus Mini Pointer   N25F   2002

523	WA	NA52AWF	530	WA	NA52AWP	537	WN	NA52AWZ	543	WN	NA52AXH
524	WA	NA52AWG	531	WA	NA52AWR	538	WN	NA52AXB	544	SD	NA52AXJ
525	WA	NA52AWH	532	WA	NA52AWU	539	WN	NA52AXC	545	SD	NA52AXK
526	WA	NA52AWJ	533	WA	NA52AWV	540	WN	NA52AXD	546	SD	NA52AXM
527	WA	NA52AWM	534	WA	NA52AWW	541	WN	NA52AXF	547	SD	NA52AXN
528	WA	NA52AWN	535	WA	NA52AWX	542	WN	NA52AXG	548	SD	NA52AXO
529	WA	NA52AWO	536	WA	NA52AWY						

549-574   TransBus Dart 8.8m   TransBus Mini Pointer   N29F   2003

549	SD	NK53TKD	556	SD	NK53TKU	563	WA	NK53TLN	569	WA	NK53TMO
550	SD	NK53TKE	557	SD	NK53TKV	564	WA	NK53TLO	570	WA	NK53TMU
551	SD	NK53TKF	558	SD	NK53TKX	565	WA	NK53TLU	571	CR	NK53TMV
552	SD	NK53TKJ	559	SD	NK53TKY	566	WA	NK53TLV	572	CR	NK53TMX
553	SD	NK53TKN	560	SD	NK53TKZ	567	WA	NK53TLX	573	CR	NK53TMY
554	SD	NK53TKO	561	SD	NK53TLF	568	WA	NK53TLY	574	CR	NK53TMZ
555	SD	NK53TKT	562	SD	NK53TLJ						

575-585   Dennis Dart SLF 8.8m   Marshall Capital   N28F   1999   Go-Ahead London, 2004

575	CR	T101KGP	578	CR	T104KGP	581	SD	T272RMV	584	SD	T114KGP
576	CR	T102KGP	579	CR	T105KGP	582	SD	T112KGP	585	SD	T115KGP
577	CR	T103KGP	580	SD	T110KGP	583	SD	T113KGP			

586-598   Dennis Dart SLF 9.9m   Marshall Capital   N30F   1999   Go-Ahead London, 2004

586	SY	T407AGP	590	SY	T421AGP	593	SY	T424AGP	596	SY	T427AGP
587	SY	T409AGP	591	SY	T422AGP	594	SY	T425AGP	597	SY	T428AGP
588	SY	T413AGP	592	SY	T423AGP	595	SY	T426AGP	598	SD	T429AGP
589	SY	T416AGP									

599-602

				Optare Solo M850			Optare			N25F	2004		
599	WN	NK54DEU		600	WN	NK54DFA	601	WN	NK54DFC	602	WN	NK54DFD	

603-606

				ADL Dart 8.8m			ADL Mini Pointer			N29F	2004		
603	SD	NK54NTX		604	SD	NK54NTY	605	SD	NK54NUA	606	SD	NK54NUB	

3676	u	G675TCN	Leyland Olympian ONCL10/1RZ	Alexander RH		B45/29F	1989		
3677	u	G677TCN	Leyland Olympian ONCL10/1RZ	Alexander RH		B45/29F	1989		
3801	CR	V801EBR	Dennis Trident	East Lancs Lolyne		N47/30F	2000		
3802	CR	V802EBR	Dennis Trident	East Lancs Lolyne		N47/30F	2000		
3803	NT	V803EBR	Dennis Trident	East Lancs Lolyne		N47/30F	2000		
3804	NT	V804EBR	Dennis Trident	East Lancs Lolyne		N47/30F	2000		
3806	SY	F106UEF	Leyland Olympian ONCL10/2R	Northern Counties Palatine		B47/35F	1989	OK Travel, 1995	
3807	CR	F107UEF	Leyland Olympian ONCL10/2R	Northern Counties Palatine		B47/35F	1989	OK Travel, 1995	
3808	CR	K108YVN	Leyland Olympian ON2R56C16Z4	Northern Counties Palatine		B47/35F	1992	OK Travel, 1995	
3809	CR	K109YVN	Leyland Olympian ON2R56C16Z4	Northern Counties Palatine		B47/35F	1992	OK Travel, 1995	
3810	CR	K110YVN	Leyland Olympian ON2R56C16Z4	Northern Counties Palatine		B47/35F	1992	OK Travel, 1995	

3811-3833

Volvo Olympian — Northern Counties Palatine II — B47/30F — 1998

3811	SY	S811FVK	3817	WA	S817FVK	3823	WA	S823OFT	3829	WA	S829OFT
3812	SY	S812FVK	3818	WA	S818OFT	3824	WA	S824OFT	3830	WA	S830OFT
3813	SY	S813FVK	3819	WA	S819OFT	3825	WA	S825OFT	3831	WA	S831OFT
3814	SY	S814FVK	3820	WA	S820OFT	3826	G	S826OFT	3832	NT	S832OFT
3815	SY	S815FVK	3821	WA	S821OFT	3827	G	S827OFT	3833	NT	S833OFT
3816	SY	S816FVK	3822	WA	S822OFT	3828	G	S828OFT			

3834-3857

DAF DB250 — Optare Spectra — B44/27F — 1992-93 — London Central, 2000

3834	CR	K301FYG	3840	NT	K308FYG	3847	NT	K315FYG	3853	CR	K321FYG
3835	CR	K303FYG	3841	NT	K309FYG	3848	NT	K316FYG	3854	NT	K322FYG
3836	CR	K304FYG	3842	NT	K310FYG	3849	NT	K317FYG	3855	NT	K323FYG
3837	NT	K305FYG	3843	NT	K311FYG	3850	CR	K125PGO	3856	NT	K324FYG
3838	NT	K306FYG	3844	NT	K312FYG	3851	CR	K124PGO	3857	CR	K159PGO
3839	NT	K307FYG	3845	NT	K313FYG	3852	CR	K160PGO			

3858-3880

Dennis Trident — East Lancs Lolyne — N47/30F — 2000

3858	NT	V858EGR	3864	NT	W864PNL	3870	WN	W174SCU	3876	CR	W186SCU
3859	NT	W859PNL	3865	NT	W865PNL	3871	WN	W181SCU	3877	CR	W187SCU
3860	NT	W806PNL	3866	NT	W866PNL	3872	WN	W182SCU	3878	CR	W188SCU
3861	NT	W861PNL	3867	NT	W177SCU	3873	WN	W183SCU	3879	CR	W189SCU
3862	NT	W862PNL	3868	NT	W178SCU	3874	WN	W184SCU	3880	CR	W176SCU
3863	NT	W863PNL	3869	WN	W179SCU	3875	CR	W185SCU			

3881-3895

Dennis Trident — Plaxton President — N47/28F — 2001

3881	CR	NK51UCH	3885	CR	NK51UCN	3889	NT	NK51UCS	3893	CR	NK51UCW
3882	CR	NK51UCJ	3886	CR	NK51UCO	3890	NT	NK51UCT	3894	CR	NK51UCX
3883	CR	NK51UCL	3887	CR	NK51UCP	3891	NT	NK51UCU	3895	CR	NK51UCY
3884	CR	NK51UCM	3888	CR	NK51UCR	3892	CR	NK51UCV			

3896-3940

Volvo Olympian — Northern Counties Palatine — B43/31F* — 1997-98 — Seating varies; London, 2002

3896	SY	R254LGH	3908	WA	R266LGH	3919	G	R567LGH	3930	SY	R389LGH
3897	SY	R255LGH	3909	CR	R267LGH	3920	SD	R558LGH	3931	SY	R390LGH
3898	SD	R256LGH	3910	WN	R553LGH	3921	SD	R559LGH	3932	SY	R391LGH
3899	SD	R257LGH	3911	WN	R269LGH	3922	SY	R281LGH	3933	G	R392LGH
3900	SD	R549LGH	3912	WN	R270LGH	3923	SY	R282LGH	3934	G	R393LGH
3901	SD	R550LGH	3913	WN	R271LGH	3924	SY	R283LGH	3935	CR	R394LGH
3902	SD	R551LGH	3914	WN	R554LGH	3925	SY	R284LGH	3936	CR	R395LGH
3903	CR	R261LGH	3915	WN	R355LGH	3926	SD	R285LGH	3937	CR	R396LGH
3904	CR	R262LGH	3916	CR	R274LGH	3927	SY	R286LGH	3938	CR	R397LGH
3905	CR	R263LGH	3917	CR	R556LGH	3928	SY	R287LGH	3939	G	R398LGH
3906	WA	R264LGH	3918	CR	R276LGH	3929	G	R288LGH	3940	G	R399LGH
3907	CR	R265LGH									

3941	G	NK05GZO	Volvo B7TL 10.1m	Wrightbus Eclipse Gemini	N41/27F	2005	
3942	G	NK05GZP	Volvo B7TL 10.1m	Wrightbus Eclipse Gemini	N41/27F	2005	
3943	G	NK05GZR	Volvo B7TL 10.1m	Wrightbus Eclipse Gemini	N41/27F	2005	
3944	SD	R469RRA	Volvo Olympian	East Lancashire Pyoneer	B49/33F	1998	City of Nottingham, 2005
3945	SD	R470RRA	Volvo Olympian	East Lancashire Pyoneer	B49/33F	1998	City of Nottingham, 2005
3946	SD	R477RRA	Volvo Olympian	East Lancashire Pyoneer	B49/33F	1998	City of Nottingham, 2005

Carrying branding for route 724, Volvo B7TL 3963, NK06JXD, is seen in Chester-le-Street while heading for Bishop Auckland. The B7TL is fitted with a Euro 3 specification engine and Volvo has advised that the new model to Euro 4 specification will be the B9TL model. *Keith Lee*

3947	u	H481PVW	Leyland Olympian ON2R50C13Z4	Alexander RH	B47/31F	1991	Isle of Man Transport, 2005
3948	u	H485PVW	Leyland Olympian ON2R50C13Z4	Alexander RH	B47/31F	1991	Isle of Man Transport, 2005
3949	SD	H589EGU	Leyland Olympian ON2R50C13Z4	Alexander RH	B47/31F	1991	Isle of Man Transport, 2005
3950	SY	G183WGX	Leyland Olympian ON2R50C13Z4	Alexander RH	B47/31F	1991	Dublin Bus, 2005
3951	SY	H551PVW	Leyland Olympian ON2R50C13Z4	Alexander RH	B47/31F	1991	Dublin Bus, 2005
3952	SY	H550PVW	Leyland Olympian ON2R50C13Z4	Alexander RH	B47/31F	1991	Dublin Bus, 2005

3953-3961			Leyland Olympian ON2R50C13Z4		Northern Counties		B47/31F	1990	Arriva London, 2006	
3953	u	G522VBB	3956	u	G529VBB	3958	SY	G549VBB	3960	u	G546VBB
3954	u	G527VBB	3957	SY	G548VBB	3959	u	G544VBB	3961	u	G545VBB
3955	SY	G528VBB									

3962-3965			Volvo B7TL 10.1m			Wrightbus Eclipse Gemini		N41/33F	2005		
3962	CR	NK06JXE	3963	CR	NK06JXD	3964	CR	NK06JXC	3965	CR	NK06JXB

4756-4761			DAF SB220			Optare Delta		B49F	1993		
4756	CR	K756SBB	4758	SY	K758SBB	4760	CR	K760SBB	4761	CR	K761SBB
4757	CR	K757SBB	4759	CR	K759SBB						

4768	WN	J110SPB	Dennis Lance 11m	Alexander PS	B50F	1992	Dennis demonstrator, 1993

4769-4773			Dennis Lance 11m			Wright Pathfinder		B40F	1994		
4769	NT	L469YVK	4771	NT	M471FJR	4772	NT	M472FJR	4773	NT	M473FJR
4770	NT	M470FJR									

4774	G	L141YTY	Dennis Lance 11m	Plaxton Verde	B49F	1994	

4775-4788			Dennis Lance 11m			Optare Sigma		B47F	1994		
4775	SD	L475CFT	4779	G	L479CFT	4783	G	L483CFT	4786	G	L486CFT
4776	WN	L476CFT	4780	G	L470YVK	4784	G	L484CFT	4787	G	L487CFT
4777	SD	L477CFT	4781	G	L481CFT	4785	G	L485CFT	4788	G	L488CFT
4778	G	L478CFT	4782	WA	L482CFT						

The 2006-07 Go-Ahead Bus Handbook

A major order for new buses has just been placed and Go North East aims to be 100% low-floor on all mainstream services before the end of 2007. Some of the early low-floor models for this fleet were six Northern Counties-bodied DAF SB220s currently allocated to Chester-le-Street. 4824, P324AFT is shown. *Phillip Stephenson*

4789-4793			DAF SB220			Optare Delta		B49F	1995		
4789	CR	M489HCU	4791	CR	M491HCU	4792	WN	M492HCU	4793	WN	M493HCU
4790	CR	M490HCU									
4805	CR	J205VHN	DAF SB220			Optare Delta		B51F	1992	OK Travel, 1995	
4809-4812			Volvo B10B-58			Alexander Strider		B51F	1994	OK Travel, 1995	
4809	WN	L209KEF	4810	WN	L210KEF	4811	WN	L211KEF	4812	WN	L212KEF
4813	SD	N813WGR	Volvo B10B			Plaxton Verde		B51F	1996		
4814	SD	N814WGR	Volvo B10B			Plaxton Verde		B51F	1996		
4815	SD	N815WGR	Volvo B10B			Plaxton Verde		B51F	1996		
4816	SD	N816WGR	Volvo B10B			Plaxton Verde		B51F	1996		
4820-4825			DAF SB220			Northern Counties Paladin		N42F	1997		
4820	CR	P320AFT	4822	CR	P322AFT	4824	CR	P324AFT	4825	CR	P325AFT
4821	CR	P321AFT	4823	CR	P323AFT						
4837-4855			Volvo B10BLE			Wright Renown		N44F	1998		
4837	G	R837PRG	4842	G	R842PRG	4847	G	R847PRG	4852	SY	R852PRG
4838	G	R838PRG	4843	SY	R843PRG	4848	SY	R848PRG	4853	SY	R853PRG
4839	G	R839PRG	4844	G	R844PRG	4849	SY	R849PRG	4854	SY	R854PRG
4840	G	340GUP	4845	G	R845PRG	4850	SY	R856PRG	4855	SY	R855PRG
4841	G	R841PRG	4846	G	R846PRG	4851	SY	R851PRG			
4862-4870			DAF SB220			Plaxton Prestige		N41F	1998		
4862	CR	S862ONL	4865	CR	S865ONL	4867	SY	S867ONL	4869	SY	S869ONL
4863	CR	S863ONL	4866	CR	S866ONL	4868	SY	S868ONL	4870	SY	S870ONL
4864	CR	S864ONL									

Pictured at Heworth Metro, having just arrived from Easington Lane is Scania 4957, NL52WVN, type L94UB. Its Wrightbus Solar body carries the new branding for Metro-Link route M1. *Keith Lee*

4875	SD	N950TVK	Volvo B10B			Alexander Strider		B51F	1995		Redby, Sunderland, 2002
4890-4895			DAF SB220			Plaxton Prestige		N41F	1999		
4890	CR	S890ONL	4892	CR	S892ONL	4894	CR	S894ONL	4895	CR	S895ONL
4891	CR	S891ONL	4893	CR	S893ONL						
4896-4925			Volvo B10BLE			Wright Renown		N44F	2000		
4896	SY	V986ETN	4904	SY	W904RBB	4912	G	X912WGR	4919	G	X919WGR
4897	SY	V987ETN	4905	SY	W905RBB	4913	G	X913WGR	4920	G	X492WGR
4898	SY	V988ETN	4906	SY	W906RBB	4914	G	X914WGR	4921	G	X921WGR
4899	SY	V989ETN	4907	SY	W907RBB	4915	G	X915WGR	4922	G	X922WGR
4900	SY	V990ETN	4908	SY	W908RBB	4916	G	X916WGR	4923	G	X923WGR
4901	SY	W901RBB	4909	SY	W909RBB	4917	G	X917WGR	4924	G	X924WGR
4902	SY	W902RBB	4910	SY	W491SCU	4918	G	X918WGR	4925	G	X935WGR
4903	SY	W903RBB	4911	SY	W411SCU						
4926-4949			Scania L94UB			Wrightbus Solar		N42F	2001		
4926	G	Y926ERG	4932	G	Y932ERG	4938	SD	NK51OKX	4945	G	NK51OLJ
4927	G	Y927ERG	4933	G	Y933ERG	4940	SD	NK51OLB	4946	G	NK51OLM
4928	G	Y928ERG	4934	G	Y934ERG	4941	SD	NK51OLC	4947	G	NK51OLN
4929	G	Y929ERG	4935	G	Y935ERG	4942	G	NK51OLE	4948	G	NK51OLO
4930	G	Y493ETN	4936	G	Y936ERG	4943	G	NK51OLG	4949	G	NK51OLP
4931	G	Y931ERG	4937	SD	NK51OKW	4944	G	NK51OLH			
4950	G	NK51OLR	Scania L94UA			Wrightbus Solar Fusion		AN56D	2001		
4951	G	NK51OLT	Scania L94UA			Wrightbus Solar Fusion		AN56D	2001		
4952	G	NK51OLU	Scania L94UA			Wrightbus Solar Fusion		AN56D	2001		
4953	G	NK51OLV	Scania L94UA			Wrightbus Solar Fusion		AN56D	2001		
4954-4966			Scania L94UB			Wrightbus Solar		N42F	2002		
4954	G	NL02ZRX	4958	WA	NL52WVO	4961	WA	NL52WVS	4964	WA	NL52WVV
4955	NT	NA02NVL	4959	WA	NL52WVP	4962	WA	NL52WVT	4965	WA	NL52WVW
4956	WA	NL52WVM	4960	WA	NL52WVR	4963	WA	NL52WVU	4966	WA	NL52WVX
4957	WA	NL52WVN									

The 2006-07 Go-Ahead Bus Handbook

Many new livery themes have been introduced during 2006, and the Scania L94s predominate. Pictured at the Gateshead Interchange is 5206, NK54NVA, which carries *fabfiftysix* colours for the high-frequency route that connects the town with Sunderland. *Keith Lee*

4967-4976			Scania L94UB		Wrightbus Solar		N42F	2004		
4967	SD	NK53UNT	4970	G	NK53UNW	4973	NT	NK53UNZ	4975	NT	NK53UOB
4968	SD	NK53UNU	4971	NT	NK53UNX	4974	NT	NK53UOA	4976	NT	NK53UOC
4969	SD	NK53UNV	4972	NT	NK53UNY						

4978-4982			Volvo B7RLE			Wrightbus Eclipse Urban		N43F	2004		
4978	SD	NK54NUH	4980	SD	NK54NUM	4981	SD	NK54NUO	4982	SD	NK54NUP
4979	SD	NK54NUJ									

4983-4988			DAF SB220			Northern Counties Paladin		N42F	1997	BAA Edinburgh, 2005
										4986 Airlinks, Heathrow
4983	SY	R971FNW	4985	SY	R975FNW	4987	SY	R982FNW	4988	SY	R983FNW
4984	SY	R972FNW	4986	SY	R979FNW						

4989	CR	YN51MKV	Scania L94UB	Wrightbus Solar	N43F	2001	Ludlows, Halesowen, 2005
4990	CR	NK51OLT	Scania L94UB	Wrightbus Solar	N43F	2001	Ludlows, Halesowen, 2005
4991	SD	YR02ZYK	Scania L94UB	Wrightbus Solar	N43F	2002	Anglian, Beccles, 2006
4992	SD	YR02ZYM	Scania L94UB	Wrightbus Solar	N43F	2002	Anglian, Beccles, 2006
4993	G	S590KJF	Volvo B10BLE	Alexander ALX300	N45F	1998	Felix, Stanley, 2006

5201-5228			Scania L94UB			Wrightbus Solar		N43F	2004		
5201	SD	NK54NUU	5208	SD	NK54NVC	5215	SD	NK54NVL	5222	CR	NK54NVV
5202	SD	NK54NUV	5209	SD	NK54NVD	5216	SD	NK54NVM	5223	CR	NK54NVW
5203	SD	NK54NUW	5210	SD	NK54NVE	5217	SD	NK54NVN	5224	CR	NK54NVX
5204	SD	NK54NUX	5211	SD	NK54NVF	5218	G	NK54NVO	5225	CR	NK54NVY
5205	SD	NK54NUY	5212	SD	NK54NVG	5219	G	NK54NVP	5226	CR	NK54NVZ
5206	SD	NK54NVA	5213	SD	NK54NVH	5220	G	NK54NVT	5227	CR	NK54NWA
5207	SD	NK54NVB	5214	SD	NK54NVJ	5221	G	NK54NVU	5228	CR	NK54NWB

5229-5233			Scania L94UB			Wrightbus Solar		N43F	2006		
5229	SD	NK55OLG	5231	SD	NK55OLJ	5232	SD	NK55OLM	5233	SD	NK55OLN
5230	SD	NK55OLH									

Go-Ahead provides several coaches for the National Express network, the latest examples being the rear-engined Volvo B12B with Plaxton Panther bodywork. Some of the older Plaxton Expressliners are now used on normal service, and 7062, GSK962, is seen here in the new *redArrows* colours applied to the vehicles on the Sunderland - Washington - Newcastle express service. *Keith Lee*

| 7058 | WA | M58LBB | Volvo B10M-60 | | Plaxton Expressliner II | | C49FT | 1995 | | |
| 7059 | WA | M59LBB | Volvo B10M-60 | | | Plaxton Expressliner II | | C49FT | 1995 | | |

7062-7079			Volvo B10M-62			Plaxton Expressliner II		C49FT	1997-98		
7062	WA	GSK962		7075	WA	YSU875	7077	CR	S977ABR	7079	CR	S979ABR
7074	WA	YSU874		7076	CR	YSU876	7078	CR	S978ABR			

7080-7085			Volvo B10M-62			Plaxton Paragon		C49FT	2001		
7080	CR	Y808MFT		7082	CR	Y782MFT	7084	CR	Y784MFT	7085	CR	Y785MFT
7081	CR	Y781MFT		7083	CR	Y783MFT						

7086	CR	JCN822	Volvo B12M		Plaxton Paragon Expressliner	C49FT	2002
7087	CR	FCU190	Volvo B12M		Plaxton Paragon Expressliner	C49FT	2002
7088	CR	524FUP	Volvo B12M		Plaxton Paragon Expressliner	C49FT	2003
7089	CR	564CPT	Volvo B12M		Plaxton Paragon Expressliner	C49FT	2003
7090	CR	CU6860	Volvo B12B		Plaxton Panther	C49FT	2004
7091	CR	CU7661	Volvo B12B		Plaxton Panther	C49FT	2004
7092	CR	K2VOY	Volvo B12B		Plaxton Panther	C49FT	2006
7093	CR	K3VOY	Volvo B12B		Plaxton Panther	C49FT	2006

8094-8109			Dennis Dart 9.8m			Marshall C37		B40F	1994		
8094	SY	M804GFT		8097	SY	M807GFT	8103	SY	M813GFT	8108	u	M818GFT
8095	G	M805GFT		8099	u	M809GFT	8105	G	M809GFT	8109	G	M819GFT
8096	SY	M806GFT		8102	G	M812GFT						

| 8110 | u | M810HCU | Dennis Dart 9.8m | | Plaxton Pointer | | B40F | 1994 | |

The 2006-07 Go-Ahead Bus Handbook

8117-8124

Dennis Dart 9.8m — Marshall C37 — B40F — 1995

8117	CR	N117WBR	8119	WA	N119WBR	8121	u	N121WBR	8123	SD	N123WBR
8118	WA	N118WBR	8120	u	N120WBR	8122	SY	N122WBR	8124	SD	N124WBR

8158-8175

Dennis Dart SLF — Plaxton Pointer SPD — N41F — 1999

8158	G	S358ONL	8163	G	S363ONL	8168	G	S368ONL	8172	G	S372ONL
8159	G	S359ONL	8164	G	S364ONL	8169	G	S369ONL	8173	G	S373ONL
8160	G	S360ONL	8165	G	S365ONL	8170	G	S370ONL	8174	G	S374ONL
8161	G	S361ONL	8166	G	S366ONL	8171	G	S371ONL	8175	G	S375ONL
8162	G	S362ONL	8167	G	S367ONL						

8186-8200

Dennis Dart SLF 8.8m — Plaxton Pointer MPD — N25F — 1999

8186	SD	V186ERG	8190	SD	V190ERG	8194	SD	V194ERG	8198	WN	V198ERG
8187	SD	V187ERG	8191	WN	V191ERG	8195	WN	V195ERG	8199	SD	V199ERG
8188	SD	V188ERG	8192	SD	V192ERG	8196	WN	V196ERG	8200	WN	V820ERG
8189	SD	V189ERG	8193	SD	V193ERG	8197	WN	V197ERG			

8201-8222

Dennis Dart SLF 11.3m — Plaxton Pointer SPD — N41F — 1999-2000

8201	NT	V201ERG	8207	NT	V207ERG	8213	SD	V213ERG	8218	SD	V218ERG
8202	NT	V202ERG	8208	NT	V208ERG	8214	G	V214ERG	8219	WN	V219ERG
8203	NT	V203ERG	8209	NT	V209ERG	8215	G	V215ERG	8220	WN	V210ERG
8204	NT	V204ERG	8210	NT	V210ERG	8216	SD	V216ERG	8221	WN	V221ERG
8205	NT	V205ERG	8211	NT	V211ERG	8217	SD	V217ERG	8222	SD	V822ERG
8206	NT	V206ERG	8212	NT	V212ERG						

8223-8241

Dennis Dart SLF 11.3m — Plaxton Pointer SPD — N41F — 2000-01

8223	WN	X223FBB	8228	WN	X228FBB	8233	NT	X233FBB	8238	NT	NK51MKM
8224	WN	X224FBB	8229	WN	X229FBB	8234	NT	NK51MKF	8239	NT	NK51MKN
8225	WN	X822FBB	8230	WN	X823FBB	8235	NT	NK51MKG	8240	NT	NK51MKO
8226	WN	X226FBB	8231	WN	X231FBB	8236	NT	NK51MKJ	8241	NT	NK51MKP
8227	WN	X227FBB	8232	WN	X232FBB	8237	NT	NK51MKL			

8242-8252

DAF SB120 — Wrightbus Cadet — N39F — 2002

8242	WN	NA52BUU	8245	WN	NA52BVB	8248	WN	NA52BVE	8251	SD	NA52BVH
8243	WN	NA52BUV	8246	WN	NA52BVC	8249	SD	NA52BVF	8252	SD	NA52BVJ
8244	WN	NA52BUW	8247	WN	NA52BVD	8250	SD	NA52BVG			

8253-8273

VDL Bus SB120 — Wrightbus Cadet — N39F — 2004

8253	SD	NK04FOP	8259	SD	NK04FPD	8264	G	NK04ZLE	8269	G	NK04NKW
8254	SD	NK04FOT	8260	SD	NK04FPE	8265	G	NK04ZND	8270	NT	NK04NKX
8255	SD	NK04FOU	8261	G	NK04ZNC	8266	G	NK04ZNE	8271	NT	NK04NKZ
8256	SD	NK04FOV	8262	G	NK04ZKY	8267	G	NK04NKT	8272	NT	NK04NLC
8257	SD	NK04FPA	8263	G	NK04ZKZ	8268	G	NK04NKU	8273	NT	NK04NLD
8258	SD	NK04FPC									

8274	SD	Y291HUA	DAF SB120	Wrightbus Cadet	N39F	2001	Teamdeck, Honley, 2005
8275	SD	Y292HUA	DAF SB120	Wrightbus Cadet	N39F	2001	Teamdeck, Honley, 2005
8276	SD	T403LGP	Dennis Dart SLF	Caetano Compass	N39F	1999	Centra, Hounslow, 2005
8277	SD	T407LGP	Dennis Dart SLF	Caetano Compass	N39F	1999	Centra, Hounslow, 2005
8278	SD	T413LGP	Dennis Dart SLF	Caetano Compass	N39F	1999	Centra, Hounslow, 2005

8279-8287

Dennis Dart SLF — Caetano Compass — N39F — 1999 — East Thames, Victoria, 2005

8279	SD	T426LGP	8282	SD	T429LGP	8284	SD	V434KGF	8286	SD	V436KGF
8280	SD	T427LGP	8283	SD	T430LGP	8285	SD	V435KGF	8287	SD	V437KGF
8281	SD	T428LGP									

8288	SY	X94FOR	Dennis Dart SLF	Caetano Compass	N44F	2000	Cheney, Banbury, 2005
8289	SY	Y558KUX	Dennis Dart SLF	Plaxton Pointer 2	N37F	2001	Elcock Reisen, Telford, 2005
8290	SY	S726KNV	Dennis Dart SLF	Plaxton Pointer 2	N39F	1999	Supertravel, Speke, 2006
8291	SY	S783RNE	Dennis Dart SLF	Plaxton Pointer 2	N36F	1998	Supertravel, Speke, 2006
8292	SY	T438EBD	Dennis Dart SLF	Plaxton Pointer 2	N39F	1999	Supertravel, Speke, 2006

TransBus Mini Pointer Dart 545, NA52AXK, is shown carrying bespoke branding for the *Doxford Clipper* in Sunderland. Wholesale changes to the fleet in recent months have seen the demise of the Leyland Tiger, the Leyland National and MCW MetroRiders. *Keith Lee*

Ancillary vehicles:

416	SD	P416VRG	Optare MetroRider MR17	Optare	B25F	1996
417	SD	P417VRG	Optare MetroRider MR17	Optare	B25F	1996
4736	G	G736RTY	DAF SB220LC550	Optare Delta	TV	1989
4752	G	G752UCU	DAF SB220LC550	Optare Delta	TV	1990
4753	G	G753UCU	DAF SB220LC550	Optare Delta	TV	1990
4754	G	G754UCU	DAF SB220LC550	Optare Delta	TV	1990
7060	G	N760RCU	Volvo B10M-62	Plaxton Expressliner II	TV	1996
7061	G	N761RCU	Volvo B10M-62	Plaxton Expressliner II	TV	1996

Previous registrations:

340GUP	--	K159PGO	K325FYG, WLT625
G183WGX	90D1001	K160PGO	20CLT
GSK962	JSK346	K317FYG	K317FYG, 170CLT
H481PVW	90D1024, DMN17R	N760RCU	N760RCU, CU6860
H485PVW	90D1027, DMN20R	N761RCU	N761RCU, CU7661
H550PVW	91D1085	N950TVK	N21OCU, 5SFS
H551PVW	91D1065	S726KNV	S726KNV, 99D81371, S8STM
H589EGU	90D1026, DMN19R	S783RNE	S783RNE, 99D68554, S10STM
K124PGO	19CLT	T438EBD	T438EBD, 99D80529, S9STM
K125PGO	18CLT		

On order: 41 Scania OmniCity and 9 Mercedes-Benz O530 Citaro.

Depots and allocations:

Chester-le-Street (Picktree Lane) - Go Northern - CR

Dart	571	572	573	574	575	576	577	578
	579	8117						
DAF SB220	4756	4757	4759	4760	4761	4789	4790	4791
	4805	4820	4821	4822	4823	4824	4825	4862
	4863	4864	4865	4866	4867	4890	4891	4892
	4893	4894	4895					
Scania	4989	4990	5222	5223	5224	5225	5226	5227
	5228							
Volvo B10M coach	7076	7077	7078	7079	7080	7081	7082	7083
	7084	7085						
Volvo B12M	7086	7087	7088	7089				
Volvo B12B	7090	7091	7092	7093				
Olympian	3807	3808	3809	3810	3903	3904	3905	3907
	3909	3916	3917	3918	3935	3936	3937	3938
Trident	3801	3802	3875	3876	3877	3878	3879	3880
	3881	3882	3883	3884	3885	3886	3887	3888
	3892	3893	3894	3895				
Volvo B7TL	3962	3963	3964	3965				
Spectra	3834	3835	3836	3850	3851	3852	3853	3857

Gateshead (Sunderland Road) - Go Gateshead - G

Dart	8095	8102	8105	8109	8158	8159	8160	8161
	8162	8163	8164	8165	8166	8167	8168	8169
	8170	8171	8172	8173	8174	8175	8214	8215
VDL SB120/Cadet	8261	8262	8263	8264	8265	8266	8267	8268
	8269							
Lance	4774	4778	4779	4780	4781	4783	4784	4785
	4786	4787	4788					
Volvo B10B	4837	4838	4839	4840	4841	4842	4844	4845
	4846	4847	4912	4913	4914	4915	4916	4917
	4918	4919	4920	4921	4922	4923	4924	4925
	4993							
Scania	4926	4927	4928	4929	4930	4931	4932	4933
	4934	4935	4936	4942	4943	4944	4945	4946
	4947	4948	4949	4954	4970	5218	5219	5220
	5221							
Scania articulated	4950	4951	4952	4953				
Olympian	3811	3826	3827	3828	3919	3929	3933	3934
	3939	3940						
Volvo B7TL	3941	3942	3943					

Percy Main (Norham Road) - Go Gateshead - NT

Solo	448	449	450	451	456	457	458	459
	460	463	464	465	466	467	468	469
Dart	514	8201	8202	8203	8204	8205	8206	8207
	8208	8209	8210	8211	8212	8233	8234	8235
	8236	8237	8238	8239	8240	8241		
DAF/VDL SB120	8270	8271	8272	8273				
Lance	4769	4770	4771	4772	4773			
Scania	4955	4971	4972	4973	4974	4975	4976	
Olympian	3832	3833						
Spectra	3837	3838	3839	3840	3841	3842	3843	3844
	3845	3847	3848	3849	3854	3855	3856	
Trident	3803	3804	3858	3859	3860	3861	3862	3863
	3864	3865	3866	3867	3868			

Stanley (Chester Road) - Go Northern - SY

Solo	452	453	454	455	461	462		
Dart	586	587	588	589	590	591	592	593
	594	595	596	597	8094	8096	8097	8103
	8122	8288	8289	8290	8291	8292		
Volvo B10BLE	4843	4848	4849	4850	4851	4852	4853	4854
	4855	4896	4897	4898	4899	4900	4901	4902
	4903	4904	4905	4906	4907	4908	4909	4910
	4911							
DAF SB220	4758	4868	4869	4870	4983	4984	4985	4986
	4987	4988						
Olympian	3806	3812	3813	3814	3815	3816	3896	3897
	3922	3923	3924	3925	3927	3928	3930	3931
	3932	3950	3951	3952	3955	3957	3958	

Sunderland (Deptford) - Go Wear Buses - SD

Dart	501	502	503	509	510	511	512	513
	515	516	519	522	544	545	546	547
	548	549	550	551	552	553	554	555
	556	557	558	559	560	561	562	580
	581	582	583	584	585	598	603	604
	605	606	8123	8124	8186	8187	8188	8189
	8190	8192	8193	8194	8199	8213	8216	8217
	8218	8222	8276	8277	8278	8279	8280	8281
	8282	8283	8284	8285	8286	8287		
Lance	4775	4777						
Volvo B10B	4813	4814	4815	4816	4875			
Volvo B7RLE	4978	4979	4980	4981	4982			
DAF/VDL SB120	8249	8250	8251	8252	8253	8254	8255	8256
	8257	8258	8259	8260	8274	8275		
Scania L94	4937	4938	4940	4941	4967	4968	4969	4991
	4992	5201	5202	5203	5204	5205	5206	5207
	5208	5209	5210	5211	5212	5213	5214	5215
	5216	5217	5229	5230	5231	5232	5233	
Olympian	3898	3899	3900	3901	3902	3920	3921	3926
	3944	3945	3046	3949				

Washington (Industrial Road) - Go Wear Buses - WA

Solo	517	518	520	521	523	524	525	526
	527	528	529	530	531	532	533	534
	535	536	563	564	565	566	567	568
	569	570						
Dart	8118	8119						
Lance	4782							
Scania	4956	4957	4958	4959	4960	4961	4962	4963
	4964	4965	4966					
Volvo coach	7058	7059	7062	7074	7075			
Olympian	3817	3818	3819	3820	3821	3822	3823	3824
	3825	3829	3830	3831	3906	3908		

Low-floor Dennis Dart 8289, Y558KUX, carries *Stanley Shuttle* branding for the very frequent bus links that are provided between Stanley, MetroCentre and Newcastle. *Keith Lee*

Winlaton (Cromwell Place) - Go Gateshead - WN

Solo	599	600	601	602				
Dart	504	505	506	507	508	537	538	539
	540	541	542	543	8191	8195	8196	8197
	8198	8200	8219	8220	8221	8223	8224	8225
	8226	8227	8228	8229	8230	8231	8232	
DAF/VDL SB120	8242	8243	8244	8245	8246	8247	8248	
Volvo B10B	4809	4810	4811	4812				
DAF SB220	4792	4793						
Lance	4768	4776						
Olympian	3910	3911	3912	3913	3914	3915		
Trident	3869	3871	3872	3873	3874			

Unallocated/trainers - u/w

Dart	8099	8108	8110	8120	8121			
Olympian	3676	3677	3678	3947	3948	3853	3954	3956
	3959	3960	3961					

DIAMOND

Go West Midlands Ltd, Cross Quays, Hallbridge Way, Tipton Road, Tividale, B69 3HW

Birmingham Coach Company commenced business in April 1984, providing private hire services. In October 1986, the company commenced commercial bus operation in Birmingham and the Black Country. The Company was incorporated in 1991, and a further business The Birmingham Omnibus Company Limited was incorporated in 1993. Following an expansion of both bus and coach activity the business moved into new premises at a purpose built site at Tividale.

In November 1995, the business commenced National Express operations as a result of the withdrawal of Express Travel from the National Express network. Many of these services continue today, with the company operating over 3.2 million kilometres annually on these contracts.

Bus operation is primarily commercial within the Centro area. However, more recently, several supported services have been acquired. In 2000, the Diamond Bus trading name was introduced which more accurately reflected the main principle of the business, complete with a new livery applied to both new and the large number of modern second-hand vehicles entering the fleet at that time. The ultimate holding company, Birmingham Passenger Transport Services Limited was acquired by The Go-Ahead Group in December 2005, with trading taking place through The Birmingham Coach Company Limited.

In March 2006, the business assets and operations of Probus Management Limited trading as People's Express were acquired.

Today, the enlarged business operates a fleet of over 230 vehicles from two depots within the West Midlands providing commercial and supported services. The latter are provided on behalf of Worcestershire, Warwickshire and Staffordshire authorities as well as Centro.

In August 2006 Birmingham Coach Company was renamed Go West Midlands Ltd, the trading name was simplified to Diamond and the whole fleet underwent a renumbering exercise.

30	TI	W30DTS	Scania K124IB4	Van Hool Alizée	C49FT	2000	Durham Travel, 2003
32	TI	W432RBB	Scania K124IB4	Van Hool Alizée	C49FT	2000	Durham Travel, 2003
41	TI	X421WVO	Scania K124IB4	Van Hool T9 Alizée	C49FT	2001	
42	TI	X422WVO	Scania K124IB4	Van Hool T9 Alizée	C49FT	2001	
43	TI	X423WVO	Scania K124IB4	Van Hool T9 Alizée	C49FT	2001	
46	TI	YP02AAV	Scania K114EB4	Van Hool T9 Alizée	C49FT	2002	
47	TI	YP02AAX	Scania K114EB4	Van Hool T9 Alizée	C49FT	2002	
48	TI	YJ03PGX	DAF SB4000	Van Hool T9 Alizée	C49FT	2003	
49	TI	YJ03PGY	DAF SB4000	Van Hool T9 Alizée	C49FT	2003	
50	TI	YJ03PGZ	DAF SB4000	Van Hool T9 Alizée	C49FT	2003	
51	TI	YJ03PKK	DAF SB4000	Van Hool T9 Alizée	C49FT	2003	
52	TI	YJ03PNN	DAF SB4000	Van Hool T9 Alizée	C49FT	2003	
53	TI	YJ53VHF	VDL Bus SB4000	Van Hool T9 Alizée	C49FT	2003	
56	TI	R259DWL	Volvo B10M-62	Plaxton Excalibur	C49FT	1998	City of Oxford, 2006

101-110			Optare Excel L1070	Optare	N35F	1997	Metrobus, Orpington, 2002
101	TI	P501OUG	104	TI	P504OUG	107	TI	P507OUG	109	TI	P509OUG
102	TI	P502OUG	105	TI	P505OUG	108	TI	P508OUG	110	TI	P510OUG
103	TI	P503OUG	106	TI	P506OUG						

Fourteen DAF SB120s with Wrightbus Cadet bodywork joined the Diamond fleet at the end of 2001. All are allocated to Tividale and 214, YD02PZO is seen in Old Square, Birmingham in June 2006. *Paul Gooding*

201-214   DAF SB120   Wrightbus Cadet   N39F   2001-02

201	TI	YJ51EKA	205	TI	YJ51EKE	209	TI	YD02PZJ	212	TI	YD02PZM
202	TI	YJ51EKB	206	TI	YJ51EKF	210	TI	YD02PZK	213	TI	YD02PZN
203	TI	YJ51EKC	207	TI	YJ51EKG	211	TI	YD02PZL	214	TI	YD02PZO
204	TI	YJ51EKD	208	TI	YJ51EKH						

301-331   Dennis Lance 11m   Northern Counties Paladin   B38D   1993   Metroline, Harrow, 2000

301	TI	K301YJA	308	TI	K308YJA	316	TI	K316YJA	325	TI	K325YJA
302	TI	K302YJA	310	TI	K310YJA	317	TI	K317YJA	327	TI	K327YJA
303	TI	K303YJA	311	TI	K311YJA	318	TI	K318YJA	328	TI	K328YJA
304	TI	K304YJA	312	TI	K312YJA	320	TI	K320YJA	330	TI	K330YJA
305	TI	K305YJA	313	TI	K313YJA	321	TI	K321YJA	331	TI	K331YJA
306	TI	K306YJA	314	TI	K314YJA	323	TI	K323YJA			

332-341   Dennis Lance 11m   Plaxton Verde   B47F   1994   Stagecoach, 2005

332	TI	L201YAG	334	TI	L204YAG	337	TI	L207YAG	340	TI	L211YAG
333	TI	L202YAG	336	TI	L206YAG	339	TI	L209YAG	341	TI	L942RJN

342	TI	N901PFC	Dennis Lance 11m	Plaxton Verde	B50F	1996	City of Oxford
343	TI	N902PFC	Dennis Lance 11m	Plaxton Verde	B50F	1996	City of Oxford
344	TI	N903PFC	Dennis Lance 11m	Plaxton Verde	B50F	1996	City of Oxford
345	TI	P452BPH	Dennis Lance 11m	Northern Counties Paladin	B49F	1996	Arriva North West, 2001
346	TI	P453BPH	Dennis Lance 11m	Plaxton Verde	B49F	1996	Stagecoach South East, 2001
347	TI	P87BPL	Dennis Lance 11m	Northern Counties Paladin	B49F	1996	Stagecoach North East, 2001

401-404   Dennis Dart SLF   Plaxton Pointer   N39F   1996

401	HT	N606WND	402	HT	P741HND	403	HT	P742HND	404	HT	P748HND

405	HT	P827BUD	Dennis Dart SLF	Wright Crusader	N35F	1997	Dawsonrentals, 2006
406	TI	P829BUD	Dennis Dart SLF	Wright Crusader	N35F	1997	Dawsonrentals, 2006
407	HT	R85XNE	Dennis Dart SLF 11.3m	Plaxton Pointer SPD	N39F	1997	Dukes Travel, Berry Hill, 2001
408	HT	R86XNE	Dennis Dart SLF 11.3m	Plaxton Pointer SPD	N39F	1997	Munro's, Jedburgh, 2001
409	HT	R87XNE	Dennis Dart SLF 11.3m	Plaxton Pointer SPD	N39F	1997	Airlinks, West Drayton, 2001
410	HT	R91XNE	Dennis Dart SLF 11.3m	Plaxton Pointer SPD	N41F	1997	Epsom Buses, 2001
411	HT	R92XNE	Dennis Dart SLF 11.3m	Plaxton Pointer SPD	N41F	1997	Epsom Buses, 2001

The Diamond fleet contains just two types of double-deck buses, all with Northern Counties bodywork. The chassis split is between Volvo Citybus and Olympians, and all were latterly with the London fleet. Carrying the now to be phased out People's Express colours is Citybus 994, G130PGK, which is seen with its former fleet number while operating route 50 to Druids Heath. *Phillip Stephenson*

412-416			Dennis Dart SLF		Wright Crusader		N41F	1997	Dawsonrentals, 2005
412	HT	R527YRP	414	HT	R530YRP	415	HT	R531YRP	416	HT	R532YRP
413	HT	R529YRP									

417	HT	R438FTU	Dennis Dart SLF		Plaxton Pointer 2		N39F	1998	Shropshire, Craven Arms, '01
418	HT	R970MGB	Dennis Dart SLF		Plaxton Pointer 2		N39F	1998	A1A, Birkenhead, 2001
419	HT	R954JYS	Dennis Dart SLF		Plaxton Pointer 2		N39F	1998	A1A, Birkenhead, 2001
420	HT	R659GCA	Dennis Dart SLF		Plaxton Pointer 2		N41F	1998	Shropshire, Craven Arms, '01
421	HT	R660GCA	Dennis Dart SLF		Plaxton Pointer 2		N41F	1998	Shropshire, Craven Arms, '01
422	HT	R810WJA	Dennis Dart SLF		UVG Urban Star		N38F	1997	
423	HT	S771RNE	Dennis Dart SLF		Plaxton Pointer SPD		N39F	1998	
424	HT	S772RNE	Dennis Dart SLF		Plaxton Pointer SPD		N39F	1998	
425	HT	S773RNE	Dennis Dart SLF		Plaxton Pointer SPD		N39F	1998	
426	HT	S397HVV	Dennis Dart SLF		Plaxton Pointer 2		N39F	1999	
427	HT	S404JUA	Dennis Dart SLF		Plaxton Pointer 2		N39F	1998	
428	HT	S405JUA	Dennis Dart SLF		Plaxton Pointer 2		N39F	1998	
429	HT	S920SUM	Dennis Dart SLF		Plaxton Pointer 2		N42F	1999	Dawsonrentals, 2006

430-434			Dennis Dart SLF		Wright Crusader		N40F	1999	Dawsonrentals, 2005
430	HT	T441EBD	432	HT	T443EBD	433	HT	T445EBD	434	HT	T447EBD
431	HT	T442EBD									

435	HT	V385JWK	Dennis Dart SLF		Plaxton Pointer 2		N41F	1999	A-Line, Bedworth, 2001
436	HT	V386JWK	Dennis Dart SLF		Plaxton Pointer 2		N41F	1999	A-Line, Bedworth, 2001
437	u	V377SVV	Dennis Dart SLF		Plaxton Pointer 2		N39F	1999	
438	HT	V391SVV	Dennis Dart SLF		Plaxton Pointer 2		N39F	1999	
439	u	W567JVV	Dennis Dart SLF		Plaxton Pointer 2		N39F	1999	

440-445			Dennis Dart SLF		Alexander ALX200		N38F	2000	
440	HT	W901JNF	442	HT	W903JNF	444	HT	W906JNF	445	HT	W906JNF
441	HT	W902JNF	443	HT	W904JNF						

446-455

							Dennis Dart SLF			Plaxton Pointer 2	N39F	1999-2000
446	HT	X631AKW	449	HT	X636AKW	452	HT	X639AKW	454	HT	Y211HWJ
447	HT	X632AKW	450	HT	X637AKW	453	HT	X641AKW	455	HT	Y212HWJ
448	HT	X634AKW	451	HT	X638AKW						

456	HT	PJ02RGX	Dennis Dart SLF	Plaxton Pointer 2	N37F	2002	
457	HT	PJ02RGY	Dennis Dart SLF	Plaxton Pointer 2	N37F	2002	
458	HT	PJ02RHA	Dennis Dart SLF	Plaxton Pointer 2	N37F	2002	

459-469

Dennis Dart SLF   Plaxton Pointer 2   N37F   2002

459	HT	KU52RXV	462	HT	KU52RYF	465	HT	KU52RYJ	468	HT	KU52RYN
460	HT	KU52RXW	463	HT	KU52RYG	466	HT	KU52RYK	469	HT	KU52RYO
461	HT	KU52RXT	464	HT	KU52RYH	467	HT	KU52RYM			

470	TI	P736RYL	Dennis Dart SLF	Plaxton Pointer 2	N36F	1996	London General, 2000
471	u	P739RYL	Dennis Dart SLF	Plaxton Pointer 2	N36F	1996	London General, 2006

501	HT	S758RNE	Dennis Dart SLF 8.8m	Plaxton Pointer MPD	N28F	1999
502	HT	S759RNE	Dennis Dart SLF 8.8m	Plaxton Pointer MPD	N28F	1999
503	HT	T71JBA	Dennis Dart SLF 8.8m	Plaxton Pointer MPD	N28F	1999
504	HT	V266BNV	Dennis Dart SLF 8.8m	Plaxton Pointer MPD	N28F	1999
505	HT	V267BNV	Dennis Dart SLF 8.8m	Plaxton Pointer MPD	N28F	1999
506	HT	V941DNB	Dennis Dart SLF 8.8m	Plaxton Pointer MPD	N28F	1999
507	HT	V942DNB	Dennis Dart SLF 8.8m	Plaxton Pointer MPD	N28F	1999
508	u	KP02PUE	Dennis Dart SLF 8.8m	Plaxton Pointer MPD	N28F	2002

701-714

Dennis Dart 9.8m   Marshall C37*   B40F   1994   *HCU buses are Plaxton

701	HT	M803GFT	705	HT	M812HCU	709	HT	M816GFT	712	HT	M891GBB
702	HT	M808GFT	706	HT	M813HCU	710	HT	M817GFT	713	HT	M892GBB
703	HT	M810GFT	707	HT	M814GFT	711	HT	M890GBB	714	HT	M811HCU
704	HT	M811GFT	708	HT	M815HCU						

715-721

Dennis Dart 9m   Plaxton Pointer   B34F   1991   London Central, 2000

715	TI	J601XHL	717	TI	J604XHL	719	TI	J606XHL	721	TI	J610XHL
716	TI	J603XHL	718	TI	J605XHL	720	TI	J607XHL			

722	TI	M442BLC	Dennis Dart 9m	Plaxton Pointer	B25F	1995	NCP, Birmingham, 2001
723	TI	M443BLC	Dennis Dart 9m	Plaxton Pointer	B25F	1995	NCP, Birmingham, 2001
724	TI	M445BLC	Dennis Dart 9m	Plaxton Pointer	B25F	1995	NCP, Birmingham, 2001

725-729

Dennis Dart 8.5m   Plaxton Pointer   B32F   1991   Metrobus, Crawley, 2002

725	TI	J701EMX	727	TI	J705EMX	728	TI	J706EMX	729	TI	J707EMX
726	TI	J703EMX									

730-737

Dennis Dart 8.5m   Plaxton Pointer   B28F   1991   Arriva London, 2002

730	TI	H122THE	732	TI	H125THE	734	TI	H128THE	736	TI	H130THE
731	TI	H123THE	733	TI	H126THE	735	TI	H129THE	737	TI	H131THE

738	HT	M105BLE	Dennis Dart	Plaxton Pointer	B40F	1994	Metroline, Harrow, 2006
739	HT	M109BLE	Dennis Dart	Plaxton Pointer	B40F	1994	Metroline, Harrow, 2006

771-780

Mercedes-Benz Vario O814   Alexander ALX100   B27F   1997   Arriva Midlands, 2003

771	HT	P101HCH	774	HT	P106HCH	777	HT	P112HCH	779	HT	P114HCH
772	HT	P102HCH	775	HT	P108HCH	778	HT	P113HCH	780	HT	P117HCH
773	TI	P105HCH	776	HT	P109HCH						

781	HT	P169PVM	Mercedes-Benz Vario O814	Plaxton Beaver 2	B31F	1997	Jim Stones, Leigh, 1999
782	HT	P206PVM	Mercedes-Benz Vario O814	Plaxton Beaver 2	B31F	1997	Jim Stones, Leigh, 1999
783	HT	P207PVM	Mercedes-Benz Vario O814	Plaxton Beaver 2	B31F	1997	Jim Stones, Leigh, 1999
784	HT	P620NKF	Mercedes-Benz Vario O814	Plaxton Beaver 2	B31F	1997	Jim Stones, Leigh, 1999
785	HT	R932AMB	Mercedes-Benz Vario O810	Plaxton Beaver 2	B31F	1997	York Pullman, 1997
786	TI	N771EWG	Mercedes-Benz 609D	Alexander Sprint	B26F	1996	
787	HT	P687HND	Mercedes-Benz Vario O810	Plaxton Beaver 2	B27F	1997	
788	HT	P697HND	Mercedes-Benz Vario O810	Plaxton Beaver 2	B27F	1997	

904	TI	P904RYO	Volvo Olympian YN2RV18Z4	Northern Counties Palatine	B47/27F	1996	Go-Ahead London, 2005
907	TI	P907RYO	Volvo Olympian YN2RV18Z4	Northern Counties Palatine	B47/27F	1996	Go-Ahead London, 2005
929	TI	P929RYO	Volvo Olympian YN2RV18Z4	Northern Counties Palatine	B47/27F	1997	Go-Ahead London, 2005
930	TI	N530LHG	Volvo Olympian YN2RV18Z4	Northern Counties Palatine	B47/27F	1996	Go-Ahead London, 2005
943	TI	N543LHG	Volvo Olympian YN2RV18Z4	Northern Counties Palatine	B47/27F	1996	Go-Ahead London, 2005

Apart from a batch of DAF SB120s and Excels from Metrobus, Dennis Lance and Dart models comprise the bulk of the single-deck fleet. The first of the Excel buses is 101, P501OUG, seen in Birmingham. The network of routes is quite extensive, one of the furthest from its current base is the Bridgnorth to Shrewsbury service. The fleet was re-numbered during August 2006 after this photograph was taken. *Phillip Stephenson*

961	TI	R361LGH	Volvo Olympian YN2RV18Z4	Northern Counties Palatine	B47/26F	1997	Go-Ahead London, 2005
963	TI	R363LGH	Volvo Olympian YN2RV18Z4	Northern Counties Palatine	B47/26F	1998	Go-Ahead London, 2005
964	TI	R364LGH	Volvo Olympian YN2RV18Z4	Northern Counties Palatine	B47/26F	1998	Go-Ahead London, 2005
980	TI	R380LGH	Volvo Olympian YN2RV18Z4	Northern Counties Palatine	B47/26F	1998	Go-Ahead London, 2005
981	TI	R381LGH	Volvo Olympian YN2RV18Z4	Northern Counties Palatine	B47/26F	1998	Go-Ahead London, 2005
992	HT	229CLT	Volvo Citybus B55-10	Northern Counties Palatine	B47/38F	1990	London General, 2002
993	HT	G123NGN	Volvo Citybus B55-10	Northern Counties Palatine	B47/38F	1989	London General, 2002
994	HT	G130PGK	Volvo Citybus B55-10	Northern Counties Palatine	B47/38F	1990	London General, 2002
995	HT	G647SGT	Volvo Citybus B55-10	Northern Counties Palatine	B47/35D	1989	London General, 2002
996	HT	G850WGW	Volvo Citybus B55-10	Northern Counties Palatine	B47/35D	1989	London General, 2002
Vehicles not in service							
-	u	L104EPA	Volvo B6-50	Northern Counties Paladin	B40F	1994	Tillingbourne, Cranleigh, 2001
-	u	M101BLE	Dennis Dart	Plaxton Pointer	B40F	1994	Metroline, Harrow, 2006
-	u	M106BLE	Dennis Dart	Plaxton Pointer	B40F	1994	Metroline, Harrow, 2006
-	u	G110NGN	Volvo Citybus B55-10	Northern Counties Palatine	B47/38F	1989	London General, 2002
-	u	G112NGN	Volvo Citybus B55-10	Northern Counties Palatine	B47/38F	1989	London General, 2002
-	u	G122NGN	Volvo Citybus B55-10	Northern Counties Palatine	B47/38F	1989	London General, 2002
-	u	WLT920	Volvo Citybus B55-10	Northern Counties Palatine	B47/38F	1989	London General, 2002
-	u	KV51KZG	Optare Solo M850	Optare	N29F	2001	
603	u	N603FJO	Volvo B10B	Plaxton Verde	B51F	1995	
612	u	N612FJO	Volvo B10B	Plaxton Verde	B51F	1995	

Previous registrations:

229CLT	G129PGK		R530YRP	R530YRP, 97D64217
G647SGT	G111NGN, WLT311		R532YRP	R532RYP, 97D63724
G850WGW	G125NGN, 125CLT		T441EBD	T441EBD, 99D80528
P169PVM	BUS1N		WLT920	G/PGK
P206PVM	B1JYM		Y211HWJ	99D80597
P207PVM	J5BUS		Y212HWJ	99D80591
P748HND	P748HND, 97P63335			

The 2006-07 Go-Ahead Bus Handbook

Depots:

Tipton Road, Tividale (TI)

Mercedes-Benz Dart	773	778	786					
	406	470	471	715	716	717	718	719
	720	721	722	723	724	725	726	727
	728	729	730	731	732	733	734	735
	736	737						
Excel	101	102	103	104	105	106	107	108
	109	110						
DAF SB120	201	202	203	204	205	206	207	208
	209	210	211	212	213	214		
Lance	301	302	303	304	305	306	308	310
	311	312	313	314	316	317	318	320
	321	323	325	327	328	330	331	332
	333	334	336	337	338	339	340	341
	342	343	344	345	346	347		
Scania coach	30	32	41	42	43	46	47	
DAF coach	48	49	50	51	52	53		
Volvo coach	56							
Olympian	904	907	929	930	943	961	963	980

Howard Street, West Bromwich (HT).

Mercedes-Benz	771	772	774	775	776	777	779	780
	781	782	783	784	785	787	788	
Dart	401	402	403	404	405	406	407	408
	409	410	411	412	413	414	415	416
	417	418	419	420	421	422	423	424
	425	426	427	428	429	430	431	432
	433	434	435	436	438	440	441	442
	443	444	445	446	447	448	449	450
	451	452	453	454	455	456	457	458
	459	460	461	462	463	464	465	466
	467	468	501	502	503	504	505	506
	507	701	702	703	703	705	706	707
	708	709	710	711	712	713	714	
Volvo Citybus	992	993	994	995	996			

Unallocated and stored:

Remainder

One of the many Lance buses operated by Diamond is 321, K321YJA, a Northern Counties model acquired from Metroline in 2000 which is seen on the Erdington Circular.
Paul Gooding

OXFORD BUS COMPANY

The Oxford Bus Company - Park & Ride - the airline - oxford espress

The City of Oxford Motor Services Ltd, Cowley House, Watlington Road, Oxford, OX4 6GA

The company began life in 1908 as the operator of horse tramways in Oxford. The intention was to electrify the system but this proved impossible and instead motor buses were introduced in 1913. Through an agreement with Oxford City Council, the company was the only operator of local bus services in the city, although it expanded into other areas during the 1930s to cover an operating territory of approximately 30 kilometres radius of Oxford. In the 1940s longer distance services were introduced to Newbury, Stratford and Swindon.

The ownership of the company was changing, too. It was owned by the National Electric Company (and the Great Western Railway bought an interest in 1930), until 1931 when BET took over NEC. It remained in BET ownership until the creation of the National Bus Company in 1969. The company was not directly involved in express work until after the formation of NBC. It then took over the Oxford-based services of Thames Valley to London, Southsea and Worcester. In the 1970s, the company began to work closely with local authorities, including operation of the UK's first permanent Park & Ride service.

The Oxford Bus Company operates several services that link the city with London and its Airports. The London services use the *espress* name as shown here on Plaxton Excalibur number 17, V17OXF. *Mark Lyons*

In 1984, the company was split into two divisions: City of Oxford took Oxford City, local services to the east of Oxford and the former express operations, whilst a new company, South Midland, took over the remaining rural routes. Both companies were sold to their management teams under NBC privatisation, with Oxford becoming part of the Go-Ahead Group in 1994.

In recent years, Oxford Bus Company has expanded its business through an innovative approach. High frequency city routes and partnership with the local authorities have helped to double the number of people travelling by bus in Oxford since 1986. The express coach services from Oxford to London and Oxford to Heathrow and Gatwick airports have been transformed by high quality vehicles, 24-hour operation and intensive marketing, while air-conditioned Mercedes Citaro buses are attracting new customers along the busy Abingdon-Oxford and Kidlington-Oxford corridors.

1-5			Scania K114EB4			Irizar Century 12.35		C46FT	2004		
1	OX	AF53OXF	3	OX	CF53OXF	4	OX	DF53OXF	5	OX	EF53OXF
2	OX	BF53OXF									

8-12			Volvo B10M-62			Plaxton Excalibur		C53F	1998		
8	OX	R8OXF	10	u	R288DWL	11	OX	R11OXF	12	u	R289DWL
9	u	R287DWL									

14-26			Volvo B10M-62			Plaxton Excalibur		C45FT*	1999-2001	*23-26 are C45F	
14	OX	V14OXF	18	OX	V18OXF	21	OX	W21OXF	24	OX	Y24OXF
15	OX	V15OXF	19	OX	W19OXF	22	OX	W22OXF	25	OX	Y25OXF
16	OX	V16OXF	20	OX	W20OXF	23	OX	Y23OXF	26	OX	Y26OXF
17	OX	V17OXF									

51-56			Volvo B12B			Jonckheere Mistral 50		C46FT	2002		
51	OX	OA02OXF	53	OX	OC02OXF	55	OX	OE02OXF	56	OX	OF02OXF
52	OX	OB02OXF	54	OX	OD02OXF						

57-63			Scania K114EB4			Irizar Century 12.35		C46FT	2003		
57	OX	J1OXF	59	OX	L1OXF	61	OX	N1OXF	63	OX	R1OXF
58	OX	K1OXF	60	OX	M1OXF	62	OX	P1OXF			

67	OX	Y27OXF	Volvo B10M-62			Plaxton Excalibur		C49FT	2001		
68	OX	Y28OXF	Volvo B10M-62			Plaxton Excalibur		C49FT	2001		
69	OX	R810NUD	Volvo B10M-62			Plaxton Excalibur		C49FT	1998		
70	OX	R809NUD	Volvo B10M-62			Plaxton Excalibur		C49FT	1998		
71	OX	R808NUD	Volvo B10M-62			Plaxton Excalibur		C49FT	1998		

101-120			Dennis Trident			Alexander ALX400		N47/24D	1999		
101	OX	T101DBW	106	OX	T106DBW	111	OX	T111DBW	116	OX	T116DBW
102	OX	T102DBW	107	OX	T107DBW	112	OX	T112DBW	117	OX	T117DBW
103	OX	T103DBW	108	OX	T108DBW	113	OX	T113DBW	118	OX	T118DBW
104	OX	T104DBW	109	OX	T109DBW	114	OX	T114DBW	119	OX	T119DBW
105	OX	T105DBW	110	OX	T110DBW	115	OX	T115DBW	120	OX	T120DBW

401-410			Dennis Dart SLF			Wright Crusader		N30D	1998		
401	OX	R401FFC	404	OX	R4OXF	407	OX	R7OXF	409	OX	R9OXF
402	OX	R2OXF	405	OX	R5OXF	408	OX	R408FFC	410	OX	R10OXF
403	OX	R3OXF	406	OX	R6OXF						

411	OX	P732RYL	Dennis Dart SLF		Plaxton Pointer		N36D	1996	Go-Ahead London, 2004
412	u	P739RYL	Dennis Dart SLF		Plaxton Pointer		N36D	1996	Go-Ahead London, 2004

The Oxford Bus Company has provided the city's Park & Ride service for many years, early vehicles being former London Fleetlines. One of the vehicles currently used on the service is Dennis Trident 120, T120DBW.
Mark Lyons

601-620 Volvo B10B Plaxton Verde B51F 1995-96

601	OX	N601FJO	608	OX	N608FJO	612	u	N612FJO	617	OX	N617FJO
603	u	N603FJO	609	OX	N619FJO	613	OX	N613FJO	618	OX	N618FJO
604	OX	N604FJO	610	OX	N610FJO	615	OX	N615FJO	619	OX	N619FJO
605	OX	N605FJO	611	OX	N611FJO	616	OX	N616FJO	620	OX	N620FJO
607	OX	N607FJO									

629-643 Volvo B10B Plaxton Verde B45D 1997

629	OX	P629FFC	633	OX	P633FFC	637	OX	P637FFC	641	OX	P641FFC
630	OX	P630FFC	634	OX	P634FFC	638	OX	P638FFC	642	OX	P642FFC
631	OX	P631FFC	635	OX	P635FFC	639	OX	P639FFC	643	OX	P643FFC
632	OX	P632FFC	636	OX	P636FFC	640	OX	P640FFC			

| 646 | u | K120BUD | Volvo B10B | | | Northern Counties Paladin | | B43D | 1993 | | London General, 1997 |

801-821 Volvo B10BLE Wright Renown N39F 1999-2000

801	OX	T801CBW	807	OX	T807CBW	812	OX	T812CBW	817	OX	W817FBW
802	OX	T802CBW	808	OX	T808CBW	813	OX	T813CBW	818	OX	W818FBW
803	OX	T803CBW	809	OX	T809CBW	814	OX	T814CBW	819	OX	W819FBW
804	OX	T804CBW	810	OX	T810CBW	815	OX	T815CBW	820	OX	W20FWL
805	OX	T805CBW	811	OX	T811CBW	816	OX	W816FBW	821	OX	W821FBW
806	OX	T806CBW									

822-827 Mercedes-Benz Citaro O530 Mercedes-Benz N35F 2002

822	OX	MA52OXF	824	OX	MC52OXF	826	OX	ME52OXF	827	OX	MF52OXF
823	OX	MB52OXF	825	OX	MD52OXF						

828-838 Mercedes-Benz Citaro O530 Mercedes-Benz N42F 2003

828	OX	X28OXF	831	OX	X31OXF	834	OX	X4OXF	837	OX	X7OXF
829	OX	X29OXF	832	OX	X2OXF	835	OX	X5OXF	838	OX	X8OXF
830	OX	X13OXF	833	OX	X3OXF	836	OX	X6OXF			

The integral Mercedes-Benz Citaro was introduced into the Oxford fleet in 2002, and further batches have subsequently arrived. Illustrating the branding used on the city services is 825, MD52OXF. *Mark Lyons*

839-848			Mercedes-Benz Citaro O530		Mercedes-Benz		N37D	2005		
839	OX	AF55OXF	842	OX	DF55OXF	845	OX	GF55OXF	847	OX	JF55OXF
840	OX	BF55OXF	843	OX	EF55OXF	846	OX	HF55OXF	848	OX	KF55OXF
841	OX	CF55OXF	844	OX	FF55OXF						
898	OX	HF06FTO	Mercedes-Benz Citaro O530		Mercedes-Benz		N39F	2006	on loan from Go South Coast		
899	OX	HF06FTY	Mercedes-Benz Citaro O530		Mercedes-Benz		N39F	2006	on loan from Go South Coast		

Ancillary vehicles:							
951	OX	EX54DYB	Ford Transit	Ford		Crew	2004	
952	OX	EX54DYC	Ford Transit	Ford		Crew	2004	
953	OX	EX54DYD	Ford Transit	Ford		Crew	2004	
954	OX	EX54DYF	Ford Transit	Ford		Crew	2004	
962	OX	K119BUD	Volvo B10B	Northern Counties Paladin		TV	1993	London General, 1997
971	OX	C63HOM	Leyland Lynx LX1126LXCTFR1	Leyland		TV	1986	Travel West Midlands, 2001

Previous registrations:

K120BUD	K3KLL	R10OXF	R410FFC
R2OXF	R402FFC	R287DWL	R9OXF
R3OXF	R403FFC	R288DWL	R12OXF
R4OXF	R404FFC	R289DWL	R10OXF
R5OXF	R405FFC	R808NUD	R7OXF
R6OXF	R406FFC	R809NUD	R6OXF
R7OXF	R407FFC	R810NUD	R5OXF
R9OXF	R409FFC		

On order: 12 Mercedes-Benz Citaro O530 buses.

Allocation

Oxford (Cowley Road) - OX

Dart SLF	401	402	403	404	405	406	407	408
	409	410	411					
Volvo B10B Verde	601	603	604	605	607	608	609	610
	611	613	615	616	617	618	619	620
	629	630	631	632	633	634	635	636
	637	638	639	640	641	642	643	
Volvo B10BLE Renown	801	802	803	804	805	806	807	808
	809	810	811	812	813	814	815	816
	817	818	819	820	821			
Citaro O530	822	823	824	825	826	827	828	829
	830	831	832	833	834	835	836	837
	838	839	840	841	842	843	844	845
	846	847	848	898	899			
Volvo B10M coach	8	11	14	15	16	17	18	19
	20	21	22	23	24	25	26	67
	68	69	70	71				
Volvo B12B Mistral	51	52	53	54	55	56		
Scania/Irizar	1	2	3	4	5	57	58	59
	60	61	62	63				
Trident/ALX400	101	102	103	104	105	106	107	108
	109	110	111	112	113	114	115	116
	117	118	119	120				
Ancillary	951	952	953	954	962	971		

Unallocated and stored - u/w

Dart	412			
Volvo B10B	603	612	646	
Volvo B10M	9	10	12	(currently on loan to Diamond)

Early low-floor buses for the Oxford Bus Company were Volvo B10BLEs with dual-door Wright Renown bodies. Seen with branding for the *city15* is 821, **W821FBW**. *Mark Lyons*

GO-AHEAD LONDON

London Central Bus Co Ltd; London General Transport Services Ltd
18 Merton High Street, London, SW19 1DN

London Central and London General are relatively new bus companies, being formed in 1989 in preparation for the privatisation of London Buses Limited. However, the origins of both companies can be traced back to one of the original pioneers of bus operations in the capital, the London General Omnibus Company Limited (LGOC).

LGOC or "General" as it was known locally, operated services throughout the capital and was absorbed into the new London Transport Executive in 1933. London Transport became synonymous with the red London bus until the bus operation was segregated in 1985, becoming London Buses Ltd and London Underground Ltd.

Upon privatisation in autumn 1994, London Central was purchased by the Go-Ahead Group, which is based in Newcastle, itself being formed on the privatisation of Northern General Transport Ltd, previously part of the National Bus Company. London General was initially purchased by an employee/management team, being subsequently acquired by the Go-Ahead Group in the summer of 1996.

London Central and London General provide nearly 15% of the London market, and account for approximately 260 million bus journeys annually on about one hundred day and night routes.

Repainted into the pre-London Transport colours of London General is Routemaster RML887, 202UXJ, which occasionally sees use on special service. Here it rounds Hyde Park Corner while heading for Putney on route 14. Mark Lyons

Go-Ahead has been one of the early customers for the new Alexander-Dennis Enviro 400. Based on the newly introduced Trident 2 chassis, and carrying the Enviro 400 body, thirty-nine are now in service from Stockwell depot. Illustrating the type is E3, SN06BND, seen operating route 196. *Mark Lyons*

AVL1-46			Volvo B7TL			Alexander ALX400		N43/20D		1999-2000	*23/9/34 are B43/17D
1	Q	V101LGC	13	Q	V113LGC	25	PM	V125LGC	36	PM	V136LGC
2	Q	V102LGC	14	Q	V114LGC	26	PM	V126LGC	37	PM	V137LGC
3	Q	V103LGC	15	PM	V115LGC	27	PM	V127LGC	38	PM	V138LGC
4	Q	V104LGC	16	Q	V116LGC	28	PM	V128LGC	39	PM	V139LGC
5	Q	V105LGC	17	PM	V117LGC	29	PM	V129LGC	40	PM	V140LGC
6	Q	V106LGC	18	Q	V118LGC	30	PM	V130LGC	41	PM	V141LGC
7	Q	V107LGC	19	PM	V119LGC	31	PM	V131LGC	42	PM	V142LGC
8	Q	V108LGC	20	Q	V120LGC	32	PM	V132LGC	43	PM	V143LGC
9	Q	V109LGC	21	Q	V221LGC	33	PM	V133LGC	44	PM	V144LGC
10	Q	V110LGC	22	PM	V122LGC	34	PM	V134LGC	45	PM	V145LGC
11	Q	V211LGC	23	PM	V223LGC	35	PM	V135LGC	46	PM	V146LGC
12	Q	V112LGC	24	PM	V124LGC						
B9	-	BX06BTF	Volvo B9TL			Wrightbus Gemini Eclipse		N41/21D	2006		
DML1-20			Dennis Dart SLF 9.3m			Marshall Capital		N31F	1999		
1	BX	T401AGP	5	BX	T455AGP	11	BX	T411AGP	17	BX	T417AGP
2	BX	T402AGP	6	BX	T406AGP	12	BX	T412AGP	18	BX	T418AGP
3	BX	T403AGP	8	BX	T408AGP	14	BX	T414AGP	19	BX	T419AGP
4	BX	T404AGP	10	BX	T410AGP	15	BX	T415AGP	20	BX	T392AGP
DMS6-9			Dennis Dart SLF 8.9m			Marshall Capital		N29F	1999		
6	BX	T106KGP	7	BX	T107KGP	8	BX	T108KGP	9	BX	T109KGP
E1-39			ADL Trident 2			ADL Enviro 400		N41/26D	2006		
1	SW	SN06BNA	11	SW	SN06BNV	21	SW	LX06EZR	31	SW	LX06EZF
2	SW	SN06BNB	12	SW	SN06BNX	22	SW	LX06EZS	32	SW	LX06EZG
3	SW	SN06BND	13	SW	SN06BNY	23	SW	LX06EZT	33	SW	LX06EZH
4	SW	SN06BNE	14	SW	SN06BNZ	24	SW	LX06EYY	34	SW	LX06ECT
5	SW	SN06BNF	15	SW	SN06BOF	25	SW	LX06EYZ	35	SW	LX06ECV
6	SW	SN06BNJ	16	PM	LX06EZL	26	SW	LX06EZA	36	SW	LX06FKL
7	SW	SN06BNK	17	PM	LX06EZM	27	SW	LX06EZB	37	SW	LX06FKM
8	SW	SN06BNL	18	PM	LX06EZN	28	SW	LX06EZC	38	SW	LX06FKN
9	SW	SN06BNO	19	PM	LX06EZO	29	SW	LX06EZD	39	SW	LX06FKO
10	SW	SN06BNU	20	PM	LX06EZP	30	SW	LX06EZE			

The 2006-07 Go-Ahead Bus Handbook

EVL1-52　　Volvo B7TL 10.4m　　East Lancs Vyking　　N45/23D　　2002

1	A	PL51LGA	14	A	PL51LGX	27	A	PN02XCL	40	A	PJ02PYX
2	A	PL51LGC	15	A	PN02XCB	28	A	PN02XCM	41	A	PJ02PYY
3	A	PL51LGD	16	A	PN02XCC	29	A	PN02XCO	42	A	PJ02PYZ
4	A	PL51LGE	17	A	PN02XCD	30	A	PN02XCP	43	A	PJ02PZA
5	A	PL51LGF	18	A	PN02XCE	31	A	PN02XCR	44	A	PJ02PZB
6	A	PL51LGG	19	A	PL51LFE	32	A	PN02XCS	45	A	PJ02PZC
7	A	PL51LGJ	20	A	PN02XCF	33	A	PN02XCT	46	A	PJ02PZD
8	A	PL51LGK	21	A	PL51LFG	34	A	PN02XBX	47	A	PJ02PZE
9	A	PL51LGN	22	A	PN02XCG	35	A	PN02XBY	48	A	PJ02PZF
10	A	PL51LGO	23	A	PL51LFJ	36	A	PN02XBZ	49	A	PJ02PZG
11	A	PL51LGU	24	A	PN02XCH	37	A	PJ02PYU	50	A	PJ02PZH
12	A	PN02XCA	25	A	PN02XCJ	38	A	PJ02PYV	51	A	PJ02PZK
13	A	PL51LGW	26	A	PN02XCK	39	A	PJ02PYW	52	A	PJ02PZL

LDP1-16　　Dennis Dart SLF 9.2m　　Plaxton Pointer　　N32F　　1996

1	A	P501RYM	4	BX	P504RYM	7	BX	P507RYM	14	A	P514RYM
2	SW	P502RYM	5	BX	P505RYM	8	A	P508RYM	15	u	P515RYM
3	Q	P503RYM	6	BX	P506RYM	9	A	WLT379	16	BX	P516RYM

LDP32-44　　Dennis Dart SLF 10m　　Plaxton Pointer　　N36F　　1996

32	u	P732RYL	36	u	P736RYL	40	A	P740RYL	43	A	P743RYL
34	u	P734RYL	37	A	P737RYL	41	A	P741RYL	44	A	P744RYL
35	u	P735RYL	39	A	P739RYL	42	A	P742RYL			

LDP45-89　　Dennis Dart SLF 10m　　Plaxton Pointer　　N35F*　　1997　　*61 is N36F

45	A	R445LGH	57	BX	R457LGH	67	Q	R467LGH	78	AL	R478LGH
46	A	R446LGH	58	u	R458LGH	68	Q	R468LGH	81	Q	R481LGH
47	A	R447LGH	59	AL	R459LGH	69	NX	R469LGH	82	Q	R482LGH
48	A	R448LGH	60	AL	R460LGH	70	Q	R470LGH	83	Q	R483LGH
49	A	R449LGH	61	AL	R461LGH	71	Q	R471LGH	84	Q	R484LGH
51	A	R451LGH	62	AL	R462LGH	72	Q	R472LGH	85	AL	R485LGH
52	A	R452LGH	63	u	R463LGH	73	u	R473LGH	86	Q	R486LGH
53	A	R453LGH	64	Q	R464LGH	74	A	R474LGH	87	Q	R487LGH
54	AL	R454LGH	65	A	R465LGH	76	NX	R476LGH	88	w	R488LGH
55	AL	R455LGH	66	Q	R466LGH	77	BX	R477LGH	89	AL	R489LGH
56	AL	R456LGH									

The last of the fifty-two attractive East Lancs Vyking-bodied buses supplied to Go-Ahead London in 2002 is EVL52, PJ02PZL. The vehicle is seen operating route 93 while heading for North Cheam.
Mark Lyons

LDP90-128 — Dennis Dart SLF 10.1m — Plaxton Pointer 2 — N30D* — 1998-99 — *118-128 are N32D

90	AL	S638JGP	101	AL	S101EGK	111	BX	S954JGX	120	BX	T120KGP
91	AL	S91EGK	102	AL	S102EGK	112	BX	S112EGK	121	BX	T521AGP
92	AL	S92EGK	103	AL	S103EGK	113	BX	S113EGK	122	BX	T122KGP
93	AL	S93EGK	104	AL	S104EGK	114	BX	S114EGK	123	BX	T523AGP
94	AL	S94EGK	105	AL	S105EGK	115	BX	S115EGK	124	BX	T124KGP
95	AL	S95EGK	106	AL	S106EGK	116	BX	S116EGK	125	BX	T125KGP
96	AL	S96EGK	107	BX	S107EGK	117	BX	S117EGK	126	BX	T126KGP
97	AL	S97EGK	108	BX	S108EGK	118	BX	T118KGP	127	BX	T127KGP
98	AL	S98EGK	109	BX	S109EGK	119	BX	T119KGP	128	BX	T128KGP
99	AL	S955JGX	110	BX	S110EGK						

LDP129-133 — Dennis Dart SLF 8.8m — Plaxton Pointer MPD — N29F — 2001

129	AF	Y829TGH	131	AF	Y831TGH	132	AF	Y832TGH	133	AF	Y833TGH
130	AF	Y803TGH									

LDP134-141 — Dennis Dart SLF 10.7m — Plaxton Pointer 2 — N35D — 2001

134	AL	Y834TGH	136	AL	Y836TGH	138	AL	Y838TGH	140	AL	Y840TGH
135	AL	Y835TGH	137	AL	Y837TGH	139	AL	Y839TGH	141	AL	Y841TGH

LDP142-152 — Dennis Dart SLF 8.8m — Plaxton Pointer MPD — N30F — 2001

142	NX	Y842TGH	145	NX	Y845TGH	148	NX	Y848TGH	151	A	Y851TGH
143	NX	Y843TGH	146	NX	Y846TGH	149	A	Y849TGH	152	A	Y852TGH
144	NX	Y844TGH	147	NX	Y847TGH	150	A	Y805TGH			

LDP153-190 — Dennis Dart SLF 9.3m — Plaxton Pointer 2 — N29F — 2001

153	Q	Y853TGH	163	Q	Y863TGH	172	PM	Y972TGH	182	Q	Y982TGH
154	Q	Y854TGH	164	Q	Y864TGH	173	PM	Y973TGH	183	Q	Y983TGH
155	Q	Y705TGH	165	Q	Y865TGH	174	PM	Y974TGH	184	Q	Y984TGH
156	Q	Y856TGH	166	Q	Y866TGH	175	PM	Y975TGH	185	Q	Y985TGH
157	Q	Y857TGH	167	PM	Y967TGH	176	PM	Y976TGH	186	Q	Y986TGH
158	Q	Y858TGH	168	PM	Y968TGH	178	PM	Y978TGH	187	Q	Y987TGH
159	Q	Y859TGH	169	PM	Y969TGH	179	PM	Y979TGH	188	Q	Y988TGH
160	Q	Y806TGH	170	PM	Y907TGH	180	PM	Y908TGH	189	Q	Y989TGH
161	Q	Y861TGH	171	PM	Y971TGH	181	PM	Y981TGH	190	Q	Y909TGH
162	Q	Y862TGH									

Apart from the experimental Electrocity buses the sole midibus model operated by Go-Ahead London is the low-floor Dart with Pointer bodywork. Examples of each name change through the transformation of Dennis and Plaxton into and out of the TransBus group are represented. Pictured heading for Mitcham is LDP193, SN51UAF. *Mark Lyons*

LDP191-237 — Dennis Dart SLF 10.1m — Plaxton Pointer 2 — N31D — 2002-03

191	AL	SN51UAD	203	AL	SN51UAS	215	SW	SK52MOF	227	AF	SK52MME
192	AL	SN51UAE	204	AL	SN51UAT	216	AL	SK52MOU	228	AF	SK52MMF
193	AL	SN51UAF	205	AL	SN51UAU	217	AL	SK52MOV	229	AF	SK52MMJ
194	AL	SN51UAG	206	AL	SN51UAV	218	SW	SK52MPE	230	AF	SK52MMO
195	AL	SN51UAH	207	AL	SN51UAW	219	SW	SK52MPF	231	AF	SK52MKX
196	AL	SN51UAJ	208	AL	SN51UAX	220	SW	SK52MPO	232	AF	SK52MKZ
197	AL	SN51UAK	209	AL	SN51UAY	221	SW	SK52MLU	233	AL	SK52MRO
198	AL	SN51UAL	210	AL	SN51UAZ	222	AF	SK52MLV	234	AF	SK52MRU
199	AL	SN51UAM	211	SW	SK52MMU	223	AF	SK52MLX	235	AF	SK52MRV
200	AL	SN51UAO	212	SW	SK52MMV	224	AF	SK52MLY	236	AF	SK52MRX
201	A	SN51UAP	213	SW	SK52MMX	225	AF	SK52MLZ	237	AF	SK52MRY
202	A	SN51UAR	214	SW	SK52MOA	226	AF	SK52MMA			

LDP238-262 — TransBus Dart 10.1m — TransBus Pointer — N30D — 2003

238	SW	SN53ETT	245	SW	SN53EVB	251	AL	SN53KKH	257	AL	SN53KKR
239	SW	SN53ETU	246	SW	SN53EVC	252	AL	SN53KKJ	258	AL	SN53KKT
240	SW	SN53ETV	247	SW	SN53EVD	253	AL	SN53KKL	259	AL	SN53KKU
241	SW	SN53ETX	248	SW	SN53EVE	254	AL	SN53KKM	260	AL	SN53KKV
242	SW	SN53ETY	249	AL	SN53KKF	255	AL	SN53KKO	261	AL	SN53KKW
243	SW	SN53ETZ	250	AL	SN53KKG	256	AL	SN53KKP	262	AL	SN53KKX
244	SW	SN53EVA									

LDP263-273 — ADL Dart 8.8m — ADL Pointer — N29F — 2005-06

263	SW	LX05EYP	266	SW	LX05EYT	269	SW	LX05EYW	272	SW	LX05EYA
264	SW	LX05EYR	267	SW	LX05EYU	270	SW	LX05EYY	273	NX	LX06EYT
265	SW	LX05EYS	268	SW	LX05EYV	271	SW	LX05EXZ			

LDP274-280 — ADL Dart 10.1m — ADL Pointer — N28D — 2006

274	NX	LX05EYU	276	NX	LX05EYW	278	NX	LX05FBE	280	NX	LX05FAF
275	NX	LX05EYV	277	NX	LX05FBD	279	NX	LX05FFA			

LDP281-291 — ADL Dart 8.8m — ADL Pointer — N23F — 2006

281	NX	LX06FAJ	284	NX	LX06FAO	287	SW	LX06FBB	290	SW	LX06EZV
282	NX	LX06FAK	285	NX	LX06FAU	288	SW	LX06FBC	291	SW	LX06EZW
283	NX	LX06FAM	286	NX	LX06FBA	289	SW	LX06EZU			

LDP292-294 — ADL Dart 10.1m — ADL Pointer — N28F — 2006

292	AF	LX06EZZ	293	AF	LX06EZJ	294	AF	LX06EZK

Go-Ahead London is one of the leaders in the use of articulated buses in the capital with almost one hundred now in service. Illustrating the three-door arrangement is MAL45, BD52LMY, an example with London Central names, seen while passing through Lewisham en route for Paddington rail station. *Mark Lyons*

The sight of an elephant in the top right-hand corner of the picture gives an indication that MAL62, BX54EFC, is at the stop of the same name while operating route 12.   *Mark Lyons*

MAL1-61   Mercedes-Benz O530G   Mercedes-Benz Citaro   AN49T   2002-04

1	RA	BX02YZE	17	RA	BX02YZA	32	NX	BN52GWC	47	NX	BD52LNC
2	RA	BX02YZG	18	RA	BX02YZB	33	NX	BN52GWD	48	NX	BD52LNE
3	RA	BX02YZH	19	RA	BX02YZC	34	NX	BN52GWE	49	NX	BD52LNF
4	RA	BX02YZJ	20	RA	BX02YZD	35	NX	BN52GVU	50	NX	BD52LNG
5	RA	BX02YZK	21	RA	BX02YYJ	36	NX	BX04NBD	51	NX	BU04EZK
6	RA	BX02YZL	22	RA	BX02YYK	37	NX	BD52LNO	52	NX	BD52LMO
7	RA	BX02YZM	23	RA	BX02YYL	38	NX	BD52LNP	53	NX	BL52ODK
8	RA	BX02YZN	24	RA	BX02YYM	39	NX	BD52LNR	54	NX	BL52ODM
9	RA	BX02YZO	25	RA	BX02YYN	40	NX	BD52LNT	55	NX	BL52ODN
10	RA	BX02YZP	26	RA	BX02YYO	41	NX	BD52LNU	56	NX	BL52ODP
11	RA	BX02YYS	27	RA	BX02YYP	42	NX	BD52LMU	57	NX	BL52ODR
12	RA	BX02YYT	28	RA	BX02YYR	43	NX	BD52LMV	58	NX	BU04UTM
13	RA	BX02YYU	29	RA	BX02YZR	44	NX	BD52LMX	59	NX	BL52ODT
14	RA	BX02YYV	30	RA	BX02YZS	45	NX	BD52LMY	60	NX	BL52ODU
15	RA	BX02YYZ	31	RA	BX02YZT	46	NX	BD52LNA	61	NX	BL52ODV
16	RA	BX02YYW									

MAL62-94   Mercedes-Benz O530G   Mercedes-Benz Citaro   AN49T   2004

62	Q	BX54EFC	71	Q	BX54UCV	79	Q	BX54UDJ	87	Q	BX54UDU
63	Q	BX54EFD	72	Q	BX54UCW	80	Q	BX54UDK	88	Q	BX54UDV
64	Q	BX54UCM	73	Q	BX54UCZ	81	Q	BX54UDL	89	Q	BX54UDW
65	Q	BX54UCN	74	Q	BX54UDB	82	Q	BX54UDM	90	Q	BX54UDY
66	Q	BX54UCO	75	Q	BX54UDD	83	Q	BX54UDN	91	Q	BX54UDZ
67	Q	BX54UCP	76	Q	BX54UDE	84	Q	BX54UDO	92	Q	BX54UEA
68	Q	BX54UCR	77	Q	BX54UDG	85	Q	BX54UDP	93	Q	BX54UEB
69	Q	BX54UCT	78	Q	BX54UDH	86	Q	BX54UDT	94	Q	BX54EFB
70	Q	BX54UCU									

The 2006-07 Go-Ahead Bus Handbook

The Go-Ahead NV class of Northern Counties bodied Volvos is now retained for training or commercial services. The training buses are adorned with dedicated special liveries while the others are used for private hire or specific events. These include the special routes at the Epsom Derby, for the Wimbledon tennis tournament, and, as depicted here by open-top NV 176, R376LGH, for the annual Chelsea Flower Show.
Colin Lloyd

MD1-17
DAF SB220 12m   East Lancs Myllennium   N33D   1999   MD8-10 use LPG fuel.

1	BX	V1GMT	6	BX	V6GMT	10	BX	V10GMT	14	BX	V14GMT
2	BX	V2GMT	7	BX	V7GMT	11	BX	V11GMT	15	BX	V15GMT
3	BX	V3GMT	8	BX	V8GMT	12	BX	V12GMT	16	BX	V16GMT
4	BX	V4GMT	9	BX	V9GMT	13	BX	V13GMT	17	BX	V17GMT
5	BX	V5GMT									

NV104	u	P904RYO	Volvo Olympian YN2RV18Z4	Northern Counties Palatine	B47/27D	1997
NV107	u	P907RYO	Volvo Olympian YN2RV18Z4	Northern Counties Palatine	B47/27D	1997

NV161-187
Volvo Olympian   Northern Counties Palatine II   *Seating varies 1997-98 *65,170/1/6 are CO47/24D

161	u	R361LGH	168	A	R368LGH	176	A	R376LGH	182	NX	R382LGH
162	SW	R362LGH	170	SW	WLT470	177	Q	VLT277	183	A	R383LGH
163	u	R363LGH	171	AL	R371LGH	178	AL	78CLT	184	A	VLT284
164	u	R364LGH	173	NX	R373LGH	179	A	VLT179	185	u	R385LGH
165	NX	R365LGH	174	AL	R374LGH	180	u	R380LGH	186	A	R386LGH
166	Q	166CLT	175	A	R375LGH	181	PM	R381LGH	187	A	197CLT
167	A	R367LGH									

PDL1-27
Dennis Trident 9.9m   Plaxton President   N41/23D   2000-02

1	SW	X601EGK	8	SW	X608EGK	15	SW	PJ02PZN	22	SW	PJ02PZV
2	u	X602EGK	9	SW	X609EGK	16	SW	PJ02PZO	23	SW	PJ02PZW
3	SW	X603EGK	10	u	X701EGK	17	SW	PJ02PZP	24	SW	PJ02PZX
4	SW	X604EGK	11	SW	X611EGK	18	SW	PJ02PZR	25	SW	PJ02PZY
5	SW	X605EGK	12	SW	X612EGK	19	SW	PJ02PZS	26	SW	PJ02PZZ
6	u	X606EGK	13	SW	X613EGK	20	SW	PJ02PZT	27	SW	PJ02RHF
7	u	X607EGK	14	SW	PJ02PZM	21	SW	PJ02PZU			

PDL28-50
TransBus Trident 9.9m   TransBus President   N41/23D   2003

28	SW	PN03ULK	34	SW	PN03ULT	40	SW	PN03ULZ	46	SW	PN03UMF
29	SW	PN03ULL	35	SW	PN03ULU	41	SW	PN03UMA	47	SW	PN03UMG
30	SW	PN03ULM	36	SW	PN03ULV	42	SW	PN03UMB	48	SW	PN03UMH
31	SW	PN03ULP	37	SW	PN03ULW	43	SW	PN03UMC	49	SW	PN03UMJ
32	SW	PN03ULR	38	SW	PN03ULX	44	SW	PN03UMD	50	SW	PN03UMK
33	SW	PN03ULS	39	SW	PN03ULY	45	SW	PN03UME			

PVL1-38 Volvo B7TL 10m Plaxton President N41/21D 2000

1	BX	V301LGC	11	BX	V311LGC	21	BX	V921KGF	30	BX	V330LGC
2	BX	V302LGC	12	BX	V312LGC	22	BX	V322LGC	31	BX	V331LGC
3	BX	V303LGC	13	BX	V313LGC	23	BX	V392KGF	32	BX	V332LGC
4	BX	V304LGC	14	BX	V314LGC	24	BX	V324LGC	33	BX	V233LGC
5	BX	V305LGC	15	BX	V315LGC	25	BX	V325LGC	34	BX	V334LGC
6	BX	V306LGC	16	BX	V816KGF	26	BX	V226LGC	35	BX	V335LGC
7	BX	V307LGC	17	BX	V317LGC	27	BX	V327LGC	36	BX	V336LGC
8	BX	V308LGC	18	BX	V218LGC	28	BX	V228LGC	37	BX	V337LGC
9	BX	V209LGC	19	BX	V319LGC	29	BX	V329LGC	38	BX	V338LGC
10	BX	V310LGC	20	BX	V220LGC						

PVL39-143 Volvo B7TL 10m Plaxton President *N41/21D 2000 *58 is N41/19D

39	BX	W439WGH	66	SW	W466WGH	92	AL	W492WGH	118	AL	W518WGH
40	BX	W840WGH	67	AL	W467WGH	93	AL	W493WGH	119	AL	W519WGH
41	BX	W441WGH	68	AL	W468WGH	94	AL	W494WGH	120	BX	W402WGH
42	BX	W442WGH	69	AL	W469WGH	95	AL	W495WGH	121	AL	W521WGH
43	BX	W443WGH	70	AL	W578DGU	96	AL	W496WGH	122	AL	W522WGH
44	BX	W544WGH	71	PM	W471WGH	97	AL	W497WGH	123	AL	W523WGH
45	BX	W445WGH	72	PM	W472WGH	98	AL	W498WGH	124	AL	W524WGH
46	BX	W446WGH	73	PM	W473WGH	99	AL	W399WGH	125	AL	W425WGH
47	BX	W447WGH	74	AL	W474WGH	100	AL	W997WGH	126	AL	W526WGH
48	BX	W448WGH	75	NX	W475WGH	101	AL	W501WGH	127	AL	W527WGH
49	BX	W449WGH	76	AL	W476WGH	102	AL	W502WGH	128	AL	W428WGH
50	BX	W499WGH	77	AL	W477WGH	103	AL	W503WGH	129	AL	W529WGH
51	BX	W451WGH	78	SW	W478WGH	104	AL	W504WGH	130	AL	W403WGH
52	BX	W452WGH	79	NX	W479WGH	105	AL	W905WGH	131	AL	W531WGH
53	BX	W453WGH	80	A	W408WGH	106	AL	W506WGH	132	AL	W532WGH
54	BX	W454WGH	81	AL	W481WGH	107	AL	W507WGH	133	AL	W533WGH
55	BX	W998WGH	82	BX	W482WGH	108	AL	W508WGH	134	AL	W534WGH
56	AL	W956WGH	83	BX	W483WGH	109	AL	W509WGH	135	AL	W435WGH
57	AL	W457WGH	84	AL	W484WGH	110	AL	W401WGH	136	AL	W536WGH
58	AL	W458WGH	85	AL	W485WGH	111	AL	W511WGH	137	AL	W537WGH
59	Q	W459WGH	86	AL	W486WGH	112	AL	W512WGH	138	AL	W538WGH
60	BX	W996WGH	87	AL	W487WGH	113	AL	W513WGH	139	AL	W539WGH
61	A	W461WGH	88	NX	W488WGH	114	AL	W514WGH	140	AL	W404WGH
62	SW	W462WGH	89	NX	W489WGH	115	AL	W415WGH	141	AL	W541WGH
63	AL	W463WGH	90	NX	W409WGH	116	AL	W516WGH	142	AL	W542WGH
64	SW	W464WGH	91	NX	W491WGH	117	AL	W517WGH	143	AL	W543WGH
65	PM	W465WGH									

One of a batch of seventeen standard-length single-decks delivered in 1999 featured the East Lancs Myllennium body on low-floor DAF SB220 chassis. All the batch is currently allocated to Bexleyheath, and MD11, V11GMT, is seen working route 486. *Colin Lloyd*

The President design was the last to be built at the former Northern Counties facility in Wigan. Launched after the factory had been acquired by the Henley Group, it took on the Plaxton name, with sales mostly to London-based operators. The model was available on Volvo, DAF and Dennis chassis and one of the latter, PDL50, PN03UMK, is seen operating route 133 in Brixton. *Mark Lyons*

PVL144-207 — Volvo B7TL 10m — Plaxton President N41/23D 2000

144	AL	X544EGK	160	PM	X616EGK	176	Q	X576EGK	192	A	X592EGK
145	AL	X745EGK	161	PM	X561EGK	177	Q	X577EGK	193	A	X593EGK
146	AL	X546EGK	162	PM	X562EGK	178	Q	X578EGK	194	A	X594EGK
147	AL	X547EGK	163	PM	X563EGK	179	A	X579EGK	195	u	X595EGK
148	AL	X548EGK	164	PM	X564EGK	180	A	X508EGK	196	u	X596EGK
149	AL	X549EGK	165	PM	X656EGK	181	A	X581EGK	197	u	X597EGK
150	AL	X599EGK	166	Q	X566EGK	182	A	X582EGK	198	u	X598EGK
151	AL	X551EGK	167	Q	X567EGK	183	A	X583EGK	199	u	X699EGK
152	AL	X552EGK	168	Q	X568EGK	184	A	X584EGK	200	u	X502EGK
153	AL	X553EGK	169	NX	X569EGK	185	A	X585EGK	201	u	X501EGK
154	AL	X554EGK	170	NX	X707EGK	186	A	X586EGK	202	u	X702EGK
155	AL	X615EGK	171	NX	X571EGK	187	A	X587EGK	203	u	X503EGK
156	NX	X556EGK	172	NX	X572EGK	188	A	X588EGK	204	u	X504EGK
157	NX	X557EGK	173	NX	X573EGK	189	A	X589EGK	205	u	X705EGK
158	NX	X558EGK	174	NX	X574EGK	190	A	X509EGK	206	AL	X506EGK
159	NX	X559EGK	175	NX	X575EGK	191	A	X591EGK	207	AL	X507EGK

PVL208-272 — Volvo B7TL 10m — Plaxton President N41/23D 2000

208	NX	Y808TGH	225	NX	Y825TGH	241	NX	Y741TGH	257	BX	PL51LDY
209	NX	Y809TGH	226	NX	Y826TGH	242	NX	Y742TGH	258	BX	PL51LDZ
210	NX	Y801TGH	227	NX	Y827TGH	243	NX	Y743TGH	259	BX	PL51LEF
211	NX	Y811TGH	228	NX	Y828TGH	244	NX	Y744TGH	260	BX	PN02XBH
212	NX	Y812TGH	229	NX	Y729TGH	245	NX	Y745TGH	261	BX	PN02XBJ
213	NX	Y813TGH	230	NX	Y703TGH	246	NX	Y746TGH	262	PM	PN02XBK
214	NX	Y814TGH	231	NX	Y731TGH	247	NX	Y747TGH	263	SW	PN02XBL
215	NX	Y815TGH	232	NX	Y732TGH	248	NX	Y748TGH	264	NX	PN02XBM
216	NX	Y816TGH	233	NX	Y733TGH	249	NX	Y749TGH	265	A	PN02XBO
217	NX	Y817TGH	234	NX	Y734TGH	250	BX	PL51LDJ	266	A	PN02XBP
218	NX	Y818TGH	235	NX	Y735TGH	251	A	PL51LDK	267	BX	PN02XBR
219	NX	Y819TGH	236	NX	Y736TGH	252	A	PL51LDN	268	BX	PN02XBS
220	NX	Y802TGH	237	NX	Y737TGH	253	A	PL51LDO	269	BX	PN02XBT
221	NX	Y821TGH	238	NX	Y738TGH	254	BX	PL51LDU	270	BX	PN02XBU
222	NX	Y822TGH	239	NX	Y739TGH	255	BX	PL51LDV	271	BX	PN02XBV
223	NX	Y823TGH	240	NX	Y704TGH	256	BX	PL51LDX	272	BX	PN02XBW
224	NX	Y824TGH									

While the Go-Ahead London fleet operates fifty Dennis Tridents with President bodywork, it also has over four hundred built on the Volvo's competing product. With Somerset House in the background, PVL314, PJ52LVR, crosses Waterloo Bridge bound for Brockley Rise. *Mark Lyons*

PVL273-354   Volvo B7TL 10m   Plaxton President   N41/23D   2002-03

273	BX	PJ02RAU	294	Q	PJ02RDZ	315	NX	PJ52LVS	336	PM	PJ52LWR
274	BX	PJ02RAX	295	Q	PJ02REU	316	NX	PJ52LVT	337	PM	PJ52LWS
275	BX	PJ02RBF	296	Q	PJ02RFE	317	NX	PJ52LVU	338	PM	PJ52LWT
276	SW	PJ02RBO	297	Q	PJ02RFF	318	NX	PJ52LVV	339	PM	PJ52LWU
277	SW	PJ02RBU	298	Q	PJ02RFK	319	NX	PJ52LVW	340	PM	PJ52LWV
278	SW	PJ02RBV	299	Q	PJ02RFL	320	NX	PJ52LVX	341	PM	PJ52LWW
279	SW	PJ02RBX	300	Q	PJ02RFN	321	NX	PJ52LVY	342	PM	PJ52LWX
280	SW	PJ02RBY	301	Q	PJ02RFO	322	NX	PJ52LVZ	343	NX	PF52WPT
281	Q	PJ02RBZ	302	Q	PJ02RFX	323	NX	PJ52LWA	344	NX	PF52WPU
282	Q	PJ02RCF	303	Q	PJ02RFY	324	NX	PJ52LWC	345	NX	PF52WPV
283	Q	PJ02RCO	304	Q	PJ02RFZ	325	NX	PJ52LWD	346	NX	PF52WPW
284	Q	PJ02RCU	305	Q	PJ02RGO	326	Q	PJ52LWE	347	NX	PF52WPX
285	Q	PJ02RCV	306	Q	PJ02RGU	327	Q	PJ52LWF	348	NX	PF52WPY
286	Q	PJ02RCX	307	Q	PJ02RGV	328	Q	PJ52LWG	349	NX	PF52WPZ
287	Q	PJ02RCY	308	Q	PJ02TVN	329	Q	PJ52LWH	350	NX	PF52WRA
288	Q	PJ02RCZ	309	Q	PJ02TVO	330	Q	PJ52LWK	351	NX	PF52WRC
289	Q	PJ02RDO	310	Q	PJ02TVP	331	NX	PJ52LWL	352	NX	PF52WRD
290	Q	PJ02RDU	311	Q	PJ02TVT	332	PM	PJ52LWM	353	NX	PF52WRE
291	Q	PJ02RDV	312	Q	PJ02TVU	333	PM	PJ52LWN	354	NX	PF52WRG
292	Q	PJ02RDX	313	NX	PJ52LVP	334	PM	PJ52LWO			
293	Q	PJ02RDY	314	NX	PJ52LVR	335	PM	PJ52LWP			

PVL355-389   Volvo B7TL 10m   TransBus President   N41/23D   2003

355	NX	PL03AGZ	364	BX	PJ53SOU	373	AL	PJ53NKK	382	AL	PJ53NKW
356	Q	PJ53NJZ	365	BX	PJ53SPU	374	AL	PJ53NKL	383	AL	PJ53NKX
357	Q	PJ53NKA	366	BX	PJ53SPV	375	AL	PJ53NKM	384	AL	PJ53NKZ
358	Q	PJ53NKC	367	BX	PJ53SPX	376	AL	PJ53NKN	385	AL	PJ53NLA
359	Q	PJ53NKD	368	BX	PJ53SPZ	377	AL	PJ53NKO	386	AL	PJ53NLC
360	Q	PJ53NKE	369	BX	PJ53SRO	378	AL	PJ53NKP	387	AL	PJ53NLD
361	Q	PJ53NKF	370	BX	PJ53SRU	379	AL	PJ53NKR	388	AL	PJ53NLE
362	BX	PJ53SOF	371	AL	PJ53NKG	380	AL	PJ53NKS	389	AL	PJ53NLF
363	BX	PJ53SOH	372	AL	PJ53NKH	381	AL	PJ53NKT			

Six Wrightbus Electrocity bodied VDL Bus SB120s were acquired in the winter of 2005-06 for evaluation on London Central route 360 that links the Elephant & Castle with Queens Gate in Kensington. These hybrid vehicles are powered by electric batteries driving a traction motor which is supported by a generator, comprising of a 120kW electric motor, coupled with a 1.9 litre turbo diesel, common-rail Euro 4 engine. Energy harnessed from braking is recycled as kinetic energy back into the battery pack. This regenerates the battery and in turn assists in improving fuel economy, which initial tests have proved to be by as much as forty per cent. Here WHY6, LX55EAJ shows its dedicated branding. *Colin Lloyd*

PVL390-419 — Volvo B7TL 10m — Alexander Dennis President — N41/23D — 2004-5

390	NX	LX54HAA	398	NX	LX54GZK	406	NX	LX54GYV	413	NX	LX54GZE
391	NX	LX54HAE	399	NX	LX54GZL	407	NX	LX54GYW	414	NX	LX54GZF
392	NX	LX54HAO	400	NX	LX54GZM	408	NX	LX54GYY	415	NX	LX54GZU
393	NX	LX54HAU	401	NX	LX54GZN	409	NX	LX54GYZ	416	NX	LX54GZV
394	NX	LX54HBA	402	NX	LX54GZO	410	NX	LX54GZB	417	NX	LX54GZW
395	NX	LX54HBB	403	NX	LX54GZP	411	NX	LX54GZC	418	NX	LX54GZY
396	NX	LX54GZG	404	NX	LX54GZR	412	NX	LX54GZD	419	NX	LX54GZZ
397	NX	LX54GZH	405	NX	LX54GZT						

RM9 — AEC Routemaster R2RH — Park Royal — B36/28R — 1959

RM9	Q	VLT9

RML887-2604 — AEC Routemaster R2RH1 — Park Royal — B40/32R — 1961-67   *2516 is DRM and B40/32RD

887	AF	202UXJ	2305	SW	CUV305C	2472	NX	JJD472C	2520	AF	JJD520D
283	SW	CUV283C	2318	SW	CUV318C	2516	Q	WLT516	2604	AL	NML604E

WHY1-6 — VDL Bus SB120 — Wrightbus Cadet Electrocity — N26D — 2005-06

1	Q	LX06ECN	3	Q	LX55EAE	5	Q	LX55EAG	6	Q	LX55EAJ
2	Q	LX55EAC	4	Q	LX55EAF						

VWL1 — Volvo B7L 12m — Wrightbus Eclipse — N31D — 2002

VWL1	BX	LF51CYC

Until 2001 Wrightbus built only single-deck vehicles, and following the reorganisation and name change from Wright a new facility with capacity for double deck buses was opened in Ballymena. The Eclipse Gemini was initially available on Volvo and DAF/VDL Bus chassis and a model on Scania chassis has been announced. Operating with London Central names is WVL266, LX06EBV, which was photographed on South Norwood Hill. *Mark Lyons*

WVL1-121

Volvo B7TL 10.1m Wrightbus Eclipse Gemini 4.2m N41/23D 2002-03

1	SW	LG02KGP	32	AF	LF52ZRO	62	AF	LF52ZTG	92	SW	LF52ZND
2	SW	LG02KGU	33	AF	LF52ZRP	63	AF	LF52ZTH	93	SW	LF52ZNE
3	SW	LG02KGV	34	AF	LF52ZRR	64	AF	LF52ZTJ	94	SW	LF52ZNG
4	SW	LG02KGX	35	AF	LF52ZRT	65	AF	LF52ZTK	95	SW	LF52ZNH
5	SW	LG02KGY	36	AF	LF52ZRU	66	AF	LF52ZTL	96	SW	LF52ZNJ
6	SW	LG02KGZ	37	AF	LF52ZRV	67	AF	LF52ZTM	97	SW	LF52ZNK
7	SW	LG02KHA	38	AF	LF52ZRX	68	AF	LF52ZTN	98	SW	LF52ZNL
8	SW	LG02KHE	39	AF	LF52ZRY	69	AF	LF52ZTO	99	SW	LF52ZNM
9	SW	LG02KHF	40	AF	LF52ZRZ	70	AF	LF52ZTP	100	SW	LF52ZNN
10	SW	LG02KHH	41	AF	LF52ZSD	71	AF	LF52ZTR	101	SW	LF52ZNO
11	SW	LG02KHJ	42	AF	LF52ZPZ	72	SW	LF52ZPB	102	SW	LF52ZLZ
12	SW	LG02KHK	43	AF	LF52ZRA	73	SW	LF52ZPC	103	SW	LF52ZMO
13	SW	LG02KHL	44	AF	LF52ZRC	74	SW	LF52ZPD	104	SW	LF52ZMU
14	AF	LG02KHM	45	AF	LF52ZRD	75	SW	LF52ZPE	105	SW	LX03EXV
15	AF	LG02KHO	46	AF	LF52ZRE	76	SW	LF52ZPG	106	SW	LX03EXW
16	AF	LG02KHP	47	AF	LF52ZRG	77	SW	LF52ZPH	107	SW	LX03EXZ
17	AF	LG02KHR	48	AF	LF52ZRJ	78	SW	LF52ZPJ	108	SW	LX03EXU
18	AF	LG02KHT	49	AF	LF52ZRK	79	SW	LF52ZPK	109	SW	LX03EDR
19	AF	LG02KHU	50	AF	LF52ZRL	80	SW	LF52ZPL	110	SW	LX03EDU
20	AF	LG02KHV	51	AF	LF52ZRN	81	SW	LF52ZPM	111	SW	LX03EDV
21	AF	LG02KHW	52	AF	LF52ZPN	82	SW	LF52ZNP	112	SW	LX03EEA
22	AF	LG02KHX	53	AF	LF52ZPO	83	SW	LF52ZNR	113	SW	LX03EEB
23	AF	LG02KHY	54	AF	LF52ZPP	84	SW	LF52ZNS	114	SW	LX03EEF
24	AF	LG02KHZ	55	AF	LF52ZPR	85	SW	LF52ZNT	115	SW	LX03EEG
25	AF	LG02KJA	56	AF	LF52ZPS	86	SW	LF52ZNU	116	SW	LX03EEH
26	AF	LG02KJE	57	AF	LF52ZPU	87	SW	LF52ZNV	117	SW	LX03EEJ
27	AF	LG02KJF	58	AF	LF52ZPV	88	SW	LF52ZNW	118	SW	LX03EEM
28	AF	LF52ZSO	59	AF	LF52ZPW	89	SW	LF52ZNX	119	SW	LX03ECV
29	AF	LF52ZSP	60	AF	VLT60	90	SW	LF52ZNY	120	SW	LX03ECW
30	AF	LF52ZSR	61	AF	LF52ZPY	91	SW	LF52ZNZ	121	SW	LX03ECY
31	AF	LF52ZST									

The 2006-07 Go-Ahead Bus Handbook

WVL122-159   Volvo B7TL 10.1m   Wrightbus Eclipse Gemini 4.2m N41/23D 2003-04

122	SW	LX53AZP	132	SW	LX53AZD	142	SW	LX53AYP	151	SW	LX53BJU
123	SW	LX53AZR	133	SW	LX53AZF	143	SW	LX53AYT	152	SW	LX53BEY
124	SW	LX53AZT	134	SW	LX53AZG	144	SW	LX53AYU	153	SW	LX53BGE
125	SW	LX53AZU	135	SW	LX53AZJ	145	SW	LX53AYV	154	SW	LX53BFK
126	SW	LX53AZV	136	SW	LX53AZL	146	SW	LX53AYW	155	SW	LX53BDY
127	SW	LX53AZW	137	SW	LX53AZN	147	SW	LX53AYY	156	SW	LX53BBZ
128	SW	LX53AZZ	138	SW	LX53AZO	148	SW	LX53AYZ	157	SW	LX53BAA
129	SW	LX53AZA	139	SW	LX53AYM	149	SW	LX53BJK	158	SW	LX53BDO
130	SW	LX53AZB	140	SW	LX53AYN	150	SW	LX53BJO	159	SW	LX53BAO
131	SW	LX53AZC	141	SW	LX53AYO						

WVL160-211   Volvo B7TL 10.1m   Wrightbus Eclipse Gemini 4.2m N41/23D 2005

160	SW	LX05FBY	173	AF	LX05FBN	186	AF	LX05FAU	199	AF	LX05EZR
161	SW	LX05FBZ	174	AF	LX05FBO	187	AF	LX05FBA	200	AF	LX05EZS
162	SW	LX05FCA	175	AF	LX05FBU	188	AF	LX05FBB	201	AF	LX05EZT
163	SW	LX05FCC	176	AF	LX05EZJ	189	AF	LX05FBC	202	AF	LX05EZU
164	SW	LX05FCD	177	AF	LX05EYM	190	AF	LX05EZV	203	AF	LX05EYZ
165	SW	LX05FCE	178	AF	LX05EYO	191	AF	LX05EZW	204	AF	LX05EZA
166	SW	LX05FCF	179	AF	LX05FBV	192	AF	LX05EZZ	205	AF	LX05EZB
167	SW	LX05FBD	180	AF	LX05FAA	193	AF	LX05EZK	206	AF	LX05EZC
168	AF	LX05FBE	181	AF	LX05FAF	194	AF	LX05EZL	207	AF	LX05EZD
169	SW	LX05FBF	182	AF	LX05FAJ	195	AF	LX05EZM	208	AF	LX05EZE
170	AF	LX05FBJ	183	AF	LX05FAK	196	AF	LX05EZN	209	AF	LX05EZF
171	AF	LX05FBK	184	AF	LX05FAM	197	AF	LX05EZO	210	AF	LX05EZG
172	AF	LX05FBL	185	AF	LX05FAO	198	AF	LX05EZP	211	AF	LX05EZH

WVL212-273   Volvo B7TL 10.1m   Wrightbus Eclipse Gemini 4.2m N41/21D 2006

212	Q	LX06DXS	228	Q	LX06DZL	244	Q	LX06EAG	259	Q	LX06EBK
213	Q	LX06DXT	229	Q	LX06DZM	245	Q	LX06EAJ	260	Q	LX06EBL
214	Q	LX06DXU	230	Q	LX06DZN	246	Q	LX06EAK	261	Q	LX06EBM
215	Q	LX06DXV	231	Q	LX06DZO	247	Q	LX06EAL	262	Q	LX06EBN
216	Q	LX06DXW	232	Q	LX06DZP	248	Q	LX06EAM	263	Q	LX06EBO
217	Q	LX06DXY	233	Q	LX06DZR	249	Q	LX06EAO	264	Q	LX06EBP
218	Q	LX06DZA	234	Q	LX06DZS	250	Q	LX06EAP	265	Q	LX06EBU
219	Q	LX06DZB	235	Q	LX06DZT	251	Q	LX06EAW	266	Q	LX06EBV
220	Q	LX06DZC	236	Q	LX06DZU	252	Q	LX06EAY	267	Q	LX06EBZ
221	Q	LX06DZD	237	Q	LX06DZV	253	Q	LX06EBA	268	Q	LX06ECA
222	Q	LX06DZE	238	Q	LX06DZW	254	Q	LX06EBC	269	Q	LX06ECC
223	Q	LX06DZF	239	Q	LX06DZY	255	Q	LX06EBD	270	Q	LX06ECD
224	Q	LX06DZG	240	Q	LX06DZZ	256	Q	LX06EBE	271	Q	LX06ECE
225	Q	LX06DZH	241	Q	LX06EAA	257	Q	LX06EBG	272	Q	LX06ECF
226	Q	LX06DZJ	242	Q	LX06EAC	258	Q	LX06EBJ	273	Q	LX06ECJ
227	Q	LX06DZK	243	Q	LX06EAF						

Ancillary vehicles:

LDP75	PLt	R475LGH		Dennis Dart SLF 10m		Plaxton Pointer		TV	1997		

NV109-127   Volvo Olympian YN2RV18Z4   Northern Counties Palatine TV 1997

109	SWt	P909RYO	112	PLt	P912RYO	116	PLt	P916RYOO	124	Qt	P924RYO
110	Qt	P910RYO	113	PLt	P913RYO	117	Qt	P917RYO	127	NXt	P927RYO
111	Qt	P911RYO	114	PLt	P914RYO						

NV131-152   Volvo Olympian   Northern Counties Palatine TV 1998

131	PLt	R331LGH	137	PLt	R337LGH	143	PLt	R343LGH	147	PLt	R347LGH
132	PLt	R332LGH	138	PLt	R338LGH	144	PLt	R344LGH	148	At	WLT548
133	PLt	R433LGH	141	NXt	R341LGH	145	PLt	545CLT	152	PLt	352CLT
134	Qt	R334LGH	142	PLt	R342LGH						

NV166	Qt	R366LGH	Volvo Olympian	Northern Counties Palatine II	TV	1997	

Previous registrations:

78CLT	R378LGH	R474LGH	R474RGH, 174CLT
166CLT	R366LGH	R476LGH	R476LGH, 176CLT
197CLT	R387LGH	R552LGH	R552LGH, 352CLT
202UXJ	WLT887	S954JGX	WLT311
LF52ZNG	LF52ZNG, WLT694	S955JGX	S955JGX, WLT599
LF52ZPX	VLT60, LF52ZPX	V146LGC	V146LGC, 46CLT
N427JBV	N427JBV, WLT527	V332LGC	V332LGC, WLT532
P508RYM	P508RYM, 188CLT	VLT179	R379LGH
P509RYM	P509RYM, WLT379	VLT277	R377LGH
P908RYO	P908RYO, 698DYE	VLT284	R384LGH
PL51LDY	PL51LDY, 257CLT	W425WGH	W425WGH, WLT625
R345LGH	R345LGH, 545CLT	W578DGU	170CLT
R346LGH	R346LGH, WLT346	WLT470	R370LGH
R366LGH	R346LGH, 166CLT	WLT516	CUV283C
R472LGH	R472LGH, WLT872		

Depots and allocations:

Bexleyheath (Erith Road) - BX - London Central

Dart	DML1	DML2	DML3	DML4	DML5	DML6	DML8	DML10	
	DML11	DML12	DML14	DML15	DML17	DML18	DML19	DML20	
	DMS6	DMS7	DMS8	DMS9	LDP4	LDP5	LDP6	LDP7	
	LDP16	LDP57	LDP77	LDP107	LDP108	LDP109	LDP110	LDP111	
	LDP112	LDP113	LDP114	LDP115	LDP116	LDP117	LDP118	LDP119	
	LDP120	LDP121	LDP122	LDP123	LDP124	LDP125	LDP126	LDP127	
	LDP128								
DAF SB220	MD1	MD2	MD3	MD4	MD5	MD6	MD7	MD8	
	MD9	MD10	MD11	MD12	MD13	MD14	MD15	MD16	
	MD17								
Volvo B7L	VWL1								
Olympian	NV72	NV128	NV135	NV139					
Volvo B7TL	PVL1	PVL2	PVL3	PVL4	PVL5	PVL6	PVL7	PVL8	
	PVL9	PVL10	PVL11	PVL12	PVL13	PVL14	PVL15	PVL16	
	PVL17	PVL18	PVL19	PVL20	PVL21	PVL22	PVL23	PVL24	
	PVL25	PVL26	PVL27	PVL28	PVL29	PVL30	PVL31	PVL32	
	PVL33	PVL34	PVL35	PVL36	PVL37	PVL38	PVL39	PVL40	
	PVL41	PVL42	PVL43	PVL44	PVL45	PVL46	PVL47	PVL48	
	PVL49	PVL50	PVL51	PVL52	PVL53	PVL54	PVL55	PVL60	
	PVL82	PVL83	PVL120	PVL171	PVL226	PVL250	PVL254	PVL255	
	PVL257	PVL258	PVL259	PVL260	PVL261	PVL267	PVL268	PVL269	
	PVL270	PVL271	PVL272	PVL273	PVL274	PVL275	PVL362	PVL363	
	PVL364	PVL365	PVL366	PVL367	PVL368	PVL369	PVL370		

A recent arrival with London Central is an early example of the new Euro4-compliant Volvo B9TL. Bodied by Wrightbus it is seen in service on route 87. The bus carries the appropriate fleet identity of B9, BX06BTF.
Mark Lyons

Camberwell (Warner Road) - Q - London Central

Dart	LDP3	LDP64	LDP65	LDP67	LDP68	LDP70	LDP71	LDP72	
	LDP73	LDP79	LDP81	LDP82	LDP83	LDP84	LDP86	LDP87	
	LDP88	LDP153	LDP154	LDP155	LDP156	LDP157	LDP158	LDP159	
	LDP160	LDP161	LDP162	LDP163	LDP164	LDP165	LDP166	LDP182	
	LDP183	LDP184	LDP185	LDP186	LDP187	LDP188	LDP189	LDP190	
VDL Bus SB120	WHY1	WHY2	WHY3	WHY4	WHY5	WHY6			
Citaro	MAL62	MAL63	MAL64	MAL65	MAL66	MAL67	MAL68	MAL69	
	MAL70	MAL71	MAL72	MAL73	MAL74	MAL75	MAL76	MAL77	
	MAL78	MAL79	MAL80	MAL81	MAL82	MAL83	MAL84	MAL85	
	MAL86	MAL87	MAL88	MAL89	MAL90	MAL91	MAL92	MAL93	
	MAL94								
Routemaster	RML2516	RML2520							
Volvo B7TL	AVL1	AVL2	AVL3	AVL4	AVL5	AVL6	AVL7	AVL8	
	AVL9	AVL10	AVL11	AVL12	AVL13	AVL14	AVL16	AVL18	
	AVL20	AVL21	PVL59	PVL281	PVL282	PVL283	PVL284	PVL285	
	PVL286	PVL287	PVL288	PVL289	PVL290	PVL291	PVL292	PVL293	
	PVL294	PVL295	PVL296	PVL297	PVL298	PVL299	PVL300	PVL301	
	PVL302	PVL303	PVL304	PVL305	PVL306	PVL307	PVL308	PVL309	
	PVL310	PVL311	PVL312	PVL326	PVL327	PVL328	PVL329	PVL330	
	PVL356	PVL357	PVL358	PVL359	PVL360	PVL361	WVL212	WVL213	
	WVL214	WVL215	WVL216	WVL217	WVL218	WVL219	WVL220	WVL221	
	WVL222	WVL223	WVL224	WVL225	WVL226	WVL227	WVL228	WVL229	
	WVL230	WVL231	WVL232	WVL233	WVL234	WVL235	WVL236	WVL237	
	WVL238	WVL239	WVL240	WVL241	WVL242	WVL243	WVL244	WVL245	
	WVL246	WVL247	WVL248	WVL249	WVL250	WVL251	WVL252	WVL253	
	WVL254	WVL255	WVL256	WVL257	WVL258	WVL259	WVL260	WVL261	
	WVL262	WVL263	WVL264	WVL265	WVL266	WVL267	WVL268	WVL269	
	WVL270	WVL271	WVL272	WVL273					
Trainers	NV110	NV111	NV114	NV117	NV124	NV126	NV134	NV166	

*Buses in mauve are allocated to private hire duties

Merton (High Street) - AL - London General

Dart	LDP54	LDP55	LDP56	LDP59	LDP60	LDP61	LDP62	LDP78	
	LDP85	LDP89	LDP90	LDP91	LDP92	LDP93	LDP94	LDP95	
	LDP96	LDP97	LDP98	LDP99	LDP101	LDP102	LDP103	LDP104	
	LDP105	LDP106	LDP134	LDP135	LDP136	LDP137	LDP138	LDP139	
	LDP140	LDP141	LDP191	LDP192	LDP193	LDP194	LDP195	LDP196	
	LDP197	LDP198	LDP199	LDP200	LDP201	LDP202	LDP203	LDP204	
	LDP205	LDP206	LDP207	LDP208	LDP209	LDP210	LDP216	LDP217	
	LDP249	LDP250	LDP251	LDP252	LDP253	LDP254	LDP255	LDP256	
	LDP257	LDP258	LDP259	LDP260	LDP261	LDP262			
Routemaster	RML2604								
Olympian	NV171	NV174	NV178						
Volvo B7TL	PVL56	PVL57	PVL58	PVL63	PVL66	PVL67	PVL68	PVL69	
	PVL70	PVL74	PVL76	PVL77	PVL78	PVL81	PVL84	PVL85	
	PVL86	PVL87	PVL92	PLV93	PVL95	PVL96	PVL97	PVL98	
	PVL99	PVL100	PVL101	PVL102	PVL103	PVL104	PVL105	PVL106	
	PVL107	PVL108	PVL109	PVL110	PVL111	PVL112	PVL113	PVL114	
	PVL115	PVL116	PVL117	PVL118	PVL119	PVL121	PVL122	PVL123	
	PVL124	PVL125	PVL126	PVL127	PVL128	PVL129	PVL130	PVL131	
	PVL132	PVL133	PVL134	PVL135	PVL136	PVL137	PVL138	PVL139	
	PVL140	PVL141	PVL142	PVL143	PVL144	PVL145	PVL146	PVL147	
	PVL148	PVL149	PVL150	PVL151	PVL152	PVL153	PVL154	PVL155	
	PVL195	PVL206	PVL207	PVL251	PVL253	PVL371	PVL372	PVL373	
	PVL374	PVL375	PVL376	PVL377	PVL378	PVL379	PVL380	PVL381	
	PVL382	PVL383	PVL384	PVL385	PVL386	PVL387	PVL388	PVL389	

New Cross (New Cross Road) - NX - London Central

Dart	LDP69	LDP76	LDP142	LDP143	LDP144	LDP145	LDP146	LDP147
	LDP148	LDP273	LDP274	LDP275	LDP276	LDP277	LDP278	LDP279
	LDP280	LDP281	LDP282	LDP283	LDP284	LDP285	LDP286	
MB Citaro O530G	MAL32	MAL33	MAL34	MAL35	MAL36	MAL37	MAL38	MAL39
	MAL40	MAL41	MAL42	MAL43	MAL44	MAL45	MAL46	MAL47
	MAL48	MAL49	MAL50	MAL51	MAL52	MAL53	MAL54	MAL55
	MAL56	MAL57	MAL58	MAL59	MAL60	MAL61		
Routemaster	RM9	RML2472						
Olympian	NV165	NV173	NV182					
Volvo B7TL	PVL65	PVL71	PVL72	PVL73	PVL75	PVL78	PVL79	PVL88
	PVL89	PVL90	PVL91	PVL94	PVL156	PVL157	PVL158	PVL159
	PVL166	PVL167	PVL168	PVL169	PVL170	PVL172	PVL173	PVL174
	PVL175	PVL176	PVL177	PVL208	PVL209	PVL210	PVL211	PVL212
	PVL213	PVL214	PVL215	PVL216	PVL217	PVL218	PVL219	PVL220
	PVL221	PVL222	PVL223	PVL224	PVL225	PVL226	PVL227	PVL228
	PVL229	PVL230	PVL231	PVL232	PVL233	PVL234	PVL235	PVL236
	PVL237	PVL238	PVL239	PVL240	PVL241	PVL242	PVL243	PVL244
	PVL245	PVL246	PVL247	PVL248	PVL249	PVL264	PVL313	PVL314
	PVL315	PVL316	PVL317	PVL318	PVL319	PVL320	PVL321	PVL322
	PVL323	PVL324	PVL325	PVL331	PVL343	PVL344	PVL345	PVL346
	PVL347	PVL348	PVL349	PVL350	PVL351	PVL352	PVL353	PVL354
	PVL355	PVL390	PVL391	PVL392	PVL393	PVL394	PVL395	PVL396
	PVL397	PVL398	PVL399	PVL400	PVL401	PVL402	PVL403	PVL404
	PVL405	PVL406	PVL407	PVL408	PVL409	PVL410	PVL411	PVL412
	PVL413	PVL414	PVL415	PVL416	PVL417	PVL418	PVL419	
Trainers	NV127	NV141						

Peckham (Blackpool Road) - PM - London Central

Dart	LDP167	LDP168	LDP169	LDP170	LDP171	LDP172	LDP173	LDP174
	LDP175	LDP176	LDP177	LDP178	LDP179	LDP180	LDP181	
Olympian	NV181							
Volvo B7TL	AVL19	AVL22	AVL23	AVL24	AVL25	AVL26	AVL27	AVL28
	AVL29	AVL30	AVL31	AVL32	AVL33	AVL34	AVL35	AVL36
	AVL37	AVL38	AVL39	AVL40	AVL41	AVL42	AVL43	AVL44
	AVL45	AVL46	PVL160	PVL161	PVL162	PVL163	PVL164	PVL165
	PVL262	PVL332	PVL333	PVL334	PVL335	PVL336	PVL337	PVL338
	PVL339	PVL340	PVL341	PVL342				
Trident 2/Enviro	E16	E17	E18	E19	E20	E21	E22	E23
	E24	E25	E26	E27	E28	E29	E30	E31
	E32	E33	E34	E35	E36	E37		

Putney (Chelverton Road) - AF - London General

Dart	LDP129	LDP130	LDP131	LDP132	LDP133	LDP222	LDP223	LDP224
	LDP225	LDP226	LDP227	LDP228	LDP229	LDP230	LDP231	LDP232
	LDP233	LDP234	LDP235	LDP236	LDP237	LDP292	LDP293	LDP294
Routemaster	RML887							
Volvo B7TL	WVL14	WVL15	WVL16	WVL17	WVL18	WVL19	WVL20	WVL21
	WVL22	WVL23	WVL24	WVL25	WVL26	WVL27	WVL28	WVL29
	WVL30	WVL31	WVL32	WVL33	WVL34	WVL35	WVL36	WVL37
	WVL38	WVL39	WVL40	WVL41	WVL42	WVL43	WVL44	WVL45
	WVL46	WVL47	WVL48	WVL49	WVL50	WVL51	WVL52	WVL53
	WVL54	WVL55	WVL56	WVL57	WVL58	WVL59	WVL60	WVL61
	WVL62	WVL63	WVL64	WVL65	WVL66	WVL67	WVL68	WVL69
	WVL70	WVL71	WVL168	WVL170	WVL171	WVL172	WVL173	WVL174
	WVL175	WVL176	WVL177	WVL178	WVL179	WVL180	WVL181	WVL182
	WVL183	WVL184	WVL185	WVL186	WVL187	WVL188	WVL189	WVL190
	WVL191	WVL192	WVL193	WVL194	WVL195	WVL196	WVL197	WVL198
	WVL199	WVL200	WVL201	WVL202	WVL203	WVL204	WVL205	WVL206
	WVL207	WVL208	WVL209	WVL210	WVL211			

*Buses in mauve are allocated to private hire duties

The 2006-07 Go-Ahead Bus Handbook

Stockwell (Binfield Road) - SW - London General

Dart	LDP2	LDP211	LDP212	LDP213	LDP214	LDP215	LDP218	LDP219
	LDP220	LDP221	LDP238	LDP239	LDP240	LDP241	LDP242	LDP243
	LDP244	LDP245	LDP246	LDP247	LDP248	LDP263	LDP264	LDP265
	LDP266	LDP267	LDP268	LDP269	LDP270	LDP271	LDP272	LDP287
	LDP288	LDP289	LDP290	LDP291				
Routemaster	RML2305	RML2318						
Olympian	NV162	NV170						
Trident	PDL1	PDL3	PDL4	PDL5	PDL8	PDL9	PDL11	PDL12
	PDL13	PDL14	PDL15	PDL16	PDL17	PDL18	PDL19	PDL20
	PDL21	PDL22	PDL23	PDL24	PDL25	PDL26	PDL27	PDL28
	PDL29	PDL30	PDL31	PDL32	PDL33	PDL34	PDL35	PDL36
	PDL37	PDL38	PDL39	PDL40	PDL41	PDL42	PDL43	PDL44
	PDL45	PDL46	PDL47	PDL48	PDL49	PDL50		
Trident 2/Enviro	E1	E2	E3	E4	E5	E6	E7	E8
	E9	E10	E11	E12	E13	E14	E15	E38
	E39							
Volvo B7TL	PVL62	PVL64	PVL263	PVL276	PVL277	PVL278	PVL279	PVL280
	WVL1	WVL2	WVL3	WVL4	WVL5	WVL6	WVL7	WVL8
	WVL9	WVL10	WVL11	WVL12	WVL13	WVL72	WVL73	WVL74
	WVL75	WVL76	WVL77	WVL78	WVL79	WVL80	WVL81	WVL82
	WVL83	WVL84	WVL85	WVL86	WVL87	WVL88	WVL89	WVL90
	WVL91	WVL92	WVL93	WVL94	WVL95	WVL96	WVL97	WVL98
	WVL99	WVL100	WVL101	WVL102	WVL103	WVL104	WVL105	WVL106
	WVL107	WVL108	WVL109	WVL110	WVL111	WVL112	WVL113	WVL114
	WVL115	WVL116	WVL117	WVL118	WVL119	WVL120	WVL121	WVL122
	WVL123	WVL124	WVL125	WVL126	WVL127	WVL128	WVL129	WVL130
	WVL131	WVL132	WVL133	WVL134	WVL135	WVL136	WVL137	WVL138
	WVL139	WVL140	WVL141	WVL142	WVL143	WVL144	WVL145	WVL146
	WVL147	WVL148	WVL149	WVL150	WVL151	WVL152	WVL153	WVL154
	WVL155	WVL156	WVL157	WVL158	WVL159	WVL160	WVL161	WVL162
	WVL163	WVL164	WVL165	WVL166	WVL167	WVL169		
Trainer	NV109							

Sutton (Bushey Road) - A - London General

Dart	LDP1	LDP8	LDP9	LDP14	LDP37	LDP40	LDP41	LDP42
	LDP43	LDP44	LDP45	LDP46	LDP47	LDP48	LDP49	LDP51
	LDP52	LDP53	LDP74	LDP149	LDP150	LDP151	LDP152	
Olympian	NV167	NV168	NV175	NV176	NV179	NV183	NV184	NV185
	NV186	NV187						
Volvo B7TL	EVL1	EVL2	EVL3	EVL4	EVL5	EVL6	EVL7	EVL8
	EVL9	EVL10	EVL11	EVL12	EVL13	EVL14	EVL15	EVL16
	EVL17	EVL18	EVL19	EVL20	EVL21	EVL22	EVL23	EVL24
	EVL25	EVL26	EVL27	EVL28	EVL29	EVL30	EVL31	EVL32
	EVL33	EVL34	EVL35	EVL36	EVL37	EVL38	EVL39	EVL40
	EVL41	EVL42	EVL43	EVL44	EVL45	EVL46	EVL47	EVL48
	EVL49	EVL50	EVL51	EVL52	PVL61	PVL80	PVL179	PVL180
	PVL181	PVL182	PVL183	PVL184	PVL185	PVL186	PVL187	PVL188
	PVL189	PVL190	PVL191	PVL192	PVL193	PVL194	PVL252	PVL265
	PVL266							
Trainer	NV148							

*Buses in mauve are allocated to private hire duties

In 2002 the Red Arrow routes operating from Waterloo lost their Leyland National Greenways in favour of new Mercedes-Benz Citaros. Thirty-one carry Red Arrow names, and MAL3, BX02YZH, is seen crossing Lambeth Bridge. *Mark Lyons*

Waterloo (Cornwall Street) - RA - Red Arrow

MB Citaro O530G	MAL1	MAL2	MAL3	MAL4	MAL5	MAL6	MAL7	MAL8
	MAL9	MAL10	MAL11	MAL12	MAL13	MAL14	MAL15	MAL16
	MAL17	MAL18	MAL19	MAL20	MAL21	MAL22	MAL23	MAL24
	MAL25	MAL26	MAL27	MAL28	MAL29	MAL30	MAL31	

Wimbledon (Plough Lane) - PL - London General

Olympian	NV164	NV177						
Trainers	NV112	NV113	NV116	NV131	NV132	NV133	NV137	NV138
	NV142	NV143	NV144	NV145	NV147	NV152		

Several training buses are allocated to Driving Instructors rather than depots.
Buses in mauve are allocated to private hire duties

unallocated/stored - u

Dart	PDL2	PDL6	PDL7	PDL10	LDP15	LDP58	LDP66	LDP75
On loan:								
Oxford Bus Comapny	LDP32	LDP39						
Go South Coast	LDP36							
Diamond	NV104	NV107	NV161	NV163	NV180			
East Thames Buses	LDP34	LDP63	PVL196	PVL197	PVL198	PVL199	PVL200	PVL201
	PVL202	PVL203	PVL204	PVL205				

The 2006-07 Go-Ahead Bus Handbook

METROBUS

Metrobus Ltd, Wheatstone Close, Crawley, RH10 9UA

Metrobus was formed in 1983 to operate the bus and coach services previously provided by Tillingbourne (Metropolitan) Ltd; the business consisted of six vehicles based at Green Street Green near Orpington, Kent.

The opportunity to expand was soon realised and the company was to benefit from the London tendering system set up in 1985. Expansion on London Transport contracts and commercial initiatives increased the fleet to 120 buses by 1997.

The opportunity to expand outside of London was taken in June 1997 with the acquisition of East Surrey Bus Services of South Godstone with a portfolio of mainly County Council tendered work in the East Grinstead and Edenbridge areas.

At much the same time, the company set up a base in Lewes, East Sussex to operate many of the services previously provided by Leisurelink of Newhaven.

In September 1999, the Company joined the Go-Ahead Group and steady expansion continued both inside and outside of London.

The prestigious Gatwick Direct service started in May 2000 as a precursor to the proposed Fastway network of services planned for the Gatwick and Crawley areas in 2003.

In March 2001, Arriva gave up the operation of bus services in Crawley and Metrobus stepped in with a replacement network.

At the same time Surrey County Council had invited tenders for most of the work from the Arriva Merstham depot in East Surrey and Metrobus was successful with a bid for most of this work.

Further growth occurred from August 2003, when the Company was successful in gaining more London Buses contracts. Additionally, the long awaited Fastway service started in Crawley and this involved the first guided busway in Southern England.

In 2006, the Company acquired a new operating base at Croydon and the opportunity was taken to relocate services from the Godstone depot.

The Company now operates a fleet of over 350 buses from its three operating sites and employs 1100 staff.

117	CY	N417MPN	Dennis Lance 11m		Optare Sigma	B47F	1996	Brighton & Hove, 2003	
118	CY	N418MPN	Dennis Lance 11m		Optare Sigma	B47F	1996	Brighton & Hove, 2003	
158	CY	L58UNS	Volvo B10B		Alexander Strider	B51F	1993	Whitelaw, Stonehouse, 2002	
159	CY	L59UNS	Volvo B10B		Alexander Strider	B51F	1993	Whitelaw, Stonehouse, 2002	

201-219			TransBus Dart 10.7m		TransBus Pointer		N36F	2003	
201	CY	SN03WKU	206	CY	SN03WLH	211	C	SN03WLZ	216	MB	SN03WMP
202	CY	SN03WKY	207	CY	SN03WLL	212	C	SN03WMC	217	MB	SN03WMT
203	CY	SN03WLA	208	CY	SN03WLP	213	C	SN03WMF	218	MB	SN03WMV
204	CY	SN03WLE	209	C	SN03WLU	214	C	SN03WMG	219	MB	SN03WMY
205	CY	SN03WLF	210	C	SN03WLX	215	MB	SN03WMK		

220-223			TransBus Dart 10.5m		Caetano Nimbus		N32F	2004	Tellings-Golden Miller, 2005
220	MB	KX04HRD	221	MB	KX04HRE	222	MB	KX04HRF	223	MB	KX04HRG

224-227			Dennis Dart SLF 10m		Plaxton Pointer		N36F	1996	London General, 2002
224	CY	P724RYL	225	CY	P725RYL	226	CY	P726RYL	227	CY	P727RYL

While Metrobus vehicles on Transport for London (TfL) routes are liveried in the red scheme, buses outside the TfL area can still be found with the blue and yellow livery although this too has been superceeded by a new two-tone livery. Dennis Dart 303, P303HDP, is seen arriving in Brighton on route 87. *Mark Lyons*

241-245			Dennis Dart SLF 10m		Plaxton Pointer		N35F*	1998	*241 is N32F	
241	CY	R741BMY	243	CY	R743BMY	244	CY	R744BMY	245	CY	R745BMY
242	CY	R742BMY									
246	CY	R746FGX	Dennis Dart SLF 10m		Plaxton Pointer		N35F	1998		
247	CY	R747FGX	Dennis Dart SLF 10m		Plaxton Pointer		N35F	1998		

251-256			ADL Dart 8.8m		ADL Mini Pointer		N29F	2004		
251	MB	SN54GPV	253	MB	SN54GPY	255	MB	SN54GRF	256	MB	SN54GRK
252	MB	SN54GPX	254	MB	SN54GPZ						

257-268			ADL Dart 8.8m		East Lancs Myllennium*		N24F	2006	*Esteem fronts are fitted	
257	MB	PN06UYL	260	C	PN06UYP	263	C	PN06UYT	266	C	PN06UYW
258	MB	PN06UYM	261	C	PN06UYR	264	C	PN06UYU	267	C	PN06UYX
259	MB	PN06UYO	262	C	PN06UYS	265	C	PN06UYV	268	C	PN06UYY

271-289			TransBus Dart 8.8m		TransBus Pointer		N29F	2003		
271	C	SN03YBA	276	C	SN03YBK	281	MB	SN03YBY	286	MB	SN03YCK
272	C	SN03YBB	277	C	SN03YBR	282	MB	SN03YBZ	287	MB	SN03YCL
273	C	SN03YBC	278	MB	SN03YBS	283	MB	SN03YCD	288	MB	SN03YCM
274	C	SN03YBG	279	MB	SN03YBT	284	MB	SN03YCE	289	MB	SN03YCT
275	C	SN03YBH	280	MB	SN03YBX	285	MB	SN03YCF			

291-299			Dennis Dart SLF 8.8m		Plaxton Pointer MPD		N29F	2000		
291	CY	W791VMV	294	CY	W794VMV	296	CY	W796VMV	298	CY	W798VMV
292	CY	W792VMV	295	CY	W795VMV	297	CY	W797VMV	299	CY	W799VMV
293	CY	W793VMV									

301-308			Dennis Dart SLF 10m		Plaxton Pointer 2		N33F	1997	Limebourne, 1999	
301	CY	P301HDP	303	CY	P303HDP	305	CY	P305HDP	307	CY	P307HDP
302	CY	P302HDP	304	CY	P304HDP	306	CY	P306HDP	308	CY	P308HDP

In 2001 three 10m and fifteen 11m Darts with Caetano Nimbus bodies were delivered. Since 1998 Caetano bus bodies for the British market have been built in the former Wadham Stringer factory in Waterlooville. Pictured on the Tesco contract service 377, Y377HMY. *Phillip Stephenson*

309	CY	T309SMV	Dennis Dart SLF 10.2m		Alexander ALX200		N32F	1999		
310	CY	T310SMV	Dennis Dart SLF 10.2m		Alexander ALX200		N32F	1999		
311	CY	T311SMV	Dennis Dart SLF 10.2m		Alexander ALX200		N32F	1999		
312-319			Dennis Dart SLF 8.8m		Plaxton Pointer MPD		N29F	1999-2000		
312	MB	T312SMV	314	CY	T314SMV	316	C	T316SMV	319	C	W319VGX
313	MB	T313SMV	315	C	T315SMV	317	C	W317VGX		
320	CY	LX03OJP	TransBus Dart SLF 10.7m		TransBus Pointer		N37F	2003		
321	CY	LX03OJN	TransBus Dart SLF 10.7m		TransBus Pointer		N37F	2003		
322-338			Dennis Dart SLF 10.7m		Plaxton Pointer 2		N31D	1999-2000		
322	C	V322KMY	326	C	V326KMY	330	C	V330KMY	335	MB	W335VGX
323	C	V323KMY	327	C	V327KMY	331	C	V331KMY	336	MB	W336VGX
324	C	V324KMY	328	C	V328KMY	332	MB	V332VGX	337	MB	W337VGX
325	C	V325KMY	329	C	V329KMY	334	MB	V334VGX	338	MB	W338VGX
339-344			Dennis Dart SLF 8.8m		Plaxton Pointer MPD		N29F	2000		
339	C	W339VGX	342	MB	W342VGX	343	MB	W343VGX	344	CY	X344YGU
341	MB	W341VGX								
348-358			Dennis Dart SLF 8.8m		Plaxton Pointer MPD		N21F*	2001	*356-8 are N27F
348	MB	Y348HMY	352	MB	Y352HMY	354	MB	Y354HMY	357	MB	Y357HMY
349	MB	Y349HMY	353	MB	Y353HMY	356	MB	Y356HMY	358	MB	Y358HMY
351	MB	Y351HMY								
359-376			Dennis Dart SLF 11m		Caetano Nimbus		N38F	2001		
359	CY	Y359HMY	364	CY	Y364HMY	368	CY	Y368HMY	373	CY	Y373HMY
361	CY	Y361HMY	365	CY	Y365HMY	369	CY	Y369HMY	374	CY	Y374HMY
362	CY	Y362HMY	366	CY	Y366HMY	371	CY	Y371HMY	376	CY	Y376HMY
363	CY	Y363HMY	367	CY	Y367HMY	372	CY	Y372HMY		

The double-deck version of the Scania OmniCity, the OmniDekka, has seen increasing orders in recent years. Until now the bodywork on the double-deck has been assembled by East Lancs, although a new, Polish-built integral body has recently become available. Pictured in Croydon is 436, YV03PZF. *Mark Lyons*

377	CY	Y377HMY	Dennis Dart SLF 10m			Caetano Nimbus		N34F	2001		
378	CY	Y378HMY	Dennis Dart SLF 10m			Caetano Nimbus		N34F	2001		
379	CY	Y379HMY	Dennis Dart SLF 10m			Caetano Nimbus		N34F	2001		

381-393			Dennis Dart SLF 8.8m			Plaxton Pointer MPD		N27F	2001		
381	MB	Y381HKE	384	MB	Y384HKE	387	MB	Y387HKE	391	MB	Y391HKE
382	MB	Y382HKE	385	MB	Y385HKE	388	MB	Y388HKE	392	MB	Y392HKE
383	MB	Y383HKE	386	MB	Y386HKE	389	MB	Y389HKE	393	MB	Y393HKE

| 398 | MB | BU04UTN | Mercedes-Benz Sprinter 411Cdi | | | Koch | | N16F | 2004 | Tellings-Golden Miller, 2005 | |
| 399 | MB | BU04UTP | Mercedes-Benz Sprinter 411Cdi | | | Koch | | N16F | 2004 | Tellings-Golden Miller, 2005 | |

417-428			Dennis Trident 9.9m			East Lancs Lolyne 4.4m		N45/23D	2001-02		
417	MB	LV51YCC	420	MB	LV51YCF	423	MB	LV51YCJ	426	MB	LV51YCM
418	MB	LV51YCD	421	MB	LV51YCG	424	MB	LV51YCK	427	MB	LV51YCN
419	MB	LV51YCE	422	MB	LV51YCH	425	MB	LV51YCL	428	MB	LV51YCO

431-447			Scania N94UD OmniDekka 10.6m			East Lancs 4.4m		N45/29D	2003		
431	C	YV03PZW	436	C	YV03PZF	440	C	YV03PZK	444	C	YV03RCZ
432	C	YV03PZX	437	C	YV03PZG	441	C	YV03PZL	445	C	YV03RAU
433	C	YV03PZY	438	C	YV03PZH	442	C	YV03PZM	446	C	YV03RAX
434	C	YV03PZZ	439	C	YV03PZJ	443	C	YV03RCY	447	C	YV03RBF
435	C	YV03PZE									

451-471			Scania N94UD OmniDekka 10.6m			East Lancs 4.4m		N45/29D	2003		
451	C	YU52XVK	457	C	YU52XVR	462	C	YN03DFK	467	MB	YN03DFX
452	C	YU52XVL	458	C	YN03DFD	463	C	YN03DFL	468	C	YN03DFY
453	C	YU52XVM	459	C	YN03DFE	464	C	YN03DFP	469	MB	YV03RBU
454	C	YU52XVN	460	C	YN03DFG	465	C	YN03DFU	470	C	YV03RBX
455	C	YN03DFA	461	C	YN03DFJ	466	C	YN03DFV	471	MB	YV03RBY
456	C	YN03DFC									

With the exception of a 2002 example and five from 2005, the Scania OmniCity buses operated by Metrobus are dual door. The single-door examples are to be found on route X26 which links London Heathrow with Croydon. Of the latter, 545, YN05HFJ, illustrates this layout. *Mark Lyons*

472-497			Scania N94UD OmniDekka 10.6m East Lancs 4.4m				N45/29D	2003-05	
472	MB	YN53RYA	479	MB	YN53RYM	486	MB	YN53RYY	492	MB	YN53RZE
473	MB	YN53RYB	480	MB	YN53RYP	487	MB	YN53RYZ	493	MB	YN53RZF
474	MB	YN53RYC	481	MB	YN53RYR	488	MB	YN53RZA	494	MB	YN54AJU
475	MB	YN53RYD	482	MB	YN53RYT	489	MB	YN53RZB	495	MB	YN54AJV
476	MB	YN53RYF	483	MB	YN53RYV	490	MB	YN53RZC	496	MB	YN54AJX
477	MB	YN53RYH	484	MB	YN53RYW	491	C	YN53RZD	497	MB	YN54AJY
478	MB	YN53RYK	485	MB	YN53RYX						

513	CY	YP52CTO	Scania OmniCity CN94UB 12m		Scania			N42F	2002	

514-530			Scania OmniCity CN94UB 12m		Scania			N37D	2003	
514	MB	YN53RXF	519	MB	YN53RXL	523	MB	YN53RXR	527	MB	YN53RXW
515	MB	YN53RXG	520	MB	YN53RXM	524	MB	YN53RXT	528	MB	YN53RXX
516	MB	YN53RXH	521	MB	YN53RXO	525	MB	YN53RXU	529	MB	YN53RXY
517	MB	YN53RXJ	522	MB	YN53RXP	526	MB	YN53RXV	530	MB	YN53RXZ
518	MB	YN53RXK								

531-545			Scania OmniCity CN94UB 12m		Scania			N37D*	2003-05	*541-5 are N36F
531	CY	YN03UWU	535	CY	YN03WPR	539	CY	YN03WRL	543	C	YN05HFG
532	CY	YN03UWY	536	CY	YN03WRF	540	CY	YN03WRP	544	C	YN05HFH
533	CY	YN03UPM	537	CY	YN03WRG	541	C	YN05HFE	545	C	YN05HFJ
534	CY	YN03WPP	538	CY	YN03WRJ	542	C	YN05HFF			

546-558			Scania OmniCity CN94UB 12m		Scania			N37D*	2005	*552-558 are N34D
546	CY	YN05HCA	550	CY	YN05HCF	553	CY	YN55PWK	556	CY	YN55PWU
547	CY	YN05HCC	551	CY	YN05HCG	554	CY	YN55PWL	557	CY	YN55PWV
548	CY	YN05HCD	552	CY	YN55PWJ	555	CY	YN55PWO	558	CY	YN55PWX
549	CY	YN05HCE									

Recently arrived with Metrobus is a batch of Scania OmniTowns with East Lancs Myllennium bodywork. However, as the batch was about to enter build, the new Esteem body was announced and it was decided that the batch would incorporate this new frontal design on the Myllennium body. The result is seen on 604, YM55SWX. *Mark Lyons*

601-623   Scania OmniTown N94UB 10.6m   East Lancs Myllennium*   N29D   2006   *Esteem fronts are fitted

601	MB	YM55SWU	607	MB	YM55SXA	613	MB	YN06JXT	619	MB	YM55SXO
602	MB	YM55SWV	608	MB	YM55SXB	614	MB	YM55SXH	620	MB	YM55SXP
603	MB	YN06JXR	609	MB	YM55SXC	615	MB	YN06JXU	621	MB	YM55SXR
604	MB	YM55SWX	610	MB	YM55SXD	616	MB	YN06JXV	622	MB	YN06JXY
605	MB	YM55SWY	611	MB	YM55SXE	617	MB	YN06JXW	623	MB	YN06JXZ
606	MB	YN06JXS	612	MB	YM55SXF	618	MB	YN06JXX			

721	u	M721CGO	Dennis Dart 9.8m	Plaxton Pointer	B35F	1995	
726	u	N726KGF	Dennis Dart 9.8m	Plaxton Pointer	B35F	1995	
757	u	P895PWW	Dennis Dart 9.8m	Plaxton Pointer	B40F	1997	Ambermile, Honley, 1998
758	u	R58GNW	Dennis Dart 9.8m	Plaxton Pointer	B40F	1997	

817-829   Volvo Olympian YN2RV18Z4   Northern Counties Palatine   B47/29F   1996

817	CY	P817SGP	821	CY	P821SGP	824	CY	P824SGP	828	CY	P828SGP
818	CY	P818SGP	822	CY	P822SGP	825	CY	P825SGP	829	CY	P829SGP
819	CY	P819SGP	823	CY	P823SGP	826	CY	P826SGP			

830-845   Volvo Olympian   East Lancs Pyoneer   B47/25D   1997

830	CY	R830MFR	834	CY	R834MFR	838	CY	R838MFR	843	CY	R843MFR
831	CY	R831MFR	835	CY	R835MFR	839	CY	R839MFR	844	CY	R844MFR
832	CY	R832MFR	836	CY	R836MFR	841	CY	R841MFR	845	CY	R845MFR
833	CY	R833MFR	837	CY	R837MFR	842	CY	R842MFR			

901-927   Scania N94UD OmniDekka 10.6m   East Lancs 4.4m   N45/26D   2006

901	MB	YN55PZC	908	MB	YN55PZL	915	MB	YN55PZW	922	C	YN06JYG
902	MB	YN55PZD	909	MB	YN55PZM	916	MB	YN55PZX	923	C	YN06JYH
903	MB	YN55PZE	910	MB	YN55PZO	917	C	YN06JYB	924	C	YN06JYJ
904	MB	YN55PZF	911	MB	YN55PZP	918	C	YN06JYC	925	C	YN06JYK
905	MB	YN55PZG	912	MB	YN55PZR	919	C	YN06JYD	926	C	YN06JYL
906	MB	YN55PZH	913	MB	YN55PZU	920	C	YN06JYE	927	C	YN06JYO
907	MB	YN55PZJ	914	MB	YN55PZV	921	C	YN06JYF			

The 2006-07 Go-Ahead Bus Handbook

Special Event vehicle:

RML2317	CY	CUV317C	AEC Routemaster R2RH1	Park Royal	B40/32R	1965	London Central, 2004

Ancillary vehicles:

7762	LR	M502VJO	Dennis Dart 9.8m	Marshall C37	TV	1995	Oxford Citybus, 2004
7763	LR	M511VJO	Dennis Dart 9.8m	Marshall C37	TV	1995	Oxford Citybus, 2004
7764	LR	M516VJO	Dennis Dart 9.8m	Marshall C37	TV	1995	Oxford Citybus, 2004
7765	LR	M520VJO	Dennis Dart 9.8m	Marshall C37	TV	1995	Oxford Citybus, 2004
7766	CY	M506VJO	Dennis Dart 9.8m	Marshall C37	TV	1995	Oxford Citybus, 2004
7767	CY	M507VJO	Dennis Dart 9.8m	Marshall C37	TV	1995	Oxford Citybus, 2004
7768	CY	M508VJO	Dennis Dart 9.8m	Marshall C37	TV	1995	Oxford Citybus, 2004
7769	CY	M518VJO	Dennis Dart 9.8m	Marshall C37	TV	1995	Oxford Citybus, 2004

8001-8015 — Ford Transit — Ford — Crew — 2003

8001	MB	GV53RHU	8005	MB	GV53RJO	8010	C	GV53MDX	8013	C	GP53CLV
8002	MB	GV53RHY	8006	MB	GV53RJX	8011	C	GP53CPY	8014	CY	GP53RBX
8003	MB	GV53RHZ	8007	C	GV53RJY	8012	C	GP53COJ	8015	CY	AM03AGU
8004	MB	GV53RJJ	8009	C	GV53RKF						

8017	C	RO06TUU	Mercedes-Benz Vito 111cdi	Mercedes-Benz	Crew	2005

On order: 228-236 ADL Dart 8.8m/East Lancs and 928-946 Scania OmniDekka N94UD/East Lancs

Depots and allocations:

Crawley (Wheatstone Close) - CY

Dart	757	758						
Dart SLF	201	202	203	204	205	206	207	208
	224	225	226	227	241	242	243	244
	245	246	247	291	292	293	294	295
	296	297	298	299	301	302	303	304
	305	306	307	308	309	310	311	314
	320	321	344	359	361	362	363	364
	365	366	367	368	369	370	371	372
	373	374	375	376	377	378	379	
Lance	117	118						
Volvo B10B	158	159						
Scania OmniCity	513	531	532	533	534	535	536	537
	538	539	540	546	547	548	549	550
	551	552	553	554	555	556	557	558
Routemaster	RM2317							
Volvo Olympian	817	818	819	820	821	822	823	824
	825	826	827	828	829	830	831	832
	833	834	835	836	837	838	839	841
	842	843	844	845				
Ancillary	7766	7767	7768	7769	8014	8015		

Croydon (Beddington Lane) - C

Dart	209	210	211	212	213	214	260	261
	262	263	264	265	266	267	268	271
	272	273	274	275	276	277	315	316
	317	318	319	322	323	324	325	326
	327	328	328	330	331	339		
Scania OmniCity	541	542	543	544	545			
Scania OmniDekka	431	432	433	434	435	436	437	438
	439	440	441	442	443	444	445	446
	447	451	452	453	454	455	456	457
	458	459	460	461	462	463	464	465
	466	468	491	917	918	919	920	921
	922	923	924	925	926	927		
Ancillary	8007	8009	8010	8011	8012	8013	8017	

Featuring the *Fastway* livery is Crawley depot's Scania OmniCity 534, YN03WPP. This is one of the vehicles fitted with guide wheels for the Crawley to Gatwick *Fastway* route 10 introduced in 2003. *Mark Lyons*

Orpington (Farnborough Hill, Green Street Green) - MB

Mercedes-Benz	398	399						
Dart SLF	215	216	217	218	219	220	221	222
	223	251	252	253	254	255	256	257
	258	259	278	279	280	281	282	283
	284	285	286	287	288	289	312	313
	332	334	335	336	337	338	341	342
	343	348	349	351	352	353	354	356
	357	358	381	382	383	384	385	386
	387	388	389	391	392	393	721	726
Scania OmniCity	514	515	516	517	518	519	520	521
	522	523	524	525	526	527	528	529
	530							
Scania OmniTown	601	602	603	604	605	606	607	608
	609	610	611	612	613	614	615	616
	617	618	619	620	621	622	623	
Trident	417	418	419	420	421	422	423	424
	425	426	427	428				
Scania OmniDekka	467	469	470	471	472	473	474	475
	476	477	478	479	480	481	482	483
	484	485	486	487	488	489	490	492
	493	494	495	496	497	901	902	903
	904	905	906	907	908	909	910	911
	912	913	914	915	916			
Ancillary	8001	8002	8003	8004	8005	8006		

Orpington (Lagoon Road, St Mary Cray) - LR

Ancillary	7762	7763	7764	7765	
Dart	723				

The 2006-07 Go-Ahead Bus Handbook

BRIGHTON & HOVE

Brighton & Hove Bus and Company Ltd, 43 Conway Street, Hove, BN3 3LT

The Company began life as Brighton, Hove and Preston United running regular horse bus services across the town in 1884 from the site of the current head office and garage in Conway Street, Hove. In 1916 these operations became a division of the privately owned Tilling Group that had already commenced bus operation in the towns.

The Company was established as a separate legal entity within Tilling's as Brighton, Hove & District Omnibus Company Ltd in 1935, with a change of ownership, when absorbed by the British Transport Commission in 1948 and the Transport Holding Company in 1962.

The state-owned National Bus Company took over in 1969 and Brighton, Hove & District Omnibus Company became dormant with its operations merged into the neighbouring Southdown bus company.

The dormant Company began trading again in 1986 and was renamed Brighton & Hove Bus and Coach Company Ltd. Privatised through a management buy-out in 1987, it was acquired by Go-Ahead in 1993, which in turn was floated as a plc in 1994.

The Group has gone on to acquire other bus companies, including Brighton Transport Ltd in 1997 (whose origins can be traced back to the start of tram operations in Brighton in 1901), which it merged with Brighton & Hove that year.

Since then, the enlarged Brighton & Hove has gone from strength to strength achieving up to 5% passenger growth year on year. Key initiatives such as real time information, a citywide flat fare and frequent Metro services have attracted many new customers, making the bus in Brighton an essential feature of city life.

In September 2005, the company acquired the neighbouring business interests of Stagecoach in the Lewes, Uckfield, Seaford and Eastbourne areas to expand its geographic coverage more extensively into East Sussex.

5-20			Dennis Dart 9.8m			Marshall C37		B40F*	1995	*14 is B41F	
5	LR	N505KCD	9	LR	N509KCD	12		B40F*	15	WK	N515KCD
7	WK	N507KCD	10	LR	N510KCD	14	WK	N514KCD	20	LR	N520KCD
65-79			Dennis Dart 9.8m			Plaxton Pointer		B40F	1995	Brighton Blue Bus, 1997	
65	u	M65CYJ	71	LR	M71CYJ	76	LR	M76CYJ	79	CS	M79CYJ
68	u	M68CYJ	73	LR	M73CYJ	78	CS	M78CYJ			
81	w	M95WBW	Dennis Dart 9.8m			Plaxton Pointer		B37D	1995	Stagecoach, 2005	
82	w	M96WBW	Dennis Dart 9.8m			Plaxton Pointer		B37D	1995	Stagecoach, 2005	
83	w	M97WBW	Dennis Dart 9.8m			Plaxton Pointer		B37D	1995	Stagecoach, 2005	
84	w	L720UMV	Dennis Dart 9.8m			Plaxton Pointer		B35F	1994	Metrobus, Crawley, 2005	
96	WK	N216NPN	Dennis Dart 9.8m			Plaxton Pointer		B40F	1996	Brighton Blue Bus, 1997	
97	WK	N217NPN	Dennis Dart 9.8m			Plaxton Pointer		B40F	1996	Brighton Blue Bus, 1997	
98	WK	N218NPN	Dennis Dart 9.8m			Plaxton Pointer		B40F	1996	Brighton Blue Bus, 1997	

In September 2005, the company acquired the neighbouring business interests of Stagecoach in the Lewes, Uckfield, Seaford and Eastbourne areas. The vehicles acquired with the operation were principally Lances, Darts and Tridents. The low-floor Lance buses carry Berkhof 2000 bodies. Seen shortly after gaining fleet livery is 282, M405OKM, although the type has since been taken out of service. *Dave Heath*

101-120			Dennis Lance 11m		Optare Sigma		B47F*	1996	119/20 are BC47F
101	u	N401MPN	106	LR	N406MPN	110	u	N410MPN	115	LR	N415MPN
102	CS	N402MPN	107	LR	N407MPN	112	LR	N412MPN	116	LR	N416MPN
103	WK	N403MPN	108	WR	N408MPN	113	LR	N413MPN	119	CS	N419MPN
104	LR	N404MPN	109	u	N409MPN	114	LR	N414MPN	120	LR	N420MPN
105	WK	N405MPN									

201-215			Dennis Dart SLF		Plaxton Pointer		N39F	1996	Brighton Blue Bus, 1997
201	CS	N201NNJ	205	CS	N205NNJ	209	CS	N209NNJ	213	LR	N213NNJ
202	WK	N202NNJ	206	CS	N206NNJ	210	CS	N210NNJ	214	LR	N214NNJ
203	LR	N203NNJ	207	CS	N207NNJ	211	CS	N211NNJ	215	LR	N215NNJ
204	CS	N204NNJ	208	WK	N208NNJ	212	LR	N212NNJ			

216-236			Volvo B10BLE		Wright Renown		N46F	1997-98	
216	CS	R216HCD	222	CS	R322HCD	227	LR	R227HCD	232	CS	R232HCD
217	CS	R217HCD	223	CS	R223HCD	228	LR	R228HCD	233	CS	R233HCD
218	CS	R218HCD	224	CS	R224HCD	229	LR	R229HCD	234	CS	R234HCD
219	CS	R219HCD	225	CS	R225HCD	230	CS	R230HCD	235	CS	R235HCD
220	CS	R220HCD	226	CS	R226HCD	231	CS	R231HCD	236	LR	R236HCD

246	LR	X346YGU	Dennis Dart SLF 8.8m	Plaxton Pointer MPD	N29F	2000	Metrobus, Crawley, 2003
247	LR	X347YGU	Dennis Dart SLF 8.8m	Plaxton Pointer MPD	N29F	2000	Metrobus, Crawley, 2003

281-285			Dennis Lance SLF		Berkhof 2000		N40F	1994	Stagecoach, 2005
281	u	M404OKM	283	u	M406OKM	284	u	M407OKM	285	u	M408OKM
282	u	M405OKM									

301	GD	LW52AFA	Optare Solo M850		Optare		N27F	2002	
401	CS	YN06NYK	Scania N94UD OmniDekka 10.6m	East Lancs 4.4m		NC51/33F	2006	Metrobus, Crawley, 2006
402	CS	YN06NYL	Scania N94UD OmniDekka 10.6m	East Lancs 4.4m		NC51/33F	2006	
503	CS	T503RPN	Volvo B10M-62		Plaxton Excalibur		C49FT	1999	
504	CS	T504RPN	Volvo B10M-62		Plaxton Excalibur		C49FT	1999	

The 2006-07 Go-Ahead Bus Handbook

Unusual among the major operators, Brighton & Hove has continued to run a small modern coach fleet. Recent additions have been Irizar Century-bodied Scanias. New in 2004, 509, YN04ANU, shows how the corporate style has been incorporated on this model. *Phillip Stephenson*

505	CS	W605OCD	Volvo B10M-62	Plaxton Excalibur	C49FT	2000		
506	CS	W606OCD	Volvo B10M-62	Plaxton Excalibur	C49FT	2000		
507	CS	Y867GCD	Volvo B10M-62	Plaxton Paragon	C49FT	2001		
508	CS	GX02ATF	Volvo B12M	Plaxton Paragon	C49FT	2002		
509	CS	YN04ANU	Scania K114IB4	Irizar Century 12.5	C49FT	2004		
510	CS	YN05GZS	Scania K114IB4	Irizar Century 12.5	C49FT	2005		

601-618   Scania OmniDekka N94UD   East Lancs   N47/32F*   2003   *617/8 are CO47/32F

601	WK	GX03SVF	606	CS	GX03SUF	611	CS	GX03SVA	615	CS	GX03SSU
602	WK	GX03SVG	607	CS	GX03SUH	612	CS	GX03SVC	616	CS	GX03SSV
603	WK	GX03SVJ	608	CS	GX03SUU	613	CS	GX03SVD	617	CS	GX03SSZ
604	CS	GX03SVK	609	CS	GX03SUV	614	CS	GX03SVE	618	CS	GX03STZ
605	CS	GX03SUA	610	CS	GX03SUY						

619-654   Scania N94UD   East Lancs Cityzen   N47/32F   2004-05

619	WK	YN04GJE	628	WK	YN04GKA	637	WK	YN54AOM	646	WK	YN54AOY
620	WK	YN04GJF	629	WK	YN04GKC	638	WK	YN54AOO	647	WK	YN05GZK
621	WK	YN04GJG	630	WK	YN04GKD	639	WK	YN54AOP	648	WK	YN05GZM
622	WK	YN04GJJ	631	WK	YN04GJX	640	WK	YN54AOR	649	LR	YN05GZH
623	WK	YN04GJK	632	WK	YN04GKE	641	WK	YN54AOT	650	LR	YN05GZJ
624	WK	YN04GJU	633	WK	YN04GKF	642	WK	YN54AOU	651	LR	YN05GZL
625	WK	YN04GJV	634	WK	YN04GKG	643	WK	YN54AOV	652	LR	YN05GZO
626	WK	YN04GJY	635	WK	YN04GKJ	644	WK	YN54AOW	653	LR	YN05GZP
627	WK	YN04GJZ	636	WK	YN04GKK	645	WK	YN54AOX	654	LR	YN05GZR

655-670   Scania N94UD OmniDekka 10.6m East Lancs 4.4m   N47/32F   2005-06

655	LR	YN55NFF	659	LR	YN55NFL	663	WK	YN55NFJ	667	WK	YN06SZW
656	LR	YN55NFO	660	LR	YN55NFM	664	WK	YN55NFC	668	WK	YN06SZX
657	LR	YN55NFH	661	LR	YN55NFE	665	WK	YN55NFD	669	WK	YN06SZY
658	LR	YN55NFK	662	LR	YN55NFA	666	WK	YN55NFG	670	LR	YN06SZZ

One of the promotional 'I'm on the bus' displays is seen on Plaxton President 866, PK02RDO. It is seen in Cornfield Road in Eastbourne. *Mark Lyons*

712-729			Scania N113DRB		East Lancs		B47/32F	1989-90	
712	WK	F712LFG	726	LR	G726RYJ	728	u	G728RYJ	729	LR	G729RYJ
725	WK	G725RYJ	727	LR	G727RYJ					

751-781			Scania N113DRB		East Lancs Cityzen		B47/31F	1996-98	*761-4/78-81 are BC47/31F
751	LR	N751OAP	759	LR	N759OAP	767	LR	P867VFG	775	WK	P875VFG
752	LR	N752OAP	760	LR	N760OAP	768	LR	P868VFG	776	WK	P876VFG
753	LR	N753OAP	761	LR	P861VFG	769	LR	P869VFG	777	WK	P877VFG
754	LR	N754OAP	762	LR	P862VFG	770	LR	P870VFG	778	LR	R878HCD
755	LR	N755OAP	763	CS	P863VFG	771	LR	P871VFG	779	LR	R879HCD
756	LR	N756OAP	764	CS	P864VFG	772	LR	P872VFG	780	LR	R880HCD
757	LR	N757OAP	765	LR	P865VFG	773	WK	P873VFG	781	CS	R881HCD
758	LR	N758OAP	766	LR	P866VFG	774	WK	P874VFG			

801-820			Dennis Trident		East Lancs Lolyne		N47/31F*	1999	*819-20 are CO47/32F
801	CS	T801RFG	806	CS	T806RFG	811	WK	T811RFG	816	WK	T816RFG
802	CS	T802RFG	807	CS	T807RFG	812	CS	T812RFG	817	WK	T817RFG
803	CS	T803RFG	808	CS	T808RFG	813	WK	T813RFG	818	WK	T818RFG
804	CS	T804RFG	809	CS	T809RFG	814	WK	T814RFG	819	CS	T819RFG
805	CS	T805RFG	810	CS	T810RFG	815	WK	T815RFG	820	CS	T820RFG

821-840			Dennis Trident		East Lancs Lolyne		N47/31F	1999-2000	
821	WK	W821NNJ	826	LR	W826NNJ	831	LR	W831NNJ	836	LR	W836NNJ
822	WK	W822NNJ	827	LR	W827NNJ	832	LR	W832NNJ	837	LR	W837NNJ
823	LR	W823NNJ	828	CS	W828NNJ	833	LR	W833NNJ	838	LR	W838NNJ
824	LR	W824NNJ	829	LR	W829NNJ	834	LR	W834NNJ	839	LR	W839NNJ
825	LR	W825NNJ	830	CS	W830NNJ	835	LR	W835NNJ	840	LR	W840NNJ

841-864			Dennis Trident		Plaxton President		N47/30F	2001	
841	CS	Y871GCD	847	CS	Y877GCD	853	CS	Y853GCD	859	CS	Y859GCD
842	CS	Y872GCD	848	CS	Y878GCD	854	CS	Y854GCD	860	CS	Y869GCD
843	CS	Y873GCD	849	CS	Y879GCD	855	CS	Y865GCD	861	CS	Y861GCD
844	CS	Y874GCD	850	CS	Y866GCD	856	CS	Y856GCD	862	CS	Y862GCD
845	CS	Y875GCD	851	CS	Y851GCD	857	CS	Y857GCD	863	CS	Y863GCD
846	CS	Y876GCD	852	CS	Y852GCD	858	CS	Y858GCD	864	WK	Y864GCD

The 2006-07 Go-Ahead Bus Handbook

865-876			Dennis Trident			Plaxton President		N47/30F	2002	
865	CS	PK02RCZ	868	CS	PK02RDV	871	CS	PK02RDZ	874	LR	PK02RFF
866	CS	PK02RDO	869	WK	PK02RDX	872	CS	PK02REU	875	LR	PK02RFJ
867	CS	PK02RDU	870	CS	PK02RDY	873	CS	PK02RFE	876	LR	PK02RFL

881-887			Dennis Trident 10.5m			Alexander ALX400 4.2m		N51/26F	1999	Stagecoach, 2005
881	WK	T669KPU	883	WK	T671KPU	885	WK	T673KPU	887	WK	T677KPU
882	WK	T670KPU	884	WK	T672KPU	886	WK	T675KPU			

901-918			Scania N94UD OmniDekka 10.6m			East Lancs 4.4m		N51/37F	2006	
901	-	YN56FFA	906	-	YN56FFG	911	-	YN56FFM	915	-	YN56FFS
902	-	YN56FFB	907	-	YN56FFH	912	-	YN56FFO	916	-	YN56FFT
903	-	YN56FFC	908	-	YN56FFJ	913	-	YN56FFP	917	-	YN56FFU
904	-	YN56FFD	909	-	YN56FFK	914	-	YN56FFR	918	-	YN56FFV
905	-	YN56FFE	910	-	YN56FFL						

Ancillary vehicles:					
69	M69CYJJ	Dennis Dart 9.8m	Plaxton Pointer	TV	1995
111	N411MPN	Dennis Lance 11m	Optare Sigma	TV	1996
221	R221HCD	Volvo B10BLE	Wright Renown	TV	1998
T1	J980JNJ	Dennis Dart 9.8SDL3017	Plaxton Pointer	TV	1992	Brighton Blue Bus, 1997
T2	J984JNJ	Dennis Dart 9.8SDL3017	Plaxton Pointer	TV	1992	Brighton Blue Bus, 1997

Heritage vehicle:					
6447	HAP985	Bristol KSW6G	Eastern Coach Works	H32/28R	1953	preservation 1986

Web: www.buses.co.uk

Depots and allocations:

Brighton (Lewes Road) - LR

Outstation: Uckfield

Dart	5	9	10	12	20	71	73	76
	203	212	213	214	215	246	247	
Lance	104	106	107	112	113	114	115	116
Volvo B10BLE	227	228	229	236				
Scania DD	649	650	651	652	653	654	655	656
	657	658	659	660	670	726	727	729
	751	752	753	754	755	756	757	758
	759	760	761	762	765	766	767	768
	769	770	771	772	778	779	780	
Trident	823	824	825	826	827	831	832	833
	834	835	836	837	838	839	840	874
	875	876						
Heritage	6447							

Brighton (Whitehawk Road): - WK

Outstations: Eastbourne and Newhaven

Dart	7	14	15	96	97	98	202	203
Lance	103	105	106	108				
Scania	601	602	603	619	620	621	622	623
	624	625	626	627	628	629	630	631
	632	633	634	635	636	637	638	639
	640	641	642	643	644	645	646	647
	648	661	662	663	664	665	666	667
	668	669	712	725	773	774	775	776
	777							
Trident	811	813	814	815	816	817	818	821
	822	864	869	881	882	883	884	885
	886	887						

As we go to press a further eighteen Scania OmniDekkas are being delivered. From the 2004 order, 834, YN04GKG, is seen in Palmeira Square in Hove, while operating route 1 for which it is route branded.
Mark Lyons

Hove (Conway Street): - CS

Outstation: Worthing

Solo	301							
Dart	78	79	201	204	205	206	207	209
	210	211						
Volvo B10BLE	217	218	219	220	222	223	224	230
	231	232	233	234	235			
Lance	102	119	120					
Volvo coach	503	504	505	506	507	508		
Scania coach	401	402	509	510	781			
Scania	604	605	606	607	608	609	610	611
	612	613	614	615	616	617	618	763
	764							
Trident	801	802	803	804	805	806	807	808
	809	810	812	819	820	828	829	830
	841	842	843	844	845	846	847	848
	849	850	851	852	853	854	855	856
	857	858	859	860	861	862	863	865
	866	867	868	870	871	872	873	

Unallocated/stored: u

Lance	101	109	110	281	282	283	284	285
Scania	728	730						
Heritage	6447							
Trainers	T1	T2	69	111	221			

GO SOUTH COAST

Wilts & Dorset - Damory Coaches - Tourist Coaches
Bell's Coaches - Kingston Coaches - Solent Blue Line - Southern Vectis

Wilts & Dorset Bus Co Ltd; Hants & Dorset Motor Services Ltd; Tourist Coaches Ltd;
Towngate House, Parkstone Road, Poole, BH15 2PR
Solent Blue Line Ltd, Barton Park, Eastleigh, SO50 6RR
Southern Vectis Omnibus Co Ltd, Nelson Road, Newport, PO31 1RD

The name Wilts & Dorset was first seen on the sides of buses in 1915, when a service commenced between Salisbury and Amesbury. Meanwhile on the South Coast, a company founded as Bournemouth and District Motor Services changed its name to Hants & Dorset in 1920 as its network of routes expanded. The 1920s and 1930s were a period of development and growth for the companies, while the Second World War brought vastly increased traffic to the Wilts & Dorset fleet in particular, which served the many military establishments on Salisbury Plain.

Both companies were nationalised in 1948, and from January 1969 became part of the National Bus Company. The name Wilts & Dorset disappeared in 1972 when the Company was subsumed into Hants & Dorset.

Go South Coast is the name given to the Go-Ahead management group that covers the area from Dorset to the Isle of Wight. Pictured on the island is Plaxton President Volvo B7TL 106, HW52EPV. *Mark Lyons*

Thirty-eight Volvo B7RLEs with Wrightbus Eclipse Urban bodies were supplied in 2004. Most carry the *More* livery, seen here on 113, HF54HGD, which carries route lettering for the service between Poole and Christchurch. *Dave Heath*

In April 1983 Wilts & Dorset was re-born with an operating area now including Poole, Swanage, Lymington, Ringwood, Salisbury and Pewsey. Privatised in 1987, during the 1990s the company acquired five local coach operators: Damory, Tourist, Kingston, Bell's and Lever's. Wilts & Dorset became part of the Go-Ahead Group in August 2003.

2004 saw a fresh start for Wilts & Dorset with a new identity developed to take the company forward into the future. The livery and image capture the valued heritage of the company while modernising it for today's discerning customers.

The biggest outward sign of a new and innovative commercial approach is the fleet of new Volvo buses for more routes in Poole and Bournemouth. Believed to be the most highly specified urban buses in the UK, they are designed to challenge the perception that in-town transport simply requires a basic vehicle. To date, 25% passenger growth has been achieved, with many people attracted from the private car.

Wilts and Dorset

101-138			Volvo B7RLE			Wrightbus Eclipse Urban	N40F	2004		
101	BM	HF54HFO	111	BM	HF54HGA	121	P	HF54HGO	130	P	HF54HHE
102	BM	HF54HFP	112	BM	HF54HGC	122	P	HF54HGP	131	S	HF54HHJ
103	BM	HF54HFR	113	BM	HF54HGD	123	P	HF54HGU	132	S	HF54HHK
104	BM	HF54HFT	114	BM	HF54HGE	124	P	HF54HGX	133	S	HF54HHL
105	BM	HF54HFU	115	BM	HF54HGG	125	P	HF54HGY	134	S	HF54HHM
106	BM	HF54HFV	116	BM	HF54HGJ	126	P	HF54HHA	135	S	HF05HXD
107	BM	HF54HFW	117	BM	HF54HGK	127	P	HF54HHB	136	S	HF05HXE
108	BM	HF54HFX	118	BM	HF54HGL	128	P	HF54HHC	137	S	HF05HXG
109	BM	HF54HFY	119	BM	HF54HGM	129	P	HF54HHD	138	S	HF05HXH
110	BM	HF54HFZ	120	P	HF54HGN						

The order for new vehicles for 2006 was placed with Mercedes-Benz to supply thirty Citaro O530 buses. Pictured on Salisbury *pulseline* route is 158, HF55JZG. As can be seen on the bus, the service crosses the town from Bemerton Heath to the District Hospital. *Dave Heath*

151-178			Mercedes-Benz Citaro O530		Mercedes-Benz		N39F	2006		
151	P	HF55JYX	158	S	HF55JZG	165	P	HF55JZP	172	P	HF06FTP
152	S	HF55JYY	159	S	HF55JZJ	166	P	HF55JZR	173	P	HF06FTT
153	S	HF55JYZ	160	S	HF55JZK	167	P	HF55JZT	174	P	HF06FTU
154	S	HF55JZA	161	P	HF55JZL	168	P	HF55JZU	175	P	HF06FTV
155	S	HF55JZC	162	S	HF55JZM	169	P	HF55JZV	176	P	HF06FTX
156	S	HF55JZD	163	S	HF55JZN	170	P	HF55JZW	177	u	HF06FTY
157	S	HF55JZE	164	P	HF55JZO	171	u	HF06FTO	178	P	HF06FTZ

401-413			Volvo B7TL		East Lancs Vyking		CO49/29F	2005	*401-4 are N49/29F	
401	P	HF54KXT	405	L	HF05GGE	408	u	HF05GGO	411	L	HF05GGV
402	P	HF54KXU	406	L	HF05GGJ	409	u	HF05GGP	412	L	HF05GGX
403	P	HF54KXV	407	L	HF05GGK	410	L	HF05GGU	413	L	HF05GGY
404	P	HF54KXW									

2228-2241			Optare Metrorider MR15		Optare		B31F	1995-96	Trent Buses, 2000	
2228	S	P228CTV	2232	S	P232CTV	2236	S	P236CTV	2239	S	P239CTV
2229	S	P229CTV	2233	S	P233CTV	2237	S	P237CTV	2240	S	P240CTV
2230	S	P230CTV	2234	S	P234CTV	2238	S	P238CTV	2241	S	P241CTV
2231	S	P231CTV	2235	S	P235CTV						

2515	S	R221HCD	Optare MetroRider MR05		Optare		B31F	1992		

2535-2545			Optare MetroRider MR15		Optare		B31F	1995-96		
2535	S	M535JLJ	2537	S	M537JLJ	2541	S	M541LEL	2545	S	N545UFX
2536	S	M536JLJ	2539	S	M539LEL	2544	S	N544UFX			

The open-top bus has long been a feature of operations in coastal towns in Britain. In 2005 Wilts and Dorset took the unusual step of purchasing nine new low-floor, open-top buses. These were East Lancs Vyking-bodied Volvo B7TLs. Showing the splendour of these buses is 407, HF05GGK. *Dave Heath*

2602-2632   Optare Solo M850   Optare   N30F   1998

2603	P	R603NFX	2614	R	R614NFX	2621	S	R621NFX	2627	S	S627JRU
2604	P	R604NFX	2615	P	R615NFX	2622	S	R622NFX	2628	S	S628JRU
2605	P	R905NFX	2616	R	R616NFX	2623	S	S623JRU	2629	S	S629JRU
2609	P	R609NFX	2617	S	R617NFX	2624	S	S624JRU	2630	S	S630JRU
2610	P	R610NFX	2618	S	R618NFX	2625	S	S625JRU	2631	S	S631JRU
2612	P	R612NFX	2619	S	R619NFX	2626	S	S626JRU	2632	S	S632JRU
2613	P	R613NFX	2620	S	R620NFX						

2633-2688   Optare Solo M850   Optare   N30F   1999-2001

2633	L	T633AJT	2647	P	T647AJT	2662	P	V662DFX	2676	L	V676FEL
2634	L	T634AJT	2648	P	T648AJT	2663	P	V663DFX	2677	R	V677FEL
2635	L	T635AJT	2649	P	T649AJT	2664	B	V665DFX	2678	R	V678FEL
2636	P	T636AJT	2651	S	V651DFX	2665	S	V664DFX	2679	R	V679FEL
2637	P	T637AJT	2652	S	V653DFX	2666	S	V966DFX	2680	R	V680FEL
2638	P	T638AJT	2653	P	V652DFX	2667	B	V667DFX	2681	L	V681FEL
2639	P	T639AJT	2654	R	V654DFX	2668	B	V668DFX	2682	L	V682FEL
2640	P	T640AJT	2655	R	V655DFX	2669	B	V669DFX	2683	L	V683FEL
2641	P	T641AJT	2656	S	V656DFX	2670	B	V670DFX	2684	L	V684FEL
2642	P	T642AJT	2657	S	V657DFX	2671	S	V671FEL	2685	L	V685FEL
2643	P	T643AJT	2658	S	V658DFX	2672	S	V672FEL	2686	R	V686FEL
2644	P	T644AJT	2659	B	V659DFX	2673	S	V673FEL	2687	S	X687XJT
2645	P	T645AJT	2660	S	V660DFX	2674	L	V674FEL	2688	S	X688XJT
2646	P	T646AJT	2661	P	V661DFX	2675	L	V675FEL			

3101-3147   DAF DB250   Optare Spectra   B48/29F*   1993-95   *3136-9 are BC45/28F

3101	S	K101VLJ	3114	P	L114ALJ	3127	L	L127ELJ	3137	S	M137KRU
3103	R	K103VLJ	3115	R	L115ALJ	3128	L	L128ELJ	3138	S	M138KRU
3104	R	K104VLJ	3116	R	L116ALJ	3129	S	L129ELJ	3139	S	M139KRU
3105	S	K105VLJ	3117	R	L117ALJ	3130	S	L130ELJ	3140	SW	M140KRU
3106	S	K106VLJ	3118	B	L118ALJ	3131	S	L131ELJ	3141	R	M141KRU
3107	S	K107VLJ	3120	S	L120ALJ	3132	S	M132HPR	3143	SW	M143KRU
3108	S	K108VLJ	3122	B	L122ELJ	3133	B	M133HPR	3144	B	M144KRU
3110	S	K110VLJ	3123	B	L123ELJ	3134	B	M134HPR	3145	SW	M145KRU
3111	P	L711ALJ	3124	B	L124ELJ	3135	B	M135HPR	3146	SW	M146KRU
3112	P	L112ALJ	3126	L	L126ELJ	3136	S	M136KRU	3147	SW	M947KRU
3113	P	L113ALJ									

The 2006-07 Go-Ahead Bus Handbook

One of the classic buses of the 1970s was the Bristol VR and Wilts & Dorset retains eighteen of the thirty-three in the Go South Coast fleet. Illustrating the model is 4449, KRU849W. *Phillip Stephenson*

3148	SW	M17WAL	DAF DB250		Northern Counties Palatine II		CO47/30F	1995	Wall's of Manchester, 1997
3149	SW	M18WAL	DAF DB250		Northern Counties Palatine II		CO47/30F	1995	Wall's of Manchester, 1997
3150	SW	M19WAL	DAF DB250		Northern Counties Palatine II		CO47/30F	1995	Wall's of Manchester, 1997
3151	SW	M20WAL	DAF DB250		Northern Counties Palatine II		CO47/30F	1995	Wall's of Manchester, 1997
3152	SW	N13WAL	DAF DB250		Northern Counties Palatine II		CO47/30F	1995	Wall's of Manchester, 1997
3153	SW	N14WAL	DAF DB250		Northern Counties Palatine II		CO47/30F	1995	Wall's of Manchester, 1997
3154	S	R154NPR	DAF DB250		Optare Spectra		N50/28F	1998	
3155	S	R155NPR	DAF DB250		Optare Spectra		N50/28F	1998	
3156	S	R156NPR	DAF DB250		Optare Spectra		N50/28F	1998	
3157	SW	M645RCP	DAF DB250		Northern Counties Palatine		CO47/30F	1995	A Bus, Brislington, 1998

3158-3166   DAF DB250   Optare Spectra   N50/28F   1999-2000

3158	S	T158ALJ	3161	R	W161RFX	3163	L	W163RFX	3165	S	W165RFX
3159	S	T159ALJ	3162	L	W162RFX	3164	S	W164RFX	3166	S	W166RFX
3160	S	T160ALJ								

3167-3175   DAF DB250   Optare Spectra   N50/27F   2001

3167	S	Y167FEL	3170	P	Y199FEL	3172	R	Y172FEL	3174	R	Y174FEL
3168	S	Y168FEL	3171	P	Y171FEL	3173	R	Y173FEL	3175	S	Y975FEL
3169	R	Y169FEL								

3176-3185   DAF DB250   Optare Spectra   N50/26F   2002-03

3176	P	HJ02WDK	3179	P	HJ02WDN	3182	S	HJ52VFY	3184	S	HJ52VGA
3177	P	HJ02WDL	3180	S	HJ52VFW	3183	S	HJ52VFZ	3185	P	HF03AEG
3178	P	HJ02WDM	3181	S	HJ52VFX					

3214	S	R214NFX	DAF SB3000	Plaxton Première 320	C53F	1998	
3215	S	R215NFX	DAF SB3000	Plaxton Première 320	C53F	1998	
3216	S	T216REL	DAF SB3000	Plaxton Prestige	C49FT	1999	
3217	S	T217REL	DAF SB3000	Plaxton Prestige	C49FT	1999	
3218	S	T218REL	DAF SB3000	Plaxton Prestige	C49FT	1999	
3233	S	R807NUD	Volvo B10M-62	Plaxton Première 350	C53F	1997	City 0f Oxford, 2004
3234	S	R812NUD	Volvo B10M-62	Plaxton Première 350	C53F	1997	City 0f Oxford, 2004
3235	S	R813NUD	Volvo B10M-62	Plaxton Première 350	C53F	1997	City 0f Oxford, 2004

Optare produced some five hundred and eighty Excel buses and the type is to be found in most of the Go-Ahead fleets. The fifteen with Wilts & Dorset are the 11.8 metre version represented here by the last to arrive, 3615, HF03HKA. *Phillip Stephenson*

3501-3506			DAF SB220			Optare Delta		B48F	1993		
3501	L	L501AJT	3503	S	L503AJT	3505	R	L505AJT	3506	S	L506AJT
3502	L	L502AJT	3504	S	L504AJT						
3507	R	N10WAL	DAF SB220			Ikarus CitiBus		B49F	1995	Wall's of Manchester, 1997	
3601-3604			Optare Excel L1180			Optare		N43F	2000		
3601	BM	W601PLJ	3602	BM	W602PLJ	3603	BM	W603PLJ	3604	BM	W604PLJ
3605-3609			Optare Excel L1180			Optare		N43F*	2000	*3609 is N42F	
3605	S	X605XFX	3607	S	X607XFX	3608	S	X608XFX	3609	P	X609WLJ
3606	S	X606XFX									
3610-3615			Optare Excel L1180			Optare		N42F	2002-03		
3610	P	HJ02WDE	3612	P	HJ02WDG	3614	S	HF03HJZ	3615	S	HF03HKA
3611	P	HJ02WDF	3613	S	HF03HJY						
4004	S	G94RGG	Volvo B10M-60			Plaxton Paramount 3500 III		C49F	1990	Park's of Hamilton, 1995	
4422-4456			Bristol VRT/SL3/6LXB			Eastern Coach Works		B43/31F	1977-78	Hants & Dorset, 1983	
4422	P	ELJ214V	4429	P	GEL679V	4448	L	KRU848W	4453	L	KRU853W
4423	P	ELJ215V	4430	P	GEL680V	4449	L	KRU849W	4454	P	KRU854W
4424	P	ELJ216V	4431	R	GEL681V	4450	L	KRU850W	4455	L	KRU855W
4426	P	ELJ218V	4432	R	GEL682V	4451	L	KRU851W	4456	L	KRU856W
4427	P	ELJ219V	4437	S	GEL687V						
4901	P	A901JPR	Leyland Olympian ONLXB/1R			Eastern Coach Works		B45/32F	1984		
4903	S	A903JPR	Leyland Olympian ONLXB/1R			Eastern Coach Works		B45/32F	1984		
4923	S	A175VFM	Leyland Olympian ONLXB/1R			Eastern Coach Works		B45/32F	1984	Crosville Cymru, 1990	
5168	P	P319DOP	LDV Pilot			LDV		M8	1996		

Damory Coaches

5011	BH	N45FWU	DAF SB3000	Plaxton Première 350	C53F	1996	
5012	BH	LIL3748	DAF SB3000	Plaxton Première 350	C51FT	1996	Armchair, Brentford, 1999
5013	BH	M574RCP	DAF SB3000	Van Hool Alizée HE	C55F	1994	North Kent Express, 2001
5014	BH	M746RCP	DAF SB3000	Van Hool Alizée HE	C55F	1994	North Kent Express, 2001
5015	BH	M577RCP	DAF SB3000	Van Hool Alizée HE	C55F	1994	North Kent Express, 2002
5016	BH	M578RCP	DAF SB3000	Van Hool Alizée HE	C55F	1994	North Kent Express, 2002
5018	BH	M580RCP	DAF SB3000	Van Hool Alizée HE	C55F	1994	North Kent Express, 2002
5023	BH	UEL489	Volvo B10M-60	Plaxton Première 320	C53F	1993	Thamesdown, 1999
5026	BH	LIL2665	Volvo B10M-62	Plaxton Première 320	C53F	1996	Woodstones, K'minster, 2002
5027	BH	VUV246	Volvo B10M-62	Plaxton Excalibur	C49FT	1996	Flights, Birmingham, 2002
5032	BH	XXI8502	Volvo B10M-62	Plaxton Première 350	C53F	1997	City of Oxford, 2004
5033	BH	G373GJT	Volvo B10M-60	Plaxton Paramount 3200 III	C57F	1990	Thamesdown, 1998
5034	BH	E313OMG	Volvo B10M-61	Plaxton Paramount 3200 III	C57F	1988	Limebourne, Battersea, 1994
5035	BH	G392GJT	Volvo B10M-61	Plaxton Paramount 3200 III	C53F	1990	Excelsior, Bournemouth, 1995
5036	BH	K750RHR	Volvo B10M-60	Plaxton Première 350	C53F	1993	Bell, Winterslow, 1999
5044	BH	M15WAL	DAF SB220	Ikarus CitiBus	B48F	1994	Wall's of Manchester, 1997
5046	BH	N15WAL	DAF SB220	Ikarus CitiBus	B49F	1995	Wall's of Manchester, 1997
5047	BH	N16WAL	DAF SB220	Ikarus CitiBus	B49F	1995	Wall's of Manchester, 1997
5058	BH	L52UNS	Volvo B10B	Northern Counties Paladin	B51F	1993	Whitelaw, Stonehouse, 2001
5059	BH	L53UNS	Volvo B10B	Northern Counties Paladin	B51F	1993	Whitelaw, Stonehouse, 2001
5063	BH	URU691S	Bristol VRT/SL3/6LXB	Eastern Coach Works	B43/31F	1978	Hants & Dorset, 1983
5066	BH	URU673S	Bristol VRT/SL3/6LXB	Eastern Coach Works	B43/31F	1977	Hants & Dorset, 1983
5069	BH	GEL655V	Bristol VRT/SL3/6LXB	Eastern Coach Works	B43/31F	1978	Hants & Dorset, 1983
5070	BH	GEL686V	Bristol VRT/SL3/6LXB	Eastern Coach Works	B43/31F	1978	Hants & Dorset, 1983
5072	BH	BFX666T	Bristol VRT/SL3/6LXB	Eastern Coach Works	B43/31F	1976	Hants & Dorset, 1983
5073	BH	UDL671S	Bristol VRT/SL3/6LXB	Eastern Coach Works	B43/31F	1978	Hants & Dorset, 1983
5074	BH	ELJ220V	Bristol VRT/SL3/6LXB	Eastern Coach Works	B43/31F	1978	
5076	BH	URU690S	Bristol VRT/SL3/6LXB	Eastern Coach Works	B43/31F	1978	
5090	BH	N602FJO	Volvo B10B	Plaxton Verde	B51F	1995	City of Oxford, 2006
5091	BH	N608FJO	Volvo B10B	Plaxton Verde	B51F	1995	City of Oxford, 2006
5092	BH	N416NRG	Volvo B10B	Plaxton Verde	B51F	1995	City of Oxford, 2006
5124	BH	P94DOE	LDV Convoy	LDV	M8	1996	
5125	BH	R710YFL	LDV Convoy	LDV	M16	1997	private owner, 1998
5126	BH	R815UOK	LDV Convoy	LDV	M16	1997	private owner, 1998
5133	u	J503RPR	Optare MetroRider MR05	Optare	B31F	1992	
5135	BH	J505RPR	Optare MetroRider MR05	Optare	B31F	1992	
5138	BH	J508RPR	Optare MetroRider MR05	Optare	B31F	1992	
5141	BH	M540LEL	Optare MetroRider MR15	Optare	B31F	1995	
5143	BH	N543UFX	Optare MetroRider MR15	Optare	B31F	1996	
5146	BH	N226VRC	Optare Metrorider MR15	Optare	B31F	1995	Trent Buses, 2000
5147	BH	N546UFX	Optare MetroRider MR15	Optare	B31F	1996	
5148	BH	N547UFX	Optare MetroRider MR15	Optare	B31F	1996	
5166	BH	N614HRV	LDV 200	LDV	M8	1996	MoD (FD64AA), 1997
5169	BH	DX03UBP	LDV Pilot	LDV	M8	2003	
5170	BH	R37GDE	LDV Pilot	LDV	M8	1998	Coupland, Wyre, 1999
5601	BH	R601NFX	Optare Solo M850	Optare	N30F	1998	
5602	BH	R602NFX	Optare Solo M850	Optare	N30F	1998	
6114	BH	J512RPR	Optare MetroRider MR05	Optare	B31F	1992	

The Damory Coaches operation is based at Blandford where it is planned to open a new depot shortly. Pictured in the summer of 2006 at the Alton transport rally is Bristol VR 5072, BFX666T.
Richard Godfrey

Tourist Coaches (including Kingston and Bell's)

6003	TC	BU03LXX	Mercedes-Benz Touro 1836RL	Mercedes-Benz	C49FT	2003	Hemmings, Holsworthy, 2006
6009	TC	SIL7914	DAF MB230	Van Hool Alizée	C49FT	1995	Wilson, Bonnyrigg, 2000
6010	TC	SIB5373	DAF MB230	Van Hool Alizée	C51F	1994	Hallmark, Luton, 2001
6015	TC	HJI2615	DAF MB230	Van Hool Alizée	C53F	1993	Wootten, Northampton, 2000
6016	TC	HSV342	DAF SB3000	Van Hool Alizée HE	C49FT	1996	Couplands, Wyre, 1999
6017	TC	TJI9462	DAF MB230	Van Hool Alizée	C57F	1993	First Lowland, 2001
6019	TC	381VHX	DAF SB3000	Van Hool Alizée HE	C49FT	1996	Wood, Barnsley, 2000
6026	TC	R126XWF	Dennis Javelin	Plaxton Première 320	C51F	1998	Stort Valley, Stansted, 2000
6027	TC	UJI2507	Dennis Javelin	Plaxton Première 320	C53F	1998	Stort Valley, Stansted, 2000
6029	TC	RJI6055	Dennis Javelin	Plaxton Première 320	C53F	1998	Stort Valley, Stansted, 2000
6030	TC	R130XWF	Dennis Javelin	Plaxton Première 320	C53F	1998	Stort Valley, Stansted, 2000
6035	TC	LSV749	Volvo B10M-60	Plaxton Première 350	C49F	1993	Spirit of London, 1996
6043	TC	NXI5358	Volvo B10M-60	Plaxton Paramount 3200 III	C57F	1990	Thamesdown, 1998
6048	TC	OIJ1875	Volvo B10M-62	Plaxton Première 350	C53F	1995	Woodstones, K'minster, 2002
6051	TC	SJI8751	Dennis Javelin 8.5SDA1915	Plaxton Paramount 3200 III	C33F	1989	Kingston, Salisbury, 1991
6054	TC	W254KDO	Mercedes-Benz Vario O814	Autobus Nouvelle 2	C29F	2000	Benson, Seaton, 2002
6061	TC	AT02CJT	Volvo B7R	Jonckheere Modulo	C52F	2002	Turner, Bristol, 2006
6062	TC	BT02CJT	Volvo B7R	Jonckheere Modulo	C53F	2002	Turner, Bristol, 2006
6164	TC	M817ARV	LDV 200	LDV	M8	1995	Adams, Ringwood, 1995
6166	TC	P693UAE	LDV Pilot	LDV	M8	1997	Churchfields, Salisbury, 1998
6213	TC	701GOO	DAF SB3000	Plaxton Première 350	C51FT	1996	Carplan, Rossall, 1999
6214	TC	MJI7514	DAF MB230	Van Hool Alizée	C51FT	1993	First Lowland, 2000
6222	TC	N322WCH	Optare Metrorider MR15	Optare	B31F	1995	Trent Buses, 2000
6224	TC	N324VRC	Optare Metrorider MR15	Optare	B31F	1995	Trent Buses, 2000
6225	TC	N325VRC	Optare Metrorider MR15	Optare	B31F	1995	Trent Buses, 2000
6227	TC	P227CTV	Optare Metrorider MR15	Optare	B31F	1996	Trent Buses, 2000
6318	TC	YMW843	DAF SB3000	Van Hool Alizée HE	C53F	1997	Berkley, Hemel Hempstead, 01
6322	TC	USV115	Toyota Coaster HZB50R	Caetano Optimo III	C21F	1994	Bell, Winterslow, 1999
6323	TC	N711WJL	Mercedes-Benz 711D	Autobus Classique Nouvelle	C24F	1995	Bell, Winterslow, 1999
6346	TC	XAM152	Volvo B10M-60	Plaxton Paramount 3500 III	C53F	1993	Bell, Winterslow, 1999
6347	TC	XAA299	Volvo B10M-62	Plaxton Première 320	C53F	1996	Bell, Winterslow, 1999
6349	TC	V37KWO	Volvo B10M-62	Plaxton Première 350	C57F	2000	Woodstones, K'minster, 2002
6352	TC	T35RJL	Mercedes-Benz O1120L	Optare/Ferqui Solera	C35F	1999	Atlantic, Heywood, 2001

One of the few coaches to carry Bell's colours, and one of the four from that firm still in use, is Plaxton Première 320-bodied Volvo B10M XAA299. Now carrying fleet number 6347 it operates alongside the orange-liveried Tourist coaches. *Phillip Stephenson*

Bluestar is the brand name for Solent Blue Line's key inter-urban and commuter routes into Southampton from Winchester, Eastleigh, Romsey and Hedge End. Solent Blue Line and Southern Vectis operations joined the Go-Ahead Group in 2005 and now form part of the Go-South Coast management unit. One of eight Dennis Tridents with East Lancs bodywork based at Eastleigh is 747, T747JPO. *Dave Heath*

Solent Blue Line - Blue Star

240	E	P240VDL	Iveco TurboDaily 59-12	Marshall C31		BC23F	1996	Southern Vectis, 2005	
241	E	P241VDL	Iveco TurboDaily 59-12	Marshall C31		BC23F	1996	Southern Vectis, 2005	
242	E	P242VDL	Iveco TurboDaily 59-12	Marshall C31		BC23F	1996	Southern Vectis, 2005	
243	E	P243VDL	Iveco TurboDaily 59-12	Marshall C31		BC23F	1996	Southern Vectis, 2005	
244	E	P244VDL	Iveco TurboDaily 59-12	Marshall C31		BC23F	1996	Southern Vectis, 2005	

401-410			Mercedes-Benz Citaro O530	Mercedes-Benz		N39F	2006		
401	H	HX06EZA	404	H	HX06EZD	407	H	HX06EZG	409	H	HX06EZJ
402	H	HX06EZB	405	H	HX06EZE	408	H	HX06EZH	410	H	HX06EYZ
403	H	HX06EZC	406	H	HX06EZF						

571-582			TransBus Dart 8.8m	TransBus Mini Pointer		N29F	2003		
571	E	SN03EBP	574	E	SN03EBX	577	E	SN03ECC	580	E	SN03LDK
572	E	SN03EBU	575	E	SN03EBZ	578	E	SN03ECD	581	E	SN03LDL
573	E	SN03EBV	576	E	SN03ECA	579	E	SN03LDJ	582	E	SN03LDU

583	E	XIL8583	Dennis Dart 8.5m	Plaxton Pointer	B28F	1992	Metroline, 2004
584	E	XIL8584	Dennis Dart 8.5m	Plaxton Pointer	B28F	1992	Metroline, 2004
585	E	K716PCN	Dennis Dart 9.8m	Alexander Dash	B40F	1992	Go-Ahead London, 2004
586	E	K719PCN	Dennis Dart 9.8m	Alexander Dash	BC32F	1992	Go-Ahead London, 2004

621-630			Volvo B10B	Northern Counties Paladin		B43D	1993	City of Oxford, 2006	
621	E	K121BUD	624	E	K124BUD	627	E	K127BUD	629	E	K129BUD
622	E	K122BUD	625	E	K125BUD	628	E	K128BUD	630	E	K130BUD
623	E	K123BUD	626	E	K126BUD						

631	E	L526YDL	Volvo B10B	Alexander Strider	B51F	1994	
632	E	L527YDL	Volvo B10B	Alexander Strider	B51F	1994	
633	E	L528YDL	Volvo B10B	Alexander Strider	B51F	1994	
706	E	F706RDL	Leyland Olympian ONCL10/1RZ	Leyland	BC39/29F	1989	
707	E	F707RDL	Leyland Olympian ONCL10/1RZ	Leyland	BC39/29F	1989	
708	E	F708SDL	Leyland Olympian ONCL10/1RZ	Leyland	BC39/29F	1989	
709	E	F709SDL	Leyland Olympian ONCL10/1RZ	Leyland	BC39/29F	1989	

Solent Blue Line was established in 1987 by Southern Vectis, the Isle of Wight operator, initially as a venture to compete on services in Southampton. One of the buses that was transferred within the fleet is 706, F706RDL, an all-Leyland Olympian constructed at the Workington factory where the National was built. *Dave Heath*

721-734			Leyland Olympian ON2R50C13Z5 Leyland					B47/31F*	1989-91	*721/2 are BC39/29F
721	E	G721WDL	728	E	H728DDL	731	E	H731DDL	733	E	H733DDL
722	E	G722WDL	729	E	H729DDL	732	E	H732DDL	734	E	H734DDL
735	E	M735BBP	Volvo Olympian YN2RC16Z5			East Lancs		BC41/29F	1995	
736	E	M736BBP	Volvo Olympian YN2RV18Z4			East Lancs		BC41/29F	1995	
742-749			Dennis Trident			East Lancs Lolyne		N47/27F	1999	
742	E	T742JPO	744	E	T744JPO	746	E	T746JPO	748	E	T748JPO
743	E	T743JPO	745	E	T745JPO	747	E	T747JPO	749	E	T749JPO
750-757			Volvo B7TL			East Lancs Vyking		N46/27F	2001	
750	E	HX51ZRA	752	E	HX51ZRD	754	E	HX51ZRF	756	E	HX51ZRJ
751	E	HX51ZRC	753	E	HX51ZRE	755	E	HX51ZRG	757	E	HX51ZRK
817	E	F817URN	Leyland Olympian ONCL10/1RZ			Leyland		B47/31F	1989	Leyland demonstrator, 1990
818	E	N539LHG	Volvo Olympian YN2RV18Z4			Northern Counties		B47/27F	1996	Metrobus, 2004
819	E	N411JBV	Volvo Olympian YN2RV18Z4			Northern Counties		B47/30F	1996	Go-Ahead London, 2004
820	E	N413JBV	Volvo Olympian YN2RV18Z4			Northern Counties		B47/30F	1996	Go-Ahead London, 2004
901	E	UFX857S	Bristol VRT/SL3/6LXB			Eastern Coach Works		CO43/31F	1977	Bath Bus Co, 2003
902	E	WTG360T	Bristol VRT/SL3/6LXB			Alexander AL		CO43/31F	1979	Bath Bus Co, 2003

Southern Vectis

100-106			Volvo B7TL			Plaxton President		N51/28F	2002	
100	N	HW52EPK	102	N	HW52EPN	104	N	HW52EPP	106	N	HW52EPV
101	N	HW52EPL	103	N	HW52EPO	105	N	HW52EPU			
246	N	P246VDL	Iveco TurboDaily 59-12			Marshall C31		BC23F	1997	
247	N	P247VDL	Iveco TurboDaily 59-12			Marshall C31		BC23F	1997	
260	N	L445FFR	Iveco TurboDaily 59-12			Mellor Duet		B27F	1994	Stagecoach Devon, 2001
300	N	HW52EPX	Dennis Dart SLF			Plaxton Pointer		N37F	2002	

The 2006-07 Go-Ahead Bus Handbook

Southern Vectis was formed in 1929 following the Southern Railway's acquisition of the Vectis Bus Company, and stayed in the ownership of large national concerns until 1970 when the company became part of the National Bus Company. The company was purchased by its then management team in 1986 and remained independent until acquired by Go-Ahead Group in July 2005. Liveried for the Needles Tour is partial open-top 743, K743ODL, an Olympian with Northern Counties bodywork. *Mark Lyons*

301-314			ADL Dart 8.8m		ADL Mini Pointer		N27F	2004-05		
301	N	HW54BTU	305	N	HW54BTZ	309	N	HW54BUH	312	N	HW54BUP
302	N	HW54BTV	306	N	HW54BUA	310	N	HW54BUJ	313	N	HW54BUU
303	N	HW54BTX	307	N	HW54BUE	311	N	HW54BUO	314	N	HW54BUV
304	N	HW54BTY	308	N	HW54BUF						

502	N	CDL899	Bristol K5G		Eastern Coach Works		O30/26R	1939		
503	N	XDL872	Bristol VRT/SL3/6LXB		Eastern Coach Works		CO43/31F	1977		
504	N	WDL655	Bristol VRT/SL3/6LXB		Eastern Coach Works		CO43/31F	1977		
681	N	ODL447	Bristol VRT/SL3/6LXB		Eastern Coach Works		O43/31F	1980		
682	N	VDL744	Bristol VRT/SL3/6LXB		Eastern Coach Works		O43/31F	1980		
683	N	934BDL	Bristol VRT/SL3/6LXB		Eastern Coach Works		B43/31F	1981		
710	N	TIL6710	Leyland Olympian ONCL10/1RZ		Leyland		BC41/29F	1989		
711	N	TIL6711	Leyland Olympian ONCL10/1RZ		Leyland		BC41/29F	1989		
712	N	TIL6712	Leyland Olympian ONCL10/1RZ		Leyland		BC41/29F	1989		

713-727			Leyland Olympian ON2R50C13Z5		Leyland		BC41/29F	1989-90	*720/6 are B45/31F	
713	N	TIL6713	717	N	TIL6717	720	N	TIL6720	725	N	TIL6725
714	N	TIL6714	718	N	TIL6718	723	N	TIL6723	726	N	TIL6726
715	N	TIL6715	719	N	TIL6719	724	N	TIL6724	727	N	TIL6727
716	N	TIL6716									

735-743			Leyland Olympian ON2R50C13Z5 Northern Counties				B48/29*	1993	*742/3 are PO41/29F	
735	N	K735ODL	738	N	K738ODL	740	N	K740ODL	742	N	K742ODL
736	N	K736ODL	739	N	K739ODL	741	N	K741ODL	743	N	K743ODL
737	N	K737ODL									

744-751			Volvo Olympian YN2R50C18Z4		Northern Counties		BC41/29F	1995		
744	N	M744HDL	746	N	M746HDL	749	N	M749HDL	751	N	M751HDL
745	N	M745HDL	748	N	M748HDL	750	N	M750HDL			

752-759			Volvo Olympian		Northern Counties Palatine I		BC41/29F	1998		
752	N	R752GDL	754	N	R754GDL	756	N	R756GDL	758	N	R758GDL
753	N	R753GDL	755	N	R755GDL	757	N	R757GDL	759	N	R759GDL

One of fourteen Mini Pointer Darts from Alexander-Dennis, 301, HW54BTU, illustrates the latest network livery for Southern Vectis, a creation from Best Impressions. 301 is the first vehicle in the batch and it is seen in Whippingham Road in Osborne. *Mark Lyons*

760	N	R741XRV	Volvo Olympian		Northern Counties Palatine	BC41/29F	1998		
761	N	R739XRV	Volvo Olympian		Northern Counties Palatine	BC41/29F	1998		
762	N	R738XRV	Volvo Olympian		Northern Counties Palatine	BC41/29F	1998		
763	N	R737XRV	Volvo Olympian		Northern Counties Palatine	BC41/29F	1998		

810-815   Dennis Dart 8.5m   UVG Urban Star   BC31F   1996

810	N	N810PDL	812	N	N812PDL	814	N	N814PDL	815	N	N815PDL
811	N	N811PDL	813	N	N813PDL					

816	N	G516VYE	Dennis Dart 8.5m	Duple Dartline	B31F	1990	London United, 2000
817	N	G526VYE	Dennis Dart 8.5m	Duple Dartline	B31F	1990	London United, 2000
818	N	J382GKH	Dennis Dart 8.5m	Plaxton Pointer	B31F	1992	Rehill, Birstall, 2003
819	N	K244PAG	Dennis Dart 8.5m	Plaxton Pointer	B31F	1992	Rehill, Birstall, 2003

Ancillary vehicles:

020	N	C877CYX	Volvo B10M-61	Plaxton Paramount 3200	TV	1986	
259	E	N259FOR	Iveco TurboDaily 59-12	Mellor	B29F	1995	
529	E	L227THP	Volvo B10B	Alexander Strider	TV	1993	Volvo demonstrator, 1994
574	N	MIL9574	Dennis Javelin	Plaxton Paramount III	TV	1989	Southern Vectis, 2005
575	N	MIL9575	Dennis Javelin	Plaxton Paramount III	TV	1989	Southern Vectis, 2005
9085	P	B201REL	Leyland Tiger TRCTL11/3RH	Duple Laser 2	TV	1984	
9087	P	B203REL	Leyland Tiger TRCTL11/3RH	Duple Laser 2	TV	1984	
9089	P	OEL232P	Bristol VRT/SL3/501	Eastern Coach Works	Tree Lopper	1976	Hants & Dorset, 1983
9096	-	F40KRO	Dennis Lancet SDA523	Wadham Stringer Vanguard	Classroom	1989	
9100	E	S35NRG	Optare Excel L1150	Optare	TV	1998	
9102	E	S157OCU	Optare Excel L1150	Optare	TV	1998	
9502	BH	F423RRD	Mercedes-Benz 308D	Coachwork Walker	M8	1989	

The 2006-07 Go-Ahead Bus Handbook

Previous registrations:

381VHX	N89FWU	MJI7514	K537RJX
701GOO	N61FWU	N45FWU	N45FWU, VUV246
G373GJT	G508EFX, A8EXC, SIB5373	N411WJL	N411WJL, VJI9368
G391GJT	G507EFX, A7EXC, PJI7002	NXI5358	G509EFX, A9EXC, G358GJT
G392GJT	G510EFX, A10EXC, UJI2507	OIJ1875	XEL24, M376MRU
HJI2615	K529RJX	PJI7002	G609THR
HSV342	N68FWU	R130XWF	R130XWF, LSV749
K121BUD	K4KLL	RJI6155	R129XWF
K122BUD	K5KLL	SIB5373	L526EHD
K123BUD	K6KLL	SIL7914	K547RJX
K124BUD	K7KLL	SJI8751	F910UPR, XIB3910
K125BUD	K8KLL	TJI9462	K535RJX
K126BUD	K9KLL	UEL489	K728JWX
K127BUD	K10KLL	UJI2507	R127XWF
K128BUD	K11KLL	USV115	L396YAM
K129BUD	K12KLL	VJI3968	-
K130BUD	K13KLL	VUV246	A3FTG, R435MEH
K208XFX	K855BUR, HSV342, LSV349	WIL2574	E745JAY, KGL803
K716PCN	K716PCN, NFX667	XAA299	A11XEL, N225THO
K719PCN	K719PCN, XYK976	XAM152	K727JWX
K750RHR	H750RHR, RJI6155	XIL8583	J393GKH
LIL2665	G138MNH	XIL8584	J394GKH
LIL3748	N983FWT	XXI8502	R811NUD
LSV749	K208XFX	YMW843	P890PWW

Depots and allocations:

Blandford (Salisbury Road) - Wilts & Dorset - B

Outstation - Shaftesbury

Optare Solo	2659	2664	2667	2668	2669	2670	
DAF/Spectra	3118	3122	3123	3124	3133	3134	3135

Blandford (Clump Farm, Blandford Heights Ind Est) - Damory Coaches - BH

Outstations: Sunrise Business Park, Blandford; Verwood; Poole and Shaftesbury

LDV	5124	5125	5126	5169	5170			
MetroRider	5133	5135	5137	5141	5143	5146	5147	5148
Optare Solo	5601							
DAF/Ikarus	5044	5046	5047					
Volvo B10B	5058	5059	5090	5091	5092			
DAF coach	3219	3220	3221	5011	5012	5013	5014	5016
	5018							
Volvo coach	5023	5026	5027	5032	5033	5034	5035	5036
	5066	5068	5069	5070	5071	5072	5073	5074
	5076							
Bristol VR	5063							

Bournemouth (Southcote Road) - Wilts & Dorset - BM

Optare Excel	3601	3602	3603	3604				
Volvo B7RLE	101	102	103	104	105	106	107	108
	109	110	111	112	113	114	115	116
	117	118	119					

Eastleigh (Barton Park) - Solent Blue Line - E

Outstation: Romsey

Iveco	240	241	242	243	244			
Dart	571	572	573	574	575	576	577	578
	579	580	581	582	583	584	585	586
Volvo B10B	631	632	633					
Bristol VR	901	902						
Olympian	706	707	708	709	721	722	723	724
	735	736	817	818	819	820		
Trident	742	743	744	745	746	747	748	749
Volvo B7TL	750	751	752	753	754	755	756	757

Pictured while passing through the village of Godshill on the Isle of Wight is 714, TIL6714, an all-Leyland Olympian. Reflecting the islands proximity to France the bus it is painted in *Route Rouge* colours, and the sign advises that Euro notes are accepted on the service. *Mark Lyons*

Figheldean - Tourist Coaches - Kingston Coaches - Bell's - TC

Outstations - Salisbury and Winterslow

LDV	6164	6166	6168					
Mercedes-Benz mini	6054	6323	6352					
MetroRider	6111	6112	6114					
Toyota/Optimo	6322							
Javelin	6026	6027	6029	6030	6051			
DAF coach	6009	6010	6015	6016	6017	6019	6213	6214
	6318							
Volvo coach	6035	6043	6048	6245	6346	6347	6349	
Mercedes-Benz Touro	6003							

Hythe (Berkeley Garage) - Solent Blue Line - H

Mercedes-Benz Citaro	401	402	403	404	405	406	407	408
	409	410						

Lymington (Station Road) - Wilts & Dorset - L

Outstation - Lyndhurst

Solo	2633	2634	2635	2674	2675	2676	2681	2682
	2683	2684	2685					
DAF/Delta	3501	3502						
Bristol VR	4448	4449	4450	4451	4453	4455	4456	
DAF/Spectra	3126	3127	3128	3162	3163			
Volvo B7TL/Vyking	405	406	407	410	411	412	413	

Newport (Nelson Road) - Southern Vectis - N

Iveco	246	250						
Dart	300	301	302	303	304	305	306	307
	308	309	310	311	312	313	314	810
	811	812	813	814	815	816	817	818
	819							
Bristol K	502							

The 2006-07 Go-Ahead Bus Handbook

Bristol VR	503	504	681	682	683			
Olympian	710	711	712	713	714	715	716	717
	718	719	720	723	724	725	726	727
	735	736	737	738	739	740	741	742
	743	744	745	746	748	749	750	751
	752	753	754	755	756	757	758	759
	760	761	762	763				

Poole (Kingland Road) - Wilts & Dorset - P

Solo	2603	2604	2605	2609	2610	2611	2612	2613
	2614	2615	2636	2637	2638	2639	2640	2641
	2642	2643	2644	2645	2646	2647	2648	2649
	2653	2661	2662	2663	5601			
Excel	3609	3610	3611	3612				
Volvo B7RLE	120	121	122	123	124	125	126	127
	128	129	130					
Mercedes-Benz Citaro	151	164	165	166	167	168	169	170
	172	173	174	175	176	178		
Bristol VR	4422	4423	4424	4426	4427	4429	4430	
DAF/Spectra	3111	3112	3113	3114	3170	3171	3176	3177
	3178	3179	3185					
Volvo V7TL/Vyking	401	404	403	404				

Ringwood (West Street) - Wilts & Dorset - R

Solo	2616	2654	2655	2677	2678	2679	2680	2686
DAF SB220	3505	3507						
Bristol VR	4431	4432						
DAF/Spectra	3103	3104	3115	3116	3117	3141	3161	3169
	3172	3173	3174					

Salisbury (Castle Street) - Wilts & Dorset - S

Outstations - Amesbury; Bowerchalke; Devizes; Downton; Hindon; Pewsey; Porton; Ringwood; Romsey; Shaftesbury; Swallow Cliffe; Warminster and Yeovil

MetroRider	2230	2231	2232	2233	2234	2235	2236	2237
	2238	2239	2240	2241	2515	2535	2536	2537
	2539	2541	2544	2545				
Solo	2617	2618	2619	2620	2621	2622	2623	2624
	2625	2626	2627	2628	2629	2630	2631	2632
	2651	2652	2656	2657	2658	2660	2665	2666
	2671	2672	2673	2687	2688			
Volvo B7RLE	131	132	133	134	135	136	137	138
Mercedes-Benz Citaro	152	153	154	155	156	157	158	159
	160	161	162	163				
Excel	3605	3606	3607	3608	3613	3214	3615	
DAF/Delta	3503	3504	3506					
Volvo coach	3233	3234	3235	4004				
DAF coach	3214	3215	3216	3217	3218			
Bristol VR	4437							
Olympian	4903	4923						
DAF/Spectra	3101	3105	3106	3107	3108	3110	3120	3129
	3130	3131	3132	3136	3137	3138	3139	3154
	3155	3156	3158	3159	3160	3164	3165	3166
	3167	3168	3175	3180	3181	3182	3183	3184

Swanage (Kings Road West) - Wilts & Dorset - SW

Spectra	3140	3143	3145	3146	3147			
DAF/Palatine	3148	3149	3150	3151	3152	3153	3157	

Unallocated and stored - u

MetroRider	5133		
Volvo B7TL	407	409	
Mercedes-Benz Citaro	171	177	(on loan to Oxford Citybus)

METEOR

Meteor - Pink Elephant - Park 1

Meteor Parking Ltd, Bassingbourne House, Thremhall Avenue, Stansted Airport, CM24 1PZ

Go-Ahead expanded its operations in car park management through the acquisition of a leading UK car park operator, Meteor Parking Limited.

Established in 1992, Meteor is now the second largest off-street parking company in the UK by turnover and was acquired by Go-Ahead in 2002.

On behalf of BAA plc, Meteor operates 33,000 car parking spaces at Heathrow, Stansted and Southampton airports, where it uses its unique branding strategy with the creation of Pink Elephant Parking, Park 1 and, most recently, eparking.uk.com (its Internet based pre-booking product). The company's emphasis is on rail stations, shopping centres, airports, hospitals, Park & Ride schemes and other locations where large parking volumes require top quality parking management.

Significant improvements have also been made in Meteor's security division, including increased reception and concierge facilities, enhanced CCTV monitoring, remote CCTV monitoring and 24-hour manned guarding services.

In addition to car park management, Meteor also provides design, build, finance and operate capabilities, passenger and staff transportation, manpower services, and management of bus services.

Meteor's proven skills in this area will help to exploit carpark related opportunities in Go-Ahead's existing transport activities, together with actively seeking new potential areas of growth.

6-11		Optare Solo M850	Optare		N19F	2006	
6	LHR YJ06FYA	8	LHR YJ06FYC	10	LHR YJ06FYE	11	LHR YJ06FYF
7	LHR YJ06FYB	9	LHR YJ06FYD				
	STN P714MLD	Iveco TurboDaily 59.12	Marshall C31		BC16F	1997	
	EDI P135LNF	Dennis Dart SLF	East Lancs Spryte		N43F	1997	Stuarts, Hyde, 1998
	STN P136LNF	Dennis Dart SLF	East Lancs Spryte		N43F	1997	Stuarts, Hyde, 1998
	STN P215OLC	Mercedes-Benz Sprinter 312	Advanced Conversion		M8	1997	Alamo, 2000
	STN P216OLC	Mercedes-Benz Sprinter 312	Advanced Conversion		M8	1997	Alamo, 2000
	STN P218OLC	Mercedes-Benz Sprinter 312	Advanced Conversion		M8	1997	Alamo, 2000
		Dennis Dart SLF	East Lancs Spryte		N25D*	1997-98	*86/7 are N23D
	STN R286OFV		SOU P989AFV		STN P991AFV		EDI P993AFV
	STN R287OFV		SOU P990AFV		STN P992AFV		EDI P994AFV
	EDI R986RBY	Mercedes-Benz Sprinter 312	Mercedes-Benz		M8	1997	
	LHR R708SLU	Iveco TurboDaily 59.12	Marshall C31		BC16F	1997	
	LHR R709SLU	Iveco TurboDaily 59.12	Marshall C31		BC16F	1997	
	STN R41BYG	LDV Convoy	LDV		M16	1998	
	STN R42BYG	LDV Convoy	LDV		M16	1998	
	STN R43BYG	LDV Convoy	LDV		M16	1998	

Anyone on a visit to London's Heathrow Airport will be familiar with the Pink Elephant courtesy buses that ply between the terminals and its car parks. One of three Optare Solo buses is, YA02YRR, which carries local number 13, is seen on the north side of the airport. *Mark Lyons*

			NAW Cobus 3000			Caetano		N15T	1997-2000		
	SOU	MET1		STN	MET3		STN	MET5		STN	MET6
	SOU	MET2		STN	MET4						
			Optare Solo M920			Optare		N25F	1999		
	LHR	T412OUB		LHR	T415OUB		LHR	T418OUB		LHR	T420OUB
	LHR	T413OUB		LHR	T416OUB		LHR	T419OUB		LHR	T421OUB
	LHR	T414OUB		LHR	T417OUB						
	LHR	V675JWC	Mercedes-Benz Vito 108			Mercedes-Benz		M6	1999		
	LHR	V676JWC	Mercedes-Benz Vito 108			Mercedes-Benz		M6	1999		
	STN	V118LVH	Optare Excel L1150			Optare		N18D	1999		
	STN	V119LVH	Optare Excel L1150			Optare		N18D	1999		
30	EDI	V930VUB	Optare Excel L1070			Optare		N25F	1999		
36	EDI	V936VUB	Optare Excel L1070			Optare		N25F	1999		
	NCL	V937VUB	Optare Excel L1070			Optare		N25F	1999		
	NCL	V938VUB	Optare Excel L1070			Optare		N25F	1999		
	SOU	V939VUB	Optare Excel L1070			Optare		N25F	1999		
	SOU	V618EVU	Dennis Dart SLF			Plaxton Pointer 2		N29F	2000		
	STN	W96AJN	Mercedes-Benz Vito 108			Mercedes-Benz		M6	2000		
	STN	W428OWX	Optare Excel L1150			Optare		N18D	2000		
	STN	W429OWX	Optare Excel L1150			Optare		N18D	2000		
			Neoplan Centroliner N4421			Neoplan		AB28T	2001		
	STN	YN51XMC		STN	YN51XME		STN	YN51XMG		STN	YN51MLZ
	STN	YN51XMD		STN	YN51XMF						
13	LHR	YA02YRR	Optare Solo M920			Optare		N25F	2002		
	LHR	YA02YRS	Optare Solo M920			Optare		N25F	2002		
	NCL	YA02YRT	Optare Solo M920			Optare		N25F	2002		
	LHR	KX02CWG	Dennis Dart SLF			Plaxton Beaver		N22F	2002	Airparks, Birmingham, 2006	

One of two Optare Excel buses at Edinburgh to carry the Meteor name is V930VUB. It is also identified as local fleet number 30. It is seen outside the main terminal. *Mark Doggett*

		Mercedes-Benz Vito 108	CoTrim		M6	2002	
LHR	EJ02OVU	LHR	EJ02OVX	LHR	EJ02OVZ	LHR	EO52HZU
LHR	EJ02OVV	LHR	EJ02OVY	LHR	EJ02OWA	LHR	EO52HZV
LHR	EJ02OVW						
		Mercedes-Benz Citaro O530G	Mercedes-Benz		AB28T	2003	
STN	BU53AXN	STN	BU53AXP	STN	BU53AXT	STN	BU53AXV
STN	BU53AXO	STN	BU53AXR				
SOU	CO1	NAW Cobus 3000	Caetano		N15T	2004	
SOU	CO2	NAW Cobus 3000	Caetano		N15T	2004	
STN	EU54MEV	Irisbus			N16	2005	
SOU	EA05KXF	Ford Transit	Ford		M8	2005	
SOU	EA05KZB	Ford Transit	Ford		M8	2005	
SOU	EA05KZC	Ford Transit	Ford		M8	2005	
LHR	AE55MVC	MAN 14.220	MCV Evolution		N28D	2005	
LHR	YJ55YFH	Optare Solo M920	Optare		N25F	2006	
LHR	YJ55YGE	Optare Solo M920 Hybrid	Optare		N25F	2005	
LHR	YJ55YGF	Optare Solo M920 Hybrid	Optare		N25F	2005	

Airport allocation codes:

BFZ	Belfast International	LGW	London Gatwick
BHX	Birmingham	LHR	London Heathrow
CWL	Cardiff Wales	LTN	London Luton
DUB	Dublin	MAN	Manchester
EDI	Edinburgh	MME	Durham Tees Valley
GLA	Glasgow	STN	London Stansted
HF	Hatfield	NCL	Newcastle
LBA	Leeds/Bradford	SOU	Southampton

The 2006-07 Go-Ahead Bus Handbook

AVIANCE

Aviance plc, 3rd Floor, First Point, Buckingham Gate, Gatwick Airport, RH6 0NT

LBA	L262PKU	Ford Transit	Ford	M8	1994	British Midland Handling, 2002
SOU	M209VKU	Ford Transit	Ford	M8	1995	Reed Aviation, 2002
LGW	P36HEW	Ford Galaxy	Ford	M8	1996	British Midland Handling, 2002
DUB	98D75120	Optare Excel L1150	Optare	N--F	1998	Go-Ahead Northern, 2005
DUB	98D75123	Optare Excel L1150	Optare	N--F	1998	Go-Ahead Northern, 2005
DUB	98D75124	Optare Excel L1150	Optare	N--F	1998	Go-Ahead Northern, 2005
LHR	LF02OHB	Ford Transit Tourneo	Ford	M8	2002	
LGW	LF02OHC	Ford Transit Tourneo	Ford	M8	2002	
LHR	LF02OHD	Ford Transit Tourneo	Ford	M8	2002	
LTN	LF02OHE	Ford Transit Tourneo	Ford	M8	2002	
MAN	LF02OHG	Ford Transit Tourneo	Ford	M8	2002	
LTN	EA52GDY	Ford Transit Tourneo	Ford	M8	2002	
LTN	EA52GDZ	Ford Transit Tourneo	Ford	M8	2002	
EDI	PV03GVT	Ford Transit Tourneo	Ford	M8	2002	
GLA	MT53NHG	Ford Transit Tourneo	Ford	M8	2002	
BHX	EA04FZT	Ford Transit Tourneo	Ford	M8	2002	
BHX	EF04TFY	Ford Transit Tourneo	Ford	M8	2002	
BFS	EG04MLY	Ford Transit Tourneo	Ford	M8	2002	
LTN	EA05KWX	Ford Transit Tourneo	Ford	M8	2002	
GLA	EA05KZS	Ford Transit Tourneo	Ford	M8	2002	
NME	EF05YBU	Ford Transit Tourneo	Ford	M8	2002	
LGW	EF05YBV	Ford Transit Tourneo	Ford	M8	2002	
LHR	GY55OMF	Ford Galaxy	Ford	M8	2005	

Previous registrations:

98D75120	S152OCU		98D75124	S153OCU
98D75123	S154OCU			

Airport allocation codes - see page 83

Park 1 is a business parking service dedicated to terminal 1 at Heathrow and offers the quickest service for users of that terminal. One of the Park 1 minibuses is Mercedes-Benz Vito EO52HZU. Aviance plc also operates five larger vehicles at Cardiff Wales International airport. Three of these are owned by the airport authority and two by sister-company Meteor. However, as these operate exclusively air-side they are not included above. *Mark Lyons*

Vehicle index

Reg	Operator	Reg	Operator	Reg	Operator	Reg	Operator
78CLT	London	BX02YYU	London	EA52GDZ	Aviance	GEL680V	South Coast
89D75120	Aviance	BX02YYV	London	EF04TFY	Aviance	GEL681V	South Coast
89D75123	Aviance	BX02YYW	London	EF05YBU	Aviance	GEL682V	South Coast
89D75124	Aviance	BX02YYZ	London	EF05YBV	Aviance	GEL686V	South Coast
166CLT	London	BX02YZA	London	EF53OXF	Oxford	GEL687V	South Coast
197CLT	London	BX02YZB	London	EF55OXF	Oxford	GF55OXF	Oxford
202UXJ	London	BX02YZC	London	EG04MLY	Aviance	GP53CLV	Metrobus
229CLT	Diamond	BX02YZD	London	EJ02OVU	Meteor	GP53COJ	Metrobus
340GUP	North East	BX02YZE	London	EJ02OVV	Meteor	GP53CPY	Metrobus
352CLT	London	BX02YZG	London	EJ02OVW	Meteor	GP53RBX	Metrobus
381VHX	South Coast	BX02YZH	London	EJ02OVX	Meteor	GSK962	North East
524FUP	North East	BX02YZJ	London	EJ02OVY	Meteor	GV53MDX	Metrobus
545CLT	London	BX02YZK	London	EJ02OVZ	Meteor	GV53RHU	Metrobus
548VBB	North East	BX02YZL	London	EJ02OWA	Meteor	GV53RHY	Metrobus
564CPT	North East	BX02YZM	London	ELJ214V	South Coast	GV53RHZ	Metrobus
701GOO	South Coast	BX02YZN	London	ELJ215V	South Coast	GV53RJJ	Metrobus
934BDL	South Coast	BX02YZO	London	ELJ216V	South Coast	GV53RJO	Metrobus
A175VFM	South Coast	BX02YZP	London	ELJ218V	South Coast	GV53RJX	Metrobus
A718ABB	North East	BX02YZR	London	ELJ219V	South Coast	GV53RJY	Metrobus
A901JPR	South Coast	BX02YZS	London	ELJ220V	South Coast	GV53RJZ	Metrobus
A903JPR	South Coast	BX02YZT	London	EO52HZU	Meteor	GV53RKF	Metrobus
AE55MVC	Meteor	BX04NBD	London	EO52HZV	Meteor	GX02ATF	Brighton & H
AF53OXF	Oxford	BX54EFB	London	EU54MEV	Meteor	GX03SSU	Brighton & H
AF55OXF	Oxford	BX54EFC	London	EX54DYB	Oxford	GX03SSV	Brighton & H
AP03AGU	Metrobus	BX54EFD	London	EX54DYC	Oxford	GX03SSZ	Brighton & H
AT02CJT	South Coast	BX54UCM	London	EX54DYD	Oxford	GX03STZ	Brighton & H
B201REL	South Coast	BX54UCN	London	EX54DYF	Oxford	GX03SUA	Brighton & H
B203REL	South Coast	BX54UCO	London	F40KRO	South Coast	GX03SUF	Brighton & H
BD52LMO	London	BX54UCP	London	F106UEF	North East	GX03SUH	Brighton & H
BD52LMU	London	BX54UCR	London	F107UEF	North East	GX03SUU	Brighton & H
BD52LMV	London	BX54UCT	London	F423RRD	South Coast	GX03SUV	Brighton & H
BD52LMX	London	BX54UCU	London	F706RDL	South Coast	GX03SUY	Brighton & H
BD52LMY	London	BX54UCV	London	F707RDL	South Coast	GX03SVA	Brighton & H
BD52LNA	London	BX54UCW	London	F708SDL	South Coast	GX03SVC	Brighton & H
BD52LNC	London	BX54UCZ	London	F709SDL	South Coast	GX03SVD	Brighton & H
BD52LNE	London	BX54UDB	London	F712LFG	Brighton & H	GX03SVE	Brighton & H
BD52LNF	London	BX54UDD	London	F817URN	South Coast	GX03SVF	Brighton & H
BD52LNG	London	BX54UDE	London	FCU190	North East	GX03SVG	Brighton & H
BD52LNO	London	BX54UDG	London	FF55OXF	Oxford	GX03SVJ	Brighton & H
BD52LNP	London	BX54UDH	London	FTN707W	North East	GX03SVK	Brighton & H
BD52LNR	London	BX54UDJ	London	FTN710W	North East	GY55OMF	Aviance
BD52LNT	London	BX54UDK	London	FTN711W	North East	H122THE	Diamond
BD52LNU	London	BX54UDL	London	G94RGG	South Coast	H123THE	Diamond
BF53OXF	Oxford	BX54UDM	London	G110NGN	Diamond	H125THE	Diamond
BF55OXF	Oxford	BX54UDN	London	G122NGN	Diamond	H126THE	Diamond
BFX666T	South Coast	BX54UDO	London	G123PGK	Diamond	H128THE	Diamond
BL52ODK	London	BX54UDP	London	G130PGK	Diamond	H129THE	Diamond
BL52ODM	London	BX54UDT	London	G183WGX	North East	H130THE	Diamond
BL52ODN	London	BX54UDU	London	G373GJT	South Coast	H131THE	Diamond
BL52ODP	London	BX54UDV	London	G392GJT	South Coast	H481PVW	North East
BL52ODR	London	BX54UDW	London	G516VYE	South Coast	H485PVW	North East
BL52ODT	London	BX54UDY	London	G522VBB	North East	H550PVW	North East
BL52ODU	London	BX54UDZ	London	G526VYE	South Coast	H551PVW	North East
BL52ODV	London	BX54UEA	London	G527VBB	North East	H589EGU	North East
BN52GVU	London	BX54UEB	London	G528VBB	North East	H728DDL	South Coast
BN52GWC	London	C63HOM	Oxford	G529VBB	North East	H729DDL	South Coast
BN52GWD	London	C102PCN	North East	G544VBB	North East	H731DDL	South Coast
BN52GWE	London	C103PCN	North East	G545VBB	North East	H732DDL	South Coast
BT02CJT	South Coast	C104PCN	North East	G546VBB	North East	H733DDL	South Coast
BU03LXX	South Coast	C682JGR	North East	G549VBB	North East	H734DDL	South Coast
BU04UTM	London	C877CYX	South Coast	G647SGT	Diamond	HAP985	Brighton & H
BU04UTN	London	CDL899	South Coast	G675TCN	North East	HF03AEG	South Coast
BU04UTP	Metrobus	CF53OXF	Oxford	G677TCN	North East	HF03HJY	South Coast
BU53AXN	Metrobus	CF55OXF	Oxford	G678TCN	North East	HF03HJZ	South Coast
BU53AXO	Meteor	CU6860	North East	G721WDL	South Coast	HF03HKA	South Coast
BU53AXP	Meteor	CU7661	North East	G722WDL	South Coast	HF05GGE	South Coast
BU53AXR	Meteor	CUV305C	London	G725RYJ	Brighton & H	HF05GGJ	South Coast
BU53AXT	Meteor	CUV317C	Metrobus	G726RYJ	Brighton & H	HF05GGK	South Coast
BU53AXV	Meteor	CUV318C	London	G727RYJ	Brighton & H	HF05GGO	South Coast
BX02YYJ	London	DF53OXF	Oxford	G728RYJ	Brighton & H	HF05GGP	South Coast
BX02YYK	London	DF55OXF	Oxford	G729RYJ	Brighton & H	HF05GGU	South Coast
BX02YYL	London	DX03UBP	South Coast	G736RTY	North East	HF05GGV	South Coast
BX02YYM	London	E313OMG	South Coast	G751UCU	North East	HF05GGX	South Coast
BX02YYN	London	EA04FZT	Aviance	G752UCU	North East	HF05GGY	South Coast
BX02YYO	London	EA05KWX	Aviance	G753UCU	North East	HF05HXD	South Coast
BX02YYP	London	EA05KXF	Meteor	G754UCU	North East	HF05HXE	South Coast
BX02YYR	London	EA05KZB	Meteor	G755UCU	North East	HF05HXG	South Coast
BX02YYS	London	EA05KZC	Meteor	G850WGW	Diamond	HF05HXH	South Coast
BX02YYS	London	EA05KZS	Aviance	GEL655V	South Coast	HF06FTO	Oxford
BX02YYT	London	EA52GDY	Aviance	GEL679V	South Coast	HF06FTO	South Coast

HF06FTP	South Coast	HW52EPL	South Coast	K124BUD	South Coast	KU52RYF	Diamond
HF06FTT	South Coast	HW52EPN	South Coast	K124PGO	North East	KU52RYG	Diamond
HF06FTU	South Coast	HW52EPO	South Coast	K125BUD	South Coast	KU52RYH	Diamond
HF06FTV	South Coast	HW52EPP	South Coast	K125PGO	North East	KU52RYJ	Diamond
HF06FTX	South Coast	HW52EPU	South Coast	K126BUD	South Coast	KU52RYK	Diamond
HF06FTY	Oxford	HW52EPV	South Coast	K127BUD	South Coast	KU52RYM	Diamond
HF06FTY	South Coast	HW52EPX	South Coast	K128BUD	South Coast	KU52RYN	Diamond
HF06FTZ	South Coast	HW54BTU	South Coast	K129BUD	South Coast	KU52RYO	Diamond
HF06FUA	South Coast	HW54BTV	South Coast	K130BUD	South Coast	KV51KZG	Diamond
HF06FUB	South Coast	HW54BTX	South Coast	K159PGO	North East	KX02CWG	Meteor
HF54HFO	South Coast	HW54BTY	South Coast	K160PGO	North East	KX04HRD	Metrobus
HF54HFP	South Coast	HW54BTZ	South Coast	K244PAG	South Coast	KX04HRE	Metrobus
HF54HFR	South Coast	HW54BUA	South Coast	K301FYG	North East	KX04HRF	Metrobus
HF54HFT	South Coast	HW54BUE	South Coast	K301YJA	Diamond	KX04HRG	Metrobus
HF54HFU	South Coast	HW54BUF	South Coast	K302YJA	Diamond	L1OXF	Oxford
HF54HFV	South Coast	HW54BUH	South Coast	K303FYG	North East	L52UNS	South Coast
HF54HFW	South Coast	HW54BUJ	South Coast	K303YJA	Diamond	L53UNS	South Coast
HF54HFX	South Coast	HW54BUO	South Coast	K304FYG	North East	L58UNS	Metrobus
HF54HFY	South Coast	HW54BUP	South Coast	K304YJA	Diamond	L59UNS	Metrobus
HF54HFZ	South Coast	HW54BUU	South Coast	K305FYG	North East	L104EPA	Diamond
HF54HGA	South Coast	HW54BUV	South Coast	K305YJA	Diamond	L112ALJ	South Coast
HF54HGC	South Coast	HX06EYZ	South Coast	K306FYG	North East	L113ALJ	South Coast
HF54HGD	South Coast	HX06EZA	South Coast	K306YJA	Diamond	L114ALJ	South Coast
HF54HGE	South Coast	HX06EZB	South Coast	K307FYG	North East	L115ALJ	South Coast
HF54HGG	South Coast	HX06EZC	South Coast	K308FYG	North East	L116ALJ	South Coast
HF54HGJ	South Coast	HX06EZD	South Coast	K308YJA	Diamond	L117ALJ	South Coast
HF54HGK	South Coast	HX06EZE	South Coast	K309FYG	North East	L118ALJ	South Coast
HF54HGL	South Coast	HX06EZF	South Coast	K310FYG	North East	L120ALJ	South Coast
HF54HGM	South Coast	HX06EZG	South Coast	K310YJA	Diamond	L122ELJ	South Coast
HF54HGN	South Coast	HX06EZH	South Coast	K311FYG	North East	L123ELJ	South Coast
HF54HGO	South Coast	HX06EZJ	South Coast	K311YJA	Diamond	L124ELJ	South Coast
HF54HGP	South Coast	HX51ZRA	South Coast	K312FYG	North East	L126ELJ	South Coast
HF54HGU	South Coast	HX51ZRC	South Coast	K312YJA	Diamond	L127ELJ	South Coast
HF54HGX	South Coast	HX51ZRD	South Coast	K313FYG	North East	L128ELJ	South Coast
HF54HGY	South Coast	HX51ZRE	South Coast	K313YJA	Diamond	L129ELJ	South Coast
HF54HHA	South Coast	HX51ZRF	South Coast	K314YJA	Diamond	L130ELJ	South Coast
HF54HHB	South Coast	HX51ZRG	South Coast	K315FYG	North East	L131ELJ	South Coast
HF54HHC	South Coast	HX51ZRJ	South Coast	K316FYG	North East	L141YTY	North East
HF54HHD	South Coast	HX51ZRK	South Coast	K316YJA	Diamond	L201YAG	Diamond
HF54HHE	South Coast	J1OXF	Oxford	K317FYG	North East	L202YAG	Diamond
HF54HHJ	South Coast	J110SPB	North East	K317YJA	Diamond	L204YAG	Diamond
HF54HHK	South Coast	J205VHN	North East	K318YJA	Diamond	L206YAG	Diamond
HF54HHL	South Coast	J382GKH	South Coast	K320YJA	Diamond	L207YAG	Diamond
HF54HHM	South Coast	J503RPR	South Coast	K321FYG	North East	L208KEF	North East
HF54KXT	South Coast	J505RPR	South Coast	K321YJA	Diamond	L209KEF	North East
HF54KXU	South Coast	J508RPR	South Coast	K322YJA	Diamond	L209YAG	Diamond
HF54KXV	South Coast	J512RPR	South Coast	K323FYG	North East	L210KEF	North East
HF54KXW	South Coast	J601XHL	Diamond	K323YJA	Diamond	L211KEF	North East
HF55JYX	South Coast	J603XHL	Diamond	K324FYG	North East	L211YAG	Diamond
HF55JYY	South Coast	J604XHL	Diamond	K325YJA	Diamond	L212KEF	North East
HF55JYZ	South Coast	J605XHL	Diamond	K327YJA	Diamond	L227THP	South Coast
HF55JZA	South Coast	J606XHL	Diamond	K328YJA	Diamond	L262PKU	Aviance
HF55JZC	South Coast	J607XHL	Diamond	K330YJA	Diamond	L417KEF	North East
HF55JZD	South Coast	J610XHL	Diamond	K331YJA	Diamond	L445FFR	South Coast
HF55JZE	South Coast	J701EMX	Diamond	K716PCN	South Coast	L469YVK	North East
HF55JZG	South Coast	J703EMX	Diamond	K719PCN	South Coast	L470YVK	North East
HF55JZJ	South Coast	J705EMX	Diamond	K735ODL	South Coast	L471YVK	North East
HF55JZK	South Coast	J706EMX	Diamond	K736ODL	South Coast	L475CFT	North East
HF55JZL	South Coast	J707EMX	Diamond	K737ODL	South Coast	L476CFT	North East
HF55JZM	South Coast	J980JNJ	Brighton & H	K738ODL	South Coast	L477CFT	North East
HF55JZN	South Coast	J984JNJ	Brighton & H	K739ODL	South Coast	L478CFT	North East
HF55JZO	South Coast	JCN822	North East	K740ODL	South Coast	L479CFT	North East
HF55JZP	South Coast	JF55OXF	Oxford	K741ODL	South Coast	L481CFT	North East
HF55JZR	South Coast	JJD472D	London	K742ODL	South Coast	L482CFT	North East
HF55JZT	South Coast	JJD520D	London	K743ODL	South Coast	L483CFT	North East
HF55JZU	South Coast	K1OXF	Oxford	K750RHR	South Coast	L484CFT	North East
HF55JZV	South Coast	K2VOY	North East	K756SBB	North East	L485CFT	North East
HF55JZW	South Coast	K3VOY	North East	K757SBB	North East	L486CFT	North East
HF55OXF	Oxford	K101VLJ	South Coast	K758SBB	North East	L487CFT	North East
HJ02WDE	South Coast	K103VLJ	South Coast	K759SBB	North East	L488CFT	North East
HJ02WDF	South Coast	K104VLJ	South Coast	K760SBB	North East	L501AJT	South Coast
HJ02WDG	South Coast	K105VLJ	South Coast	K761SBB	North East	L502AJT	South Coast
HJ02WDK	South Coast	K106VLJ	South Coast	KF55OXF	Oxford	L503AJT	South Coast
HJ02WDL	South Coast	K107VLJ	South Coast	KRU848W	South Coast	L504AJT	South Coast
HJ02WDM	South Coast	K108VLJ	South Coast	KRU849W	South Coast	L505AJT	South Coast
HJ02WDN	South Coast	K108YVN	North East	KRU850W	South Coast	L506AJT	South Coast
HJ52VFW	South Coast	K109YVN	North East	KRU851W	South Coast	L526YDL	South Coast
HJ52VFX	South Coast	K110VLJ	South Coast	KRU853W	South Coast	L527YDL	South Coast
HJ52VFY	South Coast	K110YVN	North East	KRU854W	South Coast	L528YDL	South Coast
HJ52VFZ	South Coast	K119BUD	Oxford	KRU855W	South Coast	L711ALJ	South Coast
HJ52VGA	South Coast	K120BUD	Oxford	KRU856W	South Coast	L720UMV	Brighton & H
HJI2615	South Coast	K121BUD	South Coast	KU52RXT	Diamond	L942RJN	Diamond
HSV342	South Coast	K122BUD	South Coast	KU52RXV	Diamond	LF02OHB	Aviance
HW52EPK	South Coast	K123BUD	South Coast	KU52RXW	Diamond	LF02OHC	Aviance

Reg	Location	Reg	Location	Reg	Location	Reg	Location
LF02OHD	Aviance	LG02KGY	London	LX05EZL	London	LX06EBA	London
LF02OHE	Aviance	LG02KGZ	London	LX05EZM	London	LX06EBC	London
LF02OHG	Aviance	LG02KHA	London	LX05EZN	London	LX06EBD	London
LF51CYC	London	LG02KHE	London	LX05EZO	London	LX06EBE	London
LF52ZLZ	London	LG02KHF	London	LX05EZP	London	LX06EBG	London
LF52ZMO	London	LG02KHH	London	LX05EZR	London	LX06EBJ	London
LF52ZMU	London	LG02KHJ	London	LX05EZS	London	LX06EBK	London
LF52ZND	London	LG02KHK	London	LX05EZT	London	LX06EBL	London
LF52ZNE	London	LG02KHL	London	LX05EZU	London	LX06EBM	London
LF52ZNG	London	LG02KHM	London	LX05EZV	London	LX06EBN	London
LF52ZNH	London	LG02KHO	London	LX05EZW	London	LX06EBO	London
LF52ZNJ	London	LG02KHP	London	LX05EZZ	London	LX06EBP	London
LF52ZNK	London	LG02KHR	London	LX05FAA	London	LX06EBU	London
LF52ZNL	London	LG02KHT	London	LX05FAF	London	LX06EBW	London
LF52ZNM	London	LG02KHU	London	LX05FAF	London	LX06EBZ	London
LF52ZNN	London	LG02KHV	London	LX05FAJ	London	LX06ECA	London
LF52ZNO	London	LG02KHW	London	LX05FAK	London	LX06ECC	London
LF52ZNP	London	LG02KHX	London	LX05FAM	London	LX06ECD	London
LF52ZNR	London	LG02KHY	London	LX05FAO	London	LX06ECE	London
LF52ZNS	London	LG02KHZ	London	LX05FAU	London	LX06ECF	London
LF52ZNT	London	LG02KJA	London	LX05FBA	London	LX06ECJ	London
LF52ZNU	London	LG02KJE	London	LX05FBB	London	LX06ECN	London
LF52ZNV	London	LG02KJF	London	LX05FBC	London	LX06ECT	London
LF52ZNW	London	LIL2665	South Coast	LX05FBD	London	LX06ECV	London
LF52ZNX	London	LIL3748	South Coast	LX05FBD	London	LX06EYT	London
LF52ZNY	London	LSV749	South Coast	LX05FBE	London	LX06EYY	London
LF52ZNZ	London	LV51YCC	Metrobus	LX05FBE	London	LX06EYZ	London
LF52ZPB	London	LV51YCD	Metrobus	LX05FBF	London	LX06EZA	London
LF52ZPC	London	LV51YCE	Metrobus	LX05FBJ	London	LX06EZB	London
LF52ZPD	London	LV51YCF	Metrobus	LX05FBK	London	LX06EZC	London
LF52ZPE	London	LV51YCG	Metrobus	LX05FBL	London	LX06EZD	London
LF52ZPG	London	LV51YCH	Metrobus	LX05FBN	London	LX06EZE	London
LF52ZPH	London	LV51YCJ	Metrobus	LX05FBO	London	LX06EZF	London
LF52ZPJ	London	LV51YCK	Metrobus	LX05FBU	London	LX06EZG	London
LF52ZPK	London	LV51YCL	Metrobus	LX05FBV	London	LX06EZH	London
LF52ZPL	London	LV51YCM	Metrobus	LX05FBY	London	LX06EZJ	London
LF52ZPM	London	LV51YCN	Metrobus	LX05FBZ	London	LX06EZK	London
LF52ZPN	London	LV51YCO	Metrobus	LX05FCA	London	LX06EZL	London
LF52ZPO	London	LW52AFA	Brighton & H	LX05FCC	London	LX06EZM	London
LF52ZPP	London	LX03ECV	London	LX05FCD	London	LX06EZN	London
LF52ZPR	London	LX03ECW	London	LX05FCE	London	LX06EZO	London
LF52ZPS	London	LX03ECY	London	LX05FCF	London	LX06EZP	London
LF52ZPU	London	LX03EDR	London	LX05FFA	London	LX06EZR	London
LF52ZPV	London	LX03EDU	London	LX06DXS	London	LX06EZS	London
LF52ZPW	London	LX03EDV	London	LX06DXT	London	LX06EZT	London
LF52ZPY	London	LX03EEA	London	LX06DXU	London	LX06EZU	London
LF52ZPZ	London	LX03EEB	London	LX06DXV	London	LX06EZV	London
LF52ZRA	London	LX03EEF	London	LX06DXW	London	LX06EZW	London
LF52ZRC	London	LX03EEG	London	LX06DXY	London	LX06EZZ	London
LF52ZRD	London	LX03EEH	London	LX06DZA	London	LX06FAJ	London
LF52ZRE	London	LX03EEJ	London	LX06DZB	London	LX06FAK	London
LF52ZRG	London	LX03EEM	London	LX06DZC	London	LX06FAM	London
LF52ZRJ	London	LX03EXU	London	LX06DZD	London	LX06FAO	London
LF52ZRK	London	LX03EXV	London	LX06DZE	London	LX06FAU	London
LF52ZRL	London	LX03EXW	London	LX06DZF	London	LX06FBA	London
LF52ZRN	London	LX03EXZ	London	LX06DZG	London	LX06FBB	London
LF52ZRO	London	LX03OJN	London	LX06DZH	London	LX06FBC	London
LF52ZRP	London	LX03OJP	London	LX06DZJ	London	LX06FKL	London
LF52ZRR	London	LX05EXZ	London	LX06DZK	London	LX06FKM	London
LF52ZRT	London	LX05EYA	London	LX06DZL	London	LX06FKN	London
LF52ZRU	London	LX05EYM	London	LX06DZM	London	LX06FKO	London
LF52ZRV	London	LX05EYO	London	LX06DZN	London	LX53AYM	London
LF52ZRX	London	LX05EYP	London	LX06DZO	London	LX53AYN	London
LF52ZRY	London	LX05EYR	London	LX06DZP	London	LX53AYO	London
LF52ZRZ	London	LX05EYS	London	LX06DZR	London	LX53AYP	London
LF52ZSD	London	LX05EYT	London	LX06DZS	London	LX53AYT	London
LF52ZSO	London	LX05EYU	London	LX06DZT	London	LX53AYU	London
LF52ZSP	London	LX05EYU	London	LX06DZU	London	LX53AYV	London
LF52ZSR	London	LX05EYV	London	LX06DZV	London	LX53AYW	London
LF52ZST	London	LX05EYV	London	LX06DZW	London	LX53AYY	London
LF52ZTG	London	LX05EYW	London	LX06DZY	London	LX53AYZ	London
LF52ZTH	London	LX05EYW	London	LX06DZZ	London	LX53AZA	London
LF52ZTJ	London	LX05EYY	London	LX06EAA	London	LX53AZB	London
LF52ZTK	London	LX05EYZ	London	LX06EAC	London	LX53AZC	London
LF52ZTL	London	LX05EZA	London	LX06EAF	London	LX53AZD	London
LF52ZTM	London	LX05EZB	London	LX06EAG	London	LX53AZF	London
LF52ZTN	London	LX05EZC	London	LX06EAJ	London	LX53AZG	London
LF52ZTO	London	LX05EZD	London	LX06EAK	London	LX53AZJ	London
LF52ZTP	London	LX05EZE	London	LX06EAL	London	LX53AZL	London
LF52ZTR	London	LX05EZF	London	LX06EAM	London	LX53AZN	London
LG02KGP	London	LX05EZG	London	LX06EAO	London	LX53AZO	London
LG02KGU	London	LX05EZH	London	LX06EAP	London	LX53AZP	London
LG02KGV	London	LX05EZJ	London	LX06EAW	London	LX53AZR	London
LG02KGX	London	LX05EZK	London	LX06EAY	London	LX53AZT	London

The 2006-07 Go-Ahead Bus Handbook

LX53AZU	London	M151HPL	Metrobus	MJI7514	South Coast	N605FJO	Oxford
LX53AZV	London	M209VKU	Aviance	MT53NHG	Aviance	N606WND	Diamond
LX53AZW	London	M404OKM	Brighton & H	N1OXF	Oxford	N607FJO	Oxford
LX53AZZ	London	M405OKM	Brighton & H	N10WAL	South Coast	N608FJO	Oxford
LX53BAA	London	M406OKM	Brighton & H	N13WAL	South Coast	N608FJO	South Coast
LX53BAO	London	M407OKM	Brighton & H	N14WAL	South Coast	N610FJO	Oxford
LX53BBZ	London	M408OKM	Brighton & H	N15WAL	South Coast	N611FJO	Oxford
LX53BDO	London	M442BLC	Diamond	N16WAL	South Coast	N612FJO	Oxford
LX53BDY	London	M443BLC	Diamond	N45FWU	South Coast	N613FJO	Oxford
LX53BEY	London	M445BLC	Diamond	N117WBR	North East	N614HRV	South Coast
LX53BFK	London	M470FJR	North East	N118WBR	North East	N615FJO	Oxford
LX53BGE	London	M471FJR	North East	N119WBR	North East	N616FJO	Oxford
LX53BJK	London	M472FJR	North East	N120WBR	North East	N617FJO	Oxford
LX53BJO	London	M473FJR	North East	N121WBR	North East	N618FJO	Oxford
LX53BJU	London	M489HCU	North East	N122WBR	North East	N619FJO	Oxford
LX54GYV	London	M490HCU	North East	N123WBR	North East	N619FJO	Oxford
LX54GYW	London	M491HCU	North East	N124WBR	North East	N620FJO	Oxford
LX54GYY	London	M492HCU	North East	N201NNJ	Brighton & H	N726KGF	Metrobus
LX54GYZ	London	M493HCU	North East	N202NNJ	Brighton & H	N751OAP	Brighton & H
LX54GZB	London	M502VJO	Metrobus	N203NNJ	Brighton & H	N752OAP	Brighton & H
LX54GZC	London	M506VJO	Metrobus	N204NNJ	Brighton & H	N753OAP	Brighton & H
LX54GZD	London	M507VJO	Metrobus	N205NNJ	Brighton & H	N754OAP	Brighton & H
LX54GZE	London	M508VJO	Metrobus	N206NNJ	Brighton & H	N755OAP	Brighton & H
LX54GZF	London	M511VJO	Metrobus	N207NNJ	Brighton & H	N756OAP	Brighton & H
LX54GZG	London	M516VJO	Metrobus	N208NNJ	Brighton & H	N757OAP	Brighton & H
LX54GZH	London	M518VJO	Metrobus	N209NNJ	Brighton & H	N758OAP	Brighton & H
LX54GZK	London	M520VJO	Metrobus	N210NNJ	Brighton & H	N759OAP	Brighton & H
LX54GZL	London	M535JLJ	South Coast	N211NNJ	Brighton & H	N760OAP	Brighton & H
LX54GZM	London	M536JLJ	South Coast	N212NNJ	Brighton & H	N760RCU	North East
LX54GZN	London	M537JLJ	South Coast	N213NNJ	Brighton & H	N760RCU	North East
LX54GZO	London	M539LEL	South Coast	N214NNJ	Brighton & H	N761RCU	North East
LX54GZP	London	M540LEL	South Coast	N215NNJ	Brighton & H	N771EWG	Diamond
LX54GZR	London	M541LEL	South Coast	N216NPN	Brighton & H	N810PDL	South Coast
LX54GZT	London	M574RCP	South Coast	N217NPN	Brighton & H	N811PDL	South Coast
LX54GZU	London	M577RCP	South Coast	N218NPN	Brighton & H	N812PDL	South Coast
LX54GZV	London	M578RCP	South Coast	N226VRC	South Coast	N813PDL	South Coast
LX54GZW	London	M580RCP	South Coast	N259FOR	South Coast	N813WGR	North East
LX54GZY	London	M645RCP	South Coast	N322WCH	South Coast	N814PDL	South Coast
LX54GZZ	London	M721CGO	Metrobus	N324VRC	South Coast	N814WGR	North East
LX54HAA	London	M735BBP	South Coast	N325VRC	South Coast	N815PDL	South Coast
LX54HAE	London	M736BBP	South Coast	N401MPN	Brighton & H	N815WGR	North East
LX54HAO	London	M744HDL	South Coast	N402MPN	Brighton & H	N816WGR	North East
LX54HAU	London	M745HDL	South Coast	N403MPN	Brighton & H	N901PFC	Diamond
LX54HBA	London	M746HDL	South Coast	N404MPN	Brighton & H	N902PFC	Diamond
LX54HBB	London	M746RCP	South Coast	N405MPN	Brighton & H	N903PFC	Diamond
LX55EAC	London	M748HDL	South Coast	N406MPN	Brighton & H	N950TVK	North East
LX55EAE	London	M749HDL	South Coast	N407MPN	Brighton & H	NA02NVL	North East
LX55EAF	London	M750HDL	South Coast	N408MPN	Brighton & H	NA52AWF	North East
LX55EAG	London	M751HDL	South Coast	N409MPN	Brighton & H	NA52AWG	North East
LX55EAJ	London	M803GFT	Diamond	N410MPN	Brighton & H	NA52AWH	North East
M1OXF	Oxford	M804GFT	North East	N411JBV	South Coast	NA52AWJ	North East
M15WAL	South Coast	M805GFT	North East	N411MPN	Brighton & H	NA52AWM	North East
M17WAL	South Coast	M806GFT	North East	N411NTN	North East	NA52AWN	North East
M18WAL	South Coast	M807GFT	North East	N412MPN	Brighton & H	NA52AWO	North East
M19WAL	South Coast	M808GFT	Diamond	N413JBV	South Coast	NA52AWP	North East
M20WAL	South Coast	M809GFT	North East	N413MPN	Brighton & H	NA52AWR	North East
M58LBB	North East	M810GFT	Diamond	N414MPN	Brighton & H	NA52AWU	North East
M59LBB	North East	M810HCU	North East	N415MPN	Brighton & H	NA52AWV	North East
M65CYJ	Brighton & H	M811GFT	Diamond	N416MPN	Brighton & H	NA52AWW	North East
M68CYJ	Brighton & H	M811HCU	Diamond	N416NRG	South Coast	NA52AWX	North East
M69CYJ	Brighton & H	M812GFT	Diamond	N417MPN	Metrobus	NA52AWY	North East
M71CYJ	Brighton & H	M813GFT	Diamond	N418MPN	Metrobus	NA52AWZ	North East
M73CYJ	Brighton & H	M814GFT	Diamond	N419MPN	Brighton & H	NA52AXB	North East
M76CYJ	Brighton & H	M815GFT	Diamond	N420MPN	Brighton & H	NA52AXC	North East
M78CYJ	Brighton & H	M816GFT	Diamond	N505KCD	Brighton & H	NA52AXD	North East
M79CYJ	Brighton & H	M817ARV	South Coast	N507KCD	Brighton & H	NA52AXF	North East
M101BLE	Diamond	M817GFT	Diamond	N509KCD	Brighton & H	NA52AXG	North East
M105BLE	Diamond	M818GFT	North East	N510KCD	Brighton & H	NA52AXH	North East
M106BLE	Diamond	M819GFT	Diamond	N512KCD	Brighton & H	NA52AXJ	North East
M109BLE	Diamond	M890GBB	Diamond	N514KCD	Brighton & H	NA52AXK	North East
M132HPR	South Coast	M891GBB	Diamond	N515KCD	Brighton & H	NA52AXM	North East
M133HPR	South Coast	M892GBB	Diamond	N520KCD	Brighton & H	NA52AXN	North East
M134HPR	South Coast	M947KRU	South Coast	N530LHG	Diamond	NA52AXO	North East
M135HPR	South Coast	M95WBW	Brighton & H	N539LHG	South Coast	NA52BUU	North East
M136KRU	South Coast	M96WBW	Brighton & H	N543LHG	Diamond	NA52BUV	North East
M137KRU	South Coast	M97WBW	Brighton & H	N543UFX	South Coast	NA52BUW	North East
M138KRU	South Coast	MA52OXF	Oxford	N544UFX	South Coast	NA52BVB	North East
M139KRU	South Coast	MB52OXF	Oxford	N545UFX	South Coast	NA52BVC	North East
M140KRU	South Coast	MC52OXF	Oxford	N546UFX	South Coast	NA52BVD	North East
M141KRU	South Coast	MD52OXF	Oxford	N547UFX	South Coast	NA52BVE	North East
M143KRU	South Coast	ME52OXF	Oxford	N601FJO	Oxford	NA52BVF	North East
M144KRU	South Coast	MF52OXF	Oxford	N602FJO	South Coast	NA52BVG	North East
M145KRU	South Coast	MIL9574	South Coast	N603FJO	Oxford	NA52BVH	North East
M146KRU	South Coast	MIL9575	South Coast	N604FJO	Oxford	NA52BVJ	North East

NK04FOP	North East	NK53TKV	North East	NL52WVW	North East	P417VRG	North East
NK04FOT	North East	NK53TKX	North East	NL52WVX	North East	P452BPH	Diamond
NK04FOU	North East	NK53TKY	North East	NML604E	London	P453BPH	Diamond
NK04FOV	North East	NK53TKZ	North East	NML604E	London	P501OUG	Diamond
NK04FPA	North East	NK53TLF	North East	NML605E	London	P501RYM	London
NK04FPC	North East	NK53TLJ	North East	NML606E	London	P502OUG	Diamond
NK04FPD	North East	NK53TLN	North East	NML612E	London	P502RYM	London
NK04FPE	North East	NK53TLO	North East	NML615E	London	P503OUG	Diamond
NK04NKT	North East	NK53TLU	North East	NML618E	London	P503RYM	London
NK04NKU	North East	NK53TLV	North East	NML626E	London	P504OUG	Diamond
NK04NKW	North East	NK53TLX	North East	NML631E	London	P504RYM	London
NK04NKX	North East	NK53TLY	North East	NML637E	London	P505OUG	Diamond
NK04NKZ	North East	NK53TMO	North East	NML640E	London	P505RYM	London
NK04NLC	North East	NK53TMU	North East	NML644E	London	P506OUG	Diamond
NK04NLD	North East	NK53TMV	North East	NML654E	London	P506RYM	London
NK04ZKY	North East	NK53TMX	North East	NXI5358	South Coast	P507OUG	Diamond
NK04ZKZ	North East	NK53TMY	North East	OA02OXF	Oxford	P507RYM	London
NK04ZLE	North East	NK53TMZ	North East	OB02OXF	Oxford	P508OUG	Diamond
NK04ZNC	North East	NK53UNT	North East	OC02OXF	Oxford	P508RYM	London
NK04ZND	North East	NK53UNU	North East	OD02OXF	Oxford	P509OUG	Diamond
NK04ZNE	North East	NK53UNV	North East	ODL447	South Coast	P510OUG	Diamond
NK05GZO	North East	NK53UNW	North East	OE02OXF	Oxford	P514RYM	London
NK05GZP	North East	NK53UNX	North East	OEL232P	South Coast	P515RYM	London
NK05GZR	North East	NK53UNY	North East	OF02OXF	Oxford	P516RYM	London
NK06JXB	North East	NK53UNZ	North East	OIJ1875	South Coast	P620NKW	Diamond
NK06JXC	North East	NK53UOA	North East	P1OXF	Oxford	P629FFC	Oxford
NK06JXD	North East	NK53UOB	North East	P36HEW	Aviance	P630FFC	Oxford
NK06JXE	North East	NK53UOC	North East	P87BPL	Diamond	P631FFC	Oxford
NK51MJU	North East	NK54DEU	North East	P94DOE	South Coast	P632FFC	Oxford
NK51MJV	North East	NK54DFA	North East	P101HCH	Diamond	P633FFC	Oxford
NK51MJX	North East	NK54DFC	North East	P102HCH	Diamond	P634FFC	Oxford
NK51MJY	North East	NK54DFD	North East	P106HCH	Diamond	P635FFC	Oxford
NK51MKA	North East	NK54NTX	North East	P108HCH	Diamond	P636FFC	Oxford
NK51MKC	North East	NK54NTY	North East	P109HCH	Diamond	P637FFC	Oxford
NK51MKD	North East	NK54NUA	North East	P112HCH	Diamond	P638FFC	Oxford
NK51MKE	North East	NK54NUB	North East	P113HCH	Diamond	P639FFC	Oxford
NK51MKF	North East	NK54NUH	North East	P114HCH	Diamond	P640FFC	Oxford
NK51MKG	North East	NK54NUJ	North East	P115HCH	Diamond	P641FFC	Oxford
NK51MKJ	North East	NK54NUM	North East	P117HCH	Diamond	P642FFC	Oxford
NK51MKL	North East	NK54NUO	North East	P135LNF	Meteor	P643FFC	Oxford
NK51MKM	North East	NK54NUP	North East	P136LNF	Meteor	P687HND	Diamond
NK51MKN	North East	NK54NUU	North East	P169PVM	Diamond	P693UAE	South Coast
NK51MKO	North East	NK54NUV	North East	P206PVM	Diamond	P697HND	Diamond
NK51MKP	North East	NK54NUW	North East	P207PVM	Diamond	P714MLD	Meteor
NK51OKW	North East	NK54NUX	North East	P215OLC	Meteor	P724RYL	Metrobus
NK51OKX	North East	NK54NUY	North East	P216OLC	Meteor	P725RYL	Metrobus
NK51OLB	North East	NK54NVA	North East	P218OLC	Meteor	P726RYL	Metrobus
NK51OLC	North East	NK54NVB	North East	P227CTV	South Coast	P727RYL	Metrobus
NK51OLE	North East	NK54NVC	North East	P228CTV	South Coast	P732RYL	Oxford
NK51OLG	North East	NK54NVD	North East	P229CTV	South Coast	P732RYL	London
NK51OLH	North East	NK54NVE	North East	P230CTV	South Coast	P734RYL	London
NK51OLJ	North East	NK54NVF	North East	P231CTV	South Coast	P735RYL	London
NK51OLM	North East	NK54NVG	North East	P232CTV	South Coast	P736RYL	Diamond
NK51OLN	North East	NK54NVH	North East	P233CTV	South Coast	P736RYL	London
NK51OLO	North East	NK54NVJ	North East	P234CTV	South Coast	P737RYL	London
NK51OLP	North East	NK54NVL	North East	P235CTV	South Coast	P739RYL	Oxford
NK51OLR	North East	NK54NVM	North East	P236CTV	South Coast	P739RYL	London
NK51OLT	North East	NK54NVN	North East	P237CTV	South Coast	P740RYL	London
NK51OLT	North East	NK54NVO	North East	P238CTV	South Coast	P741HND	Diamond
NK51OLU	North East	NK54NVP	North East	P239CTV	South Coast	P741RYL	London
NK51OLV	North East	NK54NVT	North East	P240CTV	South Coast	P742HND	Diamond
NK51UCH	North East	NK54NVV	North East	P240VDL	South Coast	P742RYL	London
NK51UCJ	North East	NK54NVV	North East	P241CTV	South Coast	P743RYL	London
NK51UCL	North East	NK54NVW	North East	P241VDL	South Coast	P744RYL	London
NK51UCM	North East	NK54NVX	North East	P242VDL	South Coast	P748HND	Diamond
NK51UCN	North East	NK54NVY	North East	P243VDL	South Coast	P817SGP	Metrobus
NK51UCO	North East	NK54NVZ	North East	P244VDL	South Coast	P818SGP	Metrobus
NK51UCP	North East	NK54NWA	North East	P246VDL	South Coast	P819SGP	Metrobus
NK51UCR	North East	NK54NWB	North East	P301HDP	Metrobus	P821SGP	Metrobus
NK51UCS	North East	NK55OLG	North East	P302HDP	Metrobus	P822SGP	Metrobus
NK51UCT	North East	NK55OLH	North East	P303HDP	Metrobus	P823SGP	Metrobus
NK51UCU	North East	NK55OLJ	North East	P304HDP	Metrobus	P824SGP	Metrobus
NK51UCV	North East	NK55OLM	North East	P305HDP	Metrobus	P825SGP	Metrobus
NK51UCW	North East	NK55OLN	North East	P306HDP	Metrobus	P826SGP	Metrobus
NK51UCX	North East	NL02ZRX	North East	P307HDP	Metrobus	P827BUD	Diamond
NK51UCY	North East	NL52WVM	North East	P308HDP	Metrobus	P828SGP	Metrobus
NK53TKD	North East	NL52WVN	North East	P319DOP	South Coast	P829BUD	Diamond
NK53TKE	North East	NL52WVO	North East	P320AFT	North East	P829SGP	Metrobus
NK53TKF	North East	NL52WVP	North East	P321AFT	North East	P861VFG	Brighton & H
NK53TKJ	North East	NL52WVR	North East	P322AFT	North East	P862VFG	Brighton & H
NK53TKN	North East	NL52WVS	North East	P323AFT	North East	P863VFG	Brighton & H
NK53TKO	North East	NL52WVT	North East	P324AFT	North East	P864VFG	Brighton & H
NK53TKT	North East	NL52WVU	North East	P325AFT	North East	P865VFG	Brighton & H
NK53TKU	North East	NL52WVV	North East	P416VRG	North East	P866VFG	Brighton & H

The 2006-07 Go-Ahead Bus Handbook

P867VFG	Brighton & H	PJ02RCO	London	PJ53NLA	London	PN02XCS	London
P868VFG	Brighton & H	PJ02RCU	London	PJ53NLC	London	PN02XCT	London
P869VFG	Brighton & H	PJ02RCV	London	PJ53NLD	London	PN03ULK	London
P870VFG	Brighton & H	PJ02RCX	London	PJ53NLE	London	PN03ULL	London
P871VFG	Brighton & H	PJ02RCY	London	PJ53NLF	London	PN03ULM	London
P872VFG	Brighton & H	PJ02RCZ	London	PJ53SOF	London	PN03ULP	London
P873VFG	Brighton & H	PJ02RDO	London	PJ53SOH	London	PN03ULR	London
P874VFG	Brighton & H	PJ02RDU	London	PJ53SOU	London	PN03ULS	London
P875VFG	Brighton & H	PJ02RDV	London	PJ53SPU	London	PN03ULT	London
P876VFG	Brighton & H	PJ02RDX	London	PJ53SPV	London	PN03ULU	London
P877VFG	Brighton & H	PJ02RDY	London	PJ53SPX	London	PN03ULV	London
P895PWW	Metrobus	PJ02RDZ	London	PJ53SPZ	London	PN03ULW	London
P904RYO	London	PJ02REU	London	PJ53SRO	London	PN03ULX	London
P904RYO	Diamond	PJ02RFE	London	PJ53SRU	London	PN03ULY	London
P907RYO	London	PJ02RFF	London	PK02RCZ	Brighton & H	PN03ULZ	London
P907RYO	Diamond	PJ02RFK	London	PK02RDO	Brighton & H	PN03UMA	London
P909RYO	London	PJ02RFL	London	PK02RDU	Brighton & H	PN03UMB	London
P910RYO	London	PJ02RFN	London	PK02RDV	Brighton & H	PN03UMC	London
P911RYO	London	PJ02RFO	London	PK02RDX	Brighton & H	PN03UMD	London
P912RYO	London	PJ02RFX	London	PK02RDY	Brighton & H	PN03UME	London
P913RYO	London	PJ02RFY	London	PK02RDZ	Brighton & H	PN03UMF	London
P914RYO	London	PJ02RFZ	London	PK02REU	Brighton & H	PN03UMG	London
P916RYOO	London	PJ02RGO	London	PK02RFE	Brighton & H	PN03UMH	London
P917RYO	London	PJ02RGU	London	PK02RFF	Brighton & H	PN03UMJ	London
P924RYO	London	PJ02RGV	London	PK02RFJ	Brighton & H	PN03UMK	London
P927RYO	London	PJ02RGX	Diamond	PK02RFL	Brighton & H	PN06UYL	Metrobus
P929RYO	Diamond	PJ02RGY	Diamond	PL03AGZ	London	PN06UYM	Metrobus
P989AFV	Meteor	PJ02RHA	Diamond	PL51LDJ	London	PN06UYO	Metrobus
P990AFV	Meteor	PJ02RHF	London	PL51LDK	London	PN06UYP	Metrobus
P991AFV	Meteor	PJ02TVN	London	PL51LDN	London	PN06UYR	Metrobus
P992AFV	Meteor	PJ02TVO	London	PL51LDO	London	PN06UYS	Metrobus
P993AFV	Meteor	PJ02TVP	London	PL51LDU	London	PN06UYT	Metrobus
P994AFV	Meteor	PJ02TVT	London	PL51LDV	London	PN06UYU	Metrobus
PF52WPT	London	PJ02TVU	London	PL51LDX	London	PN06UYV	Metrobus
PF52WPU	London	PJ52LVP	London	PL51LDY	London	PN06UYW	Metrobus
PF52WPV	London	PJ52LVR	London	PL51LDZ	London	PN06UYX	Metrobus
PF52WPW	London	PJ52LVS	London	PL51LEF	London	PN06UYY	Metrobus
PF52WPX	London	PJ52LVT	London	PL51LFE	London	PV03GVT	Aviance
PF52WPY	London	PJ52LVU	London	PL51LFG	London	R1OXF	Oxford
PF52WPZ	London	PJ52LVV	London	PL51LFJ	London	R2OXF	Oxford
PF52WRA	London	PJ52LVW	London	PL51LGA	London	R3OXF	Oxford
PF52WRC	London	PJ52LVX	London	PL51LGC	London	R4OXF	Oxford
PF52WRD	London	PJ52LVY	London	PL51LGD	London	R5OXF	Oxford
PF52WRE	London	PJ52LVZ	London	PL51LGE	London	R6OXF	Oxford
PF52WRG	London	PJ52LWA	London	PL51LGF	London	R7OXF	Oxford
PJ02PYU	London	PJ52LWC	London	PL51LGG	London	R8OXF	Oxford
PJ02PYV	London	PJ52LWD	London	PL51LGJ	London	R9OXF	Oxford
PJ02PYW	London	PJ52LWE	London	PL51LGK	London	R10OXF	Oxford
PJ02PYX	London	PJ52LWF	London	PL51LGN	London	R11OXF	Oxford
PJ02PYY	London	PJ52LWG	London	PL51LGO	London	R41BYG	Meteor
PJ02PYZ	London	PJ52LWH	London	PL51LGU	London	R42BYG	Meteor
PJ02PZA	London	PJ52LWK	London	PL51LGW	London	R43BYG	Meteor
PJ02PZB	London	PJ52LWL	London	PL51LGX	London	R85XNE	Diamond
PJ02PZC	London	PJ52LWM	London	PN02XBH	London	R86XNE	Diamond
PJ02PZD	London	PJ52LWN	London	PN02XBJ	London	R87XNE	Diamond
PJ02PZE	London	PJ52LWO	London	PN02XBK	London	R91XNE	Diamond
PJ02PZF	London	PJ52LWP	London	PN02XBL	London	R92XNE	Diamond
PJ02PZG	London	PJ52LWR	London	PN02XBM	London	R126XWF	South Coast
PJ02PZH	London	PJ52LWS	London	PN02XBO	London	R130XWF	South Coast
PJ02PZK	London	PJ52LWT	London	PN02XBP	London	R154NPR	South Coast
PJ02PZL	London	PJ52LWU	London	PN02XBR	London	R155NPR	South Coast
PJ02PZM	London	PJ52LWV	London	PN02XBS	London	R156NPR	South Coast
PJ02PZN	London	PJ52LWW	London	PN02XBT	London	R214NFX	South Coast
PJ02PZO	London	PJ52LWX	London	PN02XBU	London	R215NFX	South Coast
PJ02PZP	London	PJ53NJZ	London	PN02XBV	London	R216HCD	Brighton & H
PJ02PZR	London	PJ53NKA	London	PN02XBW	London	R217HCD	Brighton & H
PJ02PZS	London	PJ53NKC	London	PN02XBX	London	R218HCD	Brighton & H
PJ02PZT	London	PJ53NKD	London	PN02XBY	London	R219HCD	Brighton & H
PJ02PZU	London	PJ53NKE	London	PN02XBZ	London	R220HCD	Brighton & H
PJ02PZV	London	PJ53NKF	London	PN02XCA	London	R221HCD	Brighton & H
PJ02PZW	London	PJ53NKG	London	PN02XCB	London	R221HCD	South Coast
PJ02PZX	London	PJ53NKH	London	PN02XCC	London	R223HCD	Brighton & H
PJ02PZY	London	PJ53NKK	London	PN02XCD	London	R224HCD	Brighton & H
PJ02PZZ	London	PJ53NKL	London	PN02XCE	London	R225HCD	Brighton & H
PJ02RAU	London	PJ53NKM	London	PN02XCF	London	R226HCD	Brighton & H
PJ02RAX	London	PJ53NKN	London	PN02XCG	London	R227HCD	Brighton & H
PJ02RBF	London	PJ53NKO	London	PN02XCH	London	R228HCD	Brighton & H
PJ02RBO	London	PJ53NKP	London	PN02XCJ	London	R229HCD	Brighton & H
PJ02RBU	London	PJ53NKR	London	PN02XCK	London	R230HCD	Brighton & H
PJ02RBV	London	PJ53NKS	London	PN02XCL	London	R231HCD	Brighton & H
PJ02RBX	London	PJ53NKT	London	PN02XCM	London	R232HCD	Brighton & H
PJ02RBY	London	PJ53NKW	London	PN02XCO	London	R233HCD	Brighton & H
PJ02RBZ	London	PJ53NKX	London	PN02XCP	London	R234HCD	Brighton & H
PJ02RCF	London	PJ53NKZ	London	PN02XCR	London	R235HCD	Brighton & H

Reg	Operator	Reg	Operator	Reg	Operator	Reg	Operator	Reg	Operator
R236HCD	Brighton & H	R448LGH	London	R742BMY	Metrobus	S105EGK	London
R254LGH	North East	R449LGH	London	R743BMY	Metrobus	S106EGK	London
R255LGH	North East	R451LGH	London	R744BMY	Metrobus	S107EGK	London
R256LGH	North East	R452LGH	London	R745BMY	Metrobus	S108EGK	London
R257LGH	North East	R453LGH	London	R746FGX	Metrobus	S109EGK	London
R259DWL	Diamond	R454LGH	London	R747FGX	Metrobus	S110EGK	London
R261LGH	North East	R455LGH	London	R752GDL	South Coast	S112EGK	London
R262LGH	North East	R456LGH	London	R753GDL	South Coast	S113EGK	London
R263LGH	North East	R457LGH	London	R754GDL	South Coast	S114EGK	London
R264LGH	North East	R458LGH	London	R755GDL	South Coast	S115EGK	London
R265LGH	North East	R459LGH	London	R756GDL	South Coast	S116EGK	London
R266LGH	North East	R460LGH	London	R757GDL	South Coast	S117EGK	London
R267LGH	North East	R461LGH	London	R758GDL	South Coast	S157OCU	South Coast
R269LGH	North East	R462LGH	London	R759GDL	South Coast	S248KNL	North East
R270LGH	North East	R463LGH	London	R807NUD	South Coast	S249KNL	North East
R271LGH	North East	R464LGH	London	R808NUD	Oxford	S250KNL	North East
R274LGH	North East	R465LGH	London	R809NUD	Oxford	S251KNL	North East
R276LGH	North East	R466LGH	London	R810NUD	Oxford	S252KNL	North East
R281LGH	North East	R467LGH	London	R810WJA	Diamond	S253KNL	North East
R282LGH	North East	R468LGH	London	R812NUD	South Coast	S254KNL	North East
R283LGH	North East	R469LGH	London	R813NUD	South Coast	S255KNL	North East
R284LGH	North East	R469RRA	North East	R815UOK	South Coast	S358ONL	North East
R285LGH	North East	R470LGH	London	R830MFR	Metrobus	S359ONL	North East
R286LGH	North East	R470RRA	North East	R831MFR	Metrobus	S35NRG	South Coast
R286OFV	Meteor	R471LGH	London	R832MFR	Metrobus	S360ONL	North East
R287DWL	Oxford	R472LGH	London	R833MFR	Metrobus	S361ONL	North East
R287LGH	North East	R473LGH	London	R834MFR	Metrobus	S362ONL	North East
R287OFV	Meteor	R474LGH	London	R835MFR	Metrobus	S363ONL	North East
R288DWL	Oxford	R475LGH	London	R836MFR	Metrobus	S364ONL	North East
R288LGH	North East	R476LGH	London	R837MFR	Metrobus	S365ONL	North East
R289DWL	Oxford	R477LGH	London	R837PRG	North East	S366ONL	North East
R322HCD	Brighton & H	R477RRA	North East	R838MFR	Metrobus	S367ONL	North East
R331LGH	London	R478LGH	London	R838PRG	North East	S368ONL	North East
R332LGH	London	R481LGH	London	R839MFR	Metrobus	S369ONL	North East
R334LGH	London	R482LGH	London	R839PRG	North East	S370ONL	North East
R337LGH	London	R483LGH	London	R841MFR	Metrobus	S371ONL	North East
R338LGH	London	R484LGH	London	R841PRG	North East	S372ONL	North East
R341LGH	London	R485LGH	London	R842MFR	Metrobus	S373ONL	North East
R342LGH	London	R486LGH	London	R842PRG	North East	S374ONL	North East
R343LGH	London	R487LGH	London	R843MFR	Metrobus	S375ONL	North East
R344LGH	London	R488LGH	London	R843PRG	North East	S397HVV	Diamond
R347LGH	London	R489LGH	London	R844MFR	Metrobus	S404JUA	Diamond
R355LGH	North East	R527YRP	Diamond	R844PRG	North East	S405JUA	Diamond
R360LHG	Diamond	R529YRP	Diamond	R845MFR	Metrobus	S590KJF	North East
R361LGH	London	R530YRP	Diamond	R845PRG	North East	S623JRU	South Coast
R362LGH	London	R531YRP	Diamond	R846PRG	North East	S624JRU	South Coast
R363LGH	London	R532YRP	Diamond	R847PRG	North East	S625JRU	South Coast
R363LHG	Diamond	R549LGH	North East	R848PRG	North East	S626JRU	South Coast
R364LGH	London	R550LGH	North East	R849PRG	North East	S627JRU	South Coast
R365LGH	London	R551LGH	North East	R851PRG	North East	S628JRU	South Coast
R366LGH	London	R553LGH	North East	R852PRG	North East	S629JRU	South Coast
R367LGH	London	R554LGH	North East	R853PRG	North East	S630JRU	South Coast
R368LGH	London	R556LGH	North East	R854PRG	North East	S631JRU	South Coast
R371LGH	London	R558LGH	North East	R855PRG	North East	S632JRU	South Coast
R373LGH	London	R559LGH	North East	R856PRG	North East	S638JGP	London
R374LGH	London	R567LGH	North East	R878HCD	Brighton & H	S726KNV	North East
R375LGH	London	R58GNW	Metrobus	R879HCD	Brighton & H	S758RNE	Diamond
R376LGH	London	R601NFX	South Coast	R880HCD	Brighton & H	S759RNE	Diamond
R37GDE	South Coast	R602NFX	South Coast	R881HCD	Brighton & H	S771RNE	Diamond
R380LGH	London	R603NFX	South Coast	R905NFX	South Coast	S772RNE	Diamond
R380LHG	Diamond	R604NFX	South Coast	R932AMB	Diamond	S773RNE	Diamond
R381LGH	London	R609NFX	South Coast	R954JYS	Diamond	S783RNE	North East
R382LGH	London	R610NFX	South Coast	R970MGB	Diamond	S811FVK	North East
R383LGH	London	R612NFX	South Coast	R971FNW	North East	S812FVK	North East
R385LGH	London	R613NFX	South Coast	R972FNW	North East	S813FVK	North East
R386LGH	London	R614NFX	South Coast	R975FNW	North East	S814FVK	North East
R389LGH	North East	R615NFX	South Coast	R979FNW	North East	S815FVK	North East
R390LGH	North East	R616NFX	South Coast	R982FNW	North East	S816FVK	North East
R391LGH	North East	R617NFX	South Coast	R983FNW	North East	S817FVK	North East
R392LGH	North East	R618NFX	South Coast	R986RBY	Meteor	S818OFT	North East
R393LGH	North East	R619NFX	South Coast	RJI6055	South Coast	S819OFT	North East
R394LGH	North East	R620NFX	South Coast	RO06TUU	Metrobus	S820OFT	North East
R395LGH	North East	R621NFX	South Coast	S91EGK	London	S821OFT	North East
R396LGH	North East	R622NFX	South Coast	S92EGK	London	S822OFT	North East
R397LGH	North East	R659GCA	Diamond	S93EGK	London	S823OFT	North East
R398LGH	North East	R660GCA	Diamond	S94EGK	London	S824OFT	North East
R399LGH	North East	R708SLU	Meteor	S95EGK	London	S825OFT	North East
R401FFC	Oxford	R709SLU	Meteor	S96EGK	London	S826OFT	North East
R408FFC	Oxford	R710YFL	South Coast	S97EGK	London	S827OFT	North East
R433LGH	London	R737XRV	South Coast	S98EGK	London	S828OFT	North East
R438FTU	Diamond	R738XRV	South Coast	S101EGK	London	S829OFT	North East
R445LGH	London	R739XRV	South Coast	S102EGK	London	S830OFT	North East
R446LGH	London	R741BMY	Metrobus	S103EGK	London	S831OFT	North East
R447LGH	London	R741XRV	South Coast	S104EGK	London	S832OFT	North East

The 2006-07 Go-Ahead Bus Handbook

S833OFT	North East	SN03WMG	Metrobus	SN53KKX	London	T413OUB	Meteor
S862ONL	North East	SN03WMK	Metrobus	SN54GPV	Metrobus	T414AGP	London
S863ONL	North East	SN03WMP	Metrobus	SN54GPX	Metrobus	T414OUB	Meteor
S864ONL	North East	SN03WMT	Metrobus	SN54GPY	Metrobus	T415AGP	London
S865ONL	North East	SN03WMV	Metrobus	SN54GPZ	Metrobus	T415OUB	Meteor
S866ONL	North East	SN03WMY	Metrobus	SN54GRF	Metrobus	T416AGP	North East
S867ONL	North East	SN03YBA	Metrobus	SN54GRK	Metrobus	T416OUB	Meteor
S868ONL	North East	SN03YBB	Metrobus	T35RJL	South Coast	T417AGP	London
S869ONL	North East	SN03YBC	Metrobus	T71JBA	Diamond	T417OUB	Meteor
S870ONL	North East	SN03YBG	Metrobus	T101DBW	Oxford	T418AGP	London
S890ONL	North East	SN03YBH	Metrobus	T101KGP	North East	T418OUB	Meteor
S891ONL	North East	SN03YBK	Metrobus	T102DBW	Oxford	T419AGP	London
S892ONL	North East	SN03YBR	Metrobus	T102KGP	North East	T419OUB	Meteor
S893ONL	North East	SN03YBS	Metrobus	T103DBW	Oxford	T420OUB	Meteor
S894ONL	North East	SN03YBT	Metrobus	T103KGP	North East	T421AGP	North East
S895ONL	North East	SN03YBX	Metrobus	T104DBW	Oxford	T421OUB	Meteor
S920SVM	Diamond	SN03YBY	Metrobus	T104KGP	North East	T422AGP	North East
S954JGX	London	SN03YBZ	Metrobus	T105DBW	Oxford	T423AGP	North East
S955JGX	London	SN03YCD	Metrobus	T105KGP	North East	T424AGP	North East
S977ABR	North East	SN03YCE	Metrobus	T106DBW	Oxford	T425AGP	North East
S978ABR	North East	SN03YCF	Metrobus	T106KGP	London	T426AGP	North East
S979ABR	North East	SN03YCK	Metrobus	T107DBW	Oxford	T426LGP	North East
SIB5373	South Coast	SN03YCL	Metrobus	T107KGP	London	T427AGP	North East
SIL7914	South Coast	SN03YCM	Metrobus	T108DBW	Oxford	T427LGP	North East
SJI8751	South Coast	SN03YCT	Metrobus	T108KGP	London	T428AGP	North East
SK52MKX	London	SN06BNA	London	T109DBW	Oxford	T428LGP	North East
SK52MKZ	London	SN06BNB	London	T109KGP	London	T429AGP	North East
SK52MLU	London	SN06BND	London	T110DBW	Oxford	T429LGP	North East
SK52MLV	London	SN06BNE	London	T110KGP	North East	T430LGP	North East
SK52MLX	London	SN06BNF	London	T111DBW	Oxford	T438EBD	North East
SK52MLY	London	SN06BNJ	London	T112DBW	Oxford	T441EBD	Diamond
SK52MLZ	London	SN06BNK	London	T112KGP	North East	T442EBD	Diamond
SK52MMA	London	SN06BNL	London	T113DBW	Oxford	T443EBD	Diamond
SK52MME	London	SN06BNO	London	T113KGP	North East	T445EBD	Diamond
SK52MMF	London	SN06BNU	London	T114DBW	Oxford	T447EBD	Diamond
SK52MMJ	London	SN06BNV	London	T114KGP	North East	T455AGP	London
SK52MMO	London	SN06BNX	London	T115DBW	Oxford	T456BCN	North East
SK52MMU	London	SN06BNY	London	T115KGP	North East	T457BCN	North East
SK52MMV	London	SN06BNZ	London	T116DBW	Oxford	T458BCN	North East
SK52MMX	London	SN06BOF	London	T117DBW	Oxford	T459BCN	North East
SK52MOA	London	SN51UAD	London	T118DBW	Oxford	T460BCN	North East
SK52MOF	London	SN51UAE	London	T118KGP	London	T461BCN	North East
SK52MOU	London	SN51UAF	London	T119DBW	Oxford	T462BCN	North East
SK52MOV	London	SN51UAG	London	T119KGP	London	T463BCN	North East
SK52MPE	London	SN51UAH	London	T120DBW	Oxford	T464BCN	North East
SK52MPF	London	SN51UAJ	London	T120KGP	London	T465BCN	North East
SK52MPO	London	SN51UAK	London	T122KGP	London	T466BCN	North East
SK52MRO	London	SN51UAL	London	T124KGP	London	T467BCN	North East
SK52MRU	London	SN51UAM	London	T125KGP	London	T468BCN	North East
SK52MRV	London	SN51UAO	London	T126KGP	London	T469BCN	North East
SK52MRX	London	SN51UAP	London	T127KGP	London	T503RPN	Brighton & H
SK52MRY	London	SN51UAR	London	T128KGP	London	T504RPN	Brighton & H
SMK669F	London	SN51UAS	London	T158ALJ	South Coast	T521AGP	London
SMK673F	London	SN51UAT	London	T159ALJ	South Coast	T523AGP	London
SMK680F	London	SN51UAU	London	T160ALJ	South Coast	T633AJT	South Coast
SMK693F	London	SN51UAV	London	T216REL	South Coast	T634AJT	South Coast
SMK725F	London	SN51UAW	London	T217REL	South Coast	T635AJT	South Coast
SMK732F	London	SN51UAX	London	T218REL	South Coast	T636AJT	South Coast
SMK736F	London	SN51UAY	London	T272RMY	North East	T637AJT	South Coast
SN03EBP	South Coast	SN51UAZ	London	T309SMV	Metrobus	T638AJT	South Coast
SN03EBU	South Coast	SN53ETT	London	T310SMV	Metrobus	T639AJT	South Coast
SN03EBV	South Coast	SN53ETU	London	T311SMV	Metrobus	T640AJT	South Coast
SN03EBX	South Coast	SN53ETV	London	T312SMV	Metrobus	T641AJT	South Coast
SN03EBZ	South Coast	SN53ETX	London	T313SMV	Metrobus	T642AJT	South Coast
SN03ECA	South Coast	SN53ETY	London	T314SMV	Metrobus	T643AJT	South Coast
SN03ECC	South Coast	SN53ETZ	London	T315SMV	Metrobus	T644AJT	South Coast
SN03ECD	South Coast	SN53EVA	London	T316SMV	Metrobus	T645AJT	South Coast
SN03LDJ	South Coast	SN53EVB	London	T392AGP	London	T646AJT	South Coast
SN03LDK	South Coast	SN53EVC	London	T401AGP	London	T647AJT	South Coast
SN03LDL	South Coast	SN53EVD	London	T402AGP	London	T648AJT	South Coast
SN03LDU	South Coast	SN53EVE	London	T403AGP	London	T649AJT	South Coast
SN03WKU	Metrobus	SN53KKF	London	T403LGP	North East	T669KPU	Brighton & H
SN03WKY	Metrobus	SN53KKG	London	T404AGP	London	T670KPU	Brighton & H
SN03WLA	Metrobus	SN53KKH	London	T406AGP	London	T671KPU	Brighton & H
SN03WLE	Metrobus	SN53KKJ	London	T407AGP	North East	T672KPU	Brighton & H
SN03WLF	Metrobus	SN53KKL	London	T407LGP	North East	T673KPU	Brighton & H
SN03WLH	Metrobus	SN53KKM	London	T408AGP	London	T675KPU	Brighton & H
SN03WLL	Metrobus	SN53KKO	London	T409AGP	North East	T677KPU	Brighton & H
SN03WLP	Metrobus	SN53KKP	London	T410AGP	London	T742JPO	South Coast
SN03WLU	Metrobus	SN53KKR	London	T411AGP	London	T743JPO	South Coast
SN03WLX	Metrobus	SN53KKT	London	T412AGP	London	T744JPO	South Coast
SN03WLZ	Metrobus	SN53KKU	London	T412OUB	Meteor	T745JPO	South Coast
SN03WMC	Metrobus	SN53KKV	London	T413AGP	North East	T746JPO	South Coast
SN03WMF	Metrobus	SN53KKW	London	T413LGP	North East	T747JPO	South Coast

T748JPO	South Coast	V17GMT	London	V218LGC	London	V676FEL	South Coast
T749JPO	South Coast	V17OXF	Oxford	V219ERG	North East	V676JWC	Meteor
T801CBW	Oxford	V18OXF	Oxford	V220LGC	London	V677FEL	South Coast
T801RFG	Brighton & H	V37KWO	South Coast	V221ERG	North East	V678FEL	South Coast
T802CBW	Oxford	V101LGC	London	V221LGC	London	V679FEL	South Coast
T802RFG	Brighton & H	V102LGC	London	V223LGC	London	V680FEL	South Coast
T803CBW	Oxford	V103LGC	London	V226LGC	London	V681FEL	South Coast
T803RFG	Brighton & H	V104LGC	London	V228LGC	London	V682FEL	South Coast
T804CBW	Oxford	V105LGC	London	V233LGC	London	V683FEL	South Coast
T804RFG	Brighton & H	V106LGC	London	V266BNV	Diamond	V684FEL	South Coast
T805CBW	Oxford	V107LGC	London	V267BNV	Diamond	V685FEL	South Coast
T805RFG	Brighton & H	V108LGC	London	V301LGC	London	V686FEL	South Coast
T806CBW	Oxford	V109LGC	London	V302LGC	London	V801EBR	North East
T806RFG	Brighton & H	V110LGC	London	V303LGC	London	V802EBR	North East
T807CBW	Oxford	V112LGC	London	V304LGC	London	V803EBR	North East
T807RFG	Brighton & H	V113LGC	London	V305LGC	London	V804EBR	North East
T808CBW	Oxford	V114LGC	London	V306LGC	London	V816KGF	London
T808RFG	Brighton & H	V115LGC	London	V307LGC	London	V820ERG	North East
T809CBW	Oxford	V116LGC	London	V308LGC	London	V822ERG	North East
T809RFG	Brighton & H	V117LGC	London	V310LGC	London	V858EGR	North East
T810CBW	Oxford	V118LGC	London	V311LGC	London	V921KGF	London
T810RFG	Brighton & H	V118LVH	Meteor	V312LGC	London	V930VUB	Meteor
T811CBW	Oxford	V119LGC	London	V313LGC	London	V936VUB	Meteor
T811RFG	Brighton & H	V119LVH	Meteor	V314LGC	London	V937VUB	Meteor
T812CBW	Oxford	V120LGC	London	V315LGC	London	V938VUB	Meteor
T812RFG	Brighton & H	V122LGC	London	V317LGC	London	V939VUB	Meteor
T813CBW	Oxford	V124LGC	London	V319LGC	London	V941DNB	Diamond
T813RFG	Brighton & H	V125LGC	London	V322KMY	Metrobus	V942DNB	Diamond
T814CBW	Oxford	V126LGC	London	V322LGC	London	V966DFX	South Coast
T814RFG	Brighton & H	V127LGC	London	V323KMY	Metrobus	V986ETN	North East
T815CBW	Oxford	V128LGC	London	V324KMY	Metrobus	V987ETN	North East
T815RFG	Brighton & H	V129LGC	London	V324LGC	London	V988ETN	North East
T816RFG	Brighton & H	V130LGC	London	V325KMY	Metrobus	V989ETN	North East
T817RFG	Brighton & H	V131LGC	London	V325LGC	London	V990ETN	North East
T818RFG	Brighton & H	V132LGC	London	V326KMY	Metrobus	VDL744	South Coast
T819RFG	Brighton & H	V133LGC	London	V327KMY	Metrobus	VLT9	London
T820RFG	Brighton & H	V134LGC	London	V327LGC	London	VLT60	London
TIL6710	South Coast	V135LGC	London	V328KMY	Metrobus	VLT179	London
TIL6711	South Coast	V136LGC	London	V329KMY	Metrobus	VLT277	London
TIL6712	South Coast	V137LGC	London	V329LGC	London	VLT284	London
TIL6713	South Coast	V138LGC	London	V330KMY	Metrobus	VUV246	South Coast
TIL6714	South Coast	V139LGC	London	V330LGC	London	W19OXF	Oxford
TIL6715	South Coast	V140LGC	London	V331KMY	Metrobus	W20FWL	Oxford
TIL6716	South Coast	V141LGC	London	V331LGC	London	W20OXF	Oxford
TIL6717	South Coast	V142LGC	London	V332LGC	London	W21OXF	Oxford
TIL6718	South Coast	V143LGC	London	V334LGC	London	W22OXF	Oxford
TIL6719	South Coast	V144LGC	London	V335LGC	London	W30DTS	Diamond
TIL6720	South Coast	V145LGC	London	V336LGC	London	W96AJN	Meteor
TIL6723	South Coast	V146LGC	London	V337LGC	London	W161RFX	South Coast
TIL6724	South Coast	V186ERG	North East	V338LGC	London	W162RFX	South Coast
TIL6725	South Coast	V187ERG	North East	V385JWK	Diamond	W163RFX	South Coast
TIL6726	South Coast	V188ERG	North East	V386JWK	Diamond	W164RFX	South Coast
TIL6727	South Coast	V189ERG	North East	V391SUV	Diamond	W165RFX	South Coast
TJI9462	South Coast	V190ERG	North East	V392KGF	London	W166RFX	South Coast
TJR718Y	North East	V191ERG	North East	V434KGF	North East	W174SCU	North East
UDL671S	South Coast	V192ERG	North East	V435KGF	North East	W176SCU	North East
UEL489	South Coast	V193ERG	North East	V436KGF	North East	W177SCU	North East
UFX857S	South Coast	V194ERG	North East	V437KGF	North East	W178SCU	North East
UJI2507	South Coast	V195ERG	North East	V618EVU	Meteor	W179SCU	North East
UPT681V	North East	V196ERG	North East	V651DFX	South Coast	W181SCU	North East
URU673S	South Coast	V197ERG	North East	V652DFX	South Coast	W182SCU	North East
URU690S	South Coast	V198ERG	North East	V653DFX	South Coast	W183SCU	North East
URU690S	South Coast	V199ERG	North East	V654DFX	South Coast	W184SCU	North East
URU691S	South Coast	V201ERG	North East	V655DFX	South Coast	W185SCU	North East
USV115	South Coast	V202ERG	North East	V656DFX	South Coast	W186SCU	North East
V#1GMT	London	V203ERG	North East	V657DFX	South Coast	W187SCU	North East
V2GMT	London	V204ERG	North East	V658DFX	South Coast	W188SCU	North East
V3GMT	London	V205ERG	North East	V659DFX	South Coast	W189SCU	North East
V4GMT	London	V206ERG	North East	V660DFX	South Coast	W254KDO	South Coast
V5GMT	London	V207ERG	North East	V661DFX	South Coast	W317VGX	Metrobus
V6GMT	London	V208ERG	North East	V662DFX	South Coast	W319VGX	Metrobus
V7GMT	London	V209ERG	North East	V663DFX	South Coast	W332VGX	Metrobus
V8GMT	London	V209LGC	London	V664DFX	South Coast	W334VGX	Metrobus
V9GMT	London	V210ERG	North East	V665DFX	South Coast	W335VGX	Metrobus
V10GMT	London	V210ERG	North East	V667DFX	South Coast	W336VGX	Metrobus
V11GMT	London	V211ERG	North East	V668DFX	South Coast	W337VGX	Metrobus
V12GMT	London	V211LGC	London	V669DFX	South Coast	W338VGX	Metrobus
V13GMT	London	V212ERG	North East	V670DFX	South Coast	W339VGX	Metrobus
V14GMT	London	V213ERG	North East	V671FEL	South Coast	W341VGX	Metrobus
V14OXF	Oxford	V214ERG	North East	V672FEL	South Coast	W342VGX	Metrobus
V15GMT	London	V215ERG	North East	V673FEL	South Coast	W343VGX	Metrobus
V15OXF	Oxford	V216ERG	North East	V674FEL	South Coast	W399WGH	London
V16GMT	London	V217ERG	North East	V675FEL	South Coast	W401WGH	London
V16OXF	Oxford	V218ERG	North East	V675JWC	Meteor	W402WGH	London

The 2006-07 Go-Ahead Bus Handbook

Reg	Location	Reg	Location	Reg	Location	Reg	Location
W403WGH	London	W524WGH	London	W997WGH	London	X577EGK	London
W404WGH	London	W526WGH	London	W998WGH	London	X578EGK	London
W408WGH	London	W527WGH	London	WDL655	South Coast	X579EGK	London
W409WGH	London	W529WGH	London	WLT379	London	X581EGK	London
W411SCU	North East	W531WGH	London	WLT470	London	X582EGK	London
W415WGH	London	W532WGH	London	WLT516	London	X583EGK	London
W425WGH	London	W533WGH	London	WLT548	London	X584EGK	London
W428OWX	Meteor	W534WGH	London	WTG360T	South Coast	X585EGK	London
W428WGH	London	W536WGH	London	X2OXF	Oxford	X586EGK	London
W429OWX	Meteor	W537WGH	London	X3OXF	Oxford	X587EGK	London
W432RBB	DiamonD	W538WGH	London	X4OXF	Oxford	X588EGK	London
W435WGH	London	W539WGH	London	X5OXF	Oxford	X589EGK	London
W439WGH	London	W541WGH	London	X6OXF	Oxford	X591EGK	London
W441WGH	London	W542WGH	London	X7OXF	Oxford	X592EGK	London
W442WGH	London	W543WGH	London	X8OXF	Oxford	X593EGK	London
W443WGH	London	W544WGH	London	X13OXF	Oxford	X594EGK	London
W445WGH	London	W578DGU	London	X28OXF	Oxford	X595EGK	London
W446WGH	London	W601PLJ	South Coast	X29OXF	Oxford	X595FBB	North East
W447WGH	London	W602PLJ	South Coast	X31OXF	Oxford	X596EGK	London
W448WGH	London	W603PLJ	South Coast	X94FOR	North East	X597EGK	London
W449WGH	London	W604PLJ	South Coast	X223FBB	North East	X598EGK	London
W451WGH	London	W605OCD	Brighton & H	X224FBB	North East	X599EGK	London
W452WGH	London	W606OCD	Brighton & H	X226FBB	North East	X601EGK	London
W453WGH	London	W711WJL	South Coast	X227FBB	North East	X602EGK	London
W454WGH	London	W791VMV	Metrobus	X228FBB	North East	X603EGK	London
W457WGH	London	W792VMV	Metrobus	X229FBB	North East	X604EGK	London
W458WGH	London	W793VMV	Metrobus	X231FBB	North East	X605EGK	London
W459WGH	London	W794VMV	Metrobus	X232FBB	North East	X605XFX	South Coast
W461WGH	London	W795VMV	Metrobus	X233FBB	North East	X606EGK	London
W462WGH	London	W796VMV	Metrobus	X344YGU	Metrobus	X606XFX	South Coast
W463WGH	London	W797VMV	Metrobus	X346YGU	Brighton & H	X607EGK	London
W464WGH	London	W798VMV	Metrobus	X347YGU	Brighton & H	X607XFX	South Coast
W465WGH	London	W799VMV	Metrobus	X421WVO	Diamond	X608EGK	London
W466WGH	London	W806PNL	North East	X422WVO	Diamond	X608XFX	South Coast
W467WGH	London	W816FBW	Oxford	X423WVO	Diamond	X609EGK	London
W468WGH	London	W817FBW	Oxford	X492WGR	North East	X609WLJ	South Coast
W469WGH	London	W818FBW	Oxford	X501EGK	London	X611EGK	London
W471WGH	London	W819FBW	Oxford	X501WRG	North East	X612EGK	London
W472WGH	London	W821FBW	Oxford	X502EGK	London	X613EGK	London
W473WGH	London	W821NNJ	Brighton & H	X502WRG	North East	X615EGK	London
W474WGH	London	W822NNJ	Brighton & H	X503EGK	London	X616EGK	London
W475WGH	London	W823NNJ	Brighton & H	X503WRG	North East	X631AKW	Diamond
W476WGH	London	W824NNJ	Brighton & H	X504EGK	London	X632AKW	Diamond
W477WGH	London	W825NNJ	Brighton & H	X504WRG	North East	X634AKW	Diamond
W478WGH	London	W826NNJ	Brighton & H	X506EGK	London	X636AKW	Diamond
W479WGH	London	W827NNJ	Brighton & H	X506WRG	North East	X637AKW	Diamond
W481WGH	London	W828NNJ	Brighton & H	X507EGK	London	X638AKW	Diamond
W482WGH	London	W829NNJ	Brighton & H	X507WRG	North East	X639AKW	Diamond
W483WGH	London	W830NNJ	Brighton & H	X508EGK	London	X641AKW	Diamond
W484WGH	London	W831NNJ	Brighton & H	X508WRG	North East	X656EGK	London
W485WGH	London	W832NNJ	Brighton & H	X509EGK	London	X687XJT	South Coast
W486WGH	London	W833NNJ	Brighton & H	X509WRG	North East	X688XJT	South Coast
W487WGH	London	W834NNJ	Brighton & H	X511WRG	North East	X699EGK	London
W488WGH	London	W835NNJ	Brighton & H	X512WRG	North East	X701EGK	London
W489WGH	London	W836NNJ	Brighton & H	X513WRG	North East	X702EGK	London
W491SCU	North East	W837NNJ	Brighton & H	X514WRG	North East	X705EGK	London
W491WGH	London	W838NNJ	Brighton & H	X544EGK	London	X707EGK	London
W492WGH	London	W839NNJ	Brighton & H	X546EGK	London	X745EGK	London
W493WGH	London	W840NNJ	Brighton & H	X547EGK	London	X822FBB	North East
W494WGH	London	W840WGH	London	X548EGK	London	X823FBB	North East
W495WGH	London	W859PNL	North East	X549EGK	London	X912WGR	North East
W496WGH	London	W861PNL	North East	X551EGK	London	X913WGR	North East
W497WGH	London	W862PNL	North East	X551FBB	North East	X914WGR	North East
W498WGH	London	W863PNL	North East	X552EGK	London	X915WGR	North East
W499WGH	London	W864PNL	North East	X553EGK	London	X916WGR	North East
W501WGH	London	W865PNL	North East	X554EGK	London	X917WGR	North East
W502WGH	London	W866PNL	North East	X556EGK	London	X918WGR	North East
W503WGH	London	W901JNF	Diamond	X557EGK	London	X919WGR	North East
W504WGH	London	W901RBB	North East	X558EGK	London	X921WGR	North East
W506WGH	London	W902JNF	Diamond	X559EGK	London	X922WGR	North East
W507WGH	London	W902RBB	North East	X561EGK	London	X923WGR	North East
W508WGH	London	W903JNF	Diamond	X562EGK	London	X924WGR	North East
W509WGH	London	W903RBB	North East	X563EGK	London	X935WGR	North East
W511WGH	London	W904JNF	Diamond	X564EGK	London	XAA299	South Coast
W512WGH	London	W904RBB	North East	X566EGK	London	XAM152	South Coast
W513WGH	London	W905JNF	Diamond	X567EGK	London	XDL872	South Coast
W514WGH	London	W905RBB	North East	X568EGK	London	XIL8583	South Coast
W516WGH	London	W905WGH	London	X569EGK	London	XIL8584	South Coast
W517WGH	London	W906RBB	North East	X571EGK	London	XXI8502	South Coast
W518WGH	London	W907RBB	North East	X572EGK	London	Y23OXF	Oxford
W519WGH	London	W908RBB	North East	X573EGK	London	Y24OXF	Oxford
W521WGH	London	W909RBB	North East	X574EGK	London	Y25OXF	Oxford
W522WGH	London	W956WGH	London	X575EGK	London	Y26OXF	Oxford
W523WGH	London	W996WGH	London	X576EGK	London	Y27OXF	Oxford

One of the Mercedes-Benz Citaro buses used by City of Oxford on the Park & Ride service is 823, MB52OXF. This batch features the new version of the 'Select' marks with the OXF letters being applied. *Mark Lyons*

Y28OXF	Oxford	Y493ETN	North East	Y827TGH	London	Y868PWT	Diamond
Y167FEL	South Coast	Y558KUX	North East	Y828TGH	London	Y869GCD	Brighton & H
Y168FEL	South Coast	Y703TGH	London	Y829TGH	London	Y871GCD	Brighton & H
Y169FEL	South Coast	Y704TGH	London	Y831TGH	London	Y872GCD	Brighton & H
Y171FEL	South Coast	Y705TGH	London	Y832TGH	London	Y873GCD	Brighton & H
Y172FEL	South Coast	Y729TGH	London	Y833TGH	London	Y874GCD	Brighton & H
Y173FEL	South Coast	Y731TGH	London	Y834TGH	London	Y875GCD	Brighton & H
Y174FEL	South Coast	Y732TGH	London	Y835TGH	London	Y876GCD	Brighton & H
Y199FEL	South Coast	Y733TGH	London	Y836TGH	London	Y877GCD	Brighton & H
Y211HWJ	Diamond	Y734TGH	London	Y837TGH	London	Y878GCD	Brighton & H
Y212HWJ	Diamond	Y735TGH	London	Y838TGH	London	Y879GCD	Brighton & H
Y291HUA	North East	Y736TGH	London	Y839TGH	London	Y907TGH	London
Y292HUA	North East	Y737TGH	London	Y840TGH	London	Y908TGH	London
Y348HMY	Metrobus	Y738TGH	London	Y841TGH	London	Y909TGH	London
Y349HMY	Metrobus	Y739TGH	London	Y842TGH	London	Y926ERG	North East
Y351HMY	Metrobus	Y741TGH	London	Y843TGH	London	Y927ERG	North East
Y352HMY	Metrobus	Y742TGH	London	Y844TGH	London	Y928ERG	North East
Y353HMY	Metrobus	Y743TGH	London	Y845TGH	London	Y929ERG	North East
Y354HMY	Metrobus	Y744TGH	London	Y846TGH	London	Y931ERG	North East
Y356HMY	Metrobus	Y745TGH	London	Y847TGH	London	Y932ERG	North East
Y357HMY	Metrobus	Y746TGH	London	Y848TGH	London	Y933ERG	North East
Y358HMY	Metrobus	Y747TGH	London	Y849TGH	London	Y934ERG	North East
Y359HMY	Metrobus	Y748TGH	London	Y851GCD	Brighton & H	Y935ERG	North East
Y361HMY	Metrobus	Y749TGH	London	Y851TGH	London	Y936ERG	North East
Y362HMY	Metrobus	Y781MFT	North East	Y852GCD	Brighton & H	Y967TGH	London
Y363HMY	Metrobus	Y782MFT	North East	Y852TGH	London	Y968TGH	London
Y364HMY	Metrobus	Y783MFT	North East	Y853GCD	Brighton & H	Y969TGH	London
Y365HMY	Metrobus	Y784MFT	North East	Y853TGH	London	Y971TGH	London
Y366HMY	Metrobus	Y785MFT	North East	Y854GCD	Brighton & H	Y972TGH	London
Y367HMY	Metrobus	Y801TGH	London	Y854TGH	London	Y973TGH	London
Y368HMY	Metrobus	Y802TGH	London	Y856GCD	Brighton & H	Y974TGH	London
Y369HMY	Metrobus	Y803TGH	London	Y856TGH	London	Y975FEL	South Coast
Y371HMY	Metrobus	Y805TGH	London	Y857GCD	Brighton & H	Y975TGH	London
Y372HMY	Metrobus	Y806TGH	London	Y857TGH	London	Y976TGH	London
Y373HMY	Metrobus	Y808MFT	North East	Y858GCD	Brighton & H	Y978TGH	London
Y374HMY	Metrobus	Y808TGH	London	Y858TGH	London	Y979TGH	London
Y376HMY	Metrobus	Y809TGH	London	Y859GCD	Brighton & H	Y981TGH	London
Y377HMY	Metrobus	Y811TGH	London	Y859TGH	London	Y982TGH	London
Y378HMY	Metrobus	Y812TGH	London	Y861GCD	Brighton & H	Y983TGH	London
Y379HMY	Metrobus	Y813TGH	London	Y861TGH	London	Y984TGH	London
Y381HKE	Metrobus	Y814TGH	London	Y862GCD	Brighton & H	Y985TGH	London
Y382HKE	Metrobus	Y815TGH	London	Y862TGH	London	Y986TGH	London
Y383HKE	Metrobus	Y816TGH	London	Y863GCD	Brighton & H	Y987TGH	London
Y384HKE	Metrobus	Y817TGH	London	Y863TGH	London	Y988TGH	London
Y385HKE	Metrobus	Y818TGH	London	Y864GCD	Brighton & H	Y989TGH	London
Y386HKE	Metrobus	Y819TGH	London	Y864TGH	London	YA02YRR	Meteor
Y387HKE	Metrobus	Y821TGH	London	Y865GCD	Brighton & H	YA02YRS	Meteor
Y388HKE	Metrobus	Y822TGH	London	Y865TGH	London	YA02YRT	Meteor
Y389HKE	Metrobus	Y823TGH	London	Y866GCD	Brighton & H	YD02PZJ	Diamond
Y391HKE	Metrobus	Y824TGH	London	Y866TGH	London	YD02PZK	Diamond
Y392HKE	Metrobus	Y825TGH	London	Y867GCD	Brighton & H	YD02PZL	Diamond
Y393HKE	Metrobus	Y826TGH	London	Y867PWT	Diamond	YD02PZM	Diamond

The 2006-07 Go-Ahead Bus Handbook

YD02PZN	Diamond	YN04GJJ	Brighton & H	YN53RXG	Metrobus	YN55PWV	Metrobus
YD02PZO	Diamond	YN04GJK	Brighton & H	YN53RXH	Metrobus	YN55PWX	Metrobus
YJ03PGX	Diamond	YN04GJU	Brighton & H	YN53RXJ	Metrobus	YN55PZC	Metrobus
YJ03PGY	Diamond	YN04GJV	Brighton & H	YN53RXK	Metrobus	YN55PZD	Metrobus
YJ03PGZ	Diamond	YN04GJX	Brighton & H	YN53RXL	Metrobus	YN55PZE	Metrobus
YJ03PKK	Diamond	YN04GJY	Brighton & H	YN53RXM	Metrobus	YN55PZF	Metrobus
YJ03PNN	Diamond	YN04GJZ	Brighton & H	YN53RXO	Metrobus	YN55PZG	Metrobus
YJ06FYA	Meteor	YN04GKA	Brighton & H	YN53RXP	Metrobus	YN55PZH	Metrobus
YJ06FYB	Meteor	YN04GKC	Brighton & H	YN53RXR	Metrobus	YN55PZJ	Metrobus
YJ06FYC	Meteor	YN04GKD	Brighton & H	YN53RXT	Metrobus	YN55PZL	Metrobus
YJ06FYD	Meteor	YN04GKE	Brighton & H	YN53RXU	Metrobus	YN55PZM	Metrobus
YJ06FYE	Meteor	YN04GKF	Brighton & H	YN53RXV	Metrobus	YN55PZO	Metrobus
YJ06FYF	Meteor	YN04GKG	Brighton & H	YN53RXW	Metrobus	YN55PZP	Metrobus
YJ51EKA	Diamond	YN04GKJ	Brighton & H	YN53RXX	Metrobus	YN55PZR	Metrobus
YJ51EKB	Diamond	YN04GKK	Brighton & H	YN53RXY	Metrobus	YN55PZU	Metrobus
YJ51EKC	Diamond	YN05GZH	Brighton & H	YN53RXZ	Metrobus	YN55PZV	Metrobus
YJ51EKD	Diamond	YN05GZJ	Brighton & H	YN53RYA	Metrobus	YN55PZW	Metrobus
YJ51EKE	Diamond	YN05GZK	Brighton & H	YN53RYB	Metrobus	YN55PZX	Metrobus
YJ51EKF	Diamond	YN05GZL	Brighton & H	YN53RYC	Metrobus	YN56FFA	Brighton & H
YJ51EKG	Diamond	YN05GZM	Brighton & H	YN53RYD	Metrobus	YN56FFB	Brighton & H
YJ51EKH	Diamond	YN05GZO	Brighton & H	YN53RYF	Metrobus	YN56FFC	Brighton & H
YJ53VHF	Diamond	YN05GZP	Brighton & H	YN53RYH	Metrobus	YN56FFD	Brighton & H
YJ55YFH	Meteor	YN05GZR	Brighton & H	YN53RYK	Metrobus	YN56FFE	Brighton & H
YJ55YGE	Meteor	YN05GZS	Brighton & H	YN53RYM	Metrobus	YN56FFG	Brighton & H
YJ55YGF	Meteor	YN05HCA	Metrobus	YN53RYP	Metrobus	YN56FFH	Brighton & H
YM52TOU	North East	YN05HCC	Metrobus	YN53RYR	Metrobus	YN56FFJ	Brighton & H
YM55SWU	Metrobus	YN05HCD	Metrobus	YN53RYT	Metrobus	YN56FFK	Brighton & H
YM55SWV	Metrobus	YN05HCE	Metrobus	YN53RYV	Metrobus	YN56FFL	Brighton & H
YM55SWX	Metrobus	YN05HCF	Metrobus	YN53RYW	Metrobus	YN56FFM	Brighton & H
YM55SWY	Metrobus	YN05HCG	Metrobus	YN53RYX	Metrobus	YN56FFO	Brighton & H
YM55SXA	Metrobus	YN05HFE	Metrobus	YN53RYY	Metrobus	YN56FFP	Brighton & H
YM55SXB	Metrobus	YN05HFF	Metrobus	YN53RYZ	Metrobus	YN56FFR	Brighton & H
YM55SXC	Metrobus	YN05HFG	Metrobus	YN53RZA	Metrobus	YN56FFS	Brighton & H
YM55SXD	Metrobus	YN05HFH	Metrobus	YN53RZB	Metrobus	YN56FFT	Brighton & H
YM55SXE	Metrobus	YN05HFJ	Metrobus	YN53RZC	Metrobus	YN56FFU	Brighton & H
YM55SXF	Metrobus	YN06JXR	Metrobus	YN53RZD	Metrobus	YN56FFV	Brighton & H
YM55SXH	Metrobus	YN06JXS	Metrobus	YN53RZE	Metrobus	YP02AAV	Diamond
YM55SXO	Metrobus	YN06JXT	Metrobus	YN53RZF	Metrobus	YP02AAX	Diamond
YM55SXP	Metrobus	YN06JXU	Metrobus	YN54AJU	Metrobus	YP52CTO	Metrobus
YM55SXR	Metrobus	YN06JXV	Metrobus	YN54AJV	Metrobus	YR02ZYK	North East
YMW843	South Coast	YN06JXW	Metrobus	YN54AJX	Metrobus	YR02ZYM	North East
YN03DFA	Metrobus	YN06JXX	Metrobus	YN54AJY	Metrobus	YSU874	North East
YN03DFC	Metrobus	YN06JXY	Metrobus	YN54AOM	Brighton & H	YSU875	North East
YN03DFD	Metrobus	YN06JXZ	Metrobus	YN54AOO	Brighton & H	YSU876	North East
YN03DFE	Metrobus	YN06JYB	Metrobus	YN54AOP	Brighton & H	YU52XVK	Metrobus
YN03DFG	Metrobus	YN06JYC	Metrobus	YN54AOR	Brighton & H	YU52XVL	Metrobus
YN03DFJ	Metrobus	YN06JYD	Metrobus	YN54AOT	Brighton & H	YU52XVM	Metrobus
YN03DFK	Metrobus	YN06JYE	Metrobus	YN54AOU	Brighton & H	YU52XVN	Metrobus
YN03DFL	Metrobus	YN06JYF	Metrobus	YN54AOV	Brighton & H	YU52XVR	Metrobus
YN03DFP	Metrobus	YN06JYG	Metrobus	YN54AOW	Brighton & H	YV03PZE	Metrobus
YN03DFU	Metrobus	YN06JYH	Metrobus	YN54AOX	Brighton & H	YV03PZF	Metrobus
YN03DFV	Metrobus	YN06JYJ	Metrobus	YN54AOY	Brighton & H	YV03PZG	Metrobus
YN03DFX	Metrobus	YN06JYK	Metrobus	YN55NFA	Brighton & H	YV03PZH	Metrobus
YN03DFY	Metrobus	YN06JYL	Metrobus	YN55NFC	Brighton & H	YV03PZJ	Metrobus
YN03UPM	Metrobus	YN06JYO	Metrobus	YN55NFD	Brighton & H	YV03PZK	Metrobus
YN03UWU	Metrobus	YN06NYK	Brighton & H	YN55NFE	Brighton & H	YV03PZL	Metrobus
YN03UWY	Metrobus	YN06NYL	Brighton & H	YN55NFF	Brighton & H	YV03PZM	Metrobus
YN03UXW	North East	YN06SZW	Brighton & H	YN55NFG	Brighton & H	YV03PZW	Metrobus
YN03WPP	Metrobus	YN06SZX	Brighton & H	YN55NFH	Brighton & H	YV03PZX	Metrobus
YN03WPR	Metrobus	YN06SZY	Brighton & H	YN55NFJ	Brighton & H	YV03PZY	Metrobus
YN03WRF	Metrobus	YN06SZZ	Brighton & H	YN55NFK	Brighton & H	YV03PZZ	Metrobus
YN03WRG	Metrobus	YN51MKV	North East	YN55NFL	Brighton & H	YV03RAU	Metrobus
YN03WRJ	Metrobus	YN51MLZ	Meteor	YN55NFM	Brighton & H	YV03RAX	Metrobus
YN03WRL	Metrobus	YN51XMC	Meteor	YN55NFO	Brighton & H	YV03RBF	Metrobus
YN03WRP	Metrobus	YN51XMD	Meteor	YN55PWJ	Metrobus	YV03RBU	Metrobus
YN04ANU	Brighton & H	YN51XME	Meteor	YN55PWK	Metrobus	YV03RBX	Metrobus
YN04GJE	Brighton & H	YN51XMF	Meteor	YN55PWL	Metrobus	YV03RBY	Metrobus
YN04GJF	Brighton & H	YN51XMG	Meteor	YN55PWO	Metrobus	YV03RCY	Metrobus
YN04GJG	Brighton & H	YN53RXF	Metrobus	YN55PWU	Metrobus	YV03RCZ	Metrobus

ISBN 1 904875 36 X

© Published by *British Bus Publishing Ltd* , September 2006

**British Bus Publishing Ltd, 16 St Margaret's Drive, Telford, TF1 3PH
Telephone: 01952 255269 - Facsimile: 01952 222397**

www.britishbuspublishing.co.uk - E-mail sales@britishbuspublishing.co.uk